THE OXFORD HISTORY OF

SOUTH AFRICA

EDITED BY MONICA WILSON
AND LEONARD THOMPSON

II

SOUTH AFRICA
1870–1966

OXFORD
AT THE CLARENDON PRESS

Oxford University Press, Walton Street, Oxford OX2 6DP

OXFORD LONDON GLASGOW
NEW YORK TORONTO MELBOURNE WELLINGTON
IBADAN NAIROBI DAR ES SALAAM LUSAKA CAPE TOWN
KUALA LUMPUR SINGAPORE JAKARTA HONG KONG TOKYO
DELHI BOMBAY CALCUTTA MADRAS KARACHI

ISBN 0 19 821656 4

© *Oxford University Press 1975*

First published 1971
Reprinted 1971, 1974, 1978

Printed in Great Britain
at the University Press, Oxford
by Vivian Ridler
Printer to the University

ACKNOWLEDGEMENTS

T HE editors gratefully acknowledge research support from the University of California, Los Angeles, the University of Cape Town, and Yale University.

Thanks are also due to Miss M. A. Hennings who made the Index for both volumes of this History.

Acknowledgements to other individuals will be found at the beginnings of appropriate chapters.

CONTENTS

LIST OF MAPS

LIST OF TABLES

LIST OF FIGURES

THE AUTHORS AND EDITORS

D. HOBART HOUGHTON, *Honorary Research Fellow, the Institute of Social and Economic Research, Rhodes University, Grahamstown*

LEO KUPER, *Professor of Sociology and Director of the African Studies Center, University of California, Los Angeles*

JACK SPENCE, *Professor of Politics, University of Leicester*

LEONARD THOMPSON, *Professor of African History, Yale University*

DAVID WELSH, *Professor of Comparative African Government and Law, School of African Studies, University of Cape Town*

FRANCIS WILSON, *Lecturer in Economics, University of Cape Town*

MONICA WILSON, *Professor of Social Anthropology, School of African Studies, University of Cape Town. Honorary Fellow, Girton College, Cambridge*

RENÉ DE VILLIERS, *Editor,* The Star, *Johannesburg*

LIST OF ABBREVIATIONS

AYB	*Archives Year Book for South African History*
CGH	Cape of Good Hope
CHBE	*Cambridge History of the British Empire*
H.A.D.	*House of Assembly Debates*
JAH	*Journal of African History*
N.G.K.	Nederduitse Gereformeerde Kerk
OFS	Orange Free State
SABRA	Suid Afrikaanse Buro vir Rasse-Aangeleenthede
SAIRR	South African Institute of Race Relations
SAJE	*South African Journal of Economics*
SAR	South African Republic
SEPC	Social and Economic Planning Council
TP	Transvaal Province
VR of NRC	*Verbatim Reports of Natives Representative Council*
VRS	Van Riebeeck Society

I

ECONOMIC DEVELOPMENT, 1865–1965

1. *South Africa in the Eighteen-Sixties*

IN the 1860s there were the two British colonies on the coast—the Cape of Good Hope and Natal—separated from one another by some 300 miles of African territory where, apart from a few hunters, missionaries, and traders, the modern way of life had made little impact. The British colonies were poor, and economic progress was slow; but the essentials of a modern administration had been established. Inland, beyond the Orange River, were the two Boer republics—the Orange Free State and the Transvaal—and various independent African chiefdoms of which Lesotho was the most important. All had ill-defined frontiers and were engaged in a struggle for survival made more difficult by the vacillations of British policy. Griqualand and the lower Orange River area were politically confused and economically stagnant. Even the Boer republics, in spite of the presence there of some 50,000 people of European descent, lacked the basic structure to support a viable modern economy.

Of the four territories which later combined to form the Union of South Africa, the Cape Colony was much the most economically advanced. It had a recorded population of just under half a million persons of whom 181,600 were white[1] and all but 28,024 were South African born.[2] During the previous two centuries the white settlement had expanded slowly carrying with it many of the concepts of an exchange economy; but although the original settlers had come from what were among the most commercially advanced nations of the world at that time, the economic structure of the Colony was largely moulded by the African environment. Land was abundant, capital and skilled labour were scarce, markets were far-distant and the means of transport rudimentary. Thus it was that the descendants of men from the great trading cities of northern Europe, and from the intensive agriculture of France and the Netherlands, found themselves transformed in a generation or two into semi-nomadic stock farmers living deep in the interior where small-scale units consisting of the farmer, his family, servants, and retainers provided for most of their wants by

---

[1] CGH *Census, 1865*, p. 11.
[2] Ibid., p. 45. Born in Europe 26,310; elsewhere outside South Africa 1,714.

their own direct efforts, having relatively little contact with markets, or with the changes in manufacturing techniques which at that time were transforming the economies of Europe and bringing about the industrial revolution.

Tenuous though it was, the link with the market should not be over-looked[1] for in the immediate hinterland of the ports production for export or for revictualling passing ships had continued from the foundation of the settlement. Even from the interior, cattle (which carried themselves to market, often being driven great distances), ivory, hides, skins, and wool formed important exports. Nevertheless, in the 1860s, the vast majority of the white population was engaged in farming which was largely self-subsistence. The African tribesmen were stock-farmers and hunters; and sorghum and maize were grown under hoe cultivation. Their efforts were, however, even less market-oriented than those of the whites, although the impact of an exchange economy was beginning to make itself felt through barter and the gradual expansion of the use of money; but even on the farms of the white people few received cash wages, and many workers were paid in kind.

The population was mainly rural. In 1865 only one town in the Cape Colony had a population of over 10,000—Cape Town—where 28,457 were recorded in the municipality.[2] Of these 13,118 were white. Next in size were Port Elizabeth (8,700) and Grahamstown (5,949).[3] Of the total population of the Colony of 496,381 only about 20,000 were employed in manufacture and commerce.[4]

Cape Town was the main centre for both, and about seventy manu-facturing concerns were recorded in 1860 with fifteen brickfields heading the list, followed by nine establishments for curing fish for export, seven steam flour-mills, six soap and candle factories, six snuff mills, five iron and brass foundries, etc.[5] But manufacture was by no means confined to Cape Town, and nearly all districts of the Colony had some factories, either processing agricultural products, like the distilleries of the vineyard areas, wool-washing in the sheep-grazing districts,[6] and milling; or manufactures to supply a local need, like wagon-building, furniture-making, brick-making, and stone-quarrying. Compared with neighbouring African territories the Colony might be described as industrially advanced, but compared with the situation

[1] This is rightly stressed by S. D. Neumark, *Economic Influences on the South African Frontier, 1652–1836.*
[2] CGH *Census, 1865*, p. 5.   [3] Ibid., pp. 6 and 9.
[4] Ibid., p. viii: total employed in manufacture 13,186, and in commerce 6,887.
[5] CGH *Blue Book, 1860*, p. FF 1–21.
[6] Ibid. There were thirteen wool-washing establishments in the Eastern Division: four at Cradock, three at Port Elizabeth, two at Uitenhage, Colesberg, and Victoria East respec-tively.

a century later it was primitive and at a rudimentary stage of development. Industrial activity was small-scale and widely dispersed. This dispersal was largely the result of the inadequacies of the transport system; and, as this improved, industry tended to be more highly concentrated in a few major centres.

Except in times of drought, food was plentiful; but the standard of living of all races was low, and even the farmer with large herds of stock enjoyed few of the amenities of civilized life. In 1865 there were estimated to be nearly ten million sheep (of which over eight million were woolled-sheep), nearly 700,000 cattle, and 226,000 horses in the Colony.[1] In 1860 the average wage paid to white farm overseers and head shepherds was £3. 2*s*. 1*d*. per month, with board and lodging, and to Coloured £1. 8*s*. 0*d*. Daily rates with food were 2*s*. 9*d*. for white and 1*s*. 6*d*. for Coloured farm labourers. Skilled journeymen's daily wages without food averaged, for white and Coloured workers respectively: smiths, 8*s*. 7*d*. and 6*s*. 8*d*.; carpenters, 8*s*. and 6*s*.; and masons, 8*s*. 4*d*. and 6*s*. 6*d*.[2] The price of foodstuffs appears to have been high relative to these wages.[3]

Commerce was concentrated at the ports, and large wholesale concerns had developed a lucrative two-way trade, importing manufactures of all kinds, and exporting wool, hides, skins, ivory, and other local products. They had representatives and buyers in Britain; and in South Africa their commercial travellers visited smaller inland towns selling the imported goods to the local store-keepers who also acted as agents in the collection of South African produce for export. Banking had developed greatly since the establishment of the first commercial bank in 1837, and by 1860 there were twenty-three different banks in existence, spread widely through the country,[4] but they were all small unit-banks whose aggregate capital was £1,319,000 and whose note issue was only £374,000. The next few decades were to bring about a

[1] CGH *Census, 1865*, p. 153.

[2] CGH *Blue Book, 1860*, p. CC 3.

[3] Ibid., pp. CC 2–3. Average prices of certain commodities were:

Bread (per lb.)	4½*d*.
Mutton (per lb.)	6½*d*.
Beef (per lb.)	6¼*d*.
Butter, fresh (per lb.)	2*s*. 0¾*d*.
Butter, salt (per lb.)	1*s*. 5¼*d*.
Tea (per lb.)	4*s*. 0¾*d*.
Coffee (per lb.)	1*s*. 1½*d*.
Brandy (per gallon)	6*s*. 5½*d*.
Milk (per bottle)	4¼*d*.
Shirts (labourers) (per dozen)	28*s*. 9¾*d*.
Shoes (per pair)	9*s*. 5¾*d*.
Jackets (each)	13*s*. 0¾*d*.
Trousers (per pair)	10*s*. 3¾*d*.

[4] There were five in Cape Town, two each in Port Elizabeth, Grahamstown, Graaff-Reinet, and Paarl, and ten others in the larger country towns. CGH *Blue Book, 1860*, p. Z 2.

reduction in the number of banks and greater consolidation and concentration through the advent of the so-called 'imperial' banks with
access to the London capital and money markets and operating a
system of branch banking.

Some 1,014 ships called at Cape ports in 1860 with an aggregate
tonnage of 330,000 tons, and the value of imports was £2,665,000 and
of exports £2,080,000 (of which wool accounted for 53 per cent).[1]

Inland transport was very primitive. South Africa lacked navigable
rivers, and in 1860 there were only two miles of railway, so that the ox-
wagon was still the main means of conveying merchandise. The condition of the roads evoked constant criticism, and the situation tended
to deteriorate as the traffic increased. The Chief Commissioner for
Roads reported that, as the inland districts were becoming an important
wool-producing area, the roads, which had been adequate for military
traffic, no longer sufficed for the large quantities of goods they were now
required to carry; and he stressed the need to adapt the roads for the
increasing volume of traffic.[2] Extensive railway construction was out of
the question for financial reasons. Total Government revenue for the
year 1860 was only £742,000 and expenditure £729,000,[3] and the
share of this available even for road maintenance was woefully inadequate.

The general character of the economy of the Colony was that of a
sparsely populated country largely engaged in pastoral farming and
self-subsistence agriculture, too poor to advance rapidly by domestic
capital formation, and lacking any exploitable resources to attract
foreign capital. Nevertheless some of the essential requirements for
further development were in process of creation. The economic impact
of international markets was carried into the interior, not in the wagons
of the Voortrekkers, but upon the backs of the merino sheep. It was a
slow process and a contemporary account of the movement of this
economic frontier into the northern Cape division of Colesberg in
1860 is worth quoting.[4]

The most striking circumstance is the great impetus given to the prosperity of the division by the introduction of the woolly-fleeced Merino as a
substitute for the heavy thick-tailed Cape sheep, a change which, although
the former was naturalized in the Colony upwards of 25 years ago, and ex-
tensively bred in parts of it a few years later, has been chiefly brought about
in this division during the last 10 years.

That the introduction of the Merino gave a great and permanent impulse

---

[1] CGH *Blue Book, 1860*: summary of customs returns.
[2] *Report of the Chief Commissioner of Roads, Cape of Good Hope, 1860.*
[3] CGH *Blue Book, 1860.*
[4] Ibid., p. JJ 39. Addendum: Extracts from reports of Civil Commissioners, Colesberg.

to the prosperity of the community is obvious. In the first place, then, wool more than doubled the farmers' income; and, being a ready-money transaction, gave him annually the command of a considerable amount of cash. In the next place, the purchase of imported stock for the improvement of his flock, the disposal of his clip of wool, and last though not least, the indulgence of the good wife's craving to invest some of the superfluous cash brought in by it in the various tempting articles of personal adornment and domestic refinement, which the well-filled *winkels* [shops] of the *dorp* [village] exhibit, brought him more frequently into contact with the inhabitants of the towns,—an intercourse which not only tended to enlighten his previous crude notions of the usages of civilized life, but greatly to benefit the trading portion of the community . . .

The value of landed property has increased rapidly since the introduction of Merino sheep into the division. Two farms have changed hands lately at 32s., and 33s. 4d., per morgen respectively, that ten years ago would have been considered well sold at 8s. . . .

Two pleasing events may be recorded which are pregnant with good for the future; and which with the new year is to be inaugurated: one is the establishment of a bank, and the other that of a newspaper; both of which will almost immediately be accomplished facts.

In the Cape Colony, trade, banking, transport, education, and market-oriented farming were gradually extended into the interior from the ports. Law and order were effectively maintained, except along the frontiers where unstable conditions impeded economic advance. The occupation of British Kaffraria under military government had done much to stabilize conditions on the eastern border; and, when Kaffraria was incorporated in the Cape in 1865, the Colony's boundary was extended to the Kei River. In the north the boundary lay along the Orange River. In this vast area of 160,000 square miles, the population of half a million persons was increasingly aware of a steady, if slow, advance in their economic circumstances.

A similar process was at work in Natal spreading out in the hinterland of Durban. Although the Natal Fire Assurance and Trust Company had been operating since 1849 as a deposit and lending institution, the first true bank—the Natal Bank—was opened in 1854 and was soon followed by several others. A visitor to Natal remarked in 1861 that:

We were impressed by what we saw. . . . Natal, though very much younger than some of the settled portions of South Africa, was already, in 1861, in the 'van' as regards material progress and was becoming an 'object lesson' to its older neighbours—the Cape Colony—in the enterprise and 'go' manifested by its people; for instance, in the employment of Steam power, and cultivation, for even in this year (1861) it could show a short line of Railway, running from the Town of Durban to the 'Point', and on this line it was a pleasure for us to travel; it had also made a good beginning in Tea and

Sugar production. . . . The country as a whole, and especially the larger Towns, was at the time of our visit showing signs of rapid advancement— some thought the people a little too go-a-head.[1]

The total population of Natal was, however, only about half that of the Cape Colony, and its white inhabitants numbered under 18,000 contrasted with ten times that number in the Cape.[2]

The presence of persons of European descent was an important, if not decisive, factor in promoting economic progress, when these people maintained political, cultural, and economic links with Europe;[3] for they provided a seed-bed where the imported innovations could be cultivated and acclimatized to the African environment. These innovations ranged from the biological theories of Darwin to modern methods of transport, from new educational techniques and the establishment of newspapers to joint-stock banking and the limited liability company, and from the application of power in the manufacturing process to the introduction of new skills and the organization of labour. Above all, it made Africa aware of advances in preventive and curative medicine for both man and beast. In the terminology of a later century, it can be said that although these African territories were poor and relatively undeveloped, in the Cape and parts of Natal, the 'preconditions for the take-off'[4] were effectively established by the 1860s, and further economic progress was impeded mainly by lack of capital and exploitable natural resources. Indeed, the Cape Colony was relatively well prepared to take full advantage of the mineral discoveries of the following decades.[5]

Elsewhere in southern Africa the situation was much less stable and unpropitious for economic progress. North of the Orange River the somewhat amorphous Orange River Sovereignty had given place to the Orange Free State without any precise demarcation of the frontiers between it and the territory of Moshweshwe or the areas occupied by the Griqua chiefs Adam Kok and Waterboer. Further north, beyond the Vaal River, the several small Boer republics, often in conflict with neighbouring tribes and notoriously ineffective in co-operating with

[1] W. W. Collins, *Free Statia*, pp. 187–8.

[2] Natal *Census, 1867*: total population, 278,806; whites, 17,836.

[3] The development of Natal with only 18,000 whites, but closely linked to Britain, contrasts strongly with the Free State and Transvaal with larger white populations, but lacking close ties with Europe.

[4] W. W. Rostow, *Stages of Economic Growth*, pp. 17, 35.

[5] C. G. W. Schumann makes this point in *Structural Changes and Business Cycles in South Africa*, pp. 36–7, where he writes '. . . with regard to an important part of the Cape Colony and to a lesser extent of Natal, there was essentially no sudden economic transformation after the discovery of gold and diamonds; it may be said that the *rate* of economic advance received a new stimulus in these parts, but the gradual economic transformation had started earlier, and the essential character of the economic system was not fundamentally altered after 1870.'

one another, finally achieved political unity by 1860, but administration in the South African Republic remained at a rudimentary level.

No accurate information is available about the population of these areas because the first official censuses did not occur until two or more decades later.[1] It may, however, be estimated that in the 1860s the white population of the Orange Free State was about 25,000,[2] and that of the Transvaal between 25,000 and 30,000,[3] making the total white population north of the Orange River not much more than 50,000. No figures of the African population of the Transvaal and the Orange Free State are available.

The Orange Free State was more advanced than the Transvaal, because those economic forces which were seen to be transforming the district of Colesberg were also having an influence in the Free State, but they had not significantly penetrated beyond the Vaal. In the early 1850s fairly rapid advance had taken place as immigrants from the Cape Colony came in. The abandonment of the Sovereignty in 1854 was a considerable economic setback, but Bloemfontein had acquired a high school[4] and a newspaper.[5] The British garrison withdrew, but the merino sheep continued to advance: wool production increased from about 50 bales in 1850 to 5,000 bales (valued at £50,000) in 1856.[6] Farmers had much to contend with. 'The large number of wolves, wild dogs and jackals, which infested the country were a very serious evil to the stock farmers.'[7] The mail from Bloemfontein to the Cape Colony and abroad had to be dispatched before 4 p.m. lest the post-riders on their way to Colesberg be attacked by lion which roamed freely in the neighbourhood of the capital.[8] Farmers on the eastern border complained of ·repeated stock theft, and similar accusations against the Free Staters were made by Moshweshwe: both complaints appear to have been well founded. A Free State police force was established in 1862 but was too small to maintain effective control of the frontier, numbering, as it did, only twenty-five men,[9] and cattle raids and retaliatory forays developed into war.

Trade and commerce were advancing slowly and some Cape banks

---

[1] OFS *Census, 1880*. Total population, 133,518; white, 61,022. SAR *Census, 1890*: whites only, 119,128; *Census, 1892*: other than whites, 649,560.

[2] E. A. Walker, *A History of South Africa*, p. 352, gives a figure of 15,000 in 1854. M. H. de Kock, *Selected Subjects in the Economic History of South Africa*, p. 139, gives 35,000 for 1865 but, commenting on this, Schumann says (p. 39) he thinks de Kock's figure too high.

[3] De Kock, p. 141, 30,000 in 1872: Walker, p. 352, 25,000 in 1854 and 40,000 in 1873.

[4] Grey College, established in 1856.

[5] *The Friend of the Orange Free State and Bloemfontein Gazette*, established by Messrs. Godlonton and White of Grahamstown in 1850 as *The Friend of the Orange River Sovereignty*.

[6] Collins, p. 84.   [7] Ibid., p. 17.   [8] Ibid., p. 16.

[9] Ibid., pp. 191–2. A force of 114 white men and 60 Coloured men had been authorized by the *Volksraad*, but, as an economy measure, this was reduced to a Commandant and 24 men.

had established agencies. British currency was introduced during the Sovereignty and circulated along with the rix-dollar (value 1s. 6d.), but the legal position was obscure. Two local banks were established in 1862, the Bloemfontein Bank and the short-lived Fauresmith Bank, and in the following year the London and South African Bank and the Standard Bank of South Africa opened branches in the Orange Free State. Conditions were, however, difficult; and in December 1864 the London and South African Bank closed its branch in Bloemfontein 'owing to the disturbed times and the risk of being commandeered against the Basutos'.[1] The Standard Bank had come into competition and conflict with the Bloemfontein Bank and, after a *Volksraad* resolution prohibiting foreign banks from operating in the Orange Free State except under various restrictive provisions, it too withdrew from operations in the territory in 1868.[2] The war against Moshweshwe strained the Republic's resources to the limit, and the *Volksraad* borrowed from the Bloemfontein Bank, and issued paper money to meet the public deficit of £42,948, when the accounts for 1866 showed expenditure of £106,477 as against revenue of £63,529.[3] The small size of the annual national budget was indicative of the low administrative level of the country.

The self-subsistence character of much of the economic activity presented grave fiscal difficulties because it made direct taxation well-nigh impossible. Customs revenue was a major support of government in the Cape and Natal, where it could be collected cheaply and effectively at the ports, but the long land frontiers of the inland states made this source of revenue impracticable. Repeated requests from the republics for a *pro rata* share of the customs levied at the ports were brushed aside by the seaboard colonies, which were well aware of their strong strategic position; but their action was short-sighted and lacking in statesmanship, for it generated an ill will and mistrust which militated against subsequent attempts to unify South Africa.[4] The difficulties of creating a modern administrative machine without trained staff or adequate finance proved almost insuperable in both the Orange Free State and the Transvaal.

The extension of white rule in southern Africa drastically reduced the areas of independent African occupation, and this had important

[1] E. H. D. Arndt, *Banking and Currency Development in South Africa*, p. 309.

[2] Ibid., pp. 305–17; also G. T. Amphlett, *History of the Standard Bank of South Africa*, pp. 49–54.   [3] Arndt, p. 74.

[4] See Collins, pp. 178–9: 'The question naturally occurs here to the dispassionate reader, would it not have been better, and more honourable, in this enlightened age, for our big overgrown neighbour to have dealt fairly towards us, by handing over to the young and struggling State, her legitimate share of those duties,—by so doing, to help us establish a more stable administration.'

consequences for the traditional economy. (See I, 252–6, 416–46.) Contact between black and white had two aspects: the competitive and the co-operative,[1] but during the first half of the nineteenth century competition was uppermost because white and black were both primarily stock farmers. Except in the neighbourhood of the ports, intensive agriculture was impossible owing to the lack of a domestic market and inadequate transport. General economic development was slow, and employment opportunities to match the growing population were lacking because the labour requirements of the staple export, wool, were limited to a few shepherds. Hence the bitterness of the conflict over land, and the insatiable land-hunger of both white and black graziers. The co-operative aspect associated with expanding labour requirements, which later played such a vital role in drawing together people of all races in the creation of a modern economy, was largely dormant before the 1860s, and had to await the advent of wholly new production functions of large-scale mining and manufacturing activities. Experiments with new crops like tea, cotton, and sugar were made in Natal; and, when the last-named proved successful, expansion was limited by the inability to secure labour. The Africans showed little desire to accept wage-employment, and Indians were imported as indentured workers on the sugar plantations. Thus the rise of the sugar industry, instead of drawing Africans into the modern market-oriented economy, merely added a new racial element to the South African scene.

In the 1860s the economic auspices were far from favourable. The 'Imperial Factor' was in temporary retreat, and the British Government reluctant to spend money on a poor and struggling outpost of the Empire. The prospect of the opening of the Suez Canal caused apprehension to farmers and merchants in the Cape and Natal, who feared a major decline in shipping which would affect their revictualling trade with ships travelling between Europe and the Orient.[2] The price of wool, South Africa's major export, slumped after the end of the American Civil War. There was a recession in Britain in 1866; and in South Africa the prosperity of the fifties gave place to depression, highlighted by the crisis of 1865 with its bankruptcies and bank failures. A serious drought had affected the greater part of the country. South Africa appeared to have little to offer save toil and sweat, and the number of persons leaving the country exceeded the number arriving. This was the state of affairs when the economic prospects of southern Africa were suddenly transformed by spectacular mineral discoveries.

---

[1] For a brilliant development of this theme see H. M. Robertson, '150 Years of Economic Contact between Black and White', *SAJE*, 1934 and 1935.

[2] That the Jeremiahs were confounded is seen from Fig. 1.

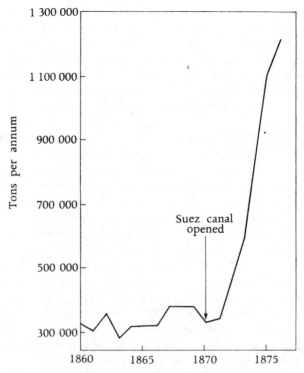

FIG. 1. Inward Shipping at Cape Ports, 1860–75.
Source: *Statistical Register: Colony of Cape of Good Hope; 1886*, p. vi.

2. *The Mining Revolution, 1866–1918*

Minerals had been worked by the indigenous African peoples for centuries (see Vol. I, Ch. IV), but their operations were essentially small-scale.[1] A belief that fabulous mineral wealth existed in southern Africa played a part in stimulating Portuguese exploration, and after van Riebeeck's landing the quest for minerals continued. Several centuries of white occupation of southern Africa failed to elicit any significant mineral deposits capable of economic exploitation. The economy, therefore, continued to rest upon a foundation of extensive ranching on the relatively unpropitious veld. A copper mine was

[1] Comparison of scale between different cultures and different centuries presents real difficulty. Thus R. Summers in his article in *JAH*, 1961, p. 1, 'The Southern Rhodesian Iron Age', suggests that mining operations were carried on for a period of 1,500 years before the European impact in the nineteenth century, and that there were more than 3,000 workings, some of which reached a depth of 100 feet. How is this to be compared with modern mining to depths of over 10,000 feet? Is it fantastic to suggest that one week's mining operation in 1965 might equal the whole output during the 1,500 years of the Rhodesian Iron Age?

opened at Springbokfontein in the north-west Cape in 1852[1] but, although it gave rise to a speculative boom, it made little difference to the basic economic structure of the country. Coal was found in Natal in the 1840s, and in the north-eastern Cape in the 1850s, but lack of transport prevented its exploitation.[2] By the 1860s auriferous formations were known to be present north of the Vaal, and a feverish search for gold began at Tati, Lydenburg, and elsewhere.

It was the discovery of diamonds, however, which triggered off the mineral revolution. After a diamond had been found near the Orange River in 1867, diggers poured into Griqua territory, and alluvial workings sprang up along the Orange and Vaal rivers. Then, three years later, diamonds were found at the site where Kimberley now stands, and miners in their thousands flocked to what were described as the 'dry diggings'. When it was discovered that the 'blue ground' of some volcanic pipes was diamondiferous, and that the precious stones were to be secured by mining in depth, this was something wholly new in the world's experience of diamond recovery, and meant that diamonds had ceased to be merely a fortune-hunter's gamble, but had become the stable foundation for a large-scale modern industry. Although gold was subsequently to overshadow diamonds, the oft-quoted words of the Colonial Secretary when he laid one of the earliest stones on the table of the Cape House of Assembly in 1867[3]—'Gentlemen, this is the rock on which the future success of South Africa will be built'—were no mere rhetoric, but a sober statement of fact. Within five years over £1,600,000 worth of diamonds was being exported annually, and during the following century no less than £700,000,000 worth of diamonds was recovered.

From being a forgotten no-man's-land inhabited by a few hundred Griqua under their chief Waterboer, Griqualand suddenly became a focus of world interest. Within a few years there were some 45,000 on the diggings[4] which represented a concentration of population second only to Cape Town, although totally lacking those amenities usually associated with an urban area.[5] Sovereignty over the area was in dispute and administration was almost non-existent[6] until a British magistrate

[1] De Kock, p. 265.

[2] A Select Committee found that it cost twice as much to transport coal forty miles overland to Durban as to bring it 7,000 miles by sea from Britain. L. Knowles, *Economic Development of the Overseas Empire*, iii. 217.

[3] *Cape of Good Hope: House of Assembly Annexure* 126, 1867, 'message on discovery of diamonds'. Quoted in Knowles, iii. 204, and in S. H. Frankel, *Capital Investment in Africa*, p. 52.

[4] 'Population thought to be 15,000 whites, 10,000 coloured and 20,000 natives', Knowles, iii. 206. A lesser figure of 'about 18,000' is given by S. van der Horst, *Native Labour in South Africa*, p. 86.

[5] For a vivid description of conditions in the early days see J. W. Matthews, *Incwadi Yami or Twenty Years Personal Experience in South Africa*, pp. 131 ff.

[6] The diggers had set up their own independent government and elected a former seaman

was appointed in 1870 and the territory annexed by Britain in 1871. It was incorporated in the Cape Colony in 1880. Whatever the moral and legal rights of the case, it was economically advantageous that the diamond fields should come under British control for this facilitated the forging of economic ties with the Cape Colony, which was, administratively, the most advanced territory in southern Africa.

For the general economic advance of the country as a whole, it was fortunate that the diamond fields (like the Witwatersrand discoveries which followed later) lay deep in the interior of the continent, since in the process of developing the necessary infra-structure for the mines, large areas of southern Africa were opened up to trade and commerce.

The importance of the diamond discovery lies in its effects upon the whole economic structure of the country. Diamond-mining provided a new source of wealth which dramatically altered the pattern of economic life by offering lucrative employment, other than in agriculture, to people of all races: the lure of diamonds attracted both capital and immigrants; the concentration of people on the diggings required food, and a new market was opened to the farmer; new forms of transport became essential, and the revenue from diamonds helped to finance railway construction. The consequential changes are, however, more appropriately discussed later for they were reinforced by gold-mining and together these minerals transformed the economy of southern Africa.

The immediate effect was to lift the Cape out of the recession of the 1860s and the newly found prosperity facilitated the granting of responsible government in 1872. There was a minor recession in 1876–7,[1] but optimism again prevailed in spite of disturbing political events. The Anglo-Boer War of 1880–1[2] together with a reaction to over-extension of credit and excessive speculation in diamond-mining shares, led to a crisis in 1881, followed by a general depression in South Africa from 1882 to 1886, described by Schumann as 'the most severe South Africa had to endure during the 19th century'.[3] The situation was intensified by recession in England and America, which illustrated the growing inter-dependence between South Africa and the world's commodity and money markets.

In the diamond-mining industry itself major technical difficulties had been encountered. Large numbers of individual claim-holders, who could operate satisfactorily on alluvial diggings, were wholly unsuited to undertake operations involving deep-level mining. This was obvious

of Her Majesty's Navy, Stafford Parker, as president, but its effectiveness was limited. See Walker, p. 342, and Collins, pp. 280 ff.

[1] For details see Schumann, pp. 81–2.
[2] Usually referred to by Afrikaans writers as 'The First War of Independence'.
[3] C. G. W. Schumann, pp. 84 ff.

to all, but Kimberley had drawn together men of quite exceptional financial and administrative genius. After the epic struggle for power between Cecil Rhodes and Barney Barnato,[1] De Beers Consolidated Mines Ltd. finally emerged to reorganize mining as a highly capitalized and concentrated modern industry, employing the latest scientific techniques, and establishing a world monopoly of sales through the London Diamond Syndicate. Kimberley was in the nature of a dress rehearsal for the Witwatersrand, and the financial strength and mining experience acquired at Kimberley were available to tackle the much greater technical difficulties of gold-mining in the Transvaal.

After five years of recession, the Witwatersrand was proclaimed a gold-mining area in 1886, and the whole of southern Africa was drawn into the new mining boom which exceeded anything yet experienced. It soon became clear that the Witwatersrand was no mere flash in the pan, but was a huge auriferous formation, although few at that time would have believed that after eighty years some of the mines would still have been in production, and that the Witwatersrand would have yielded a total of over £6,000 million worth of gold. The Witwatersrand lay deep in the Transvaal, the poorest, most backward, and administratively least competent of the four white territories. Great technical difficulties had to be overcome. The gold content of the ore was extremely low by international comparison with other gold-mining areas, and the highest technical and administrative skills were necessary to render it a paying proposition. The value of large-scale mining units had been learned at Kimberley, and the 'group system', whereby a financial 'house' controlled a number of mines, soon developed; and it gave financial strength and higher quality technical knowledge than a single mine could have obtained on its own. Deep-level mining encountered many difficulties—heat, dust, ventilation, water-disposal, so that underground engineering and ore recovery called for the application of scientific knowledge on a vast scale. The story of how the difficulties were one by one overcome is an epic of applied science, of which perhaps the most important single event was the introduction of the MacArthur-Forrest cyanide process of gold recovery.

Moreover, the provision of the infra-structure for a modern industry in a wholly undeveloped area called for organizational abilities of the first order. Labour, housing, water, power, and transport—all these had to be developed from scratch. Coal deposits were conveniently located near the gold-mines, and coal-mining was developed to supply the power for deep-level gold-mining and for the railways.

Foreigners poured into the Transvaal, and Johannesburg rose mushroom-like almost overnight. These *uitlanders* with their foreign capital

[1] L. Michell, *Cecil John Rhodes*, i, chs. 5, 6.

developed the gold-mining industry at great speed and, by 1888, forty-four mines were in operation with a nominal capital of £6,800,000 and a gold output worth £1,300,000 per annum.[1] This huge influx of foreigners and foreign capital (most of it British) was seen by the Transvaalers as a threat to their newly regained independence and their traditional way of life. They believed that the British, and Cecil Rhodes in particular, had set covetous eyes upon their wealth, and they welcomed friendly advances from Holland and Germany. Their improved financial position enabled them to negotiate for a railway to Delagoa Bay which, besides being a shorter line to the coast, would free them of their bondage to the Cape and Natal ports. After 1886, customs tariffs, railway freight rates, and political and military strategy were closely linked.[2]

The foreign miners, with a variety of international experience behind them, found the Transvaal administration inefficient, obscurantist, and sometimes corrupt, and some resented the franchise laws which precluded the majority of them from participation in the government of the country. The mining companies found the system by which the state granted monopoly rights to manufacturers most irksome and particularly resented the dynamite concession.

However, the gold boom continued up to 1889 when, initiated by a stock-market collapse in which Transvaal shares on the London Stock Exchange shed over half their value, a banking crisis, followed by general recession, engulfed South Africa.[3] Renewed proposals for a customs union came to naught, but gold-mining continued to expand and by 1890 was employing over 100,000 men.

In 1892 the railway from the Cape ports reached the Transvaal, and the Netherlands South African Railway Company established the link with Delagoa Bay in 1895. Railway competition became intense,[4] and economic and political forces became fused in the *Realpolitik* which led up to the Anglo-Boer war of 1899–1902. Because the Republic favoured the development of traffic through Delagoa Bay, the reduction in the Cape rates was counteracted by higher charges on the Transvaal section of the line to the Cape. Attempts by the Cape to circumvent the higher railway rates by using ox-wagon transport from the Vaal River to Johannesburg, were frustrated by the closing of the drifts across the river. The Reform Committee was formed in Johannesburg to press the claims of the *uitlanders* in 1895, and Jameson invaded the Transvaal in December of the same year. Milner arrived as High Commissioner

[1] De Kock, p. 247.

[2] For a scholarly analysis of this see J. van der Poel, *Railway and Customs Policies in South Africa 1885–1910*.

[3] Schumann, pp. 88–91.   [4] Van der Poel, chs. IV, V. and VI.

in 1897, and war broke out two years later. These events are described elsewhere (Chapter VI).

The immediate results of the outbreak of war were the almost complete cessation of gold-mining, and the disruption of farming in the Republics due to the absence of the men on military service. In contrast, the Cape and Natal experienced hectic prosperity, and the inflationary effects of British expenditure on maintaining an army of a quarter of a million men in Africa. Exports from the Cape and Natal ports fell from £26 million in 1898 to £9 million and £12 million in 1900 and 1901 respectively. Imports, however, increased from £22 million in 1898 to £23 million and £31 million in 1900 and 1901.[1] Towards the end of the war Kitchener's attempts to combat guerrilla warfare by a scorched-earth policy led to the wholesale destruction of farms, and the situation of farmers and their families in the subjugated Transvaal and Orange River Colony was desperate at the conclusion of hostilities in 1902.

At the end of the war there was a short period of boom, and capital and immigrants poured in. Over 114,000 people landed in South Africa in the two years after hostilities ceased, but recession came in 1903.

Milner tackled the problem of rehabilitation with his usual energy and ability, but he soon realized that, in spite of a British loan of £35 million for reconstruction, little progress could be made until the gold-mines were back in production. The labour force of 119,000 in 1899 had vanished: the 12,000 white miners had been absorbed into the war efforts of one or other of the belligerents, as were some of the 107,000 African miners, the remainder having retired to their homes in the country. The labour situation in 1902 was critical as the demand for labour for public works, railways, the reconstruction of the farms, and mining far exceeded the supply.[2] It was found possible to muster 10,000 white miners, but only 45,000 Africans, or less than half the number employed in 1899. In desperation Milner decided upon the importation of indentured Chinese workers:[3] and, by 1906 the mines were in full production with a labour force of 163,000 (18,000 whites, 94,000 Africans, and 51,000 Chinese).

The depression continued, however, and lasted till 1909 because of the problems of rehabilitating the farming areas of the Transvaal and the Orange River Colony, and because of the difficulties of reaching agreement on railways and customs. Moreover the world trade recession of 1907 retarded recovery.[4] 'The Cape and Natal had hoped that the establishment of British rule in the Transvaal would see an end to the

[1] De Kock, p. 122.
[2] *Report of Transvaal Labour Commission, Majority Report* (Cd. 1896), 1904, para. 101.
[3] *The Milner Papers*, C. Headlam (ed.), ii. 458.   [4] Schumann, p. 96.

privileged treatment given to the Portuguese harbour and railway by Kruger's Government', but Milner was faced with a grave labour shortage for his reconstruction programme, and the Portuguese intimated that recruitment of African labour would be permitted only if the railway and harbour privileges were continued. Milner therefore had no choice but to renew the agreement for a further term, although his action angered the Cape and Natal, and led to a renewal of the commercial rivalry which had been so strong before the war.[1]

The railways of the Transvaal and the Orange River Colony had been united in a single system—the Central South African Railways— in the hope that this would ease the general railway problem by loosening the Transvaal ties with Delagoa Bay and giving it a greater interest in the other ports. After preliminary negotiations in 1902, conferences on customs tariffs and railways met in Bloemfontein in 1903 where all four colonies, Rhodesia, and Mozambique were represented. The railway conference revealed the deep cleavage between the Cape, Natal, and the Portuguese, and it was saved from breaking up in disorder only through the personal intervention of Lord Milner; and a tentative agreement, subject to review a year later, was reluctantly accepted. The customs conference found the going somewhat easier, and a customs union embracing the Cape, Natal, the Transvaal, the Orange River Colony, Rhodesia, and the High Commission Territories[2] was brought into being.

Before six months had elapsed the railway agreement ran into difficulties and protracted and unfruitful negotiations led to increased tensions.[3] The prospect of the granting of responsible government to the Transvaal made a settlement more urgent as the coastal colonies feared the resurgence of the Transvaal–Mozambique alliance of before the war. Natal gave notice to withdraw from the customs union, and a conference was hurriedly called in 1906. Here complete breakdown, which might have led to war, was averted by the intervention of the High Commissioner, Lord Selborne, who had succeeded Lord Milner. He secured an unstable compromise, and hammered home the realities of the situation in a memorandum on the Relations of the Colonies,[4] namely that recent experience had shown conclusively that agreement on customs and railway tariffs could never be reached save within a political association of the four territories. In the political negotiations leading to Union (described in Chapter VII) the economic rivalries and tensions that had arisen from the attempted separate development

---

[1] Van der Poel, pp. 108–10.

[2] The present Lesotho, Botswana, and Swaziland.

[3] Van der Poel, pp. 126–45.

[4] *A Review of the present mutual relations of the British South African Colonies to which is appended a memorandum on South African Railway Unification and its effect on Railway Rates.* Cd. 3564, 1907.

of the four territories played no small part. Advocates of Union were able to cite incontrovertible examples of the disasters of separation, and to advance cogent economic arguments in support of closer association. For example:

The evils of today—the inefficiency and extravagance of four Governments doing the work of one, racialism and inter-colonial bitterness, inequality in fiscal burdens and railway rates, the spectacle of South Africa thwarted in her endeavour to grapple with her most essential problems because she cannot command herself—these evils will disappear if the Constitution is carried.[1]

Union, when it came in 1910, did not unfortunately include the whole customs union, but only the Cape, Natal, the Transvaal, and the Free State. Nevertheless it provided a single political entity of 471,000 square miles and a common market of almost six million people[2] which were of the greatest significance in the subsequent industrial development of South Africa. Rhodesia and the High Commission Territories did not join the Union, although the Act had made provision for this possibility. They did, however, remain members of the customs union so that there was free movement of goods throughout the whole area.

The new state was hardly able to get into its stride when the First World War occurred. This tested its political foundations, but they stood firm. Economically the war stimulated industrial advance because shipping difficulties restricted importation during the war, and local manufacture of many goods previously imported was undertaken. Moreover the common market area was considerably extended. South African troops had conquered German South West Africa, and in the peace settlement this territory was allotted to the Union as a 'C' class mandate (i.e. to be administered as an integral part of the mandatory country). South West Africa thus became part of the customs union.

The war was followed by a short period of boom, but this soon gave place to difficult economic conditions during the nineteen-twenties, which will be considered in the next section of this chapter. A review of the major structural changes in the South African economy that occurred between 1860 and 1920 should first be attempted.

The most obvious change was the broadening of the economic base from being almost entirely agricultural to one in which mining played at least an equal part. Diamonds, gold, and coal had all become major industries and, although no estimates of the national product are available for the earlier years, the change in the structure of the economy is clearly illustrated by the graph of South African exports (1860 to

[1] *The State*, vol. i, no. 4 (1909), p. 362.
[2] Population of the Union: 5,972,757 (*Census*, May 1911).

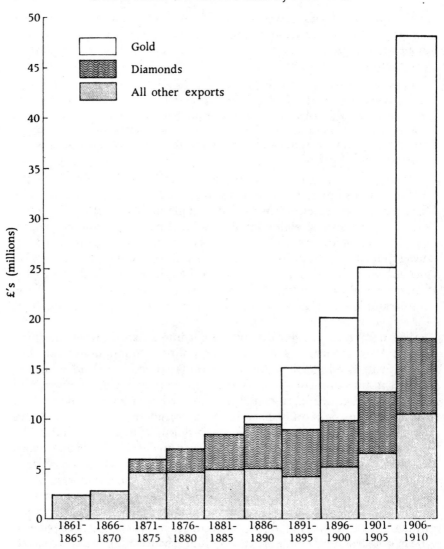

FIG. 2. Exports of South African Produce 1861–1910 (Average for five-year period).

1910) above, where the contribution of gold and diamonds stands out clearly. In 1912, over a quarter of the national product was derived from mining. Of an estimated total net national product of £133 million, £36 million (or 27·1 per cent) came from mining, £23 million (or 17·4 per cent) from agriculture, and manufacturing was a poor third at £9 million (or 6·7 per cent). Moreover, ever since the discovery of diamonds, mining had been the leading sector of the whole economy of southern Africa and much of the expansion in agriculture, manufacturing, and tertiary activities like trade, transport, and banking was induced by the growth of the mining sector.

During the fifty years from 1862 to 1912 the number of persons employed in mining had risen from practically zero to 325,000 and they formed the first large body of wage-paid workers in the country. The majority of the 36,000 white miners had been born outside South Africa and had come from Britain, Australia, the United States, Germany, and elsewhere; but many South Africans too had been drawn off the land to work on the mines. The Chinese, once numbering over 50,000, had all been repatriated. The bulk of the miners—285,000 Africans—were drawn from all parts of southern Africa: from the Transvaal, Natal, and the Cape, from the mountains of Basutoland, the plains of Bechuanaland, and from Swaziland. Many also came from further north in Nyasaland and the Rhodesias. The white miners were permanent, but the Africans were migratory workers doing their stint of six to eighteen months and then returning home. Thus over the years the actual number of Africans who had worked on the mines was far larger than the number at a given time, and the influence of *Egoli* (the African name for Johannesburg) penetrated into the remotest corners of southern Africa. This mass confrontation of the traditional African with urban life and modern industry is probably the most important cultural, social, and economic consequence of the mineral discoveries.

Although the need for more modern transport facilities was widely proclaimed in the 1860s the economic realities of railway construction in a vast territory with a sparse population engaged in stock-farming deterred even the most foolhardy. If one were to build a railway, where would it go? All areas except in the immediate vicinity of Cape Town and Durban were likely to prove unremunerative. With the advent of Kimberley and Johannesburg, railway construction had a specific destination, an economic *raison d'être*, and a good prospect of raising the necessary finance, but the distances were so great[1] that private enterprise was reluctant to undertake it. Railway construction and operation thus became state functions at an early stage in both the Cape and Natal. In the 1870s railway construction commenced from Cape Town, Port Elizabeth, East London, and Durban, all lines heading for the diamond fields; and after 1886 they were pushed on to the Witwatersrand as rapidly as possible. De Kock shows the rate of new railway construction by decades:[2]

---

[1] Cape Town to Kimberley 647 miles, and to Johannesburg 957 miles, with little prospect of picking up remunerative traffic *en route*.
[2] De Kock, p. 351.

1860–69	68 miles
1870–79	781 miles
1880–89	1,065 miles
1890–99	2,046 miles
1900–09	2,977 miles
1910–19	2,605 miles.

This gives a total of over 9,500 miles of railway opened during these sixty years, and the greater part of the construction was the direct consequence of the mineral discoveries. During the periods of rapid construction large numbers of skilled and unskilled workers were employed on railway-building, and this added significantly to the process of adaptation from farming to industrial employment, but it was never of the same magnitude as mining. Road construction too made rapid strides, especially in the matter of bridges, fords, and the cutting of mountain passes, but in the open veld the ox-wagons were often left free to find their own way, and hillsides scarred by a score or more parallel, abandoned roads are still visible in aerial photographs. Before the railway reached Kimberley and the Witwatersrand millions of tons of food and mining equipment were transported from the ports by ox-wagon, and thousands of South Africans of all races were employed in transport-riding. This played a very important role in the transformation of farming, because it drew the landless away from the land, and indeed some landowners as well, for good money was to be made if one could gather together sufficient capital to purchase a wagon and a span of oxen. When the railways reached the mining centres these people were destitute, and this contributed to the problems of rural poverty and the migration to the towns. On the more positive side, however, many country folk, impressed by the fantastic prices paid for food[1] in the mining area, adapted their farming to satisfy this vast new market. In the development of farming (see Chapter III) a major role was played by mining, both by creating these urban concentrations and by stimulating the improved transport which, though initially created for the mines, was also available for carrying farm produce to the inland towns and to the ports for export.

At the end of the First World War South Africa had 47,000 miles of proclaimed provincial roads[2] and many more miles of what were described as 'farm roads'. The former were generally of sound construction although the surface left much to be desired. Bituminous roads did not make their appearance until motor transport became more generally used.

---

[1] Collins, p. 310, states that butter in Bloemfontein in 1873 was 8s. 1d. per lb.; and Matthews, p. 132, states that on the diggings cauliflowers fetched £1 each.

[2] *Union Statistics for Fifty Years*, p. O-17.

There had been some manufacturing activity from earliest times, but most African utensils such as mats and pots were handcrafts until well on in the nineteenth century; and many things used on the farms like candles, soap, clothes, and rough shoes were home-made. (Figures of manufacturing concerns in the Cape in 1860 are given at p. 2.) Little real advance in manufacturing activity could be expected before urban concentrations of population had come to provide a worthwhile market. Mining activity provided just such a market; and the manufacture of dynamite, certain mining equipment, and miners' boots soon made an appearance. There were other factories of importance[1] but, in general, it is true that mining absorbed so much of the capital, skilled labour, and entrepreneurial ability that the development of manufacturing took place on a large scale only after the First World War had given an initial impulse in this direction.

The population of southern Africa increased very rapidly as a result of the mining. It is not possible to give accurate figures because, except in the Cape and Natal, no census had been taken in the 1860s. Natural increase was probably high and very considerable immigration, far exceeding anything experienced in the past, occurred. Whites came from overseas, and Africans from all neighbouring countries in the southern part of the continent, both attracted by the economic opportunities offered at Kimberley and on the Witwatersrand. By 1918 there were nearly half a million employed in industrial activities of whom 80,000 were white workers, the remainder being African or Coloured.

Industrial Employment in 1918

	White workers	All workers
Mining[2]	32,000	291,000
Private Manufacturing[3]	44,000	124,000
Railways[4]	35,000	72,000
Total	111,000	487,000

When diamonds and gold were first discovered, skilled workers were scarce and high wages had to be offered to attract immigrants from abroad; unskilled labour was relatively plentiful at rates of pay set by the opportunity cost of their earnings in agriculture. This was only a small fraction of the rate necessary to secure skilled workers. Thus a wide disparity between the earnings of skilled and unskilled arose

[1] See H. Schauder, 'The Chemical Industry in South Africa before Union (1910)', *SAJE*, 1946, p. 277.
[2] *Union Statistics for Fifty Years*, p. G-4.   [3] Ibid., p. G-6.   [4] Ibid., p. G-15.

initially in response to the economic forces of supply and demand, the wages of unskilled being somewhere between 10 and 20 per cent of those of skilled. The wage structure in mining tended to be carried over to other industrial activities. One might have expected that this disparity would have tended to disappear in the course of time as unskilled workers acquired new skills. This has not been the case. Initially skilled workers were mostly white, and unskilled were Coloured or African, and for a variety of reasons this racial division has been perpetuated. Various obstacles, some legislative, but up to 1918 mainly customary, made it difficult for any but white people to acquire skills. In the nineteen-twenties, however, the customary barriers were reinforced by legislation.[1]

Geographically, the main structural change was the shift of the centre of economic gravity from the ports to the Witwatersrand where the heavy population concentrations associated with the gold-mining industry soon provided the most important market in the country. This attracted new industries to this area, which in turn still further increased the wealth and population of the southern Transvaal. Initiated by diamond-mining and gold-mining, economic advance gathered momentum from the mid sixties up to the end of the First World War, and the achievement was the more remarkable in view of the unpropitious political environment in a divided sub-continent almost continuously engaged in war. In almost half of the fifty-three years from 1865 to 1918, war, rebellion, or annexation of territory was recorded.[2] In spite of this, population, wealth, and living standards increased greatly.

3. *The Unstable Years, 1919–1932*

The short post-war boom was followed by a slump in 1922. Then came five years of slow recovery, but in 1928 the forces of world recession reversed this trend. Over this period as a whole there was no economic progress; and, as seen from Fig. 3 below, the national income in 1932 differed little from what it had been in 1919. Population had, however, increased, so that *per capita* income actually declined (see Fig. 4). Unfavourable economic conditions were fairly general throughout the world. The international economy had been shattered by the war, and attempts to rebuild it were only partly successful. Even the restoration of the international gold standard failed to bring stability,

---

[1] For an analysis of this process and its effect see van der Horst, *Native Labour in South Africa;* and G. V. Doxey, *The Industrial Colour Bar in South Africa.*

[2] Some of the wars and rebellions were: 1864–6 Sotho, 1876 Pedi, 1877–8 Gcaleka–Ngqika, 1878–9 Zulu, 1880 Sotho, 1881 Anglo-Boer, 1893 Ndebele, 1896 Ndebele and Shona, 1895 Jameson raid, 1899–1902 Anglo-Boer, 1906 Zulu rebellion, 1914–1918 First World War.

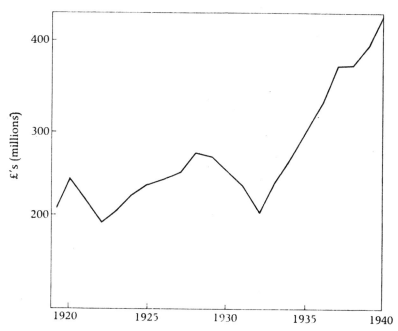

FIG. 3. Net National Income at Factor Cost, 1920–40.
Source: *Union Statistics for Fifty Years*, p. S–3.

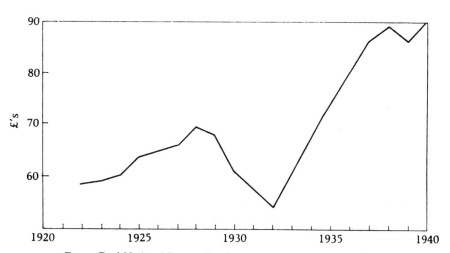

FIG. 4. Real National Income *Per Capita*, 1920–40 (at 1958–9 prices).
Source: *Union Statistics for Fifty Years*, p. S–6.

and international economic disintegration culminated in the Great
Depression with its world-wide repercussions. Some countries were
more severely affected than others, and the international impact was

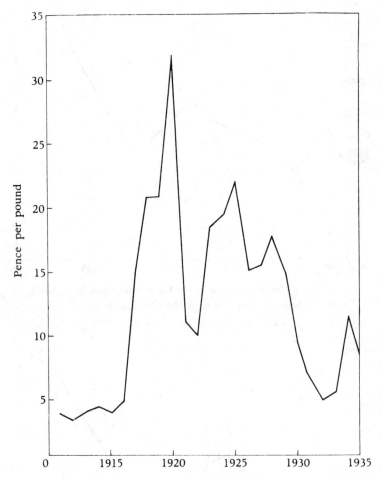

FIG. 5. Annual Average Price of South African Wool, 1912–35.
Source: *Union Statistics for Fifty Years*, p. I–26.

particularly severe on both South Africa's major economic sectors—
agriculture and gold-mining.

World prices of agricultural products fluctuated violently, and the
general trend was downward. The prices of wool, still South Africa's
major agricultural export, are shown in Fig. 5. In a single year between
1920 and 1921, the average price of wool fell from a peak of 32·9 pence
per pound to 10·7 pence, so that, assuming production to have been

unchanged, the farmers' incomes were reduced by two-thirds.[1] Prices rose in 1925 to 21·6 pence, only to fall again to 4·5 pence in 1932. Most other farm products showed similar price instabilities, and frustration and despair were widespread in the farming community. Moreover, it was generally the most progressive farmers who were worst affected, having turned from self-subsistence farming to market production. The less enterprising white farmers and the majority of the Africans, who still produced to satisfy directly the needs of their own households, were less affected by the fall in prices.

The low level of agricultural prices combined with the fact that the world prices of manufactured goods did not fall to anything like the same extent, changed the real terms of trade to the detriment of countries like South Africa, which exported primary products and received most of their manufactured goods from abroad. This stimulated a demand for greater diversification of the national economy, and gave rise, if not to positive economic nationalism, at least to a more critical view of the theory of free trade, which had up to then been adopted almost without question as part of the heritage of British ideas.

The price fluctuations are to be seen against a general background of rural impoverishment and frustration, for the 'poor white problem', as it was then called, was rising like a thundercloud and casting an ominous shadow across the political and economic landscape. Rural impoverishment was not solely the result of the instability in world prices for it had its roots in history. In part it was due to the difficult process of adapting farming methods to the requirements of a market economy (see Chapter III). But other elements too played a part— the effects of the destruction of farms in the Anglo-Boer war; the uneconomic sub-division of land, encouraged by the Roman-Dutch law of inheritance; the limited employment opportunities in urban areas; and the inadequacy of educational facilities for children on the farms.

Poor whites were estimated to number between 200,000 and 300,000[2] or about one in eight of the entire white population. Most of the poor whites were Afrikaners, and they were flocking to the towns without any training to fit them for employment in an urban environment, where they found they had to compete as unskilled labourers with Coloured and African workers. Moreover, mining, manufacturing, and commerce were at that time largely dominated by the English-speaking section, and Afrikaans-speakers were often at a disadvantage. In the country areas there was widespread poverty and discontent, which was being

---

[1] The fall in the aggregate value of wool sold was even greater, from £22·6 millions in 1920 to £5·2 millions in 1921. *Union Statistics for Fifty Years*, pp. 1–26.

[2] J. F. W. Grosskopf, *Rural Impoverishment and Rural Exodus*, pp. vii and viii.

carried into the towns, where the migrants found their situation as hopeless as it had been on the farms.

Urban society was in process of adapting itself to the sweeping industrial changes brought about by the growth of the mining industry. Even in relatively homogeneous European nations the industrial revolution had been accompanied by many difficulties of adjustment, and to these were added, in South Africa, the complications arising from the diverse cultural, linguistic, racial, and historical backgrounds of the people.

Industrial unrest had begun to show itself in 1913, when a series of strikes and disaffection among white workers culminated in a general strike. In the same year a young Indian lawyer, M. K. Gandhi, subsequently famous as Mahatma Gandhi, the liberator of India, called a general strike of all Indian workers in Natal which was conducted according to his philosophy of 'passive resistance'. After the 1914–18 war, industrial unrest was intensified, and an element of violence became manifest as strikes by both white and African workers increased in number. An all-African union, the Industrial and Commercial Workers Union, or I.C.U. as it was called, was launched by Clements Kadalie in 1920, and had a meteoric career. African strikers in Port Elizabeth were fired upon by white civilians, and the tragic affair at Bulhoek occurred in the next year. The Witwatersrand, however, became the focal point of the industrial unrest, and it was precipitated by Britain's monetary policy, as South Africa's currency was linked to sterling.

During the war the depreciation of sterling had raised the price of gold in South Africa, and the gold mines enjoyed a premium which reached 50 per cent above the statutory price of 85 shillings an ounce. In 1922 the British Government notified its intention to return to the gold standard *at the pre-war parity*. The mining companies were faced with a fall of about 35 per cent in the price of their product.[1] Costs, however, had risen, and it was estimated that, unless they could be reduced, 'twenty-four out of the thirty-nine producing mines, might be expected to make losses which would drive them to discharge 10,000 white miners and many thousands of blacks'.[2] The Chamber of Mines hoped to effect the necessary reduction of costs by increasing the ratio of black workers to white, for although the latter's wages had risen 60 per cent, African wages had increased only 9 per cent.[3]

It had always been the custom that skilled work was done by white

---

[1] In fact Britain did not reach the old parity until 1925, but knowing the intention, the Chamber of Mines had to prepare for a fall in the price of gold from the peak of £6·5 to the statutory gold-standard price of £4·248 per ounce.

[2] E. A. Walker, p. 584.   [3] Doxey, p. 124.

men, and this was reinforced by legislation when Chinese labourers were introduced under the Milner regime. The situation had been frozen for the duration of the war by the '*status quo* agreement', by which the Chamber of Mines agreed not to alter the over-all ratio of white to black workers. When, faced with the prospect of a fall in the price of gold, the Chamber gave notice to terminate the *status quo* agreement, the white miners reacted strongly. Anything looking like 'dilution' is always resented by skilled workers, and on the Witwatersrand, differences in colour, standards of living, and cultural background increased the white skilled workers' fears.

In protracted negotiations with the South African Industrial Federation, which represented the white miners, the Chamber offered a 1 to 10·5 ratio of white to black. This the Federation countered by demanding a ratio of 1 to 3·5, not only in gold-mining, but in all industries in the country. Negotiations broke down when in February 1922 the Action Group, some of whom were members of the Third International, seized control, armed the white miners and set up barricades. It was civil war, and the miners were in control of the greater part of the Witwatersrand. The army was called in and, by use of infantry, artillery, and aircraft, the Rand Rebellion was crushed after fierce fighting.[1] Four of the leaders were condemned to death, and went to the gallows singing 'The Red Flag'.[2] To the majority of the Labour Party there was nothing incongruous in communists calling upon the workers of the world to unite to protect the privileged position of the white workers, and the leader of the Party, Colonel F. H. Creswell, stated that he believed the white miners to be in the right in opposing the attempt to restrict 'the opportunities of civilized men to earn a living in the industries of the country'.[3]

The effect of rising costs and industrial strife on gold production is shown in Fig. 6. The miners returned to work, and gold production again increased, but the political consequences of the Rand Rebellion, and resentment at the harsh measures invoked to suppress it, together with the frustrations of the farmers and the mounting poor white population, led to the overthrow of the South African Party which had governed the country since 1910. The National Party led by General J. B. Hertzog, supported by republican-minded Afrikaners, with its strength mainly in the rural areas; and the Labour Party, mainly English-speaking and professedly socialist, with its membership drawn from skilled urban workers, formed an election pact, and came into power in 1924. Commenting on this Professor Eric Walker writes:[4]

[1] Casualties exceeded those in the whole South West Africa campaign. E. A. Walker, p. 586.
[2] I. L. Walker and B. Weinbren, *2000 Casualties*, p. 157.
[3] Ibid., p. 101.   [4] E. A. Walker, p. 599.

It was the end of a chapter. Men of British and Afrikaner stock stood shoulder to shoulder in the country, and sat together on either side of the house. The old 'racial' lines of division were cut clean across by the economic. The re-alignment of parties was a proof that the two sections of the Europeans had realized that the issues on which they had hitherto divided were as nothing to the issues raised by their contact with non-Europeans.

Whether the feud between Boer and Briton was indeed ended, or not, the new alignment certainly gave greater emphasis to economic forces

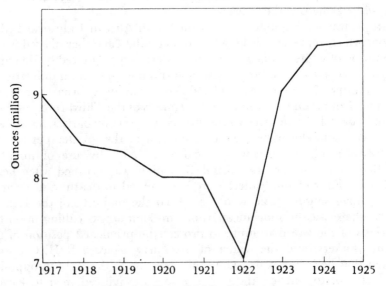

FIG. 6. South African Gold Production, 1917–25.
Source: *Union Statistics for Fifty Years*, p. K–4.

in the House of Assembly, and to an increasingly national orientation in commercial and trade policy. From the composition of its electoral support, the new government was under strong pressure to concern itself with three major issues: the plight of the farming community, the provision of jobs in towns for the poor whites, and the protection of the skilled white workers in mining and industry.

The Government embarked upon its task with energy and determination, and the next few years saw a series of far-reaching measures which influenced South Africa's economic development for many years to come. The gradual evolution of an agricultural policy based on farmers' co-operatives and a system of controlled marketing culminating in the Marketing Act[1] are described in Chapter III.

[1] Act No. 26, 1937.

The Government initiated positive state action to encourage the establishment of local manufacturing industries. In general, the intention was to give wider diversification to the national economy, and to reduce its heavy dependence upon the gold-mining industry, which from its very nature, was a wasting asset. Even as late as 1930, the Government Mining Engineer had estimated that under existing price and cost relationships, gold-mining would reach its peak in 1932, and thereafter decline fairly rapidly in importance. Manufacturing, it was hoped, could be developed to take its place in the national economy, and, more specifically, to provide a new field of employment for white men and women who were moving into the towns in such large numbers.

The Board of Trade and Industries, established in 1921, was reconstituted after the change of government, and protective duties were increased and extended to new commodities. A report of twenty years later[1] treats 1925 as an important landmark in the industrialization of South Africa. As in many countries embarking on industrialization it was the final stages of production which came first, and the new factories were mostly engaged in manufacturing final consumer goods from imported materials. Clothing factories used imported textiles, footwear factories obtained much of their leather from abroad, and the motor-car assembly works used imported components. The reasons for this lay in technical factors, in the size of the market, and in the relative capital requirements for the manufacture of consumer goods and intermediate products. An important exception to this was the iron and steel industry.

By 1920 there were several small iron and steel foundries using scrap-iron, and experiments in smelting South African ores had been successful. Attempts by private enterprise between 1920 and 1924 to amalgamate and form a large-scale iron and steel works using local ores failed for various reasons, but principally because of the difficulty in raising the necessary capital. The new government favoured the establishment of the industry under State auspices. After bitter controversy,[2] the Iron and Steel Corporation of South Africa (ISCOR) was established by Act of Parliament in 1928 as a public utility corporation in which the government held the controlling power. Subsequent history has proved the sceptics were wrong, and ISCOR has made an immense contribution to the industrial development of the country and has become the foundation for an expanding iron, steel, and engineering group of industries.

[1] Board of Trade and Industries, Report 282, *Investigation into Manufacturing Industries in the Union of South Africa*, 1945, para. 329.
[2] *House of Assembly Debates, 1927*, cols. 2091, 2160, 2164, 2681, 2854.

Employment in manufacturing increased by 26,000 from 115,000 in 1924/5 to 141,000 in 1928/9, but the advent of the world depression inhibited growth for the next few years. Nevertheless, the foundations had been laid for the rapid industrial development of the following decades. The policy initiated to combat white unemployment was so successful that by the later 1930s the 'poor white problem' had ceased to exist; indeed, industrialization was so great that it transcended its original purpose, and ever-increasing numbers of other racial groups were drawn to the cities. By 1966, the industrial labour force numbered over 1,000,000 of whom white people accounted for only a quarter.[1]

Returning to the Government's third major concern in 1924—the protection of the white skilled worker—action was soon taken. Legislative discrimination on the grounds of race had its origin in a Transvaal ordinance[2] designed to reassure the white miners that they would not be endangered by the importation of Chinese workers. An early Union statute had permitted discrimination on racial grounds in the mining industry.[3] After the events of 1922 the labour leaders demanded further protection for skilled labour, not only in the mines, but also in manufacturing industry; and three important Acts were passed. The first was the Industrial Conciliation Act of 1924[4] which set up machinery for consultation between employers' organizations and trade unions for the determination of wages and conditions of work by collective bargaining. Each industry had its Industrial Council and the Act also made provision for mediation and arbitration when employers' and employees' representatives might fail to reach agreement. It was an admirable piece of labour legislation in many respects, and it gave South Africa a remarkable degree of industrial peace and freedom from strikes. There was no overt reference to race in the Act, but the definition of an employee was such as to exclude the vast majority of African workers who therefore had no part in the consultative process which determined their wages and conditions of service.

The Wage Act[5] followed in the next year, and was complementary to the Industrial Conciliation Act; the latter applied to industries where employers and employees were organized, the former to industries which were not organized. The Wage Act established a Wage Board to recommend minimum wages and conditions of employment which, when approved by the Minister of Labour, had the force of law.

---

[1] *Statistical Year Book, 1966*, pp. H–33 and H–39.
[2] Ordinance 17 of 1904, 'To regulate the introduction into the Transvaal of unskilled non-European Labourers'. It was passed before the granting of responsible government while the Transvaal was still under British administration. It prohibited the employment of non-European immigrants in skilled jobs.
[3] The Mines and Works Act, No. 12, 1911.
[4] Act No. 11, 1924.   [5] Act No. 27, 1925.

The main deficiencies in the Wage Act machinery were administrative
— the time taken by the Board to make the necessary investigations,
and the lack of sufficient inspectors to ensure compliance with the
determinations.

The third Act was the Mines and Works Act Amendment Act of
1926, which reiterated and reinforced the principle of the original Act
of 1911, after certain regulations promulgated under it had been
declared *ultra vires* in the courts. The new Act firmly established the
principle of a colour bar in certain jobs in mining.

These three Acts were, of course, only a part of a wider legislative
and administrative framework,[1] which included the Native Labour
Regulation Act (1911), the Land Act (1913), various Natives (Urban
Areas) Acts; and in the administrative field, preference in the granting
of government contracts and tariff protection to firms employing a high
proportion of 'civilized labour'. The cumulative effect of these measures
has been analysed and discussed by many economists.[2] In the late
twenties and early thirties they undoubtedly gave some protection to
white workers at the expense of workers of other races, but the general
world recession was the major cause of the increasing poverty and
declining national income (see Fig. 3, and Fig. 4, p. 23) whose
impact affected workers of all races.

The Government was, however, so concerned with the poor-white
problem that little attention was paid to the poverty of other races.
The extent to which Africans had been drawn into the industrial
economy was not fully realized despite an excellent government
commission report,[3] and there was a widespread belief that if they were
thrown out of work in town they could always return to their subsistence economy in the country without suffering great hardship. This was
not the case even in the late 1920s, and it ignored the needs of Coloured
people and urbanized Africans.

In September 1931 the United Kingdom abandoned the gold
standard. Britain was at once followed by many other countries. South
Africa, however, decided to remain upon the gold standard,[4] and for a
further sixteen months endured the hardships inflicted by falling prices
and competition from countries whose currencies had been devalued,
until, at the end of 1932, the Government was forced by public opinion
to resign, and a coalition government came into power.

[1] The wider political framework as presented in Hertzog's bills of 1926 is dealt with in
Chapter VIII.

[2] e.g. van der Horst, *Native Labour in South Africa*, and in G. Hunter (ed.), *Industrialization
and Race Relations*; and G. V. Doxey, op. cit.

[3] *Report of Economic and Wage Commission*, U.G. 14, 1926.

[4] For reasons see *Report of Select Committee on the Gold Standard*, S.C.-9, 1932.

4. *The Making of a Modern Industrial Economy, 1933–1965*

The abandonment of the gold standard immediately reversed the downward trend in the economy, and gold-mining once again provided a powerful upward thrust.[1] It initiated a long period of almost uninterrupted prosperity which, even after thirty-two years, showed no sign of abating. There were a few hesitations and temporary set-backs, but between 1933 and 1965 the real national product grew at an average rate of about 5 per cent. With population increasing at about 2·3 per cent, there was an average rise of over 2 per cent per annum in *per capita* incomes.

Progress was not confined to mining, and expansion and diversification has been almost continuous. New industries have been established, and older ones modernized and made more efficient. Two great structural changes have occurred. Firstly, more and more South Africans of all races have been drawn into the industrial market-oriented sectors of the economy. Secondly, and closely related with the first, there has been the expansion of manufacturing relative to agriculture and mining. Its position has changed from third place, accounting for less than 13 per cent of the national product in the nineteen-twenties, to first place, generating a quarter of the greatly increased national income of the sixties. These processes are not yet (at the time of writing) complete, for there are still pockets of low productivity particularly in the African peasant areas. Modernization of the whole economy appears, however, to be merely a matter of time, for a stage has been reached when economic progress is self-generating, and South Africa has the capacity to maintain a rate of capital formation adequate to provide rising *per capita* income for its whole population. The progress from 1933 to 1965 was a continuous process; but, for ease in exposition, it is convenient to divide it into four phases: the nineteen-thirties, the Second World War, the post-war period to 1960, and the great boom of the sixties.

The five years after 1933 are particularly important, for the upsurge which then occurred would appear to have been the Rostow 'take-off' into sustained economic growth.[2] This period has not received the careful analytic study which it merits, although some pioneer work was done by S. H. Frankel.[3] Between 1932 and 1937, the gross national product rose from £217 million to £370 million, an increase of £153

---

[1] The price of gold jumped immediately from £4·25 an ounce to £6·23, and by 1939 had reached £7·7.

[2] Rostow does not mention South Africa, but see his *Stages of Economic Growth*, p. 38, for other 'take-off' dates.

[3] S. H. Frankel, 'An Analysis of the Growth of the National Income of the Union in the Period of Prosperity before the War', *SAJE*, 1944.

million (or 70 per cent) in five years. There was relatively little increase in the cost of living, so that the real gain was substantial (see Figs. 3 and 4, p. 23). Growth was facilitated by a large inflow of foreign capital, but capital formation was also sustained by a rise in domestic saving.

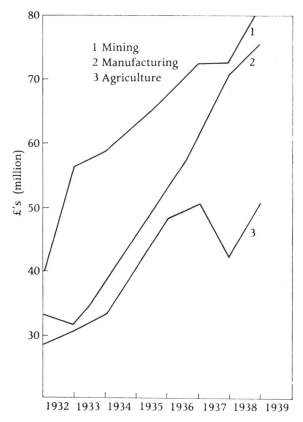

FIG. 7. Value of Output of Major Sectors, 1932–9.
Source: *Union Statistics for Fifty Years*, p. S-3.

Investment was not confined to mining, but was widely extended in the manufacturing and construction industries.

Gold-mining was undoubtedly the leading sector in the advance. The increase in price of gold caused an immediate expansion of mining because ores, previously sub-marginal, were brought within the pay limit. After a very short time lag, prosperity spread to other sectors of the economy (see Fig. 7). Increased mining activity led to higher capital investment in both the private and the public sectors leading eventually to increased consumer outlay. The demand for agricultural and manufactured products rose, and factories benefited from fuller utilization of their plant. The iron and steel mills at Pretoria came into production in 1933 and provided a source of raw materials for the metal engineering industries which expanded rapidly. Farmers were, however, adversely affected by drought, and, in the 1937/8 season the physical output of arable farming fell by 14 per cent.[1] For this, and other reasons,[2] agricultural employment showed little increase.

Employment in the mining industry (including quarrying) rose from 308,000 in 1932 to 475,000 in 1939. Manufacturing, construction, electricity, water, and gas showed an even larger increase, from 161,000 to 331,000; while in the transport sector, railway employment rose from 86,000 to 123,000. Employment in trade, commerce, and other services undoubtedly expanded rapidly at the same time, but statistics are not available. The expansion of employment for people of all races was very rapid, and the incomes generated as a result of this played a large part in raising living standards and alleviating poverty. The situation in mining, manufacturing, and railways was as follows:

	Industrial employment 1000s		Increase 1932–9 1000s		
	1932	1939	All races	White	Others
Mining and quarries[3]	308	475	167	21	146
Manufacturing and Construction[4]	161	331	170	56	114
Railways[5]	86	123	37	5	32
	555	929	374	82	292

Taking into account the increased employment in trade, commerce and services, well over 100,000 additional white workers found employment in the expanding economy between 1932 and 1939, and the 'poor white problem', which had dominated the economic and political scene for two decades, disappeared in the space of seven years of rapid growth.

In the same period nearly 300,000 Africans, Coloureds, and Indians were drawn into industrial employment, and, if account is taken of trade and commerce, the figure must have been over 400,000. When the economy was stagnant in the nineteen-twenties, the competition for the

---

[1] *Union Statistics for Fifty Years*, pp. 1–28.

[2] Chiefly because modernization of agriculture required the introduction of more capital-intensive methods, and agriculture was more prone to shed its 'surplus labour' than take on more people (see Chapter III).

[3] *Union Statistics for Fifty Years*, p. G–4.

[4] Ibid., pp. G–6, 7, 13.   [5] Ibid., p. G–15.

limited jobs available was intense, and various measures mentioned earlier were taken to protect the white workers. Although these measures remained on the statute-book, their positive impact declined because, with the high rate of growth of the thirties, white and black labour ceased to be so competitive, and became largely complementary. Even in manufacturing, whose growth was fostered with the specific aim of employing whites, the rate of growth was such that a high rate of intake of white workers (56,000) was accompanied by the intake of double that number of other workers (114,000) without whom the growth could not have been maintained.

The Coloured, Indian, and African sections of the community all benefited from the expansion of the economy, but their case differed from that of the whites in that expansion was not sufficient to overcome poverty. Indeed South Africa had been so concerned with the poor whites that it was only in the thirties that the poverty of other groups received national attention. After some pioneering work in the twenties,[1] the Native Economic Commission was appointed and its report in 1932[2] revealed the deteriorating condition of agriculture in the areas reserved for African occupation where over-population and poverty were widespread, and soil destruction, due to bad farming, was assuming alarming proportions. This had led to mass migrations of workers to the towns seeking employment in mining and manufacturing to enable them to support their families in the reserves. Some of them took up their permanent abode in town bringing their families to join them there, and in spite of many hindrances imposed by Government policy, the African population of the large industrial towns rose rapidly. The majority, particularly the mine workers, were temporary migrants, circulating throughout their working lives between town and country. They have been described as 'men of two worlds', because they had close and inseparable ties both with their peasant society and with the modern industrial world.[3] The existence of this vast army of perpetual migrants indicated an imbalance in the national economy and exercised a disturbing effect upon labour stability and the industrial wage-structure typical of a state of economic dualism as described by many writers in this field.[4] The influx of many thousands of workers from outside the Union of South Africa also exerted a depressing effect upon the level of African wages, preventing any marked increase in wage-rates in spite of the economic expansion.

[1] J. Henderson, 'The Economic Condition of the Native People', *South African Outlook*, (1927 and 1928); W. M. MacMillan, *Complex South Africa*.

[2] U.G. 22, 1932.

[3] D. Hobart Houghton, *The South African Economy*, pp. 79–111.

[4] In particular W. A. Lewis, 'Economic Development with Unlimited Supplies of Labour', *The Manchester School*, May 1954.

The outbreak of the Second World War in 1939 found the South African economy much stronger and more diversified than it had been in 1914. The drastic cutting off of imports presented both a challenge and an opportunity to the developing manufacturing industries, and bold experiments and improvisations occurred, particularly in the iron, steel, and engineering sectors. National output continued to increase, but an acute labour shortage soon developed, especially in the skilled ranks, because of the increased demands upon the limited resources and the fact that over 300,000 men[1] were in the armed forces. The value of manufacturing output increased by 116 per cent between 1939 and 1945, but inflationary pressures developed, and the retail price index (all items) rose by 32 per cent in the same period. The industrial labour force grew by 53 per cent during the war, but of the increase of 125,000 persons, only 19,000 were white, the remaining 106,000 being drawn from the other races. Moreover, many of them moved into skilled and semi-skilled jobs formerly performed by whites. Had it not been for their contribution, South Africa could not both have expanded output and maintained its war effort.

In 1945 the South African economy was in a strong position. More diversified than it had been in 1939 it was well placed for further expansion. The discovery of a new gold-field in the Orange Free State, and of extensions both to the east and west of the original Witwatersrand, stimulated heavy investment in mining. Capital and immigrants poured into the country and boom conditions continued. Manufacturing was expanded in various directions, particularly in metals and engineering, textiles, and the chemical industry.

The Net National Income (at factor cost), for the years 1940 to 1965, is shown in *rand*[2] at current prices in Fig. 8A. This figure which is a continuation of Fig. 3 on p. 23, shows that the strong upward trend, which commenced in 1933, continues without a break, although steps or hesitations are discernible in 1948, 1952, and 1958. Real income grew during this period at an average rate of between $4\frac{1}{2}$ and 5 per cent per annum, and *per capita* incomes, though showing a dip in 1949, 1952, and 1958 maintained an upward movement of well over 2 per cent per

[1] 186,000 white and 123,000 non-white. Source: *The Union of South Africa and the War*, Government Printer, Pretoria, 1948.

[2] Although South Africa did not adopt a decimal currency until 1960, it will facilitate comparisons if a single currency is used. For the remainder of this chapter, therefore, all money values will be expressed in *rand* rather than in pounds. The rate of conversion is £1 = R2. It should also be noted that all national accounts and foreign trade statistics relate to the Southern African Customs Union, i.e. the Union (Republic) of South Africa, Basutoland (Lesotho), Bechuanaland (Botswana), Swaziland, and South West Africa. Of the Gross Domestic Product (at factor cost) of R6,800 million in 1964, the Republic accounted for R6,547 million and the other four countries for only R253 million. Source: calculated from data in the *Quarterly Bulletin* of the South African Reserve Bank, Dec. 1966, pp. S–53 and 55.

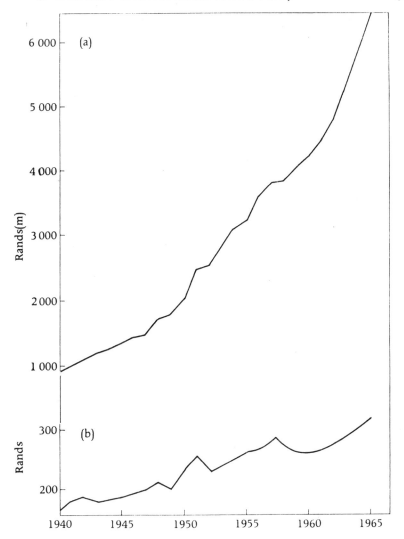

FIG. 8 (a). Net National Income at Factor Cost, 1940–65; (b) *Per Capita* Income, 1940–65.

annum (Fig. 8B). This high and long-sustained rate of growth would not have been possible but for a high rate of domestic saving and an elastic supply of labour as more Africans were drawn from self-subsistence farming into the industrial labour force.

None the less, pressures manifested themselves from time to time, particularly in periodic crises in the balance of payments. These may

be conveniently indicated on the graph of the gold and foreign exchange reserves (Fig. 9) where five troughs are to be seen.

South Africa ended the war in a strong financial position with considerable reserves which were augmented by a large capital inflow from
Britain.[1] In 1948–9 there was a rapid increase in imports due partly to
pent-up consumer demand and to the importation of machinery and
capital equipment for the development of the Free State gold-mines

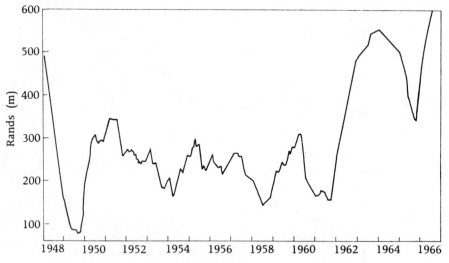

FIG. 9. Gold and Foreign Exchange Reserves, 1948–66.

and for general industrial expansion. The spending spree was so great
that even a capital inflow of R681 million between 1947 and 1949 did
not offset the deficit on the current trading account. Sterling was
devalued in 1949, and, this time, South Africa immediately followed.
This redressed the balance of payments by checking non-sterling imports, and the enhanced price of gold and higher wool prices boosted
the value of exports, so that the country's reserves increased by R142
million in 1950.

The crises of 1954 and 1958 were in many respects similar. All three
had their origin in an adverse balance on current account, but the last
two were caused primarily by heavy importations of capital goods as a
result of the high level of public and private investments. They were, in
fact, the direct consequence of the rapid expansion of the national
economy. In both cases the fiscal and monetary measures were applied
to restore the balance of payments.

---

[1] Partly genuine investment funds, partly money brought in by immigrants, and partly
'flight capital' scared by the possibility of a capital levy in the United Kingdom.

The crisis of 1960/1 was of a very different character from those which had gone before, because in this case the current balance was in a strong position. The 1960 crisis was caused by a large flight of capital from the country induced by political, rather than economic, fears.[1] This capital outflow of over R12 million per month in 1960 and the first half of 1961 halved the country's reserves and placed the stability of the currency in jeopardy. In addition to normal monetary and fiscal measures, strict control over capital movements was imposed and the rand was no longer freely convertible. These measures checked the capital drain and, assisted by a favourable balance of R190 million on current account, the nation's reserves rose rapidly. Interest rates were reduced and public investment outlays of considerable size initiated a new upsurge of the national economy comparable only with the period following devaluation in 1933. Between 1960 and 1966 the Gross Domestic Product at current prices rose from R5,335 million to R8,788 million—a rise of R3,453 million in six years.[2]

The real Gross Domestic Product (at 1958 prices) increased from R5,153 million to R7,426 million, an increase of 44 per cent or an average real growth-rate of about 7 per cent per annum over the six-year period.[3] In 1963 the real growth-rate reached 9·4 per cent, but by 1965 various bottlenecks appeared, and inflationary pressure became strong. The *Economic Development Programme, 1964–69*,[4] estimated that South Africa's resources were adequate to maintain real growth at a rate of 5½ per cent per annum, but that a rate exceeding this would encounter balance-of-payments difficulties and cause a shortage of skilled labour. This proved to be the case, and an adverse balance of payments on current account led to the depletion of the reserves in 1965. The balance of payments was again restored through fiscal and monetary measures, assisted by a strong inflow of foreign funds. Although helpful in restoring the international balance these funds had an inflationary effect within the country and offset, to some extent, the restrictive monetary measures which the Reserve Bank was seeking to impose.

Private capital movements during the post-war period are presented in Fig. 10. In the immediate post-war years foreign investment in South Africa was large, but it tended to decline after 1954. It then became strongly negative up to 1964, and the outflow of capital would

---

[1] The 'wind of change' was sweeping through the continent; the Congo eruptions, the break-up of the Rhodesian Federation, riots with bloodshed in South Africa, the declaration of a republic, and the imposition of a state of emergency, all combined to shake the confidence of investors.

[2] South African Reserve Bank *Quarterly Bulletin*, Dec. 1966, p. S–53.

[3] Ibid., June 1967, p. S–61.

[4] *Economic Development Programme for the Republic of South Africa, 1964–69*, Government Printer, Pretoria, 1965.

have been greater had it not been for controls. A change came in 1965, and large amounts of capital began to enter the country again. The trend of the capital movements would appear to indicate a lack of confidence in the political and economic stability of South Africa on the part of the foreign investor during the years immediately preceding and following 1960. The subsequent demonstration of renewed confidence must be attributed to the manifest strength and growth of the South

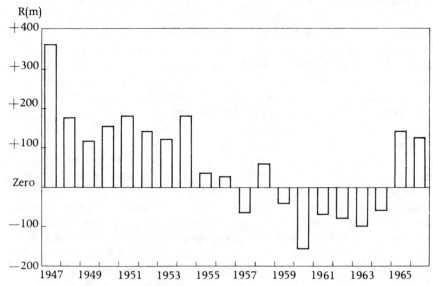

Fig. 10. Net Private Capital Inward (+) and Outward (−) Movement, 1947–66.
Source: *Quarterly Bulletin*, South African Reserve Bank.

African economy and, perhaps, to the realization that its government was unlikely to capitulate to the forces of African nationalism. Increased prosperity and expanding employment opportunities eased social tensions within the country.

South Africa's foreign trade expanded more than four-fold during the post-war period. The change in 20 years is shown by the figures below:

	1946 (R millions)	1965 (R millions)
Imports	433	1,814
Merchandise exports	156	1,073
Gold production	203	775
Total exports	359	1,848

The greater diversification of the South African economy is seen from the fact that, although gold output increased from R203 million to R775 million, its importance as a proportion of total exports has declined. Nevertheless, gold together with other mining and agricultural products is still the main earner of foreign exchange. Manufacturing, which accounts for a quarter of the Gross Domestic Product, as yet exports only a fraction of the imports which it requires. J. C. du Plessis's figures are illuminating:

Net Contributions to South Africa's Current Balance 1964[1]

(R millions)	
Gold mining	+ 701
Other mining	+ 144
Agriculture	+ 249
Manufacturing industries	− 515
Individuals	− 278
Government	− 102
Commerce	− 98

South Africa's trade has become more widely spread than formerly, but Britain still holds first place both in exports and imports.[2] The six leading countries are shown below with the value of trade in 1964.

South African Trade, 1964[3]

Exports to (R millions)		Imports from (R millions)	
(1) United Kingdom	321	(1) United Kingdom	438
(2) Japan	118	(2) United States	292
(3) United States	102	(3) German Fed. Repub.	165
(4) German Fed. Repub.	58	(4) Japan	81
(5) Rhodesia	51	(5) Italy	46
(6) Italy	40	(6) Canada	46

Political pressures against South Africa became strong after 1958, and many countries signified their intention of placing an embargo upon imports from South Africa. These measures, whether governmental or voluntary, have not prevented the expansion of South Africa's foreign trade, except in the case of the African continent; and, even here, the decline was partly due to a slowing up in the rate of growth in some

[1] J. C. du Plessis, 'Investment and the Balance of Payments', *SAJE*, Dec. 1965, p. 329.
[2] For recent analysis of this see D. Austin, *Britain and South Africa*.
[3] *Statistical Year Book, 1966*, pp. Q-12, Q-13.

South African Exports (R millions)[1]

	1958	1964
Europe	358	530
America	61	102
Asia	35	118
Africa	134	114
Oceania	10	14
Other (i.e. ships' stores, gold and uranium).	550	812
Total	1,148	1,690

African territories. It would be wrong to say that the embargoes had no effect because, had it not been for them, South Africa's trade expansion might have been greater. Sanctions, and the threat of sanctions, also played an important part in stimulating the domestic economy, because they accelerated the development of import-replacement industries like automobile manufacturing, the aircraft industry, shipbuilding, chemical manufacturing (including synthetic rubber); and they stimulated the search for natural oil.

The rapid industrialization in the period since 1933 was not, of course, without its difficulties, and certain problems have exercised the minds of economists and politicians. One of these is the uneven geographical distribution of the industrial expansion, which has been concentrated very largely in the southern Transvaal. This area accounts for approximately half the industrial output of the whole country, and together with Cape Town, Durban, and Port Elizabeth, for 80 per cent of the Republic's total. In spite of the general growth of the economy, most rural areas and smaller towns have experienced economic stagnation and population decline. Since the early 1960s, the Government has embarked upon a plan (forming part of the general policy of 'separate development' for various races) for the wider dispersal of manufacturing industry, motivated initially by the desire to establish industries in or near the areas of African land-ownership. In these areas rural population densities were highest and poverty most in evidence. Methods to induce industrialists to select these areas included provision of the infra-structure, tax remission, assistance in the building of factories, preferential railway rates, and less restrictive labour regulations governing the employment of Africans in skilled and semi-skilled jobs.

Another persistent problem has been the wide disparity between the earnings of skilled and unskilled workers. As the majority of the white

[1] *Statistical Year Book, 1966*, pp. Q–12, Q–13.

group are in skilled or managerial jobs this is reflected in a disparity between the average incomes of white people and people of other races. Three sets of forces interact to perpetuate this situation: the legislative and customary hindrances to the vertical mobility of non-white workers;[1] the differences in productivity due partly to inadequate technical training; and the constant augmentation of the supply of unskilled labour, resulting from the movement of Africans out of self-subsistence agriculture, and from the relatively high rate of natural increase.[2] Recent legislation has ostensibly increased vertical immobility[3] but, in spite of it, the acute shortage of skilled labour has enabled African, Coloured, and Indian workers to move into more highly skilled jobs in manufacturing and distributive services.

There is need for reliable statistical information about income distribution, but accurate up-to-date data about earnings of the various racial groups are difficult to obtain.[4]

At the time of writing, there are, broadly speaking, three main tiers or income levels: the white people are the wealthiest, but even within this group there is a wide range from the wealthy property-owning minority to the wage-earning majority; Coloureds, Indians, and urban African workers form the middle tier; while rural Africans form the poorest section of the population. During the boom of the nineteen-sixties the earnings of the first two groups rose significantly,[5] but the rural Africans benefited little, if at all, except in so far as their earnings as migrant workers were increased. It has been estimated that the average income of the whites is about five times that of the other racial groups.[6]

This disparity in incomes has caused concern on both humanitarian

---

[1] Mentioned above, pp. 55–8.

[2] Percentage of persons under 10 years of age, 1960 census: Whites 22·3, Africans 29·65, Coloureds 32·6, Asians 30·0.

[3] Industrial Conciliation Act, No. 28 of 1956.

[4] See, however, W. F. J. Steenkamp, 'The Bantu Wage Problem', *SAJE*, Mar. 1962; S. van der Horst, 'The Economic Implications of Political Democracy', supplement to *Optima*, 1960; F. P. Spooner, *The South African Predicament*; J. de Gruchy, *The Cost of Living for Urban Africans in Johannesburg, 1959*; and the publications of the Bureau of Market Research (University of South Africa): *Income and Expenditure Patterns of Urban Bantu Households*, Research Reports Nos. 3 (Pretoria), 6 (Johannesburg), 8 (Cape Town), 13 (Durban); *Income and Expenditure Patterns of Urban Coloured Households, Durban Survey* (Research Report No. 11); *Income and Expenditure Patterns of Urban Indian Households, Durban Survey* (Research Report No. 12); *Income and Expenditure Patterns of Coloured Households, Cape Peninsular* (Research Report No. 9).

[5] The increase in the average monthly income of African households in Pretoria between 1960 and 1965 was 32 per cent. Allowing for the rise in prices the real increase was 17·86 per cent over five years, or about 3·6 per cent per annum. See Bureau of Market Research (University of South Africa) *Comparative Income Patterns of Urban Bantu: Pretoria, 1960–1965* (Research Report No. 14), p. 102.

[6] S. Enke, 'South African Growth: a Macro-economic Analysis', *SAJE*, Mar. 1962, p. 37.

and economic grounds. Although extreme poverty, such as is found in some Asian and African countries, is not present in the Republic, many people live at a bare subsistence level and there is malnutrition. Moreover, the disparity between the living standards of the white and other groups is there for all to see, and may be a cause of social discontent and political instability. From the industrial point of view, the relative poverty of fourteen million out of a population of eighteen million[1] restricts the size of the domestic market. Were it possible to raise the average incomes of all to the level at present enjoyed by the whites, this great increase in demand would enable factories to benefit more fully from the economies of large-scale production, and to install more highly specialized machinery. In spite of all these considerations many economists are reluctant to press for rapid wage increases for the lower-paid workers unless justified by increases in productivity. They believe that the expansion of employment opportunities to provide jobs for the increasing population and for those moving out of subsistence agriculture should take precedence over more equitable distribution. Any too rapid increase in wages might restrict the rate of growth of the economy with dire consequences. It was estimated that, in 1964, there were some 200,000 new entrants to the labour market per annum of whom 20,000 were white and 180,000 other races.[2] These problems were discussed in a series of articles in the *South African Journal of Economics*;[3] and the forces operating in the labour market in gold-mining is the subject matter of a forthcoming book.[4] The Government's attitude to the problem was conveyed in a statement issued in 1962 by the Prime Minister, Dr. Verwoerd, in which he weighs the pros and cons of legislation to bring about a rapid general increase in minimum wages.[5] He stated that:

the desirability and necessity of an increase in non-white wages were emphasised by studies made of the average income of non-white families in Johannesburg, Durban and Pretoria. While certain findings of these family studies may be criticised, it can hardly be denied that they revealed extreme poverty towards which neither the employers nor the Government can adopt

[1] Mid-year estimated population of the Republic in 1965: Whites, 3,398,000; Coloured 1,751,000; Asian, 533,000; African, 12,186,000; Total, 17,867,000. *Statistical Year Book, 1966*, p. A-11.

[2] *Economic Development Programme for the Republic of South Africa, 1964–69*, Table 3.

[3] L. H. Katzen, 'The Case for Minimum Wage Legislation in South Africa', *SAJE*, 1961, pp. 195–217; S. P. Viljoen, 'Higher Productivity and Higher Wages for Native Labour in South Africa', *SAJE*, 1961, pp. 35–44; O. P. F. Horwood, 'Is Minimum Wage Legislation the Answer for South Africa?', *SAJE*, 1962, pp. 119–39; W. F. J. Steenkamp, 'Bantu Wages in South Africa', *SAJE*, 1962, pp. 93–118.

[4] F. Wilson, *The Economics of Labour in the South African Gold Mines*.

[5] 'Statement issued by the Honourable the Prime Minister, in connection with the meeting of the Economic Advisory Council, held at Cape Town on 15th and 16th March, 1962.' Press release, 26 Apr. 1962.

an attitude of indifference. . . . Although all the members of the Economic Advisory Council in principle strongly support an increase in Bantu wages, there is a difference of opinion as to the methods to be adopted to achieve this object as well as to the rate and extent to which wages should be increased.

He concluded by stating that 'the Government supports the endeavours to establish a wage level which will enable all low-paid workers (whites as well as non-whites) to meet at least their minimum subsistence requirements', and that 'to achieve this objective the existing machinery for the determination of minimum wages is being used to an increasing extent'. Better facilities for the industrial training of workers of all races received special attention in the *Economic Development Programme*.[1]

The great industrial development of the hundred years 1865–1965 could not have been achieved without an appropriate expansion of the infra-structure. Space does not permit a full account of the stages through which communications, transport, power, banking and finance, and the social infra-structure of health and education have been developed to keep pace with the transformation of a predominantly farming community into the most industrialized country in Africa.

Reference was made earlier to the advent of the railway, and to the importance of unified control after Union in 1910. In 1965, the railways carried over 64 million tons of goods and 425 million passengers.[2] An ever-increasing volume of persons and goods was also being carried by road transport over the 115,000 miles of the national and provincial road system. In 1965 there were 1,540,000 registered motor vehicles.[3] Air services, both domestic and to other parts of the world, expanded greatly in the twenty-five years to 1965 and carried a total of about 700,000 passengers in that year.[4] Ocean transport, both abroad and coastwise, carried some 30 million tons in the same year.[5] The general transport system of the country successfully kept pace with economic expansion, but during periods of rapid growth it temporarily lagged behind demand, and bottlenecks appeared from time to time.

Electricity generation is a sensitive indicator of industrial progress. In South Africa it is mainly undertaken by a public utility corporation —the Electricity Supply Commission. The total generated increased from 3,308 million kilowatt-hours in 1934 to 26,969 million in 1963, and *per capita* consumption rose from a little over 600 kilowatt-hours in 1945 to over 1,600 in 1965.[6]

The history of banking and financial institutions shows the evolution of a modern financial structure from the small local banks of the nine-teenth century to the highly concentrated commercial banks of the

[1] *Economic Development Programme for the Republic of South Africa 1965–70*, pp. 86–8.
[2] *Statistical Year Book, 1966*, p. R–9.   [3] Ibid., p. R–13.
[4] Ibid., p. R–10.   [5] Ibid., p. R–12.   [6] Ibid., pp. O–3 and O–5.

twentieth.[1] An important landmark was the establishment of a central bank—the South African Reserve Bank—in 1920,[2] and after 1949 a short-term money market came into being.[3] Other financial institutions were set up to meet specific needs: the Land Bank, the discount and accepting houses, hire-purchase institutions and the building societies, and the Johannesburg Stock Exchange.

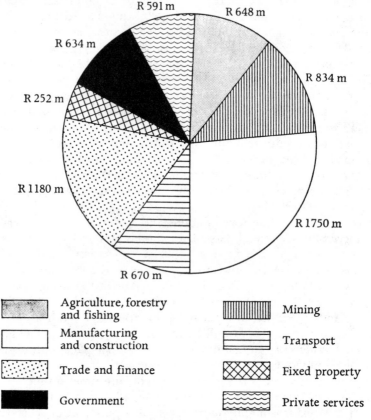

FIG. 11. Gross Domestic Product of Republic of South Africa, 1964 (Excluding Botswana, Lesotho, Swaziland, and South West Africa).

Source: *Quarterly Bulletin*, South African Reserve Bank, December 1966, p. S-55.

The general picture of the national economy in 1965 is very different from what it was a century before. Then sheep-farming and self-

[1] See in particular Arndt, op. cit.

[2] G. de Kock, *A History of the South African Reserve Bank (1920–52)*.

[3] See G. F. D. Palmer, 'The Development of a South African Money Market', *SAJE*, 1958, and G. F. D. Palmer and A. B. Dickman, 'The South African Money Market', *SAJE*, 1960.

THE SOUTH AFRICAN LABOUR FORCE -1960

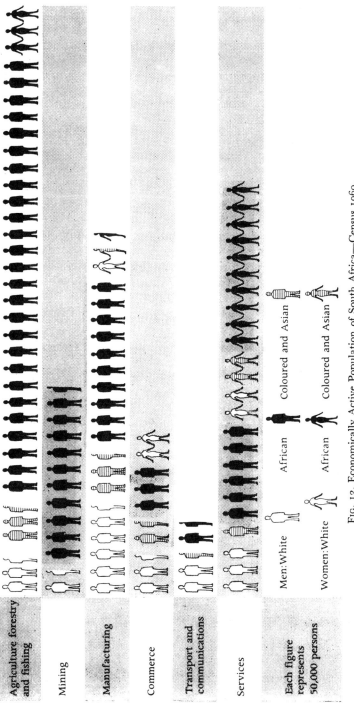

FIG. 12. Economically Active Population of South Africa—Census 1960.

Source: Houghton, *The South African Economy*.

subsistence agriculture were the principal sources of income. A century later, a much more productive and scientific type of farming ensures the food supply for the increasing population for the foreseeable future, but it represents only a small part of the Gross National Product. Mining, manufacturing, and a variety of tertiary activities have arisen. In 1964 the gross domestic product was valued at R6,547 million, and its derivation is shown in Fig. 11.

Similarly the occupations of the people have become more diverse, and the economic expansion has drawn men and women of all races together in a great productive effort which has raised the average standard of living far above the most optimistic expectations of a century ago. The composition of the economically active population of the Republic at the 1960 census, and its distribution between the main sectors of the economy is depicted in Fig. 12.[1] The remarkable prosperity which the country enjoyed during the years 1933–65 has transmuted economics in South Africa from the 'dismal science' into the contemplation of expanding horizons and rising expectations. Great expectations remaining unfulfilled may lead to social discontent and political instability. High hopes seem destined to disappointment in many parts of Africa, but in the Republic the degree of economic sophistication already attained, the high rate of domestic capital-formation, and the great resources, both physical and human, not yet fully developed, augur well for continued prosperity. It has been estimated that, if the Republic can maintain the growth-rate of the last half-century, the average real *per capita* income of the whole population in the year 2000 would be equal that of Britain in 1960.[2] To achieve this, however, full use will have to be made of all available manpower through better training facilities and unrestricted employment opportunities for South Africans of all races.

---

[1] Since then employment in manufacturing and construction has increased from 957,000 to 1,181,000 in Jan. 1966; of these workers 25 per cent were white. Source: *Bulletin of Statistics*, June 1967.

[2] S. P. Viljoen, 'Higher Productivity and Higher Wages of Native Labour in South Africa', *SAJE*, Mar. 1961.

II

THE GROWTH OF PEASANT COMMUNITIES[1]

1. *Genesis*

PEASANT communities, in the sense in which the term is used in this book, began in 1738 with the foundation of the first mission station in South Africa. A Moravian missionary, George Schmidt, began work in Baviaans kloof, near Caledon, among the Khoikhoi, and after an interruption between 1744 and 1792 his station grew, and became the pattern for missions that followed. It was named Genadendal.[2] The missionary gathered round him a community of people who settled on land eventually granted to the mission. A church and school were established. The people were taught to plough and to build substantial cottages for themselves, wheat and fruit-trees were introduced, and crafts such as carpentry and shoe-making started. The community lived within the framework of government and trade created by the Dutch East India Company.

From early in the nineteenth century mission stations were established by a number of societies and denominations—notably the London, Glasgow, Paris, Rhenish, Berlin, Norwegian, and American societies, and by Wesleyan and Anglican Churches—among Khoikhoi, San, Nguni, and Sotho. Before the end of the century mission stations spread from the Cape to Rehoboth (far north of the Orange), to Shoshong in Bechuanaland, Inyati in Ndebele country, Elim in the Soutpansberg, and Eshowe in Zululand. In 1911 there were well over five hundred stations south of the Limpopo, and westward among the Tswana and Nama.[3]

Although certain differences in mission policies, and in the peoples among whom missionaries worked, created variations between stations, there was a basic similarity in all of them which far exceeded the

---

[1] I am particularly indebted to Professor Hobart Houghton, Professor Leonard Thompson, Dr. Francis Wilson, Dr. Archie Mafeje, and Mr. David Welsh for criticism of this chapter, and to Mrs. M. Pimstone for sterling work as a research assistant.

[2] *Georg Schmidt en sy Opvolgers, 1737–1937* (Hernhutt, 1937).

[3] The precise number turns on the definition of 'mission station' and the line between 'central station' and 'outstation' with an elementary school and regular services, but no resident missionary. *The World Atlas of Christian Missions*, S. S. Dennis *et al.* (eds.), marks 418 mission stations in South Africa (as defined). These do *not* include Roman Catholic stations, but do include Protestant missions in towns which differ in character from rural mission stations.

differences. The centre was the church and school; the converts and adherents lived as a community; the missionaries—notably the Moravians, Rhenish,[1] and Scottish missions (see Vol. I, pp. 239–40)—stressed the moral value of work and struggled to build up communities of peasant farmers and craftsmen. Families were urged to settle; the hunters were pressed to become herders; the herders were taught to cultivate; the cultivators were taught to use a plough and irrigate; and all came into much closer relationship with the outside world. Since great importance was attached to abandoning the traditional skin clothing and replacing it by some form of European dress, a trading store on the mission, or near to it, was welcomed,[2] and in church and school people quickly began to learn a second language—Dutch or English—as well as to read.

Trade was welcomed by missions but did not arise from them; it grew independently because it was profitable, and ivory and cattle-traders often preceded the missionaries. Similarly, the shelter of a European administration was welcomed by most missionaries, and they played a part in extending control by Great Britain (see Vol. I, pp. 267, 400–1), but they established themselves through the greater part of South Africa ahead of any government, and did not invariably support those seeking to exercise authority. Missionary, trader, and administrator all played a part in the establishment of a peasantry. Neither trade nor government, nor even a missionary working in isolation from these forces, alone created it.

Peasant communities began around mission stations, but as churches, schools, and trading stations were established, and external political control was enforced throughout what had been independent chief-doms, the peasant communities spread. The mission remained one focus of community life; the trading store and administrative office provided other centres; only on the mission reserves occupied by Coloured people, and in large Tswana settlements, were church, store, and administrative centre concentrated.

The characteristics of peasants as defined here were first, that they were landowners or tenants, producing on a small scale for their own consumption and for trade with a town. The peasant is distinguished on the one hand from the tribesman who lived in isolation with only a trickle of trade, and on the other from the farmer and his paid servants who combined in larger-scale production for a market.

Secondly, literacy, and adherence to a church had begun. In a tribal society the art of writing is unknown, but the peasant community includes some members who are literate and aware of a long tradition in time, as well as wide links in space. Those who lived on mission stations

---

[1] J. du Plessis, *A History of Christian Missions in South Africa*, pp. 202–3.
[2] J. Philip, *Researches in South Africa*, i. 204–5.

were 'people of the book', since the Bible was read and expounded daily, and the prime object of school was to teach people to read it for themselves.

Thirdly, some political authority existed wider than that of a chief ruling an independent unit of, at the most, a hundred thousand men, and commonly less than a tenth of that, and some portion of the peasants' surplus helped to maintain a dominant group.[1]

Most of the white settlers who became farmers began as small-scale producers (see I, pp. 196, 279, 282), and up to the nineteenth century they were repeatedly referred to as 'peasants' by travellers from Europe, but they differed from peasants elsewhere in that they were slave-owners or employers. Successive governments tried to establish a white peasantry, tilling their own fields, and they failed. They failed with the Dutch Free Burghers in the seventeenth, with the British and German settlers in the nineteenth, and with poor Afrikaners in the twentieth century. Each time white families were settled on the land they began to employ Coloured or African labourers, no matter what the regulations prohibiting this, and the trend has been away from small-scale agricultural production to large-scale farming. The small farmers of Malmsbury, Franschhoek, Swellendam, Long Kloof, Albany, Berlin, Frankfort, and Kakamas are not, therefore, included in our examples of 'peasants'.[2] Those who have continued to work land for themselves, not depending substantially on paid servants, have almost all been Coloured or African.

How first the Khoikhoi and San, and then Xhosa, Zulu, and Sotho lost much of the land they had occupied has already been described (see I, 65, 252–6, 416–46). What Coloured people held on individual tenure, including the land-holdings allocated to them in the fertile Kat river valley from 1837 onwards, and the rich farm lands occupied by the Griqua around Kokstad in 1863, they gradually lost. Farms were mortgaged, often to pay for a wagon and oxen, sometimes for clothes and food and brandy, and eventually sold.[3] The land Coloured communities continued to occupy was mostly that allocated to missions.[4] These areas continued to be administered by missionary societies until, in 1909, provision was made for 'the granting of titles to the inhabitants of such stations or reserves' and a white magistrate became chairman of

---

[1] Cf. R. Redfield, *Peasant Society and Culture*; J. Pitt-Rivers (ed.), *Mediterranean Country Men*; E. R. Wolf, *Peasants*; L. A. Fallers, 'Are African Cultivators to be called Peasants?', *Current Anthropology* 2 (1961), 108–10.

[2] J. F. W. Grosskopf, *Rural Impoverishment and Rural Exodus*; R. W. Wilcocks, *The Poor White*; E. G. Malherbe, *Education and the Poor White*; E. L. G. Schnell, *For Men Must Work*; D. Hobart Houghton, *Economic Development in a Plural Society*, pp. 65–70.

[3] *Report of the Government Commission on Native Laws and Customs, 1883* (hereafter *1883 Report*), ii, 374; *South African Native Affairs Commission, 1903–5, Report*, (hereafter *1903–5 Report*), ii. 1100; J. S. Marais, *The Cape Coloured People*, pp. 49–73; 216–45.

[4] Marais, pp. 32; 246–55.

each local Management Board. In 1952 administration of them was taken over by the Division of Coloured Affairs.[1]

Most Khoikhoi and Coloured families settled as farm labourers on white-owned farms, or as workers in the growing towns and villages. By 1965 the total number of Coloured people living in reserves was under forty-one thousand, less than three per cent of the Coloured population.[2]

A great deal more land was left in African occupation than had been put aside for the Khoikhoi and San, and land allocated to Africans on freehold and quitrent title, both west and east of the Kei, as well as land held on communal tenure, was secured by a clause prohibiting sale to any non-African. In the Cape and Natal up to 1913, and in the Transvaal and Orange River Colony between 1902 and 1913, Africans who could afford to do so could buy land, and others rented land from whites, paying either in cash or in a share of the crop. In the Transvaal, and in Natal, particularly along the foothills of the Drakensberg, a considerable number of farms were bought either by individual Africans or by groups under the leadership of chiefs,[3] and some of the cash and share tenants were relatively better off than farm servants.[4]

Then, in 1913, a Land Act was passed which entrenched territorial segregation between white and black throughout the Union. Certain areas occupied by Africans were 'scheduled' as 'reserves', and Africans were prohibited from purchasing or hiring land from whites, pending the demarcation of areas within which sale might be permitted. The Act was declared *ultra vires* in the Cape,[5] but operated elsewhere; sales almost ceased, and cash tenants and share-croppers were forced to move.[6] The law confining Africans to 'scheduled' and 'released' areas became effective in the Cape from 1936, and 'released' areas within which land to be occupied by Africans might be bought were defined (see map 2). Between 1936 and 1966 about half of the 'released' areas were bought by the Bantu Trust or individual Africans, but there was also a gradual process of expropriation and expulsion of Africans from land they held outside the main reserves and 'released' areas. This land had sometimes been held on freehold through several generations, or in communal tenure for much longer, and driving families 'from the graves of their fathers' created deep bitterness.

---

[1] W. P. Carstens, *The Social Structure of a Cape Coloured Reserve*, pp. 25–36, 134–49.

[2] Population figures for Coloured reserves by courtesy of the Department of Coloured Affairs. *Republic of South Africa Population Census, 1960*, Pretoria.

[3] *1903–5 Report*, iv. 428–30; *Development of the Bantu Areas within the Union of South Africa, Official Summary* (hereafter *Tomlinson Report*), p. 51.

[4] M. Hunter, *Reaction to Conquest*, p. 518.

[5] *Thompson and Stilwell* v. *Kama*, South African Law Reports, 1917, Appellate Division, 209.

[6] W. M. Macmillan, *Complex South Africa*, pp. 125–6, 194; Hunter, p. 557.

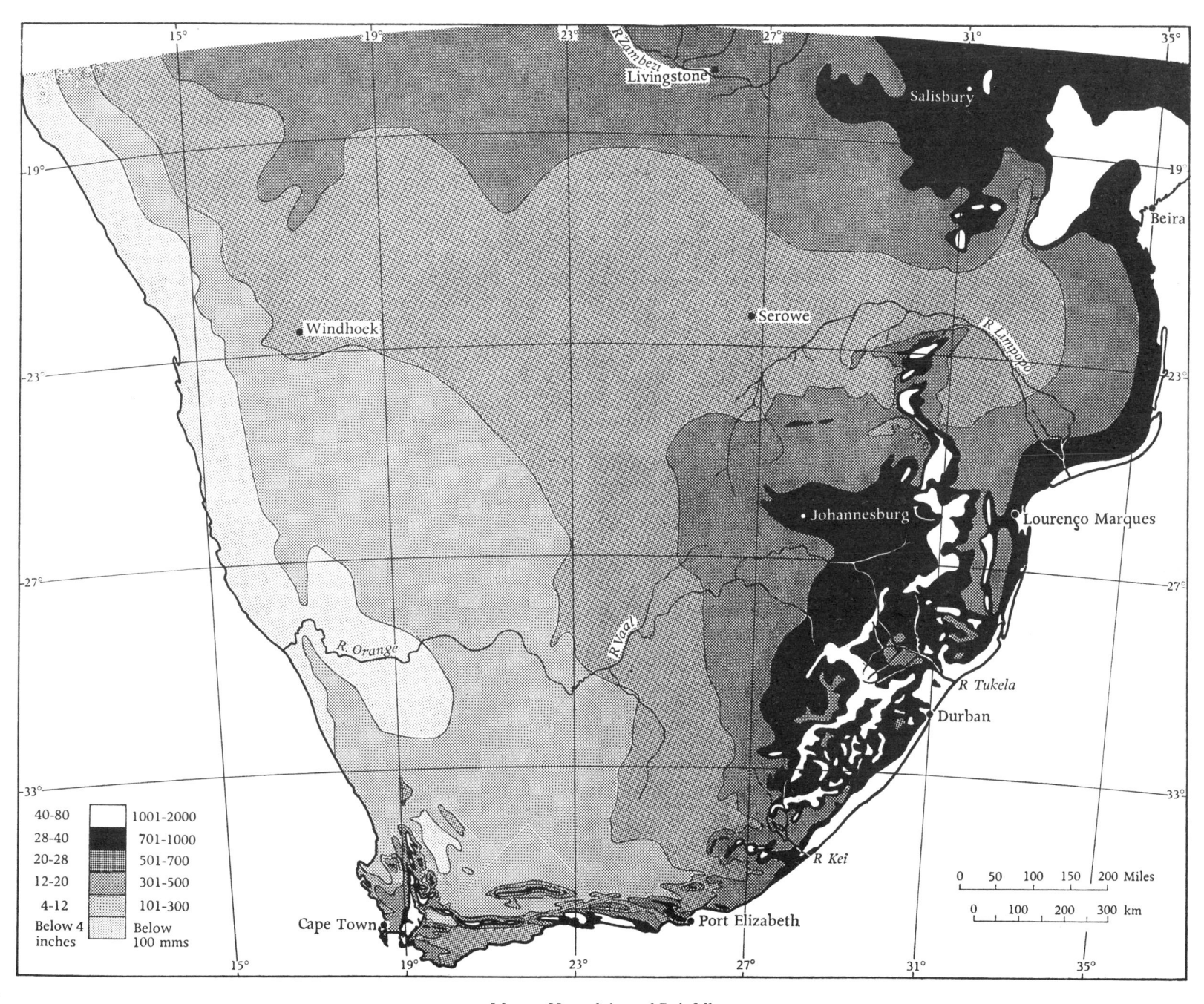

40-80		1001-2000
28-40		701-1000
20-28		501-700
12-20		301-500
4-12		101-300
Below 4 inches		Below 100 mms

MAP 1. Normal Annual Rainfall

Source: Republic of South Africa, Weather Bureau (map) (Government Printer, Pretoria, 1959)

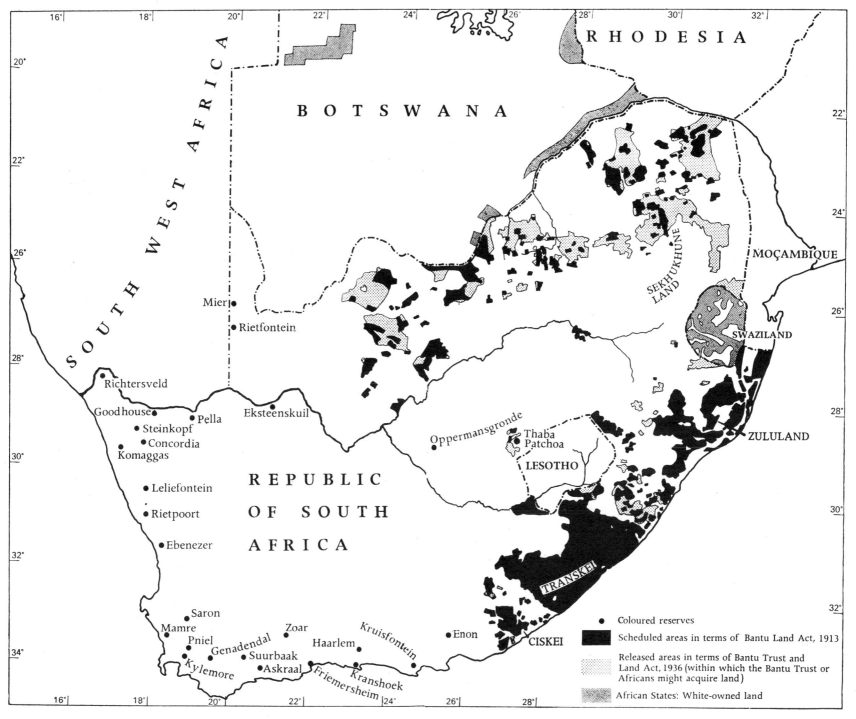

MAP 2. African and Coloured Reserves in the Republic of South Africa: White-owned land in Botswana and Swaziland

Sources: South African Institute of Race Relations: Scheduled and Released Bantu Areas, 1966 (map)
Coloured Affairs Department: Coloured Reserves, 1966 (map)
I. Schapera, *Native Land Tenure in the Bechuanaland Protectorate* (Lovedale, 1943)
H. Kuper, *The Uniform of Colour* (Johannesburg, 1947)

Forced expropriation of both white and black is the price of territorial segregation.[1] But in spite of population removals the reserves for
Africans, as well as the fragments of land held by Coloured communities, are still, in 1966, dispersed, as map 2 shows. By far the largest
single area is the Transkei, 15,000 square miles.

The value of land in Africa depends largely on rainfall, and therefore
it is instructive to compare a map of the reserves with a rainfall map.
The Transkei, Ciskei, Zulu, Venda, and some of the Sotho reserves fall
within the better watered parts of South Africa, averaging twenty-five
to forty inches of rain annually, with some coastal and mountain areas
exceeding forty inches, but the greater part of the Sotho reserves of the
northern and western Transvaal have less than twenty-five inches, and
those in the northern Cape, and some Coloured reserves, are arid, with
under fifteen inches a year (see maps 1 and 2).

In 1915 the proportion of Africans in the Union living in reserves or
on African-owned farms was fifty-five per cent. In 1951 it was forty-
three per cent.[2] No more recent official figures are available (astonish-
ingly, since a census was taken in 1960) but a calculation made from the
agricultural census suggests that in 1964 the proportion of Africans in
reserves probably was about thirty-seven per cent, that is the fall
continued in so far as the 'reserves' are conceived of as territorially
separate areas. The present policy (1966) is for African suburbs of towns
such as Durban and East London to be designated 'reserves'. This is
little more than a legal fiction (see pp. 192–3).

Over 3·5 million Africans live in reserves within the Republic, and a
further 1·3 million live under somewhat similar conditions in Lesotho,
Botswana, and Swaziland. Less than forty-one thousand Coloured
people live in reserves. Therefore it is with Africans that this chapter
chiefly deals, but comparison with Coloured reserves is of particular
interest since it was on the Coloured mission stations that peasant
communities (as here defined) began in South Africa, and the development on Coloured and African reserves shows marked similarities.
There evolved a customary way of life which owed as much to Christian
Europe as to the tribal societies of Africa.

The peasants described differed in one important respect from those
to whom the name is commonly applied: they were radicals who could
and did adapt to a new world. They were not cultural last-ditchers,

[1] For an analysis of the very complicated situation see: M. Horrell, *Survey of Race Relations
in South Africa, 1966*, pp. 141–6. On removals see Horrell, *Survey, 1961*, pp. 103–6; *1962*,
pp. 88–92, 95; *1963*, pp. 112–13; *1964*, pp. 154–60; *1965*, pp. 129–31, 136; *1966*, p. 197. Alan
Paton, *The People Wept*. Official statements on the area of 'black spots' have varied with
changes in policy. The figure given in the *Tomlinson Report* (pp. 45–6) was 188,660 morgen
(Horrell, *1966*, p. 141).
[2] *Report of the Natives Land Commission* (Beaumont Commission) p. 9; *Tomlinson Report*, p. 28.

withdrawing into isolation as some small groups of hunters did, and as some communities of cultivators attempted to do. This chapter is concerned with the development of a peasantry. The process is a gradual one and it is not possible to define a point in time at which the peasant replaced the tribesman, but it is possible to show when and how, in a given area, isolation diminished and interaction with the outside world grew. Our theme is a study of increase in scale. It is examined in the economic, religious, intellectual, political, domestic, and symbolic aspects.

The sources of evidence for peasant communities are mission and government reports and, most important, the minutes of debates of the Transkeian Territories General Council[1] (commonly known as the Bunga), since for nearly fifty years it discussed the issues which most concerned the peasantry of the largest African reserve, the Transkei. Minutes of the shorter-lived and less lively Ciskeian General Council are also available. Books and newspapers which have been used in addition to the official sources are cited in footnotes.

Because no material comparable to the Bunga debates is available for the smaller reserves, the argument is developed largely in terms of the Transkei and Ciskei, which together contain between a half and a third of the Africans living in reserves in the Republic.[2] Official reports and independent investigators all indicate that, in the smaller reserves, trends were closely similar to those in the Transkei, though the pace of change varied.[3] Particular attention is paid to the adjoining territories of Basutoland, Bechuanaland, and Swaziland in an attempt to discover how far differences in political structure affected their development.

[1] See particularly: *Report of the Native Economic Commission, 1930–2 (Economic Commission)*; *Third Interim Report of the Industrial and Agricultural Requirements Commission (Van Eck Report)*; *Report of the Witwatersrand Mine Native Wages Commission, 1943 (Mine Wages Commission)*; *Social and Economic Planning Council, Report No. 9, The Native Reserves and their Place in the Economy of the Union of South Africa (Report No. 9)*; *Report of the Native Laws Commission, 1946–8 (Fagan Report)*; *Union Statistics for Fifty Years, 1910–1960*; *Republic of South Africa, Population Census, 1960*; *Basutoland 1956 Population Census*; *Basutoland, Annual Reports*; *Transkeian Territories General Council, Proceedings and Reports (Bunga Reports)*; *Ciskeian Territories General Council, Proceedings and Reports (Ciskei Bunga Reports)*. (Short titles used in reference are given in brackets. Reference numbers are to volumes and pages, not paragraphs.)

[2]
	Population (Tomlinson Report, p. 49)	*Area in square miles*
Transkei (1951)	1,202,197	214,596 (adjoining)
Ciskei	264,481	3,366 (dispersed)
Natal (including Zululand)	925,610	11,211 ,,
'Northern Areas' (Transvaal)	926,569	16,325 ,,
'Western Areas' (Transvaal)	314,402	12,436 ,,

Census, 1960, gives Transkei population as 1,387,682. Later figures for other reserves are not available.

[3] A. Vilakazi, *Zulu Transformation*; D. H. Reader, *Zulu Tribe in Transition*; B. A. Pauw, *Religion in a Tswana Chiefdom*; M. Horrell, *Visit to Bantu Areas of the Northern Transvaal*; P. Ruopp (ed.), *Approaches to Community Development*, pp. 97–120.

2. *Economic Interdependence*

Although the ideal of the missionaries was self-supporting communities of farmers and craftsmen, in practice their followers often earned a living by hunting and herding, or by outside employment. The mixed groups of herders along the Orange, and at Theopolis in Alexandria district, earned a cash income by shooting elephant or buffalo, and selling the ivory and pelts.[1] The Griqua, who were 'the voortrekkers of civilization on the northern frontier',[2] were slow to settle down as cultivators; they preferred to continue living as semi-nomadic hunters and pastoralists;[3] and the Coloured descendants and followers of Coenraad de Buys (see Vol. I, p. 240) who settled at Mara near the Soutpansberg, well ahead of Louis Trichardt's party of Voortrekkers, traded ivory, and salt from the deposit nearby. Other Coloured men who owned wagons found employment as transport riders from Port Elizabeth to Grahamstown after 1820, in Namaqualand during the copper-boom of the eighteen-fifties, and from the coast to Kimberley after the discovery of diamonds.[4]

Some early mission communities, using ploughs and leading water for irrigation, were indeed successful in producing grain over and above their needs, for with ploughs families could cultivate more than the two acres per adult which is about the limit in Africa with hoe culture.[5] Some men also began to breed sheep for wool (see Vol. I, p. 263). They sold the surplus grain and wool, together with skins, to buy the clothes which converts were required to wear, and the ploughs and harrows which were the farmer's tools. These successes were achieved both in Coloured and African communities, and on mission stations such as Shiloh, on the eastern Cape frontier, where different groups mingled.

From one community after another, however, there is evidence of a fall in productivity after a period of early prosperity. The tale is one of increasing pressure of population on deteriorating land, and the fall was not only in productivity per head, but in the total crop produced. In Victoria East, a district of the Ciskei, a population of under 6,000 Africans sold produce worth £19,000 in 1875; but in 1925 double that population (12,000) sold produce worth only £10,000 at current prices. The fall was chiefly in grain and wool.[6] The date at which the decline

---

[1] H. Lichtenstein, *Travels in Southern Africa, 1803–6*, ii. 301–2
[2] Marais, p. 43.   [3] Lichtenstein, ii. 305–6; Marais, pp. 43–4, 47, 150 n.
[4] Marais, pp. 81 n, 150 n.
[5] Ibid., pp. 76, 150; D. Biebuyck (ed.), *African Agrarian Systems*, pp. 68–9, 148, 377.
[6] J. Henderson, 'The Economic Condition of the Native People', *South African Outlook*, 57 (1927), 130. Evidence of Livingstone Moffat speaking in House of Assembly, *South African Outlook*, 57 (1927), 101.

began varied with the area: in the Coloured reserves of Namaqualand and Griqualand West, and in the Ciskei, it began before the end of the nineteenth century;[1] in the Transkei it was conspicuous after 1930.

Pressure on the land was due both to a rapid increase in population and the cultivation of a larger area by each family. Many complaints of land shortage were made to the Native Affairs Commission of 1903–5.[2] By 1928 a 'considerable number' of families in the Ciskei were without fields; Professor W. M. Macmillan found the proportion to be between 10 and 20 per cent of the adult men in Herschel district.[3] In 1936, Councillor Ntlatla from Idutywa in the Transkei told the Bunga that: 'the people who are landless in the surveyed districts are equal to those who have lands, if not more . . .'.[4] By 1946 it was certain that 20 per cent of the married men in the Ciskei and 25 per cent in the surveyed districts of the Transkei had no land to cultivate.[5] The population density on African land in the Ciskei was 79 to the square mile—83 in one district. In Natal and the Transkei it was 82 to the square mile, or 94 if migrants (who also wanted land for their families) were considered.[6] Crops were shrinking owing to erosion and the fall in fertility. Between 1921 and 1930, 640 million pounds of mealies were produced by Africans, and between 1931 and 1939 this fell to 490 million pounds, though production by white farmers rose steeply during the same period.[7] There was no longer room to move when land became exhausted, and most peasants did not practise new methods of rotation and fertilizing, which alone could have maintained communities with fixed, as opposed to shifting, cultivation. Moreover, in most areas fuel was so scarce that the dung and herbage required for compost was burnt on cooking fires. Therefore increasing agricultural production partly depended, and still depends, on the distribution of cheap fuel, whether coal, oil, or electricity.

The food shortage was exacerbated because some peasants, needing ready cash or goods from traders, or unable to store their grain securely, sold more than they could afford to do, and had to buy it back again at

[1] J. Henderson, 'Ciskei Missionary Council: Report on the Economic Condition of the Native People', *South African Outlook*, 58 (1928), 48. (Information was collected for this Report by eighty-one missionaries, White, African, and Coloured.)

[2] *1903–5 Report*, ii. 502–4, 571, 840, 931; iii. 402.

[3] *South African Outlook*, 57 (1927), 101.

[4] *Bunga Reports, 1936*, p. 101. In 1937, 14,560 married men in seven surveyed districts of the Transkei were landless. *Bunga Reports, 1937*, p. 167.

[5] W. R. Norton, Assistant Director of Native Agriculture, evidence given in a private capacity to Native Laws Commission. Reported in East London *Daily Dispatch*, Oct. 1946; *Report No. 9*, p. 57 (evidence of Chief Magistrate, Transkei); cf. M. E. Elton Mills and M. Wilson, *Land Tenure*, pp. 128–9.

[6] D. Hobart Houghton and E. M. Walton, *The Economy of a Native Reserve*, p. 22. *Tomlinson Report*, p. 49.

[7] E. Hellmann (ed.), *Handbook on Race Relations in South Africa*, p. 184.

double the price or more later in the season.[1] Storage of maize is costly, but the increase in price was also due to the scarcity of food during the spring. Whatever their origin may be, people are often improvident with new forms of wealth, and grain and cash were new forms of wealth to Coloured families whose ancestors had been hunters and pastoralists. So long as they had cash or grain the leaders were expected to be lavish in entertaining.[2] The Xhosa also found it more difficult to conserve grain and cash than cattle.

The values of nomadic pastoralists, which made them conserve breeding stock (which hunters would have eaten) were, indeed, out of date among a peasantry on limited land. Overstocking became so acute in some areas that what had once been good pasture became semi-desert.[3] This process has not yet been halted in all reserves, though it has been reversed in some districts, and Nguni and Sotho have been bitterly criticized for not selling cattle when they should.[4] Thus the same people were sometimes condemned for being 'improvident' and 'hoarding stock'.

There is no certainty as to the number of stock in proportion to population owned by Nguni in the early nineteenth century but such figures as we have indicate that cattle far exceeded the human population.[5] Xhosa herds were almost annihilated in the cattle-killing of 1857 (see Vol. I, p. 258) and herds throughout the country by the rinderpest epidemic of 1896. In 1918, in the Transkei, the proportion of cattle to people was 0·7 : 1. By 1930 it reached 1·4 : 1;[6] but overstocking

---

[1] *1903–5 Report*, ii. 1088; Marais, p. 81; *Bunga Reports, 1924*, pp. 95–8; 1937, p. 87. Most Tswana chiefs forbade their people to sell sorghum (kaffircorn) without permission but allowed sale of maize. I. Schapera, *Native Land Tenure in the Bechuanaland Protectorate*, p. 19.

[2] Marais, pp. 45–6.

[3] *Economic Commission*, pp. 11, 38; *Tomlinson Report*, pp. 75; Houghton and Walton, p. 165. In 1844 grass was twelve feet high on the road between Fort Beaufort and Alice, an area now almost bare. *The Narrative of Private Buck Adams* (ed. A. Gordon-Brown), p. 45; observation by the author over a period of fifty years.   [4] *Economic Commission*, p. 16; *Tomlinson Report*, p. 82.

[5] Cattle captured by colonists nearly equalled the estimated Xhosa population (see I, 242, 255). In 1824 in Graaff Reinet district the proportion of cattle to people (white, slave, and Khoikhoi) was 5 : 1, and small stock 63 : 1. *1903–5 Report*, iii. 20. W. Govan, *Memorials of the Rev. James Laing*, p. 33. Laing found the master of a homestead 'singular in the small number of his cattle, having no more than seven head'.

[6] *Economic Commission*, Annexure 13. *Union Statistics for Fifty Years*, 1910–60. The full figures are:

1918.	Transkei	Cattle to people	0·7 : 1
		Sheep to people	2·0 : 1
		Goats to people	1·2 : 1
		Horses and donkeys to people	0·1 : 1
		i.e. stock units to people	1·1 : 1
1930.	Transkei	Cattle to people	1·4 : 1
		Sheep to people	3·0 : 1
		Goats to people	1·0 : 1
		Horses and donkeys to people	0·1 : 1
		i.e. stock units to people	2·4 : 1

was already serious in all the reserves save some parts of Zululand and Pondoland, and stock in proportion to population began to fall. In 1950, after drought, the cattle:people ratio in Keiskammahoek district was 0·5:1, the cattle being almost the same in number as in 1925, but the human population having increased.[1] In 1955 Professor F. R. Tomlinson noted that stock units per family were falling for the reserves as a whole: the average number of units owned by a family (with 6·3 members) in 1939 was 9·1, in 1946, 7·9, and in 1954, 7·1.[2]

The milk supply per family fell drastically, both because cattle were fewer in proportion to the population, and because the milk produced by each cow diminished as pastures were eroded. In Keiskammahoek district in 1834 a missionary visiting homesteads was constantly offered curds,[3] but by 1928 in only 13 per cent of the Ciskeian districts was there commonly milk,[4] though in Pondoland (not yet seriously over-stocked) milk was available even in winter in 75 per cent of the home-steads, and in summer every homestead was well supplied.[5]

The decrease in the number of cattle and their bad condition also affected production of grain, since few families in the Ciskei had a full plough-team,[6] and successful farming turns on quick ploughing after rain. This problem is met when cultivation, as well as transport, is mechanized. Ploughing by tractor, privately owned or hired from the state, had begun in the Ciskei by 1948.

Not only did the peasant communities cease to export grain: they ceased to grow sufficient to feed themselves. One district after another in the reserves reached the point at which it was no longer self-support-ing in food but was dependent on imports of basic grain—maize, sorghum (kaffir-corn), wheat—as well as 'luxuries' like sugar, coffee, and tinned or dried milk. Precise evidence is lacking, but in 1903, following a drought, 'the whole . . . country . . . lived on American mealies for several months.'[7] At that date Zulu in Natal ordinarily grew their own food and the coastal districts of Pondoland still exported maize and tobacco in good seasons.[8] By 1932 estimated production in the Transkei was about three-fifths of requirements in maize;[9] by 1943

---

[1]
1946. Keiskammahoek District
Stock units to people   1·0:1
1950. Keiskammahoek District (after drought)
Stock units to people   0·5:1
Houghton and Walton, pp. 13, 164–75.
A 'stock unit' is one bovine or equine, or four sheep or goats (*Tomlinson Report*, p. 78 n.) or, in Keiskammahoek, five sheep or goats (Houghton and Walton, p. 165, n. 3).

[2] *Tomlinson Report*, pp. 54, 78–80.   [3] Govan, pp. 27, 30–1.
[4] Henderson, *Outlook*, 58 (1928), 48.   [5] Hunter, pp. 68–9.
[6] M. Wilson, S. Kaplan, T. Maki, E. M. Walton, *Social Structure*, pp. 18–20.
[7] *1903–5 Report*, ii. 1088.   [8] Ibid. ii. 1088–9; iii. 406, 407.
[9] *Economic Commission*, p. 41; *Census, 1926*, p. ix. Requirements are calculated at 3½ bags per head, per annum.

it was not much more than half;[1] by 1950, in Keiskammahoek district, production in a good season was less than half the requirements, and in a year of drought only one-twentieth.[2] In 1933 in the Transkei 25 per cent of the sales in stores was food (including mealies, sugar, and tea) and tobacco: 50 per cent blankets and clothing. In 1947–8 in Keiskammahoek the comparable figures were 55 per cent food and tobacco, and 32 per cent clothing.[3] Thus 'peasants' as well as townsmen came to depend upon farmers for their daily bread.

Food production was falling and at the same time potential consumption was rising fast, and still (in 1966) it continues to rise. In the traditional societies a man with 50 head of cattle, and wives and daughters to cultivate, and sons to herd and hunt, had more choice food than his family could consume. They built their own huts and made their own clothes and utensils, and opportunity for trading was very limited. The rich man distributed his wealth, and gained prestige by doing so, just as a millionaire distributes wealth and gains prestige in contemporary society. But once trade with the outside world developed, potential consumption, beginning with beads and blankets and expanding to include fine houses and pianos, education, and overseas travel, was enormously greater. He who had felt himself rich in possession of cattle was now poor in terms of new wants.

The consumption of 'school people' rose faster than that of conservative 'reds' (see I, p. 265) largely because of their requirements in clothing. In 1903 a Transkei trader reported that 'a red' man spent on the average £1 a month in stores, and a 'school' man £2 a month, and thirty years later, pagans in Pondoland sometimes objected to members of the family becoming Christian on the ground that they would 'always be poor'.[4]

As pressure on land grew the natural increase began to emigrate, at first to the less populated reserves. Mfengu from the Ciskei moved east of the Kei in 1866–8, and fifty to sixty years later they were moving from the western Transkei into the less densely populated Pondoland, and the mountains of Basutoland.[5] But most of the movement was to the growing towns. The doubling of population in Victoria East between 1875 and 1911 was followed by a decline,[6] and much the same happened in Keiskammahoek district. The movement was directly due to

[1] *Mine Wages Report*, p. 11; *Report of the Commission on Native Education 1949–1951*, p. 194, put Transkei imports at an average of 35,286 tons (357,000 bags) a year between 1932 and 1949. Curiously, an average of 4,064 tons per annum were exported over the same period.
[2] Houghton and Walton, pp. 157–60.
[3] Howard Pim, *A Transkei Enquiry, 1933*, p. 21; Houghton and Walton, p. 80.
[4] *1903–5 Report*, ii. 1088; Hunter, p. 142.
[5] Ibid., p. 7; Macmillan, p. 152.
[6] Henderson, *Outlook*, 57 (1927), 130–3.

hunger.[1] After 1921, in South Africa as a whole, Africans were moving to town faster than whites (see pp. 173, 188).

Individual tenure for Africans began with the settlement of Mfengu refugees in the Cape Colony. On their arrival in 1837 they were placed in 'locations' held on communal tenure, but individual holdings were pressed for by missionaries, and in 1855 the first grants of land on free-hold were made to twenty-nine 'mission Natives' in an area adjoining Lovedale.[2] Sir George Grey, following a policy of 'civilization through mingling', favoured individual tenure, and Cecil Rhodes pressed it forward in Glen Grey in 1894. It gradually extended through all the districts of the Ciskei, seven magisterial districts of the Transkei, and two in Natal. Each married man who wished to take up individual tenure was granted an arable plot of about eight acres and a building site, on freehold or quitrent tenure, together with grazing rights on pasture-land demarcated for the village or 'location' in which he built. Those villages in which the majority opposed survey remained on land held under communal tenure.[3]

In 1923 the extension of survey, which had been proceeding slowly, was halted. Individual tenure had not worked as the originators of the scheme had intended: land held individually was treated as lineage land, rather than the holding of one individual, and it was sub-divided in practice if not in law;[4] productivity of individual holdings was scarcely higher, in later generations, than on communally held land;[5] transfers were not legally effected and there was confusion over the legal status of holdings.[6] Individual tenure was liked by many of the land-owners but opposed by others, for it diminished the powers of the chiefs,[7] and people linked land-shortage with the survey which pre-ceded allocation of individual plots. Survey made plain to the villagers that there was not sufficient land for every family to own a holding, whereas, so long as communal tenure prevailed, additional allotments were taken from the pasture, and fields were shared out. Survey was also expensive.[8] To the villagers access to land for cultivation and pasture was a natural right: every married man was entitled to a field for cultivation, a homestead site, and grazing for stock on the village com-mon, and a widow retained these rights after her husband's death. The

---

[1] Houghton and Walton, pp. 10–12, 176.

[2] *1883 Report*, ii. 374; J. Ayliff and J. Whiteside, *History of the Abambo*, p. 45; *Report on Native Location Surveys, Cape Town*, p. 1.

[3] *1883 Report*, ii. 366–77. Individual grants were also made to 'Natives' in the districts of Port Elizabeth, Oudtshoorn, George, and Swellendam; *Native Location Surveys*.

[4] Elton Mills and Wilson, pp. 20–3, 44, 50–8, 81–2, 129–30, 136, 147; *1903–5 Report*, ii. 724.

[5] Elton Mills and Wilson, pp. 104, 130.   [6] Ibid., pp. 56, 72, 146, 148.

[7] *1883 Report*, ii. 373–7; Hunter, p. 117; Elton Mills and Wilson, p. 134.

[8] *Bunga Reports, 1924*, p. 62; *1883 Report*, ii. 375–6. A district that applied for survey was refused on the ground that 'the cost was prohibitive'.

administration, for their part, were anxious to settle as many Africans as possible in the reserves and individual tenure hampered the attempt to do this. The native commissioners followed the policy (approved by chiefs and headmen) of making the land go as far as possible by dividing large holdings and allocating only one arable plot—in theory eight acres but often much less—to each man.[1]

From the nineteenth century onwards, there have been passionate complaints of landlessness from African leaders. The Nguni and Sotho chiefs Sandile, Sarili, Cetshwayo, and Moshweshwe spoke bitterly of it; the Mfengu refugees began to complain of it before the end of the nineteenth century; and the educated leaders of the twentieth century reverted to the problem again and again.[2] The underlying (but rarely explicit) assumption was that every family was entitled to land, and the discrepancy between the land-holding of whites who formed a fifth of the population and held over eighty per cent of the land, and that of Africans, was repeatedly emphasized. The shift from a society in which most people have land rights, to one in which a diminishing proportion are farmers and sell food to the others, has been a difficult one almost everywhere, and the poor have commonly suffered, losing what land they had to the rich. In South Africa the problem has been exacerbated by the colour cleavage. Not only were Africans unable to acquire farming land, owing to the limitations imposed in 1913 and 1936 (see p. 52), but property rights and the rights of domicile in town have been closely restricted, and in 1966 the restrictions were growing still more, rather than less, stringent (see pp. 191–202). Pressure on land in the reserves is therefore directly related to territorial segregation as established in 1913, and the restriction on movement to town.

Since pressure on land was so great, and both the administration and most Africans favoured sub-division of land to allow a field to as many families as possible, very few men had sufficient land to grow a cash crop and become full-time farmers. The exceptions were a few Xhosa-speakers with considerable flocks of sheep which they grazed on the common pasture; some Zulu living on the coastal belt of Natal who grew sugar cane; and Sotho settlers in irrigated areas in the northern Transvaal. Sugar production and the areas under irrigation are increasing, and plantations producing fibre (sisal, *phormium tenax*,

---

[1] Ibid. ii. 35, 47; *1903–5 Commission*, iv, 430.

[2] *Bunga Reports, 1924*, pp. 55–8, 175; *1927*, pp. 80–4; *1931*, pp. 138–9; *1933*, pp. 95–6; *1936*, pp. 101–2, 115–17; *1937*, pp. 167, 182–5; *1938*, p. 238; *1939*, p. 112; *1940*, pp. 110–11; S. M. Molema, *The Bantu Past and Present*, pp. 250, 353, 385–6; A. B. Xuma, *Reconstituting the Union of South Africa*, pp. 7–8; D. D. T. Jabavu, *Native Disabilities in South Africa*, pp. 8–9; D. D. T. Jabavu, *The Findings of the All African Convention*, pp. 11–15; D. D. T. Jabavu (ed.), *Minutes of the All African Convention*, p. 30; Hunter, pp. 554–7, 560–1; on areas held see Hellman, (ed.), *Handbook on Race Relations*, pp. 171–5.

and *furcreae*) have been established in reserves,[1] but taken as a whole, the reserves are no nearer being self-supporting. Economists have repeatedly pressed for a change in policy which would allow a competent farmer to acquire more land,[2] but their recommendations have not been implemented.

The deterioration of land already referred to (pp. 55–6) has been met by state-aided schemes for rehabilitation. This involves the replanning of a given area, and the laying out of 'economic units', that is units large enough for a family just to support itself, but because there are twice or three times too many people on the land, and there is nowhere for the surplus population to go (the families not being admitted to towns) the new allocations are of half-units or less. In a Ciskeian conservation area Dr. Christopher Board found as many men going out to work as before. 'Betterment . . . has the effect of freezing the traditional pattern.'[3]

What is proceeding is limitation of stock, paddocking of grazing commons, contouring of arable land, sinking boreholes, and building dams. If erosion, and in some reserves the total destruction of the soil, is to be checked, limitation of stock with paddocking and contouring is essential, but culling of stock and fencing have been bitterly opposed in many areas[4] and the opposition linked with African nationalism. Conflicts in Witzieshoek between 1946 and 1951, and in eastern Pondoland between 1953 and 1961, were local manifestations of widespread and long-continuing tension. Individuals saw the animals on which they depended for milk and ploughing, as well as for sacrifices and for marriage, disappearing, and their remaining cattle excluded from their accustomed pastures, and they argued that the cure was not reduction of stock or fencing, but allocation of more land. Moreover, rehabilitation schemes were associated with the imposition of 'Bantu Authorities' (see pp. 89–93.) The recommendation of the official 'Commission of Enquiry into the Disturbances in Witzieshoek Native Reserve in 1951' that pressure on land in the reserves be relieved by providing security of tenure for African industrial workers in town, has never been implemented, and Government policy in 1966 is directly contrary to it. Opposition to new agricultural techniques (which are desperately needed to save the soil and provide more food for the people working it) thus became identified with opposition to a hated form of government.

Deep bitterness over land continues, but there is some evidence that

---

[1] *Tomlinson Report*, p. 112–13; Horrell, *Survey, 1965*, pp. 140–1; *1966*, pp. 136–7.

[2] *Economic Commission*, p. 22; *Report No. 9*, p. 57; *Tomlinson Report*, p. 114.

[3] C. Board, 'The Rehabilitation Programme in Bantu Areas', *SAJE*, 32 (1964), 48.

[4] *Report of the Commission of Enquiry into the Disturbance in the Witzieshoek Native Reserve*; direct observation.

the practical advantages of paddocking and contouring are recognized by landholders, and water-conservation has been generally accepted. Again and again in history the building of reservoirs and aqueducts has been one of the lasting monuments created by wealthy empires in the countries they ruled, and no one flying over southern Africa can doubt that the innumerable dams, small and large, are a major contribution of this generation of South Africans—white and black—to posterity. Contour walls and banks have also been valuable investments pressed by rulers on reluctant villagers, even before Europeans came to Africa.

But other reforms are debatable. For example, as part of their agricultural policy the Government has sought to concentrate scattered homesteads, and this has been strongly resisted. Administrators, whether the Dutch East Indian Company dealing with Free Burghers, or a Tswana chief with his followers, always prefer the people they rule to be concentrated, for then control is easier, but while some concentration may be necessary where surface water is scarce, it is hard to discern the economic advantage, in a country full of streams, of concentrating peasants so that they may be up to four miles from their fields, as some families are reported to be in newly established villages in Herschel district. With the increasing density of population, and a growing tendency for each married man to establish his own independent homestead, rather than live in that of his father or senior brother, homesteads among the Nguni generally are smaller and closer together than they were (see Vol. I, p. 116). The landscape of the Ciskei in 1945, even before villagers were forced to conform to any imposed pattern of settlement, was considerably different from that of conservative and less densely populated Pondoland in 1931, or Swaziland in 1936,[1] but the gradual emergence of villages of 300 to 2,000 people, spread out over a mile, is very different from compulsory settlement on half-acre plots, laid out in streets. It is noticeable that Nguni people, when left to themselves, prefer to scatter. Xhosa and Mfengu complained in 1883 of the disadvantage of being required to live close together on surveyed lots; the converts settled in the mission village of Burnshill around the church scattered within a generation; and freeholders in the Ciskei built their homesteads in long lines between field and pasture, rather than closely adjacent.[2] Concentration is more likely to be acceptable among the Sotho-speakers who have a tradition of living in compact villages, but some of them, also, tend to scatter when they are free to choose (see Vol. I, p. 153). Elsewhere settlement patterns have persisted through centuries and they may well do so in Africa.[3]

[1] Direct observation.   [2] *1883 Report*, i. 121–2, 196; Elton Mills and Wilson, pp. 134–5.
[3] G. C. Homans, *English Villagers in the Thirteenth Century*, pp. 23–8.

Apart from controversy over settlement patterns peasant farming is not flourishing. In the reserves the agricultural revolution (described in the next chapter) has not taken place, and there is little indication that it will soon begin. The development of peasant farming in Africa has everywhere depended upon Government initiative, because the returns on investment were nowhere sufficient to attract private capital.[1] It is no accident that those territories in which cash crops were developed by peasant farmers with effective government aid (notably cocoa in Ghana, coffee in Tanganyika, and cotton in Sudan) were territories in which competition between African peasants and white settlers did not exist, or territories (such as Tanganyika) in which the interests of Africans were held to be paramount.[2] The South African Government has not carried out the recommendation of its own Tomlinson Commission that very large capital investment be made for the development of the reserves, and it rejected the Commission's recommendation that private entrepreneurs, even though white, be encouraged to establish industries in the Transkei.[3]

The pull of towns is strong in Africa as elsewhere, and opportunity of urban employment has been greater in the south than in the west or east. At the same time, inducements for peasants to grow cash crops have been much less, and the small number of men who choose to remain permanently in the reserves do so for other than economic reasons.[4]

Opportunity of paid employment in the reserves is extremely limited. Virtually the only employers are the Government and missions, and the small number of white traders and hotel keepers. Motions were repeatedly brought up in the Bunga asking that Africans rather than whites be appointed to such posts as dipping supervisors, postal officials, health inspectors, court messengers, and clerks; that they be trained as court interpreters, lawyers, doctors, surveyors, and engineers; and that industries be established to provide employment.[5] Nevertheless manufacture had scarcely begun in 1966 and opportunity of local employment remains meagre. Since the establishment of Bantu Authorities there has been much talk of more posts being open to Africans in the reserves. In practice, in the Transkei until 1960, trade remained largely in the hands of whites though there were repeated recom-

[1] I am indebted to Professor John Gallagher of Balliol College, Oxford, for making this point clear to me.

[2] W. K. Hancock, *Survey of British Commonwealth Affairs*, ii, part ii (London, 1942), 109–12.

[3] *Government Decisions on the Recommendations of the Commission for the Socio-Economic Development of the Bantu Areas within the Union of South Africa*, p. 8.

[4] Direct observation of contrast between Pondoland and Ciskei, and Nyakyusa country, 1931–8.

[5] *Bunga Reports, 1928*, pp. 83–5; *1930*, pp. 64–5, 118–20; *1934*, pp. 99–107, 296; *1936*, 139–42; *1937*, pp. 90–6, 188–9; *1939*, pp. 133–5; *1955*, p. 106.

mendations that licences be given to Africans more readily than whites, and African traders were encouraged to establish themselves.[1] Since 1959 the Government-controlled Development Corporation has bought a number of trading stations and some are managed by Africans. By 1966, 297 Africans were trading on their own account and fourteen managing stores, in a population of 1,400,000.[2]

As the food supply declined more and more men, and some women, took the only alternative open to them and went out to work in mines, in towns, and on European-owned farms. Migrant labour had begun as early as 1707—Kolb speaks of the 'Hessequas' (Khoikhoi men from near the modern Caledon)—taking service with white farmers and using their wages to buy cattle,[3] and men from Coloured mission stations and reserves have continued to go out as migrant workers for two centuries.[4] It has been shown how employment of Xhosa and refugees from Natal developed on the eastern Cape frontier, and received a great impetus from the cattle-killing of 1857 (see Vol. I, p. 258). The second leap in employment of migrants came in 1870 when owners of claims on the new diamond fields were avid for labour, and when Xhosa, Sotho, and Zulu realized that guns, as well as horses and blankets, might be earned by working there. Rhodes, himself a large-scale employer and sympathetic to the needs of employers, devised a system of land-tenure for Glen Grey district, which was designed to force a portion of the men to work as migrant labourers. 'The intention was to locate then resident natives on these surveyed allotments, and to make no provision for the natural increase of the population, the surplus to find work elsewhere: so that . . . during the coming generation a limited number will be agriculturalists, i.e. native farmers—and the the rest will have to go out and work.'[5] The argument that land should be limited, so that African men might not 'live in idleness' but go out to work for Europeans has been repeated again and again in the history of southern Africa: Rhodesians were using it as late as 1951.[6] Peasant production was 'idleness' to the white man in need of labour.

Migrant labour began with a few of the young unmarried men from a village going out to work for some months. Its character changed as the proportion of men increased, as it included older married men, and as the periods of employment away from home became longer and longer. The proportion of adult men (tax-payers) away rose to 71·7 per cent in Middledrift district (an eroded area of the Ciskei) and 67 per cent in Sekhukhuneland in the Transvaal in 1928-9.[7] By 1953 in

[1] Ibid., *1922*, pp. 74–6; *1931*, pp. 129–32; Pim, p. 22.
[2] Horrell, *Survey, 1966*, pp. 137–8.
[3] P. Kolb, *The Present State of the Cape of Good Hope*, i. 75.
[4] Marais, p. 255; Carstens, p. 211.   [5] *Native Location Surveys*, p. 5.
[6] *1903–5 Report*, iii. 409, 449. Direct observation.   [7] *Economic Commission*, p. 173.

Keiskammahoek district (adjoining Middledrift) it had dropped to 53 per cent, but by then an appreciable proportion of the population had moved permanently to town, and was not included in this figure. Thirty-five per cent of the total population (including migrants) had emigrated more or less permanently from the district.[1]

The periods of employment on the mines rose and the periods spent at home dropped, and those moving into secondary industry spent longer at work and much shorter periods at home than the miners.[2] The Tomlinson Commission found that migrants spent 62 per cent of their working lives away from home, and in Keiskammahoek district in 1950 41 per cent had been away for five years or more without returning.[3] Government policy since 1952, particularly in the Western Cape, has been directed towards increasing the number of migrants and decreasing the number of those who settle in town.

Far fewer women go out to work in town than men, but the proportion was rising until further restrictions on women entering towns were imposed from 1952 onwards. In Keiskammahoek, in 1950, 39 per cent of the women of working age were away: of these over a third were living with their husbands in town, over a third were unmarried, and the rest were widows, abandoned wives, or unmarried mothers.[4]

Those who go out to work are the able-bodied. In the country there are a disproportionate number of the very young, the old, the unfit, and women with children to tend. The masculinity rate (males to a hundred females) in Keiskammahoek villages in 1946 was 73·8; the corresponding figure for the Transkei in 1960 was 70·8.[5]

The importance of outside employment to the reserves was reflected in Bunga debates.[6] Anxiety about employment was often expressed; so was opposition to the 'civilized labour' policy which reserved jobs for whites, and to the employment of Africans from north of the Limpopo; and motions demanding a minimum wage were debated.[7] The same problems are discussed in the Transkei Legislative Assembly which succeeded the Bunga.

Detailed investigation of budgets of Keiskammahoek district in 1949

[1] Houghton and Walton, pp. 111–35.

[2] *Mine Wages Report*, pp. 15, 55; I. Schapera, *Migrant Labours and Tribal Life*, pp. 57–8; *Tomlinson Report*, p. 96.

[3] Houghton and Walton, p. 127.   [4] Ibid., pp. 129–32.

[5] Ibid., pp. 24–41; *Census, 1960*, v. 38.

[6] In 1921, total sums coming into Transkei were estimated at £700,000. *Bunga Reports, 1921*, p. 161. From 1926 to 1930 deferred pay from Johannesburg mines was in the region of £200,000 a year. *Economic Commission*, p. 135. In 1965, 258,000 Transkeians were officially reported to be employed outside Transkei, and the money remitted or saved and bought home during the year was estimated at R9,000,000. Horrell, *1966*, pp. 139–40.

[7] *Bunga Reports, 1921*, pp. 159–64; *1923*, pp. 46–7, 74–7, 142–3; *1930*, p. 95; *1931*, pp. 100–2; *1932*, p. 115; *1933*, p. 89–91; *1934*, pp. 78, 164–6, 174–5; *1935*, pp. 171–3; *1937*, p. 229; *1938*, pp. 149–52.

showed the average annual income of a family of six to be about £50 a year in cash and kind. Of this only about £9 a year came from farming in produce consumed or sold; well over a third came from wages earned outside the district, and the rest from earnings in the district. The well-to-do families were those with more than one wage-earner in the district,[1] for they had only one home to maintain, whereas migrants must maintain two.

The food of most Nguni families is probably less nutritious and less plentiful than it used to be, though fewer die from famine during drought. Even though their consumption in clothing, furniture, housing, and tools has risen, poverty—how to obtain the barest necessities—remains the problem of the great majority of peasant families. There is no sense of steadily increasing wealth as there is in some African communities elsewhere, with lucrative cash crops and ample land.[2]

Economists have long agreed that the movement of a large section of the African population into industry is a condition of increasing productivity in South Africa:[3] the agriculturists are agreed that agricultural development in the reserves depends upon the removal of between one-third and two-thirds of the families there;[4] but the policy of separation between white and black, which has been held to be paramount, has delayed, though it has not prevented, the process.

Families which would willingly move to town dare not do so since they fear that later they may be excluded, and no longer have a country home to fall back on. The official policy of encouraging the growth of industry near the borders of reserves (see p. 42) does not obviate the problem of split families since the labourers can rarely live at home (though some may week-end at home if they can afford the cost of transport); nor does it provide more than a very small proportion of jobs required. A lifetime of moving from country home to town job and back, and of separation of husband from wife and children is the way of life which South Africa imposes on a quarter or more of its population. The implication of the land reform in progress in 1966 is that while a third of the families now in the reserves may become full-time farmers, the others become solely dependent upon the earnings of bread-winners working away from home.

It may well be asked whether a rural community, so dependent on urban earning, is indeed a peasant community. Is it not rather an industrial proletariat domiciled in the country? Peasant communities

[1] Houghton and Walton, pp. 91–110.

[2] D. Brokensha, *Social Change at Larteh, Ghana*, pp. 19–20, 35–45, 60–6, 78.

[3] *Report No. 9*, pp. 58–61; *Tomlinson Report*, p. 131.

[4] D. Hobart Houghton, 'Men of Two Worlds', *SAJE*, 28 (1960), 177–90; 'Land Reform in Bantu Areas', *SAJE*, 29 (1961), 165–75.

have frequently supplemented their income by sending out migrant labourers[1] and the point at which they cease to be defined as 'peasant' is arbitrary. We take it to be the point at which most families in a community no longer have land of their own or which they work as tenants. Those settled in villages without land-rights other than over the half-acre on which the home is built, are not, in our terms, peasants: they are the dependants of urban workers, and the 'village' is a 'dormitory suburb', though very far from any centre of employment. The occupants of new landless villages, which the Department of Bantu Development is fostering, are in this category. Many of them would live in town near employment if they could. But the majority of families in reserves, still having a fragment of land or the hope of inheriting one, is classified here as 'peasant'.

The changes described in some detail for the Ciskei and Transkei occurred also in the reserves of the northern Cape, Natal, and the Transvaal, and the two small reserves of the Orange Free State. Pressure of population and consequent movement of large numbers of men as migrant labourers, occurred later in Zululand and the northern Transvaal than elsewhere, and the education of women developed there slowly, but there is no indication of any appreciable difference in trends in different reserves. The overall picture is one of pressure on land, decline in productivity, and dependence on bread-winners in town, but the movement of families to industrial centres (which alone would relieve pressure on land) is delayed by the policy of apartheid. As already noted (p. 51) no peasants have been successful as small-scale agriculturists in South Africa—not even the hard-working and skilful German settlers whose land-grants were more than twice the proposed 'economic holding' for Africans in the same area.[2] In the climate and conditions of South Africa the trend is towards large-scale farming and industry.

What of developments in the adjoining territories of Basutoland, Bechuanaland, and Swaziland?[3] There expressed policy differed from that in the Union, and it grew yet more different after the Union became a Republic in 1961, and Basutoland and Bechuanaland became the independent states of Lesotho and Botswana in 1966. Nevertheless in demographic trends and in economy these two countries have

---

[1] Pitt-Rivers, passim; W. I. Thomas and F. Znaniecki, The Polish Peasant in Europe and America.   [2] Houghton, Economic Development, p. 87.

[3] Basutoland, Report for the Year, 1956, pp. 6–37; 1962, pp. 18–53; 1963, pp. 10, 22–34, 41–57, 72; Basutoland 1956 Population Census, pp. 28–30, 68–9; V. Sheddick, Land Tenure in Basutoland; Report (1945–6) of the Commission on Education in Basutoland, p. 11; I. Schapera, Migrant Labour, and Tribal Life; Native Land Tenure in the Bechuanaland Protectorate; H. Kuper, The Uniform of Colour; J. F. Holleman (ed.), Experiment in Swaziland.

developed step by step in the same way as the Transkei. In Lesotho no land is owned by whites, mineral resources are limited, and industry has scarcely begun (in 1966). In Botswana a very limited amount of land is owned by white farmers and industrial development has scarcely begun. Swaziland is different for there African-owned land is interspersed with European-owned farms (see map II); moreover Swaziland has rich mineral resources which began to be developed in 1937, a flourishing timber industry, good roads, and a fast growing tourist trade. Its economy is more comparable to that of Natal than to Lesotho or Botswana. Climatically Swaziland resembles Zululand, and Lesotho the inland parts of the Transkei, while most of Botswana is arid like the reserves of the northern Cape (see map I).

In population the independent states are small—the three combined probably had a slightly smaller population in 1966 than the Transkei[1]— and despite the resources of Swaziland they are very weak in comparison with the Republic. Their economies, like that of the Transkei, have been shaped by the growth of industry and markets in the Cape and the Transvaal (and later Natal and the Orange Free State) where wages could be earned and food bought. Like the Transkei, the three independent states supply labour and buy both food and manufactured goods.

In all three countries initial increases in areas cultivated by each family, through the introduction of ploughs, were followed by rapid population growth and pressure on land or, in Bechuanaland, pressure on land with accessible water. They all ceased to be self-supporting in food, and became dependent upon the earnings of migrant labourers in the cities and on the farms of the Union, and on the import of grain. The analogies are closest between the Transkei and Basutoland, and they changed simultaneously. In Basutoland, the rapid increase of population between 1891 and 1921 was followed by a period (1936–46) when population (with a density of 70 to the square mile) became nearly static, the natural increase moving out to employment within the Union. Thereafter, when restriction on movement of Africans into town became more rigid in the Union (notably after 1952), the population of Basutoland began to rise again.

In 1837 the Sotho of Basutoland (which then stretched west of the Caledon) had grain stored for four to eight years: in 1844 white farmers 'flocked' to them to buy grain. During 1872 (*after* the loss of their most fertile land west of the Caledon) the Sotho exported 100,000 muids of grain (wheat, mealies, and kaffir-corn),[2] and in 1877 when the demand

---

[1] Census Reports are not available for the same dates. The most recent show: Swaziland (1956), 229,744; Bechuanaland (1964), 514,378; Basutoland (1958), 638,857; total, 1,382,979. Transkei (1960), 1,387,682.

[2] One muid was about 185 lb. See also vol. i, p. 206.

for grain on the diamond fields had fallen 'large quantities' were held by producers and shopkeepers in Basutoland; but once shifting cultivation became impossible, owing to the pressure of population, there was a 'downward trend in production'. In 1903, during a drought, Basutoland, like the Transkei, began importing grain from overseas. In 1775 there were 1·7 cattle for every person in Basutoland and 2·8 stock units (cattle, horses, sheep, and goats). The numbers of stock increased until 1931, but thereafter fell, and stock in relation to people has declined markedly. In 1946 the figure (1·8 stock units per person) was little more than half that of 1875.[1] Since the proportion of cattle is now (1966) smaller than elsewhere, and the pastures are overstocked, milk is correspondingly scarce. Wool and mohair are the chief exports of the territory, and the proportion of horses, mules, and donkeys is high because roads do not exist through most of the territory, and transport (even of supplies to the mountain trading stations) is largely by pack animals, for which equines are preferred to oxen. Mechanization of transport and cultivation is beginning, and the potential in spray irrigation for pastures,[2] and hydro-electric power (which could replace dung as fuel, releasing it for compost) is enormous.

A third of the male population of Basutoland was working in South Africa as migrant labourers in 1936, and by 1956 the figure was forty-two per cent.[3] Corresponding figures for women were seven and eleven per cent. One characteristic of the districts adjoining the Orange Free State[4] is that families—men, women, and children—go out for short periods as reapers on European-owned farms, and are paid in grain, which (added to their own crops) provides subsistence for the greater part of the year.

The Tswana population probably doubled between 1911 and 1936 and then increased more slowly, but after 1956 rapid increase again occurred, exactly following the pattern of the Ciskei and Basutoland.[5] Bechuanaland had a short period of agricultural prosperity after the introduction of ploughs. In 1878 Shoshong had forty ploughs and by 1890 enterprising men were growing maize for sale to the whites moving into Rhodesia, but before 1943 pressure on land near the larger settlements was apparent and grain was imported. The majority of families 'reaped too little, or barely sufficient' to support themselves each year.

[1] R. C. Germond, *Chronicles of Basutoland*, pp. 439, 444, 478; CGH, *Blue Book of Native Affairs, 1874; 1876; 1877; Basutoland Population Census, 1956*, table I; Sheddick, p. 36; *Annual Reports*, especially *1955*.

[2] R. C. Germond, 'Economic Development and Land Reform in Basutoland', *South African Outlook*, 95 (1965), 186–8.

[3] *Basutoland 1956 Population Census*, p. 73.

[4] This includes Herschel district which is geographically part of Lesotho though politically part of the Ciskei.

[5] *Census of the Bechuanaland Protectorate, 1964*, p. 1. 'The accuracy of census figures prior to 1946 is doubtful', and therefore conclusions drawn are not certain.

Poor seasons exceeded the good or moderate. The average annual import between 1927 and 1941 was 26,000 bags.[1]

Throughout southern Africa, but most conspicuously in Botswana, rainfall, and consequently yields of grain, are very variable, and bulk storage for more than one season is a difficult technical problem. So long as a people remained isolated, population was limited by what could be produced or collected within a restricted area, in the worst years (see Vol. I, p. 254); increase in population is immediately related to import of food from a much wider area, during famine years. When crops failed throughout South Africa in 1903 the Transkei lived on American mealies as already noted (see p. 58), and during the drought of 1962–6 Bechuanaland, Basutoland, and the northern Transvaal were dependent on grain not only from the rest of South Africa but even from overseas.

The imports to Bechuanaland (as to Basutoland and the Transkei) were paid for chiefly by migrant labourers working in the towns of South Africa. In 1942–3 over sixty per cent of the able-bodied men were away from the eastern districts of Bechuanaland, some of them in the army, but many in the Union. The proportion of adult women migrants was five per cent. Census figures show that the number of short-term migrants quadrupled between 1946 and 1964 but the number of men away for one to five years, and the number of women away, changed little.[2]

Swaziland does not show either the early rapid increase in population or the flattening in increase which is evident elsewhere (if official figures are remotely correct), and in 1960 African families were much nearer to being self-supporting in food than those in the Ciskei, Transkei, and Basutoland. The ratio of cattle per person was 1·9 : 1; it had not fallen markedly since a peak in 1921, and had probably quadrupled since 1904 when herds had been destroyed by rinderpest and 'east coast fever'. Though overstocking existed it was not as acute as in the Ciskei and Basutoland, and milk must have been available. Three-quarters of the homesteads purchased some of their requirements in maize but the African population as a whole came 'close to providing food requirements'. With a population density of forty-four to the square mile there were no landless families but 'abundant space for extending cultivation'. Forty per cent of the homesteads had no income from wages, nevertheless wage-earning was a much more important source of cash than the sale of any crop, or even of cattle, and some cash income was a necessity. Half the homesteads had a cash income of over R50 a year.[3]

---

[1] Schapera, *Land Tenure*, pp. 19, 118–20. Professor Schapera calculates two bags of grain per annum per person. In the Ciskei and Transkei, two and a half bags are allowed.
[2] Schapera, *Migrant Labour*, pp. 34, 65–8; *Bechuanaland Protectorate Census 1964*, p. 26.
[3] Holleman, pp. 35–6, 224, 235–52.

In none of the three territories discussed has individual tenure of land been introduced on tribal land, though farms, individually held, exist in Swaziland and on the fringes of Botswana. Chiefs retained power in all three countries until 1964 and, as has been shown, chiefs consistently opposed individual tenure, since it undermined their power. Some educated Tswana have been very critical of the administering authority for failing to establish individual tenure,[1] and it will be interesting to see what policy the independent states follow. Development of industry depends upon security of tenure, and this is difficult to achieve on communally held land. Therefore the industrial development, so badly needed in densely populated areas, tends to create new forms of tenure.

Trade in all three territories has been largely in the hands of whites, though in 1956 the issue of new licences to whites or Asians ceased in Basutoland. Basutoland co-operative societies have lagged as they have done in the Transkei. An officer was appointed to foster them in Basutoland in 1948 and such success as they have had has been in marketing the chief products of Basutoland, wool and mohair.[2] This fits with experience elsewhere in Africa; co-operatives have flourished only in marketing cash crops.

Two questions emerge: Will political independence in Lesotho and Botswana now outweigh economic dependence upon the Republic or will they long remain economic colonies, exporting chiefly labour like the Transkei? And secondly, how fast and far will Swaziland, with a mixed community and considerable capital investment, outstrip them in production?

3. Church and School

The Church was a new type of organization which had not existed traditionally among San, Khoikhoi, and Bantu-speakers. It brought together people not necessarily related by kinship or locality in a worshipping group under a leader whose primary function was the worship of God, the teaching of his followers, and, in the light of this teaching, changing the kind of society in which they lived. In practice the Christians did form local groups, converts and adherents settling in villages on mission land with the church building as the centre. In some of the early Moravian stations, notably Genadendal, Mamre, and Clarkson, large and beautiful churches were erected and, in most of the missions settled by Khoikhoi, school and store were built near the church building, and it remained physically and socially the centre of a village. Richard Freislich illustrates this vividly in his account of how the

[1] S. M. Molema, *Montshiwa, 1814–96*, pp. 166–8.
[2] *Basutoland Annual Report, 1956*, pp. 45, 57; *1948*, pp. 36–9, 57–8; *1954*, pp. 43–6.

Bondelswarts, a Coloured group living north of the Orange who rebelled against the administration in 1922, repeatedly gathered at their church; and it is clear in Peter Carsten's study of Steinkopf.[1] In the Coloured reserves virtually everyone is a Christian.[2]

The Berlin mission, which worked among the Pedi, gathered its converts during persecution by the chief Sekhukhune, and continued to encourage them to build together,[3] and so Pedi Christians, like the Coloured people, formed discrete local groups; but among the Nguni, who traditionally lived in scattered homesteads, the mission station was less important as a centre. Tiyo Soga, the first Xhosa ordained as a Christian minister, and a man of great influence, was opposed to converts moving from their homes on to mission land (see Vol. I, pp. 265–6), so after the initial years Christian families mostly lived dispersed.

Besides creating a new type of organization, the missionaries introduced a new conception of time. They established a seven-day week. They laid enormous stress on Sunday observance, and taboos on work, already customary during mourning and after a thunderstorm, were readily assimilated. The Christian requirement of Sunday observance and celebration of Christmas was re-enforced by employment patterns with Sunday as a day of rest, or lighter work, and a holiday over Christmas. Thus a totally new division of time—the week—was so integrated into Nguni and Sotho communities that the rhythm of pagan (as well as Christian) work and recreation has come to be determined by the seven-day week, and a great feast at Christmas.[4]

Since the Nguni lived scattered, the missionaries working among them were concerned to establish a network of schools in the neighbourhood surrounding a central mission station, and a seminary to train teachers for these schools was founded in 1842 (see Vol. I, pp. 239, 262). Parents were pressed to send their children to school and the teacher (who might be man or woman) became the leader of a local Christian group[5] This system of seminary, mission station, and 'out-station' schools was found effective and spread even among people who lived less scattered than the Nguni.

The writing of Gona, Nama, Tswana, Xhosa, Sotho, and Zulu began with the arrival of the missionaries, and translations of gospels, catechisms, and reading primers were the first publications. J. T. van der Kemp prepared a catechism in Gona at Bethelsdorp before his death

[1] R. Freislich, *The Last Tribal War*, pp. 12, 15–17; W. P. Carstens, *The Social Structure of a Coloured Reserve*, pp. 4, 21–35, 150–64.

[2] *Census, 1960*, vi 16, 18. Ninety-two per cent of the Coloured population is Christian, 6 per cent (largely urban) Mohammedan.

[3] T. Wangemann (trans. J. F. W. Grosskopf), *Maléo en Sekoekoeni, passim*.

[4] Hunter, pp. 356–7; Wilson *et al.*, *Social Structure*, pp. 160–2.

[5] Govan, pp. 72–4; 343–5.

in 1811; Robert Moffat published his Tswana translation of St. Luke's Gospel in 1830, working on it himself as a compositor in the office of the Government Printer in Cape Town;[1] his translation of the New Testament into Tswana appeared in 1840; and J. W. Appleyard's translation into Xhosa in 1854. By 1883 the whole Bible appeared in Tswana, Xhosa, Sotho, Zulu, and a New Testament in Nama—fifty-three years of astonishing achievement.[2]

Ability to read had to be nourished, and *Ikwezi* (the Morning Star), a Xhosa/English magazine, was started in 1841. It lasted only a short time but it was followed by *Indaba* (the News) in 1862, and *Isigidimi sama Xosa* (the Xhosa Messenger) in 1876. In 1888 the first vernacular newspaper, *Imvo Zabantsundu* (Opinion of the Brown People), began in King William's Town with J. Tengo Jabavu as editor, and it was followed in 1904 by a Zulu newspaper, *Ilanga laseNatal* (the Natal Sun), edited by the Revd. J. L. Dube.[3]

Literacy grew with the growth of the church, since converts in most of the missions were required to learn to read a gospel, but the profession of Christianity outstripped education. In 1960 two thirds of the African population called themselves Christians, but less than a third had passed the lowest school class. Ninety per cent of the Coloured population was professing Christian but only fifty-four per cent had passed the lowest school class.[4] The discrepancy is partly accounted for by the large number of children of pre-school age, and by the fact that in census returns many more people claim to be Christian than churches recognize as members, but it is also likely that a number of independent churches do not require literacy of their converts.

The cleavage already referred to (see Vol. I, p. 265) between the followers of the missionaries and the conservatives, the 'school' people and the 'reds' who used red ochre on their blankets, developed most conspicuously among the Xhosa. Many of the Mfengu refugees accepted the new teaching quickly and, returning eastward across the Kei in 1865, they formed the nucleus of 'school' communities in a number of areas.[5] So convinced were they of the advantage of education they subscribed £3,000 towards the foundation of a new seminary in the area they settled—'Fingoland'—east of the Kei, hence the secondary school and teachers' training institution of Blythswood, which opened in 1877.[6]

[1] T. Hahn, *Tsuni-Goam*, p. 48; R. Moffat, *Missionary Labours*, pp. 561–3.

[2] R. H. W. Shepherd, *Lovedale and Literature for the Bantu*, pp. 5–10; J. du Plessis, p. 209. The whole Bible was translated into Nama before 1888, but only the New Testament was published.

[3] Shepherd, *Lovedale and Literature*, pp. 11–12; C. L. S. Nyembezi, *A Review of Zulu Literature*. Four short-lived papers were published in Zulu between 1861 and 1904.

[4] *Census, 1960*, vi, 29; vii, 42–72.   [5] Govan, pp. 248–52, 259–61.

[6] *The Christian Express*, vii. 83 (1877), 15. One family even went from Lovedale to Morija in Lesotho to help start the printing press in Lesotho.

In 1931 Mfengu were still moving eastward and settling in the less heavily populated Pondoland, where they formed an important part of Christian congregations. As so often in history, the refugees became innovators, for once having been compelled to leave their homes they were more open to new ideas. The depth of the cleavage between 'school' and 'red' in Pondoland in 1931 was reflected in verbal usage: neither group referred to an individual of the other group by the intimate term 'a person' (umntu) but specifically as 'a red' or 'a convert',[1] in the same way as someone of another race was 'a white' rather than 'a person': however, in the following thirty years the cleavage diminished in many districts. By 1966 some leading Christian women in the Ciskei were wearing 'red' dress on festive occasions as an assertion of 'national' identity.

The proportion of 'school' and 'red' has, of course, changed in time and it also varies with locality. In 1881 the proportion of 'red' to 'school' in King William's Town district was estimated at 4:1; in 1933 in the Transkei at 7:3. About the same time a few 'reds' remained in the Upper Tyhume valley in the Ciskei, but by 1950 none was left there or in the neighbouring Keiskammahoek district.[2] Professor Philip Mayer's estimate of 85 per cent 'red' in East London district in 1958 is atypical: his figure of 45 per cent for King William's Town is more representative. According to the 1960 census, 48 per cent of the Africans in the Transkei west of Mzimvubu, 77 per cent east of it, and 46 per cent in the rural Ciskei, claim attachment to a church.[3] No full analysis of the percentage of Christians and the literacy rate in different areas is possible on the figures available, but it is clear that Xhosa (Gcaleka and Ngqika) living in coastal districts, especially those on European-owned farms, were slower to send children to school and join churches than other Xhosa-speakers in the Ciskei and Transkei, and the Sotho. This can be directly related to the frontier wars and the widespread feeling among the Xhosa that acceptance of Christianity and education was a betrayal of national identity. James Laing, who began work near the 'great place' of the Ngqika chiefdom in 1831, wrote: 'The Gospel had to encounter the jealousy of a people proud of their nationality, and instinctively feeling, and that not without reason, that it was seriously threatened by the encroachments of the people that were bringing the Gospel to them.' And William Govan (the first principal of Lovedale) referred to 'that systematic, and so to speak patriotic, opposition to the Gospel'.[4] In the Republic as a whole, the 1960 figures suggest a predominance of

[1] Hunter, pp. 6–7, 129, 176, 351, 432.
[2] 1833 Report, i. 173; Pim, p. 8; direct observation; Wilson et al., Social Structure, p. 129.
[3] P. Mayer, Tribesmen or Townsmen, pp. 298–9; Census, 1960, vi. 31, 34.
[4] Govan, pp. 12, 14.

professing Christians among Africans in towns (81 per cent Christian as against the country (60 per cent Christian).[1]

'School' people are the typical peasants, having closer links with the outside world, with a distant past, and with a 'great tradition' than conservative pagans, but even the pagans are no longer 'tribesmen' in any precise sense. 'Red' families also depend upon bread-winners in town, and buy much of their food from traders; for a hundred years they have used blankets and cloth and beads, and to these are now added bicycles and guitars, and occasionally radios. Though not literate themselves, they depend upon literate neighbours—black or white—for assistance. Every man must carry his pass and preserve his tax receipts; none is still a member of a pre-literate society.

Compulsory education for African children has long been discussed. As early as 1905 the conservative Bhaca and Xesibe chiefs in the Transkei were asking for it, and motions for free, compulsory education came up again and again in the Bunga, and party congresses, as well as in church assemblies.[2] The inadequacy of funds for African education and the disparity in public moneys spent on White, Coloured, and African children was criticized.[3]

A pattern was established very early among Nguni and Sotho Christians of sending at least one child in a family away to boarding-school for further education, and for this both parents often struggled and saved. An older brother or sister, having become a teacher or clerk, often helped a younger member of the family. Education was something sought after, and a dozen mission boarding-schools, and after 1916 the University College of Fort Hare, provided the base from which the new leaders were drawn.

The first hospital primarily serving Africans was established by the Government in 1856 (see Vol. I, p. 263). It was followed in 1898 by a mission hospital at Lovedale, and the training of African girls as nurses began, at Lovedale, in 1903.[4] The number of mission and government hospitals steadily grew, and besides providing for the care of the sick, they were important in changing attitudes towards disease. In the traditional tribal societies almost all disease was thought of as being caused by an ill-disposed person: the field of natural causation was a very narrow one (see Vol. I, pp. 269–70). One effect of hospitals, and of medical training for African men and women, has been to extend the field within which the ordinary villager attributes disease to natural

---

[1] *Census, 1960*, vi. 31.

[2] *1903–5 Commission*, ii. 1277–8; *Bunga Reports, 1908*, pp. xiii–xviii; *1910*, pp. 2, 70–3; *1911*, p. 3; *1922*, pp. 162–4; *1923*, pp. 149–56; *1933*, pp. 159–61; *Report of Native Affairs Commission, 1924*, p. 17.

[3] *Bunga Reports, 1930*, pp. 67–72; *1931*, pp. 217–21.

[4] R. H. W. Shepherd, *Lovedale, South Africa*, pp. 346–7.

causes. Most peasants still fear witches and to a lesser degree the shades of their ancestors, and they think that some diseases (particularly mental disorders) are 'not understood' by western trained doctors and cannot be cured by them. But their reliance on Western science is proved by the large numbers of patients coming from villages—often far distant—to mission and state hospitals, and the demand for more hospitals, clinics, and nurses. It is instructive to listen to country folk citing proximity to a hospital as one of the advantages of living in a particular village, and distance from a doctor as the disadvantage of another. The shift from a personal to an impersonal view of causation proceeds very slowly, and the same people speak of 'infection' when a neighbour has typhus, but think in terms of witchcraft when they themselves are very ill with pneumonia. Nevertheless a shift is apparent.[1]

The role of the church in creating new social groups, in fostering agriculture and writing, in establishing schools, and caring for the sick was nothing new. For a thousand years in Europe it had 'educated the barbarians'. Professor Herbert Butterfield tells how:

the Church presided over the evolution of political ideas, the conduct of craft-guilds, the rise of literature, art, and historical writing . . . the Church promoted the idea of property, the use of title deeds, the resurrection of Roman legal concepts. It conducted education and schools, built universities, and it gave its protection to the men who were opening the path to modern science.[2]

In Europe, as in Africa, the church was the pioneer in many fields, and in Europe, as now in Africa, the state gradually took over the services which the church alone had once recognized as necessary. This is most apparent in education.

From the mid-nineteenth century some mission schools received grants in aid (see Vol. I, p. 261). These gradually increased[3] and a state-controlled inspectorate was established. The explicit aim was to provide Africans with the same education as whites. Mr. J. McLaren, representing the Education Department, told the 1908 session of the Bunga:

The aim of the Education Department was to give the Natives the same education as the Europeans were getting. The same kind of instruction, on the same lines, and on the same standards. The reason for this was that a very large number of Europeans as well as Natives had to work together and they would work much better if they had a common foundation and basis of knowledge. If they were educated in different directions they would not understand each other.[4]

---

[1] *Bunga Reports, 1920*, pp. 91, 113–17; *1927*, pp. 98–101; *1930*, pp. 107–9; *1936*, pp. 145–61; *1937*, pp. 124–6; A. Barker, *Giving and Receiving*, pp. 89–91, 112–17.

[2] H. Butterfield, *Christianity in European History*, p. 21.

[3] M. Horrell, *African Education: Some Origins, and Development until 1953*.

[4] *Bunga Reports, 1908*, p. xiii.

McLaren took the problem of communication so seriously that he himself published a Xhosa-English dictionary, and a Xhosa grammar.

Since education for the various racial groups was not differentiated, interchange of children was possible. Mission schools in the Cape had been attended by white and Coloured children, and a few by white and African (see Vol. I, pp. 261–3), and this continued even when the schools received state aid. Certain schools helped to fuse together people of different languages and customs, as Khoikhoi, San, Coloured, and Tswana in Griquatown; Griqua and white in Ugie; Coloured and white in Natal; Sotho, Nguni, Coloured and white in Zonnebloem, Cape Town.[1] Lovedale drew pupils from all over southern Africa, and there Swazi, Tswana, and Lozi heirs to chiefdoms rubbed shoulders with Xhosa and Sotho commoners, Coloured and white; townsmen mixed with countrymen. A son of Lobengula distinguished himself, and even Kenya, Tanganyika, and Nyasaland were represented. Other schools also, notably Adams, Healdtown, and St. Peters' and, most conspicuously, the University College of Fort Hare, drew students from all over southern African, and the opportunity to mix with people of different groups was something valued.[2] For example, Tengo Jabavu deliberately sent his Xhosa-speaking sons to Morija that they might mix with Sotho speakers, though he had a choice of good schools nearer home.

In 1954 all this was changed. The Government announced its intention of taking control of all African schools in receipt of state aid. The responsibility of the state for providing education was generally acknowledged, and its acceptance of that responsibility welcomed, but there was bitter conflict over three issues: the kind of education to be provided; the right of schools to admit pupils of different groups; and the right of established mission schools to continue, with or without grants in aid.

The Government policy was explicitly to provide Africans with education for a subordinate position in South Africa as a whole, with opportunity for a small number to qualify in professions to serve reserves—'Bantu areas'—only. In 1954 the then Minister of Native Affairs, Hendrik Verwoerd, stated in the House of Assembly that 'the much greater number of Natives . . . should have a training in accordance with their opportunities in life'. In the Senate he criticized the former system as having created a class of Africans which 'feels that its spiritual, economic and political home is among the civilized community of South Africa'.[3] The new syllabus was bitterly opposed

---

[1] M. T. R. Smit, *The Romance of the Village Ugie*, p. 83; H. F. Dickie-Clark, *The Marginal Situation*, pp. 55–6; *1903–5 Report*, ii. 194–207.

[2] The Principal, Lovedale, 'Where Lovedale Pupils Come From', *South African Outlook*, 57 (Apr. 1927); direct observation by the writer as a schoolgirl at Lovedale, a student and staff member at Fort Hare, and a field-worker in Pondoland and the Ciskei.

[3] *House of Assembly Debates*, 1953, col. 3585; *Senate Debates*, 1954, col. 2611. See also full

by most Africans on the ground firstly that it required mother-tongue instruction up to standard six (eight years of schooling) and most teachers considered it more efficient to use English as the sole medium of instruction, particularly in subjects like arithmetic, from an earlier stage; secondly that it neglected subjects like mathematics which were essential for children who wished to continue to university education; thirdly that it required a knowledge, from early classes, of two 'official' languages in place of one (African schools in the Ciskei, Transkei, and Zululand were required to teach Afrikaans which they had not hitherto done); and fourthly, that the emphasis was excessively parochial. Adequate training in English was particularly desired not only as an aid to getting a job, but because 'the whole world speaks English' and isolation was what the educated leaders feared most.

Schools were demarcated as belonging to one or another 'ethnic group' and they were permitted to enrol only pupils of that group. This sort of segregation (extended also to university education) is regarded as a technique of isolation, designed to foster 'tribalism', that is local as opposed to national loyalties, and it is bitterly resented. Nguni and Sotho people have shown no desire for cultural isolation partly because, being numerically strong, they are not afraid of being swamped by any other group. It is the Afrikaner, not the Xhosa, or Zulu, or Sotho, who fears to lose his own language and so cherishes a school or university in which that language alone is used. What is bitterly resented is the refusal to admit Africans to full participation in 'the civilized community of South Africa'. The effort of the Government to foster Bantu languages and culture in schools in itself sets up an opposition to that policy, as was plain during the debates at a conference on Christian Education in Africa in Salisbury in 1959. A Ghanaian delegate spoke of the need to foster African languages in schools and replace English; South Africans of various complexions replied that such a policy, if compulsory, was cramping and divisive.

Under the new system of 'Bantu Education' African teachers were required to work two shifts a day, teaching two classes, each for four hours, though white and Coloured teachers did not do so, and this, it was argued, immediately reduced the quality of education provided for Africans.[1] The control of schools, hitherto exercised by missionaries and ministers, was vested in local 'school committees'.[2] Some mission

debate, *H.A.D.*, 1953, cols. 3575–672; *Senate Debates*, cols. 2595–620; *H.A.D.*, 1959, col. 8318; *Report of the Commission on Native Education, 1949–1951*.

[1] D. G. S. M'Timkulu, 'The African and Education', *Race Relations Journal*, 16 (1949), 56–63; *Report of Proceedings of National Conference on Report of the Commission on Native Education*, for the official view on the medium of instruction see: *Department of Bantu Education, Report of the Commission of Inquiry into the Teaching of the Official Languages and the use of the Mother Tongue as Medium of Instruction in Transkeian Primary Schools*.   [2] M. Horrell, *A Decade of Bantu Education*.

schools (including St. Peter's in Johannesburg) closed rather than accept the new conditions, and in 1956 permits to continue were refused to certain others, notably Adams College in Natal, even though they were prepared to work without government subsidy.[1]

The enforcement of the new system roused more bitter feeling among ordinary villagers than any legislation except the laws excluding labourers who lacked permits from town. Many African teachers, and at least one white Inspector of Schools, resigned; other teachers known to oppose the policy were dropped (school committees were told that certain posts would no longer be subsidized); the morale of teaching staffs slumped; and so did the proportion of children passing public examinations. Innumerable parents believed the changes meant poorer opportunities for their children and were bitterly critical. In 1965, the Transkei Authority, having secured control of local education, resolved to change the syllabus and revert to instruction through English in primary schools. This was one of the few motions warmly supported by all parties.

In one respect the 1954 legislation had an effect which was welcomed. The number of African schools rose considerably, and the proportion of school-age children attending school (on the two-shift system) increased, but this had less effect in the reserves than on white-owned farms. A large proportion of the new schools established have been on farms. The legislation was passed with an eye on farmers (who were finding that the quality of labourers they could retain depended partly on opportunities for schooling) and specific provision was made for farm-school teachers to work on the farm with their pupils, when required. Still, in 1965, despite the wealth of the Republic, only forty per cent of African children were in school,[2] and there was no indication that provision was being made for the majority who *could not* attend school because there were no places for them. Africans argue cogently that education for blacks should not be financed and administered separately from education for whites, and both should be under one Minister of Education.[3] Between 1930 and 1953 the gap in expenditure per head of the population of different races narrowed: after 1953 it widened,[4] and in 1963 nearly twelve times as much was spent per head of the white population as was spent per head for Africans.

 'The church' referred to here was not the single hierarchy of medieval Europe. It consisted of a number of 'missions' sent by churches of

[1] G. C. Grant, *The Liquidation of Adams College* (Private circulation, n.d.).

[2] N. Hurwitz, *The Economics of Bantu Education in South Africa*, pp. 11, 26–30, 74.

[3] *Bunga Reports, 1934*, pp. 234–41; *1939*, pp. 129–31.

[4] Horrell, *African Education*; The 1961 Education Panel, *Education and the South African Economy*, 1966, p. 77; Horrell, *Decade of Bantu Education*, p. 41.

Europe and America, which worked more or less independently, each of the other, and from 1884 of independent African churches, groups which broke away from these missions under the leadership of some outstanding men. The characteristic of these groups was that they consisted solely of Africans, and in the initial splits the colour issue was dominant—Africans felt that they were not being treated as equals within the church. But colour was never the only issue—control over finance was repeatedly a ground of conflict also—and independent African churches continued to fragment.[1] In 1932, 293 were listed; in 1938, 511; in 1966, 2,400.[2] The majority of the new churches were offshoots from independent churches, not from missions, proof that colour ceased to be the major cause of splits. Moreover, attempts to create one independent African church failed.[3]

Fragmentation of this sort is not peculiar to Africa. Independent churches are widespread as part of the reaction to conquest by western technical superiority, military power, and religious ideas presented in the clothes of another culture. Vittorio Lanternari in a perceptive analysis, typifies them as seeking 'freedom and salvation: freedom from subjection and servitude to foreign powers, as well as from adversity, and salvation from the possibility of having the traditional culture destroyed'.[4] But the independent churches are themselves evidence of the impact of Christian teaching: it cannot be wholly rejected, and the illiterate and conservative seek somehow to translate it into their own terms.

The independent churches have varied greatly in character. They range in size from the 6,500 communicant members and 20,000 adherents claimed by the Revd. Mpambane Mzimba in 1904, or 30,000 members claimed by Shembe II in Natal, and 600,000 claimed by the Zionist Bishop Lekganyane of the northern Transvaal, both in 1966, to tiny personal followings. One self-styled church was found by the late Professor Jabavu to consist only of the leader and his wife. The total membership of about 1,500,000 in 1960 (20 per cent of the African Christians in the Republic) suggested an average size of about 600.[5]

[1] *Report of Native Churches Commission*; J. Wells, *Stewart of Lovedale*, pp. 295–6; A. Lea, *The Native Separatist Church Movement in South Africa*; B. G. M. Sundkler, *Bantu Prophets in South Africa*, references are to the second edition; M. Wilson and A. Mafeje, *Langa*, pp. 91–100; 'Death of Doctor L. M. Mzimba', *The South African Outlook*, 89 (1959), 82.

[2] Hunter, p. 562; Christian Council of South Africa, *The Christian Handbook of South Africa*, pp. 145–58; Sundkler, p. 307; Horrell, *Survey, 1966*, p. 28.

[3] D. D. T. Jabavu, *An African Independent Church*; Sundkler, pp. 50–3, 306.

[4] V. Lanternari, *The Religions of the Oppressed*, p. 239.

[5] Lea, p. 39. I am indepted to the Revd. A.-I. Berglund for figures on the membership of Shembe's 'Church of the Nazarites', and to Miss Horrell, Research Officer of the South African Institute of Race Relations, for membership of Lekganyane's. Cf. Horrell, *Survey, 1965*, p. 19. The membership of Limba's church was given at about 1,500 in 1942. L. Mqotsi and N. Mkele, 'A Separatist Church, Ibandla, lika-Krestu', *African Studies* 5 (1946), 111. Revd.

Some independent churches retained the organization, discipline, dogma, and ritual of the church from which they had sprung—the Presbyterian Church of Africa which dates from the Revd. Mpambane Mzimba's secession in 1896 from the Free Church of Scotland is an example—but others combined traditional customs and belief with a modicum of Christian teaching, and existed as the personal following of one leader, more like the following of a traditional diviner, than an organized church. The universality of the Christian gospel is asserted in the teaching of the 'mission' churches even though the colour bar is apparent within the church in everyday practice. The idea of universality is less apparent in small Zionist groups, or a 'Church of Christ for the Union and Protection of Bantu Customs' or those which assert the revelation of a black messiah.[1]

There is a clear connection between church affiliation and class, and the independent churches generally—particularly those of the Zionist type—tend to attract the less educated and less sophisticated.[2] The leaders of three of the earliest splits (1884, 1892, and 1896) were ordained ministers of the Methodist (Wesleyan) Church—the Revd. Nehemiah Tile, the Revd. M. M. Mokoni, and the Revd. James Dwane—and were among the better educated Africans of that period, but leaders of many later splinter groups have been illiterate or only just literate—men with less than four years schooling, or sometimes none at all. The son of a successful leader is, however, educated, and the church is likely to change its character if (as often happens) he is chosen to succeed his father.[3]

The Revd. Bengt Sundkler has argued that the proliferation of independent churches was partly a result of the Land Act of 1913, and that one of the attributes of a successful prophet was to lead his followers to land on which to settle.[4] The people primarily affected by the Act were not families already domiciled in reserves, but those living as cash or labour tenants, or share-farmers on white-owned farms, and it is significant to note that Isaiah Shembe, the founder of one of the most successful independent churches in Zululand, was the son of a farm labourer in the Orange Free State,[5] and Enoch Mgijima, leader of the 'Israelites', though himself a resident of Ntab' elanga (Bulhoek) in the Kamastone reserve near Queenstown, came into conflict with the authorities because he gathered round him on Ntab' elanga (Bulhoek)

N. B. H. Bhengu's 'Assemblies of God' Church seated 2,500 in 1962. B. A. Pauw, *The Second Generation*, p. 23. Sundkler, p. 306, cites a union about 1960 between the Ethiopian Catholic Church of Zion with 30,000, and the New Mission Church with 10,000 members.

[1] Sundkler, pp. 323–37; *Native Churches Commission*, p. 28.
[2] Wilson and Mafeje, p. 149.   [3] Lea, pp. 23–33; Sundkler, pp. 121–6, 308–9.
[4] Ibid., pp. 69, 91, 104, 129.
[5] G. C. Oosthuizen, *The Theology of a South African Messiah*, pp. 1, 3.

commonage families from other places, and they refused to move after celebrating their 'passover'.[1] The reserve is surrounded by white-owned farms. It would be instructive to inquire what proportion of the followers of independent churches indeed come from farms as opposed to reserves —it may well be large—but the Land Act itself can be no more than a contributing cause of proliferation among independent churches since they are conspicuous in Swaziland which lay beyond the scope of the Act.

In the early stages of the independent church movement a link existed between some of the churches and the beginnings of African nationalism. Several of those who initiated splits (notably James Dwane and John Msikinya) had visited the United States and had links with American negro churches, and the Government repeatedly expressed anxiety at the growth of 'Ethiopianism' in a religious form. In 1920 there were rumours that Enoch Mgijima's followers were making arms, and eventually in 1921 when his men, armed with swords and spears, charged the police sent to disperse them, 163 were shot.[2] As the secular political movements and trade unions developed, however, these organizations tended to separate more and more from any church. By 1960, it seemed that independent churches were on the wane and nationalist fervour was flowing into secular channels. Whether the banning of the two strongest political movements (see p. 468) and the harrying of trade union leaders will give a further impetus to the growth of independent churches remains to be seen.

In the reserves, therefore, not only is a cleavage between Christians and non-Christians apparent, but there is differentiation among the Christians by denomination. Sometimes the religious cleavage coincides with other cleavages and acute tension exists; but often ties of kinship, neighbourhood, and personal friendship cut across denomination, and members of different denominations (particularly the women's *manyano*) combine for prayer meetings and other purposes. The present world trend towards the growth of co-operation between all Christians in a World Council of Churches impinges even on some remote congregations of independent African churches as their leaders seek further theological education through an African Independent Churches Association, which co-operates with the multi-racial Christian Institute.[3]

In Basutoland, Bechuanaland, and Swaziland, missions and education developed in much the same way as in the reserves of the Union, with mission schools, which later received government grants in aid and

---

[1] *Reports of the Native Affairs Commission, 'Israelites' at Bulhoek and Occurrences in May, 1921; Native Churches Commission*, pp. 7–17.

[2] Hunter, pp. 563–4; *Report of the Native Affairs Commission, 'Israelites'*.

[3] Horrell, *1965*, p. 19; *1966*, p. 29.

were inspected by a government-appointed officer. Eventually, governments began to establish schools on their own initiative which were not attached to any missions, but support was not withdrawn from mission schools, which continue to provide by far the largest number of school places. The Paris Evangelical Mission, which began work in 1833 among the Sotho (see I, p. 401), fostered education assiduously, and later the administration did so also. By 1945 twenty per cent of the annual revenue was being spent on education—twice as much as the average for African territories[1]—and in 1957 Basutoland claimed to have the highest literacy rate for Africans in any state in southern Africa (50 to 55 per cent over the age of fifteen)[2] and had overtaken the Transkei where, in 1960, 59 per cent over the age of fourteen, had not passed the lowest form in school, though in 1903 the Cape Colony was ahead of Basutoland.[3] In 1956 Lesotho also had a slightly higher proportion of African Christians (71 per cent) than the Union (66·6 per cent).[4]

In Swaziland and Bechuanaland the proportion of children in school and the literacy rate was lower—36 per cent of those over ten years of age in Swaziland in 1963, and about 30 per cent of those over ten years of age in Bechuanaland in 1964[5]—but more than half the Swazi population (56 per cent) professed Christianity. Nearly half of these belonged to independent African churches for though the independent movement began very early in Basutoland—in 1872—it was in Swaziland, with the lower level of education, that it flourished, and there it has been closely linked with the royal house.[6]

Until 1954, high schools and universities of the Union of South Africa attracted advanced students from Basutoland, Bechuanaland, and Swaziland. In education, as in the economic sphere, the Union played the typical role of a metropolitan area towards its 'colonies' within and beyond its borders.[7] After 1954 the flow dried up, and indeed reversed, as educated Africans from within the Republic sought jobs abroad and, above all, sought to educate their children abroad.[8]

4. Government and Law

The change from tribal to peasant society was marked by the establishment of administrative control from outside, which began in 1835

---

[1] *Report of the Commission on Education in Basutoland*, p. 21.
[2] Holleman, p. 174 (quoting *World Illiteracy at Mid-Century*, UNESCO, 1957).
[3] *Census, 1960*, vii. 86–7; *1903–5 Commission*, i. 69.
[4] *Basutoland 1956 Population Census*, p. 99.
[5] *Swaziland Report, 1963*; Holleman, pp. 173–4, gives a figure of 27·6 per cent literate for rural Swaziland. Literacy in Tswana towns may reach 35–45 per cent. *Bechuanaland Report, 1964*, p. 79; *Census, 1964*.
[6] Holleman, pp. 152, 155; Sundkler, pp. 38, 313–19.
[7] L. Marquard, *South Africa's Colonial Policy*.   [8] Direct observation.

among the Xhosa with a British 'Government Agent' 'advising' an independent chief, and gradually became more and more effective and pervasive, as territories were annexed and administered by 'native commissioners' or magistrates. How the British vacillated between alliance with strong independent chiefs, and destruction of chiefly power which represented a military danger, has already been described (see I, pp. 240, 250, 264). A policy of using commoner headmen, directly dependent upon the administering authority, in place of chiefs, was initiated by Sir George Grey in the Ciskei. In Natal refugees from the Zulu kingdom were settled on defined 'locations' by Sir Theophilus Shepstone, under leaders recognized by him, and not all of these were heirs to traditional chiefdoms. Hariette Colenso told the 1903–5 Commission that: 'numbers of so called Kafir chiefs have been appointed whom the people only recognize as Government officials'. The tendency to establish hereditary authority was strong, and many a lineage head, recognized as a local headman, has fathered a line of headmen, but they never achieved the prestige of the direct descendants of royal lines, and became more and more dependent on the support of white administration.[1]

Village councils were established in 1894 in Glen Grey district. These were gradually extended through the Transkei and Ciskei territories and a General Council, or Bunga (originally proposed in 1883), was established for each territory. A Bunga was composed of delegates from each magisterial district, some of them elected and some nominated, certain hereditary chiefs, the 'native commissioner' or magistrate for each district, and the chief magistrate of the territory as *ex officio* chairman. It has at its disposal a local tax (10s. per adult male) which was used for the construction and maintenance of roads, bridges, and dams; for agricultural schools and demonstrators; for clinics or hospitals, and scholarships for general education.[2]

The double ties of the peasant community—to a tribal past and to a wider contemporary world—were apparent in law. From 1833 onwards, traditional Xhosa law was recognized in some chiefdoms on the eastern Cape frontier, and Zulu law in Natal, in so far as these traditional systems governed relationships between Africans, and were not judged to be 'contrary to natural justice';[3] and even where traditional law had no statutory recognition many families continued to act in matters of marriage and inheritance as if they were bound by traditional law. But changes springing from assumptions of the

[1] *1883 Report*, i. 15–19; *1903–5 Report*, iii. 1–11, 18–20, 405, 412, 419.

[2] R. W. Rose-Innes, *The Glen Grey Act and the Native Question*; Hunter, pp. 430–3; Wilson et al., *Social Structure*, pp. 38–45; *Bunga Reports*; *Ciskei Bunga Reports*.

[3] E. R. Garthorne, 'Application of Native Law', *Bantu Studies*, 3 (1927–9), pp. 245 ff.; *1903–5 Report*, iii. 1–2, 11–16.

governing authority about 'natural justice' were far-reaching. Imputation of witchcraft was a criminal offence, and this radically changed the traditional law which allowed the 'smelling out' of witches (see I, pp. 269–70). The criminal code which was introduced in the Cape and Natal punished much the same actions as had been punished by the chiefs court, but imprisonment for criminal offences replaced the customary fine in cattle. The customary law which (except in Natal) was not codified, changed considerably. Local divergences were gradually obliterated; property rights of women under customary law diminished; but the right of a woman to choose her husband—or at least reject an unwelcome suitor—was upheld, and the custom of widow-inheritance (where it existed, as among Zulu and Mpondo, and in communities of refugees from Natal (Mfengu)) gradually fell into disuse.[1]

Civil marriages between Africans were recognized within the Cape Colony from 1838. Moreover, by the turn of the century very many 'school people' were marrying by Christian rites, and their marriages were governed by the Roman-Dutch Law of the Colony. This considerably modified the legal status of women, particularly when marriage was in community of property, and conflict of law was common.[2] For example, while customary law permitted polygyny, Roman-Dutch law did not, and the Bunga councillors sought to prevent those who married by Christian or civil rites from also contracting customary marriages.[3]

The concern of ordinary villagers with what the law should be and how in fact it was adapted, is reflected in the frequent debates in the Bunga on the law of marriage and inheritance, and the authority of a father over his children.[4] One of the controversial issues was whether or not marriage cattle should be returned if a wife died childless:[5] another was the extent of a father's responsibility for a child over twenty-one years of age.[6] It was proposed repeatedly that Africans should serve on juries in cases in which Africans were concerned,[7] and limitations on the freedom of movement of Africans were constantly criticized.[8]

During a hundred years, conflict concerning chieftainship has been

---

[1] *1883 Report*, i. 37–8; Hunter, pp. 119–20, 210–12, 237, 240; *Bunga Reports, 1935*, pp. 86–9.

[2] The leading authority, Professor H. J. Simons, cannot be quoted in South Africa as he is banned. M. Hunter, 'The Effects of Contact with Europeans on the Status of Pondo Women', *Africa*, 6 (1933), 259–76; *Bunga Reports, 1927*, pp. 65–71.

[3] *Bunga Reports, 1922*, pp. 68–9; *1924*, pp. 69–70, 164–5; *1930*, pp. 92–4; *1934*, pp. 96–7; *1937*, p. 61.

[4] Ibid. *1920*, pp. 65–7, 77–9, 80–2, 111–13; *1922*, pp. 64–8, 127; *1923*, pp. 109–12; *1925*, 136–44; *1928*, pp. 53–5; *1930*, pp. 96–7; *1933*, pp. 172–8; *1936*, pp. 84–7.

[5] Ibid. *1920*, pp. 153–5; *1922*, pp. 83–6; *1923*, pp. 127–31.

[6] Ibid. *1920*, pp. 70–9; *1921*, p. 83; *1933*, pp. 194–6.

[7] Ibid. *1924*, pp. 93–7; *1931*, pp. 118–23; *1934*, pp. 121–2.

[8] Ibid. *1921*, p. 92; *1930*, pp. 121–4; *1927*, pp. 45–9, 50–6.

evident not only in the policies of white administrators but among African villagers. Opposing views were repeatedly expressed in Bunga debates: the 'school people' generally, though not invariably, favoured decrease in chiefly power, and the conservative pagans its increase. In 1920 one councillor in the Bunga spoke of how 'people at home laughed at the Chiefs and Headmen whom they regarded simply as officers appointed by the Government' and another replied that: 'He was sorry members of the Council who were school teachers should speak against cases being tried by Headmen.'[1] In 1923 another councillor expressed the view that: 'The time had come when the chiefs should get away from the Bunga . . . because many of the Councillors . . . would like to see Chieftainship put an end to.'[2] But in 1924 a motion requesting the reintroduction of the hereditary principle in the appointment of headmen was carried.[3] In 1927 a magistrate introduced a motion that judicial powers be conferred on all Government headmen, that failure to attend a headman's meeting be a punishable offence, and that contempt of the headman's court be punishable with a fine not exceeding one head of small stock. The motion was carried in the Bunga but not enforced.[4] A similar motion was carried in 1935,[5] but in 1939 a motion again requiring compulsory attendance at headman's meetings was lost.[6]

The conflict over chieftainship was reflected in the attitude towards chiefs' courts. In Pondoland, in 1931–2, the courts of subordinate chiefs regularly heard cases of dispute and gave judgements which were executed, though these courts had no legal status in the eyes of the Government. The only chiefs' courts recognized were those of the Mpondo paramount chiefs at Nyandeni and Qawukeni, and recognition of these dated from 1931 and 1932 respectively. Conservatives took civil disputes to their district chief as a matter of course, and if not satisfied with the decision there might proceed to the court of the superior chief at Nyandeni or Qawukeni, and only then, if still dis-satisfied, did a conservative litigant proceed to the court of a commis-sioner or magistrate. But 'school people' often by-passed the chiefs altogether and went direct to the magistrate's court.[7] For this they were bitterly criticized by their conservative fellows.

For forty-eight years, from 1908, the Transkeian Territories General Council (the Bunga) was lively, but there was increasing discontent among the members because they had so little power. Important decisions taken were not implemented because the Bunga lacked the

[1] Ibid. *1920*, p. 144; *1921*, pp. 46–8.   [2] Ibid. *1923*, p. 55.
[3] Ibid. *1924*, pp. 99–103.   [4] Ibid. *1927*, pp. 155–66.   [5] Ibid. *1935*, pp. 211–12.
[6] Ibid. *1939*, p. 95. For other debates on the powers of the chiefs and headmen see *1930*, pp. 131–9; *1931*, pp. 178–84; *1933*, pp. 189–90; *1936*, pp. 89–92; *1937*, pp. 168–70; *1939*, pp. 92–3.   [7] Hunter, pp. 425–6.

power to carry them out. 'Things were discussed by the Council (Bunga) but the Government paid no attention to them.'[1] Motions were brought proposing that: 'Magistrates should not meet alone afterwards', or at least their review of Bunga resolutions be published;[2] that Bunga resolutions refused by the Government and passed for a second time by the Bunga be subject to a referendum and then, if favoured generally, be implemented;[3] that 'the Minister' (of Native Affairs) should hold only one portfolio;[4] that the Native Affairs Commission should visit the Transkei annually 'to hear what they [Bunga councillors] had to say';[5] that the Bunga be consulted before the promulgation of a proclamation affecting 'Native Territories'.[6] As the councillors knew, effective power lay neither with the Bunga, nor the chiefs, but with the magistrates or 'native commissioners', and the Minister of Native Affairs whose Department appointed and controlled the commissioners.

At least some members of the Bunga were keenly aware of the wider political issues, and anxiously watching the trend in legislation. In 1925 application was made to present a petition at the Bar of the House of Assembly on the provisions of the Mines and Works Amendment Bill, but the application was rejected.[7] Opposition to the whole segregation policy of the Government was repeatedly expressed.[8] Councillor Qamata of Xalanga said: 'Under the old Cape Government the maxim had been "equal rights for all civilized people . . ."' It would appear that the policy of the Union Government was to have two nations in South Africa. . . . The Natives desired to be regarded as one nation with the white people. Nobody would ever solve the Native problem without working together with the Natives . . .'[9] And Councillor Sopela of Nqamakwe stated roundly that: 'They had not yet made claim to social equality, but they wanted justice.'[10] In 1937 the Native Laws Amendment Bill was bitterly criticized on the ground that 'it makes a Native in an urban area a temporary resident'[11] (see pp. 187 ff.).

At the same time the Bunga dissociated itself from the African National Congress's appeal to boycott celebrations welcoming the Prince of Wales, and the value of the British link in providing protection for Africans was repeatedly stressed. Fear lest franchise rights be lost if South Africa became independent and 'the protection of the British crown . . . interfered with . . .' were explicit.[12]

In the Cape Province, from 1853, there was a colour-blind franchise,

---

1 *Bunga Reports, 1920*, p. 73.
2 Ibid. *1921*, pp. 117–21, 126–37; *1924*, p. 93; *1925*, pp. 97–113.
3 Ibid. *1920*, p. 151.   4 Ibid. *1923*, pp. 41–6.   5 Ibid. *1923*, p. 39.
6 Ibid. *1920*, pp. 79–80.   7 Ibid. *1925*, pp. 118–22, 206, 227–8; *1926*, pp. ii, iii.
8 Ibid. *1925*, pp. 122–4; *1927*, pp. 118–24.   9 Ibid. *1928*, pp. 212–13.
10 Ibid. *1925*, p. 121.   11 Ibid. *1937*, pp. 96–8.
12 Ibid. *1925*, pp. 202–4; *1928*, pp. 211–14; *1930*, pp. 212–14, *1934*, pp. 200–6.

but as the numbers of African voters increased their rights were gradually whittled away (see p. 437). This was bitterly resented. In 1936 the Bunga, aware of what was happening, passed a unanimous resolution opposing any legislation which would abolish the existing franchise. Councillor Qamata said in supporting it: 'I cannot see how Western civilization and Christianity can be defended at the expense of other people.'[1] A motion recommending the extension of the franchise to African women was passed in the 1938 session, with two dissentients; Chief Victor Poto expressed a general attitude when he said: 'I think the Pondo people may be taken as a backward people, yet they all admitted it was right and proper that women should have the vote.'[2]

A Natives' Representative Council was established in 1936 as part of the plan to replace the common franchise in the Cape. It consisted of twelve elected African representatives, four nominated Africans, five European officials, and the Secretary for Native Affairs as chairman. African leaders from the Transkei were very critical of segregated political representation but agreed to serve on the council in the hope that something might be achieved. It had advisory functions only, and its advice was disregarded as soon as it passed resolutions on the matters most concerning peasants—land and freedom of movement to seek work. Its influence on the reserves was negligible, but it was of importance in bringing together African representatives from different parts of the country, and men from town as well as country.[3] Twenty years later it was abolished because it did not fit in to the new pattern of developing 'separate national units' each in isolation from the other.

In 1956 the existing councils in the Transkei and Ciskei were disestablished by proclamation and replaced in the Transkei by a 'Territorial Authority' and 'District Authorities'. These were later subdivided into 'Tribal' or 'Community Authorities' and a Transkei Legislative Assembly and Executive were established in 1963. Similar 'Bantu Authorities' were established in the Ciskei and other reserves but only the Transkei has a Legislative Assembly and Executive. By 1966 there were six Territorial Authorities: Tswana, Lebowa (north Sotho), Matshangana (Tsonga), Thoho Ya Ndou (Venda), Transkei, and Ciskei. In Natal, the Orange Free State, and part of the Transvaal there were 'Tribal' and 'Regional Authorities' but the Territorial Authorities originally planned for Zulu, South Sotho, and Swazi were not yet established in 1966.

In structure these various authorities differ from the old system of councils in that far greater power has been given to hereditary chiefs

[1] Ibid. *1936*, pp. 281–6.
[2] Ibid. *1938*, p. 68. For opposing views see *1937*, pp. 103–5.
[3] J. K. Ngubane, *Should the Native Representative Council be Abolished?*, p. 15.

and the elective element is smaller, and at the same time the native commissioners, who had sat and voted as full members of the previous councils have now lost their seats.[1] In the old Transkei Bunga the ratio of *ex officio* members (chiefs and native commissioners) to elected members was 30:78. In the new Transkei Legislature the ratio is 64:45, all the 64 *ex officio* members being Government-paid chiefs.[2] All Africans (men and women) born in the Transkei, or resident for five years, have the franchise. Whites are excluded. Under the 1963 constitution the Transkei Assembly has a Cabinet consisting of a Chief Minister and five other ministers controlling six portfolios: Finance, Justice, the Interior, Education, Agriculture and Forestry, Roads and Works. The ministers are Africans, but white officials of the Bantu Affairs Department have been seconded to act as Secretaries to these Departments, and three-quarters of the Transkei budget comes as a direct grant from the Government of the Republic. There is considerable criticism in the Transkei at the slow pace of Africanization of the civil service: senior posts are in fact still held by whites, and up to the end of 1966 no African had been appointed as a 'Bantu commissioner' though there were three African 'assistant Bantu commissioners' outside the Transkei.

Members of the National Government which set up the new system of Bantu Authorities suggested that the Bunga had represented the educated people only, and that the conservative peasantry had no interest in it. In fact, as has been shown, both conservative and radical viewpoints were expressed in Bunga debates, and the chief criticism was not that it represented sectional interests, but that it was 'a talking shop'. It did not have power over the issues that concerned people most, such as more land for African occupation, freedom to seek work, more jobs within the Transkei itself, wages, and political representation on a national body. The new Transkeian Authority is also operated by 'school people', and is also powerless in these same issues. In 1963 the chief Minister publicly laid claim to more land—the whole territory between the Fish river and Zululand[3]—and four years later he appealed for the total relaxation of influx control, but these are issues settled by the Government of the Republic, not by the Transkei. A third contentious issue, investment in the Transkei on a scale which might create employment for some of the many men and women seeking work, is also subject to controls by the Government of the Republic.

The development of local government with responsibility for local affairs is generally welcomed, and the suggestion by two Transkeian

[1] Horrell, *1955–1956*, pp. 59–67; *1965*, pp. 131–6.
[2] D. Hammond-Tooke, 'Chieftainship in Transkeian Political Development', *The Journal of Modern African Studies*, 2 (1964), 517, 525; Horrell, *1963*, pp. 80–106.
[3] Horrell. *1963*, p. 90.

leaders, Chief Victor Poto and Mr. Knowledge Guzana, that the Transkei be given the status of a Province within the Republic, is logical, but local self-government cannot replace participation in national government, and the argument that the Transkeian Government can adequately represent the interests of Xhosa living not in the Transkei but in other parts of the Republic, can hardly be taken seriously.

Many of the chiefs who gained power under the new system have been extremely unpopular. Charges of corruption are continuously made.[1] The control of the commoners over chiefs which existed traditionally diminished with increasing density of population and pacification of the country. Formerly an unpopular chief lost his following—his men moved away—and this was the effective sanction against tyranny (see Vol. I, pp. 122–3). Now men cannot move away for alternative land is no longer available, and a man may even be dependent upon his local chief for a pass to go out to work. The unpopular chief is maintained in office by force exercised by the Government of the Republic. In 1959–60 a peasants' revolt in Eastern Pondoland was suppressed by military force, and Emergency Regulations proclaimed throughout the Transkei. The new constitution was brought into operation and elections held under the shelter of these regulations, and Proclamation 400 of 1960 has still, in 1966, not been withdrawn. Any meeting not specifically sanctioned by the Bantu commissioner is illegal; free speech is limited; entry and exit from the Transkei is controlled; and 'trouble makers' are banished from their homes.[2] The continuing anger of the people against the chiefs has been expressed in physical assaults: there have been murders of chiefs and headmen, and attempts to murder others, including the Chief Minister, Mantanzima. According to popular report most chiefs, with the notable exception of Chief Poto of Western Pondoland and his son, go armed, something unheard of thirty years ago when the Transkei boasted the smallest police force in proportion to its population of any area in the Commonwealth.[3]

Opposition to the new Authorities occurred also in Zeerust, Sekhukhuneland, and Tsonga country in the Transvaal, and in Zululand, but reporters have been excluded from disturbed areas, and the fullest accounts of opposition that have been published are banned in South Africa. According to a statement in Parliament, 4,769 men and women were held in custody, for varying periods, during 1960; of these less than

---

[1] Horrell, *1959–60*, p. 44; direct observation.

[2] *H.A.D.*, 1961, cols. 226, 437–9, 4999; Horrell, *1959–60*, pp. 39–52; *1961*, pp. 42–52. I regret I cannot quote Mr. Govan Mbeki or Mrs. Helen Joseph.

[3] Hunter, p. 573; Pim, pp. 7, 20, gives one policeman to 1,500+persons.

half (2,067) were brought to trial. A number of others who led the opposition were taken from their homes and banished to remote areas among people who spoke another language.[1] The other Bantu Authorities are less developed than that in the Transkei and since their territories are fragmented they have even less chance of establishing efficient local government. But whether they succeed or fail Bantu Authorities provide for local self-government of only a minority of the Africans in the Republic. The majority live and work in towns or on white-owned farms.

Development in Basutoland, Bechuanaland, and Swaziland was very different. There a great deal more power was left with the chiefs than in any reserve of the Republic, and the British Administration worked through the chiefs. The struggle of individual chiefs to retain power was reflected in Basutoland in a series of murders to secure human flesh for medicines, which shocked both Sotho and outsiders. But the swing, since 1960, has been to an elective system. In all three territories hereditary chiefs are still the leaders but in Botswana and Lesotho they hold office by virtue of election.

There are other radical differences in the trend of development: in the Transkei, social relations between black and white are becoming more rigidly segregated, whereas in Lesotho, Botswana, and Swaziland the trend is in the opposite direction. The Transkei was not left a free choice in determining its constitution: it was made clear that the Government of the Republic would not accept any form of multi-racialism, which Chief Victor Poto, who commanded a large popular following, advocated; Swaziland, however, has a multi-racial constitution. In the Transkei, hotels, cafés, libraries, theatres, schools, and receptions for Government officials are rigidly segregated. A bishop living in Umtata was refused the use of the library because he was African, and in 1962 an African university lecturer was driven from an Umtata café by the proprietor, because he dared to ask at the counter for a cup of tea. Furthermore, the proprietor complained to the police who proceeded to charge the owner of the car in which the lecturer was travelling with misparking.[2] The only Africans known to have been admitted as guests in an Umtata hotel were three delegates from Malawi visiting South Africa on a trade mission in 1966. In Lesotho, Botswana, and Swaziland the atmosphere is totally different: there hotels and other public services, including schools, have no colour bar.

A further difference is that the leaders of Botswana and Lesotho and

[1] *H.A.D.*, 1959, cols. 324–8; 1961, col. 226; Horrell, *1961*, pp. 92–6; *1962*, pp. 17–20; *1964*, p. 57; *1966*, pp. 64–6.
[2] Direct observation.

Swaziland travel abroad, negotiating with other states, and both Lesotho and Botswana are represented at UNO. Every encouragement is given to citizens to travel and study. No Bantu Authority has international links for none is an independent state, and the Republican Government has repeatedly refused passports to political leaders, prominent Churchmen, and students who have been invited to travel overseas or offered scholarships.[1] The official trend is consistently towards isolation, isolating the Bantustans both from the outside world and from each other.

The reason for separation of Bantustans from each other was made clear in a speech by the Minister of Bantu Administration and Development in the House of Assembly in 1966. He said: 'As regards all the various nations we have here, the White nation, the Coloured nation, the Indian nation, the various Bantu nations, something to which we have given too little regard is the fact that numerically the White nation is superior to all other nations in South Africa . . . It has a very wide implication for us . . . Firstly, it demonstrates our duty as guardians . . . It also demonstrates the utter folly of saying that a minority government is ruling others in South Africa . . . Our policy is based on the . . . separateness and the diversity of the various Bantu nations and other nations in South Africa as separate national entities set on separate courses to separate destinies.'[2]

5. *Kinship and Association*

A radical change in traditional kinship systems began with the opportunity for individuals to earn stock for themselves, the growth of a money economy, the Christian insistence on monogamy, and the establishment of worshipping groups which were not based on birth. In 1707 the poor Hessequa, already mentioned, preferred taking employment with white settlers rather than with rich men of their own group, and they were rewarded for their labour with cattle. The Xhosa, and refugees from the wars of Shaka and his rivals who sought employment with settlers on the East Cape frontier in the early nineteenth century, also earned stock—horses and cattle. Traditionally young men got stock with which to establish a herd and marry from two sources: their senior kinsmen and raids on neighbouring chiefdoms. Employment abroad gradually replaced raiding, and it made a man dependent upon whites who provided passes and jobs, rather than on kinsmen and fellow warriors. An analysis, made in 1931, of where marriage-cattle came from in Pondoland (then the most conservative part of the Transkei) showed that by that date a small percentage of the young men

[1] Direct observation. [2] *H.A.D.*, 1966, cols. 4132–4.

earned all their own marriage-cattle, a larger number earned a part of them, but the majority still got all their marriage-cattle from their fathers and other kinsmen.[1] From the moment migrants go out to work, relationships between the generations are modified. Traditional authority may be asserted for a time, and young men hand over their earnings to their fathers who, in turn, fulfil traditional responsibility in providing marriage-cattle, but as the use of money spreads and potential consumption in clothes and bicycles, guns, guitars, and furniture increases, sons seek economic independence. It is still usual (in 1966) for an Nguni or Sotho man to bring his bride to his father's homestead, but the period during which they live in the family homestead is getting shorter: more and more young men establish their own homesteads a year or two after marriage, and so achieve economic independence.[2]

Polygyny was traditionally the ideal among all the herders and cultivators. It was first modified by Christian teaching, and later by economic necessity. As land became scarce, and a man could secure no more than one field, and country families ceased to be self-supporting in food, an ordinary man could not afford a second wife. The incidence of polygyny in Cape Province dropped only slightly between 1911 and 1921 (from twelve to eleven per cent of the married men) and in Ngqeleni, a conservative district of Pondoland, in which land was still plentiful, fifteen per cent of the married men were still polygynists in 1932, but by the 1950s the proportion was down to four or five per cent in the districts of the Transkei and Natal then investigated, and under one per cent in the Ciskei. Among the Kgatla of Botswana it was similarly low even in 1930 (three to four per cent) but in the lowveld of Swaziland in 1960 it was twenty-five per cent.[3] Marriageable women far outnumber unmarried men in the country, not only because some of the young men who go to work in town never return to the country, but also because there is a marked difference in the marriage age of men and women (six years in Keiskammahoek district). Sonnabend has shown that seven years difference in the marriage age allows twenty per cent of the married men to have two wives.[4] Furthermore, it is probable that the survival rate differs, men dying younger than women. In 1950 in a quarter of the homesteads in Keiskammahoek

[1] Hunter, pp. 124–7.

[2] Ibid., pp. 59–60; A. Mafeje, 'Leadership and Change: A Study of Two South African Peasant Communities' (unpublished M.A. Thesis, University of Cape Town, 1964); Vilakazi, pp. 30–1; Wilson et al., Social Structure, p. 46.

[3] Hunter, p. 202; W. D. Hammond-Tooke, unpublished material kindly communicated; Reader, p. 84; Wilson et al., Social Structure p. 94; I. Schapera, Married Life in an African Tribe, pp. 99–100; Holleman, pp. 132–3.

[4] H. Sonnabend, 'Demographic Samples in the Study of Backward and Primitive Populations', SAJE, 2 (1934) 319–21.

district the heads were widows, and similar figures were reported from other areas.[1] One of the recurring themes in Bunga debates was the property rights of widows.[2] Few Nguni or Sotho women are prepared to live single and forgo childbearing, and the result of such a disproportion of the sexes in the country, and the decrease in polygyny, is a high illegitimacy rate (24 per cent in Keiskammahoek district),[3] and a very general practice of concubinage where long-term, but not legally recognized, liasons are formed. The children of such unions are brought up and cared for at the mother's home, and belong to her lineage, and a new type of mother-centred family (unknown among Nguni and Sotho traditionally) is becoming increasingly important in country as well as in town.

In spite of this decline in polygyny and increase in concubinage, the giving of cattle or some substitute for cattle by the groom to the bride's father or guardian (*lobola*) is still generally regarded as a prerequisite of a properly constituted marriage, and the status of a wife is higher in the eyes of the community if cattle have been given. In 98·7 per cent out of a sample of two thousand marriages contracted between 1880 and 1950 in Keiskammahoek district *lobola* had been given,[4] and even after 1940 it was given in 97·4 per cent of the cases. 'Shall *lobola* live or die?' is a matter of hot debate. Christians among the Ngwato dropped it two generations ago, but it is still given in most Nguni and Sotho peasant communities.[5]

The lineage diminishes in importance as its control over stock diminishes, but where land is held on freehold, there lineage members are bound together by a common interest in the land, which is generally treated as the property, not of the legal heir alone, but of all the descendants in the male line if the original holder. As land becomes scarcer the concern of individuals in lineage land increases.[6]

Traditionally, members of a lineage formed a worshipping group sacrificing together to common ancestors, and junior members were dependent upon the senior for celebration of rituals. As individuals became Christian they no longer necessarily worshipped with kinsmen. The congregation was formed of individuals who accepted a new faith, and though they founded families and brought up their children as

[1] Wilson *et al.*, *Social Structure*, pp. 89–93; Houghton and Walton, pp. 51–60; Roupp, p. 110.

[2] *Bunga Reports*, *1920*, pp. 53–5; *1925*, pp. 67–8; *1932*, pp. 96–7.

[3] Wilson *et al.*, pp. 93–106.

[4] Wilson *et al.*, p. 82.

[5] H. H. T. Marwede and G. G. Mamabolo, '*Shall Lobolo Live or Die?*'; Vilakazi, p. 65; H. Kuper 'Nurses' in L. Kuper, *An African Bourgeoisie*, p. 230; Reader, p. 215; Schapera, *Married Life*, pp. 84–91; Files in vernacular newspapers, and debates in African schools and colleges.

[6] Elton-Mills and Wilson, pp. 133–4; A. I. Richards, *The Changing Structure of a Ganda Village, 1892–1952*.

Christians, membership of a church continued to be an individual choice. It was the church which began the shift from a society based on kinship and locality to one in which association—the combination of individuals to pursue a common interest—is equally important. To the theologian the church is a *community* of believers, called by God: to the anthropologist seeking to analyse social structures, it is, in one aspect, an *association* since, though the children of members are baptized and brought up as Christians, full participation depends upon the choice and action of adults.

In the traditional societies a man was placed by his lineage, age-group or regiment, and chiefdom. Among the Xhosa, men and women were politely saluted by clan names, and a stranger, asked to identify himself, replied with clan and chiefdom. In the Xhosa peasant community identification by lineage and locality still exists, but added to this are school, church, and class. In the Coloured reserves of Rehoboth and Steinkopf position likewise depends on membership of a lineage, and on education, church affiliation, and wealth.[1]

Men seek identity as members of groups, and the telling of history plays a part in fostering a sense of identity and belonging. The history related orally by bards, and written early this century by Nguni and Sotho (see Vol. I, pp. 85–6, 137) was conceived of in terms of lineages and chiefdoms; Xhosa historians, like the chroniclers of Israel, were preoccupied with a hero's descent;[2] modern historians are concerned with events affecting nations, and the part of leaders in shaping these. The shift to a more impersonal view of causation, and a search for some general understanding of the process of change becomes apparent.[3]

Christian congregations which gathered for worship and instruction were the first associations formed by those sharing a common interest, but they were soon followed by others. Most churches have a penumbra of associations for different categories of members—women, men, girls—and for recreation and instruction. Professional associations of teachers, a health society, sports clubs, agricultural associations, co-operative societies, savings clubs, political associations,[4] all began in peasant communities, and in them began the long, slow process of training in joint-action through committees. All these associations have chairmen and secretaries; they keep minutes; they levy a subscription, and they record accounts. De Tocqueville spoke in 1848 of voluntary associations to achieve some end as characteristic of America, as

[1] Carstens, pp. 120–33.

[2] W. B. Rubusana, *Zemk' inkomo Magwalandini*; R. T. Kawa, *I-Bali lama Mfengu*, Victor Poto Ndamase, *Ama-Mpondo Ibali ne-Ntlalo*.

[3] E. H. Carr, *What is History?*; G. and M. Wilson, *The Analysis of Social Change*.

[4] Wilson *et al.*, *Social Structure*, pp. 136–44, 165–9.

distinct from France and Britain: 'Les Américains, de tous les âges, de toutes les conditions, de tous les esprits, s'unissent sans cesse. . . .'[1]

Whether or not this distinction between Europe and America is still valid, there can be no question that the voluntary association with office-bearers, formed to achieve a specific end, is a type of organization planted among Africans in South Africa by European and American missionaries, and now deep rooted. The growing number of such associations is the structural manifestation of increasing diversity of interests in peasant communities.

The associations share one feature with the traditional chiefdoms and clans: they tend to split; and this has led simple-minded observers to suppose that 'fissiparous tendencies' are peculiar to Africans, and possibly innate in negroes! The most cursory acquaintance with the history of the Christian Church, the trade union movement, international communism, or the Voortrekkers, shows that fissiparous tendencies are always present; the question is how successfully they are controlled. The conditions of control are obscure, but they are linked to the strength of purpose to combine, willingness to subordinate sectional to common interests, skill in leadership, and the realization that success is attainable through unity. Those who remain parochial in outlook continue to fragment.

One of the effects of colonial rule in Africa has been to create national states which, after gaining independence, are struggling to remain intact. Another conspicuous tendency is for states, and organizations within states such as churches, trade unions, professional associations, sports clubs, and educational and welfare associations, to seek international affiliation with like bodies. Southern Africa is no exception in this regard, and very many local bodies, from the tiny women's clubs of the reserves, and the football unions, to the churches, and African political parties have (or had until the parties were banned) international links. The isolation of tribal society has been breached at innumerable points by Africans. Those who are now driven into isolation are white racialists, for their values are unacceptable to the outside world. Because of its apartheid policy the Republic has been excluded from one international organization after another, including the Scientific Council for Africa, and is so being forced into intellectual, as well as political and social, isolation.

6. *Leaders*

Leadership in tribal societies was concentrated in the persons of chiefs who initiated action in political, economic, and religious fields,

---

[1] A. de Tocqueville, *De la démocratie en Amérique*, ii. 113–17.

as well as settling disputes. The chief was both *dux* and *rex*;[1] he was the distributor of wealth, as well as priest, judge, and commander of the army. Only the diviners and notable warriors could be singled out as specialist leaders. By contrast, peasant communities have a diversity of leaders. Hereditary chiefs may yet be of importance but there are also specialist priests and teachers; traders, craftsmen, and administrators; doctors and nurses; and the basis of their authority is not birth, but skills. They include 'outsiders' whose leadership depends upon their wider relationships.

The degree of stratification varied in traditional Nguni and Sotho chiefdoms. Everywhere it was based primarily on descent, and members of royal clans claimed a higher status than commoners; descendants of old adherents of the chief a higher status than immigrants; and control of wealth was closely linked with descent. In the peasant communities of southern Africa descent is still of very great importance, particularly the differentiation between white, and African or Coloured, but differentiation between lineages of one colour group is less important. Ownership of *land* differentiates people rather than ownership of cattle. In districts where individual tenure operates, and in other reserves also, cleavages exist between landowners or those with recognized land rights, and 'squatters'; and people from reserves generally look down on farm-labourers as 'landless wanderers'.[2]

A new ground of status emerged in education. This was reflected in the motion brought before the Bunga in 1925 proposing that a higher fine in case of seduction be levied for an educated girl than for one who was uneducated,[3] just as a higher *lobola* and seduction fine was paid traditionally for the daughter of a chief than for a commoner.[4] The motion was lost, but it typified a widespread attitude. Leadership in peasant communities is, in fact, passing to the better-educated members, who work as professional men, craftsmen, or traders. Members of families who first accepted Christianity and education have been educated at one or another of half a dozen famous schools; they have intermarried across the boundaries of chiefdom and language; and they have links of kinship and friendship spreading through the reserves and towns of southern Africa and, since many individuals have fled the country, to other African territories and overseas. The higher the status of an individual or family, the wider the social contacts; and leaders in the reserves are not isolated. Three generations of leaders who came from villages, and lived largely in the country, were educated in close

---

[1] B. de Jouvenel, *Sovereignty*, pp. 21–2, 34.

[2] Hunter, pp. 506–7; Elton-Mills and Wilson, pp. 121–2; Vilakazi, pp. 112, 142; Carstens, pp. 6, 126–31, 215–17, 228.

[3] *Bunga Reports, 1925*, pp. 90–3.

[4] Hunter, p. 376; *Bunga Reports, 1934*, pp. 97–8.

association with those of other races and languages, and were often the product of integrated schools. They included the families of Soga, Makiwane, Jabavu, Bokwe, Moroka, Molema, Xuma, Lutuli, Matthews, Zulu. The majority in the contemporary generation of leaders came from educated homes. Some individuals did not—their parents were pagan and illiterate—but most of them achieved their positions through education, and their children are educated.[1]

Leaders have become steadily more radical, as the attempts of 'moderates' to secure some participation in the government of South Africa were rejected by whites, but the leaders are still educated men, not illiterate conservatives. Many of those who have been banned in the country were professional men—teachers and lawyers; and even those who have gained power under Bantu Authorities, such as the Chief Minister, Matanzima, and members of his cabinet, are educated. If they were not they would be unable to fulfil their functions. The typical uneducated leaders have been the founders of some independent churches, mostly those of the Zionist type, but if they acquire wealth their sons are educated. For example the son of Shembe, the illiterate founder of the independent Nazarite Church in Natal, graduated at Fort Hare.

For the professional class there is no sharp cleavage between town and country.[2] A son or daughter of the village may return as teacher or minister, nurse, agriculturalist, or doctor, but the country is so poor that opportunity in business or profession is greater in town, and the country-born move citywards, as they do elsewhere.

Within the reserves one section stresses traditional custom, and identifies piety with conservatism as their ancestors did (see Vol. I, pp. 128, 265). Their leaders have been chiefs (but not all chiefs), traditional diviners, and conservative lineage heads, and they have observably diminished in numbers, in at least some areas, over thirty-five years.[3] The other section—the 'school people'—began as radicals, accepting a new religion and a new manner of life, and the majority of their descendants have continued to think in terms of 'progress'. The shift from a society in which the golden age was in the past to one with heaven or utopia in the future is apparent, and the leaders of the 'peasant' communities (as defined here) value change. They think in terms of improved education, increasing skill, participation in an expanding economy, and the development of political rights, though

[1] J. Stewart, *Lovedale Past and Present*; T. D. Mweli Skota, *The African Yearly Register*; Vilakazi, pp. 108–11, 139–40; 'Fort Hare Historical Notes', *The South African Outlook*, 91, 92, (1961–2); 'Mini-Biographies', *The South African Outlook*, 94, 95, 96 (1964–66).

[2] Wilson and Mafeje, pp. 74–5, 137–43.

[3] Direct observation. I have watched particularly two villages in the Ciskei in which I began field-work in 1931.

in practice real income may not have risen since 1911[1] and political rights have diminished. The shift in values is reflected even in toys children make for themselves. During the last thirty years wire models of motorcars have ousted the stylized clay oxen with humps.[2] That deep conservatism, generally taken as characteristic of peasants is not characteristic of the total community here defined as 'peasant'.

Nevertheless for many in Africa, as elsewhere, a nostalgia for the village remains.[3] Zulu literature is dominated by the theme of the country boy who goes to town and is corrupted.[4] To an anthropologist it seems as if the values of 'negritude' even as expressed by so eminent a writer as Leopold Senghor,[5] are the values of the small-scale society— the society in which close-knit communities existed, there was no dichotomy between sacred and profane, and personal relationships were dominant—and it is no accident that black South Africans distrust 'negritude'. They are no longer members of a small-scale society.

The magistrates or 'native commissioners' (later called 'Bantu commissioners'), like the missionaries and traders, were part of peasant communities which could not exist independently of them, but they were separated from the peasantry by the authority they exercised, by differences in custom, in some measure by language, and by colour. Even in a peasant community within a society homogeneous in race and language, where those in authority may have themselves come from peasant families, the administrator, the merchant, and the priest are differentiated from the peasants.[6] In a society which is stratified in colour castes, as South Africa is, and the administrator, trader, and priests are whites, living among Africans, the social distance is still wider. Nevertheless they are all part of one community. The work and professional interests of the 'outsider' leaders are bound up with those of the peasants.[7] Often, in South Africa, administrator, or trader, or missionary had grown up among the people with whom he worked, and spoke Xhosa, Zulu, Sotho, Tswana, or Venda as readily as his mother tongue. White South Africa as a whole has opposed close social interaction and intermarriage, yet both have occurred and recurred. Love and charity between neighbours was manifest in the Transkei during the devastating influenza epidemic of 1918 when the white population exerted itself to provide medical attention and food for

[1] Francis Wilson, *The Economics of Labour in the South African Gold Mines* (Cambridge forthcoming). Real wages in manufacturing rose after 1936, but not for Africans in gold-mining.   [2] Direct observation.

[3] G. C. Homans, *The Human Group*, pp. 453–68.   [4] Nyembezi, p. 9.

[5] L. S. Senghor, 'Negritude, A Humanism of the Twentieth Century', *Optima* 16 (1) (1966), 1–8.

[6] J. A. Pitt-Rivers, *The People of the Sierra*, pp. 15–16, 122–36.

[7] M. Gluckman, 'Analysis of a Social Situation in Modern Zululand', *Bantu Studies*, 14 (1940), 1–30, 147–74.

Africans at village schools, and to bury the dead; and white children whose parents had died on remote trading stations were rescued and adopted by African neighbours. It was apparent when, in 1906, an African minister, John Knox Bokwe, started a school for white children who were no longer permitted to attend the mixed school he managed;[1] and again in the drought of 1928 when the Transkei Bunga voted £250 from its meagre resources for the assistance of white farmers in drought-stricken areas.[2]

7. *The Reality of Interaction*

The roots of all the peoples of South Africa (save the remnant of hunters living in the Kalahari) lie deep in interaction between them. Isolation is a value—an ideal—expressed by some whites and some blacks, not a reality. The tribesman, in any precise sense, has ceased to exist; he has become a peasant, a farm-hand, or an urban labourer with a home in the country, who tries to maintain what he can of traditional custom. The extent of economic and political interdependence has been shown. Emotional interdependence is equally real. The mutual fear and love, attraction and rejection, between members of different racial groups is reflected in the so-called 'immorality laws' prohibiting both marriage and liaison between members of different racial groups. If attraction did not exist there would be no law, nor the frequent breaches of it which occur. Without rejection there would be no law either. The extent of racial intermixture goes considerably further than is legally recognized, for many individuals and families, known by local gossip to be of mixed descent, are classified either as African or white, having lived and identified themselves with one or other group. Many children of mixed descent are brought up by the mothers' kin in reserves, or on farms, or in towns. South Africans abroad, unimpeded by law and convention, quickly manifest their common interests.

The emotional interdependence is reflected also in art. Not only do artists look back to the mythology and painting of the hunters, but leading writers in English, Xhosa, Afrikaans, and Sotho are preoccupied with the struggles of men and women to assimilate the clash in tradition and values of diverse groups. *Ingqumbo Yeminyanya* [The Wrath of the Shades], *Cry the Beloved Country*, *The Blood Knot*, and *Ons die Afgod*[3] all turn on this. It is from the turmoil that drama and poetry has sprung. And perhaps it is no accident that the art in which South Africans of all complexions have excelled in the international field is dancing, for dancing was the traditional art of the country, and generations of

[1] Smit, pp. 83-4, 99. [2] *Bunga Reports, 1928*, pp. 102-3.
[3] A. C. Jordan, *Ingqumbo Yeminyanya*; Alan Paton, *Cry the Beloved Country*; A. Fugard, *The Blood Knot*; Jan Rabie, *Ons die Afgod*.

white children have been dandled by nannies who themselves could dance as soon as they could walk, and who were deeply aware that rhythm soothed a child. The influence of diverse traditions has been mutual in music as in dancing: jazz springs from Africa, and echoes of German chorales pervade the songs sung at home by Mpondo or Zulu; *King Kong* (a musical with an African cast which in 1959 took South Africa by storm) had roots in both Europe and Africa; Miriam Makeba is admired by white and black alike. Even the hunter of the desert, once having tasted interaction, can scarcely withdraw again into isolation.

Any study of reserves within the Republic, and of Lesotho and Botswana, demonstrates the unresolved contradiction between economics and politics. The reserves are not self-supporting even in the basic foods, but are dependent for their daily bread on the earnings of migrant labourers in towns or on white-owned farms to buy maize grown on white-owned farms. They have become steadily more dependent over a hundred years. The same is true of Lesotho, and in a lesser degree of Botswana (see pp. 58–9, 70–1). Economically, African peasants are dependent upon selling their labour to white industrialists and large-scale farmers, and the whites, equally, are dependent upon the peasants for labour. They cannot operate without them. Moreover mutual dependence grows steadily greater. But the Republic seeks to prevent Africans from settling in towns, or even on farms in the Western Cape, and fosters contract labour whereby men are recruited and work for a limited period and must then return to their reserve whence they came. This implies a permanent system of separating wage-earners from their families: it implies that labourers never remain in one job, or even one type of work.

The Republic rejects Africans as citizens with political rights and gives a limited measure of local self-government in 'homelands' only one of which, the Transkei, is a substantial territorial unit. 'Separate freedoms' and 'independence' are promised in the 'homelands' but are nowhere yet realized. Lesotho and Botswana are politically independent but are not economically viable, and like the reserves of the Republic they must send out labourers to the towns and white-owned farms in the Republic in order to live. Only Swaziland, with a population of African and white mingled through the territory; with a lower population density on well-watered land; with a timber industry and substantial mineral resources, shows signs of employing and feeding its population without relying on migrants working in the Republic.

Economically the area defined in this book as 'South Africa' (see Vol. I, p. xi) is a unit and its prosperity has depended upon its population becoming closer and closer knit. Politically it is divided and the explicit policy of the Republic is towards further fragmentation if promises of 'independence' for 'homelands' are to be taken seriously. Economically and politically the reserves of the Republic resemble colonies, and the period of colonial rule lingers on.[1] It has been argued that, elsewhere in Africa, imperial governments have offered little resistance to movements for independence because African colonies were of neither economic nor strategic importance to them.[2] The reserves of the Republic are of immediate importance, strategically and economically, to the Republic as a whole, and so indeed are Lesotho, Swaziland, and Botswana.

Three questions remain to be answered: Can close economic interdependence be combined with political independence? Can any country remain stable when the majority of its population—the workers who man its industries and farms—are not citizens but foreigners, exercising political rights only in other states? Can any society built on the separation of families throughout a man's working life survive?

[1] Marquard, *South Africa's Colonial Policy.*
[2] Professor John Gallagher, unpublished lecture. Cf. R. Robinson, J. Gallagher, with A. Denny, *Africa and the Victorians.*

III

FARMING, 1866–1966[1]

No ONE who wishes to understand the history of South Africa in
the century that followed the discovery of diamonds can ignore
the *platteland*.[2] For the *platteland* was the cradle of Afrikaner life
and nationalism. Indeed it was the place where most of the groups for
whom, by the 1960s, South Africa was home, had had their formative
experience. It was into the soil of the farms that the first English settlers
sent their roots, in the years before the discovery of minerals made it
possible to make money in the towns. It was as agricultural labourers
that Indians were indentured into the country. It was in the vineyards
and wheatlands of the western Cape that the shattered Khoikhoi
became the Coloured people. And it was on the *platteland* that there
evolved, during the two slow centuries of the ox-wagon, the pattern of
relationships between black and white that was to imprint itself
indelibly upon the country's political, social, and economic structure
for the first hundred years of its industrial life.

The interaction between people of diverse origins, languages,
technologies, ideologies, and social systems meeting on South African
soil is, it is maintained,[3] the central theme of the country's history. This
interaction may be divided into three broad categories, for it varied
according to its locus. In the reserves[4] Africans met missionaries and
traders. The missionaries, particularly, were people who maintained
contact with the ideas of the wider world overseas and who held an ideal
of equality which, while often paternalistic, was none the less decidedly
different from the prevailing ethos of the farming community. This
mission influence[5] which, through the schools, was particularly strong
in the Cape, Lesotho, and parts of Natal gave to the interaction between
black and white a closeness and solidarity that did not fit the pattern of

[1] I wish to acknowledge my debt to the two editors of this volume for their detailed criticisms of earlier drafts of this chapter. In like measure I thank Mr. Leo Marquard, Professor
Hobart Houghton, and Mr. Sean Archer for their help. A number of officials in Pretoria
generously provided information which is gratefully acknowledged. The chapter benefited
also from discussion with colleagues at the University of Cape Town. For constant encouragement I thank my wife.

[2] Literally meaning 'the flat land', the word '*platteland*' is commonly used when referring
to the white-occupied rural areas of the country.   [3] Vol. I, Preface.

[4] Reserves are those areas where, by the law after 1913, Africans only were allowed to own
land. See map.

[5] See, for example, J. Wells, *Stewart of Lovedale*.

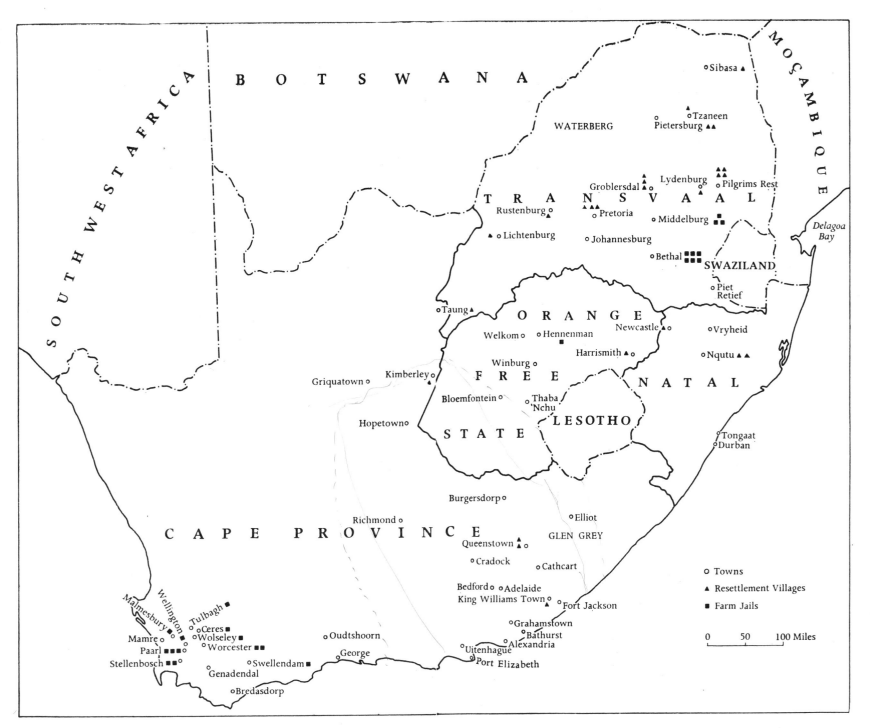

MAP 3. Farm jails and resettlement villages, 1966. Note: Farm jails and resettlement villages are shown on the map near the name of the town to which they are closest

Sources: Republic of South Africa: *House of Assembly Debates* (Hansard) (Cape Town, 1967) col. 3511

M. Horrell, *A Survey of Race Relations in South Africa*, 1967 (Johannesburg, 1968) p. 181. Bantu Administration and Development, General Circular, No. 25, 1967

C. Desmond, *The Discarded People* Christian Institute of S.A. Johannesburg, 1970.

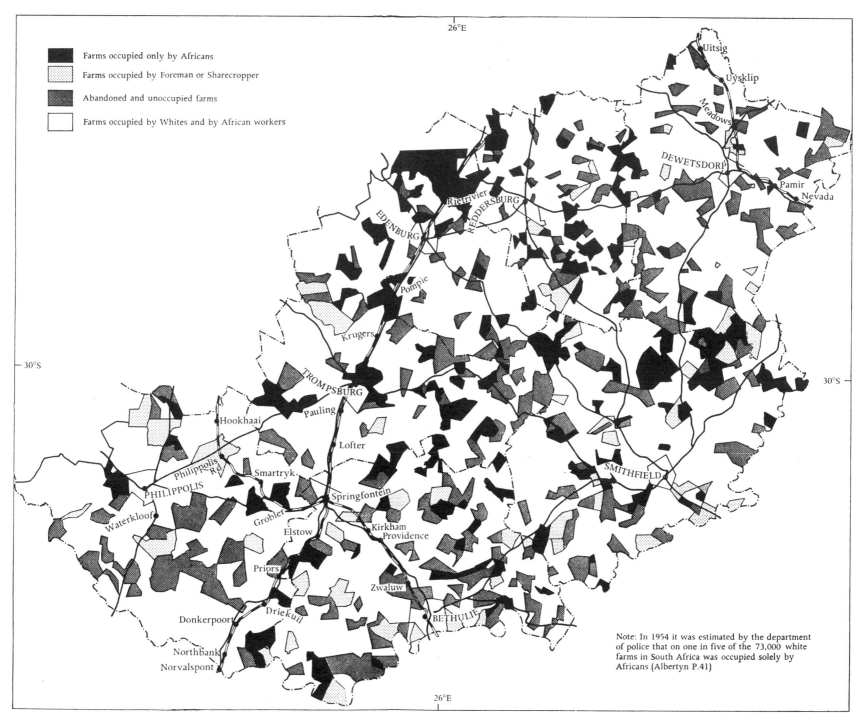

Legend:
- Farms occupied only by Africans
- Farms occupied by Foreman or Sharecropper
- Abandoned and unoccupied farms
- Farms occupied by Whites and by African workers

26°E

Uitsig
Uysklip
Meadows
DEWETSDORP
Pamir
Nevada
Rietrivier
EDENBURG
REDDERSBURG
Pompie
Krugers
30°S
TROMPSBURG
Pauling
Hookhaai
Lofter
Philippolis Rd.
Smartryk
SMITHFIELD
PHILIPPOLIS
Springfontein
Grobler
Kirkham
Elstow
Providence
Waterkloof
Priors
Zwaluw
Donkerpoort
Driekuil
BETHULIE
Northbank
Norvalspont

30°S

Note: In 1954 it was estimated by the department of police that on one in five of the 73,000 white farms in South Africa was occupied solely by Africans (Albertyn P.41)

26°E

MAP 4. The 'beswarting' of the platteland: farm occupancy in the southern districts of the Orange Free State, 1959
Source: Commission of Enquiry into the European Occupancy of the Rural Areas (Government Printer, Pretoria, 1959)

the 'traditional way of life' which was seen as ideal by successive white generations. But it had a profound influence on the evolving ideas of the blacks.

In the towns the interaction was different from that on both reserves and farms. Not only were the relationships between the diverse groups more impersonal, but also the process of urbanization came too late to influence the norms by which the politically dominant, white, group judged and to which it sought to mould social interaction as the country became industrialized. The coming of unskilled workers to the new mines and factories did not lead, as in most other countries,[1] to the emergence of a solid working-class movement against those who owned and controlled the means of production. Rather it was the pattern of the farms where white men owned the land and black men did the 'kaffir' work that influenced the manner in which urban South Africa ordered its affairs.

In short, the isolation of the farms combined with the master-servant relationships of a semi-feudal situation led to the growth of communities which not only differed from, but also greatly influenced, those developing in towns and the reserves. It is as one of the key areas of interaction that the farms of South Africa can most fruitfully be studied.

1. *The Setting*

By 1866 the whites were in control, albeit tenuous in some places, of most of the land that subsequently became consolidated into the Union of South Africa. But such control had not been won easily. On the eastern frontier alone there were nine major clashes, in the hundred years 1779–1879, between the Xhosa-speaking inhabitants and the white settlers who, after 1799, were mainly English-speaking. Further north, the descendants of pioneers from both Holland and England fought bloody battles with the Zulu in 1838 and 1879. And in the interior the movement and settlement of the Voortrekkers was hotly contested by Sotho, Tswana, Venda, and others who had numbers on their side but no guns.[2] Except in the western Cape, where prolonged military might combined with the ravages of smallpox had long since eliminated the dangers of attack, the whites, although nominally in control, still lived in fear of attack from the black enemy. Just north of the Orange river a family which, in 1849, bought a 5,000-morgen[3] farm on which the father expected to settle for life was driven off by Mosh-weshwe's warriors a year later.[4] And in the Bathurst district near

---

[1] Cf. C. Vann Woodward, *Origins of the New South*, Chap. IX.

[2] Vol. I, pp. 335 ff.

[3] 1 morgen = 2·12 acres.   [4] W. W. Collins, *Free Statia*, p. 12.

Grahamstown it was still, in 1877, too risky for white men to live on some farms.[1]

Despite this resistance on the moving frontier, it was relatively easy for whites to obtain land and it would seem that the type of tenure which they adopted as a result hindered rather than helped economic development. Prior to Sir John Cradock's reform of 1813, any white man could obtain land in the Cape merely by paying the Government an annual sum of 24 rix dollars.[2] The rent of these *leeningsplaatsen* (loan farms) was too low to force the settler to make the land productive; and land was still plentiful enough for a farmer to move his stock on to new pastures once the first farm had been grazed bare. After 1813 all new grants of land were made on a quitrent basis, and were limited to a maximum size of 3,000 morgen. The rent was fixed at anything up to 250 rix dollars a year, depending on fertility. Although not immediately effective, Cradock's proclamation had the long-term consequence of compelling farmers to take a rudimentary interest in the output of the land. Those who could not face such a commercial view of life moved on to the north-east frontier where the land was excellent and where the Government's revenue collectors were less likely to make their unwelcome appearance.[3] Inland the pattern was similar although it was not until 1858 that the Transvaal Government took over all unallotted land and not until 1871 that it began to issue title-deeds and to limit the size of farms.[4] But quitrent was by no means the only form of tenure. Some farmers owned their land, whilst, in various parts of the country, there were those who, holding no title, roamed the veld grazing their flocks wherever they could.[5]

Generally speaking farms were very large. Three thousand morgen was taken to be the standard size throughout South Africa during the nineteenth century. The consequence of this was, as Trollope points out,[6] bad for the country, particularly the Transvaal where the land was unused yet locked up and not open to newcomers. Furthermore the fact that farms were so large meant that people were extremely isolated from community life. But not all farms were of the standard size for there was little precision about measurement. It varied from walking a

---

[1] A. Trollope, *South Africa*, i. 177.

[2] The sterling value of the rix dollar fell steadily from 3s. 6d. in 1806–10 to 1s. 6d. in 1825 when the exchange rate was fixed. See R. Leslie, 'Paper Money and the Gold Standard at the Cape', *Report of the Fourteenth Annual General Meeting of the South African Association for the Advancement of Science* (Cape Town, 1917).

[3] Sir Arnold Plant, 'Economic Development 1795–1921', in *CHBE* (2nd edn.), viii. 796.

[4] *Report of the Commission of Inquiry into European Occupancy of the Rural Areas* (Pretoria, 1960), para. 8. See also C. W. de Kiewiet, *A History of South Africa, Social and Economic*, p. 185: Trollope, ii. 108.

[5] J. Mackenzie, *Ten Years North of the Orange River*, p. 14.

[6] Trollope, ii. 21, 109–10.

horse for half an hour from some central spot in each of several directions, to walking a horse round as large a circumference as possible in a day thus making a farm twice as big. Throughout the country there were farms double or treble the standard size[1] whilst on either side of the Vaal some farms of 500 morgen were measured out by the respective governments.[2] And, in some instances, men on return from Commando were rewarded with grants of only eight morgen.[3]

By 1867, notwithstanding the extent of subsistence farming in the white-controlled Transvaal and black-controlled Transkei, commercial farming in South Africa was well established. From the 1820s wool production expanded rapidly and by 1841 the Cape was exporting over one million lb. of wool annually,[4] three-fifths of this coming from the eastern frontier. The Orange Free State, which at that time contained some of the finest sheep-runs in the country,[5] was opening up for white settlement and the next generation saw an enormous expansion of wool production as sheep moved across the Orange river. By 1862 South Africa's wool exports had risen to 25 million lb. a year.[6] As Hobart Houghton points out:[7] 'The economic impact of international markets was carried into the interior, not in the wagons of the Voortrekkers, but upon the backs of the merino sheep.' The effect of this was to drive up land prices rapidly. One farm of 2,400 morgen was sold in 1848 for £63, in 1851 for £158, in 1856 for £1,350, in 1857 for £2,000, and in 1861 its estimated value was £3,000.[8] In the Transvaal, however, the land was not suitable for sheep, the ports were far away, and so it lagged behind the rest of the country in economic development. In Natal it was not sheep but sugar which gave promise of an agricultural future. After experiments with a number of different commodities, sugar production began in 1850. It started slowly, but, after the arrival of the first indentured Indians in 1860, output expanded rapidly behind the comfortable shelter of a protective tariff.

Other products already established were wheat, fruit, butter, beef, and maize (indian corn) for the internal market, together with hides, wine, and ostrich feathers for export. Most of these commodities were produced along the coastal belt where the climate was particularly suitable and where transport costs, by ship, were not prohibitive as in the interior. Farmers at this period cultivated less than one per cent of their land,[9] but most of them seem to have grown a little wheat and the country was more or less self-sufficient in food, although, in times of

[1] Ibid. i. 299; ii. 21, 108; Collins, p. 182.
[2] Ibid., p. 149; *Report of the Commission of Inquiry into European Occupancy of the Rural Areas*, para. 9.   [3] Ibid.
[4] J. C. Chase, *The Cape of Good Hope*, p. 173.   [5] Mackenzie, p. 47.
[6] Plant, in *CHBE*, viii. 298.   [7] p. 4 above.   [8] Collins, p. 182.
[9] G. C. R. Bosman, *The Industrialization of South Africa*, p. 34; Trollope, ii. 21, 236.

drought, wheat had to be imported.[1] In the western Cape, where the winter rainfall climate was particularly suited to wheat, the land was often very stony and difficult to plough, and, in a world of rapidly improving transport, South African wheat was to have no comparative advantages. With maize, it was a different matter. Although not indigenous to the country it was being cultivated by the Africans in the eastern Cape when the whites settled there early in the nineteenth century.[2] Spreading inland before the turn of the century it was later to make fortunes for farmers of the maize triangle.

Before the mineral discoveries, which made it worth while to build railways into the interior, all transport was drawn by animals. The country was huge, the farms were far apart, the roads were very bad, and the going was slow. In a period when it might take an hour to walk to one's nearest white neighbour, when it could take three months for goods to reach Bloemfontein by ox-wagon from Port Elizabeth, only 400 miles away,[3] and when a letter to England cost the equivalent of several lb. of beef,[4] life in the interior was isolated for the farmer and his family. Thus it is not surprising that the travelling *smous* (pedlar or hawker)[5] with all his wares was so eagerly welcomed, nor that *Nachtmaal* was so important an event, nor that the farm village (*boeredorp*), which grew up round the place of worship, played such a crucial role in the life of the rural community.[6]

Nachtmaal was far more than the Holy Communion which its name implied. Held four times a year, it was not unlike a Holy Fair. Rich and poor, pious and not so pious all converged by wagon. The wealthy were pulled by teams of ten horses, the others by oxen. The former, in the more settled areas, repaired to their town houses; the latter pitched their tents. All were drawn by the need for company, the desire to shop, and thirst for news.[7] At first, *Nachtmaal* was held in the wagon-shed of some centrally placed farm, but as time went on a community would begin to take root on this site. First, a small school and the store of the *smous* (who might also act as postmaster and even letter-writer) would be set up. Then a hall would be built that could serve both as church and school; and houses for the wealthier of the church-goers. Finally part of the original farm which had been bought for, or given to, the church would be laid out as a village, and the *dorp* would become fully established when it had its own pastor.[8] Such a *dorp* played a crucial role in the development of white, particularly Afrikaans-speaking, society. 'It

---

[1] Trollope, ii. 107; Plant, in *CHBE*, viii.
[2] Vol. I, p. 109.   [3] Collins, p. 179.   [4] Ibid., pp. 15, 183.
[5] See Vol. I, p. 109. Mackenzie p. 15; S. D. Neumark, *The South African Frontier*, p. 149.
[6] J. R. Albertyn, *Land en Stad*, pp. 79 ff.
[7] Mackenzie, pp. 18–24.
[8] P. Smith, *The Beadle*; Albertyn, pp. 79 ff.

was', wrote Albertyn,[1] 'the focus of light and life for the stock farmer and husbandman, the breeding ground of his noblest traditions, the protector of his own language and culture, the watchman of the people's moral fibre (*volksedes*) and the centre of worship.' The *dorps* of South Africa have been no less important as a focus for the life of Coloured and black farm-workers,[2] but in the middle of the nineteenth century the *boeredorp* had not yet become widely established. It was later that these country villages were to flower in such profusion. Only forty-five were established, predominantly in the Cape, in the two centuries after van Riebeeck's arrival but, thereafter, the number grew rapidly. By 1921 there were 369 *dorps* each with less than 2,000 white inhabitants and, over the following thirty years, the number rose to 603. In addition there were, by 1951, ninety-eight larger towns.[3]

The extent of isolation varied according to the area. In the Cape attendance at *Nachtmaal* would also, in all probability, be a visit to an established village; generally small, but also a place where the *dominees* (*predikants* or ministers) and shopkeepers had a chance to build some contact with the urban centres like Cape Town, and through them with the outside world. But in the interior, lack of communication, the absence of village life, and the rudimentary nature of education, made for an isolation which even in those days was remarkable for a people who, by virtue of the ships that docked in Table Bay, had previously been involved in a larger-scale society. On the frontiers of the Transvaal there were many who thought that the earth was flat, and who took a poor view of their better-educated *dominees* who told them differently.[4] Isolated with their Bibles, many of the Voortrekkers identified themselves with the people of Israel. There were some who seriously hoped to get to Canaan in their ox-wagons.

No-one [wrote Mackenzie in 1871] who has freely and for years mingled with this people can doubt that they have persuaded themselves by some wonderful mental process that they are God's chosen people, and that the blacks are the wicked and condemned Canaanites over whose heads the divine anger lowers continually. Accordingly in their wars with the natives, the question of religion is at once brought into continual and prominent mention.[5]

But while the Bible was interpreted in this way, it was also the source of much genuine goodness. In the matter of hospitality, for example, the New Testament injunction was taken very seriously. 'No person, black or white', reported Mackenzie, 'leaves a frontier farm without having partaken of food.'[6] White travellers dined at the master's table, while black visitors joined the farm servants.

[1] Ibid., p. 78.   [2] M. Hunter, *Reaction to Conquest*, p. 506.   [3] Albertyn, pp. 79, 83.
[4] Mackenzie, p. 51.   [5] Ibid., pp. 50–1.   [6] Ibid., p. 54.

Relationships between master and servant had all the distance of a caste society, combined with the closeness that is inevitable when human beings are thrown together in an isolated enterprise. Most farms seem to have had two or three Coloured or black families living on them, though, in the Transvaal, one observer noted that farmers would allow no Africans to make homes on their land.[1] Travelling north from Cape Town in 1858 Mackenzie found[2] that in most households it was the practice for the assembled company of whites to have their hands washed in the evening by a maidservant. In the Orange Free State farmers generally had African families living in adjacent huts—often within the precincts of the same courtyard, and here Trollope found[3] that black and white children played together, and that there seemed to be 'no feeling of repugnance by anyone at such intercourse'. Up on the Transvaal frontier, as indeed elsewhere, many whites resorted to African diviners and herbalists and the people were so closely bound up with each other that Tswana idioms were slipping into Afrikaans.[4] Although the extent is not easily documented, undoubtedly there were love-relationships across the colour line. Frequent unions, though no marriages, between white men and Coloured women, for example, were reported.[5]

But the caste system retained its rigidity and the social taboos on doing hard unskilled manual work, which were to cause such distress in later years, originated on the farms where the presence, first of slaves and, subsequently, of black serfs, combined with limited wants made it unnecessary for the white conquerors to exert themselves unduly. As early as 1743 a visitor to the Cape noted that 'the majority of farmers in the Colony are not farmers in the real sense of the word, but owners of plantations, and . . . many of them consider it a shame to work with their own hands'.[6] And in 1877 two English-speaking tramps, who needed money, but who could not bring themselves to apply for reasonably well-paid jobs alongside 'niggers', gave a foretaste of what was to come.[7] In his travels through the country Trollope found that nowhere was the white man willing to work on equal terms with a black man.[8] Everywhere it was black men not white who were doing the work on the farms.[9] No less an authority than 'Onze Jan' Hofmeyr, giving evidence to the Transvaal Indigency Commission in 1907, had this to say on the subject: 'Before the emancipation of slaves, all menial work was performed by the slaves, and the white men were in the position of a more or less non-labouring aristocracy. This tradition as to

[1] Trollope, ii. 109.   [2] Mackenzie, p. 16.   [3] Trollope, ii. 239.
[4] Mackenzie, p. 53.   [5] Ibid., p. 156.
[6] E. G. Malherbe, *Education and the Poor White*, p. 23.
[7] Trollope, i. 146.   [8] Ibid. i. 219, ii. 80.   [9] Ibid. 340.

the place of the white man has persisted more or less ever since. . . .
By menial work I mean labour for another.'[1]

This distance between master and servant was reinforced in the
religious sphere. A Scots Calvinist was shocked to notice that family
prayers, which were held in most South African farm households, were
exclusive. Servants were not invited to participate as they were in
Scotland.[2] In the Transvaal the situation was much the same, as the
following letter, written in 1876 by the wife of the French missionary
Coillard, indicates:

> As our little party were being led back to Pretoria, a lieutenant of police
> said to Onesima that they were quite mad to have been led into the delusion
> that they were preachers or catechists . . . they were neither the one nor the
> other, they were simply *Kaffirs*, and always would remain so. As for God, they
> had nothing whatever to do with Him, and if by any accident a Kaffir, even
> *one*, were to be seen in Heaven when he got there, he would pick up his hat
> and wish [the Almagtij] goodbye and walk straight out.[3]

But it would seem that there were two traditions, for Marquard writes
that 'In the Free State . . . it was customary to have the domestic
servants (not the labourers) in for family prayers. They sat on low stools
which they brought into the dining room with them, and slightly apart
from the family.'[4]

The isolation of these small communities, encapsulated in their
farms, was increased by the paucity of education. As far as most
blacks were concerned life on a white farm cut them off almost entirely
from the missionary thrust which, on the frontiers and in areas where
Africans still held the land, was providing an education that opened up
whole new worlds of awareness. It was many decades after the establishment of schools in the reserves and towns that blacks on the farms were
to be given the opportunity of learning to read and write. Many
farmers were against their labour being 'spoilt' and 'made cheeky' by
book-learning even when it was available.[5] For whites there was a
certain amount of education, albeit rudimentary, but it varied from
place to place.

Amongst the Dutch settlers it was the custom that no young man
could get married before he had been 'aangenomen' by the church. But
in order to be so confirmed the man had to pass an examination before
the *predikant*. Thus there was considerable incentive for boys to learn
to read and to become acquainted with the Bible as well as such knowledge of the church dogma as the examiners thought necessary.[6] Ritual

---

[1] *Report of the Transvaal Indigency Commission.* Minutes of Evidence, p. 196.
[2] Mackenzie, p. 17.   [3] C. W. Mackintosh, *Coillard of the Zambezi*, p. 221.
[4] L. Marquard, personal communication to the author, 1968.
[5] Hunter, pp. 526–7.   [6] Trollope, ii. 84; Mackenzie, p. 55.

was taken very seriously and even apparently minute differences, such as the type of altar-cloth, were the cause of much bitterness, and even bloodshed.[1] In order to make sure that their sons could qualify properly for marriage, the wealthier farmers would hire a schoolmaster to come and live with the family for a year or two while the children were growing up.[2] This education on the frontier was not sufficient to bridge the gap between the cultured Dutchmen of the Cape and the Boers of the Transvaal who, so Trollope tells us,[3] were regarded by the former as 'dirty, ignorant, and arrogant Savage[s]'. The Free Staters, like those in the Colony, tended to be better educated than their brethren across the Vaal. In the eastern Cape the children of English-speaking farmers were either taught at home or sent to one of the many church schools in the area. In Natal, too, the church was not far behind the settlers and provided the early education.

For Coloured people, concentrated in the western Cape, the educational opportunities were, by 1870, probably somewhat better than for whites in the Transvaal. A number of mission stations, of which Genadendal and Mr. Esselin's Institute in Worcester[4] were the most famous, provided an education for Coloured adolescents not dissimilar from that which Africans were getting on the eastern frontier in places like Lovedale, Healdtown, and St. Matthew's, and in Natal at Amanzintoti (Adams College).

What then was life like on the *platteland* at the time of the diamond discoveries? What was the standard of living? Men lived simply. Many, both black and white, dwelt in clay huts. Others lived a nomadic life, the whites amongst them owning wagons and tents which they pitched wherever they found grazing for their flocks and herds. The richest class of white farmers had houses which consisted, generally, of a front room in which the family ate and lived by day; behind this was the kitchen and on either side bedrooms.[5] Fuel varied from place to place. Cow dung seems to have been the most common, though mimosa-thorn wood was also used. Coal was something of a luxury.[6] In Natal most English-speaking farmers were found to have a wooden floor to their living room, but the Dutch-speaking Boers were content with the clay.[7] In the front room, where there was no fireplace, it was typical to find two large tables, settees with *riempie* (leather-thong) seats along the walls, and open corner-cupboards in which the crockery was kept. And, in the Free State at least, there was always a pile of books in one corner: Bibles, half a dozen hymn-books, and even, sometimes, an Anglican

---

[1] Mackenzie, p. 50. [2] Trollope, ii. 84. [3] Ibid. 115.
[4] p. 49 above; Trollope, i. 135; B. Krüger, *The Pear Tree Blossoms*.
[5] Mackenzie, p. 14. [6] Ibid., p. 13; Collins, p. 317; Trollope, ii. 20.
[7] Trollope, i. 300.

prayer book if the younger people were 'affecting the English language'[1].

Clothing was rough, partly because it was expensive and partly because the Boers saw no necessity for finery.[2] Men, women, and children all wore 'strong loose brown clothes well bestained with work',[3] and nobody bothered to spin the wool off the merino's back into stockings. Pyjamas were non-existent for 'no genuine Dutch colonist ever thinks of undressing before going to bed.'[4] The clothing of the Africans was even simpler.

The Boers ate only two meals a day. Breakfast, which was identical to dinner in the evening, consisted of stewed meat, cut to small pieces, together with bread or rice. There were seldom vegetables, but soup with flour dumplings followed the meat. Only the English ate potatoes.[5] The excellent bread was home-made from flour which the farmer had grown and ground for himself.[6] For Africans the staple diet was maize and pumpkin,[7] sour milk (amasi), and meat. Sorghum, sweet potatoes, beans, and wild herbs cooked as spinach (imifino) were common.[8]

Such then, in brief, was the picture of rural South Africa when the discovery of a diamond near Hopetown in 1866 and the rediscovery of gold on the Tati river in 1867[9] gave the first inkling of the mineral flood that was about to break upon the country and sweep it forward at a rapidly increased pace. South Africa was feeding itself and although farming was already established it was largely subsistence agriculture and it was not ready to meet the demands of the markets that were to spring up so suddenly in its midst.

2. The Impact of Minerals, 1866–1899

The discovery of diamonds marked both the birth of South Africa's industrial economy and the beginning of profound changes in the nature and pattern of her agricultural sector. The railways which reached into the interior from each of the major ports widened the market for agricultural produce. Farmers near the line who previously had produced only for their own consumption now found that they could get their products to markets many miles distant. Moreover, in the interior, farmers whose opportunity to export had been limited by insuperable transport difficulties now began to glimpse an overseas market within their reach. However, the new markets were not merely a result of better transport. The effect of the mineral discoveries was to increase the size of the already established centres and to bring into being towns

---

[1] Trollope, ii. 237.   [2] Ibid. ii. 238; Collins, p. 15.   [3] Trollope, ii. 238.
[4] Mackenzie, pp. 15, 19.   [5] Ibid., p. 16.   [6] Trollope, ii. 236.
[7] Chase, p. 151.   [8] Hunter, pp. 68, 104.   [9] Mackenzie, p. 453.

where, but a few years previously, there had been open veld. Kimberley, which in 1866 did not exist, became by 1877 a thriving community of 18,000 persons.[1] Similarly Johannesburg, whose first street was not laid out until 1886, had a population of 166,000 at the turn of the century.[2] Nor were these the only new urban markets; along the Reef many other mining towns mushroomed overnight.

It is beyond the scope of a chapter on agriculture to analyse the effects on South Africa as a whole of the rush of immigrants and capital which so disturbed the relative tranquility of the isolated farmers who, growing sufficient cattle, mealies, and wheat for their own needs, enjoying their quarterly holiday at *Nachtmaal* and satisfied with their recreations of gun and pipe, wanted nothing so much as to be left in peace to enjoy the way of life to which they were accustomed.[3] But, quite apart from political upheavals that followed in its train, the inflow of *uitlanders* (foreigners) was to cause profound changes in farming.

The farmers, who could hardly have anticipated the mineral discoveries, were in no position to increase food supplies as rapidly as they were needed. Thus prices soared. In the early diamond years it was possible to earn as much as £1 for a dozen eggs whilst cabbages were said to cost seven shillings each.[4] In Kimberley, the food, much of it brought all the way from the coast 400 miles away, left much to be desired. Butter was uneatable, meat bad, and disease was rife in the diggings.[5] But agriculture was not completely unresponsive to the changed circumstances. Gradually farmers began to realize the potential of the home market, and supplies expanded. But for some farmers the railways, far from improving their markets, were, in the short run at least, to have the opposite effect. For, as a missionary in Basutoland pointed out, the railway line from the Cape to Kimberley enabled American wheat to undercut the products of Basutoland. 'The cause of this crisis', he wrote, 'is well known: while the Basutos were fighting for their independence, favoured by the railways the Americans supplanted them on the market of the diamond fields and have flooded the country with their flour.'[6] The fact that by 1899 the country was no longer self-sufficient in basic food requirements and was importing wheat, maize, meat, eggs, milk, and butter in large quantities[7] is due, it would seem, to two distinct factors. On the one hand the rise in agricultural production was not sufficient to keep up with the growth of population whilst, on the other hand, the same railways that were

[1] Trollope, ii. 185.   [2] Johannesburg Municipality, *Minutes* (1903), p. 2061.
[3] E. B. Rose, *The Truth About the Transvaal*, p. 25.
[4] L. Marquard, *People and Policies of South Africa*, p. 16; Collins, p. 319.
[5] Ibid., pp. 318–19; Trollope, ii. 191.
[6] R. C. Germond, *Chronicles of Basutoland*, p. 470.
[7] *Statistical Register of the Colony of the Cape of Good Hope* (Cape Town, 1899).

ultimately to prove so important in the development of South African agriculture enabled foreign producers to compete effectively for the new markets. Over this period the pattern of agricultural exports did not change significantly. The main ones continued to be wool, hides and skins, mohair and to a lesser extent, wine.[1]

Despite the increased prosperity for many farmers the period was by no means a uniformly happy one. We have already seen something of the temporary effects of foreign competition. But two further problems emerged in the agricultural sector, and they were to remain the predominant difficulties for decades to come. The first might be called the vicissitudes of agriculture. The second was the shortage of labour.

Amongst the vicissitudes were, on the one hand, the scourges of pestilence and drought and, on the other, the abrupt fluctuations in market price to which so many agricultural products are prone. And South Africa at this time had its full share of both natural hazards and price fluctuations. De Kiewiet estimates[2] that, between 1882 and 1925, South Africa suffered, on average, one severe drought every six years. But the phenomenon did not begin in 1882; years before that men knew that there would be times when the essential rain would not fall. There had been a devastating drought in 1833[3], whilst the drought of 1860 which was broken by heavy cold rain and severe hail was estimated to have killed 40,000 sheep in the Winberg district alone. Two years later it was followed by another calamitous drought.[4] But the weather was not the only scourge. Indeed it is perhaps surprising that the early trekkers identified themselves with the children of Israel rather than with the Egyptians, so often were they plagued by pestilence. Horse sickness wrought havoc in 1861, and, in later years, it was estimated that in many parts of the Transvaal 90 per cent of all horses that were not stabled in the four months from January to April would die.[5] In the late 1880s horse sickness passed 'like a wave' over the Cape Colony, carrying off its victims by the thousand in almost every district.[6] Then there were locusts which descended in periodic swarms and ate every mealie and blade of grass in sight. One such visitation occurred in 1869 and was only halted some months later when birds arrived and devoured the locusts.[7] The destruction of crops by locust swarms was one of the contributory factors which led to a rebellion in Bechuanaland in 1896.[8] Meanwhile in the Western Cape although wine farmers felt reasonably secure from the locusts, whose breeding-grounds on the

[1] Ibid., pp. 165 ff.   [2] De Kiewiet, p. 189.   [3] Germond, p. 435.
[4] Collins, p. 179.   [5] Ibid., p. 183.
[6] Hon. A. Wilmot (ed.), *The Book of South African Industries*, p. 35.
[7] Collins, p. 278.
[8] H. Saker, *The Langeberg Rebellion*, unpublished B.A. (Hons.) thesis, University of Cape Town, 1965, p. 40.

edge of the Kalahari were a safe distance away, they had to cope with
another destructive insect, the phylloxera or vine-aphid. Notwithstanding the farmer who, misled by larger-than-life drawings, assured
an agricultural officer that he would be fully able to deal with the
phylloxera by means of mole traps,[1] the vines withered and died, until
eventually a protective spray was developed.

Another disease was redwater, which first appeared among cattle in
Natal in 1871 and spread throughout the rest of the country during the
next two decades. Sheep were infected by scab, as well as by internal
parasites.[2] But far the worst of the natural hazards was the rinderpest,
which, appearing first in Somaliland in 1889, swept down Africa at
the end of the century. In 1892 a Cape veterinary officer warned of the
devastation to come if proper measures were not taken to halt the
disease;[3] but it continued to baffle everybody, and four years later it
reached the northern Cape. The century ended with South African
herds greatly reduced in number. In the Transkei it was roughly
estimated that 90 per cent of the cattle, which formed the real wealth of
the people, were swept off by the disease.[4] For the Cape Colony as a
whole (including Bechuanaland but excluding the native territories
and Pondoland) it was estimated that the cattle herds were reduced by
35 per cent from 1·64 to 1·06 million.[5]

On top of all these hazards were the price fluctuations. These were
experienced most vividly by the ostrich farmers of the Little Karroo who
began catching wild birds in the late 1850s. Feathers exported in 1870
fetched a price of £3. 17s. per pound, yielding a total revenue of over
£91,000. Five years later the price had doubled, the quantity exported
was 72 per cent higher, and revenue was well over £300,000. After
another five years revenue was almost ten times what it had been a
decade earlier. But 1880 was a boom year and prices fell sharply
thereafter. By 1895 the price was so low that although the quantity
exported had more than doubled since 1880 earnings were only three-
fifths of what they had been. And the fluctuations of succeeding years
were to prove even more dislocating than those of the previous twenty-
five. The golden years, 1910–13, when prices held firm at just under £3
per pound whilst exports increased steadily from 700,000 lb. to over one
million lb., were followed by the crash that accompanied the beginning
of the First World War. By 1916 the total export earnings from ostrich
feathers were only one-sixth of what they had been in 1913. It was

[1] Cape of Good Hope Department of Agriculture, *Agricultural Miscellany* (Cape Town,
1897), p. 366.
[2] Wilmot, p. 42.
[3] Cape of Good Hope Department of Agriculture, p. 158.
[4] The South African Native Races Committee (eds.), *The Natives of South Africa*, p. 266.
[5] *Cape Hansard* (1896), p. 166, cited by Saker, p. 34

another forty years before the industry began once again to develop.[1] Nor were the feather price fluctuations the only ones to give farmers a difficult time. As early as the decade 1830–40 the price of wool exported from the eastern Cape varied from year to year by an average of 10 per cent.[2] And these early fluctuations were only a foretaste of what was to come. In the years 1910–36 wool was to have an annual price variation of no less then 28 per cent.[3]

The building of the railways was not an unmixed blessing to the farmers; for, apart from widening the market, it brought sharply into focus the second major problem with which South African farmers were to find themselves grappling over the next century. Shortage of labour was nothing new: in the early days of settlement the white farmers had partially solved the problem by importing slaves. With their emancipation in 1834 a new solution had to be found; and, as Davenport argues,[4] one of the economic origins of the Great Trek lay in the shortage of labour. As they moved north the settlers adopted several different methods to ensure an adequate supply of labour. In Natal there was the *isibalo*[5] system whereby African chiefs were compelled to find men to be labourers on public works at relatively low wages. In the eastern Cape farmers relied on a thicket of pass and vagrancy laws[6] to assist them in obtaining and controlling their labour. In the Transvaal there was 'apprenticing' of children.[7] But in all three of these areas, as well as in the Orange Free State, the most important method of ensuring a supply of labour was the 'squatter' system, whereby the white conquerors allowed some of the native inhabitants to continue living on the land in return for some tangible benefit. In some cases the squatters were required to pay rent: in others the tenants had to furnish from 90 to 180 days of labour each year. The *Plakkers Wet* (Squatter's Law) of 1895 which the respective governments passed both in the Free State and in the Transvaal was aimed at improving the supply of labour by prohibiting, 'except under special circumstances', the settlement of more than five African families upon any one farm and thus distributing them more widely over the land. The effect of the law was described to the Transvaal Labour Commission by a witness who pointed out that, 'If it were not for this, many of the natives would leave the farms on which

---

[1] P. J. du Toit, *The Farmer in South Africa*, p. 43; R. J. Beyleveld, 'Ostrich Farming in South Africa', *Agrekon*, 6 (3), 1967.

[2] Chase, p. 174. For an analysis of wool price fluctuations in the nineteenth century, see H. B. Thom, *Die geskiedenis van die skaapboerdery in Suid-Afrika* (Amsterdam, 1936) p. 201.

[3] See table on p. 140.   [4] Vol. I, p. 292.

[5] From '*isibalo*', literally meaning 'what is written'. See the South African Native Races Committee, p. 236.

[6] *Report of the Select Committee on the Pass Laws of the Colony* (A. 15/1883, Cape Town, 1883), pp. 33–40.

[7] S. T. van der Horst, *Native Labour in South Africa*, p. 57. Trollope, ii. 33.

they are engaged, and accumulate on other farms, the owners of which
have a reputation for being more liberal in the matter of pay, and for
treating boys better.'[1] The law gave Native Commissioners the power to
take families living on farms in the low country along the Lebombo
river and to scatter them over the highveld. But this caused great
dissatisfaction amongst the Africans concerned, many of whom crossed
the river and left the Transvaal.[2] Thus the government was placed in a
difficult position because one of its great fears was that the Africans living
under its jurisdiction would move elsewhere and that the Transvaal
'might lose the advantage of their labour and their presence'.[3]

In Natal, even in the days before railways, the white farmers faced
competition for labour by virtue of the fact that there was still sufficient
land available to Africans for them to support themselves independently.
And so, rather than push up local wages, the farmers resorted to the
indenturing or recruiting of labour from the Indian sub-continent.
What was unusual about this early indenture scheme (which began
in 1860) compared with those that followed was that the men were
allowed to stay in the country, and even to buy land after the contracted
five-year period was over, and their women and children were allowed
to follow them and settle.[4]

In the western Cape the shortage of labour was probably even more
acute. The density of non-white population was much less than in the
frontier districts of the eastern Cape and further north; and there was
great competition from the railway lines and the docks. Several select
committees were appointed by the Cape Parliament, during the latter
part of the nineteenth century, to inquire into the whole problem of the
labour supply and it is from the evidence given to these committees that
much of our information comes.[5] Many possibilities were examined
and the consensus of opinion was that the problem could best be solved
by the systematic recruiting of labour from far afield. During the late
1870s nearly 4,000 Africans were brought in from the eastern frontier
by the Government, and rapidly absorbed in jobs within thirty miles of
Cape Town.[6] However, few of these men wished to stay and most of
them soon ran away. As Mr. Vermaak from Burghersdorp explained in
evidence to the 1879 Select Committee, the labour problem in the west
would not be solved by bringing in men from the eastern Cape unless
the government was willing to bring the families as well. 'Single Kafirs
will never stay . . . I advise the government if they get Kafir labour to

[1] *Report of the Transvaal Labour Commission* (Johannesburg, 1903), p. 36.
[2] Ibid., p. 293.   [3] Ibid., p. 123.   [4] Vol. I, p. 387.
[5] *Report of the Select Committee on the Supply of the Labour Market* (A. 26/1879, Cape Town,
1879); *Report of the Select Committee on the Labour Question* (A. 12/1890, Cape Town, 1890);
Report of the Select Committee on the Labour Question (C. 2/1892, Cape Town, 1892).
[6] *Select Committee* (1879), p. 12.

bring the families.'[1] He suggested that an agent be employed in Kaffraria to engage families for periods of at least five years. At this time men were also brought on contract from Zanzibar, Mozambique, Delagoa Bay, and Damaraland (South West Africa) as farm hands and dock workers.[2] Under some schemes men were brought for up to three years but they did not always return home when their contract expired. Chinese and Indians were also employed.[3] One person even suggested that an agent be sent to California to recruit Chinese immigrants who could not be absorbed into agriculture there.[4] Another witness, however, felt that recruiting of large numbers of Chinese would merely add to the future problems of the country. There was the added difficulty that the Chinese were too industrious. Farmers feared that those brought in as unskilled labour would not stay long on the farms but set up shop somewhere and move off the land. There were, in 1892, a few Chinese cultivating on shares land which had previously been regarded as useless at Uitenhage where 'their industry and care in raising produce is calling forth the admiration of all the people . . . who have seen it'.[5]

Labour was recruited from as far afield as Cornwall, whilst Irishmen and Germans were also tried.[6] But there were two problems about white labourers. Firstly many of them, like the Chinese, moved out of the agricultural labouring class as quickly as they could. Secondly, as a witness explained to the 1879 Select Committee, 'It does not answer to introduce them as common labourers, because we cannot keep them separate from the blacks; and at first the blacks look down upon them owing to their not being accustomed to our work as well as themselves; and in many cases they degenerate in consequence. If they could be placed separately they would do well.'[7]

But not all labour coming to work in the western Cape was recruited. A farmer from the Worcester district told the Select Committees of both 1879 and 1892 something about the 'many thousands of Makatese' who came to work in the area in the years just prior to the diamond discoveries. 'They were the finest natives we have ever had here, and the cleanest. They were a gentlemanly set of fellows, well dressed, and walked with umbrellas when off-duty. They were honest above all things . . . They built walls in our part of the country, and very good walls too. It was then that we commenced fencing our farms.'[8] But with the discovery of diamonds, the men vanished and did not return. Exactly who they were is not certain. The witness who in 1879 said they came from

[1] Ibid., p. 14.   [2] Ibid., p. 61; *Select Committee* (1892), p. 11.
[3] *Select Committee* (1879), p. 32.
[4] *Report of the Select Committee on Colonial Agriculture and Industries*, (A. 3/1883, Cape Town, 1883), p. 113.
[5] Ibid., p. 382.   [6] *Select Committee* (1879), p. 62.   [7] Ibid., pp. 45, 52.
[8] *Select Committee* (1892), p. 49; see also *Select Committee* (1879), p. 50.

the Magaliesberg in the western Transvaal suggested to the 1892 committee that they were under Moshweshwe and so they seem more likely to have come from Lesotho.

There were two other sources of farm labour, particularly in the western Cape: white *bywoners* and Coloured men from the mission villages. Farmers around Swellendam were very anxious to get *bywoners* who, generally poor and owning little stock, worked the farms on shares and were available to help the farmer in harvest and shearing time.[1] The mission villages aroused antagonism; and not only in the western Cape. For years some farmers had complained that the practice of missionaries in granting residence rights to their followers aggravated the labour shortage.[2] Having an independent home, labourers were able, so the argument ran, to refuse work if they so wished. Some farmers in the Paarl district solved the problem by buying houses in Paarl itself which they let to labourers on condition that they worked part of the year for the landlord. But antagonism to the villages remained. 'I think', said a Cape Town merchant who owned an extensive farm near Mamre, 'the sooner these stations are done away with the better'.[3]

Despite recruiting, indenturing, pass laws, the *isibalo* system, and squatters, the shortage of labour remained an acute problem in many parts of the country.[4] 'Every farmer, every merchant, every politician I had met and spoke with since I had put my foot on South African soil,' exclaimed Trollope, 'had sworn to me that the country was a wretched country simply because labour could not be had!'[5] In Constantia and Paarl, in Natal and the Transvaal, men complained that they could not produce more, that they were crippled by lack of labour.[6] But as Trollope himself pertinently observed, the supply of labour forthcoming depends upon the level of wages paid. And he, like the various commissions, found ample evidence[7] of more intelligent farmers who had obtained all the labour they needed by paying a little more.

Nevertheless the belief amongst many employers at this time that raising wages would actually reduce the amount of labour available is a sociological phenomenon of too great significance to be dismissed so easily. It was to have important repercussions in South African history. For a shortage is a shortage and if employers did not think that wage increases would eliminate it then they had to find other methods. And, as we shall see, although money wages did go up during the years 1866–

---

[1] *Select Committee* (1879), p. 46.
[2] *Report from the Select Committee on Granting Lands in Freehold to Hottentots* (Cape Town, 1854), p. 25.   [3] *Select Committee* (1879), p. 68.
[4] The Select Committee of 1892 reported that 22 of the 76 divisions of the Cape Colony had no shortage of labour.
[5] Trollope, i. 146.   [6] Ibid. i. 83, 128, 301; ii. 80.
[7] See, for example, *Select Committee* (1892), p. vi.

1966, South African farmers tended to rely more heavily on compulsive measures for obtaining labour than they would have done under a more freely competitive market. Why then did they believe that the supply curve of labour was backward sloping? This problem has been carefully examined by others[1] and there is little to add to the analysis except to use it to reconcile the apparently conflicting evidence of individual witnesses. 'Do you think', asked the Chairman of the Select Committee in 1879, 'they would work more days than they do if they could get higher wages?' 'No, I do not think so. On the contrary, if you pay them more they will work less.'[2] And employers of Coloured labour in the western Cape, nearly a century later, were to say exactly the same thing.[3] While it seems true that, under certain circumstances, a rise in cash wages may outrun the desire for goods that can be bought with the extra money, farmers were mistaken, as Berg has pointed out,[4] in deducing from this fact that they would get less labour if they raised wages. For the supply depends not only on the number of hours or days that an individual is prepared to work but also on the number of individuals available at the different wage levels. And the overwhelming mass of evidence suggests that, imperfect though the market was, the supply of labour was directly related to the level of earnings. Farmers complained constantly of the high wages on the Public Works which were draining off labourers. They knew that the diamond mines, which during the early years paid a cash wage of ten shillings per week, plus rations, were attracting men who had previously come to the farms.[5] And the evidence, to the 1892 Select Committee, of a recruiter who had recently returned from a journey through the Transkei and Ciskei showed clearly the fallacy in the argument that raising wages would not increase the supply of labour:

'You were lately employed on a special mission for the purpose of obtaining native labour?'
'Yes, I have just returned from the Frontier.'
'Did you meet with any success?'
'Not at the lower rate of wages offered by the farmers. The natives would not think of accepting the terms offered, fifteen shillings a month with board and lodging.'
'Was that their only objection?'

---

[1] E. J. Berg, *Recruitment of a Labor Force in Sub-Saharan Africa*, unpublished Ph.D. thesis, Harvard, 1960; S. Rottenberg, 'Income and Leisure in an Under-developed Country', *Journal of Political Economy*, 60 (2), 1952; H. G. Vatter, 'On the Folklore of the Backward-sloping Supply Curve', *Industrial and Labour Relations Review*, vol. 14, 1961.
[2] *Select Committee* (1879), p. 30. See also *Report of the Transvaal Labour Commission* (1903), p. 338.   [3] Personal observation (Cape Town, 1968).
[4] E. J. Berg, 'Backward-sloping Labor Supply Functions in Dual Economies—The Africa Case', *Quarterly Journal of Economics*, Aug. 1961.
[5] Trollope, ii. 158; *Select Committee* (1879), p. 59.

'It was their main objection. It is true that they would prefer to work in large bodies, but if the wages offered by the farmers had been adequate, they would have engaged themselves as farm labourers.'

'Did you form any idea of what would satisfy them?'

'They quoted the rate of wages at the Diamond Fields, and the Gold Fields, and on the railway works, but that was beyond what the farmers were prepared to offer.'[1]

The reason why, despite this evidence, many farmers continued to believe that raising wages would not solve their problem lay partly in their ability to find other methods of ensuring that labourers worked on their farms and partly in the confusion between the amount of labour that an individual is prepared to supply at different wage rates and the total amount of labour available to an employer.

The general level of earnings in the western Cape at the end of the 1870s was of the order of one shilling per day with rations, plus wine five or six times daily. In the harvest season cash wages went up to two shillings or more, and on many farms labourers were provided with a place to live, and land to cultivate. For more skilled men, e.g. wagon drivers, wages were higher.[2] In the eastern Cape farm labourers got about ten shillings a month, plus a daily food ration. On one farm Trollope found the labourers getting as much as twenty-six shillings a month.[3] In Natal wages were lower than in the eastern Cape, and there men were paid about seven shillings a month, with a ration of maize on farms, and fourpence a day for working on the roads, compared with 2s. 6d. per day for railway labourers in the eastern Cape.[4] In the Transvaal the highest wages were a shilling per day, with mealies for day labourers, while those who worked for longer periods generally got a heifer a year, a daily allowance of maize, and sometimes a little meat.[5] But in the eastern Cape, at least, farm wages did not rise as time went on. More than a decade after Trollope's visit farm servants in the Albany district were getting six to ten shillings per month, with keep,[6] and this was a very low wage even in those days. In 1891 a sergeant from Fort Jackson wrote: 'I am convinced that in most cases of stock-stealing the owner's own servants are implicated. How a man can expect to have labourers decently dressed, honest, and generally living like other civilized people for his food and 10s. a month wherewith to feed his family, is beyond my comprehension. I am convinced that were more liberal wages offered the labour market wouldn't be in its present state.'[7]

Wages remained static in many areas despite the fact that the

---

[1] *Select Committee* (1892), p. 8.   [2] *Select Committee* (1879), p. 18.   [3] Trollope, i. 174.

[4] Ibid. i. 146, 288.   [5] *Select Committee* (1879), p. 59.

[6] *Select Committee* (1892), Appendix; evidence from Albany.

[7] Ibid., Appendix; evidence of Thomas Halifax.

productivity of the labour force appeared to be increasing. Giving evidence
in 1892 a farmer, who had been working in the Bedford district since
1853, stated that labour had improved in quality, in that many men
were now accustomed to shears, could drive, plough, and use a spade.[1]
But not all farm wages remained unaffected by competition. Men from
Mozambique, for example, who previously had been recruited on
three-year contracts starting at 15s. per month with board and lodging
for the first year, were, by 1892 only prepared to come if they began
at 20s. per month.[2] By the end of the nineteenth century the agricultural
labour market was still in a very imperfect state. Wages varied widely
from place to place, and the evidence suggests that one reason for
the differences lay in the fact that mobility for men living in the
'reserves' was considerably greater than that for people living on the
farms. Wages, it seems, were far less likely to rise for those who lived
permanently on the farms and who were less able than men in the
'reserves' to choose alternative employment.

Labour shortage in the midst of an apparently abundant supply was
not the only economic anomaly in the agricultural sector. Land seemed
to share the same fate. Thus, writing in 1899, J. P. Fitzpatrick maintained[3] that in the Transvaal there were still immense quantities of
unoccupied land, and yet land hunger was all too evident. At first
glance there would seem to be some conflict between the historians who
maintain that the interior of South Africa was by the end of the
nineteenth century excessively subdivided[4] and those who assert that
the country consisted almost entirely of farms that were too large for
purposes of efficient cultivation.[5] Yet both views are true. The contradiction is resolved when one appreciates the fact that in the Transvaal,
at least, half the farms to which whites laid claim were unoccupied by
them, while farms that were occupied by whites were often heavily
subdivided with up to as many as forty whites on them.[6] In the Free
State, however, things seem to have been more rational. In 1903 it was
estimated that almost all of the 11,000 farms were white-occupied, and
that there were about two farmers to each farm.[7] But generally despite
the existence of many large unoccupied farms, some of them owned by
mineral speculators, the process of subdivision was intensified at this
time because it was no longer possible for farmers' sons to hive off on to
new land. The closing of the frontier in South Africa coincided with the
discovery of minerals. The first Trek had ended, the second Trek was
beginning.

One of the most important social developments during this period was

---

[1] Ibid., p. 69.   [2] Ibid., p. 69.   [3] J. P. Fitzpatrick, *The Transvaal from Within*, p. 50.
[4] De Kiewiet, p. 191.   [5] Du Toit, p. 9.
[6] *Report of the Transvaal Labour Commission*, p. xiii.   [7] Ibid., p. 730.

expansion of the educational system. The most dramatic change was in the Free State where the appointment of the Revd. John Brebner as Inspector-General of Education in 1872 heralded the assumption by that Government of full responsibility for white education. Brebner was a remarkable man, and, starting with only a dozen one-teacher schools and 350 pupils, by the time he retired in 1899 there were well over 8,000 pupils and three hundred teachers in some two hundred Government schools.[1] This massive expansion of the educational system in a tiny agricultural society was partially financed by the sale of loot taken from Africans during the various raids and battles and also from the proceeds of the sale of Crown lands, which were themselves formerly held by the new farm labourers.[2] A major problem was to provide schooling for the children on remote farms. Brebner solved this by establishing a farm school system whereby the Government provided the teacher's salary and his house if the farmers provided and maintained the school. In addition Brebner adopted the Cape method of appointing itinerant teachers and hiring a room on a farm where the teacher worked for six months or a year. His salary came from the Government, his board was provided by the farmer.[3] Thus by the turn of the century Brebner had succeeded in getting the Free State to the position where it was able to introduce legislation to compel all white children between the ages of ten and sixteen to go to school.

In the Cape between 1870 and 1900 the number of pupils in elementary schools, both white and non-white, more than trebled.[4] But a serious weakness in the Cape system was that it failed to ensure that the poor and remote areas which most needed education did in fact get it. In 1882 an official report found that only one-sixth of the white children of school-going age were attending school with beneficial regularity.[5] Despite official denials of these figures, the report stimulated the founding in 1883 of a system of one-teacher farm schools similar to those in the Free State. In the Transvaal education was far less thoroughly organized than in the Cape or the Free State, and, despite the value placed on learning by many of the Transvaalers, in 1895 only 25 per cent of the white children of school age were at school.[6] In Natal, as in other areas, special provision was made for the rural areas. Here, by a 'farmhouse' system of grants, education was extended to rural whites, particularly after 1888.[7]

For Africans the picture was rather different. What seems to have been the prevalent attitude amongst farmers towards the education of

---

[1] E. G. Pells, *300 Years of Education in South Africa*, p. 57. [2] Ibid., p. 58.
[3] Ibid., p. 60. [4] Ibid., p. 35. [5] Ibid., p. 49. [6] Ibid., p. 52.
[7] *Report of the Superintendent Inspector of Schools for 1890–91*, Blue Book for the Colony of Natal, 1890–1 (Pietermaritzburg, 1891), p. u-3.

their labourers at this time was expressed by a witness to the 1890 Select Committee on the Labour Question. 'I am in favour', said Mr. Theron of Richmond, 'of teaching him [the native] what is necessary for him to know in order to become a good subject during life, and to entertain the expectation of better things hereafter: further than that I would not go.' Mr. Theron explained how, previously, masters were in the habit of imparting this kind of education to their servants in the evening when work was over. He continued: 'When I went up country I found the same system existing among many of the farmers, though it is gradually disappearing, because the servants are instructed in the schools in a contrary direction, and the masters therefore abstain from giving instruction.'[1] Although in some areas, particularly in the Cape and Natal, where Africans, Coloureds, and Indians could get education from mission schools, there were many places where education was not available. Giving evidence to the 1892 Select Committee on the Labour Question one witness pointed out that whilst every effort was being made for the education of white children on the farms in the Cape, 'Nothing whatever is done for the education and industrial training of native children on farms.'[2] And if the situation was bad in the Cape, in the interior it was even worse. Generally speaking, for Africans isolated on the farms there was little education of any sort.

It has been said earlier that Africans on the farms were more isolated than those either in the 'reserves' or in the town. This was certainly true in the Cape and in Natal where the mission schools were well established, near and in 'reserves'. But in the Transvaal where the schools had not penetrated it would seem that the contact between black and white on the farms itself provided a form of reciprocal learning which those still without contact were not getting. Thus H. M. Taberer, in evidence to the Transvaal Labour Commission in 1903, found that Africans on white-occupied Transvaal farms were, 'invariably far more advanced than those on locations. They appear to become infected with the energy of their European neighbours and masters. Their individuality seems to be developed, they build better houses, are cleaner and more law abiding, and their wants appear to increase, and they become more industrious consequently.'[3] Trollope, however, would probably have disagreed with such a judgement. During his travels he had not found the whites very energetic.

By the end of the nineteenth century the impact of the mineral discoveries had rippled through the whole fabric of the society and penetrated to the remotest rural areas. This account of some of the

[1] *Select Committee* (1890), p. 51.
[2] *Select Committee* (1892), p. 14. See also the South African Native Races Committee, p. 332.
[3] *Report of the Transvaal Labour Commission*, p. 338.

major changes that took place on the farms lends support to de Kiewiet's conclusion that 'The leading theme of South African history is the
growth of a new society in which white and black are bound together
in the closest dependence upon each other.'[1] For, whether one considers
urbanization, the shortage of labour, or the quality of rural life, it is
abundantly clear that the effect of economic development was to bind
black and white more closely together than they had ever been tied
before.

3. *Social Dislocation, 1899–1924*

The stresses set in motion by the mineral discoveries were to culmi-
nate in the Anglo-Boer War of 1899–1902 which itself marked only the
beginning of a long period of social dislocation, when South Africa
adjusted slowly and painfully to the changes that had come about.
Indeed it was not until well into the 1930s that the country began to
recover from its industrial birth pangs.

For South Africa, as for most countries in the twentieth century, the
process of urbanization was one of the main features of its development.
The steady movement from rural area to town is both part of the price
and part of the gain from economic growth. South Africa's rural
exodus which gathered momentum from this time was, as elsewhere,
the result of twin forces. On the one hand there were forces pushing
men off the land and on the other there were those attracting them to the
towns. Some South African historians have suggested that the predominant forces were those pushing men off the land,[2] others that the
pull to the towns was more important.[3] But it would seem that both
factors have been operating with approximately equal weight.

Amongst the forces pushing men off the land was the population
pressure that began with the closing of the frontier. Linked to this was
the process of subdivision. The combination of the Roman-Dutch law
of inheritance whereby every child got an equal portion of land and the
activities of the mineral speculators who were locking up vast tracks of
unoccupied land, meant that on the already settled farms subdivision
was liable to go to excessive lengths. Many a man was to write in his will
that '*Geen nakomeling van my moet ooit nodig hê om te swerwe nie; elkeen moet
sy eie sitplekkie behou.*'[4] Malherbe[5] cites cases of a hundred poor whites
being produced on a Transvaal farm in three or four generations as
a result of subdivision. The inheritance of some was less than one
thousandth of a farm. But population pressure and excessive fragmentation were by no means the only push factors. Another major one was

---

[1] De Kiewiet, p. 79.   [2] Ibid., p. 196.   [3] Albertyn, p. 17.
[4] Ibid., p. 35. 'No descendant of mine must ever need to wander; each must have his own
lot.'   [5] Malherbe, p. 21.

the rinderpest which swept through Africa in the 1890s. Fourthly there was the devastation of the war years. The British policy of laying waste farms by burning them brought a heavy toll of destitute families. At the Peace of Vereeniging, says de Kiewiet, 'Not less than ten thousand individuals had been torn loose from the land which was their way of life and the pillar of their self-respect.'[1] There were other factors too, such as the spread of jackal-proof fencing which hindered the movement of landless men with their flocks. Many of these forces worked slowly and did not become noticeable until some major event, like a drought, a war, or an epidemic brought them all to a head. It was a combination of factors that made the end of the century so difficult a time for South African farmers. For not only was there the rinderpest and the war, but also the drought of 1897 which was the first that farmers in the interior had experienced for an abnormally long time. It so happened that the discovery of gold coincided with the beginning of a decade during which the annual rainfall was no less than a quarter more than normal. In the rainfall district No. 15 which lies roughly between Cradock and Kimberley, the average annual fall over the decade 1886–95 was 26 per cent higher than it was over the whole period 1878–1958. And in other districts for which figures are available it appears that, apart from the well-watered coastal belts, the decade before 1897 was one in which the rainfall was not only abnormally high but also evenly spread so that there were no dry years. This freak weather came to an abrupt end in 1897 in most of the interior districts, and the general pattern of inter-mittent drought reasserted itself.[2]

These push-factors did not, of course, apply to whites only. Blacks too moved off the land. But for them there was an additional pressure in the form of land legislation. By the time of Union two problems were dominating the thinking of whites with regard to blacks on the farms. First was the perennial problem of labour shortage. Second was fear lest the land gained by conquest should be lost through the market; for, except in the Free State where such a thing had long been forbidden, Africans were buying farms. The Land Act of 1913 was passed in an attempt to solve both these problems at once. Looking back, the historian is tempted to interpret the Act almost exclusively as the basis of the country's future policy of apartheid, but the contemporary evidence suggests that those who agitated for the legislation were far more concerned with the problem of labour supply than with anything else. The immediate object of the Act was to abolish the system of farming-on-the-half and to eliminate squatter locations. Under the widespread practice

---

[1] De Kiewiet, p. 196.
[2] Weather Bureau, *Climate of South Africa.* W.B. 23; Part 5, District Rainfall (Pretoria, 1960).

of farming-on-the-half Africans, who owned their own ploughs and oxen, entered into a partnership with the white land-owner and worked the land, sowed their own seed, reaped the crop, and then handed over half of it to the farmer in return for the right to cultivate, graze stock, and live on his land. The system was popular; for not only did it enable whites to farm with a minimum of effort but also it permitted blacks to reap the rewards of their labours more fully than they would have done as mere farm-hands. But there were many whites who regarded the practice as a great evil. For some, the very idea of black and white undertaking a venture as partners was anathema; others argued that the system led to a destructive use of land, through ignorant methods; yet others saw it as a threat to the economic position of poor whites. The Prime Minister and his Minister of Native Affairs, Generals Botha and Hertzog, travelled up and down the country telling farmers that they should expel blacks from their farms and replace whem with poor whites. But there was little economic incentive to obey the Generals for manual labour was, as has already been shown (p. 110), an indignity to which few whites, no matter how poor, were willing to submit themselves. However, none of these reasons seems to account for the strength of feeling as evidenced, for example in the correspondence columns of the *Farmers' Weekly* in 1911, against farming-on-the-half. The fundamental objection was that the system provided far greater reward for an African working on a white farm than other farmers were prepared to pay. It is possible to regard the 1913 Land Act as being an act of collusion amongst the hirers of farm labour not to give remuneration above a certain level. At the same time as the land legislation was being discussed and passed, mine owners were working out, not for the first time, an agreement whereby the average wage of blacks on any mine would not exceed a certain maximum, and there is a sense in which the Land Act was, for farmers, what the maximum-permissible-average agreement was for the mining magnates. The unpopularity of whites who worked on shares with blacks was the unpopularity of a fellow employer who pays more than necessary to get his labour. 'The sooner a gallows is erected to hang those who work on shares with Kaffirs the better', wrote an angry farmer from the heart of the Free State in 1911.[1]

But there was another villain. The practice of 'kaffir farming' was denounced as vigorously as farming-on-the-half, and for the same basic reason: it interfered with the supply of cheap labour. In a situation where many white landowners had more morgen than they knew what to do with whilst blacks had too few, it is hardly surprising that some of the white farmers found it easier (and more profitable) to let their land to Africans rather than organize labourers to produce crops for which

[1] *Farmers' Weekly*, Aug. 1911.

there was little market. The unpopularity of 'kaffir farming' amongst whites who were not receiving rent in this manner lay in the fact that it deprived them of labour. 'A native will rather pay rent and squat, and do as he likes, than live rent free and work. This', as a correspondent of the *Farmers' Weekly* pointed out, 'is the root of our difficulty.'[1] Farms which had a large number of rent-paying tenants living on them were known as locations, and were much disapproved of by surrounding farmers. One reason for their antagonism was that the locations were widely believed to harbour stock-thieves. Another, perhaps more fundamental, objection was that the locations, like the mission villages against which employers had been protesting for the past century, gave the farm-labourer a bargaining power which if he lived on a farm he would never have. Living in a village or location, he could not only change jobs and so force farmers to bid up wages competitively, but also he could refuse to work and so exact more favourable terms from his employers. 'It will be ruination', wrote a Free State farmer in 1911, 'if we allow our natives to be placed in locations. We shall then hear of strikes, hitherto unknown here. We shall have to go daily, hat in hand, to the location if the crops are ripe, and will have a great deal of trouble.'[2] The political pressure for the passing of the Natives' Land Act came, almost entirely it seems, from those who wished to ensure a cheap supply of labour by eliminating squatters and by doing away with the system of farming-on-the-half.

The reasons behind those provisions of the Act which made it illegal for an African to buy land from a white are more obscure. The Report of the Native Affairs Commission, 1903–5, had laid great emphasis on the amount of land that Africans were buying outside the reserves. And yet examination of the figures shows that the amount of land that passed into black hands was insignificant. In the debate on the Land Bill, it was estimated that in the Transvaal, where the situation was said to be most acute, the entire African population had bought little more than 1,000 morgen of land each year for the past twelve years. There seems to have been no urgent necessity, from the white voter's point of view, to limit land sales to blacks. However, as the Native Affairs Commission had reported, the growth of a mixed rural population should be discouraged if the 'absolutely necessary social and political distinctions' were to be preserved. A few people, at any rate, hoped that the Act might serve as the basis of the, ultimately complete, partition which, over the next generation, some were to see as the only hope of a peaceful solution to the country's racial tensions.

The Act was to have far-reaching consequences. Its immediate effect was to uproot hundreds of black South Africans from white-owned

[1] Ibid.   [2] Ibid.

farms and to send them wandering round the roads of the country
seeking a new place to live. In his fascinating book *Native Life in South
Africa* Sol Plaatje paints a vivid picture of the hardships suffered by men,
women, and children thrown out of their homes in the grim winter of
1913. 'If ever there was a fool's errand,' a policeman told Plaatje who
was travelling around to observe the effects of the Act, 'it is that of a
Kafir trying to find a new home for his stock and family just now.'[1]
Hardest hit were the black *bywoners*, that wealthier class of Africans who
had built up teams of oxen and other capital and who had spent much
of their lives in farming land under the half-share system. It was these
men who, all over the country, were called before their landlords and
faced with the alternative either of becoming servants and, in many
cases, of handing over their stock, or of leaving the farm. Unaware
that it was now illegal for any white farmer to offer the terms to which
they had become accustomed Africans chose to leave in the hope of
finding another landlord who would be willing to take them on. Some
found their way into the reserves; some into Basutoland and Bechuanaland; some got back on to farms where, in a few redeeming cases, com-
passionate white farmers, spurred on by their wives,[2] chose to defy the
law. But many, with their stock either dead or sold for a song, made
their way to the towns. Few laws passed in South Africa can have
been felt with such immediate harshness by so large a section of the
population. The system of farming-on-the-half, which had flourished
ever since whites had gained control of the interior, was dealt a
blow from which it never recovered. The next three decades were to
see the almost total elimination of that class of rural African who,
in the words of Sol Plaatje's policeman, had once been 'fairly comfortable, if not rich and [who] enjoyed the possession of their stock,
living in many instances just like Dutchmen'.[3] The Act, like many
laws before it, was aimed also at the elimination of 'kaffir farming'.
But although some farmers took the opportunity to evict some of their
'squatters' (Africans who were allowed to live on their farms in return
for rent paid either in cash or labour), the Act was little more successful than its predecessors in compelling farmers to forgo the benefit
of substantial revenue from land whose opportunity cost was negligible.
Squatters continued to be 'an evil', in the eyes of farmers who did not
have them.

In the longer term, the Act served well[4] to fuse those idealists, who
felt that partition alone was a realistic means of protecting Africans from
total domination by whites, with those more selfish and more numerous

[1] S. T. Plaatje, *Native Life in South Africa* (2nd edn.), p. 66.
[2] Ibid., ch. VI.   [3] Ibid., p. 66.
[4] W. K. Hancock, *Smuts: The Sanguine Years, 1870–1919*, pp. 313–18.

people who wanted economic integration without the uncomfortable social and political consequences. For the new law set aside sufficient land to tantalize the idealists without providing enough to enable all Africans to make their living there and so to be able to exist without working for the white man on his terms. In later years much political dexterity was displayed in using the reserves to maintain a policy which simultaneously won the support of idealists—members of the Dutch Reformed Church and others—without alienating the confidence of those voters for whom Africans were primarily units of labour whose presence was essential but only tolerable so long as they ministered to the needs of the white man.[1]

One other long-term aspect of the law was that, like the Mines and Works Act of 1911, it contained an economic colour bar to protect whites. For had Africans continued to buy farms, and had they had the State support which whites enjoyed, it is possible that they would have undercut the white farmers whose income generally was far above the level at which blacks would have been prepared to farm. Economic forces cannot, however, be completely dammed up although the law can affect the manner in which they work. In this case, the law operated to prevent Africans becoming landowners and undercutting whites as independent farmers, but it was not able to prevent blacks taking the place of whites on the land as tractor-drivers and managers so that the 'blackening' (*beswarting*) of the *platteland* became[2] as much a bogey as the *beswarting* of the cities.

While the Natives' Land Act was exerting pressure, the outbreak of the First World War, and the ostrich-feather slump which accompanied it, added yet another force which pushed men from the land. For the change in fashions broke an industry which had, for a generation, provided one of the main sources of export earnings. It is no accident that one of the principal areas from which the poor whites came was that part of the country in which the ostrich industry had been most firmly established.

Thus, with population pressure, subdivision, disease, drought, war devastation, market uncertainties, and (for blacks) hostile legislation, it is little wonder that for many people life on the land became impossible. Even if the rural population had been highly educated and skilled in farming, it is unlikely that men would have been able to survive the blows that rained upon them. But they were neither. Nor did they have a marketing organization adequate to sell even the little that they were producing. The men of the land, both black and white, were ill-prepared to meet the changes that were coming. The plight of

[1] *Report of the Local Government Commission* (T.P. 1, 1922, Pretoria, 1922), para. 267.
[2] *Report of the Commission of Inquiry into European Occupancy of the Rural Areas* (1960).

poor whites and equally poor, but less politically protected, blacks was pitiable evidence of the costs of rapid social change.[1]

But, important though they were, the push factors were not the only ones operating. In South Africa the initial impetus pulling men to the towns came not as a result of increased productivity in agriculture, but rather because of the discovery of a commodity which was in demand by an external market. The nature of the demand was such that it was possible for those producing the commodity to pay a rate of wages considerably higher than the going agricultural rate. There is abundant evidence from the earlier period that men, particularly blacks, were pulled out of agriculture into mining by the attractions of higher wages (see p. 121). In later years, once the initial disequilibrium between mining and rural areas had been overcome, the increase in the economy's productivity, combined with the fact that as people became wealthier they spent a smaller proportion of their income on farm products,[2] provided the underlying economic pull to the cities. Apart from these two fundamental forces, there were also such attractions as the 'bright lights'. Men go to town not only because they are hoping to earn a higher cash wage, but also because, for many of them, the quality of life there promises to be more interesting and exciting. In addition there is what might be labelled the willingness to gamble. For whites who, in the early mining years, contemplated going to the diamond or gold fields there was no certainty that their standards of living would increase as a result. However, there was a chance that it might make a spectacular leap forward and it seems likely that many went more because they preferred the uncertainties of digging to the vicissitudes of farming than because they were sure that they would receive higher incomes. Once they were in town, even although they did not find their dream diamond, it was often easier to stay than to return to the country district whence they came. However, many people, both white and black, did retain their rural links. As late as the 1920s, 'The mass of the Afrikaans mine-workers were yet only half-miners . . ., still looking back to their fathers' farms, spending their savings on small-holdings to keep contact with their tradition as frontier Boers.'[3]

But the movement to town set in process by these push-pull forces was a painful process. It is possible, in the history of economic activity,

[1] The position of landless men trekking to the cities at this period of South African history has been far better documented for whites than for blacks. See, for example, the Report of the Carnegie Commission, *The Poor White Problem in South Africa*; also W. M. Macmillan, *Complex South Africa*; and the *Report of the Transvaal Indigency Commission* (Pretoria, 1908).

[2] See R. G. Lipsey, *An Introduction to Positive Economics* (2nd edn.), p. 149, for a technical discussion of the connection between income elasticity of demand and the process of urbanization.

[3] B. Hessian, 'An Investigation into the Causes of the Labour Agitation on the Witwatersrand, January to March 1922, unpublished M.A. thesis, Witwatersrand, 1957 p. 16.

to distinguish two broad types of urbanization: that which occurs when people living in the rural hinterland decide to move to town; and that when the migrants come from a distant land. The farm labourers moving to London typified the one; the waves of immigrants from Ireland, Italy, Poland, and Germany to the United States exemplified the other. The pattern in South Africa during this period was a combination of the two. In very broad terms it seems true to say that the blacks moving to the cities came from surrounding rural areas, albeit often many miles distant, while the influx of whites was, at first, predominantly one of immigrants from overseas. Few figures are available of the number of people who came to the country from outside Africa over the period, but such scanty evidence as there is suggests that it must have been considerable. To what extent whites already living in the country moved into town is difficult to quantify, but it seems that the Afrikaners, at any rate, were late starters in the process. Afrikaans writers have made much of the fact that the country's cities did not grow out of the midst of the indigenous rural people, but that the Afrikaners moved into towns that were, for all practical purposes, foreign; dominated by an alien language and culture.[1] By 1911 less than 80 per cent of the whites in South Africa had been born in the country: the other 260,000, who, it is reasonably safe to assume, settled in the cities, came from the United Kingdom (70 per cent) Russia (9 per cent), Germany (5 per cent), Australasia (3 per cent), and elsewhere.[2] It is estimated[3] that in the two or three years following the discovery of gold, the white population of the Transvaal almost doubled. Much of this increase came from beyond the shores of southern Africa, but by the turn of the century the increase in the white urban population was coming more and more from within the country.

Writing of the urbanization of the Afrikaans-speaking South Africans, Albertyn[4] has emphasized his belief that their experience was unique. He gives four reasons for this. Firstly that the process was so fast. At the beginning of the twentieth century hardly 10,000 Afrikaans-speaking people were living in the ten big cities of the country, whereas by 1959 there were approximately 600,000. Secondly that the Afrikaner came into a city dominated by a culture and language different from his own. Thirdly, that this urbanization was swiftly followed by a similar trek of the Africans to the industrial centres. And fourthly, that the whole process occurred in a world of upheaval. But the Afrikaner's experience was not unique. It was exactly paralleled by that of black South Africans. They too moved to town very rapidly. They came to

[1] Albertyn, Introduction.
[2] Bureau of Census and Statistics, *Union Statistics for Fifty Years* (Pretoria, 1960), p. A. 23.
[3] Rose, p. 25. J. P. R. Maud, *City Government: The Johannesburg Experiment*, p. 17.
[4] Albertyn, Introduction.

cities which were even more alien to them in that the language and
culture were different and much of the legislation was directed against
them. Their process of urbanization was also accompanied by that of a
competitive group—the Afrikaners. And they too moved in a world of
upheaval. The insecurity of both the Afrikaner, defeated in war, and
the African, excluded from power, as they moved to the cities is discussed in the next chapter. Here we seek to focus on some of the
agricultural aspects of this insecurity.

One of the most serious charges made against farmers in South Africa
is that they have destroyed the productive potential of the land. Such
devastation was not confined to whites (see Vol. I, pp. 110, 253–4,
Vol. II, pp. 55–8, 70). The great drought of 1919 brought forcibly to the
attention of the general public the extent of the destruction. 'Since the
white man has been in South Africa', wrote the Drought Investigation
Committee in 1922, 'enormous tracts of country have been entirely, or
partially denuded of their original vegetation, with the result that
rivers, vleis and water-holes described by old travellers have dried up or
disappeared'.[1] The Commission found that this process was continuing
with great rapidity, and warned that, if unchecked, it would lead to
'national suicide'.[2] One immediate cause of the devastation was the
general practice of farmers in kraaling their small stock at night. This
protected the sheep from jackals but meant that the stock was collected
regularly in one place with the result that the veld round the kraal was
grazed bare, and paths were worn in taking the animals to and fro
between the kraal and the pastures. The scarcity of drinking places
necessitated a similar congregation of animals and the wearing of more
paths, which in turn became dongas, so exacerbating the erosion.
There was overstocking and selective grazing when farmers ignorant of
proper pastoral management ·responded to falling wool prices by
increasing the number of sheep with scant regard for the long-term
consequences. Furthermore, in high rainfall areas there was the deeply
rooted practice of veld burning whereby farmers ensured fresh green
grass each spring. Controlled burning had its uses in destroying insects,
brushwood, and unpalatable grass but careless burning, such as often
occurred, destroyed the natural covering so that the soil was either
blown or washed away.

There were two reasons for these farming malpractices. First, there
was the lack of education, particularly training in farming methods.
'The bulk of the present generation of farmers', wrote the Drought
Committee, 'had little schooling, and even the most elementary facts
of science are unknown to them.'[3] In his study of education and the

[1] *Final Report of the Drought Investigation Committee* (U.G. 49, 1923, Cape Town, 1923) p. 3.
[2] Ibid., p. 15.   [3] Ibid., p. 72.

poor white, E. G. Malherbe, noting the customary reason for education in the rural areas, wrote that confirmation for church membership 'constitutes even today [1932] the great common denominator of educational qualification among the poor whites, and though it might have saved some souls, it had very little prophylactic value in opening their eyes to the economic forces that were moving them to destruction.'[1] The second reason for the poor farming methods lay in the lack of capital. Despite the ease with which farmers were able to obtain credit, or indeed perhaps because of this, they put all the money they had into buying land and livestock. Besides pushing up the price of land, this meant that farmers had little of the capital necessary for fencing, sinking bore-holes, and other fixed investment. Indeed, although what the farmer needed was capital, the availability of credit, combined with the poor education, was disastrous: for he used the credit unwisely, landing hopelessly in debt. To extricate himself he had to sell his bonded land, but having done so he had little capital left for the necessary adaptation to town life.

In terms of both veld husbandry and business management most farmers responded equivocally to economic change. But what about the responsiveness of the structure of production? It varied from place to place, and farmer to farmer. In an earlier generation the *bywoner* had been left to cultivate the land on a share basis whilst the landowner confined himself to the more profitable stock-farming.[2] Nevertheless there was positive response to change: as land became scarcer *bywoners* were squeezed off the land, and as arable farming became increasingly profitable more farmers in the interior began producing for the market. The most noticeable change was in the production of maize. Due chiefly to the reduction, in 1907, of the railway rate to the coast for export maize the overseas market was made accessible to producers and a great stimulus was given to maize cultivation. 'The industry', writes du Toit, 'was asthmatic until the export trade was established.'[3]

During the First World War South Africans became increasingly aware not only of the need to produce more for home consumption, but also of the potentialities of overseas markets. And it was during this period that, with the development of refrigeration, the export of eggs, meat, and other perishable food products began.

But despite these efforts, farming in South Africa by 1924 was still in very bad shape. Poorly educated, loosely organized, and with a pattern of land tenure that was ill suited to more modern farming methods, those left behind on the land were struggling to cope with the new world into which they had been swept. Furthermore, economic change was giving rise to acute social tensions. It is small wonder that the white

[1] Malherbe, p. 17.   [2] *Drought Investigation Committee*, p. 210.   [3] Du Toit, p. 44.

farmers of South Africa, who held the balance of political power, handed over to the State the well-nigh impossible task of trying to resolve the conflicts.

4. *The State Takes Charge, 1924–1937*

The intervention of the State was nothing new in South African agriculture. Long before 1910 the government of the day had taken upon itself the job of helping farmers to farm better. Most of the agricultural initiative had not come, as in England, from individual entrepreneurs, but rather from far-sighted public officials. As early as 1803 Governor Janssens encouraged the establishment of an Agricultural and Sheep Breeding Society. Although his coercive measures to get good sheep adopted by conservative farmers aroused much resentment, it is to his efforts that the beginning of South Africa's wool industry can be traced.[1] And, at the end of the century it was the Cape Government, too, which took the lead in seeking ways to curb and eliminate the phylloxera in the vineyards, and the scab which destroyed so many sheep. Indeed the Scab Legislation of the 1890s was not welcomed by many farmers. They resented any intrusion upon what they considered to be inalienable individual rights by the State which proposed that dipping should be compulsory in order to prevent the spread of the disease.[2]

Despite the early resistance of those independent frontiersmen there was one form of State assistance which farmers had always been happy to receive. The establishment of the Land Bank in 1912 had marked the beginning of a new stage in the farmer's approach to the State for financial credit and other assistance. The significance of the Land Bank Act lay not only in the fact that credit was made specially available to assist farmers, but even more important, that henceforth farmers were to look increasingly to the State to solve their problems. Closely related to this Act was the development of agricultural co-operatives. The Land Bank was made responsible for the financing of co-operatives and the State took the lead in setting up a number of schemes many of which came to grief because of ignorance, poor management, and lack of support by members. The early years of the co-operative movement in South Africa were disastrous and it was not until the Co-operatives Act of 1922, with its provision of limited liability, that the movement began to be effective in assisting farmers. The problems of the previous decade were not immediately solved but membership started to grow rapidly.[3]

Further intervention by the State occurred during the First World War with legislation to control the quality of various potential export

---

[1] Chase, p. 171.   [2] T. R. H. Davenport, *The Afrikaner Bond*, pp. 155–9, 291.
[3] Koöperatiewe Raad van die Suid-Afrikaanse Landbou-Unie, *Inleiding tot die Kooperasiewese*, pp. 38–58.

commodities. And the establishment of the Koöperatieve Wijnbouwers-Vereniging in 1917 followed by the Wine and Spirits Act of 1924 marked the beginning of the State's attempt to assist farmers to stabilize the prices of their products.[1] In 1923 a principle that was to have far-reaching consequences was introduced with an Act giving the State power to take a levy on locally sold meat in order to pay a bounty to exporters.[2]

The election, in 1924, of a Government formed by coalition between the National and Labour parties did not bring about a complete change of direction in South African agriculture, but it did intensify the process of State intervention in that sector. This Government, which in class terms was a coalition between farmers and urban workers, had been elected with the express purpose of tackling the dislocations of change, and it set to work both on the farms and in the towns. The Civilized Labour policy of the next decade (see p. 206) was aimed at assisting the absorption of poor whites fleeing from the land into industrial occupations. The protective tariffs, introduced by legislation in 1925, were aimed at expanding the industrial sector with the same purpose in mind.

At the rural end two things were urgently needed. First was the improvement of farming methods to prevent the appalling soil erosion, to increase output, and to make agriculture a more efficient and economic enterprise. The second was to assist the farmer by protecting him from competitive imports and encouraging his exports. The Drought Investigation Committee had stressed that, 'First and foremost the State is bound to prevent such waste of its natural resources which, if persisted in, can but lead to national suicide; so it should take action in connection with soil erosion as it has done in other directions.[3] But it was a difficult task. The farmers were very often unwilling and generally ill equipped to make the necessary adjustments to their farming methods, and it was to be more than two decades before the conservatism of farmers could be sufficiently overcome for Parliament to pass the Soil Conservation Act in 1946. However, subsidy and protection were far more acceptable to farmers than were steps to combat erosion. In 1925 the Minister of Agriculture was given power to obtain a levy on all butter sold which he could then use for promoting the dairy industry. In the same year the Fruit Export Board was set up with wide powers to regulate all fruit exports. The following year control of all dairy exports was placed under a new Perishable Products Export Board, and further measures were introduced for the control of fruit.

During these years it would seem that agricultural legislation was

[1] A. J. Beyleveld, 'The Development of Production Control in the Wine Industry', *Agrekon*, 5 (1) 1966.
[2] J. G. van der Horst, 'Two Conferences', *SAJE*, 1 (1) 1933.
[3] *Drought Investigation Committee*, p. 15.

aimed predominantly at encouraging the better organization of the industry for export purposes. But gradually the emphasis changed from one of improving organization to protecting the sector, not only from the fluctuations in the market price, to which agricultural products are prone, but also from outside competition. The Fahey sugar agreement of 1926 was the first important step towards sheltering agriculture from the violent gusts of competition. Following upon the decline in world sugar prices, the import duty on sugar was raised from £4. 10s. to £8 per ton.[1] The Great Depression of 1929–32 accelerated the process. For world prices of agricultural products fell fast and far so that already harassed South African farmers turned yet more urgently to the State for assistance. In 1930 control of the Dairy industry was further tightened with the establishment of the Dairy Industry Control Board which had powers to fix both prices and the amount that each producer must export.[2] This control, by restricting imports, paying export bounties, and keeping the local prices of butter and cheese above international prices encouraged producers to expand their output rapidly. Local consumption increased less fast and so South Africa, which before 1930 had been an importer of dairy products became, after 1932, an exporter.[3] In the same year wheat, which as far back as 1883 had been heavily protected,[4] was also brought under control. The introduction of a quantitative import control combined with powers to fix the price of imported wheat well above the international level forced up the price of the local product and led to a massive extension of wheat farming in the country and to a progressive reduction of wheat imports. Between the beginning and end of the Great Depression the area under wheat increased by 0·1 per cent in Natal, 8·7 per cent in the Transvaal, 24·6 per cent in the Orange Free State, and no less than 66·6 per cent in the Cape Province. But this was a costly exercise. Richards estimates that in 1933 the excess cost of wheat alone to South African consumers was of the order of one and three-quarter million pounds.[5] The country was paying heavily not only for the wheat it consumed but also for the uneconomic surpluses that the policy had produced.

For maize, too, control measures were introduced with export subsidies which raised the local price above the international level by between 1s. and 4s. per bag, depending on the crop. This encouraged further production, and exports at the end of the 1930s were sixteen times as high as they had been in the last three years of the 1920s.[6]

[1] *Social and Economic Planning Council* [hereafter *SEPC*] *Report No. 4, The Future of Farming in South Africa* (Pretoria, 1944), pp. 4 ff.

[2] J. G. van der Horst, p. 11.   [3] *SEPC Report No. 4.*

[4] *Select Committee of the Cape: Colonial Agriculture and Industries* (A. 3, '83, Cape Town, 1883).

[5] C. S. Richards, 'Subsidies, Quotas, Tarriffs and the Excess Cost of Agriculture in South Africa', *SAJE*, 3 (3), 1935, 391.   [6] *SEPC Report No. 4*, p. 5.

Despite the fact that by 1928/9 the country was already exporting 86,000 tons of sugar, and despite the fact that the high tariff barrier had encouraged an increase in sugar cultivation from 264,000 acres in 1927 to 336,000 acres in 1932, world prices were falling so far that in the latter year the Government was persuaded to raise the tariff first to £12. 10s. and subsequently in the same year, to £16 per ton. By 1933 South African sugar was being dumped on the international market at a price that was a fraction less than 1d. a pound. Already in that year the excess cost to South African consumers of this sugar control was estimated to be well over £1,000,000 and production was continuing its meteoric rise. Such a process could not go on indefinitely, and a halt was called in 1936 with the passing of the Sugar Act, whereby machinery was created to limit production by enforcing quotas.[1] Another major product to come under control was meat. In 1933 the Meat Board was established with power to fix not only the number of slaughtered animals sold on any day, but also the maximum prices that could be paid at any place.

The commodities for which the State found itself able to provide real assistance for farmers were those for which there was a local market, but which could also be exported whenever there was a surplus, and imported to meet a shortage.[2] But there were important products which were more difficult to help. Chief of these was wool which had always been the major agricultural export. Because the internal market was so small, wool prices could be stabilized above the international level only by means of direct subsidy, and the State did in fact undertake such subsidization between 1933 and 1937. In 1937 the subsidy amounted to well over £1,000,000.[3] Similar assistance was provided for mohair, fruit, and wattle-bark exports.[4] At the other end of the spectrum were commodities which needed no tariff protection because their perishability effectively prevented competition from outside. However, it was extremely difficult to stabilize the local prices because these products (e.g. vegetables and potatoes) could not be easily graded and lacked the homogeneity which facilitates price setting.

The agricultural legislation of the early 1930s was essentially an attempt to stabilize fluctuating prices at a level well above the international prices which had fallen so sharply in the depression. But when it became apparent that the sectoral terms of trade between agriculture and industry had moved, for a time at least, against the former, the feeling arose that a more lasting measure of State participation in

---

[1] J. K. Huntley, 'The Development of Production Control in the South African Sugar Industry', *Agrekon*, 5 (2), 1966.

[2] T. van Waasdijk, 'Agricultural Prices and Price Policy, 1933-1953', *SAJE*, 22 (1), 1954, 166.

[3] Richards, p. 374, Schedule II.   [4] *SEPC Report No. 4*, p. 4.

the marketing of agricultural goods was necessary. Thus, in 1937, the Marketing Act was passed.[1] This Act, in the words of an official report 'Contains sufficient permissive powers to enable the Department of Agriculture and the Boards to control, and even to nationalize, perhaps one-fifth of the Union's economy'.[2] The primary aim of the Marketing Act was not so much the short-term stabilization of prices in a sector subject to violent fluctuations in output due to weather conditions, but rather the long-term social aim of keeping farming incomes more in line with those in town.

Investigation of the figures suggests that the intervention of the State was remarkably successful in stabilizing prices for those products which could easily be graded, and for which there was a large local demand. The following table shows the percentage change in the price of a com-

TABLE I

Average Annual Percentage Change in Price[3]

	1911–37	1937–59
Potatoes	30	30
Wool	30	25
Maize	18	5
Wheat	13	7
Mutton	11	10
Beef	8	7
Sugar	8	2
Milk	5	4

modity over the price in the previous year averaged over a period both before and after the Marketing Act. The significance of the figures may be questioned in view of the fact that the Marketing Act, which was a piece of enabling legislation, was not applied simultaneously to all commodities. Moreover the influence of such exogenous variables as the Second World War has been ignored. None the less the figures do suggest that the State's efforts to stabilize the prices of maize, wheat, and sugar were not altogether unsuccessful but that for dairy products, mutton, beef, potatoes, and, most important of all, for wool the reduction in price fluctuations was negligible. One other effect of the Act was

[1] *SEPC Report No. 4*, p. 16; H. J. Rensburg, 'Beheer Kragtens die Bemarkingswet', *Agrekon*, 1 (1), 1962.
[2] *SEPC Report No. 4*, p. 5.
[3] Note: All prices, except milk, at wholesale. Source: Union Statistics for Fifty Years.

Derivation:
$$\% = \frac{\sum_{i=1}^{n-1}\left|100 - 100\frac{P_{i+1}}{P_i}\right|}{n-1}$$

cf. T. W. Schultz, *The Economic Organization of Agriculture*, p. 337.

to boost membership of the co-operatives (which had more than doubled since 1922) by enabling them to be used as agents of the control boards to do the physical handling and marketing of various commodities.[1]

Turning now to the nature of farm life we find that there were four major studies[2] during this period from which it is possible to gain a considerable amount of information. The Native Economic Commission which made its report in 1932 found that labour tenancy (see p. 117) was still widespread, but that it was showing signs of disintegration in many directions.[3] Land was becoming increasingly scarce, and farmers correspondingly unwilling to have labour that did not work the full year round. One of the main provisions in the 1936 Natives' Trust and Land Act (which fulfilled some of the obligations undertaken in the 1913 Land Act (see Map 2, p. 53), was to enable magisterial districts to extend, by proclamation, the period for which tenants must work from 90 to 180 days.[4] The half-shares system was, as has been shown (see p. 130), almost eliminated by the Natives' Land Act of 1913 but, even in the Free State, remnants of the system were still to be found in the 1930s.[5] 'Kaffir farming' remained; but, more and more, the tendency was for farmers to employ full-time servants who were paid a cash wage, plus rations, and who generally had some grazing rights and access to arable land. For poor whites, at the time that the Carnegie Commission made its report in 1932, the situation was still bad, but the problem was entering its last stage. The industrial expansion of the next few years (see p. 142) together with the manpower requirements of the Second World War absorbed the last of the poor whites.

The evidence from both the Orange Free State and from the eastern Cape at this time suggests that wages of farm labourers far from increasing were in real terms actually diminishing. The writer on the Orange Free State estimated that agricultural wages had fallen since the beginning of the century because the increase in cash which had occurred was not in itself sufficient to offset the decreased wages in kind which labour was getting.[6] For the eastern Cape, Monica Hunter concluded that 'It is clear that the "farm Native" has lost economically by contact with Europeans. Working very much harder than he did under tribal conditions, he has no more nourishing or varied a diet than the rawest Pondo of the reserves; a servant or "labour tenant" dismissed by his

[1] *Report of the Commission of Inquiry into Co-operative Affairs RP* 78, Pretoria, 1967.

[2] *Report of the Carnegie Commission* (1932); *Report of the Native Economic Commission 1930–1932* (U.G. 22, 1932, Pretoria, 1932); Hunter, *Reaction to Conquest* (1936 edn.); SAIRR, *Farm Labour in the Orange Free State*, 1939.

[3] *Report of the Native Economic Commission 1930–1932*, pp. 359–61.

[4] D. Hobart Houghton, *Some Economic Problems of the Bantu in South Africa*, p. 28.

[5] SAIRR, p. 34.   [6] Ibid., p. 22.

employer has no hut site or land to cultivate. No longer a member of
a tribe owning land, he has lost economic security. And withal he is no
longer his own master, but a servant. His position appears to be deteriorating, rather than improving.'[1] Farmers told her that the average
wage for a married man before the First World War in the districts
studied was six to ten shillings per month. By 1934 the customary wage
was between eight and twelve shillings per month: an increase of only
two shillings per month over twenty years. Moreover this was accompanied by a reduction in the number of stock grazed free. Both in
eastern Cape and in the Free State housing for labour was very poor.[2]
In the Free State the Race Relations investigator found that malnutrition was rife, and that for clothing the people had only rags. However,
he considered that social insurance on the farms in that area was better
than in town.

Faced with these worsening conditions, why then did men not leave the
land in greater numbers than they did? The answer lies in the barriers to
mobility. These were extremely effective. The strongest was the monetary indebtedness of farm labourers to their employers, but in addition
there were the pass laws (see pp. 197 ff.) and the reluctance of many to
give up their grazing rights thus losing any chance of owning cattle.[3]

Looking back it is possible to see that the period 1929–32 was one
of the watersheds in South Africa's farming history. First there was the
depression which sent the prices for agricultural products down to
abysmally low levels. Naturally enough the response to this was protection with the aim of isolating local prices from the depressing effects
of unremunerative exports.[4] Secondly there was the great drought of
1932–3 which killed thousands of livestock. Simultaneously with the
drought, however, came a rise by 50 per cent of the price of gold which
sparked off an enormous industrial expansion both in the mines as well as
in the manufacturing sector. Employment in the gold-mines alone rose
from 228,000 in 1932 to 391,000 in 1941[5] whilst in the building industry
employment, having fallen from 22,000 in 1930 to 11,000 in 1933, had
risen to 39,000 by 1937.[6] In that brief period both the forces pushing
men off the land and those pulling them to the cities were greatly intensified. So it is no accident that despite the State's sustained effort to
maintain the incomes of white farmers by price supports, the absolute
number of whites in the rural areas reached its peak in 1931, and from
that date started to fall.[7]

---

[1] Hunter, p. 517.   [2] Ibid., p. 514; SAIRR, p. 29.
[3] Ibid., p. 32.   [4] Van Waasdijk, p. 61.
[5] Transvaal and Orange Free State Chamber of Mines, *Annual Report*, 1964.
[6] Union Statistics for Fifty Years, p. L. 29.
[7] *SEPC Report No. 4*, p. 6. (The number of whites actually employed on farms did not start
to fall for another five or six years.)

Although warning voices against the effects of the State's measures to mitigate the pains of economic and social adjustment existed, it was not until the following period that the full consequences of the nature of the State's intervention became more easily visible.

5. *The Consequences of Control, 1937–1966*

By the beginning of the Second World War the State had become so involved in farming that it is impossible to consider the subsequent history of agriculture without first analysing the various effects of State participation. Although they interacted, it is possible to distinguish at least six major strands of Government policy in the agricultural sector.

The most obvious was the marketing policy developed during the 1930s. The State, as has been shown, took upon itself the power not only to stabilize short-term price fluctuations, but also, by means of tariffs, subsidies, export quotas, and other controls, to raise agricultural prices well above the competitive level. The result of this was, with the help of sheltered Commonwealth outlets, to encourage the uneconomic expansion of many products including sugar, wheat, maize, wine, milk, and butter.[1] More serious perhaps than the immediate costs of such subsidization was the fact that the high prices received by farmers encouraged the extension of cultivation into marginal areas, not really suitable for such crops. Indiscriminate ploughing accelerated[2] the process of soil erosion in so devastating a manner that by 1966 there were experts who considered it to be far the most serious of the country's many problems.

However, with the outbreak of the Second World War, the growth of agricultural production slowed down (see p. 163). In addition the increased consumption of food (see p. 152) led to a position where, by 1946, there were acute shortages of commodities which had previously been over-produced. However, intervention by the State once again reversed the situation. Maize was a case in point. By the end of the war it seemed that South Africa would, in future, always have to import substantial amounts to meet its needs. However wise such importation might have been in purely economic terms, it was politically impossible. Not only was the country unwilling to leave itself vulnerable by importing one of its staple foods, but the maize farmers of the interior held considerable political power within the National Party during the years immediately following its election victory in 1948 and they were able to exert effective pressure. Thus the Government decided, in 1949, to encourage production by raising prices. Within the next three years the average price per bag was raised from 21s. 3d. to 30s. For many farmers

[1] F. J. van Biljon, *State Interference in South Africa* (1939), p. 116.
[2] G. V. Jacks and R. O. White, *The Rape of the Earth*, p. 268.

this meant almost a doubling of net profits and they responded immediately to the incentive. Production increased rapidly and, after that
time, there were surpluses every year. By 1962 it was estimated that no
more than 70 per cent of the average crop was adequate for home consumption. The other one-third of the crop had to be exported at a loss.[1]
'The search for markets outside the Union', wrote van Biljon[2] in 1938,
'has been chiefly motivated by the necessity of disposing of uneconomic
surpluses.' By 1966, despite notable exceptions, the generalization remained true.

Yet deliberate bolstering of favoured products was not the only
problem caused by marketing control. Another was the lethargy and
complacency induced in some farmers by such protection. 'In South
Africa in particular', wrote a former head of the National Marketing
Council in 1966, 'the rigid maintenance of producers' prices for some
farm products has involved regimentation of marketing channels, stultifying innovations in marketing, and sheltering the producer to such a
degree that he has become unresponsive to new production and
marketing opportunities.'[3] Dr. van Biljon went on to cite the beef-rearing
industry as one in which growth and adaptation to changing consumer
preferences had been retarded by years of rigid price control.

Closely linked with marketing policy was that concerning income
distribution. As Dr. van Biljon has shown, 'The preservation in South
Africa of so many uneconomic farming units is partly traceable to the
fact that the principle of greater price stability for farm products
has become confused with the social aim of keeping farming incomes
more in line with urban incomes. In this way the valid objective
of short-term price stabilization . . . has come into conflict with the
over-riding objective of a more efficient farming system.'[4] Increased
productivity in an economy where consumers spend relatively more of
their new wealth on industrial goods than they do on food implies that
men must move off the land so that there are neither unwanted surpluses of food, nor insufficient factory workers to make the goods which
people with a rising standard of living increasingly require (see p. 132).
But for this movement to the towns to take place it is necessary that
some signal be given in the economy to tell people that this is what must
happen. If the price mechanism is not allowed to operate and indicate
to people, by virtue of the wage difference between town and country
occupations, that some movement from the one to the other is required,
then some other means must be found of reallocating the labour force.

[1] A. P. Scholtz, 'Die mieliebedryf in Suid-Africa—Gevaartekens vir die toekoms', *Agrekon*.
1(1), 1962.   [2] Van Biljon (1939), p. 117.
[3] F. J. van Biljon, 'The Economic Nature of the Challenge to South African Agriculture',
Agrekon, 5 (1), 1966.   [4] Ibid.

If there is no signal and if people do not move to town sufficiently rapidly, then not only is there liable to be over-production in the agricultural sector, but also inefficient and destructive farming may be hidden.

A third crucial area of Government involvement was that of labour. There were two aspects of this, each with its own consequences. First, the State's policy with regard to urban labour affected the farms. For the Civilized Labour policy which had so effectively maintained a colour bar in gold mines, on railways, and elsewhere in the industrial sectors of the South African economy did, as was intended, much to protect white workers from competition by blacks. But except for the Land Act which prohibited black ownership in 'white' areas (see p. 129) the policy could not be, and was not, applied to farms. This differential treatment led to a greater substitution of cheap black labour for white on South African farms than in the urban areas. As early as 1932 there was evidence of white farmers replacing unsatisfactory white managers with Africans.[1] A generation later the substitution had advanced still further. 'Previously', reported an official commission in 1960, 'the Nonwhite foreman was simply a leading labourer in charge of a gang, but . . . in numerous cases such foremen can be regarded as farm managers rather than leading labourers'.[2] But black mine managers or factory managers were inconceivable in South Africa both in the 1930s and in the 1960s. This contention that black labour was substituted for white on the farms is supported by evidence from the South African Agricultural Union to a Commission of Enquiry in May 1967. The ratio of blacks to whites in the economically active population on the land was 8:1 in 1946, 9:1 in 1951, and 13:1 in 1960.[3] Although these figures include the reserves, the number of peasant farmers there is unlikely to have increased sufficiently to account for all the change in ratios. Thus we may conclude that the movement of whites off the land, particularly since 1924, was somewhat retarded by the State's ability to raise their incomes on the land, but that, at the same time, it was accelerated by the policy of Civilized Labour in non-agricultural sectors. The second aspect of labour policy concerned the State's attempt to find methods, other than raising wages, of ensuring an adequate farm labour supply. It has already been shown that this practice dates far back into South African history, and it was one that was to continue throughout the century, 1866–1966. One major effect of the various pass laws had been to reduce, substantially, the mobility of farm labour. This in turn

[1] Hunter, p. 519.
[2] *Report of the Commission of Inquiry into European Occupancy of the Rural Areas*, p. 19.
[3] South African Agricultural Union, *Memorandum for Submission to the Commission of Enquiry into Agriculture*, p. 15.

implied that such labour was likely to be unevenly distributed, and that some farmers would have too much, while others were crying for more. During the late 1930s the problem of labour shortage, which seemed to have lain dormant for a generation after the 1913 Natives' Land Act, once again appeared in an acute form, and the Government appointed a committee[1] to investigate the matter. The shortage, which was greatest for seasonal labour, appears to have risen again when it did for two reasons. First, the enormous industrial expansion following devaluation in 1932 had drawn much labour, both black and white, to the cities. Secondly, farm wages, as always, lagged far behind. In 1952 the value of the average African farm labourer's income (including food and clothing) was just over £3 a month whilst average mine wages (including the value of food), which had not risen in real terms since the time of Union, were exactly double farm earnings.[2]

In response to the shortage there seems little doubt that many farmers did increase their wages. In 1949 the Natal farmers in the Underberg district, for example, set up a labour charter to standardize and, in many cases, to improve labour conditions.[3] But other steps were also taken to augment the supply. Of these two were most important. One was a renewed attempt to enforce the 1913 Land Act with regard to squatters more strictly than ever before. The other was the development of a prison labour system. Feeling was particularly strong against those people who, despite all laws, continued to practice 'kaffir farming'. These labour farms, explained an official report in 1944, 'are part of a particularly pernicious system and have come to be regarded as an almost essential adjunct to European farming in certain areas. Under this system whole farms are placed at the disposal of Natives to use as they see fit, with little or no control in regard to human or animal numbers or farming methods . . . in some cases it seems that the owner is less interested in the land and labour as such than in the cash rental which he is able to obtain from the Natives.'[4]

Prison labour was nothing new in South Africa. The use of convicts on the roads and docks had been adopted in the Cape as far back as the 1860s, and its employment on the docks was seen as a help to farmers.[5] In 1889 the State began hiring out convicts to wine farmers, a practice

---

[1] *Report of the Native Farm Labour Committee*, 1937–9.

[2] *Agricultural Census No. 26 (Special Report Series, No. 3)*, p. 1. F. Wilson, 'An Analysis of the Forces Operating in the Labour Market of the South African Gold Mines', Ph.D. thesis, Cambridge, 1966, p. 114.

[3] *Rand Daily Mail*, 14 Mar. 1949.

[4] *Report of the Reconstruction Committee of the Department of Agriculture and Forestry*, p. 6.

[5] *Report of the Select Committee upon the Convict Department* C. 3–1866, Cape Town, 1866, p. vii; *Select Committee* (1879), p. 386.

which had apparently continued for many years,[1] and which was expanded in 1934 with the introduction of the 'sixpenny scheme' whereby short-term prisoners could be compelled to spend their sentences working for farmers who paid sixpence a day to the Department of Prisons for each labourer. But, time-honoured though the custom was, it had never before flourished quite as it did during the decades that followed the Second World War. In 1947 two steps were taken which marked the beginning of a massive increase in the employment of non-white prisoners on white farms. The first concerned the establishment of farm jails which were eventually to house long-term convicts serving sentences of two years or more. The second was the suspension of the sixpenny system and its replacement by a 'Volunteer Scheme' whereby petty offenders might choose to work, on parole, as farm labourers.[2]

The matter of farm jails was publicly mooted by the United Party's Minister of Justice, Mr. H. G. Lawrence, who in July 1947 told a meeting of farmers at Bethal in the Eastern Transvaal that he was considering the establishment of a prison outstation in the district in order to help solve the farmers' labour problem. 'One of our difficulties', he is reported to have said, 'is to get enough work for convicts to do.'[3] One farmer at the meeting said that he was prepared to build, at his own expense, a jail on his farm to house one hundred convicts if he could be assured (which he was not) of their services of fifteen years.[4] But although the Smuts Government built a farm jail at Bellville in the western Cape, it was not until the National Party came to power that the system became fully established. The costs of building each jail were met by local farmers, each of whom bought shares and who was able to draw labour according to his proportion of total share-capital. The gaol was run by the Department of Prisons which met the running expenses including the salaries of warders and the cost of the prisoners' food, and which charged between fifteen and fifty cents a day for each prisoner hired to a shareholder.[5] By the beginning of 1952 there were four prison outstations in the Bethal area and another, with a capacity of 350, was opened during the course of the year.[6] Nor was Bethal the only area to be thus served. In the same year large jails were also built at Klein Drakenstein for the wine farmers of the Paarl district, and near Welkom in the Orange Free State where the development of the new gold-fields had drawn labour away. Two years later, another three jails

---

[1] Speech by the Minister of Justice when opening farm jail at Klein Drakenstein. *Rand Daily Mail*, 29 Aug. 1952.

[2] *Report of the Penal and Prison Reform Commission* (U.G. 47, 1947, Pretoria, 1947), pp. 82, 132, 158.

[3] *Rand Daily Mail*, 21 July 1947.   [4] *Sunday Express*, 20 July 1947.

[5] *The Star*, 5 Aug. 1952; *Evening Post*, 22 July 1967; C. Southern, *Wyksdorp: A Study of a South African Village*, pp. 10, 17, 24.   [6] Ibid., pp. 10, 17.

had been opened near Paarl alone, and by 1966 there were no less than twenty-three such prison outstations with total accommodation for more than 6,000 long-term prisoners.[1] Thirteen of the jails were in the western Cape, where the pass laws were being stringently applied in an attempt to prevent black labour moving in. Nine were in the eastern Transvaal where farmers had long found it necessary to recruit labour from as far away as Nyasaland and where, despite the model recruiting organization run by the farmers of Bethal, the unscrupulousness of some farmers had, for twenty years before the investigations of the Revd. Michael Scott and Mr. Drum, given rise to reports of ill treatment which discouraged labourers from going there.[2] And one was in the Orange Free State where mine wages were more than double what a casual labourer could expect to earn on a farm[3] (see map).

But the system remained controversial. In its defence the Minister of Justice, Mr. C. R. Swart, contended that it was sensible to relieve the overcrowded city jails by sending some of its inhabitants out into the country districts where they could work constructively.[4] Others, however, argued that the private employment of casual convict labour was a different thing from the systematic building of prisons with the primary object of providing farm labour.[5] The argument that the growth of the system led to a vested interest in crime is cogent. To have found empty a jail which cost them anything up to £25,000 would have been painful to local farmers no matter how much they deplored lawlessness. In the eastern Transvaal it was estimated that the right to draw convict labour had raised the value of the farms concerned by between £2 and £3 per morgen.[6] And in the western Cape, the right to employ prison labour was valued at R1,000 a convict.[7] The owner of a 3,000-morgen farm or a farmer with right to employ twenty prisoners stood to lose a lot of capital if the system were to collapse.

In a study of convict road work in the American South, two historians analysed the economics of prison labour as follows:

When a county has once adopted the plan of convict road work, it becomes necessary to maintain a convict road force sufficient in number to justify the overhead charges for equipment and supervision. Under such circumstances the local criminal courts tend to be looked upon as feeders for the chain gang, and there is evidence in some instances that the mill of criminal justice grinds more industriously when the convict road force needs new recruits.[8]

[1] *Hansard*, 1967, col. 3511.
[2] *Report of the Native Farm Labour Committee*, p. 66; *Rand Daily Mail*, 28 June 1947.
[3] *The Star*, 5 Aug. 1952.   [4] *Rand Daily Mail*, 29 Aug. 1952.
[5] *The Star*, Editorial, 'Investment in Crime', 12 July 1952.
[6] Shareholder of the O.F.S. farm jail, reported in *The Star*, 5 Aug. 1952.
[7] *The Star*, 11 Nov. 1965. Confirmed by personal research, 1969.
[8] F. Steiner and R. M. Brown, *The North Carolina Chain Gang, A Study of County Convict Road Work*, Chapel Hill, 1927.

South Africa did not use chain gangs, and there was no evidence that the courts were misused to fill the jails, but the fact that the large prison outstations were built in direct response to the pressure of farmers suffering from a shortage of labour showed the extent to which South African agriculture had become dependent upon crime.[1]

Besides the spread of the network of prison outstations, the pressures for labour led to the establishment and expansion of the 'Volunteer Scheme' for petty offenders, serving sentences of three months or less. And this scheme was open to abuses which the farm jail system was not. For although Africans arrested for pass or other technical offences were theoretically allowed to choose whether or not they would work on a farm rather than go to jail or, in the case of foreign Africans found on the Witwatersrand without pass or passport, bc dumped on the northern borders of the Transvaal, a great deal of evidence came to light of men being compelled to volunteer. Under the scheme, those who went to work on the farms were paid a wage of 9d. a day which they received when they were released. During 1949 no less than 38,000 petty of-fenders went from the Witwatersrand to work on farms.[2] In 1954 the scheme was extended throughout the country.[3] However, a series of habeas corpus applications which were given wide publicity in the press led to a public outcry and the scheme was suspended in 1959.[4] A new system of probationary release on parole took its place.[5]

In addition to the use of prisoners to meet the farm labour shortage, which one newspaper declared was so acute 'that some farmers are permitting recruited Natives to bring their wives with them and are providing accommodation for them and their families',[6] the State set about the establishment of labour bureaux in order to improve the distribution of farm workers. Between the establishment of these bureaux in 1951, and the middle of 1954, 79,000 men were placed in employment on farms. And a further 20,000 men were recruited in 1954 in order to assist with the bumper maize harvest.[7] This development further restricted the mobility of farm labourers, for before any African was allowed to leave a country district the local labour bureau had to satisfy itself that the labour position in the district was satisfactory.

After labour, the fourth important area of State involvement in agriculture was in the field of education where the fruit of much neglect became apparent. Despite the various colleges which had been set up

---

[1] *Rand Daily Mail*, 30 Dec. 1948; *The Star*, 5 Aug. 1952.
[2] *The Star*, 14 Dec. 1950.
[3] Department of Native Affairs, *General Circular No. 23 of 1954*.
[4] M. Horrell, *Annual Survey of Race Relations, 1958–9*, pp. 308–20; International Commission of Jurists, *South Africa and the Rule of Law*, pp. 129 ff.
[5] Horrell, *Survey, 1959–60*, p. 268.
[6] *The Star*, 12 Feb. 1948.   [7] *Rand Daily Mail*, 13 Oct. 1954.

for white farmers at the turn of the century the level of training in the agricultural sector was extremely low. Not only were an insignificant number of farmers provided with the necessary technical education but the standard of general education available in country districts left much to be desired. By the 1960s it was estimated that no less that 79 per cent of the white farmers had had less than ten years of schooling.[1] For African labour the position was incomparably worse. Far into the twentieth century many, though by no means all, farmers opposed the schooling or even technical training of their labour force.[2] The reasons for this were complex (see p. 111), but amongst them was the fact that, given the low level of agricultural wages, the more highly educated a man the more likely was he to leave the farm and move to the city. But by the 1960s it was becoming increasingly obvious that the losses of having an illiterate labour force outweighed the gains. For with the development of farming, and with the substitution of black labour for white, Africans were being required to do more highly skilled jobs than they had in the past. One of the most important of these was tractor driving. Pointing to the fact that the use of tractor spares in South Africa was inordinately high, a former head of the Marketing Council warned farmers that 'Patently the education and training of our non-European farm labour force has become inadequate for the mechanized and scientific farming age.'[3] This was an understatement: in 1960, 65 per cent of the African population over the age of nineteen had never been to school, whilst only 12 per cent of those over the age of nine had passed standard V, i.e. had at least seven years of schooling.[4] One of the most serious consequences of the low level of farm skills, particularly at the managerial level, was the soil erosion which, caused primarily by bad farming methods, continued its devastating progress (see p. 166).

Another aspect of State policy which had important consequences for farmers was that relating to agricultural credit. Over the period 1912–40 land prices remained fairly constant, but from that date they started to increase sharply. After 1951 the rise in land prices became even more rapid. This was partly due to the astronomical increase in the price of wool that year and the fact that wealthy wool farmers brought up land and left it idle, creating much bitterness in Afrikaner circles.[5] Analysing these trends van Wyk concluded that they could not be ascribed to the prevailing inflationary pressures and the profitability of farming alone, but that the ready availability of credit was one of the contributing factors.[6] Examining in detail the extraordinary rise in land values in the

[1] *Financial Mail*, 5 Apr. 1968.

[2] *Report of the Commission on Native Education: 1949–1951* (U.G. 53, 1951, Pretoria, 1951), para. 303.   [3] Van Biljon (1966).

[4] *Statistical Yearbook (1964)*, pp. A–32, A–35.   [5] Marquard, *People and Policies*, p. 72.

[6] C. A. G. van Wyk, 'Trends in Land Values in South Africa', *Agrekon*, 6 (1), 1967.

Bethal district from £9 per morgen in 1947/8 to £34 per morgen in 1964/5, he found that there was no data from which to estimate accurately the extent to which the increase in land values was due to the trend for allowing more and more land purchases to be made on credit. Although van Wyk failed to take account of the establishment of farm jails and their effect on land values in Bethal it seems reasonable to conclude that the interest on the loan with which farmers paid for land was often more than could be recovered from farming that soil. This meant that farmers who bought such land on credit found it extremely difficult to pay back what they had borrowed.[1] Van Waasdijk commented that by 1953 'although better equipped, South African farmers were more heavily burdened by debt than at any time in their history'.[2]

On the positive side, the availability of credit, combined with tax concessions, led to considerable fixed capital investment on farms, particularly after the Second World War. During this period a change became visible as farmers built dams, closed dongas, and made contour banks on hillsides. But in other areas there were signs of deterioration. The dust storms of the Orange Free State, which made it necessary for motorists to use their headlights in the middle of the day, were a grim warning of the consequences of extending maize cultivation without due regard for the necessity of trees and other covering vegetation. And the legally registered but effectively uncontrolled sinking of large numbers of boreholes served to lower the water table to such a level that many streams ceased to flow except after particularly heavy rains.

One last sphere of State influence was the excellent research which it sponsored at the various agricultural colleges. In the early years of Union, the Government had concentrated its attention on creating a well-equipped agricultural department whose research and educational propaganda were crucial to the development of scientific farming in South Africa.[3] Although the State had subsequently placed more emphasis on fiscal protection as a means of assisting agriculture, a strong foundation had been laid on which was built such internationally recognized work as that of the veterinary scientists at Onderstepoort. Excellent and practical though the research was, the resources devoted to it were pitifully small.[4] Agricultural shows, often instigated by the State, were another potent force in the improvement of agriculture.

But, of course, not all the changes that took place in the agricultural sector were due to the State's influence, although even these were not completely isolated from the effect of Government policy. Two of the

---

[1] *Report of the Native Farm Labour Committee*, p. 22.
[2] Van Waasdijk, *SAJE*, 22 (1), 1954.
[3] Van Biljon (1938), p. 115.
[4] C. van der Merwe and S. J. du Toit, 'The contribution of the Agricultural Departments to Agricultural Development', *Agrekon*, 6 (1), 1967.

most important were the changes in the pattern of consumption and the process of mechanization. The following table illustrates the manner in which the *per capita* consumption of foodstuffs increased during the Second World War up until 1952. Thereafter however, consumption levelled off, and for meat it actually declined. There would seem to be three reasons why the consumption of bread, butter, meat, and sugar increased so rapidly during the war. Many of those who joined the army were whites who had previously been too poor to eat the better food now provided by the Quartermaster-General. Also the expansion of steel and other industries combined with the absorption of men into

TABLE 2

The Pattern of Consumption (1937/9 = 100)[1]

(*Per capita*)

Year	Maize (Human)	Maize (Animal)	Wheat	Butter	Meat	Sugar
1937–9	100	100	100	100	100	100
1946	98	214	123	112	128	137
1952	99	343	138	171	132	159
1964/5	n.a.	n.a.	138	171	119	n.a.

the army drew thousands of rural Africans into wage-earning employment. Thirdly the consumption of passing ships, if not allowed for, will have inflated the figures considerably.

The process of mechanization was one of the most notable features of change in the agricultural sector between 1937 and 1966. Before the

TABLE 3

Mechanization (Index of numbers sold 1946 = 100)[2]

Year	Tractors	Combine Harvesters	Animal-drawn wagons
1926	6	n.a.	83
1937	30	34	97
1946	100	100	100
1955	431	519	43
1960	587	594	n.a.

Second World War few farmers used tractors, combine-harvesters were virtually non-existent, and the demand for animal-drawn wagons and

[1] Source: Van Waasdijk; see also South African Agricultural Union, *Memorandum* (1967), Tables VI–VIII. 1964/5 figures are preliminary.

[2] Source: *Union Statistics for Fifty Years*, p. I–22; *Statistical Yearbook 1966*, p. J–20.

trolleys was still rising. But, as the above table (3) makes clear, by the end of the war a switch towards tractors had begun, and a similar increase in the use of combine-harvesters was to follow in the next decade. Despite the fact that real wages of farm labourers do not seem to have risen during this period, there was extensive substitution of capital for labour. One reason for this was that the labour was so unevenly distributed. Farmers, faced with shortage, chose to mechanize[1] rather than raise wages in the hope of obtaining more labour. Furthermore, as Salter has shown, one effect of technical progress is to make capital goods cheaper relative to labour so that new knowledge itself generates a pressure for the substitution of labour by capital.[2]

By 1966 much had changed on the white farms over the previous hundred years. But there was much that remained remarkably unaltered. It would perhaps be instructive to consider now the century as a whole.

6. *A Century of Agriculture, 1866–1966*

The most striking difference between the beginning and the end of the century was, as in many other countries, the breakdown of isolation. Where farmers had previously travelled over bad roads or paths, on foot or on horseback, by cart or ox-wagon, they were now linked with one another, with the urban areas, and with the wider world by all-weather roads, over which they travelled in large cars. Telephones, too, which spread through the rural areas in the 1920s, served to increase the scale of interaction in the white community. The party-line system made it possible for neighbours to have long conversations at little cost. Radios, newspapers, and journals were equally important links with the wider world. And sons, coming back from university, agricultural college, or from overseas where they had gone to gain wider experience, although a minority, brought in new ideas.

This breakdown in isolation was most marked for the white group but it affected others on the farms as well. Seldom would a farmer go to town without at least one of his labourers accompanying him. And the spread of bicycles, particularly noticeable after the Second World War, facilitated the gathering of young farm labourers for their week-end parties and visits to the *dorp*. On some farms, a few labourers even began to acquire second-hand motor-cars, which enabled the community of a farm to maintain closer contact with those farther away. During the

---

[1] A Transvaal congress of the National Party in the early 1950s asked that Africans, even though they were illiterate, should be given licences to drive a tractor. It seems to have been general practice to pay a bonus to tractor drivers.

[2] W. E. G. Salter, *Productivity and Technical Change*, chs. 1–3.

1960s the extension of vernacular programmes and spread of portable transistor radios marked a radical break in the isolation of farm labourers. Nevertheless, when compared with their white employers, Africans on farms remained dispersed and out of touch. Without either the social solidarity that still existed, by virtue of traditional ties, in the reserves,[1] or the wider experiences open to those who lived in town, many farm labourers were as isolated as they had ever been.

In view of the profound changes that took place in the white farming community over the century it is surprising to find how static was the nature of black-white relationships. The social distance, the taboos, and indeed the whole caste pattern which existed before the mineral discoveries continued on the farms throughout the century. At a lively meeting of Bethal farmers held in 1947 to discuss labour problems, after allegations by the Revd. Michael Scott had focused attention on the area, one farmer complained that, 'Mr. Scott eats and lives with Natives. Is that a decent European?' Judging by the laughter, loud stamping, and applause which greeted his question[2] the answer was, 'No'. The paradox of social distance combined with intimacy (see p. 110) so familiar to those acquainted with the American Deep South, remained. In the 1960s white children, both Afrikaans- and English-speaking, still grew up on the farms with African or Coloured playmates, who, until the sons and daughters were sent away to school, romped through the house like any other child. But even this closeness was not without its ambiguities. Why, asked one small boy plaintively in the Free State at this time, could not his *kaffertjie*, who watched him go to bed every night, also have a bath with him? And, as they grew older, the white children gradually grew away from their childhood friends as they had always been taught to do. The extent of social distance is perhaps best illustrated by the number of farmers who continued to transport their farm labour in the back of a truck, even although there was no one else sitting next to them in the cab. Yet farmers and their children, together with the families of those who were traders in the reserves, remained the one group of white South Africans with a good working knowledge of the language which their labourers spoke. Interaction on the farms, while perhaps even less equal, was far deeper than on the factory floor, where inability of workers to speak either English or Afrikaans generally implied extremely poor communication with the white managers and foremen, few of whom had any knowledge of their workers' home language. On the mines communication had been greatly improved by the teaching of Fanakalo: nevertheless it remained rudimentary. Another contrast was that neither on the mines nor in the

[1] Suid Afrikaanse Buro vir Rasse-Aangeleenthede (SABRA), *Die Naturel in die Suid Afrikaanse Landbou* (1954), p. 70.   [2] *Rand Daily Mail*, 21 July 1947.

factories did the wife of the boss know anything about the families of his workers, nor care for them when they were ill, as was generally the case on farms.

Changes in the social framework may, perhaps, be most easily seen by considering the different categories of people (as listed in the following table) who, over the century, worked on farms.

TABLE 4

Categories of Farm Workers in South Africa, 1866–1966

1. Full-time worker (paid monthly)
2. Labour tenant
3. Cash tenant (squatter)
4. Half-shares man
5. Migrant: (*a*) long-term, (*b*) seasonal
6. Daily Labourer: (*a*) long term, (*b*) seasonal
7. Prison Labour: (*a*) farm jails, (*b*) volunteers on parole
8. *Isibalo* labour
9. Landless trekker
10. *Bywoner*
11. Manager
12. Farmer and his family

Full-time workers, who, by 1960,[1] were far and away the biggest group of labourers, lived on the farms with their families and were paid, as they always had been, both in cash and kind. But over the century the ratio of cash to kind increased, both as money wages went up and grazing rights and arable allotments were reduced. By the 1960s no whites belonged to this category as some had done a hundred years before. In times past labour tenants had been required to furnish from 90 to 180 days' labour each year in return for permission to live as farmers on white-owned land. The Natives' Trust and Land Act of 1936 had empowered the State to extend, by proclamation, the period of service required in any district from 90 days to six months. And, as labour and land grew scarcer, this was done in many areas. In Natal, where six months had always been required, the main change occurred after the Second World War. Up until that time the six-months-in/six-months-out labour system had been widespread, but was coming under increasing pressure as more and more men went to work in the cities for the six months 'out', leaving their families on the farms. The farmers' complaint that they were being used as 'incubators of labour for industry'[2] pointed to the fact that, by having to look after the families for all twelve months of the year, they had to bear a cost of the migrant labour system which industry did not. By the 1960s although the six-months'

---

[1] *Statistical Yearbook (1966)*, p. H–31.   [2] *The Star*, 14 Jan. 1954.

pattern still existed in some areas, it was vanishing and being replaced with full-time work paid in cash and kind. Social pressures for ending the system of cash tenants on labour farms increased steadily during the century but it continued to exist despite all laws which, as far back as 1913, made it illegal. However, it seems that labour farms as such were on the decline by 1966 although more and more farms were being left to the sole occupancy of black employees (see Map 4, p. 105). The system of ploughing on half-shares, whereby African men owning cattle and ploughs worked the land for the farmer and handed over half the crop, was common in the Free State and some parts of the eastern Cape before the First World War, but this category of worker too was, as has been shown (see p. 130), greatly reduced by the Natives' Land Act of 1913. The principle of partnership implied in this arrangement was at variance with what whites thought to be the proper place of blacks, and the resulting elimination of this category was a measure of the increasing poverty of a class who had once been relatively wealthy.

Throughout the century migrant workers were part and parcel of South African agriculture and it seems likely that they became more, rather than less, important as time wore on. In the 1860s both in the western Cape and in Natal, a great deal of farm work was done by the long-term migrants, who were brought in under contract for periods of as much as five years. Such labour did not always return home at the end of the contract period, and in Natal particularly, many indentured Indians remained behind. Although it would seem that some contract workers settled in the western Cape others returned to the Transkei, Mozambique, and other areas from which they were brought. Apart from these long-term migrants, there were also seasonal workers. During the 1860s this type of worker seems to have been confined to the teams of shearers and reapers moving through the farms of the eastern Cape and the interior.[1] With the spread of maize into the Free State and Transvaal, more reapers were required, and there grew up a pattern whereby teams of men, women, and children moved in from Basutoland, the Herschel district, and parts of the northern Cape to help with the harvest.[2] By the 1960s, although there seems to have been a decline in the long-term migrant labour coming for periods of three years or more, there was a marked increase in shorter-term migrants who, though predominantly seasonal, might stay for a full year. In the interior of the country there was a great increase in the use of foreign workers who came in without their families[3] and in some areas recruiting was organ-

[1] *Select Committee* (1879), p. 66.
[2] *Report of the Native Farm Labour Committee*, p. 53; P. Whitehead, 'When it's harvest time every-one goes', *Cape Argus*, 18 June 1966.
[3] SABRA, p. 71.

ized on a large scale.[1] In the western Cape, the rapidly expanding production of fruit for export required increasing numbers of contract workers who came predominantly from the Transkei.

Another source of labour throughout the period were the daily labourers who came from near-by villages, towns, reserves, and sometimes even from within the farm itself. Although normally classified as casual labour and generally hired at specific seasons, such as planting, weeding, and harvesting, some of these daily labourers did in fact work on the farm for most of the year. By the 1960s, although the figures varied widely from year to year, the number of African men who worked as casual employees on white farms was of the order of 300,000, while the number of permanent farm workers was approximately twice as large. For African women, however, the proportion of casual to permanent was reversed. Although only 100,000 of them worked permanently on the farms (excluding domestic servants) the number of casual employees, predominantly seasonal workers, was nearly as large as for the men.[2] It seems likely that whereas most of the casual female labour lived on the farms, most of the casual male labour came from elsewhere. Many of those classified as casual workers were in fact migrants under contract rather than daily labourers.

It is not necessary to add much to what has already been written about the remaining categories of workers. Prison labour was one of the important developments after the Second World War. The *isibalo* system of compulsory labour, so unpopular amongst those to whom it was applied in Natal in the nineteenth century, was ended at the time of Union. The landless trekker, the man who moved with his few animals and other scanty possessions from white farm to white farm, was, by the 1960s no wealthier than his great-grandfather, no longer white, and his status was considerably lower than it had once been.[3] But, although they still existed, there were not many such trekkers. The *bywoners* too, were in a class which by 1966 had virtually disappeared. There were still some 50,000 white farm employees but the evidence suggests that most of them were either managers or in some other supervisory position. The old type of *bywoner*, who farmed on shares and earned little in the way of hard cash, was a person whom economic circumstances had forced off the land in the first three decades of the twentieth century. Finally, of course, work (predominantly organizational) was also done by the white farmers themselves and their families.

This breakdown of the different categories of economically active persons on the farms has taken no account of domestic servants, of whom

[1] *The Star*, 15 July 1938; *Rand Daily Mail*, 11 July 1947.
[2] *Statistical Yearbook (1966)*, p. H–31.
[3] R. E. van der Ross, 'Misery of Farm Trekkers', *Cape Times*, 16 July 1959.

in 1960 there were 150,000, two-thirds being African and the rest
Coloured. These people, most of whom were women, were generally the
wives and daughters of men working on the farms, and their presence
in the homestead provided much of the intimacy which permeated
master-servant relationships. Many farmers' wives worked closely with
their servants upon whom they depended a great deal for company.

Apart from the differences in status which these various categories
implied there was also the wide disparity in standard of living. The
economic gap between black and white was enormous and, although it
always existed it seems that it was one which widened rather than
narrowed over the century. In 1866 the average monthly cash wage for
white foremen and head shepherds in the Cape was £2. 18s. 1d., whilst
non-white farm servants, cattle herds, and shepherds earned 12s. 10d.
cash a month. By 1952 white farm employees, including *bywoners*, earned
a monthly sum of £19. 7s. 7d. in the Cape whilst African farm labourers
earned £2. 7s. 10d. Thus, taking no account of the white owners of farms,
the ratio between white and black cash wages had increased from
approximately 5:1 in 1866 to 8:1 in 1952.[1] Few figures are available
about the white farmers' incomes, which varied considerably from farm
to farm, but it seems certain that the majority of whites left on the land
in 1966 enjoyed a far higher standard of living than did their grand-
fathers. This was to be seen most noticeably in housing which, in the
1860s consisted of rude and simple dwellings, often with mud floors.
A century later, however, farmers were living in large brick buildings,
with wooden flooring, running water, and sewerage. Many of these houses
were served with electricity, which came either from the national grid
or from small, privately owned generators. Other indicators of the
growing wealth were clothes, furniture, boarding-school education,
private tennis-courts, motor-cars, and, for a few, aeroplanes. For black
workers, however, the similarities in this regard between the beginning
and the end of the century are more striking than the differences. Despite
the fact that some farmers did a great deal to improve and ensure
adequate housing for their employees it seems true to say that, for the
vast majority, amenities were essentially the same as they had been a
hundred years before. Workers continued to live in wattle and daub
huts, in shacks and (a more recent development) in compounds. They
had no electric light; water came either from an outside tap, or, more
commonly, had to be fetched by bucket from some distance away: and
lavatories, if they existed, were of a pit type. Furniture remained simple
and sparse, and the amount of stock owned by farm workers seems,
generally, to have decreased. Bicycles, radios, and occasional old cars

---

[1] CGH *Blue Book* (1866), p. CC. 2; *Agricultural Census No. 26* (Special Report Series, No. 3),
pp. 3, 14; see also Southern, p. 12.

were the sole evidence among the vast majority of farm workers that the country was becoming wealthier.

It would be misleading to suggest that there is much reliable information about wages, because the little evidence that there is indicates wide variations (particularly in non-monetary income) from farm to farm and area to area. The following table shows the extent to which the non-

TABLE 5

Production or Ownership per African Family on White Farms, 1935/6[1]

Area	Number of families (1000s)	Maize (200 lb. bags)	Sorghum ('Kaffir corn') (200 lb. bags)	Cattle	Goats	Woolled sheep
N.W. Natal	13	1·5	0·3	3·9	2·8	..
N. Natal	13	2·1	0·7	7·3	5·5	..
S.E. Transvaal	27	3·5	0·6	5·1	3·8	0·2
N.W. Transvaal (Waterberg)	8	3·8	1·8	4·4	1·2	..
W. Transvaal (Lichtenburg)	5	10·6	2·1	2·1	0·2	0·5
Northern O.F.S.	15	9·7	..	3·5	0·03	0·9
Central O.F.S.	16	6·1	..	2·3	..	0·8
Southern O.F.S.	2	0·06	..	0·7	0·7	3·1
Eastern Cape (coastal)	11	1·6	0·2	3·7	1·1	0·002
N.E. Cape (Elliot, etc.)	5	0·003	..	1·6	0·2	3·0
Inland Cape (Cradock, etc.)	6	..	..	1·6	1·4	0·8
Griqualand West (Hay, etc.)	6	0·6	0·4	0·8	5·9	1·4

monetary incomes of African farm labourers varied between different parts of the country. In general such variations were not compensated by cash wages. Labourers, in the area lying between Queenstown and Cradock, who grew no grain and who owned very little stock were clearly far worse off than those of the western Transvaal who grew over a ton of maize per family. The table also illustrates the fact that, as the Native Farm Labour Committee pointed out,[2] in the almost exclusively sheep areas the ownership of small stock was discouraged by farmers.

Some idea of the change in income over the time may be gained from Table 6 which shows the average cash wage of a farm labourer in the

[1] Source: *Report of the Native Farm Labour Committee*, pp. 29–40.   [2] Ibid., p. 40.

TABLE 6

Monthly Cash Wages of African Farm Labourers in the Eastern Cape,
1866–1966

Date	Cash	Remarks	Source
1866	14s. 2d.	Average for farm servants, cattle herds, and shepherds in eastern divisions. With board and lodging.	Cape Blue Book (1866) p. CC. 2
1870	12s. 3d.	Ditto	Cape Book Blue (1870) p. CC. 2
1878	10s. to 12s.	Division of George. Average rate for herds and ordinary farm labourers.	Cape Blue Book (1878), Appendix, p. 20
	26s.	Figure for one ostrich farm visited by Trollope. Rations included meat and maize	Trollope, i. 174
1891	10s.	Evidence from Fort Jackson where labourers were provided with cash plus food. Police sergeant considered wages totally inadequate (see p. 122)	Select Committee (1892) Appendix p. x.
1892	6s. to 10s.	Albany district magistrate said, 'This is altogether insufficient to admit of the people clothing themselves with decency.'	Ibid., Appendix p. v
	10s.	Given as the 'ordinary rate'. Daily rations were 2 lb. meat and meal or maize.	Ibid., p. vi
1898/9	12s. 5d.	Average rate on farms in Cape Colony	S.A. Native Races Committee (ed.), p. 123
1905	12s.	Kingwilliamstown area. Wages in kind included one acre of arable land per family, food, sufficient clothing, and medical attention.	S.A. Native Affairs Commission (1903–5), vol. ii, p. 764.
1930	5s. to 15s.	Alexandria area. Food and hut site provided. According to magistrate, living standards had declined over the previous 25 years.	Native Economic Commission (1930–2), p. 189
1932	9s. to 11s.	Adelaide, Bedford, and districts. Minimum was 5s., maximum (graded) 30s. Major grievance of workers that number of stock grazed free was now greatly reduced	Hunter, pp. 508, 513
1937	10s.	'The standard wage' in the Cape Province. Sometimes increased to 15s. Graded wage of 20s. to 30s. paid to 5% of the labourers.	Native Farm Labour Committee (1937–9), p. 41
1943–4	12s.	Dairy farms, eastern Province. Cost of rations, grazing, land, etc., valued at 22s. 9d per month.	Official Year Book No. 24 (1948), p. 307
1952	30s.	Albany district. Wages in kind (excl. housing) valued at 30s. 3d.	Agricultural Census, No. 26 (Special Report Series, No. 3), p. 14

TABLE 6 (cont.)

Date	Cash	Remarks	Source
1957–8	31s. 10d.	Albany and Bathurst districts. Wages in kind (57%) included maize (27%), skim milk (5%), meat (3%) grazing for an average of 5 head of cattle (11%), arable land (3%), clothes (5%), housing (1%), and medical care (2%). Total cost of family (cash and kind) = £7. 7s. 8d (100%)	Roberts, pp. 21, 49
1966	30s. to 45s.	Cathcart district. Starting wage for ordinary labourer was 30s. (tractor driver 60s.) After 5 years it was 45s. One farmer estimated total cost (cash and kind) of each labourer on that farm to be £20 per month.	Personal communication

eastern Cape between 1866 and 1966. The most striking feature of the table is the fact that, apparently, the cash wages of the average farm labourer in the eastern Cape stayed almost constant (in monetary terms) from the discovery of diamonds until the end of the Second World War. Throughout that time, however, it would seem that there were exceptional farmers who paid 25s. a month or more. The trend in the value of wages in kind is more difficult to assess. The evidence from the early 1930s suggests that the number of cattle which labourers were allowed to graze was markedly less than it had once been. After that, however, stock-ownership rose from 3·7 head of cattle per family in 1937 to 5 head twenty years later. In considering cash wages no allowance has been made for the fact that the value of money fell considerably over the hundred years.

Whilst bearing in mind the inadequacy of the two tables (5 and 6) and the fact that they must be used with caution, it is possible to conclude that farm wages remained low. Indeed it is likely that through much of the country the standard of living of farm employees rose very little, if at all, in the century. Whether or not they remained in line with incomes in other sectors was a subject of much debate. Dr. Neethling, for example, argued forcefully[1] that, if due account were taken of earnings in kind, a farm labourer was quite as well off as his urban counterpart. In the absence of detailed statistics, it is impossible to be certain but the vociferous complaints[2] by farmers in the late nineteenth and early twentieth centuries against the mines and the railways, coupled with their anxiety

[1] SABRA (1954), pp. 60–8.
[2] Select Committee (1890), p. 12; South African Native Affairs Commission, 1903–5, vol. ii, p. 763.

at the loss, despite legal barriers, of their labour to industry after the Second World War[1] suggest that, as far as the labourers were concerned, farm incomes lagged behind those in towns throughout the period.

One important kind of wage, not mentioned in the tables, was the wine provided for Coloured farm labourers in the Western Cape. The tot system was fully established in the area by 1866 and the farmers seemed to be generally agreed that their labourers would not work without their five or six daily tots.[2] In winter, when the wine provided was strong, the ration was somewhat less, although some farmers gave a tot of brandy on cold mornings. Two sociological studies[3] at the University of Stellenbosch found the system little changed by the end of the Second World War, and in 1966 it was still firmly entrenched.

Almost as important, with regard to the supply of labour, as wages was the reputation of a farmer concerning his relations with his employees. It is difficult to generalize about those less tangible but very real considerations. However, two letters which appeared in a Johannesburg newspaper in 1947 make clear the extremes between which conditions varied. The one letter, from an Afrikaans farmer in the Orange Free State, outlined an experiment in labour co-operation, which he had begun during the 1930s. Under the scheme his labourers were provided with four-roomed cottages, a cash wage varying between fourteen shillings and two pounds per month, a monthly ration of food which included ten pounds of meat, a morgen of land ploughed and planted with maize for each worker, and a vegetable garden which the wives had to weed. In addition, a profit sharing incentive of a shilling per bag of maize harvested on the farm was paid into a common pool, which the labourers subsequently shared out. The workers were granted the right of engaging and dismissing staff. During the ten years in which the scheme had been working the farmer had had no labour troubles, and great financial success. He had enjoyed his farming. The other letter said: 'To speak of better wages and housing is nonsense. All the wages and housing schemes will not change the native. He will remain dirty, lazy, and thoroughly dishonest. He does not understand decent civilized treatment. He can, and does, understand a good hiding. If we want the natives to be law-abiding, let us speak to them in the language they understand: the language of the sjambok, administered frequently and with vigour.'[4] Twenty years later the profit-sharing scheme was still

---

[1] Cape Argus, 1 July 1964.   [2] Select Committee (1856), pp. 28, 37; Select Committee (1879), p. 18.

[3] J. B. du Toit, Plaasarbeiders: 'n Sosiologiese Studie van 'n Groep Kleurling-Plaasarbeiders in die Distrik Tulbagh, unpublished M.A. thesis, Stellenbosch, 1947; A. Uys, Plaasarbeiders: 'n Sosiologiese Studie van 'n Groep Kleurling-Plaasarbeiders in die Distrik Stellenbosch, unpublished M.A. thesis, Stellenbosch, 1947; for a discussion of the arguments for and against the tot system see Uys, pp. 193 ff.

[4] Rand Daily Mail, 8 Sept. 1947.

operating, but had not been widely emulated. Although it was by no means typical, the extent of sjambokking or whipping farm labourers, sometimes even to death, remained horrifying.

Turning now from the social framework to the economic structure of agriculture, the most striking change over the century was the increase in aggregate production. With the exception of one or two commodities, there are few figures for agricultural production in the country prior to Union, and it is difficult to assess with any accuracy what happened to output immediately after the discovery of diamonds. However, it would seem that the reponse was sluggish, and that it was not until the beginning of the twentieth century that productivity began to increase. The following table shows the change in production over the four decades that followed the First World War.

TABLE 7

Output on White-owned farms: 1916/19 to 1956/59
(1936/39 = 100)[1]

	1916/19	1926/29	1936/9	1946/9	1956/9
Maize	48	73	100	101	155
Wheat	56	49	100	120	194
Potatoes	58	71	100	152	185
Groundnuts	25	62	100	485	1,378
Fruit	27	45	100	123	253
Sugar	28	59	100	103	198
Total, Crops:	54	71	100	123	193
Wool	53	108	100	84	118
Lamb, mutton and goat's meat	73	84	100	95	112
Beef	45	79	100	149	159
Dairy products	51	67	100	144	217
Total, Livestock:	57	88	100	118	161
Total, Agriculture	54	77	100	121	178

Maize doubled in output between the two World Wars, and then remained static until 1948 when Government action in raising the price led to a rapid increase in production. Wheat output declined during the 1920s and then, following the introduction of quantitative controls upon imports in 1930, more than doubled in the next ten years, slowed down during the war years, and then went on increasing rapidly. Wool, which

[1] Source: United Nations, *Economic Survey of Africa* (E/CN/14/370, Ethiopia, n.d.) p. 194. 1916/19 is the average of the three years 1916/17; 1917/18; 1918/19: similarly for other periods.

doubled in output during the 1920s, was hard hit by the double blows of drought and depression in 1932/3 and declined steadily until the astronomical prices of the Korean War boom led to the further increase in output. Dairy products rose steadily during the period, while fruit and sugar production increased more rapidly, doubling their output in every decade except the one spanning the Second World War. The commodity which grew slowest was mutton (including lamb and goat's meat), whilst the one that grew most spectacularly was groundnuts, which, like sugar and fruit, quadrupled during the inter-war years, and then went on to increase by a multiple of thirteen in the following two decades.

Such increases in production were remarkable in a country not naturally endowed with great agricultural potential. What were the causes of this development? Ever since van Riebeeck had come to the Cape to establish a victualling station white farming had been market orientated. But, as men moved slowly inland, away from the sea routes, some of them lost touch with the agricultural (though not with the ivory) markets, and became subsistence farmers. Nevertheless, agricultural development, although slow, was taking place prior to the mineral discoveries. Wool had become a major export from as far inland as the Orange River; maize was being widely grown in the eastern Cape; and sugar had been chosen as the basis of agriculture in Natal well before the economic tempo was quickened by the discoveries of diamonds and gold. It so happened (not altogether by coincidence) that these discoveries coincided with the closing of the frontiers so that, from this time on, population density on the land began to increase steadily. Thus it would be possible to argue[1] that the change in agricultural output that took place during the following century was due to the powerful force of population pressure. Important though this was, however, it would seem that there were two other factors which were far more significant: both of them related to the minerals. The one lay in the stimulus of new markets; the other was due to the subsidization of agriculture by other sectors, notably mining. The effectiveness of a market in fostering agricultural growth in South Africa may be seen in the history of the ostrich feather industry which was one of the country's major export earners for forty years before 1913. Responding to the market stimulus, farmers acted perhaps too eagerly in their desire to meet the new demand. Land prices in Oudtshoorn district rose spectacularly and, despite warnings,[2] numbers of producers placed far too much trust in the whims of women's fashion. But before it crashed, the ostrich feather market stimulated the beginnings of irrigation as farmers had to grow lucerne to feed their birds. This, in turn, enabled dairy farming to replace ostriches.[3] Another

[1] Cf. E. Boserup, *The Conditions of Agricultural Growth.*   [2] *Farmers' Weekly*, 15 Mar. 1911.
[3] Du Toit, p. 32.

example of the effectiveness of a new market in stimulating production was the expansion of maize output due to the building of railways and the subsequent rating policy.

The history of maize also serves to illustrate the importance of subsidies in the development of the country's agriculture. It has already been shown (p. 138) that the help provided to maize farmers in the early 1930s led to a massive increase in production from an annual average of 18·7 million bags between 1927 and 1929 to an average of 25·5 million bags in 1937–9. And the rise in the maize price in 1948 led to an increase in annual production from 24·8 million bags over the three years 1946–8, to 57·1 million bags in 1961–3.[1] Subsidization was a costly policy. Between 1948 and 1966 the Department of Agricultural Economics and Marketing spent an average of R31 million a year in subsidies and rebates. Of this R13·2 million was for wheat, R10·1 million for maize, R2·9 million for dairy products, particularly butter, and R2·3 million for fertilizer.[2] By 1967 the total amount spent on subsidizing white farmers had risen to R66·8 million which was almost double the public funds being spent on African education.[3] The growth of the economy in this manner provides a fascinating contrast with those countries which used the increase in agricultural production to finance development in other sectors.

Yet a nagging question still remains. To what extent was South African agriculture, despite its enormous expansion in the half-century after the First World War, economically viable? 'South Africa', wrote a noted economic historian in 1940, 'is not an agricultural country. . . . Without subsidy and under conditions of free competition much of the land could not be economically cultivated, and many of the agricultural and pastoral products could make no headway against the products of New Zealand, Canada, the Argentine, or the United States.'[4] There is little doubt that without the special tariff policies devised in the years before the Second World War some of South Africa's important export commodities would have found international competition too keen. And other commodities, particularly wheat, would not have been able to compete, even in the home market. But to say this does not really answer the question: for there are few countries whose agricultural policy is based on purely economic considerations. The most one can say is that without the subsidies provided on exports by the home consumers of some commodities, without tariff protection against competitive imports of others, and without the direct assistance to farmers in trouble, which

---

[1] *Handbook of Agricultural Statistics*, p. 53; Statistical Year Book, 1966, p. J. 10.
[2] Supplementary Data to the Abstract of Agricultural Statistics of the Republic of South Africa (Jan. 1969), p. 104.   [3] Ibid.; Horrell, *Survey*, 1967, pp. 230–1.
[4] De Kiewiet, p. 259.

would have been more difficult without the tax revenue from the
gold-mines, South African agriculture would have expanded far less than
it did. In assessing whether this policy would provide long-term benefits
to outweigh the short-term losses it is necessary to consider some of the
weaknesses in agriculture which its very success tended to hide.

One of the most disturbing features about farming in South Africa
was the process of soil erosion. Despite the harsh warnings of the Drought
Investigation Commission in 1923 (see p. 134), despite the assessment of
independent observers in 1939 that 'A national catastrophe, due to soil
erosion, is perhaps more imminent in the Union of South Africa than in
any other country'[1] and despite the Soil Conservation Act of 1946, the
rape of the soil continued. In 1953 the Department of Agriculture published a carefully documented paper which showed the alarming pace
at which desert conditions were encroaching, in a north-easterly direction, into the heart of the country.[2] During the 1960s it was estimated
that some four hundred million tons of scarce topsoil were being lost
annually, almost enough to fill one of the country's largest reservoirs
every second year.[3] This devastation was due partly to the fact that
insufficient resources were being devoted to conservation but also, in
most areas, to wasteful and short-sighted farming practices. Over-
grazing, failure to rotate crops, and the State-subsidized extension of
commercial cultivation, particularly of maize in the Orange Free State,
with little regard to ecological balance, all played their destructive part.
Despite much good conservation work that had been done, particularly
after the passing of the soil Conservation Act and the establishment of
the Veld Trust, the evidence suggests that the country was still fighting
a losing battle. The long-term consequences remained ominous.

A second major weakness in the agricultural sector lay in the inefficiency with which labour was used. The following table shows the

TABLE 8

Efficiency of Labour in Agriculture, 1960[4]

Country	% Labour (males) in agriculture	% Share of agri- culture in G.D.P.	Ratio
U.K.	6	4	1·5:1
U.S.A.	9	4	2·3:1
Japan	26	15	1·7:1
S. Africa	35	11	3·0:1
Turkey	61	45	1·4:1

[1] Jacks and Whyte, p. 264.   [2] J. P. H. Acocks, *Veld Types of South Africa*.
[3] 'Save our Soil', *Financial Mail*, 5 Apr. 1968.
[4] South African Agricultural Union, *Memorandum* (1967), Table XVII.

extent to which the sector carried a far higher proportion of the adult male population than its share in the gross domestic product appeared to warrant. The above table does not provide an accurate measure of the efficiency with which labour was used on white South African farms as the figures include economically active males living in the reserves which, for special reasons, including oscillating migration and the pattern of land tenure (see pp. 55–62), were notoriously un-productive. Nevertheless the figures do reflect the relative under-utilization of farm labour which, in the opinion of the South African Agricultural Union, was 'probably the most important single factor . . . hampering efficiency in agriculture'.[1]

Another structural weakness was the extent of indebtedness. The aggregate debt of the agricultural sector in 1966 was estimated to be of the order of one thousand million rand[2] which was nearly 12 per cent of the gross national product in that year.[3] Whilst many of the loans were advanced to credit-worthy farmers the Government found it necessary to set up a special department of Agricultural Credit and Land Tenure, whose most important function during the 1960s was lending money to non-credit-worthy farmers in an attempt to achieve the finan-cial rehabilitation of those who, for one reason or another, found them-selves in difficulties.[4]

In addition to these weaknesses there were a number of other issues which posed questions for the future. 'The supply of the produce mar-kets', van Biljon had written in 1938, '. . . is the acme of disorganised distribution.'[5] In 1966 distribution was still a crucial problem. Evidence of widespread malnutrition[6] in the midst of an economy which was over-producing many food staples was disturbing. Piling up oranges to rot, pouring thousands of gallons of milk down the drain,[7] and exporting maize well below the home price, in a society where kwashiorkor, pel-lagra and marasmus were rampant, where gastro-enteritis and tuber-culosis were exacerbated by malnutrition, and where in one Pretoria hospital alone more than nine children died every week in 1966 from

---

[1] South African Agricultural Union, *Memorandum* (1967), p. 91.

[2] Ibid., p. 16.

[3] In the absence of an estimate of the country's stock of capital the less meaningful, but none the less instructive, comparison with G.N.P. has been used.

[4] South African Agricultural Union, *Memorandum* (1967), p. 17.

[5] Van Biljon (1939), p. 135.

[6] J. F. Potgieter, S. A. Fellingham, and M. L. Neser, 'Incidence of Nutritional Deficiency Diseases among the Bantu and Coloured Population in South Africa as Reflected by the Results of a Questionnaire Survey', *South African Medical Journal*, 40 (22), 1966; W. Wittman, A. D. Moodie, S. A. Fellingham, and J. D. L. Hansen, 'An Evaluation of the Relationship Between Nutritional Status and Infection by Means of a Field Study', ibid., 41 (27), 1967; P. J. Pretorius, 'The Clinical Nature and Extent of Protein Malnutrition in South Africa'. ibid., 42 (36), 1968.

[7] *H.A.D.*, 1968, col. 832, but cf. *Financial Mail*, 11 July, 1969, p. 109.

gastro-enteritis, broncho-pneumonia, or malnutrition, betrayed a grave
flaw in the socio-economic framework. Indeed the continuing poverty
amongst farm labourers and their families was one measure of South
Africa's failure to face the welfare consequences of rapid and disrupting
economic growth, and was also a pointer to the vast sea of unresolved
and potentially explosive tensions between those who had gained substantially over the century and those who had not.

Another source of potential conflict lay in the spectre of unemployment. In all countries the proportion of labour in the agricultural sector
has declined as a result of industrialization, and in many of them the
stage has been reached where the absolute number employed on
the land falls as well. South Africa was no exception. The proportion of
the total population living in the rural areas (including the reserves) fell
from 76 per cent in 1904 to 53 per cent in 1960. In absolute terms the
number of whites on the land fell by 20 per cent, from 637,000 in 1936
to 507,000 in 1960.[1] For blacks as the following table shows, the numbers

TABLE 9

African Farm Labourers, 1911–1952[2]

Date	Nos. employed (1000s)
1911[3]	213
1918[4]	255
1925	341
1930	361
1937	403
1946	568
1950	637
1952	592

rose steadily until 1950. By this time no less than 30 per cent of black
South Africans lived on white farms. Whether or not the fall in
employment between 1950 and 1952 marked a permanent downturn or
was merely the result of weather variations is not immediately clear.
However, subsequent figures do suggest that, by the 1960s a turning-
point had been reached. Over the five years 1954–8 the average number
of people of all races regularly employed on farms was 828,000: for the
next five-year period, 1959–63 the average annual employment was

---

[1] *Statistical Year Book, 1964* p. A–12.

[2] Numbers employed during the last month of each census year. Source: *Handbook of Agricultural Statistics, 1904–1950*, p. 11. [3] Occupiers included.

[4] Average number of labourers for the 12 months ended 30 June 1918.

826,000.[1] With improved methods of production and increasing use of machinery it seemed that South African agriculture would absorb no more labour.

Indeed, as for example in the Mississippi delta, it appeared that economic forces were pushing labourers off the land in a two-stage process. It has been shown[2] that technological innovation (e.g. tractors) results first of all in a saving of unskilled hand labour, except for the summer weeding and full harvesting seasons. Under such circumstances, as Day has argued, the maintenance of unskilled labour on farms all the year round is seen to be uneconomic, and it becomes cheaper to use a 'combination of resident wage labor, and labor hired from near-by villages'.

Thus the first consequence of this technological development is to push unskilled labourers living on the farms to some place where, while they will remain available for seasonal requirements, they will not be a drain on the farmer's resources during those portions of the year when he no longer needs them. In the light of this analysis, and given the stage which South Africa's agriculture had reached by 1966, it was not surprising to find the country's Agricultural Union arguing[3] that the solution of the labour problems in the farming sector lay in setting up a recruiting organization which would provide farms with contract labour. For in the peculiar political circumstances of South Africa labourers pushed off the land during this first stage did not, as in Mississippi, have the right to settle in near-by villages. They were compelled to go 'back to the homeland'. But the reserves were full; and there was no room for people from the farms. Thus, in response to these economic changes, the State set about the establishment of 'resettlement villages' on the borders of reserves in the remoter parts of the county (see map). In such places unemployed families from farms, small dorps, and towns, were settled in areas often far removed from the centres of economic activity.[4] However, they were a ready pool for that contract labour which the farmers required.

But although it could be argued that the expansion of a contract system would improve the distribution of farm labour which a century of pass laws and other restrictions had rendered immobile, yet the spectre of unemployment remained. For the pushing of 'redundant' people to the resettlement villages was only the first stage; the second was still to come. As new technology spread through the agricultural sector, it seemed virtually certain that the demand for labour, which by 1966 had probably declined due to mechanization in all except the weeding and

---

[1] *Agricultural Census, No. 37*, p. 2.

[2] R. H. Day, 'Technological Change and the Sharecropper', *American Economic Review*, lvii (3), 1967.

[3] South African Agricultural Union, *Memorandum* (1967), p. 70

[4] Horrell, *Survey 1967*, p. 181, supplemented by unpublished information.

harvesting seasons, would soon start to fall off in these peak periods as well. The accompanying chart[1] shows the alternative labour require- ments of maize farmers in the Transvaal highveld during 1962/3 depend- ing upon whether they used combine harvesters or unskilled labourers for reaping. It was estimated[2] that the farmers who used combines saved an average of 70 per cent of the labour involved in the harvesting and threshing process. The other peak demand, during December and January, was for labour to hoe the fields, and this labour-intensive

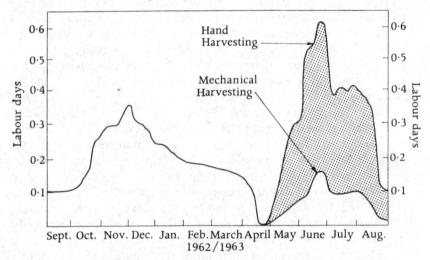

Weekly distribution of labour requirements of maize per morgen in the Transvaal Highveld. Two methods of reaping, 1962/3.

technique too was in process of being replaced by weed sprays. But where, during this second stage of the push from the land, were those made 'redundant' to go? In other countries they had tended to drift into the towns and be absorbed in the industrial expansion there, or, as in Latin America, become part of the urban under-employed. But in South Africa official policy was to discourage both the employment and settlement of blacks in the urban growth centres and to promote the substitution of capital for labour. The Government's stated solution was to move people to the distant resettlement villages and then to encourage industry to site itself near this labour. But economists remained sceptical as to whether industrialists would in fact re-locate to such places. With no rights to live in the reserves, or in the towns, or on the farms where they grew up, the unskilled sons of unskilled farm labourers were liable

[1] The chart is taken, with acknowledgement, from J. J. van Wyk et al., 'Mechanize our Maize Harvesting Process', Farming in South Africa, June 1964.
[2] Ibid., p. 17.

to find themselves unemployed. And their number, which appeared likely to increase rather than diminish, was another sign of the hidden weaknesses in an otherwise seemingly strong economy.

One of the major themes in this chapter has been to examine the way in which South Africans living on the land responded to the changes sparked off by the mineral discoveries. Although there were many remarkable agricultural developments over the century, there were also, as has been shown, a number of severe dislocations which a more perceptive assessment of the future might have mitigated. With hindsight it is easy to be wise; nevertheless one of the features of the period was the number of changes which caught the farming community unawares and ill prepared. Not all the changes could have been foreseen, but an understanding of certain trends would have enabled the society to ease its transition from a fairly simple pastoral state to a complex industrialized economy. Although considerably more was understood about South African agriculture in 1966 than had been the case a century before, it was by no means clear that the farming community as a whole was any more prepared for the future dislocating changes that seemed likely to occur than it had been when the unexpected discovery of diamonds plunged it into the swirling waters of rapid economic growth.

IV

THE GROWTH OF TOWNS

1. *Introduction*

IN 1870 South Africa was overwhelmingly an agrarian society and there were hardly twenty towns with populations exceeding 1,000 inhabitants. Of the major towns Cape Town, Durban, East London, and Port Elizabeth were ports and commercial centres, while Pietermaritzburg, Pretoria, and Bloemfontein were administrative centres. Scattered throughout the hinterland were isolated hamlets or *dorps*, many of which had arisen around churches founded mainly by the Nederduitse Gereformeerde Kerk (N. G. Kerk). By 1850 there were forty-five of these *dorps* which served the spiritual and commercial needs of rural farming communities.[1]

Kimberley was a portent of changes that were dramatically to transform the rural communities of South Africa into an industrialized society in less than two generations. After the discovery of diamonds in 1867 the arid land of Kimberley was transformed into a seething, polyglot community of fortune-seekers and labourers. By 1874 some 50,000 people of different races and nationalities made Kimberley second in size to Cape Town.[2] The discovery of gold on the Witwatersrand in 1886 led similarly to the mushrooming of a community of miners.

The growth of the mining industry, and its stimulus to the development of other industrial and commercial enterprises, was the first major impetus to large-scale urbanization. The dimensions of the demographic changes that followed are shown in the table on p. 173.

Industrialization in South Africa was attended by certain unique features. It did not arise out of a gradual improvement in mechanical techniques but came rather as a sudden irruption amidst rural peoples. In England industrialization and the growth of towns had been gradual, and an agricultural revolution had preceded the industrial revolution. Farming had been modernized and oriented towards the market, and domestic manufacture was diffused throughout the countryside. Agriculture could feed the growing towns and its surplus labour, driven off the land, could man the rising industries.[3]

---

[1] J. R. Albertyn, *Land en Stad*, p. 79.

[2] H. M. Robertson, '150 Years of Economic Contact between Black and White', *SAJE*, 3 (1935), 9.

[3] E. J. Hobsbawm, *The Age of Revolution*, p. 31.

TABLE I

Urban populations as percentages of the total population

	1890–1	1904	1911	1921	1936	1946	1951	1960
Whites	35·8	53	51·6	55·8	65·2	74·5	78·4	83·6
Africans	Not	13	12·6	12·5	17·3	23·7	27·2	31·8
Coloureds	avail-	46	46·0	45·8	53·9	60·9	64·7	68·3
Indians	able		46·0	30·9	66·3	71·3	77·5	83·2
		25	24·7	25·1	31·4	38·4	42·6	47·0

Source: Census Reports.[1]

A legacy of conflict between the different sections of the population gave urbanization in South Africa a peculiar configuration. For rural Africans and Afrikaners, industries and the towns that followed were the creation of foreigners whom they mistrusted. Africans attributed to the whites the growing landlessness and poverty that was to drive them to the towns in ever-larger numbers. It was a consequence of subjugation. Afrikaners blamed the English for rural poverty and the disruption of the *boerelewe*. This, too, was a consequence of subjugation. An Afrikaner nationalist writing in 1942 said: 'The whole problem of our impoverishment, like all our other problems, is part of the history of conflict between two cultures. . . . '[2]

Tensions that arose in other conditions, in the frontier wars between white colonists and African peoples, or from Afrikaners' attempts to free themselves from British domination, were carried over and compounded in new urban settings. These conflicts in a diverse and divided society markedly affected the process of urbanization and partially obscured the truth that the towns were co-operative enterprises that reflected the ever-closer intertwining of all groups in a common society. While the towns developed as multi-racial communities the interaction between the groups tended to be seen in competitive terms.

The nature of the contact between the colour groups was conditioned by local policies. The Cape had inherited a liberal tradition of formal equality before the law and a non-racial franchise in central and local government. Non-whites were viewed as potentially equal citizens. In the Transvaal, and the Orange Free State (the northern states), and also in Natal, there was greater emphasis on white domination. The different effects on urban life of these rival philosophies is reflected in reports on Cape Town and Johannesburg made early in the present

[1] For criticisms of census reports see H. A. Shannon, 'Urbanization, 1904–1936', *SAJE*, 5 (1937), 164–190; D. H. Reader, *The Black Man's Portion*, pp. 41–2; and S. T. van der Horst, *African Workers in Town*, p. 35.

[2] J. H. Coetzee, *Verarming en Oorheersing*, Foreword (trans.).

century. Maurice S. Evans, writing in 1911, thought that a Natal resident who visited Cape Town would see

a toleration of colour and social admixture to which he is quite unaccustomed; it is evident in the streets, on the tramcars, in the railway stations, public offices, and in places of entertainment. Should he take a walk in Plein Street on a fine Saturday evening he will witness a sight impossible in an Eastern town such as Durban or Pietermaritzburg. The street is crowded, footway and roadway alike full of strollers, all shades and all colours, but, generally speaking, all neatly dressed and well behaved. As a rule whites and coloured people keep apart and do not mix, but there are very many exceptions; he will . . . not infrequently see cases corroborative of the miscegenation between the races of which he has been informed. Young white men will be seen walking with well-dressed coloured girls, and an older European may often be seen with coloured wife and children of varying shades. . . . The doors of a Bioscope entertainment are open, and the crowd awaiting admission and jostling each other as they get tickets, includes representatives of every colour from the light-haired fair-complexioned Scandinavian sailor or English work-man to the sooty-black of the Shangaan, and if he enters the overcrowded room and braves the fœtid atmosphere, he will find no distinction made, all and every colour occupy the same seats, cheek by jowl, and sometimes on each other's knees.[1]

In Johannesburg, however, wrote a Cape journalist in 1910,

the natives . . . are already kept in their places with rigour that would surprise you. One result is that they have no footing in the public life of the community outside certain menial forms of labour. . . . 'The nigger' . . . is not tolerated, except, so to speak, as a hewer of wood and a drawer of water. . . . I am only just becoming accustomed never to seeing 'snuff-and-butter' (Mr. Merriman's expression) and mahogany-coloured complexions at public meetings, and in the various other phases of life, from which, in the Cape, the colour is rarely absent.[2]

To another visitor 'the Rand showed better than anything else the difficulty of a composite society in which the two races live side by side, depend upon one another, cannot separate and cannot fuse'.[3] Cape Town, as these accounts suggest and succeeding sections will show, was unique among South African towns in the extent to which it was racially integrated. The history of subsequent interaction between the different groups who constituted the urban communities reflects the opposition between rival policies, and the victory of the 'northern tradition'.

Economic forces drove people to the towns, and after 1870 the main arena of conflict was the industrial labour market. With the development of an organized white, skilled, labour force pressing for preferential

[1] M. S. Evans, *Black and White in South East Africa*, pp. 296–7.
[2] *New Nation*, I (5), (1910), 8–9.
[3] Dr. M. J. Bonn, in 1907. Quoted by H. M. Robertson, *South Africa—Economic and Political Aspects*, p. 31.

treatment against the competition of white and non-white unskilled workers, and, in turn, competition between the latter two groups, conflicts between classes, races, and language groups continually recur. 'Hitherto the native problem has been one of how to keep the restless kaffir tribes peaceful. Today it takes another form—that of an economic struggle for employment. It is an industrial problem often represented by the question: 'Is South Africa to be a white man's country?' For it is the people who do the work who in the long run will be masters of the land.'[1]

The history of South African towns does not easily lend itself to division into separate epochs, and for this reason the following account has been divided by topic rather than period.

The process of urbanization of all racial groups is comparable, but it started later for African than for white and Coloured people and the movement of Africans has been deliberately delayed by Government control. This chapter is concerned with movement to town, the reasons for that movement, and the growth of a distinct community. New arrivals in town and temporary migrants may live in the urban community without being townsmen in their ideas and values, but there can be no doubt that many Africans, as well as white and Coloured people, are now townsmen proper.

The drift of rural people to the towns was the combined effect of the push of rural poverty and the pull of rapidly expanding industries, thirsty for labour. The push-pull mechanism affected all groups in all parts of South Africa (see pp. 25, 34–5, 64, 131–2).

It is impossible to say how many whites forced off the land went directly to the towns, because official statistics give only the Province of origin of urban dwellers. Commenting on the preliminary 1931 Census figures Grosskopf suggested that 'there is no clear statistical evidence that the rural exodus meant that all these people went to urban areas. In earlier years many undoubtedly migrated to other farming regions.'[2] In 1918 a significant increase in population was recorded in the areas of the south coast of the Cape.[3] After 1924 some went to the diamond diggings along the Vaal River and in Lichtenburg.[4] Evidence taken by a Select Committee of the House of Assembly in 1913 showed that recruits for unskilled work on the railways came from the smaller towns and villages rather than directly from the land.[5] 'In case of failure or ejection from the land, men would first make for the nearest dorp, and later get to the towns. . . .'[6] The mobility of the rural poor was increased by the extension of railways. 'Formerly the very poorest families, who

---

[1] *The State*, 2 (1909), 15.
[2] J. F. W. Grosskopf, *Rural Impoverishment and Rural Exodus*, p. 9.
[3] W. M. MacMillan, *Complex South Africa*, p. 38.
[4] Ibid.　　　　　[5] Ibid.　　　　　[6] Ibid.

owned no means of transport, had generally not been able to get away from their birthplaces.'[1]

It has been shown that the major cause of white urbanization was an agrarian crisis of major dimensions. The pull of the towns was mainly economic but they had other attractions for some: 'Here I earn more money in a month than in a whole year on the farm. And then there are many, many facilities that I never knew in the country; a pretty house, water, light, many shops for making purchases, schools for my children, and we live near the church.'[2] There were also better medical facilities and more charitable institutions. For some town life meant an escape from the isolation of rural life.[3]

Afrikaners were the main white group affected by the rural poverty, constituting some 90 per cent of the 300,000 persons found to be 'very poor' by the Carnegie Commission in 1932.[4] Between 1936 and 1951 the Afrikaans-speaking proportion of the white rural population declined from 86 per cent to 82·2 per cent. Afrikaners became a predominantly urban people, constituting in 1960 51 per cent of the urban white population as compared with 44 per cent in 1936. By 1960 slightly less than half of the urban Afrikaners were concentrated in the smaller urban centres, many of which are *dorps*.[5]

The pattern of white townward migration was significantly different from that of Africans. 'The earning possibilities of the children, more particularly the girls, play an important part, especially in the drifts to the larger cities, for in the country the daughter of a *bywoner* is seldom able to contribute anything to the family income. The children are often the first to migrate to a town, the parents following afterwards.'[6] Between 1921 and 1951 an annual average of over 500 more females than males left the rural areas.[7] Despite frequent hankerings for return to the country, urbanization tended to be permanent.

Prior to the industrial era white agricultural interests had consistently exerted pressure to obtain African labour from the reserves. 'It seems impossible for a body of white men to live in proximity to the coloured races, without a conviction that as the dominant people, they have a right to command the services of the less civilised. . . .'[8] Complaints about the shortage of African labour were voiced in all parts of the

[1] Grosskopf, p. 38.
[2] Letter from an urban Afrikaner, quoted by J. R. Albertyn, *My Eie Boeresitplekkie*, p. 7 (trans.).   [3] Ibid., p. 8.
[4] *Joint Findings and Recommendations of the Carnegie Commission* para. 9, Grosskopf p. vii.
[5] *Report of the Commission of Inquiry into European Occupancy of Rural Areas (du Toit Commission)*, para. 137.
[6] Grosskopf, p. 184.   [7] *Du Toit Commission*, para. 129.
[8] Lieutenant-Governor Scott (of Natal) to the Secretary of State for the Colonies, Lord Stanley, 2 June 1858.

country. The farmers were later joined by the mining industry. Implicit in their demands was the assumption that Africans had no right to continue as self-sufficient and independent farmers because this conflicted with white interests.

With the rise of industry in the 1870s and a great investment of capital, the demand for labour swelled enormously. Many believed that the traditional African social system was the main obstacle to meeting the shortage.

The rise of industries in South Africa has . . . created a demand for industrial workers among nomadic or pastoral peoples, who until Europeans came into contact with them, were ignorant of the uses of money and who, therefore, cannot be dragged suddenly into the industrial labour market by the ordinary law of supply and demand. The existing labour scarcity might indeed have been expected, for it is not likely that a savage people, who before the advent of Europeans lived their own life, in which industrial employment had no place, should at once acquire the needs and habits of industrial communities and come out voluntarily to meet the labour demand which the introduction of such communities into their midst has created. The only pressing needs of a savage are those of food and sex, and the conditions of native life in Africa are such that these are as a rule easily supplied.[1]

The debate turned on how the conditions under which Africans occupied land could be changed to meet labour requirements. In the Cape, the Glen Grey Act of 1894, with its provisions for taxation and individual tenure, had been aimed at stimulating the labour supply. 'The abolition of native locations and of native reserves like Basutoland, Swaziland, etc., and the expropriation of the land for white settlements was also suggested, as well as proposals for the distribution of the natives on the land held by white owners.'[2] A conference of Colonial representatives at Bloemfontein in 1903 had recommended the creation of settlements of Africans near towns, but witnesses before the Transvaal Labour Commission of 1904 rejected the idea, 'mainly on the ground that its consequent evils would outweigh its advantageous effect on the labour supply'.[2]

The 1903–5 Native Affairs Commission considered the question of land-tenure exhaustively. While not convinced that the Glen Grey System had achieved its aims, it recommended none the less the encouragement of a movement in the direction of individual land-holdings.[3] It considered also 'that where found practicable the formation of labour locations, where the Native could reside with his family near his employment, would largely tend to diminish the number of those intermittent

[1] *Report of the Transvaal Labour Commission* (London, 1904), Cmd. 1894, para. 70.
[2] Ibid., para. 93.
[3] *South African Native Affairs Commission, 1903–5, Report*, 5 vols. (hereafter *1903–5 Report*), i. 27.

workers in whom absence from their families induces a spirit of restlessness and disinclination to remain in continuous employment'.[1]

The flow of Africans to the towns came not only from the African areas but also from the white-owned farms. The 1903–5 Commission estimated that there were 1,398,787 Africans on these farms (as opposed to 2,458,281 in reserves).[2] Farmers who gave evidence before the Commission complained that the attractions of the towns, the high wages paid in mining centres and ports, and unregulated squatting prevented them from obtaining adequate labour.[3] Competition for African labour between industry and farming had existed in the nineteenth century and was to be a recurrent theme in subsequent years.

Official statistics do not show the number of Africans migrating from farms to towns. An analysis in 1955 of patterns of townward migration among 118 East London Africans showed that eighteen had come from white-owned farms, seven of whom had originally migrated from a reserve to a farm.[4] In 1953 a study of 348 African workers in a commercial concern in Johannesburg showed, by analysis of past job histories, a shift in employment from farm-work, mine labour, and domestic service to industrial and commercial employment.[5] In 1950 a survey among 156 Durban African workers showed that a higher proportion of men from farms brought their wives to Durban than those who came from reserves.[6]

Economic necessity accounted mainly for the townward movement of Africans. The towns also provided an escape for those who found tribal life dull and its controls irksome. A study of labour migration from Bechuanaland showed that a spell of working in a town had come to be widely regarded as part of a youth's initiation into manhood. It was socially prestigious, and, further, it enhanced a man's attraction to women.[7] Of 300 African males in unskilled and semi-skilled jobs in Pretoria 84 per cent gave economic reasons for seeking town employment and there was hardly any evidence that urban earnings were sought to make improvements to rural homes.[8]

Indians and Coloured people, as the statistics show, have also been swept up in the townward migration. After completing their terms as indentured labourers on the sugar farms of Natal, Indians settled in Durban or the surrounding peri-urban areas, or in the coastal sugar towns. The peri-urban dwellers were mostly market-gardeners or small fruit farmers. 'Owing to their generally low level of income, to the restrictions upon the purchase of land by Indians, and to the absorption of market-gardening areas for industrial purposes, the land was

[1] *1903–5 Report* i. 83.   [2] Ibid.; *Annexures*, 27.   [3] Ibid., 82.
[4] B. A. Pauw, *The Second Generation*, p. 3.   [5] E. Hellmann, *Sellgoods*, p. 20.
[6] Department of Economics, University of Natal, *The African Factory Worker*, p. 108.
[7] I. Schapera, *Migrant Labour and Tribal Life*, pp. 115–21.
[8] G. M. E. Leistner, 'Patterns of Urban Bantu Labour', *SAJE*, 32 (1964), 255.

unable to support the growing Indian population.'[1] Indians who had established themselves in the later decades of the nineteenth century as market-gardeners around Durban were greatly affected by the city's expansion which caused garden land to become valuable for industrial and residential purposes. The Indians in Pietermaritzburg and other Natal towns 'abandoned gardening when their holdings became too valuable for agricultural purposes and no alternative land was available'.[2] Many moved into urban occupations, as did the younger people and those who found agricultural work too heavy and unremunerative.

The urbanization of rural Coloured people dates from the early nineteenth century. One effect of Ordinance 50 of 1828 (which abolished laws that tied 'Free Persons of Colour' to the land) was to accelerate the movement of Coloured people to the towns and villages.[3] A further townward migration resulted from the emancipation of slaves that had been completed in 1838.[4] Gradual urbanization continued throughout the nineteenth century and proceeded rapidly as agriculture sank into the crisis of the twentieth century. A summary of the causes of the movement to the towns by an official Commission in 1937 shows them to be identical to those that forced Africans and whites off the land: '(1) the attractions of higher cash wages and the desire to escape the long hours of work on the farms, (2) the reduction of farm labour required consequent to the fencing of grazing land and the increased use of agricultural machinery, (3) the desire to obtain educational facilities for the children'.[5]

The first major impetus to African industrial employment had resulted from the discovery of minerals. Even before the industrial era, however, Africans were present in many towns as servants and labourers. In 1836, for instance, Mfengu had been given ground in Uitenhage;[6] and in 1856 Sir George Grey had established the 'Fingo Location' in Grahamstown where Africans could own land.[7] A census in 1862 showed that there were 1,593 Africans in Durban.[8] In 1844 the Transvaal *Volksraad* deemed it necessary to decree that 'no natives shall be allowed to establish their residences near towns to the detriment of the inhabitants, except with the consent of the full Raad'.[9]

[1] S. Cooppan and B. A. Naidoo, 'Indian Adjustments to Urbanization', *Race Relations Journal*, 22 (2) (1955), 13.
[2] Department of Economics, Natal University College, 'Indian Agriculture', in E. Hellmann (ed.) *Handbook on Race Relations in South Africa*, p. 219.
[3] W. M. MacMillan, *The Cape Colour Question*, p. 268.
[4] J. S. Marais, *The Cape Coloured People 1652–1937*, p. 191.
[5] *Report of the Commission of Inquiry regarding the Cape Coloured Population of the Union*, para. 381.
[6] MacMillan, *Cape Colour Question*, p. 268.
[7] *Report of Commission on Native Laws and Customs*, 1883, Appendix E, p. 326.
[8] W. P. M. Henderson, *Durban—Fifty Years Municipal History*, p. 53.
[9] Article 29 of the '*Drie-en-Dertig Artikelen*' (Potchefstroom, 1844).

In 1878 Trollope mentioned Africans in Transvaal towns:

The Kafirs at Pretoria, and through all those parts of the Transvaal which I visited, are an imported population—the Dutch having made the land too hot to hold them as residents. The Dutch hated them, and they certainly have learned to hate the Dutch in return. Now they will come and settle themselves in Pretoria for a short time and be good humoured and occasionally serviceable. But till they settle themselves there permanently it is impossible to count them as a resident population.[1]

The first Africans to come to the diamond fields at Kimberley were 'target workers', temporarily detached from rural domiciles, for work periods that averaged about three months.[2] It was here that the migrant labour system developed with large concentrations of workers. In the 1880s a pattern was set which was extended to gold-mining and other industries, and it came to be regarded by many employers as the norm. Another institution that developed in Kimberley and was later adopted by other mining industries was the compound. The compound was primarily a device for combating illicit diamond buying and preventing drunkenness and desertions. It was estimated that the mines lost between £500,000 and £1,000,000 annually through illicit sales by Africans to dealers. Africans were now confined to a compound for the entire period of their service which might be from three to twelve months. Thefts were greatly reduced.[3] Kimberley traders objected to the institution because it cut away a large slice of a lucrative trade with Africans.[4] Profits on food and other necessaries sold in compound shops were appropriated by the mines. In a speech to shareholders of the De Beers Company in 1898 Rhodes reported a profit of £24,385 over two years from compound shops, none of which was used for the benefit of Africans.[5] When compounds were established on the Witwatersrand, they were not 'closed' as in Kimberley. Initially conditions were very bad. Sir Godfrey Lagden reported that chiefs in Basutoland appealed to him not to let men go to Johannesburg,[6] where Africans were free to come and go when not at work. While the mineowners of Johannesburg would have preferred closed compounds as a measure against desertions, it was impossible to establish them, owing to the strong opposition of the traders.[7]

The recommendation of the 1903–5 Commission that family settlements be encouraged was never adopted on the gold-mines, where only

---

[1] A. Trollope, *South Africa*, ii. 70.
[2] Robertson, '150 Years of Economic Contact', p. 9.
[3] A. Plant, 'Economic Development 1795–1921', *CHBE* (1936 edn.), viii. 778.
[4] O. Doughty, *Early Diamond Days*, p. 199.
[5] The South African Native Races Committee, *The Natives of South Africa*, p. 141.
[6] *Transvaal Labour Commission 1904*, Evidence, p. 93.
[7] South African Native Races Committee, p. 139.

a tiny élite were accommodated in married quarters; however, on the coal-mines of Natal and the Transvaal, where land was plentiful, Africans were at first permitted to live on the mine premises with their families. In 1914 an official of the Native Recruiting Corporation told a Commission that the desire of African miners to live under conditions of family life was increasing: 'It is not only a strongly expressed wish, it is a growing wish, especially now. You will understand that in most parts of the country they have lost their cattle through diseases . . . and they say, "Having lost my cattle there is no tie to keep me here. My home is my work, and I should like to have my wife and children with me at my work." '[1]

One effect of industrialization was that the main arena of racial conflict became the towns. The struggles of the twentieth century were foreshadowed in the early days of Kimberley. Much resentment was expressed at the right of Africans (which some exercised) to take out their own claims. 'Trusting to the liberality and elasticity of the British Constitution, the native considered he had equal rights with the white man, and by paying the usual fee for a claim licence he saw no reason why he should be debarred from becoming a full-blown digger. But the European digger pointedly declined to recognise Jim Crow's *bona fides*, and would have none of him.'[2] By 1876 the pressures of the white diggers had prevailed and Africans were henceforth confined to the status of lowly paid unskilled labourers.[3] The seed of the industrial colour bar had been sown. Also of significance was the advice of an early claim-owner: 'The raw, untutored, unclad Kafirs, fresh from their "kraals" up the mountains are by far the best and most trustworthy workmen. The contact of civilization seems to be almost invariably pernicious and demoralizing to the peculiar organization of our Kafir friends. Above all things, mistrust a Kafir who speaks English and wears trousers.'[4] Resentment and fear of Africans who 'aped the ways of the white man' was to be a powerful motive for later doctrines of segregation.

2. State Policy and Urbanization

The townward movement of whites and non-whites was an aspect of a single process, but no Government was ever to recognize the parallel. For much of the period under consideration policy aimed at prising Africans out of reserves to work on white-owned farms and in industry.

[1] *Report of the Economic Commission*, para. 52. Quoted by S. T. van der Horst, *Native Labour in South Africa*, p. 187.
[2] G. Beet, *The Grand Old Days of the Diamond Fields*, p. 140.
[3] C. de Kiewiet, *The Imperial Factor in South Africa*, pp. 58–9.
[4] Quoted by Doughty, p. 184.

African reserves were regarded by whites as 'reservoirs of labour', and congestion, landlessness, and crop-failure were welcomed as stimulants to the labour supply.[1] But similar phenomena among whites were viewed as national calamities.

The townward migration of whites became a public issue in the Transvaal in the 1890s. From the outset counsels were divided over what action should be taken, the Government not realizing that a major and irreversible process was under way. In 1893 communities of poor whites began to collect around Vrededorp (Johannesburg), and in other towns, often living in tents. On the advice of an official who noted that land had been allocated to urban Coloured people, the Government decided to grant them plots (erven) in the towns. A Commission of the Volksraad, however, disputed the idea, saying that it would be better for them 'if they were to go back to the land in order to obtain a better means of livelihood, and where the children are not exposed to the many temptations of the town'.[2] This recommendation was ignored and the granting of 'burgher right erven' proceeded. A spate of applications for these erven ensued and in 1897 the Volksraad had second thoughts, considering now that 'it does not appear . . . desirable to collect the poor round about and within the towns . . .'. They recommended resettlement of the poor whites on the land. In 1905 a Commission reported on the large number of whites who had gathered round Pretoria after the dislocation caused by the war. It described them as an 'undesirable influx' and recommended that they be resettled on the land: 'We feel strongly that these people, owing to their previous environment and their character, which has been moulded by such environment, are ill-fitted for a town life.' Moreover, said the Commission, 'the great bulk of these people have expressed . . . their willingness to go back to the land'.[3]

In the Cape in 1895 the N. G. Kerk had attempted to alleviate rural poverty by establishing a labour colony at Kakamas on the banks of the Orange River. The success of this scheme gave encouragement to the belief that rural rehabilitation schemes would curb the townward movement. The slogan 'back to the land!' summed up a widespread feeling until the late 1930s. In 1908 the Transvaal Indigency Commission rejected the idea: 'to place on the land men who are not enterprising and who have not a good knowledge of practical farming is to court disaster. If a policy of settlement is unlikely to succeed in the case of people born and bred in the country, it is an even less hopeful method of dealing with indigents who have never been in the country, or who have lived in towns for some time and have consequently acquired urban habits

---

[1] Report of the Native Affairs Commission for 1939–40, para. 14.
[2] Report of Commission in re Pretoria Indigents (Pretoria, 1905), para. 26.
[3] Ibid., para. 18.

and tastes.'[1] Such hard-headed advice was not palatable, and 'back to the land' solutions continued to be propounded regularly after Union. In 1916, for example, a Church conference in Cradock urged that white urbanization be reversed by intensive agricultural reform. One speaker considered that, apart from mining, the few existing industries would be capable of providing only a very limited number of poor whites with work.[2]

After 1910 Government policy consistently aimed at keeping as many whites on the land as possible. Official measures to assist poor whites took various forms: aid for farmers, social welfare measures such as pensions and invalidity grants, expanded educational facilities, and protection of whites against non-white competition in industry. Between 1914 and the 1930s welfare provisions expanded until in 1937 a sociologist could write: 'Today the provision for [South Africa's] European population, if still behind New Zealand, is scarcely less complete than that of Great Britain.'[3] This development occurred despite warnings such as that voiced by the Carnegie Commission that 'much of the assistance is given in such a way as to have a demoralising effect on the poor whites. . . . It causes loss of independence and may imbue them with a sense of inferiority, impairs their industry, weakens their sense of personal responsibility, and helps to make them dishonest.'

The poor white had found unskilled agricultural labour pre-empted by Africans, and in towns he was faced with non-white competition. 'The workers who are not, with the commercial return to industry what it is, worth employing at the relatively higher rate exacted for skilled European labour, have no alternative but to swell the ranks of unskilled labour and handymen; in other words, to put themselves into competition with the native.'[4] Africans had virtually the monopoly of unskilled industrial labour, and the wage-structure rested squarely on high wages paid to the skilled white worker and low wages paid to the unskilled non-white worker. In evidence to a Commission in 1925 the Federated Chamber of Industries said: 'White wages have been paid, and are being paid, largely at the expense of the native workers.' The Gold Producers' Committee of the Transvaal Chamber of Mines reported that their profits and the 'exceptionally high' wages of the European depended similarly on low African wages.[5] The urban poor white lacked skills and education, and, moreover, retained a prejudice against menial work ('*kaffirwerk*'). In the towns of a racially stratified society he was an anomaly and in the 1920s and early 1930s the poor white problem increasingly became an unemployment problem.[6]

[1] *Report of Transvaal Indigency Commission*, para. 339.
[2] Verslag van Het Kerkelik Kongres, *Het Arme Blanken Vraagstuk*, pp. 35, 69.
[3] J. L. Gray, 'The Comparative Sociology of South Africa', *SAJE*, 5 (1937), 270.
[4] *Report of the Economic and Wages Commission* (Clay Commission), para. 144.
[5] Ibid., para. 141.   [6] Grosskopf, p. 10.

The Nationalist-Labour Pact Government (1924–33) became acutely conscious of the urban poor white's plight, partly because of the so-called 'threat to civilized standards' and partly through fear of the real possibility of solidarity among workers of all races. 'If the more privileged European grudges and refuses the poor his patronage and society, the latter will associate with non-Europeans, if he finds no member of his own race to consort with.'[1] Proletarianization might mean the rejection of traditional values, 'de-nationalization', and finding common cause with non-whites in a class struggle.[2] In the towns the poor white often found himself in a multi-racial slum. Afrikaner writers emphasized the danger that inter-racial slums fostered a kind of social intimacy which eventually eliminated race consciousness. Not only did the poor white 'sink from the social and communal standards of the white community to those of the non-whites, but the non-white, as a result of these contacts and this social intimacy, lost the necessary respect for whites in general, and developed in his heart a feeling of defiance and a dangerous desire for equality with the whites.'[3]

The Government stepped in. In 1923 a statute provided for compulsory residential segregation of Africans as a means of stopping 'undesirable mixing'.[4] The Pact Government intensified the industrial colour bar and in 1924 adopted the 'Civilized Labour' Policy in terms of which non-white workers were to be replaced as far as possible with poor whites (see p. 34). Paradoxically for Afrikaners, who feared urbanization but wanted to capture urban Afrikaner votes, the Civilized Labour policy gave urbanization a considerable impetus. 'By this [policy] the ice was broken',[5] and thousands more joined those already in the towns. A further measure adopted by the Pact Government to assist poor whites was the protection of industry by tariff. In 1925 the Board of Trade and Industries considered that

the encouragement of manufacturing industries through the tariff and by all other practical means is rendered necessary by the fact that the agricultural, pastoral and mining industries have not proved to be capable of furnishing an adequate livelihood to all the European inhabitants of this country, owing, in the first place to numerous natural obstacles and disabilities which render agriculture and stock-farming in general uncertain and unprofitable in many parts of the country, and, secondly, to the employment of an unusually large percentage of low-paid coloured labour in farming and mining (90 per cent in the gold mines). In consequence, the field of employment of unskilled or

[1] J. R. Albertyn, *The Poor White and Society*, p. 106.
[2] G. D. Scholtz, *Het die Afrikaanse Volk 'n Toekoms?*, p. 116.
[3] Coetzee, pp. 41–2. (trans.)   [4] The Natives (Urban Areas) Act.
[5] J. R. Albertyn, P. du Toit and H. S. Theron, *Kerk en Stad—Verslag van die Kommissie van Ondersoek van die Gefedereerde N.G. Kerke na Kerklike en Godsdienstige Toestande in die nege stede van die Unie van S.A.*, p. 33 (trans.).

even semi-skilled labour is contracted to such an extent that the problem of a large number of permanently unemployed Europeans has come into existence.[1]

In 1932 the Carnegie Commission reported that 'the development of a number of industries resulting from a policy of import protection, has provided thousands of poor from rural areas with industrial work in the cities and elsewhere, and that this [was] one of the most potent means of bringing about their economic rehabilitation'.[2]

By the early 1930s, particularly after the rise in the price of gold in 1933 had given a further fillip to industrial expansion, it was realized that the urbanization of large numbers of Afrikaners was inevitable, even if regrettable. Rural depopulation, however, remained a matter of concern, as is shown by the report of the du Toit Commission in 1960. While not recommending 'back to the land' solutions, it saw dangers in continuing white rural depopulation: 'The Commission agrees that the land will eventually be owned by him that cultivates it in the sweat of his brow; and the Commission is convinced that, if the tide does not turn and the growth of non-white preponderance on the white *platteland* continues, this state of affairs will in the end hold out a serious threat to White civilization in this country.'[3]

Prior to Union the governments of South Africa had not given much attention to the social problems posed by the townward movement of Africans, or the wider issue of how this movement was to affect overall racial policy. Indeed, the 1903–5 Commission, apart from noting that conditions in several locations it visited left much to be desired, devoted only a few paragraphs to the subject. Urban Africans who worked, the Commission considered, 'should be encouraged to stay as useful members of the community', but 'surplus or idle Natives' should be expelled.[4]

By the turn of the century, it was officially held in most parts of South Africa that urban Africans were not permanent members of urban communities but migrants whose domiciles were in the rural areas. 'The traditional conception of our Native locations in the Free State . . . undoubtedly is that they are merely convenient reservoirs for the purpose of supplying the legitimate labour requirements of our towns and villages. . . . The old Free State Republican Volksraad . . . resolutely set its face against the recognition of locations in Urban Areas as townships. . . .'[5]

[1] Quoted by M. Kooy and H. M. Robertson, 'The South African Board of Trade and Industries; The South African Customs Tariff and the Development of South African Industries', *SAJE*, 34 (1966), 214.
[2] *Joint Findings and Recommendations*, para. 81; Grosskopf, p. xxiii.
[3] *Du Toit Commission*, para. 428.   [4] *1903–5 Report*, i. 47–8.
[5] Statement by O.F.S. Municipal Association at Kroonstad, 1932.

In Natal officials noted with disapproval the symptoms of social dislocation among town Africans. In Pietermaritzburg 'the bulk of the Native women have abandoned kraal life, and have adopted prostitution and petticoats'.[1] Others foresaw in the continuing urbanization of Africans serious racial conflict. 'Let them understand that the towns of the Colony are the special places of abode for the white men, who are the governing race. . . .'[2] Permanent residence in towns for the great majority of Africans should be 'distinctly discouraged' and the status of those in the towns should be that of 'mere visitors'.[3] Part of Natal's policy was the segregationist idea (later to be adopted by the Union Government) that Africans should 'develop along their own lines'. 'National and tribal disintegration would quickly be followed by racial amalgamation. There was evidence of this process and this result in the towns. Let us stem back and keep off the process of disintegration, both in ours as well as the interests of the natives themselves. . . .'[4]

The view that urban Africans were 'mere visitors' prevailed in the Transvaal also.[5] The conception of the towns as white preserves dated from 1844 when the *Volksraad* decreed that no Africans were to be permitted to settle near towns without official permission. Their subordinate status was emphasized by a *Volksraad* resolution of 1899 which prohibited them 'from walking on the sidewalks of the streets, or on any *stoep* serving as a sidewalk'.[6]

It is difficult to generalize about Cape policy. As has been mentioned, Africans were allowed freehold rights in Uitenhage and Grahamstown in the middle of the nineteenth century. The authorities of East London in the 1890s, however, looked upon the African population as 'temporary sojourners' and in no sense an integral part of the urban community.[7] The fact that the large majority of town Africans *were* migrant labourers no doubt confirmed this view. The migrant labour system was well entrenched and officially supported. In 1910 a Commission remarked critically upon the 'heterogeneous settlements which have sprung up in the towns where there exists no organised state of society nor recognised code of public morals'. It viewed periodic returns to rural homes as a beneficial means of rehabilitating Africans as 'reformed and law-abiding members of the community'.[8]

[1] *Reports of Resident Magistrates and Administrators of Native Law on Natives*, 1880. County of Pietermaritzburg, City Division.
[2] *Blue Book on Native Affairs*, 1904, p. 68.   [3] Ibid., p. 77.
[4] *Natal Native Affairs Commission, 1906–7, Evidence*, S. O. Samuelson (Under-Secretary for Native Affairs, Natal) p. 644.
[5] J. P. R. Maud, *The Johannesburg Experiment*, p. 59.
[6] Native Affairs Department (Transvaal), *The Laws and Regulations etc. Specially Relating to the Native Population of the Transvaal*, p. 153.
[7] Reader, p. 12.
[8] *Report of the Native Affairs Commission*, para. 36.

Despite these early views of towns as white preserves, there were no restrictions on Africans acquiring freehold land in towns, except in the Orange Free State. The stereotype of the urban African as a 'temporary sojourner' had, however, developed. In 1900 this was an accurate description of the large majority, but the stereotype was to endure into times when this was no longer so.

In the first two decades of this century several commissions criticized the conditions under which urban Africans lived.[1] Municipalities lacked both the will and the powers to remedy matters, and the Union Government lacked power to implement the recommendations of the commissions it had appointed.[2] The situation called for legislation that would enable the Government to intervene. A Bill to regulate urban African affairs was first introduced in 1912 but was shelved when war broke out in 1914. A draft Bill was circulated in 1918 but it was never introduced into Parliament because its scope was not considered sufficiently wide.[3] In the early 1920s, two commissions considered what policy ought to be, and their recommendations formed the basis of the Natives (Urban Areas) Act of 1923 which remained the foundation of policy in the 1960s. In 1921 the Native Affairs Commission reported that 'it should be understood that the town is a European area in which there is no place for the redundant Native, who neither works nor serves his or her people but forms the class from which the professional agitators, the slum landlords, the liquor sellers, the prostitutes and other undesirable classes spring'.[3] It considered that Africans were 'not by nature town dwellers' and that they had 'not yet made a success of city life . . .'.[3] Similar views were expressed by the Transvaal Local Government Commission in 1922 which recommended 'that it should be a recognised principle of government that natives—men, women and children —should only be permitted within municipal areas in so far and for so long as their presence is demanded by the wants of the white population'.[4] Moreover, 'the masterless native in urban areas is a source of danger and a cause of degradation of both black and white'.[5]

The Act of 1923, whose provisions are examined below, attempted to apply the doctrine of segregation to towns. This policy, first formulated as a conscious doctrine in Natal,[6] had been adopted by the first Union Government. It provided for only partial separation of whites and Africans. 'Economically the native will go on working in the white areas.'[7] An African leader later defined it as 'the separation of black and

---

[1] See, e.g., *The Report of the Tuberculosis Commission*, paras. 233–65.
[2] *Report of the Native Affairs Commission for 1921*, pp. 25–7.
[3] Ibid., p. 25.
[4] *Report of the Transvaal Local Government Commission*, 1921, para. 267.   [5] Ibid., para. 268.
[6] A conclusion based upon the writer's research into Natal Archival records.
[7] J. C. Smuts, 'Problems in South Africa', *Journal of the African Society*, xvi (1917), 280.

white, not with the idea of protecting each group in regard to its basic interests, but the separation of the groups in order to facilitate the subordination of the one group to the other—the exploitation of the one group by the other'.[1]

The renewed emphasis on segregation in the 1920s was a response to rapid African urbanization and the assumed threat to the white worker. (Between 1921 and 1936 the urban African population increased by 94·49 per cent.)[2] Politicians, both black and white, were aware of the revolutionary possibilities presented by the urban African masses who could be mobilized for action against a social order that denied them equality. The 1920s were the heyday of Clements Kadalie and the Industrial and Commercial Workers' Union. 'The locations in the towns are the incubators of unrighteousness, and Kadalie and his myrmidons find the locations the most fruitful place for their operations.'[3] In 1937 a leading segregationist claimed that 'the towns constitute the front trenches of our position in South Africa. It is in the towns that seige is being made against our civilized standards.'[4]

The corollary of segregation was migrant labour. 'While the native may come voluntarily out of his own area for a limited period every year to work with a white employer, he will leave his wife and children behind in their native home . . . migration of the native family, of the females and children, to the farms and the towns, . . . should be prevented.'[5]

Segregation was defended on the grounds that Africans were 'primitive' and 'barbarous'. The truth was that tribalism was eroding; Africans were becoming less 'primitive' and 'barbarous', and many demanded equality and assimilation in the urban industrial societies. Africans repeatedly pointed out that the whites themselves had created, and were perpetuating, the very conditions that forced them into the towns. The African 'had been called out of his old life and brought by the Europeans into the new life much against his will, and now he was going to adapt himself to it. . . . It was no longer the question of teaching the black man the dignity of labour but of preventing him from competing with the whites on the farms and the whites in the towns. His laziness was no longer a menace to the existence of the white race but his industry and progress were!'[6] 'Why should we now, after helping you Europeans to build your cities and your industries, not be allowed to

---

[1] Z. K. Matthews, *Verbatim Reports of the Natives Representative Council* (hereafter *VR of NRC*) (Adjourned Seventh Session), 1944, i. 162.

[2] *Report of the Native Laws Commission*, 1946–8 (*Fagan Report*), para. 7.

[3] M. L. Malan, M.P., *House of Assembly Debates* (hereafter *H.A.D.*), 1927, col. 2966.

[4] G. Heaton Nicholls, M.P., *H.A.D.* 1937, col. 6100.

[5] J. C. Smuts, *Greater South Africa*, p. 53 (the quotation is from a speech made in 1929).

[6] 'The South African Native's Point of View' (Anon.), *Round Table*, 19 (1928), 790.

derive the benefit of our labour?'[1] It was apparent to Africans that the whites paradoxically wanted their labour but objected to their presence.

While segregation was accepted by both main parliamentary parties, the Opposition Nationalist Party after 1933 continually criticized the United Party Government for failing to implement policy with sufficient rigour, thereby allegedly allowing 'surplus' Africans to accumulate in the towns and depriving farmers of labour. During the 1940s it was evident that the Government was slowly recognizing the need for reform of urban African policy. Industry expanded rapidly during the war, and the demand for labour increased dramatically. In 1941 a Commission reported that 'the proportion of the population engaged in farming is too high to enable the present low rural incomes to be raised to a level comparable with the urban. . . . a further townward movement is considered to be an economic necessity. This movement will be mainly a transfer of Natives of whom 82 per cent were still on the land in 1936 as against 33 per cent in the case of the Europeans, Coloureds and Asiatics. . . .'[2] In 1942 the Smit Committee[3] and in 1946 the Social and Economic Planning Council condemned the migrant labour system, the Planning Council reporting that 'the past half-century has witnessed a decline in the stability of Native family life which constitutes a danger to the whole nation—black and white alike—in the spheres of health, of morality and of general social structure, peace, order, reasonable contentment, goodwill, and a sense of national solidarity'.[4] The Council emphasized the need for the development of a permanent urban labour force, and would have rejected the continuation of migrant labour on the gold-mines 'were it not convinced that the mines are a disappearing asset'.[5] The Prime Minister, General Smuts, spoke eloquently of African urbanization: 'Segregation tried to stop it. It has, however, not stopped it in the least. The process has been accelerated. You might as well try to sweep the ocean back with a broom.'[6]

In Parliament the Nationalists lashed the Government for permitting the increased influx into towns and tacitly abandoning segregation. In 1947 the Minister of Native Affairs, Major P. van der Byl, claimed that the Government was doing all it could to stem the tide; but, he asked, 'can we develop our industries when we have the position that the native only works for a few months and then returns to the reserves

[1] R. V. Selope Thema, *VR of NRC* (Adjourned Seventh Session), 1944, i. 40.

[2] *Report of Industrial and Agricultural Requirements Commission* (van Eck Commission), 1941, p. 248.

[3] *Report of the Interdepartmental Committee on the Social Health and Economic Conditions of Urban Natives*, 1942 (*Smit Committee Report*), para. 8.

[4] *Social and Economic Planning Council, Report No. 9, The Native Reserves and their place in the Economy of the Union of South Africa*, para. 11.

[5] Ibid., para. 16.

[6] J. C. Smuts, *The Basis of Trusteeship*, p. 10.

for a couple of years? No, the native must be trained for his work in industry, and to become an efficient industrial worker he must be a permanent industrial worker. On that account he must live near his place of employment.' The major segregation laws of 1936, he said, had not anticipated the unprecedented industrial development of the past few years.[1]

Repeated accusations were made that many of the Africans in the towns were 'surplus' or 'idle' undesirables who were responsible for much of the violent crime that occurred in the towns.[2] A huge increase in the number of urban Africans *had* occurred (between 1936 and 1946 the number had risen by 652,570 or 57·16 per cent) but it was never proved that large numbers were unemployed. In Durban a judicial commission found in 1948 that 'the great majority of the male shack dwellers are usefully employed in the city'. Similar findings were reported of the African squatters who crowded around Johannesburg. A Commission commented that the Johannesburg Municipality's ideas as to the proportion of squatters actually employed in Johannesburg were 'hopelessly vague and, indeed, hopelessly wrong. At one time the Council was even prepared to let the Government take all the squatters away. . . .The results of the subsequent enumerations showed that, had this been done, the effect on the economic life of Johannesburg would have been like that of a major strike.'[3] The squatters stayed, and ultimately had to be given more adequate housing. They had demonstrated that they were *not* 'temporary sojourners'.

The climax of the trend towards recognizing the permanent urban African population came with the report of the 1946–8 Natives Laws (Fagan) Commission. It stated that 'the idea of total segregation is utterly impracticable; secondly, that the movement from country to town has a background of economic necessity—that it may, so one hopes, be guided and regulated, and may perhaps also be limited, but that it cannot be stopped or be turned in the opposite direction; and thirdly that in our urban areas there are not only Native migrant labourers, but there is also a settled, permanant Native population'.[4] The Commission dismissed as a 'parrot-cry' the notion that Africans could be returned to the reserves.[5] Moreover, migrant labour was 'a system which, in the long run, cannot be maintained otherwise than on a limited scale'.[6] Significantly, the Commission pointed to the parallels between African and white urbanization, noting that 'back to the land' solutions had been desired initially for whites. 'When now, in the light of later

[1] *H.A.D.*, 1947, cols. 5009–5010.
[2] See, e.g., D. F. Malan, M.P., *H.A.D.*, 1946, col. 103.
[3] *Report of the Commission appointed to Enquire into the Disturbances of the 30th August 1947 at Moroka Emergency Camp, Johannesburg*, para. 94.
[4] *Fagan Report*, para. 28.   [5] Ibid.   [6] Ibid., para. 25.

developments, we look back on that period, it is very clear that this cry called for an utterly impracticable and impossible solution.'[1] Now, there was no more talk of a poor white problem; whites who migrated to the towns had been fully absorbed in industry.

The United Party Government accepted these conclusions and those of the other reports cited above. It fought and lost the 1948 election mainly on its racial policies. The Nationalists had appealed to the electorate with the slogan 'Apartheid', the tag given to a race policy that had been drawn up by an internal commission and to which the new regime would faithfully adhere.[2] The new Government repudiated the findings of the Fagan Commission and reaffirmed the recommendation of the 1922 Stallard Commission that permanent residence in the towns was the exclusive right of whites. Indeed, it was denied that a permanently urbanized African population existed: 'All the Bantu have their permanent homes in the reserves and their entry into other areas and into the urban centres is merely of a temporary nature and for economic reasons.'[3] Nationalist spokesmen reacted sharply to allegations that apartheid meant the removal of all urban Africans to the reserves. Policy was aimed at freezing the number of 'de-tribalized' Africans in the towns, and preventing the further townward migration of African families. While the presence of African labourers in the towns was essential, their status was that of foreigners who could have 'no political, or equal social or other rights with Europeans'.[4] 'They will be like the Italians who go to France to take up employment there.'[5] Dependence upon African labour did not constitute 'integration'. According to the Prime Minister, Dr. H. F. Verwoerd, '. . . . the mere presence of larger numbers of Bantu in employment does not amount to integration. It is only when there is intermingling of those people in social life or in the political or religious spheres that one really gets integration. The mere fact that foreigners are employed in a community or in another country does not constitute integration.'[6] Total racial separation was never seriously considered. Apartheid would be implemented 'under one umbrella of a South African economy'.[7] Critics argued that the policy was a mere façade, designed to give an ethical embellishment to the continuation of an unequal society.

In 1954 the Tomlinson Commission reported that over six million

[1] Ibid., para. 8.

[2] D. W. Krüger (ed.), *South African Parties and Policies 1910–1960*, pp. 402–6.

[3] W. W. M. Eiselen (Secretary for Native Affairs), 'Harmonious Multi-Community Development', *Optima*, 9 (1), (1959), 3.

[4] E. G. Jansen (Minister of Native Affairs), *H.A.D.*, 1950, col. 4703.

[5] A. N. Pelzer (ed.), *Verwoerd Speaks*, p. 121.

[6] *H.A.D.*, 1964, col. 68.

[7] M. D. C. de Wet Nel, M.P., reported in *Cape Argus*, 24 Jan. 1958.

Africans would be in the 'white' areas by the year 2000 even if its proposals for rural rehabilitation were implemented.[1] Some two million of
this number would be in the towns. According to Dr. Verwoerd, when
Minister of Native Affairs, 'the assumption [was] unfounded that the
same persons will always be domiciled here permanently'.[2] This presumably meant that the migrant labour system would be extended as
far as possible. 'We all know that for mining labour it is the best and
presumably the only practicable system. It is my contention that the
strengthening of this system and its extension to most other fields of
labour would benefit the Bantu. . . .'[3] In 1950 a mining company proposed to house in married quarters at least ten per cent of its African
labour force on the Orange Free State mines.[4] The plans, however,
were vetoed by the Government.

In 1950 industrialists were warned against establishing labour-intensive enterprises requiring large numbers of African labourers in existing
industrial complexes, and were asked to locate such enterprises, as far
as possible, near African reserves.[5] This effort to reduce the number of
Africans required in the cities later crystallized as the 'border industries'
scheme. Border industries were to be established in 'white' areas but
near to African reserves. (Ironically, similar-looking schemes for rural
industries had been propounded earlier in an effort to curb the townward flow of whites. In 1939, for example, a speaker at the *Ekonomiese
Volkskongres* in Bloemfontein had recommended the establishment of
rural industries which, he said, 'would facilitate the inevitable transition from agriculture to industry and bring economic advantages to the
country. It would also counter rural depopulation.')[6] Between 1928 and
1967 the average ratio of Africans to whites in all South African industries had risen from 1·01:1 to 2·2:1. By restricting the expansion of
labour-intensive industries in existing complexes it was hoped to
achieve a ratio of one white worker to less than one African worker.
In 'border' industries, however, 'the ratio of Bantu workers to white
workers . . . can be unrestricted'.[7]

By 1967 the most successful 'border industries' had been established
close to pre-existing towns and were, in effect, extensions of the industrial
complexes of Durban, Pretoria, East London, and Pietermaritzburg.
Only the 'border' industrial complex at Phalaborwa in the north-eastern

[1] *Summary of the Report of the Commission for the Socio-Economic Development of the Bantu Areas
within the Union of South Africa* (Tomlinson Report), p. 179.
   [2] Pelzer, p. 183.   [3] Ibid., pp. 91–2,
   [4] H. F. Oppenheimer, 'The Orange Free State Goldfields', *SAJE*, 18 (1950), 153.
   [5] E. G. Jansen (Minister for Native Affairs), *H.A.D.*, 1950, col. 4706.
   [6] Ekonomiese Instituut van die F.A.K., '*N Volk Staan Op*, p. 120. (trans.)
   [7] M. C. Botha (Minister of Bantu Administration and Development), *H.A.D.*, 1967, col.
741.

Transvaal was an exception to the pattern of building on to existing industrial complexes. According to official statements the Phalaborwa project would provide employment for 'thousands of Bantu, making it unnecessary for them to look for work in the cities'.[1] Phalaborwa constitutes a border area by virtue of the existence of a small reserve six miles from the town. Had it not been for the development of the industry at Phalaborwa the reserve was to have been declared a 'black spot' and disestablished.[2]

It is difficult to accept official claims that 'border industries' reduce racial integration. Phalaborwa is in embryo another large town in which the traditional South African pattern of white/African interdependence is maintained. The requirements of apartheid are complied with, if African workers reside in reserves and commute on a daily or weekly basis to industries in 'white' areas, and in Natal, the northern Transvaal, and eastern Cape Africans are being moved from municipal townships and placed in new towns created in nearby reserves. But in effect, these 'homeland towns' are economically and geographically suburbs of the 'white' towns in which many of their inhabitants work. In East London, for example, all the municipal African townships are being disestablished, and the inhabitants are being moved to Mdantsane which is situated in a Ciskei reserve eleven miles from the city.[3] At present the pattern is being repeated in numerous other South African towns where African reserves are in close proximity,[4] and a pro-apartheid writer has suggested that the policy is sufficiently flexible to permit the creation of urban 'homelands' adjacent to cities like Johannesburg which are far from existing reserves.[5] However 'reserve towns' or proposed 'urban homelands' are described, the essence of the matter is they are parts of multi-racial cities.

In terms of apartheid, Africans could have 'no right of existence in the Western Cape', which is 'the natural labour field of the White man and the Coloured man'.[6] In 1955 it was announced that Africans would be gradually eliminated from the region, which comprised the area south of the Orange River and west of the magisterial districts of Gordonia, Hope Town, De Aar, Hanover, Richmond, Murraysburg, Aberdeen, Willowmore, Uniondale, and Knysna.[7]

In view of this policy, it might be noted that official returns in 1879

[1] *Bantu*, Sept. 1963.
[2] For a description of Phalaborwa see *Financial Mail Special Survey*, 'Phalaborwa', 29 Apr. 1966.
[3] Communication to the writer from the East London Municipality.
[4] M. Horrell, *Survey of Race Relations, 1966*, pp. 198-9.
[5] J. E. Holloway, *Apartheid—A Challenge*, pp. 56-7.
[6] M. Viljoen (Minister of Labour), reported in *Cape Times*, Mar. 16, 1967.
[7] W. W. M. Eiselen, *The Coloured People and the Natives*, p. 15.

showed that a total of 2,984 African men, women, and children were employed in the western Cape. 'As far as possible they shall contract and be settled in complete families, and no force shall be used in the separation of such families.'[1] In 1904 official figures showed a total of 7,492 Africans in greater Cape Town.[2] The Revd. E. Dolomba and other Africans told the 1903–5 Commission of a permanently urbanized section of the African population in Cape Town's Ndabeni Location. The claim was supported by an official.[3]

During the Second World War Cape Town's expanding industry and the construction of a new harbour and fortifications led to a greatly increased demand for African labour. A member of the Natives Representative Council said that he had been approached by his Native Commissioner to encourage Africans to go to Cape Town.[4] Between 1936 and 1946 the African population rose from 14,160 to 35,197 according to official statistics, but in 1944, the Minister of Native Affairs estimated that the figure was approximately 60,000.[5]

Members of the Langa African Vigilance Committee, in giving evidence to the Fagan Commission, expressed bitterness at the insinuation that they were intruders into the area.[6] Since 1955 the implementation of the removal scheme has meant rigorous enforcement of influx controls, removal of 'foreign' (i.e. non-South African) Africans, repatriation of families, and a widening disproportion between the numbers of men and women.[7] It has heightened feelings of insecurity among Africans in the area.

In December 1966 the Government announced details of a plan to reduce African labour complements in 'white' industrial complexes by 5 per cent per annum. The plan 'was announced more specifically for the Western Cape, but it applies to the whole of South Africa'.[8] Industrialists complained bitterly about the scheme, which, they said, would seriously affect expansion. The Johannesburg Chamber of Commerce estimated that the cost to industry of implementing the scheme would not be less than R70,000,000 per annum.[9]

In terms of apartheid African hospitals not essential in 'white' areas (*nie-plekgebonde*) and institutions such as those for the blind and the deaf, and old-age homes must be transferred to reserves, and no new ones may be established in 'white' areas.[10] The aged and the debilitated are

---

[1] *Annexures and Notes to Proceedings of the House of Assembly, Cape of Good Hope*, 1879.
[2] M. Wilson and A. Mafeje, *Langa*, p. 2.   [3] *1903–5 Report*, ii. 414 and 416.
[4] Z. K. Matthews, *VR of NRC*, 9th Session, 1945, p. 121.
[5] *H.A.D.*, 1944, col. 3965.   [6] Undated memorandum of evidence, paras. 1–4.
[7] Wilson and Mafeje, pp. 183–4.
[8] *H.A.D.*, 1967, col. 736.   [9] *Cape Argus*, Mar. 8, 1967.
[10] M. C. Botha (Deputy Minister of Bantu Administration and Education), 'Ons Stedelike Bantoebeleid Teen die Agtergrond van ons Landbeleid', *Journal of Racial Affairs*, 15 (1964), 17.

not welcome in 'white' areas. In 1941 an African leader commented: 'Today when a man is old he is chucked out of his municipal house, because he has become useless and can no longer pay his rent. He has helped to build up your towns and industries, and has worked for the Europeans, but in his old age he is chucked out of his home.'[1]

The view that all Africans in the towns are 'temporary sojourners' with a home in the country has had important consequences. It has served as a pretext for withholding from Africans political and civic rights in 'white' areas.[2] In the mining industry African wages are calculated according to the needs of a single man. It is claimed that the African has rural land and pasturage and his wages in industry are purely a supplement to a rural income.[3] This belief affected the whole structure of African wages, and only slowly and incompletely was its obsoleteness recognized.[4] The stereotype of the African as an unskilled worker who desired a migrant work-pattern has served to rationalize limits placed on African progress in industry.[5] In addition rural Africans were excluded from old-age pensions until 1944 'mainly on the assumption that Native custom makes provision for maintaining dependent persons. Urban Natives were excluded in consequence, regardless of their needs, owing to "the difficulty of applying any statutory distinction between them and other Natives".'[6] Until the 1940s the assumption that all urban Africans were 'temporary', moreover, made local authorities reluctant to finance 'temporary' housing, with the result that the housing shortage became acute.[7]

The urban African trader, too, is regarded as a 'temporary sojourner'. Government policy maintains that Africans may trade only in African townships (where whites are not allowed to trade), and that they should be discouraged from building up large businesses there. 'When a Bantu trader in a location [township] has sufficient capital to establish a large business, he must move his business to his Bantu area, where the necessary facilities exist, among them the establishment of Bantu towns. Another Bantu trader must then replace him.'[8] A circular issued to local authorities by the Department of Bantu Administration and Development in February 1963 stated that trading by Africans in urban townships was 'not an inherent primary opportunity' for them. It laid down the conditions that were to govern urban trading. It was stated that no

[1] R. H. Godlo, *VR of NRC*, 5th Session, 1941, ii. 238.
[2] M. Wilson, 'The Principle of Maintaining the Reserves for the African', *Race Relations Journal* 29 (1), (1962), 8.
[3] *Report of Witwatersrand Mine Natives Wage Commission*, 1943, para. 102.
[4] Y. Glass, *Industrial Man in Southern Africa*, p. 6.
[5] Ibid., p. 14.   [6] *Report of the Social Security Committee*, para. 129.
[7] L. Marquard, *People and Policies in South Africa*, p. 49.
[8] M. D. C. de Wet Nel (Minister of Bantu Administration and Development), reported in *The Star*, 26 Oct. 1959. Quoted by L. Reyburn, *African Traders*, p. 18.

business which does not confine itself to the provision of daily essential domestic necessities must be established. New licences for dry cleaners, garages and filling stations, for example, should not be granted. Persons already holding such licences could continue to operate until 'the opportunity arises to close' the concerns or to persuade the owner to move to his 'homeland'.[1]

The different official policies adopted in relation to the urbanization of Africans and whites (who were mainly Afrikaners) reflected the different positions in society of the two groups. The poor whites were members of the dominant group: their poverty *had* to be noticed, not only because they possessed the parliamentary vote, but also because their poverty was felt to be degrading to the white man. The Carnegie Commission strongly recommended that poor whites 'receive a favourable reception in urban industries, and that their adaption to the new conditions of life is not artificially hampered'. In general, this recommendation was complied with; but the urbanization of Africans occurred *despite* official policy. The racial divisions of the society prevented policy makers from seeing the parallels between the forces that drove country people of different races to the towns. The very term 'poor white' showed that poverty was not considered as a general phenomenon but had to be seen in a racial perspective.

The desire of whites both to absorb non-white labourers into the economy, and to treat them as subordinate aliens in 'white' areas, is illustrated by the development of those bureaucratic controls over the free movement of Africans collectively known as the 'pass laws'.[2] The following account deals with pass laws in so far as they relate to urban areas only.

The pass was a well-established institution long before the industrial era. In 1760 a Cape regulation required every slave going 'from the town to the country or from the country to town' to carry a pass authorizing the journey signed by his owner.[3] A more far-reaching measure was a proclamation of 1809 which provided that all Khoikhoi must have fixed abodes from which they might not move without a pass. The belief that the 'masterless native' was a danger accounts for the attempts of the pass laws to ensure that all Africans in towns were employed. Their entry must be regulated in accordance with labour requirements of employers in the towns and rural areas. The Transvaal

[1] Horrell, *Survey, 1963*, p. 148.
[2] The writer regrets that he is unable to refer to the writings of the leading authority on the subject, Dr. H. J. Simons, who, having been 'banned' under the Suppression of Communism Act, may not be quoted in South Africa.
[3] Marais, *Cape Coloured People*, p. 117.

regulation of 1844, requiring Africans to obtain official permission before settling near towns, has been mentioned above. The increasing entry of Africans into Natal towns in the early 1870s caused the authorities to lay down controls. In 1873 Theophilus Shepstone discerned dangers in the 'large but fluctuating native population living in the towns, but having no home in them. . . . With regard to the effect of this upon general government of the natives, it must be remembered that the towns are the points at which most contact takes place between the races. . . . They come and go when they please.'[1] The objection was that no control could be exercised over Africans after working hours 'resulting in their wandering about the Borough at night . . .'.[2] In 1874 regulations were promulgated which established control over African males in the boroughs of Pietermaritzburg and Durban. In the Orange Free State, in addition to other passes, provision was made in Law No. 8 of 1893 to compel Africans residing in urban areas to take out municipal residential passes with the object of ensuring that only people who were employed remained in the towns.[3]

Mining interests pressed for controls in Kimberley and on the Witwatersrand to prevent desertions and to exclude Africans who were not employed. An ordinance of 1872 provided for the registration of service contracts in Griqualand West. Later, however, the adoption of closed compounds overcame the problems of theft and desertion. On the Witwatersrand the complaint was against desertion. Mining pressure resulted in the passing of Law 31 of 1896 whose aim was 'to have a hold on the native whom we have brought down . . . at a considerable outlay to ourselves . . .'.[4] In the Cape, the Native Reserve Location Act, Urban Areas 1902, provided that passes might be issued to Africans entering or leaving the urban locations established by the Act, and also for the registration of all Africans in the locations.

The powerful influence of the mining industry on the development of the pass laws and, indeed, on the whole policy relating to urban Africans, is apparent. The Natives (Urban Areas) Act of 1923 was intended to perpetuate the restrictions on African workers that had developed on the Witwatersrand. The municipalities, who were compelled to provide housing for Africans in their areas, insisted on provision being made in the Act for 'influx controls' that would enable them to restrict Africans entering their areas to the numbers required by employers. This statute established the framework within which the modern system of influx control was to develop.

[1] Natal Archives Files, S.N.A. 1/1/23. [2] Henderson, pp. 81-2.
[3] H. Rogers, *Native Administration in the Union of South Africa*, p. 195.
[4] South African Native Races Committee, p. 166. The statement was made by a mining official.

The 1923 legislation provided that, at the request of the local authority, the Governor-General could 'proclaim' the urban area to be one in which certain restrictions on Africans were operative.[1] In proclaimed areas every employer of a male African had to register the service contract, and both employer and employee could be asked to show this contract to an authorized officer. Male Africans entering the area were to report their arrival to the local authority within a prescribed period, and obtain documentary evidence that they had done so. Africans who were unable to find employment within a prescribed time could be ordered to leave the area. Exempted from these provisions were holders of letters of exemption under previous legislation; registered parliamentary voters in the Cape, owners of land, chiefs and headmen, clergymen, certain teachers, and court interpreters.[2] Habitually unemployed, and 'idle, dissolute or disorderly' Africans might be removed from the area.[3] By 1948 a total of 265 urban areas had been proclaimed.[4]

After 1923 the Act was repeatedly amended, and with each amendment it became more difficult for Africans to enter towns and settle there with their families. The trend of legislation was opposite to that of economic forces which drove increasing numbers of Africans into industrial employment. In 1930 the Act was amended to give the local authorities in proclaimed areas power to exclude African women from towns unless they had a certificate to the effect that there was accommodation available for them. Previously African women had practically free access to urban areas and this, said the Minister of Native Affairs, often led to an 'undesirable state of affairs'.[5] In 1937 the Act was further amended to give the government powers to compel municipalities to remove Africans 'surplus' to labour requirements.

In both the 1930 and 1937 amendments the pressure of white agricultural interests was discernible. The farmers, unable to compete with the towns in securing and retaining labour, demanded restrictions on the townward movement of Africans. In the 1870s several Transvaal laws had been passed with the intention of curbing Africans from going to Kimberley thereby denuding Transvaal farms of labour.[6] '. . . we must keep as many people on the land as possible, because the farmer is the backbone of the country'.[7]

In March 1942 the Minister of Native Affairs, Colonel Deneys Reitz, condemned the pass laws which, he said, had resulted in the conviction of 273,790 Africans for pass law offences in the Transvaal alone in 1939, 1940, and 1941.[8] The administration of the pass laws was then relaxed

[1] Natives (Urban Areas) Act, section 12.   [2] Ibid., s. 12 (2).
[3] Ibid., s. 17 (1).   [4] Rogers, p. 171.   [5] H.A.D., 1930, col. 212.
[6] E. Kahn, 'The Pass Laws', in E. Hellmann (ed.), Handbook on Race Relations, p. 276.
[7] P. W. G. Grobler (Minister of Lands), H.A.D., 1930, col. 224.
[8] Senate Debates, 1942, col. 1583.

in Johannesburg, the Witwatersrand, Pretoria, Durban, Pietermaritz-burg, Kimberley, and Bloemfontein.[1] In 1946, however, after strident criticisms from the Nationalist Party, enforcement was resumed.

From 1948 onwards the implementation of apartheid involved drastic extensions of influx controls in the towns. In 1952 the Natives (Abolition of Passes and Co-ordination of Documents) Act abolished eleven previous laws or regulations that had provided for the carrying of passes. It introduced the 'reference book' in which was to be recorded all the information previously contained in separate documents. The Act provided that reference books were to be issued to all Africans (men and women) born in the Republic, South West Africa, Basutoland, Bechuanaland, or Swaziland, on reaching the age of sixteen. It would be an offence not to possess a reference book after dates that were to be published in the *Government Gazette*.[2] Despite the title of the Act, the reference book is a 'pass', defined by the 1946–8 Fagan Commission as a document carried by a particular race, connected with freedom of movement, and to be carried by the person concerned at all times.[3]

An amendment to the Natives (Urban Areas) Act in 1952 ensured that all urban areas were automatically proclaimed and influx controls operated in them. Provision was made for a local authority to request exemption from being proclaimed, but this has never been granted.[4] The 1952 Amendment provided that no African could remain in a pro-claimed area for more than 72 hours unless he or she complied with certain qualifications. Amendments to the principal Act in 1955, 1957, and 1964 successively made these qualifications more rigorous, thereby making it increasingly difficult for Africans to qualify for permanent residences in urban areas (now termed 'prescribed areas'). Section 10(1) of the Act, reads as follows:

No Bantu shall remain for more than 72 hours in a prescribed area unless he produces proof in the manner prescribed that

(a) he has, since birth, resided continuously in such area; or

(b) he has worked continuously in such area for one employer for a period of not less than ten years or has lawfully resided continuously in such area for a period of not less than fifteen years, and has thereafter continued to reside in such area and is not employed outside such area and has not during either period or thereafter been sentenced to a fine exceeding one hundred rand or to imprisonment for a period exceeding six months; or

(c) such Bantu is the wife, unmarried daughter or son under the age at which he would become liable for payment of general tax under the Bantu Taxation and Development Act, 1925 (Act No. 41 of 1925), of any Bantu

---

[1] *Fagan Report*, Annexure 6, p. 72.
[2] For men the date was 1 Feb. 1958, for women 1 Dec. 1960.
[3] *Fagan Report*, para. 39.
[4] To the writer's knowledge no local authority has ever applied.

mentioned in paragraph (a) or (b) of this sub-section and after lawful entry into such prescribed area, ordinarily resides with that Bantu in such area; or

(d) in the case of any other Bantu, permission so to remain has been granted by an officer appointed to manage a labour bureau in terms of the provisions of paragraph (a) of sub-section (6) of section twenty-one of the Bantu Labour Regulation Act, 1911 (Act No. 15 of 1911), due regard being had to the availability of accommodation in a Bantu residential area.

The onus is upon Africans who are prosecuted for alleged contraventions of this section to prove that they are lawfully in the area.[1]

The pass laws have been used to implement as far as possible what the Government regards as the ideal pattern of African labour: single male contract labourers who work for specified periods of up to one year and then return to the country. A contract labourer cannot send for his family to join him in the town and he can never qualify under the law to do so.[2] Despite influx controls, the numbers of Africans in the towns have continued to rise. In 1965 131,282 men and 14,475 women were admitted to the prescribed areas of Bloemfontein, Cape Town, Durban, East London, Kimberley, Pietermaritzburg, Port Elizabeth, Pretoria, and the Witwatersrand, while in the same year 66,303 men and 19,883 women were 'endorsed out' of these areas.[3]

Nothing has done more to inflame African opinion than the pass laws. To Africans the pass is a symbol of servile status. If influx controls are to achieve their stated aims they must be strictly enforced. Strict enforcement, however, involves constant checks on Africans, carried out by 'authorized officers', often taking the form of mass police raids on groups of Africans or townships. Between 1951 and 1962 an average of 339,255 Africans were convicted under various pass law offences.[4] In 1937 the Police Commission of Inquiry found 'abundant evidence that the enforcement by the police of the present laws is often marked by unnecessary harshness, lack of sympathy and even violence'.[5] It noted that the overwhelming majority of white police recruits were of rural origin and that 'Countrymen, owing to their outlook towards natives as they find them in the rural areas, are apt to arouse resentment and friction when dealing with the very different urban type of native.'[6]

In 1942 the Smit Committee, after referring to the large numbers of pass law convictions, made the following comments:

These statistics indicate the tremendous price which the country is paying in respect of these laws for, apart from the actual cost of the administration,

---

[1] Section 10 (5).

[2] For an analysis of the system see *Memorandum on the Application of the Pass Laws and Influx Control*, Black Sash (Johannesburg, 1966).

[3] Horrell, *Survey, 1966*, p. 162. (The figure excludes women in Durban.)

[4] Ibid., *1963*, p. 138.

[5] *Report of Police Commission of Inquiry, 1937*, paras. 275–6.   [6] Ibid., para. 63.

there is the vast loss of labour due to detention during arrest and imprisonment. Fines paid constitute a drain on the Native's income which it has been shown he can ill afford. Apart from these considerations the harassing and constant interference with the freedom of movement of Natives gives rise to a burning sense of grievance and injustice which has an unsettling effect on the Native population as a whole. The application of these laws also has the undesirable feature of introducing large numbers of Natives to the machinery of criminal law and makes many become familiar at an early age with prison. These laws create technical offences which involve little or no moral opprobrium. The Committee has reached the conclusion that rather than perpetuate the state of affairs described above, it would be better to face the abolition the Pass Laws.[1]

Several defences of the pass laws are advanced. It is necessary, it is said, to have influx controls to prevent urban areas being 'swamped' by rural Africans, though this argument has never been demonstrated. Port Elizabeth, for example, was not a 'proclaimed area' until 1952 and, despite the rapid growth of its African population during and after the Second World War, it had by no means an abnormally acute housing shortage. Influx controls are said to protect the wage levels of those Africans already in the towns against the competition of further migrants.[2] This proposition, however, has never been proved. A recent study of African labour forces in Cape Town showed that '... any system of influx control which confines workers to a particular industry, firm, or occupation within a firm will prevent or retard their progressing to more skilled and better paid work'.[3] Influx controls in prescribed areas do not apply to Africans recruited for mining work, which has become progressively less attractive to Africans. It is hard, dangerous, and worse-paid than many other industrial jobs. Influx control, 'by diverting men into mining, who might otherwise have sought employment in some other field, tends to increase the supply of mine workers and thus to depress wages in mining'.[4]

While supporters of influx control point with satisfaction to the development of contract or migrant labour, critics of the system condemn it for making further inroads into African family life. Innumerable cases have been reported of African women who are parted from their husbands because they do not 'qualify' under the law to join them in the towns.

The enforcement of influx controls has led to the growth of a large bureaucracy. Vast and arbitrary powers have been vested in the hands of officials who administer the system.[5] It is widely believed that bribery

[1] *Smit Committee Report*, paras. 305–6.
[2] See, e.g., W. J. P. Carr, *Influx Control as seen by an Administrator of Non-European Affairs.* (Address to SAIRR, 1961.)   [3] S. van der Horst, *African Workers*, p. 12.
[4] D. Hobart Houghton, *The South African Economy*, p. 162.
[5] D. B. Molteno, 'Urban Areas Legislation', *Race Relations Journal*, 22 (2) (1955) 26–35.

and corruption on a large scale are endemic in the system. In 1963 the Paarl Commission of Inquiry found that 'extensive corruption took place at Paarl in respect of the issuing of entrance permits to Bantu work-seekers under the Influx Control Regulations. Many such persons were required to pay bribes in order to obtain permits; others were called to work for them without wages.'[1]

3. Processes of Urbanization

Among Africans and Afrikaners, the groups with whom this chapter is mainly concerned, the towns soon acquired the reputation of being evil and undesirable places. 'The sober, honourable Afrikaner farming people [boerebevolking] detested the modern towns that had surprised them like a flood in the night. The tales of crime, gambling, drunkenness, murder and immorality on the Rand deeply shocked the Afrikaner with his strong moral and religious views. Parents would not allow their children to go there.'[2] Tengo Jabavu, an African newspaper editor, told the 1903–5 Commission that while a great number of young people who lived in rural areas near towns went to work in the towns, 'further away from the towns there is a strong desire on their part to remain on the land and to remain away from the towns as much as possible. The reason for that is that they consider the influences of the town contaminating. . . .'[3] Bitter complaints were made by rural Africans that their young folk, particularly girls, broke away from their homes and were corrupted in the towns.[4]

To the Afrikaners, towns were pre-eminently the places of the oppressor. Many attributed their rural poverty to the financial power of the English and Jewish groups. 'As the original agent of the destruction of the Boer way of life, the gold-mining industry has always retained its diabolic character for the majority of Afrikaners.'[5] The Afrikaner in the town regarded himself as a foreigner among aliens. 'He is also not welcome there. He is often regarded as an intruder and a rival.'[6] Moreover, Afrikaners saw themselves as being at the mercy of alien groups who were unsympathetic if not hostile to the *volk* and their ideals. The language of industry, commerce, and officialdom of the towns was overwhelmingly English. Even the former Trekker capitals of Pietermaritzburg, Pretoria, and Bloemfontein had been 'captured by the language and way of life of the foreigner'.[7] Poor English was a

---

[1] *Report of the Commission Appointed to Inquire into the Events on the 20th to 22nd November 1962 at Paarl (para. 205)*.

[2] Albertyn *et al.*, p. 12. (trans.)   [3] *1903–5 Report*, ii. 421.

[4] *Natal Native Affairs Commission, 1906–7*, Evidence of Gobozi, p. 824.

[5] S. Patterson, *The Last Trek*, p. 149.

[6] Albertyn *et al.*, p. 18. (trans.)   [7] Ibid., p. 11 (trans.).

considerable disadvantage in urban occupations, and difficulties in communication made the Afrikaner feel even more ill at ease in the towns. 'Being under the impression that he was unwelcome, his attitudes also handicap him; he acquits himself poorly, he is timid, comes hat-in-hand and lacks the greater self-confidence of the English workseeker. He enjoys no influence and aid from the better-off; his volk is small, poor and subordinate to the world power that lends support to the English worker. He is scorned and considered insignificant by other peoples.'[1] The struggle of Afrikaners to gain a foothold in the towns was mirrored in their efforts to obtain an equality of status for Afrikaans in the towns. 'Greater equality between the influence of English and Afrikaans [would] lead to a reduction of the inequality between the English and Afrikaners in professional life.'[2] The contempt that many English speaking town-dwellers showed for Afrikaners and their culture was bitterly resented and contributed to the growth of nationalism. This contempt was the theme of S. Bruwer's novel *Bodemvas* (published in 1935) which describes the experiences of an Afrikaner farm girl married to an Englishman in the anti-Afrikaner stronghold of Durban. Unable to stand the constant jibes and attacks on her *volk* she flees to her parents' farm. In 1912, when 85 per cent of the civil service were English speakers, a regulation was passed requiring bilingualism (English and Dutch). This was a deadletter, and only in 1925 when Afrikaans became an official language, and the Pact Government was in power, was the regulation enforced. This gave Afrikaners a considerable advantage in the civil service as many more of them were bilingual than English-speaking whites.[3]

To Afrikaner leaders the danger was that poverty and demoralisation might lead to the Afrikaner townsman's losing his identity, or becoming 'de-nationalized'. Common life and poverty in multi-racial slums would reduce the significance of racial and cultural differences. Moreover, being an Afrikaner in itself was a handicap in the alien world of the city: 'To thrive in the town, he must degenerate as an Afrikaner; to progress socially he must retrogress nationally.'[4]

Comparisons between town and country life occur frequently in commission reports and in Afrikaans literature. In 1947 an N. G. Kerk Commission reported: 'In the country, one feels dependent on God; in the town, on men, such as one's employer.' Compared with the intimacy of small-scale rural communities, towns were anonymous and this could lead to licence and debauchery. The country was homogeneous, towns were heterogeneous. Country people were attached to the old farm house and had considerable house-pride but the townsman lived in rented, temporary accommodation and never had a truly fixed abode. Money

[1] Ibid., p. 46.   [2] S. Pauw, *Die Beroepsarbeid van die Afrikaner in die Stad*, p. 180.
[3] Ekonomiese Instituut van die F.A.K., p. 73.   [4] Albertyn *et al.*, p. 217 (trans.).

was little used in the country but was all-important in the towns; it was not surprising that Afrikaners, with little traditional commercial sense, tended to become entangled in wasteful hire-purchase agreements, gambling, and the like. The countryman possessed a measure of independence but the town-dweller was reduced to servitude (*knegskap*). The country was peaceful and quiet but the towns were restless and noisy. Racial divisions were firmly maintained in the country but in the towns race-mixing occurred: 'employers were less concerned than the Afrikaner with maintaining the colour-bar because they wanted the cheapest labour. It didn't worry them that this would blunt the Afrikaner's racial consciousness.' 'Compared with the godly life of the country, in the town one encountered a total indifference to spiritual and religious sanctions.'[1] In 1960 the du Toit Commission (composed entirely of Afrikaners) reported that: town-dwellers, unlike country people, were 'increasingly dominated by machines; and they are surrounded on all sides by an artificial man-made environment'. Country families were more stable than town ones and there was less crime in the country. Moreover, 'as to religion and general attitude towards life, the country has always served as a wholesome conservative factor. In spite of all the advantages which the city offers and which enrich the spirit, the city is also the breeding ground of foreign schools of thought such as atheism, international liberalism, materialism, etc.' City-dwellers were often not property-owners and, therefore, they were more 'likely to develop leftist tendencies'.[2]

In 1904 only some 40,000 out of a total number of 630,000 Afrikaners were in the nine major towns of South Africa. The 'Second Great Trek' was under way and before them lay a painful period of adjustment to urban conditions. Little in the rural Afrikaners' background equipped them for urban life; they lacked a tradition of skilled labour; hardly any had learned a trade and, moreover, they had a disinclination for what was called 'kaffirwerk'. i.e. the rougher types of physical labour performed under supervision for a wage. Their entry into the occupational structure of the towns could only be at the lowest rungs.

It was Dr. D. F. Malan who cast the townward movement in the imagery of the Trek with its attendant conflicts and ultimate goal of conquest. 'Alas', he said in 1916, 'this trek does not lead from the narrows [*engte*] to the open spaces. This is a trek from a condition of freedom and abundance to one of poverty and want. This is the journey from Canaan to Egypt. This is the departure of the prosperous land-occupier to the land of misery.'[3] Malan's account of rural conditions may have been misleading but his idealization of the country touched a receptive

[1] Albertyn *et al.*, pp. 42–6 (trans.).
[2] *Du Toit Commission*, paras. 35–51.
[3] Malan, *De Achteruitgang van Ons Volk*, p. 21 (trans.).

chord in the minds of Afrikaners who reflected upon town life. In 1938 Malan made another speech on the theme of the Second Great Trek:

> The battle with weapons is over. That was the Voortrekkers'. But one, even more violent, more deadly than theirs is being decided now. The battle-field has shifted. Your Blood River is not here. Your Blood River lies in the town . . . at that new Blood River of our people white and non-white meet each other in much closer contact and in a much tighter wrestling-hold than one hundred years ago when the circle of white-tented wagons protected the laager and the shotgun and assegai clashed against each other. . . . Where he must stand in the breach for his people, the Afrikaner of the new Great Trek meets the non-white at his Blood River, half-armed or even completely unarmed, without a barricade, without a river between them, defenceless in the open plains of economic competition.[1]

Many deluded themselves that they would ultimately be able to return to the land. In 1930 W. M. MacMillan wrote: 'However he is placed, the poor Afrikaner always clings to the possiblity of maintaining his dignity as a property owner, if no longer in land, then in sheep, goats, donkeys, or oxen, against the day when he can return from day-labour to the semblance of independence as a full-blown *bywoner*.' Ten per cent of unskilled railwaymen in the Transvaal were reported to own some animals, and often they clubbed together to acquire an animal, envisaging some day a return to the land.[2] In 1947 the N. G. Kerk Commission received evidence that 'a very big percentage of [Afrikaner] labourers regarded themselves as only temporarily employed in industries'. A mining official told the Commission that 'many mine-workers deluded themselves that they were going to save money, and, then, later, return to the country . . .'.[3]

In the early days of the Witwatersrand the new Afrikaner town-dweller could enter only those occupations in which his lack of urban skills was not too great a disadvantage: the civil service, education, the police force, and the railways. On the mines immigrant white workers held a jealously preserved monopoly of skilled work while unskilled work was the monopoly of Africans. A breakthrough came in 1907 when white mine-workers went on strike in protest against a proposal by the mine-owners to permit African and Chinese workers to perform more skilled work. The strike was broken by replacing the strikers with un-employed Afrikaners. 'This led the mine-owners to abandon their policy of employing immigrant workers only in skilled occupations. When the strike ended after two months, hundreds of strikers had been permanently replaced by Afrikaners.'[4]

The poverty and hardship of the urban Afrikaner (even if he or she

---

[1] Malan, *Glo in U Volk!*, pp. 123–7 (trans.).   [2] MacMillan, *Complex South Africa*, p. 95.
[3] Albertyn *et al.*, p. 48 (trans.).   [4] Ekonomiese Instituut van die F.A.K., p. 53. (trans.).

were fortunate enough to find employment) is illustrated by the following account of a woman worker: 'At the beginning of 1911, I arrived in
Johannesburg and obtained employment through a school friend. . . .
She found me a job in a small workshop where she was a tailoress.
I started at ten shillings a week. The hours were from seven a.m. to
six p.m. daily, with an hour for lunch, and seven a.m. to twelve noon
on Saturdays. The workshop was terribly overcrowded and hot. . . .
Very often, we had to take work home and sit up late at night finishing
it. For this, we received no extra pay.'[1]

After 1924 the Civilized Labour policy did facilitate the entry of
Afrikaner unskilled workers into industrial employment (at the expense
of displaced non-whites) but unemployment remained a considerable
problem. Older immigrants to the towns had difficulty in adapting
themselves to urban life because they were unskilled workers and 'under
the system in force in South Africa a trade [could] only be learnt by
going through an apprenticeship which has to begin fairly early in
youth'.[2] They therefore had to remain as unskilled workers. S. Pauw
investigated 4,928 unskilled whites who sought work at the Cape Town
Labour Bureau in the few years before 1939. 57·3 per cent were of rural
origin and 83·8 per cent of the Afrikaners among them had been born
on the *platteland*. The author commented: 'Most of them were too old
to make a promising start in urban professions. They spent their youth
on the *platteland* in fruitless efforts to begin a career. There was no help,
no vocational or technical training; they had to try and fight their way
in an environment where there was no future for people like them. Even
when their own efforts took them to the town, where there were still
possibilities, state policy was aimed at getting them out of the town to
dead-end careers outside.'[3] But the Carnegie Commission could report
that a process of economic adaptation was taking place, particularly
among the younger generation which had more possibilities of receiving
a training in skilled work.[4]

In the depression years (1928–32) the demoralization and misery of
the urban poor white was immense, particularly in the smaller towns
where economic opportunities were even fewer. 'We, the undersigned
inhabitants of Vryheid, wish to bring to your notice the precarious economic position of this town and the terrible distress that is existing among
the ranks of the unemployed. All the signatories to this petition are
unemployed, and their wives and children are bordering on starvation.'[5]
C. M. van den Heever's short story *Nooit!* graphically described the

---

[1] Quoted in E. S. Sachs, *Garment Workers in Action*, p. 32.
[2] *Joint Findings and Recommendations of Carnegie Commission*, para. 79; Grosskopf, p. xxiii.
[3] S. Pauw, pp. 196–7 (trans.).
[4] *Carnegie Commission*, para. 82; Grosskopf, p. xxiii.   [5] *Cape Argus*, 21 Oct. 1931.

demoralization of the ruined farmer in Johannesburg who lived in rooms, hired from an Indian, with his wife and four children. The hero is unskilled, unemployed, and humiliated at being powerless to help his family. 'He had to set aside everything that constituted his very nature —to come and live here. He had to cut out his self-respect, he had to become a dog who licked the hands of those who gave him food.'[1]

In the years of steady industrial expansion after 1933 the urban poor white problem was being slowly overcome and by the late 1930s could hardly be said to exist. At this time Afrikaners began in earnest to organize themselves to 'conquer the towns' and 'to penetrate the existing economic structure and gain [for Afrikaners] a controlling share in the economic life of the country'.[2] In 1938 D. F. Malan had called upon the strength of Afrikaner nationalism to help those in the towns: 'Unite that strength consciously in a mighty act of rescue, and then Afrikaner-dom's future is assured and white civilization is saved.'[3] The formation of the *Reddingsdaadbond* (see pp. 301–4) in 1938 signalized the determina-tion of Afrikaner nationalists to 'rescue' their urban compatriots.

Urbanization had thrown Afrikaners into cosmopolitan cities but, as Malan had reminded his people in 1917, *'een volk is een lichaam'* ('a people is a body') and social dislocation and dispersion of Afrikaners must not be permitted to endanger national identity. Several speakers referred to the danger at the Afrikaner Economic Congress held in Bloemfontein in October 1939. C. G. W. Schumann said: 'The major task of the future is to retain these Afrikaners for the Afrikaner struggle and for the estab-lishment of an Afrikaner national identity and culture. It will pro-bably be a long time before the Afrikaner finds his feet in the town and builds up a town-tradition as he has done on the land and on the farm. Only then will he find that inner balance, that compatibility with his environment. . . .' Among the resolutions passed was one that 'the Afrikaner labour-force must be organized in such a manner that they are thereby consciously drawn into the *volkslewe* [national life] . . .'.[4]

The economic rise of urban Afrikaners from this time onward was steady. A striking feature was the growth of a prosperous and assertive entrepreneurial class, greatly assisted after 1948 by an Afrikaner nation-alist government. Their activities have been recorded in a detailed account whose title, *'n Volk Staan Op* ('A People Stand Up') is indicative of their success. Economic inequalities between English- and Afrikaans-speaking townspeople remained large, although in the 1950s and 1960s the gap was becoming perceptibly narrower. In 1951 'the annual per

[1] *Kortverhale* (Cape Town, 1942), p. 4 (trans.).
[2] *Volkshandel*, Aug. 1943 (trans.). Quoted by Laurence Salomon, 'The Economic back-ground to the Revival of Afrikaner Nationalism', J. Butler (ed.), *Boston University Papers in African History*, i. 238. [3] Malan, *Glo in U Volk!*, p. 129 (trans.).
[4] Ekonomiese Instituut van die F.A.K., pp. 108, 131.

capita income of Afrikaners in Johannesburg and nine other cities along the Witwatersrand (where Afrikaners comprised 43 per cent of the total white population) was £182, compared with £349 for English-speaking whites. A similar disparity prevailed in the other leading urban areas —Pretoria, Cape Town, Durban, Port Elizabeth; even where Afrikaners predominated among whites numerically, as in Bloemfontein (73·3 per cent), the corresponding figures are £180 and £318.'[1] An indication of the Afrikaners' progress in the towns was given by the 1960 Census figures on occupational distribution. Fifty-one per cent of white males in working towns were Afrikaans-speaking.Seventy per cent of all white mine-workers and 37 per cent of all professional and technical workers were Afrikaners. The top professional posts in commerce and industry were still over-whelmingly filled by English-speaking whites: 109 per 1,000 of English-speaking whites fell into this group as opposed to 36 per 1,000 of Afri-kaans-speaking whites.[2] The higher echelons of the civil service were, however, overwhelmingly occupied by Afrikaners. Afrikaner business houses claimed in 1960 to control ten per cent of invested capital.[3]

In politics the number of parliamentary constituencies won by the Nationalist Party in the major urban centres increased steadily after 1948. In 1944 they held four such seats; after the 1948 election, fifteen, and after the 1966 election, fifty five.[4] The growth of a settled population of Afrikaner townspeople is reflected in the increase of N. G. Kerk urban congregations: before 1920 there were not forty town churches, by 1947 there were 122, and by 1958, 229.[5] The Church had played a key role in keeping the poor white problem in the public eye, and striving to ensure that the urban Afrikaner was not lost to his *volk*. In 1947 the Dutch Reformed Churches resolved that 'urbanization is a desirable and necessary extension of Afrikaner national life [*volkslewe*]; it is a process which all other civilized nations had to undergo to reach maturity. The Afrikaner must therefore abandon his former negative and hostile attitude to town life. Not that he should adapt himself to what is alien and unwholesome in the town, but rather that he should establish himself in the town and maintain his own nature and traditions. The town is another outpost which the Afrikaner must occupy; every Afrikaner must play his part in achieving this.'[6]

By 1960 the du Toit Commission could report that 'although many

---

[1] Salomon, p. 235.
[2] S. van Wyk, *Die Afrikaner in die Beroepslewe van die Stad*, ch. 4.
[3] Marquard, *Peoples and Policies*, p. 72.
[4] The writer is indebted to Mr. Stanley Uys and Senator J. L. Horak for this information.
[5] Albertyn *et al.*, p. 32; Albertyn, *Land en Stad*, p. 144.
[6] Federale Armsorgraad van die Gefedereerde N.G.K., *Die Stadwaartse Trek van die Afrikaner-Nasie*, p. 117 (trans.).

city-dwellers still entertain hopes of being able to return to the *platteland* as farmers one day, this yearning should not always be interpreted as a real desire to brave the ups and downs of agriculture. True, in some townsfolk this longing finds expression in the acquisition and occupation of peri-urban small holdings but the real motive is seldom to find an independent and economic existence there; employment in the city remains the principal means of livelihood.'[1] In the *Huisgenoot* a journalist has described the fully urbanized Afrikaner as the 'New Afrikaner': unlike men of the previous generation who idealized rural life the 'New Afrikaner', having remained and been successful in a town, realizes that he does not belong on the *platteland*. 'Everything there is just as strange as the town was for his forefathers.' Towns were no longer hostile, anti-Afrikaner places; they had become Afrikanerized and Afrikaner communities had put down deep roots; the prejudice against Afrikaans had declined down the years.[2]

Despite the official insistence that towns were 'white man's places' and the policy of discouraging Africans from settling as permanent town-dwellers, there arose in every major South African town a hard core of Africans who regarded themselves as 'townsmen' and no longer looked upon the country as 'home'. Nat Nakasa, a Johannesburg journalist, precisely expressed the view of an educated townsman in 1966:

> I am supposed to be a Pondo, but I don't even know the language of that tribe. I was brought up in a Zulu-speaking home, my mother being a Zulu. Yet I can no longer think in Zulu because that language cannot cope with the demands of our day. . . . I have never owned an assegai or any of those magnificent shields. Neither do I propose to be in tribal war when I go to the United States this year for my scholarship. I am just not a tribesman, whether I like it or not. I am, inescapably, a part of the city slums, the factory machines and our beloved shebeens.[3]

Africans who regarded themselves as permanently urbanized were present in Cape Town in the early 1900s (see p. 194). By the 1920s the realization that not all urban Africans were 'temporary sojourners' had crept into official reports. 'Round many of the larger towns there were growing up settled Native communities among whom Native traditions or customs were only a memory.'[4] In 1932 the Native Economic Commission found that 'it is perfectly clear that a considerable number of Natives have become permanent town-dwellers'.[5] The 1939–40 Report

[1] *Du Toit Commission*, paras. 19–20.
[2] W. Hartman, 'Die Nuwe Afrikaner', *Huisgenoot*, 28 May and 4 June 1965 (trans.).
[3] 'The World of Nat Nakasa', *The Classic*, ii, 1 (1966), 50.
[4] *Report of the Native Affairs Commission for 1921*, p. 6.
[5] *Report of the Native Economic Commission 1930–1932*, paras. 500, 529 ff.

of the Native Affairs Commission estimated the number of permanently urbanized Africans to be 750,000.[1] The Broome Commission found that in 1946 nearly one quarter of Durban's African population could be regarded as permanently urbanized.[2] The findings of the 1946–8 Fagan Commission have been noted above.

Reseach workers have experienced difficulty in formulating criteria of 'urbanization'. Some employ 'objective 'tests. Ellen Hellmann, for example, considered at least ten years' permanent residence in the town, permanent residence of the wife in the town, and no land rights in the country, to warrant a person's being described as 'urbanized'.[3] Others employed 'subjective' tests, such as a man's stated intentions of remaining in town and bringing his family to join him there.[4] An incalculable factor is the effect of official policy in retarding African urbanization. One cannot know how many Africans were prevented or deterred from settling in the towns by the operation of influx controls; or how many retained a footing in the country because they disliked the constant bureaucratic surveillance and general insecurity of town life.[5] In a study of African migrants in East London, Philip Mayer reported his impression of 'regulations deflecting what would otherwise be a rather powerful drive towards urbanization'.[6]

Between the 'ideal-types' of 'town-rooted' and 'country-rooted' there existed several intermediate categories which made the classification of all town Africans on an urbanization scale very difficult. Mayer found in his East London study a large class of 'school' migrants who were 'double-rooted', being simultaneously town-rooted and urban-cultured, and country-rooted.[7] Studies of African workers on the Witwatersrand showed many to be country-rooted people who left their homes with reluctance and favoured jobs which enabled them to make periodic returns to the country. 'We now have reason to believe that rural orientation, or a low level of urbanization, may co-exist with a complete integration into industrial employment. Yet these men are not migrant. They work continuously in the urban-industrial environment returning home annually during the prescribed leave period.'[8]

Recent studies of the urban African population indicated that in Pretoria 63 per cent were settled in town,[9] in Johannesburg 50 per cent,[10]

---

[1] *Report of the Native Affairs Commission for 1939–40*, p. 16.
[2] *Report of Judicial Commission on Native Affairs in Durban* (1948), p. 18.
[3] Hellmann, *Sellgoods*, pp. 64–5.
[4] P. Mayer, *Tribesmen or Townsmen*, pp. 8 ff.
[5] S. T. van der Horst, 'The Effects of Industrialisation on Race Relations in South Africa', G. Hunter (ed.), *Industrialisation and Race Relations*, p. 112.
[6] Mayer, p. 225.   [7] Mayer, pp. 224–5.
[8] Glass, pp. 15–18.   [9] Leistner, p. 277.
[10] S. Biesheuvel, 'Some Characteristics of the African Worker', *Journal of the S.A. Institute of Personnel Management*, 15 (5), (1962), 10–11.

and in Cape Town 21 per cent, with a further 25 per cent expressing the intention of remaining in town.[1]

A rough indication of the trend towards permanent urbanization is afforded by the masculinity ratios in the major towns. In Durban, for example, in 1880 there were 23·78 men to one woman, while by 1960 the ratio was 1·5 to one.[2] In Johannesburg in 1910 the ratio was 23 to one, while in 1965 (Soweto only) it was 0·94 to one. In smaller towns such as Bloemfontein and Grahamstown, African women outnumbered the men by 1960.[3]

Like the Afrikaner, little in his traditional background equipped the African for urban conditions. While it is true that the Tswana and, to a lesser extent, other Sotho groups lived in large concentrations, these were essentially villages in no way comparable to the towns that developed in South Africa. To some white observers early manifestations of social dislocation among town Africans were symptoms of a fundamental inability to cope with urban life. Others, however, saw this as bewilderment occasioned by a foreign and hostile environment:

in the town locations the familiar restraints are almost entirely absent. The Native has no security of tenure, no garden, no incentive to improve his home. In many cases he has no home at all, but only a lodging place, which is often a miserable hovel or shanty. He has little of the social life with which he has been acquainted at his own village, and no responsibility for maintaining public order. He discovers that he is a unit, and so long as he does not commit any of the crimes in the calendar, he is left pretty much to his own devices. There is thrust upon him a freedom from social restraint for which he is wholly unprepared.[4]

But beneath this seemingly amorphous and anomic mass a new kind of social structure was rapidly emerging.

Investigations of urban African communities have revealed a basic cleavage between migrants who regarded themselves as temporarily absent from rural homes, and townsmen who looked upon the towns as home. It has been suggested that 'school' Africans took more readily to town life than 'red' Africans (see pp. 74–6 for an explanation of these terms). An official noted this division in Port Elizabeth in the 1880s. 'Red' people lived separately from 'school' people in a location outside the town and 'they make no improvement in their habits and are content to live in the most barbarous way'. But the 'school' person had 'a great desire for good clothes' and 'his power of assimilation is developing, and he allows nothing to pass unheeded which has benefited his enlightened

---

[1] Van der Horst, *African Workers*, pp. 7 ff.
[2] *Population Census, 1960. Sample Tabulation 5.*
[3] Ibid.   [4] *Christian Express*, 1 Oct. 1906.

neighbour'.[1] These remarks suggested different attitudes to Western culture, one hostile, the other receptive. While it may be true that 'school' people took to urban conditions more readily than 'red' people, there were 'school' people who remained country-rooted in outlook and deplored the ways of townspeople proper.[2] Mayer formulated the concept of 'incapsulation' to describe the apparatus of safeguards established by migrants in East London to resist urbanization. He was dealing with 'red' migrants only but it is probable that the concept has application to 'school' migrants as well, as a study of Langa (Cape Town) has shown. Migrants typically resisted becoming town-rooted and asserted the superiority of rural ways and values over those of the townsmen. Even though they spent a large portion of their lives working in towns the aspiration of eventual return and settlement in the country remained.

Studies of migrants in East London and Cape Town showed that they associated mainly with people from the same rural locality. These 'home-boy' groups were based upon a rural village, or section of a village, or even a magisterial district.[3] The groups tended to lodge and eat together, and preferred one another's company. The group socialized the newly arrived migrant, warning him against the dangers of the town. Older members regarded it as their duty to keep a watchful eye on the younger ones. 'Home-boy' groups helped members in difficulty as a result of illness, bereavement, unemployment, or other misfortune. They tried also to preserve the solidarity of the group by bringing quasi-judicial sanctions to bear against members who transgressed the unwritten code of etiquette.[4] Migrants in Cape Town and East London were found to avoid cinemas, dances, public meetings, and other associational life in the towns.[5] Their main leisure activity in East London was the companionship and affability of the drinking party, attended by fellow home-boys. In Langa there were also migrant sports and music clubs. Conversation and general interest was focused on the rural areas.[6]

A partial analogy is found in the behaviour of Afrikaner immigrants to the towns. They tended to settle in particular parts of the towns, especially in the peri-urban areas. Many Afrikaners preferred the peri-urban areas where they could retain some rural habits by having gardens and owning some poultry and perhaps a cow. Later immigrants came into an environment which was less strange than it might otherwise have

---

[1] *Blue Book on Native Affairs* (Cape Town, 1884). Observation by Civil Commissioner, Port Elizabeth.
[2] Mayer, p. 71; Wilson and Mafeje, p. 53.
[3] Mayer, pp. 99–100; Wilson and Mafeje, pp. 47–8.
[4] Mayer, pp. 127–33; Wilson and Mafeje, pp. 153–61.
[5] Mayer, pp. 116 ff.; Wilson and Mafeje, p. 16.
[6] Ibid., pp. 18–19.

been. Earlier immigrants helped the later ones finding employment and adjusting to urban life. As has been shown (see p. 205) many town Afrikaners tended to remain country-rooted. S. Pauw remarked: 'The rural immigrant to the towns retained his rural background all his life and even transfers certain elements of this to his children. The townward trek means, therefore, not only the urbanization of rustics but also contributes to the ruralization of town life.'[1] The development of semi-urban areas on the edges of town was an aspect of this. A prominent Afrikaner told the writer that in the predominantly Afrikaner northern suburbs of Cape Town features of the *boeredorp* (rural village) have been re-created. The analogy with incapsulation could be taken further: Afrikaners tended to avoid the existing associational life of the towns. They did not join the clubs and societies started by English-speaking townsmen but formed their own. They did not attend English churches. Dutch Reformed churches sprang up rapidly in the towns, and contributed greatly to the cohesion of urban Afrikaners. Moreover, Afrikaners were not absorbed and did not wish to be absorbed, in the existing English-dominated social hierarchy of the towns; they formed their own, and social status was gauged on an exclusively Afrikaner hierarchy.[2] Afrikaner élites did not, generally, reside in the parts of the town chosen by their English counterparts, but tended to form élite areas of their own.

Urbanization greatly affected the kinship systems of all the peoples who were swept up in the townward movement. The N. G. Kerk Commission of 1947 noted that the rural Afrikaner family was traditionally a self-sufficient unit whose members co-operated in running a farm. Occasionally, a large farm would support a couple and four to six of their married children with their families. The patriarchal authority of the father extended to the entire small community thus formed. The patriarch exercised religious as well as secular authority. Families were large, and divorce or separation were practically unknown. People married young and, usually, with their parents' consent. An important factor in maintaining the norms of the society was the pressure of public opinion: little could be done in small-scale rural communities without its becoming public knowledge. In towns the structure and function of the family changed and kinship ties were loosened. From being a cohesive unit the family became a group of discrete individuals, each with different interests and occupational circles. Both parents were forced to take paid employment, and members of the family saw one another only in the early mornings and evenings and 'leisure time was spent mostly out of the house. Therefore a decline of household togetherness [*samesyn*] occurs. Family members come more and more in contact with people

---

[1] S. Pauw, p. 139 (trans.).   [2] Patterson, p. 253.

who are not family members. Everyone moves in different circles. Each circle has a measure of influence. Thus the family members are not only differentiated, they are also individualized. More and more each leads his own life.'[1] The authority of the patriarch declined with the loosening of kinship ties: 'he can no longer serve as so powerful a bulwark against foreign, new-fangled ideas and concepts'.[2]

Among Africans the dislocation of the family system was even greater as a result of the migrant labour system. While Afrikaners, Coloured people, and Indians often migrated to the towns as family units and married men rarely continued for as long as migrant labourers, the opposite was true of Africans. Most men first went to town alone. Of those women who followed, many also moved back and forth between town and country. The migrant labour system inaugurated a pattern of separation of husband and wife. Separation encouraged the formation of casual liaisons in towns and weakened ties with rural families. '. . . the pattern of conduct which was established . . . has come down to the present day, partly on its own momentum and partly because it has been reinforced by wave after wave of labour migrants'.[3] Other factors also contributed to the high incidence of concubinage, and hence, illegitimacy, observed in all studies of urban African communities: by preventing a man's family from joining him, influx controls caused men to take casual 'wives'; poverty and high *lobola* demands, often coupled with the inaccessibility of a girl's guardian (whose permission was required for marriage), caused men and women to live together without formal marriage. Investigation of illicit unions in Cato Manor (Durban) showed that among many couples there was a great desire for a proper marriage that was thwarted for these reasons.[4]

While the incidence of polygyny had greatly declined in most rural areas, in the towns it nearly disappeared. Municipal accommodation did not provide the space a polygynous household required. More important, the higher status of women in the towns and their opposition to polygyny, coupled with high costs of urban *lobola* and marriage, virtually extinguished the system. Even many traditionalist women objected: 'Her husband's wages are not enough to cover her needs. It is therefore understandable when she revolts against polygamy.'[5]

Among all groups women had occupied a subordinate status in rural communities but in the towns their status rose. Many took employment and their income gave them a measure of independence. Afrikaner

[1] G. Cronje and J. D. Venter, *Die Patriargale Familie*, pp. 162–3 (trans.).
[2] Ibid., p. 163.
[3] M. B. Mbata, *The African in the City and his Family* (address to SAIRR), (Durban, 1960), p. 3.
[4] SAIRR, 'The Challenge to Urban Family Life Today' (papers presented at Natal Conference—1959), p. B3.   [5] Ibid., p. A4.

women, married and unmarried, found work quite easily because their labour was cheaper and less organized in trade unions than male labour. Evidence given to the Natal Native Affairs Commission of 1906 suggested that some African women were using the towns as escapes from the restraints imposed upon them in male-dominated rural societies. An African witness told the Commission that 'there was something wrong in their laws, which rendered it possible for their girls to run off to towns, and, under the pretext of working, lead a loose life, and bear children by all sorts of people. The girls run away, in some cases, because their father refused to allow them to marry indigent persons.'[1] African women entered paid employment in large numbers, often performing roles that were traditionally male preserves. Investigators have noted the high incidence of female-headed urban households. In a sample of 109 households among urbanized Africans in East London it was found that forty-six were headed by females, eleven of whom were unmarried mothers, the remainder being mostly widows and divorcees. A survey in Soweto showed that 1,260 out of 8,288 families had female heads. They were said to be common in Langa.[2] Even among the traditionally subordinate and secluded Indian women, urbanization was responsible for an elevation of their status, although their entry into employment outside the home came much later than that of women in other racial groups.[3]

Further evidence of the rising status of women was found in their increasing independence of choice in marriage partners. Indeed, younger people generally became more independent with the loosening of kinship ties. Afrikaner traditionalists complained that their young people found themselves thrown together in towns far from watchful parental eyes and the pressure of small community public opinion. 'The godly origin of marriage and family is being replaced by some with "romantic love" as the origin and aim of marriage.'[4] Among Africans in the towns investigators have observed a decline in the traditional concept of marriage as an alliance between groups of kin and the growth of the notion that it is a union between two individuals, often based on the idea of romantic love.[5] Similar tendencies were noticed among young Indian townspeople.[6]

Among urban Africans the traditional rules of clan exogamy or preferential marriage weakened. In Langa it was reported that many young Nguni people said clan exogamy no longer mattered.[7] In

---

[1] *Natal Native Affairs Commission, 1906–7, Evidence*, p. 723.

[2] B. A. Pauw, p. 146; estimate by Non-European Affairs Dept., Johannesburg Municipality, 21 Oct. 1966; Wilson and Mafeje, p. 79.

[3] H. Kuper, 'The South African Indian Family', SAIRR, *The Indian as a South African*, pp. 26–7.

[4] Albertyn *et al.*, p. 212 (trans.).

[5] B. A. Pauw, p. 126.

[6] H. Kuper, p. 23 (trans.).

[7] Wilson and Mafeje, p. 77.

Atteridgeville (Pretoria) it was shown that the system of preferential marriage had practically disappeared among Sotho-speakers.[1] All urban studies showed too that marriages between Africans of different linguistic groups were common.[2] In the large majority of urban marriages, whether traditional, Christian or civil, a traditional element, *lobola*, has survived, although changed in form and function.[3] Money was substituted in many cases for cattle. Several explanations for the survival of *lobola* in towns have been advanced.[4] Most Africans explain it by saying 'it is our custom', while women regard it as being the means of conferring upon them the status of properly married women.

Studies of urban African families revealed a varied pattern of household structures. B. A. Pauw concluded in his study of urbanized Africans in East London that 'the elementary family is the basic type, but it shows a strong tendency on the one hand to lose the father at a relatively early stage and on the other hand to develop a multi-generation span'.[5] In Baumannville (Durban) the characteristic family types were found to be the 'extended family' (consisting of the nuclear family augmented by individual kinsmen) and the 'joint family' (consisting of the nuclear family augmented by one or more sub-families, usually related). It was hinted that the kinds of household structures found owed much to the acute shortage of accommodation.[6] In Langa it was found that shortage of accommodation and difficulty in obtaining adjoining houses prevented kinsmen from living together even if they wanted to. Moreover, young married couples tended to prefer living on their own.[7] It is clear that marriage and family life among African townspeople are widely different from their traditional counterparts. In traditional society cohesive kinship groups based upon a particular locality were the dominant social group. With the development of labour migration kinsmen dispersed far and wide, and in the urban communities that arose corporate kinship groups came to be of little significance: 'Elementary families are important in town but the wider kinship groups are of negligible importance as corporations, and even the network of kinship relationships is modified by the need to look for a job, or the desire to associate with others of like interests. The very fact that kinsmen are so

[1] J. F. Eloff, ' 'n Sosiografiese Studie van Aanpassing en Ontwikkeling in die Gesinslewe van die Naturelle van Atteridgeville', (unpublished M.A. thesis, University of Pretoria, 1952), p. 76, cited by Anna F. Steyn, *Die Bantoe in die Stad—Die Bantoegesin*, p. 21.

[2] A summary of the evidence from several studies is contained in Steyn, p. 21; see also E. Hellmann, *Rooiyard—a Sociological Survey of an Urban Native Slum Yard*, p. 112.

[3] B. A. Pauw, pp. 128–30.

[4] M. Brandel, 'Urban Lobolo Attitudes', *African Studies*, 17 (1) (1958), 34–50; J. E. Mathewson, 'Impact of Urbanization on Lobola', *Journal of Racial Affairs*, 10 (3), (1959), 72–6.

[5] B. A. Pauw, p. 149.

[6] University of Natal, Institute for Social Research, *The Baumannville Community*, p. 24.

[7] Wilson and Mafeje, p. 75.

scattered proves that kinship is no longer dominant.'[1] Moreover, as Hilda Kuper remarked, 'marriage itself is no longer the essential preliminary qualification for social status and responsibilities. Other factors —education, skill, wealth—are of greater use for advancement in the world opened by competitive western industrialisation.'[2] Individuals, men and women, could *choose* roles and *acquire* status in a manner previously unknown.

A striking feature of the urban African communities was the development of a rich and varied associational life. This germ of a new society had been noticed among Africans in Port Elizabeth in the 1880s: 'Of societies there is no end at the Locations. The fall of one society is a signal for another to rise. The Benefit, Temperance, and Debating Societies have been attempted with marked success. Some now talk of Free Masonry as the main spring of success. A branch of the Empire League will be started at no distant date. . . .'[3]Associations were started by people with like interests in response to perceived needs, and include churches, mothers' unions, and other off shoots of church activities, recreational and sporting clubs, welfare societies, professional associations of teachers, clergy, traders, business men, social workers, and herbalists, trade unions, and associations of tenants, sub-tenants, and stand-owners. A widespread form of association is the *stokfel* which, in its several variants, is a form of savings and recreational club. Each member contributes weekly or monthly a fixed amount and the money thus collected is given to each member in rotation.[4] Political associations attracted large memberships: the towns, where racial inequalities were most starkly manifest, became the main arena of the race conflict and the crucible of African nationalism. The major movements, the African National Congress and the Pan African Congress, were declared unlawful in 1960 but continued to function underground. Allied to political associations were trade unions which, while not illegal, have never been recognized or encouraged by the State.

Studies have shown that language and chiefdom were not invariable determinants of association membership. In East London some rugby clubs were found to be closely associated with particular chiefdoms or regions, but this was not true of other sports clubs.[5] Football clubs in Durban were not based on linguistic divisions, although some were reported to be based on rural regions. In Langa it was found that sports clubs reflected the cleavage between town-rooted and country-rooted people. Most of the clubs patronized by countrymen had a 'home-boy'

[1] Ibid., p. 174.   [2] SAIRR, *The Challenge to Urban Family Life Today*, p. G4.
[3] *Blue Book on Native Affairs* (Cape Town, 1885), pp. 52–3.
[4] UNESCO, *Social Implications of Industrialisation and Urbanization in Africa South of the Sahara*, pp. 724–43.
[5] B. A. Pauw, pp. 172–3.

(i.e. regional) base, but townsmen's clubs were based on other interests.[1] Hellmann reported of Soweto that 'common tribal membership seems to be a category of growing irrelevance'.[2] Associations based on linguistic divisions have been found to be few in number and of little significance.[3]

The shift away from association membership based on locality and language can be shown by reference to the largest urban associations, the churches. In Langa it was shown that while missionary activity created territorial links with particular churches, 'these . . . appear to be growing less and less important and numerous examples can be cited to show that they do not operate consistently, but that every denomination embraces various district and tribal groups'. Investigations showed that class was emerging as a more important determinant of membership, with the educated middle-class people being members of the Anglican, Presbyterian, African Methodist Episcopal, or Methodist Churches, while the less educated and unsophisticated tended to belong to others.[4] Similar effects of the embryonic class structure were shown in the membership of sports, dancing, and other clubs in East London and Durban.[5] In Langa divisions in social clubs on the basis of age and class were reported. A recreational association started by élite, 'middle-class' people ('ooscuse-me'), was later joined by townspeople of lower status, divided on a basis of age into the categories of 'ooMac' and 'ikhaba'. The lower status groups broke away and formed their own club. With the passing of time the younger members ('ikhaba') of the lower status group graduated into the higher age category of the group, and the club became exclusively 'ooMac' in membership. The 'ikhaba' subsequently formed a similar club of their own.[6] An awareness of distinctions in social status is apparent among urbanized Africans as is shown by these labels given by Langa inhabitants to different categories.[7] Another category of people singled out are the Iibari, who are semi-urbanized people with some degree of education and who aspire to inclusion in the ranks of the fully urbanized.[8] Leo Kuper's investigation of selected occupational groups in Durban also showed a marked awareness of status distinctions among Africans. Generalizing from urban studies, status was chiefly determined by education, wealth, and occupation, and degree of westernization. In East London 'the highest status is generally accorded to persons like doctors, teachers, trained ministers and nurses, as well as prosperous business-men who are also well-educated'.[9] A similar pattern of status determinants was reported in Durban, although

[1] Wilson and Mafeje, pp. 114 ff.   [2] E. Hellmann, *Soweto—Johannesburg's African City*, p. 17.
[3] Wilson and Mafeje, pp. 34–8; L. Kuper, *An African Bourgeoisie*, p. 314; Hellmann, *Soweto*, p. 17.   [4] Wilson and Mafeje, p. 101.
[5] Mayer, p. 221; L. Kuper, p. 99.   [6] Wilson and Mafeje, pp. 131, 141.
[7] Ibid., p. 15.   [8] Ibid., p. 20.   [9] B. A. Pauw, p. 179.

different occupational groups who constituted the African 'bourgeoisie' tended to emphasize some determinants rather than others. Status differences manifested themselves in various ways: in dress, furniture, type or size of cars, consumption habits, lavishness of entertainments, weddings and funerals, and place and style of residence. Hellmann noted that Soweto's middle class is concentrated largely in Dube where Africans have been permitted to build their own homes (though not to own the land). Inhabitants of Dube are nicknamed 'Dubenheimers', with a distinct connotation of status.[1]

The tensions, upheavals, and dislocation accompanying the urbanization of any people were exacerbated for Africans by official policies directed against the stabilization of urban African communities. '. . . the impression of at once being wanted and unwanted in the urban area, makes the African live under a smarting sense of grievance and resentment'.[2] An African has written:

One feels that the urban African is a little bewildered. He makes every effort to adjust himself to urban living and to accept a western way of life; but he finds that there is a strong authoritative pressure to obstruct such a change. For instance, in a property-owning society he cannot own property, —in a society which has grown and prospered by workers organizing themselves his own organizations are restricted. In fact it seems that authority is not anxious to assist him in making adjustments from rural to urban living. He is thus uncertain and not sure of his goals.[3]

Although the urban African townships are often gay and vibrant places, insecurity of life and property are ever-present. Criminal gangs were noted even in the early days of this century and remained a marked feature of urban life. Indeed, there can be few more violent communities in the world than some of South Africa's African townships. Violence and fear have become woven into the very fabric of life. In Soweto, where some one thousand murders are committed annually,

there is an army of men fighting a bloody battle against authority and against those laws and values which the world now recognises are essential for the happiness and safety of the common man. They roam the streets in gangs, robbing, raping, killing anyone in their path. They break into houses and threaten people with the death of their children if they don't hand over their wages. In shebeens they stab customers who refuse to buy them a drink and they beat up the girls who won't 'go with' them. They march through crowded trains robbing anyone they like and pushing people out of the windows. They run protection rackets, forcing shopkeepers and men with any sign of wealth to pay for their safety. If they don't pay, they are shot or stabbed with

---

[1] Hellmann, *Soweto*, p. 19.
[2] *Report of the Proceedings of the Natives Representatives Council*, 1943, p. 6.
[3] D. G. S. M'timkulu, *African Adjustment to Urbanization*, p. 4.

the dreaded '*ntshumentshu*', a needle-sharp spoke of steel which is plunged through the spinal cord, leaving the victim paralysed. They have given South Africa the highest paraplegic rate in the world.[1]

Concern over crime on the Witwatersrand and in Pretoria led to the appointment of a Government committee in 1942. In their Report the Committee stated:

> The consequences of many years of indifference, half-measures or measures whose intellectual content never aspired to rise above the conception of more and larger prisons, more and more frequent floggings and more (or less) spare diet, have been to produce a native population of industrial serfs, called upon to perform the unskilled labour of civilisation under exacting conditions and at wages which keeps it chronically on the verge of destitution and produces, *inter alia*, the native criminal.[2]

In a minority report, the three African members of the Committee noted the link between crime and the colour bar:

> . . . Africans, like other races in South Africa, desire possession to satisfy their wants, to gain power and to satisfy 'desires of prestige' and 'social recognition'. To gain these, fair means are first earnestly and honestly attempted; but when legislative and administrative colour and racial barriers are met with, then illicit means of obtaining a livelihood such as theft, robbery, housebreaking, and illicit liquor traffic, are resorted to as a result of thwarted ambitions . . . crime among Africans in the Union of South Africa . . . is anti-social behaviour arising from bad living conditions and discriminating legislative disabilities. It is a protest of a weak section from frustrated desires.[3]

Crime is a symptom of social dislocation and a violent reaction to a social order that denies people equality. To Africans in the towns the law and those who enforce it have become synonymous with racial inequality. Many of the laws relate to passes and other restraints on Africans that do not apply to other groups. To be convicted and jailed for a technical offence carries no moral stigma, and the consequence is for the whole of the law to be brought into disrepute. The police who enforce these laws, often by means of mass raids and arrests, are to Africans the most tangible symbols of a white domination that places more stress on the regimentation and discipline of Africans than the security and peace of the townships. An African journalist commented in 1942:

> I wonder if those in authority are making any effort to exterminate the

---

[1] M. Cobden, 'The Bloodiest Place on Earth', *Rand Daily Mail*, 18 Feb. 1967.

[2] *Report of the Committee appointed by the Ministers of Justice and Native Affairs, July 1942, to investigate the position of crime on the Witwatersrand and in Pretoria* (Elliot Committee Report), para. 13.

[3] *Minority Report of Elliot Committee*, submitted by A. B. Xuma, S. P. Mqubuli, and R. V. Selope Thema, para. 19.

lawless gangs that haunt the streets of Western Native Township [Johannesburg] day and night. Is it impossible to annihilate these gangs of hooligans who prey on the law-abiding and peaceful citizens of this town and community? I personally do not think so. But so long as those in authority do not regard the attacks made on members of the Bantu society, attacks which are almost of daily occurrence, as being more serious than the infringement of local bye-laws, then I pity those who, like me, are trying to live a decent life.[1]

Like disease, crime knows no colour bar. To many whites the crime and violence of African townships was the inevitable result of an 'inherent' streak of 'barbarism'. But the sense of insecurity spilled out beyond the townships into white suburbs, manifesting itself in Johannesburg, for example, in the notices on innumerable front-gates that proclaim 'This house is protected by X's burglar alarms', and in the possession of fire-arms and watchdogs.

4. Education and the Industrial Revolution

In the towns and villages of the Cape racially mixed schools were common in the nineteenth century. Mostly these were mission schools that had replaced the slave schools after emancipation.[2] The Report for 1885 of the Superintendent-General of Education in the Cape contains the following comment:

Many writers about colonial schools have assumed that mission schools are attended only by coloured children, for the most part of mixed race; but it is noticeable that whilst very few coloured children attend the public schools, no fewer than 9235 white children are enumerated as in actual attendance in the mission schools, particularly of the larger towns, where the low fee (1d to 3d weekly), enables the European artizan to get cheap schooling for his children.[3]

A few Coloured children attended 'Public Undenominational Schools' in Cape Town, and others such as Marist Brothers and the South African College. Another racially mixed institution was Zonnebloem Training School whose origins go back to 1858. It was founded by the Anglican Church 'for the education of the children of African chiefs and of pupils of all races of South Africa'. During the last quarter of the nineteenth century about half of the number of boarders were Africans while the rest were Coloured and White. By the end of the century, however, Coloured pupils predominated, and by the 1920s the last of the African and white pupils had left.[4]

[1] *Bantu World*, 6 June 1942. [2] Marais, p. 269.
[3] *Report of Superintendent-General of Education for 1885, pp. 2–3*. Quoted by B. M. Kies, 'The Policy of Educational Segregation and some of its effects upon the Coloured People of the Cape' (unpublished B. Ed. thesis, University of Cape Town, 1939), p. 31.
[4] M. Horrell, *African Education: Some Origins, and Development until 1953*, pp. 10–11.

From 1890 onward pressure for school segregation increased, and the Cape Government implemented this largely by creating a new class of public school which made it unnecessary for whites to send their children to mission schools. The Superintendent-General's report for 1909 remarks that 'the first noteworthy differences between the school system of 1909 and that of 1891 is the separation of European and Coloured children . . . the separation between the two races though made in the interests of both was gladly welcomed by the European community, there having been a growing feeling that white children, especially girls, should not be brought daily into contact with Coloured boys of the common street type.'[1] In 1911 the Appellate Division of the Supreme Court held that racially exclusive schools were lawful as 'it was part of the policy of the Cape School Board Act of 1905 to establish separate public . . . schools' for different races. (*Moller v. Keimoes School Committee* (1911), A.D. 644.)

The rise of industry and the simultaneous agrarian crisis highlighted the shortcomings of educational facilities for whites. In 1893 leading Dutch Reformed Church clergy issued a manifesto which claimed that 'a radical change is necessary in our educational system otherwise our people with only half a year's schooling will be destined to become the hewers of wood and the drawers of water for the new arrivals from Europe'.[2] The general effect of industrialization was to place whites and non-whites in a more acutely competitive situation, and education, depending on its content and the extent to which it was made available to the different groups, might promote or prevent this competition. In the view of many whites, educational systems must harmonize with the pattern of race relations: members of different groups must be educated to fill their prescribed status in the common society. Thus in 1889 the Cape Superintendent-General of Education said: 'The first duty of the Government has been assumed to be to recognize the position of the European colonists as holding the paramount influence, social and political; and to see that the sons and daughters of the colonists, and of those who come hither to throw in their lot with them, should have at least such an education as their peers in Europe enjoy, with such local modifications as will fit them to maintain their unquestioned superiority, and supremacy in this land.'[3]

In 1911 the Natal segregationist, Maurice S. Evans, had foreseen dangers in the education of Africans and Indians: education should be designed 'to prevent overlapping of the races with its possible friction and animosities . . .'. He considered that 'agricultural education [was]

[1] *Report of the Superintendent-General for Education for 1909*, p. 6. Quoted by Kies, p. 46.
[2] E. G. Malherbe, *Education and the Poor White*, p. 49.
[3] *Special Report of Superintendent-General for Education for 1889*. Quoted by Kies, p. 33.

less likely to cause opposition, and friction between black and white, or overlapping of their spheres of activity, than either of the other great branches of instruction, the literary or the industrial'.[1] A section of white opinion opposed the education of Africans completely and preferred the 'raw Kaffir'. As The *Christian Express* explained in 1907, the defects of an uneducated man 'are balanced by the ease with which, owing to his simplicity and ignorance, he can be exploited as an economic asset'.[2] Similar views were reported by the Interdepartmental Committee on Native Education in 1936: 'There still exists opposition to the education of the Native on the grounds that (a) it makes him lazy and unfit for manual work; (b) it makes him "cheeky" and less docile as a servant; and (c) it estranges him from his own people and often leads him to despise his own culture.'[3]

If many whites were concerned that education would produce, and indeed, was producing a class of Africans who desired to rise above the station segregation prescribed for them, there was equal concern that a lack of education had caused a considerable number of whites to sink below *their* prescribed station. Education and the skills it imparted were vital weapons in the battle to maintain white supremacy in all fields. 'The system of education was inadequate, both in quantity and quality, to bring about a process of adjustment and thus to prevent the older white population from falling behind.'[4] E. G. Malherbe, a leading educationist, considered that education for rural whites was not adjusted to their environment because they received 'hardly any *ad hoc* training for that intricate and exacting occupation of farming'.[5] He argued that education systems had in the past been 'moulded to fit the requirements of the towns' and not the country. This emphasis on literary education or 'book-learning' was attributable to the whites' 'perverted conception of education and of their position as aristocrats to whom manual and industrial labour would mean a loss of prestige'.[6] Facilities for industrial and vocational training for whites had expanded before 1925 in an effort to equip poor whites with the skills required of them in a modernizing society, but, as Malherbe indicated, this type of education bore a stigma. In 1930–1 the number of whites receiving industrial and vocational training was less than one per cent of the number receiving ordinary primary and secondary education.[7]

An important measure aimed at facilitating the entry of urban whites into industry was the Apprenticeship Act of 1922. Although the Act was

[1] Evans, *Black and White in South East Africa*, pp. 112–13, 117.
[2] *Christian Express*, 1 May 1907.
[3] *Report of Interdepartmental Committee on Native Education, 1935–36*, para. 453.
[4] *Carnegie Commission*, para. 14; Grosskopf, p. viii.
[5] Malherbe, p. 334.   [6] Ibid., p. 53.
[7] Ibid., p. 51.

not ostensibly discriminatory in its provisions, its intention was to give whites a competitive advantage over non-whites and thereby enable them to pull themselves out of the ranks of unskilled labour. By stipulating minimum educational qualifications (eight years' schooling) for apprentices, it effectively prevented Africans and, to a slightly lesser extent, Coloured boys and Indians, from obtaining apprenticeships. Vocational education for whites expanded considerably in the 1920s and after. Between 1926 and 1946/7 the enrolment of students increased by over 150 per cent and considerable increases occurred in the number of white pupils taking vocational subjects in the schools. All these developments aided whites in their adjustment to urban conditions.[1] Industrial training facilities for Africans remained limited. In 1948 the de Villiers Commission stated that 'the explanation for the lack of progress in industrial training must be found mainly in the limited sphere in which the trained Native worker can find an outlet for the practical application of his skill'.[2]

In 1936 the Interdepartmental Committee on Native Education noted the link between education and social stratification: 'The education of the White child prepares him for life in a dominant society and the education of the Black child for a subordinate society.' It asked the question: 'what are we really driving at in educating the South African Native? Are we to Europeanize him as quickly as possible so that he can take his place in our pattern of Western civilization with as little trouble as possible? Or are we to prepare him for an isolated Native Civilization, or . . . to "develop him along his own lines"?'[3] Segregationists, like D. F. Malan, pointed to the political dangers of a rising, educated class of non-whites. Knowledge, he said, was power. The Voortrekkers had had to deal with uncivilized and ignorant non-whites but now 'for a white minority to face a large majority of civilized and educated non-whites, wishing to share our way of life and striving for equality in all respects, [was] something quite different. It made the fight for a white South Africa immeasurably more difficult for the present generation than it had been for the generation of Piet Retief and Sarel Cilliers.'[4] Others condemned the existing system of African education. It 'denationalized' and 'detribalized' Africans, facilitating the assimilation of black and white. Afrikaner nationalists criticized the widespread use of English in African schools for spreading English culture and making the total environment more English in character, thereby handicapping Afrikaners in their struggle against anglicization.[5]

---

[1] *Report of the Commission on Technical and Vocational Education*, paras. 138, 529.
[2] Ibid., para. 1832.   [3] Ibid., para. 455.
[4] Malan, *Glo in U Volk!*, p. 113 (trans.).
[5] See, e.g., B. F. Nel, *Naturelle-opvoeding en-onderwys*, pp. 37, 40, 62.

A reorientation of African education began in 1949 when a Commission was set up to formulate 'the principles and aims of education for Natives as an independent race, in which their past and present, their inherent racial qualities, their distinctive characteristics and aptitude, and their needs under the ever-changing social conditions are taken into consideration'. It was also to suggest how the existing system should be reformed to conform with these aims, and *'to prepare Natives more effectively for their future occupations'*. (Italics added.) The Commission's major recommendation was that all education, except in the case of a foreign language, should be through the medium of the mother-tongue for the first eight school years and mother-tongue instruction should gradually be extended upwards to secondary schools and training institutions. But both official languages should be taught from the earliest school days 'in such a way that the Bantu child will be able to find his way in European communities; to follow oral or written instructions; and to carry on a simple conversation with Europeans about his work and other subjects of common interest'. Handwork taught in the first few years of school should aim at inculcating 'the habit of doing manual work'.[1]

Critics of the Commission's report and the Bantu Education Act of 1953, which incorporated most of its recommendations, argued that an inferior type of education for Africans was being proposed, adapted to the roles expected of Africans as subordinate members of a common society (see pp. 78–9). This interpretation was strengthened by statements made in Parliament by Dr. H. F. Verwoerd, then the Minister of Native Affairs. Race relations, he said, 'cannot improve if the result of Native education is the creation of frustrated people. . . . Education must train and teach people in accordance with their opportunities in life, according to the sphere in which they live.' Furthermore, 'education should have its roots entirely in the Native areas and in the Native environment and Native community. There Bantu education must be able to give itself complete expression and there it will have to perform its real service. The Bantu must be guided to serve his own community in all respects. There is no place for him in the European community above the level of certain forms of labour. Within his own community, however, all doors are open. For that reason it is of no avail for him to receive a training which has as its aim absorption in the European community while he cannot and will not be absorbed there. Up till now he has been subjected to a school system which drew him away from his own community and partially misled him by showing him the green pastures of the European but still did not allow him to graze there.'[2]

[1] *Report of Commission on Native Education 1949–51*, paras. 1, 921, 924, 932.
[2] Pelzer, p. 83.

The anti-assimilationist and anti-urban aim of the policy was quite explicit. The emphasis on vernacular instruction was to be the main instrument to promote separateness. An educationist made the following comments on the syllabus:

In general there is far too much concentration upon tribalism and upon local environment—upon South Africa. . . . Until he reaches Standard Six, except in religious instruction, there is no hint of any continent beyond Africa. . . . Urban areas have a peculiar difficulty. The African, the stereotype of the African to the people who frame education policy, is the rural dweller, living in tribal conditions with his sleek cattle and fertile maize fields. In the syllabus the concentration is upon the rural African. There is quite insufficient attention to the environment of the city-dweller.[1]

In white schools, where education has been a powerful instrument for impressing on pupils the elements of the white group's 'social charter', it has been shown that a static view of Africans as 'primitive' tribesmen is generally presented. According to a textbook used in Transvaal high schools 'the Bantu had a splendid way of living of their own before they ever came into contact with the culture of the whites. In the cities and towns they have lost much of their old delightful way of living but fortunately much of this has been preserved in their tribal reserves.'[2]

In the towns Africans made repeated pleas for further educational facilities. In 1937, for instance, the Natives Representative Council requested this 'in view of the growing lawlessness among boys and girls . . .'. In 1940 the Chief Inspector of Native Education in the Transvaal, Dr. W. W. M. Eiselen, supported demands for compulsory education in towns saying that '. . . while Native education in the rural areas is an excellent thing, it is definitely essential in the urban areas, because in the urban areas where tribal ideas and tribal institutions have been completely revolutionized, some other disciplinary agency has to take the place of tribal control, and the most efficient agency we can think of is the school'.[3] After 1953, however, policy aimed at ensuring that African education should 'have its roots in the reserves' and in 1959 the Minister of Bantu Education announced that future expansion of secondary educational facilities would be concentrated in the reserves:

If you have to supply the Bantu in the European urban locations with higher educational facilities on a large scale—on the scale which they want such facilities there—it means that you give him training facilities there in surroundings and under circumstances which are not his own and which

---

[1] J. W. Macquarrie, *The African in the City: His Education* (address to SAIRR), (Durban, 1960).
[2] A. P. Hunter, 'South Africa', in D. G. Scanlan (ed.), *Church, State and Education in Africa*, pp. 279–80. See also F. E. Auerbach, *The Power of Prejudice in South African Education*, p. 118.
[3] *VR of NRC*, 1940, i. 38.

cannot remain his own forever, training facilities which anchor him to a greater extent than is the position at the moment, to that area. . . . To train the Bantu to be of service in the European area simply means that you then train him to come into competition with the European. . . .[1]

The Minister said subsequently that so far as education for the first four years was concerned, there would be no difference between the African and 'white' areas, but that in educational expansion above this level the stress would be laid on the African areas.[2] In 1966 the Bantu Education Department gave an indication of progress in implementing this policy: 'Our people in the cities are already complaining that they do not have a sufficient number of high schools. They will have a few high schools, but never enough, because, according to Government policy, most of these schools should be situated in the homelands. They will never get a trade school in the White cities again.'[3]

By 1964 six technical schools for Africans existed in urban areas with a total enrolment of 385 pupils.[4] Since 1942 there has also been in Johannesburg the Orlando Vocational Training Centre which was opened by the Municipality. It offered trade and other industrial subjects. In 1960, however, the centre was forced to discontinue a course for motor mechanics after pressure from white trade unionists 'who objected to the suggestion that these men should work in townships at lower rates of pay than prevailed elsewhere'.[5] In terms of legislation passed in 1959 non-whites were debarred from attending the Universities of Cape Town, Natal, and the Witwatersrand except by permit. Three University Colleges were provided for Africans in isolated rural areas, further emphasizing the policy of not offering higher educational facilities for Africans in towns. Nevertheless, despite the paucity of training facilities and official discouragement, many Africans have acquired the skills of an urban industrial society, and a small but growing group of professional men has emerged in the towns.

5. Race and the Government of Towns

A full review of the development of local government in South African towns is beyond the scope of this chapter. The focus in this section is primarily upon the manner in which local authorities have responded to the development of towns as multi-racial entities, and in particular, the relationship between African townsmen and the municipalities under whose control they came.

[1] Senate Debates, 2 June 1959, cols. 345–6.   [2] H.A.D., 20 Jan. 1960, col. 148.
[3] Bantu Education Journal, Nov. 1966, editorial.
[4] Horrell, Survey, 1964, pp. 288–9.
[5] M. Horrell, A Decade of Bantu Education, p. 107.

The differing Cape and Northern traditions of race relations are reflected in the development of local authorities. The Cape established in the 1830s a non-racial municipal franchise but in the Transvaal and Orange Free State the franchise was exclusively for whites. In Natal Coloured males and Indians could qualify as municipal voters until 1924 when Indians were debarred from the franchise. Those Indians already on the roll were not disenfranchised. In 1956 Coloured people were effectively debarred from the franchise but, again, those on the roll were not disenfranchised. The first Coloured person elected to the Cape Town Council was Dr. A. Abdurahman, who served as a Councillor from 1904 until 1940. Port Elizabeth, Kimberley, Simonstown, and other Cape municipalities have had Coloured councillors.

The view that Africans in towns were 'temporary sojourners' rationalized their exclusion from direct representation on town councils. In 1922 the Stallard Commission said: 'If the Native is to be regarded as a permanent element in municipal areas . . . there can be no justification for basing his exclusion from the franchise on the simple ground of colour.' But the Commission did not regard urban Africans as a 'permanent element' and claimed, moreover, that 'the history of the races, especially having regard to South African history, shows that the co-mingling of black and white is undesirable'.[1] Indeed, before this time, little serious attention had been paid to the problems created by the flow of Africans to the towns. In 1902 'the Natives . . . had hitherto never been considered as part of the human population of Johannesburg, still less as a permanent factor in the situation. At this time they had not even become a "problem" in the sense in which water and sewage were problems.'[2] And in 1908 the *Christian Express* remarked that 'under the present system, locations are looked upon rather as convenient sources of revenue than as objects of serious responsibility'.[3] It suggested that Africans in municipal 'locations' (i.e. areas set aside for African residence) be allowed to elect advisory councils to assist municipalities. In several towns, including Pretoria, advisory boards came into existence as an informal means whereby municipalities could sound out African opinion without having to grant Africans actual representation on councils. Under the Natives (Urban Areas) Act of 1923 local authorities were obliged to establish advisory boards in all locations under their control. The Boards were to consist of at least three Africans and a chairman who could be a European. Model regulations, issued by the Native Affairs Department in 1924 and followed by most municipalities, prescribed a board of six members, three elected by African residents

---

[1] *Stallard Commission Report*, para. 42. (For a critical analysis of the Stallard Commission's conclusions see *Fagan Report*, para. 29.)

[2] Maud, p. 59.

[3] *Christian Express*, 1 Sept. 1908.

and three nominated by the local authority, with the location super-intendent as chairman. Municipalities were charged with the duty of consulting the boards on proposed regulations dealing with African affairs.

Advisory boards were never a success: they lacked any executive power and, in many cases, the consultation between the boards and the municipalities was of a perfunctory nature. Particularly in smaller towns, the tendency was to ignore the system, or to regard the boards as nuisances.[1] 'Generally speaking the treatment meted out to the boards discourages the most intelligent and capable people in the locations from standing for election.'[2] Administrators complained that board members 'talked politics', and concerned themselves with national issues of race policy rather than confining themselves to purely local interests. The lack of interest in the boards shown by Africans is reflected in the low percentage polls recorded in elections. In 1961 the Minister of Bantu Administration and Development said that usually the percentage poll was about twenty, and sometimes only ten, or five.[3]

Africans never regarded the boards as adequate substitutes for direct municipal representation, for which they repeatedly asked. In 1942 a judge who inquired into a riot at Pretoria stated that 'there are numer-ous points of friction which continually arise between Natives in urban areas and the Municipal authorities which can be avoided or adjusted if the Council knew properly what the Native complaint is, and this information can most effectively be given—and the Native viewpoint stressed—by a Councillor in close contact with the Natives and chosen by them to represent their interests'.[4] But suggestions like this were not acceptable to local authorities: thirty-seven out of forty municipalities represented at a meeting of the Municipal Association of the Transvaal in 1942 and nearly all municipalities that submitted evidence to the 1946–8 Fagan Commission expressed opposition to the idea. In the Cape only a few Africans were enfranchised 'because of the restriction on African land acquisition and because the value of dwellings in the loca-tions is usually estimated at less than that needed for franchise qualifi-cations'.[5]

With the advent of apartheid in 1948 pressures were exerted against the Cape franchise system. In 1958 the Cape Provincial Council called for the creation of a separate roll for Coloured municipal voters. The Cape Town City Council unanimously rejected the proposal, stating in a resolution to the Administrator of the Province that '... this Council,

[1] *VR of NRC*, 1946, i. 46. [2] Ibid., 1941, i. 227.
[3] *H.A.D.*, 1961, col. 8266.
[4] *Report of Judicial Commission of Enquiry into the Pretoria Municipal Riot of 28th December, 1942*, para. 139 (printed in Proceedings of Native Representative Council, 1943, iii).
[5] Hellmann, *Handbook on Race Relations*, p. 265.

as the largest local authority in the Cape Province and representative of by far the largest number of European and non-European voters, feels that it is duty bound to place these opinions at the disposal of the Administrator—and it does so in the knowledge that the Cape Peninsula has a history of 300 years of racial peace and amity, no doubt by virtue of the fact that its local governing bodies have been representative of European as well as non-European racial groups'.[1] A committee of the Provincial Council which investigated the feasibility of removing Coloured people from the common roll concluded that there was as yet no Coloured area which could satisfactorily be proclaimed as a local authority. In 1961 the Prime Minister, Dr. H. F. Verwoerd, promised Coloured people 'their own local authorities in the Coloured towns' and estimated that in ten years' time they would have 'full control of all their cities and towns'.[2] With the implementation of the Group Areas Act (see pp. 239–40) Coloured people were being removed to separate areas in which 'consultative' and 'management' committees were being established. In the course of time it is likely that these committees will become elective and assume certain executive powers, whereupon Coloured people will be removed from the common municipal roll. The Coloured 'towns' being created will be essentially parts of wider, multi-racial cities. The Coloured people expressed little interest in the committees, and resented bitterly the prospect of losing their long-standing franchise rights which gave them effective representation on town councils and considerable bargaining power in the local-level political process.

In 1952 the Urban Bantu Authorities Bill was drafted but never enacted, allegedly because certain authorities opposed it. The principle of the Bill reflected the apartheid policy that Africans could have political rights only in relation to African areas. In 1961 a Bill enshrining similar principles was passed as the Urban Bantu Councils Act. Its object was 'the integration of the urban Bantu into the systems of government of their homelands and the extension thereof'.[3] The Act provided that municipalities could, after consultation with advisory boards or with African communities should no board exist, establish an Urban Bantu Council in its area of jurisdiction for Africans of particular 'National units' (i.e. linguistic or ethnic groups). A Council must be established if an Advisory Board so requests, or if the Minister of Bantu Administration and Development, after consultation with the African people concerned, is satisfied that they want a Council. Councils must consist of at least six members, a majority of whom must be elected. It was envisaged that in many cases Councils would consist almost

---

[1] *Cape Times*, 4 Dec. 1958.
[2] 'More Power for Coloureds', address by Prime Minister to Union Council of Coloured Affairs, Cape Town, Dec. 1961.   [3] G. F. Froneman, M.P., *H.A.D.*, 1961, col. 8157.

entirely of elected members.[1] Selected members would be nominated by officially recognized town representatives of chiefs and approved by the Minister of Bantu Administration and Development and the local authority. (In 1959 the Promotion of Bantu Self-Government Act had provided for the appointment of chiefs' 'ambassadors' in urban areas.) The Councils are to have the same functions as Advisory Boards but may be granted certain executive powers. The Minister may also confer on any member of a Council the civil and criminal jurisdiction of a chief or headman. Funds received by the Council from fines and other sources are to be paid into the Bantu Revenue Account. Budgets for African townships must be drawn up by the local authority in consultation with the Council. Advisory Boards have not been abolished, except where replaced by an Urban Bantu Council. The Act, however, provided that no further Boards were to be established. Only four Councils had been established by 1966. It was evident that many urban Africans opposed the concept embodied in the system. Chiefs or tribal representatives were felt to be inappropriate in towns. In Potchefstroom, for example, it was found that tribal 'ambassadors' were not acceptable to the African community. 'Sometimes these ambassadors are regarded as foreigners by the inhabitants of the Bantu area with the result that there is usually a struggle between the acknowledged leader and the ambassador, with the latter usually on the losing side.'[2] An analysis of a chief's visit to Cape Town in 1961 showed that townsmen and migrants held differing views on chieftainship and even migrants were very critical of particular chiefs. Westernized Africans in the community rejected traditional authority as 'unenlightened, conservative and incompetent'. Conservative, country-rooted people still supported the institution of chieftainship in principle but regarded it as having been debased and perverted by Government use of chiefs as petty administrative functionaries.[3] Similar reports of lack of enthusiasm over chiefs' visits have been reported in other towns from the 1930s onward. Writing in 1938, Phillips mentioned a visit by the Zulu Paramount Chief to Johannesburg. He was to have addressed a meeting but was 'joyously howled down by an irresponsible group of young hoodlums, advance guard of the new generation which has thrown away the old classificatory system'. In 1963 Chief Matanzima of the Transkei appointed an 'ambassador' in Soweto, Johannesburg, who subsequently resigned, saying that there was no support for the chief among educated urban Africans.[4]

[1] M. D. C. de Wet Nel (Minister of Bantu Administration and Development), *H.A.D.*, 1961, col. 8147.

[2] P. J. Riekert (Manager of Non-European Affairs, Potchefstroom), 'Skakeling van die Stedelike Bantoe met hul Tuislande', *Triomf* (SABRA Yearbook), 1966, p. 30 (trans.).

[3] A. Mafeje, 'An African Chief visits Town', *Journal of Local Administration Overseas*, ii, 2 (1963), 88–99.   [4] R. E. Phillips, *The Bantu in the City*, p. 50; Horrell, *Survey, 1964*, p. 141.

The denial of effective municipal political rights to Africans has illustrated the general tendency for unenfranchised groups to suffer discriminatory treatment. In his study of local government in Johannesburg, John P. R. Maud (later Sir John), said that

it would be difficult to name a city in any part of the world in which the governing class has either known or done what justice demanded for the poorer or more needy section of the community, so long as those sections have had no effective say in the government of the city. . . . It is hardly surprising, therefore, if the white enfranchised section of Johannesburg, unassisted by any large measure of encouragement from the central government, has not succeeded altogether in understanding or doing justice to the needs of the unenfranchised.[1]

Most local authorities saw their task as ensuring that the towns remained 'white man's places' whose African populations must be controlled and disciplined, with a minimum of expense and inconvenience to white ratepayers.

The Natives (Urban Areas) Act of 1923 attempted to achieve a measure of uniformity in urban African administration and laid down the basic structure of controls. In an effort to improve the appalling conditions prevailing in most urban areas, the Act required local authorities to provide housing and welfare amenities for Africans. It prescribed also a system of financial segregation in municipal accounting. Expenditure on African affairs and revenue from African sources (such as fines, pass or registration fees, rentals, and profits on the sale of Bantu beer) were to be reflected in a Native Revenue Account, separate from the General Revenue Account. Only services rendered by the local authority in its African areas could be charged to the Native Revenue Account. Other services could be charged to this account only if the Minister of Native Affairs certified that they were for the benefit of Africans in the area. The Act provided that deficits on the Native Revenue Account could be met from the General Revenue Account.

After a survey in 1938 two investigators concluded that

the vast majority of Urban local authorities . . . attempt to arrange the services which they perform for the benefit of the natives within their area in such a manner that (a) in no case is there a serious deficit on the Native Revenue Account; (b) a deficit when incurred can often be charged against an accumulated revenue surplus; (c) if a small regular deficit has to be incurred and it is decided to meet this out of the general rate fund, then this charge (which partakes of the nature of a subsidy), must be kept as small as possible; and (d), if possible a regular profit should be made on the Native

[1] Maud, p. 209.

Revenue Account from which a contribution towards the cost of the purchase of capital assets can be made.[1]

A calculation of the revenue and expenditure of all local authorities in 1935–6 showed that revenue from African locations was £471,421, while expenditure on locations was £380,372.[2] In 1942 the Smit Committee found that there was 'some basis' for the frequent assertion that the 'self-balancing' principle was being followed by many local authorities in their Native Revenue Accounts.[3] Where this occurred 'the essential public services required by the Native Community must fall below an adequate standard'.[4] Similar criticism of municipal parsimony was voiced by the Social and Economic Planning Council in 1945. The Council expressed its 'disapproval of the manner in which the Native section of the urban community is made to rely upon its own financial resources for its civic services and amenities'.[5]

A major source of revenue for municipalities was the profit derived from the sale of Bantu beer. The legislation of 1923 permitted local authorities who did not allow Africans to brew their own beer domestically, to have exclusive rights to make and sell beer in their areas. All profit was to be credited to the Native Revenue Account. In 1942–3 the Native Affairs Commission noted a tendency for local authorities 'to exploit beer-hall profits to meet recurring expenditure on ordinary municipal services' which, the Commission considered, ought to be charged to the General Revenue Account.[6] In 1945 the Social and Economic Planning Council estimated that beer profits amounted to almost one-fifth of the cost of services and amenities for locations and that net profits of 100 per cent were often made. The Council condemned these profits as 'a highly regressive concealed tax [which] in no way conforms to the norm of equity'.[7] In terms of existing legislation, local authorities may spend up to two-thirds of beer profits to meet losses on housing schemes, losses resulting from reductions in rentals, capital expenditure on housing schemes, and interest, redemption and maintenance costs in connection with townships. Remaining profits may be spent on social or recreational amenities and welfare for Africans in the local authority's area.[8]

Prior to 1923 African housing had been conspicuously neglected by local authorities. Several official commissions had warned against the

---

[1] P. H. Gúenalt and R. J. Randall, 'Some Financial Aspects of Urban Native Segregation in South Africa', *Race Relations Journal*, 7 (4), (1940), 96.

[2] John Burger (pseudonym of L. Marquard), *Black Man's Burden*, p. 98.

[3] *Smit Committee Report*, para. 202.   [4] Ibid., para. 11.

[5] *Social and Economic Planning Council, Report No. 8, Local Government Functions and Finances*, para. 107.   [6] *Native Affairs Commission Report on Kaffir Beer* (1942–3), para. 93.

[7] *Social and Economic Planning Council, Report No. 8*, para. 109.

[8] Bantu (Urban Areas) Consolidation Act of 1945. Section 19 (3).

consequences of this neglect.[1] In 1920 the Housing Committee said that 'so little attempt has been made to effect improvement in the directions indicated by these commissions, that we candidly confess to a feeling of the ineffectualness of our own efforts in the matter'.[2] In the past disease had sometimes jolted local authorities into action. Outbreaks of plague in some of the major cities of South Africa in the early 1900s had led to swift action in demolishing existing dwellings and removing Africans to hastily established areas on the edges of the towns.

Reluctance to spend money on building African townships meant that work on housing Africans proceeded slowly, and further slum conditions were allowed to develop. In 1902 the Cape Town Municipality had been reluctant to pay for African housing. Ndabeni 'location' was established and controlled by the Central Government but not before John X. Merriman had lambasted the Municipality for having 'shamefully neglected their duty' to provide housing. 'These men in Cape Town who had made big piles should be made to pay. They dragged these people from the farms and then they left them to go body and soul to ruin in Cape Town.'[3] Charges and counter-charges by municipalities and the Central Government over the financing of African housing provided a recurrent theme in subsequent decades.

The Natives (Urban Areas) Act of 1923 required local authorities to house Africans in their areas. Employers of more than 25 Africans (including the Central and Provincial Governments) were bound to accommodate their employees. The Minister of Native Affairs was given powers of compulsion should local authorities provide inadequate or unsuitable accommodation. Residential segregation was provided for in the Act and could be enforced by means of a proclamation requiring all Africans (except for limited exempted categories) to be accommodated in separate locations, villages, or hostels.

With the growth of substantial communities of poor whites living in urban slums, the State acted in 1920 to provide loans for economic housing for all races. Few local authorities, however, availed themselves of the opportunities to provide housing for Africans and Coloured people. The indifference of most local authorities to African housing was partly a consequence of official policy which insisted on the 'temporariness' of urban Africans. In 1941 an official of the Central Government spoke of the tendency of some local authorities to hide behind the underlying policy 'to avoid their obvious responsibility'.[4] Why incur large capital expenditure on temporary populations? The indifference

[1] Most notably, the Tuberculosis Commission of 1914.
[2] Report of the Housing Committee, p. 30.
[3] (Cape) House of Assembly Debates, 1902, p. 146.
[4] Chief Native Commissioner, Witwatersrand, VR of NRC, 1941, i. 238.

of the authorities, central and local, was shown by the Slums Act of 1934 which deliberately excluded from the purview of its remedial provisions compounds, 'locations', villages, and hostels occupied by Africans. In 1942 the Smit Committee found that many of the houses built for Africans with the intention of eradicating or preventing slums were 'from the first day of their occupation overcrowded and therefore slums as defined in the Second Schedule to the Slums Act'. It condemned the exclusion of 'locations' from the purview of the Act as 'an example of the tendency towards the adoption of dual standards of public hygiene . . .'. The Committee found also that 'except in one or two instances', municipalities debited their losses on African sub-economic housing schemes to the Native Revenue Account. This, it said, was inequitable discrimination against Africans. The Committee found, moreover, that 'comparatively few' local authorities (forty-one including sixteen of the larger ones) had availed themselves of the facilities for borrowing sub-economic housing funds.[1] Sub-economic housing was needed, of course, because most Africans were exceedingly poor and could not afford economical rentals. The costs of housing schemes were inflated by the industrial colour bar which resulted in 'the almost universal practice of building Native locations with European skilled labour'.[2]

The huge influx of Africans into the towns after 1939 exacerbated the housing shortage, and led to the growth in major urban centres of 'squatter' settlements. 'Emergency camps' were established by municipalities in most urban centres in which rough shelters and rudimentary services could be provided. The Johannesburg Municipality, for example, established Moroka which eventually accommodated 60,000 Africans.[3]

After 1948 the Nationalist Government energetically tackled the urban housing problem. A calculation in December 1951 showed that there was a shortfall of 167,328 houses and a need for an additional 185,813 more to meet the anticipated increase between 1952 and 1961. The Government encouraged the 'site-and-service' scheme whereby Africans were provided with a serviced site in newly created townships upon which they could build a temporary dwelling that was to be replaced by a more permanent structure within five years. Employers were taxed to contribute to housing schemes,[4] and, after 1953, policy was aimed at providing only economic housing (i.e. rents which would amortize the capital outlay). By the end of the decade the housing shortage had been greatly reduced. It was ironic that this should have been achieved by

[1] *Smit Committee Report*, paras. 94, 170, 173.
[2] *Report of Native Economic Commission*, 1930–2, para. 505.
[3] Non-European Affairs Department, Johannesburg Municipality, *Thousands for Houses* (1960).
[4] Under the Native Services Levy Act of 1952.

a government whose commitment to the belief that urban Africans were 'temporary sojourners' was even stronger than that of its predecessors.

For many Africans the rentals and the costs of transport from distant townships (even if subsidized) constituted a heavy burden. An African remarked in 1951:

> If municipal locations are destined to provide accommodation for people who serve the interests of Europeans in the towns, whose occupants are thereby destined to be sub-economic units for all time, it seems to me unreasonable and unfair that they should be called upon to pay rent or for any other service at all. Those who benefit and thrive on cheap labour should accept the responsibility in the same way as an owner of a horse who provides for it in stable and fodder. But if we claim ... the right of being part and parcel of the town, and that we have contributed to its development by our labour and sweat, we should not be content to live in ghettoes, to be treated as sojourners or be subjected to the whimsies of local authorities.[1]

If income, occupation, and social status are the main determinants of place of residence, it is not surprising that South African towns have tended to develop, residentially, along the lines of segregation as colour and these determinants have largely coincided. Moreover, local and central governments that were controlled by whites could give the force of law to the desires of many whites to have non-whites residentially segregated from them. Even in Cape Town, the most racially integrated of the South African towns, a survey to ascertain the 'precise ethnic character of residential areas' concluded that 'perhaps its [Cape Town's] most striking feature is the sharpness of the divide between most European and non-European areas: intermingling is confined to a few restricted tracts'. It was also found that where the cleavage between white and non-white districts was blurred, usually Coloured people had infiltrated into former white areas, although, in some cases whites had encroached on formerly Coloured areas. But there were parts of the city, like Diep River, Newlands, Woodstock, and Simonstown which contained racially mixed neighbourhoods.[2] Little research has been done on the development of Cape Town's racial ecology and therefore it is impossible to trace here the changes since 1870.

In Natal, where questions of race and residence have been public issues for longer than in any other part of the country, the Indians became special objects of white hostility in the 1870s and 1880s. Whites resented both living near them and facing their competition in business. In 1889, for example, the Superintendent of the Durban Police strongly recommended in a report to the Borough Council that 'no licences be given

---

[1] H. Selby Msimang, address to *Location Advisory Boards Congress*, Ermelo, 1951. Minutes.
[2] P. Scott, 'Cape Town: A Multi-Racial City', *Geographical Journal* cxxi, 2 (1955), 152.

to Indians for any building in our three main streets'.[1] In the Transvaal, Law No. 3 of 1885 confined members of any 'aboriginal races of Asia' to certain streets and wards, ostensibly on health grounds, and prohibited them from acquiring landed property. But the Law was not rigorously enforced, and loop-holes were discovered. Legislation in 1919 tightened up the restrictions. Anti-Indian agitation continued, and in 1920 the Lange Commission recommended, *inter alia,* a scheme of voluntary segregation in the towns. Implementation, however, was delayed. In 1922 a riot occurred when Indians attempted to buy land at a Durban sale, whereupon the Durban Municipality secured the passing of a Provincial Ordinance containing provision for racial restrictions in the sales and leases of municipal land. Attempts in 1924, 1925, and 1926 to introduce legislation for more comprehensive measures of segregation proved abortive.[2] In the Transvaal, after attempts had been made in 1932, 1935, 1936, and 1937 to restrict Indians further by statute, a far-reaching measure was passed in 1939 which provided that no Indians could hire or occupy land or premises in the Transvaal, except by permit from the Minister of the Interior, unless such land or premises had been occupied by Indians or Coloureds on 30 April 1939. The Act was a temporary measure, intended to impose restrictions until May 1941, but in 1941 it was extended until May 1943.

Whites continued to complain about alleged Indian 'penetration' into white residential areas in Natal and the Transvaal and in the 1940s investigations were made by a judicial commission. According to the Commissioner, Justice F. C. Broome, local authorities and individuals who gave evidence 'frequently took up the unfortunate attitude that the onus was upon the Indians to show why they had acquired sites in predominantly European areas'. 'Penetration', according to the Commission, was a normal part of urban development: 'When the process of area degeneration reaches a certain stage infiltration by non-Europeans begins.' The Commission noted also that ' "succession and invasion" occurred frequently in cities elsewhere in the world but in South Africa because of the colour varieties of her population, it is obvious and easily becomes a focus of racial antagonism'.[3] The phenomenon of 'succession and invasion' had been noted in other cities like Cape Town. In the suburb of Salt River, for instance, 'it would seem that as soon as Coloureds gain a foothold in a street Europeans evacuate in the mass'.[4] Added impetus to the desire for residential segregation resulted from the urban poor white question. It was unthinkable to Afrikaner nationalists

---

[1] Quoted by Henderson, p. 139.

[2] M. Webb, 'Indian Land Legislation', in Hellmann (ed.), *Handbook on Race Relations,* p. 207; *Report of Asiatic Land Laws Commission,* 1939, paras. 12–46.

[3] *Interim Report of the Commission of Enquiry into matters affecting the Indian Population in the Province of Natal,* 1945, para. 14.   [4] Scott, p. 151.

that fellow Afrikaners should have to live next to non-whites in adjacent houses, or worse, adjacent rooms and that their children should play in mixed groups. Lives were lost in 1920 and 1922 when poor whites in Vrededorp (Johannesburg) clashed with non-whites whose residence in their midst they resented.[1]

In 1940, at the instigation of the central government, an attempt was made to institute voluntary segregation. A Committee was set up consisting of representatives of the Durban Municipality and the Natal Indian Association. It was charged with trying to dissuade would-be Indian purchasers from acquiring property in predominantly white areas. The Committee collapsed after one year.[2] The second 'penetration' Commission found that in the first two months of 1943 Indians in Durban had paid more for sites in predominantly white areas than in any complete year between 1927 and 1939.[3] The result was the passing of the Trading and Occupation of Land (Transvaal and Natal) Restriction Act of 1943 (the 'Pegging' Act) which attempted to restrict the acquisition of property by Indians in predominantly white areas for a period of three years during which time, it was hoped, a negotiated agreement could be reached. An agreement was reached in Pretoria in 1944 between the Prime Minister, the Minister of the Interior, the Administrator of Natal, Mr. D. E. Mitchell, and representatives of the Natal Indian Congress. It proved impossible, however, to translate the agreement into an ordinance which would satisfy both the Indian and white communities. After continuing protest, the Asiatic Land Tenure and Indian Representation Act was passed in 1946. To Indians it was known as the 'Ghetto' Act. The Act divided Natal and the Transvaal into 'exempted' and 'unexempted' areas, and in 'unexempted' areas no Indian could buy or occupy fixed property except by permit from the Minister of the Interior.[4]

Both the Native Land Act of 1913 and the Native Land and Trust Act of 1936 had provided for a country-wide application of possessory land segregation but neither applied to land in urban areas. In many towns, big and small, Africans acquired freehold property. But in 1937 an amendment to the Natives (Urban Areas) Act restricted their right to do so. Considerable opposition from Johannesburg whites to existing African freehold areas was welling up as white suburbs expanded and reached the borders of places like Alexandra Township, Sophiatown, Martindale, Newclare, and Pageview where, for many years, Africans had owned land. In the 1930s white ratepayers formed the 'North Eastern District Protection League' which campaigned vigorously for the

[1] Malan, *Glo in U. Volk!*, p. 127; A. Coetzee, *Die Opkoms van die Afrikaanse Kultuurgedagte aan die Rand 1886–1936*, pp. 385–6.   [2] Webb, p. 208.
[3] *Report of Indian Penetration Commission, 1943*, para. 18.   [4] Webb, pp. 200–10.

abolition of Alexandra Township.[1] In 1943 and 1944 the Johannesburg Municipality, under pressure from organized white ratepayers, resolved to disestablish all these areas and to remove the African inhabitants to other areas, south-west of the city. Nothing was done to implement the plan as this would have exacerbated an already acute housing shortage.[2]

As has been shown, the belief that, for health reasons, African townships should be situated on the edges of towns, distant from white residential areas, is of long standing (see pp. 233-4). Moreover, the Natives (Urban Areas) Act of 1923 had provided for compulsory segregation of Africans, but the slow development of African housing and the huge influx of Africans delayed the implementation of complete segregation. In 1942 the Smit Committee reported that if complete segregation were envisaged one-third of the urban African population would have to be rehoused.[3]

The advent of the Nationalist Government in 1948 marked an increase in pressure for completely segregated residential areas in towns. The major instrument for achieving this was the Group Areas Act of 1950 which made previous efforts at residential segregation seem feeble: it provided for the zoning of all towns and villages into areas for the exclusive ownership and/or occupation of particular groups. For the first time, Coloured people were brought within the scope of laws enforcing residential segregation. It was not sufficient that, with the few exceptions noted above, local segregation should exist within racially mixed neighbourhoods (as in parts of Cape Town): complete segregation had to be enforced. The Group Areas Act is a complex statute that has been amended on many occasions.[4] It provides that the State President may proclaim group areas for occupation by a particular colour group and group areas for ownership by a particular colour group. Areas that are proclaimed for occupation by a specified group must be vacated by disqualified persons not less than one year after a stipulated date. Failure to move is a criminal offence. Recommendations for racial zoning are made by the Group Areas Board after a public inquiry at which interested parties may give evidence. Local authorities also present proposals for the implementation of the Act in their areas.

The Group Areas Development Act of 1955 provided for compensation to be paid to disqualified owners who were forced to sell their property, but in practice many of those compelled to move lost heavily.[5]

[1] Alexandra Health Committee, *The Future of Alexandra Township—An Open Letter to the Citizens of Johannesburg.*   [2] For background see SAIRR, *The Western Areas Removal Scheme.*
[3] *Smit Committee Report*, para. 155.
[4] L. R. Dison and I. Mohamed, *Group Areas and their Development.*
[5] L. Schlemmer, 'The Resettlement of Indian Communities in Durban and some Economic, Social and Cultural Effects on the Indian Community', SAIRR, *The Indian South African*, pp. 18–20.

When the legislation was being passed, the Government gave assurances that it would be equitably applied and no one group would suffer special hardship. In practice, the Act has affected Coloureds, Indians, and Africans to a much greater extent than whites. In the metropolitan area of Cape Town 2·6 per cent of the white population as against 25·7 per cent of the Coloured population had been affected by proclamations under the Act by the end of 1961.[1] In Pietermaritzburg, a calculation made in 1961 showed that 7,000 Indians, 1,175 Africans, and 1,000 Coloured people had been affected by a proclamation, while the number of whites affected (owning only nine properties between them) was negligible.[2] A survey of the implementation of Group Areas in the Transvaal showed that only 15·01 per cent of the Coloured population and 7·5 per cent of the Indian population in the entire province would remain unaffected by the Act. The proportion of the white population affected would be 'very small indeed'.[3] This pattern of implementation can be directly related to the structure of the society: it would be politically impossible for the Government to cause large-scale removals of whites from long-established areas.[4] Indians and Coloureds, however, are voteless and defenceless communities, whose removal, in many instances, opens up desirable areas for white settlement. In the large majority of cases, despite official assertions to the contrary, the more desirable areas have been proclaimed as white areas. The length of occupation of an area by a particular group, or the fact that they were the original inhabitants, is not decisive. For example, in the Cape Peninsula Coloured communities whose forebears had settled in particular areas anything up to 200 years previously have been required to leave. In the fishing village of Kalk Bay the Coloured community was already established by 1800. Whites infiltrated into the village only towards the end of the nineteenth century.[5]

Few legislative enactments in South Africa have caused more resentment than the Group Areas Act. The legislation was, and is, defended as a means of reducing racial friction by removing points of contact between colour groups. Its effect has been to cause bitterness and animosity, and to heighten racial tension.

After 1948 the Nationalist Government launched an attack on existing African freehold rights in the towns because these rights symbolized a permanency that was incompatible with the renewed emphasis on the conception of urban Africans as 'temporary sojourners': 'black spots' in

[1] Y. M. Maytham, *The Changing Position of the Coloured People*, p. 1.

[2] Horrell, *Survey, 1961*, p. 180.

[3] Horrell, *Group Areas in the Transvaal—The Emerging Pattern*, p. 83.

[4] *South African Outlook*, 82 (1952), 161–2.

[5] M. Ritchken, 'The Fisherfolk of Kalk Bay', *The Black Sash*, Mar.–Apr. 1965, pp. 2–6.

'white' areas must be eradicated. Pressure was exerted on the Johannesburg Municipality to implement its earlier plans to disestablish its African freehold areas. When the Municipality dragged its feet, the Government passed the Natives Resettlement Act of 1954 which provided for the removal of all Africans from the 'Western Areas' (Sophiatown, Martindale, Newclare, and Pageview) to Meadowlands and Diepkloof which were to be controlled by a Resettlement Board created by the Government. It was a bitter blow to the African residents of the Western Areas who lost freehold rights and the freedom of living in communities not subject to the rigorous controls encountered in ordinary municipal townships. Slums undoubtedly did exist, but there were also substantial houses. An African leader remarked: 'We deny that this is a slum clearance scheme, because to eliminate slum conditions you do not have to shift a whole community, nearly 60,000 people, you do not have to condemn the good with the bad, you do not have to divest people of their property rights.'[1] In 1961 African freehold rights in Lady Selborne, Eastwood, and Highlands (suburbs of Pretoria) were abolished by proclaiming the areas for white ownership and occupation under the Group Areas Act.

When new African townships were being constructed in the 1950s, great pains were taken by the Government to ensure that they were 'properly' located in accordance with apartheid ideas. According to principles laid down by Dr. H. F. Verwoerd, when Minister for Native Affairs, urban townships should ideally be: an adequate distance from the 'white' town; preferably connected with African areas of neighbouring towns; preferably separated from 'white' areas by industrial areas; within easy distance of the town, preferably by rail; and so situated that the expanding European town should not encircle it. In addition, there must be suitable 'buffer' spaces around townships, the breadth of which should depend on whether the border touches on densely or sparsely occupied white areas.[2] The effect is to ensure that Africans reside on the edge of towns, far from their places of work.

From the Government's point of view, the most desirable plan is to house urban Africans in a reserve near the town in which they work. To achieve this thousands of people are being moved from their homes in East London (see p. 193), Durban, and elsewhere.[3]

The policy of the Government is to emphasize ethnic divisions among Africans, and in 1954 it directed municipalities to apply the principle of 'ethnic grouping' in urban townships; Africans who speak different languages *must* live in separate quarters, although a recent survey in Soweto showed that 83 per cent of the respondents were opposed to

---

[1] SAIRR, *Western Areas Removal Scheme*, p. 25. [2] Pelzer, pp. 42, 132.
[3] Horrell, *Survey, 1966*, pp. 196, 198–9.

this.[1] After a riot in Dube (Soweto) in September 1957 in which more than forty Africans were killed, the Johannesburg Municipality appointed a commission under the chairmanship of ex-Chief Justice A. van de Sandt Centlivres, to investigate the causes. The Commission reported that 'there can to our mind be no doubt that the implementation of the policy of ethnic grouping was one of the causes which led to and facilitated the rioting'.[2]

6. Conclusion

Urbanization undermined the master/servant relationship between white and non-white that had been established in the pre-industrial era. It opened up a much more competitive situation between the groups. But industry was forced to defer to traditional white attitudes and, with the consolidation of segregation from the 1920s onward, the traditional pattern was re-established though, it is suggested, on a more insecure foundation. It is seemingly paradoxical that the more Africans moved to the towns and settled as urban dwellers the more stridently whites asserted that their 'proper' place was in the reserves; the more interdependent white and non-white grew in the towns, the more fearful the majority of whites became of non-white competition.

The difference in official policies towards the movement of Afrikaners and Africans to town has been described. The adjustment of Afrikaners to town life was facilitated by official policies, but Africans have had to contend with the efforts of successive governments to isolate them, and to limit their townward movement rather than to foster the growth of urban communities and educate country people for town life. The activities of various private agencies which sought to facilitate the adjustment of Africans (e.g. through night schools) have been prohibited.

Urbanization promoted an increasing degree of homogeneity between the various peoples caught up in the process. People grew closer in values, ideas, and customs; but this increasing homogeneity could not be made the basis of a democratic urban civilization because the dominant white group assumed that the interests of people who differed in race were necessarily opposed. If cultural homogeneity *between* groups increased, differentiation *within* each group increased as well. The urban revolution produced the 'New Afrikaner' of the towns: he might be an artisan or a financier, but he was widely different in style of life and values from his *platteland* compatriot. The town African was different

---

[1] Hellmann, *Soweto*, p. 17.

[2] *Report of the Commission Appointed by the City Council of Johannesburg to enquire into the causes and circumstances of the riots which took place in the vicinity of the Dube Hostel in the South-Western Native Townships over the weekend 14th/15th September 1957* (Johannesburg, 1958), para. 177.

from the country-rooted migrant in the town, or the reserve peasant. Within each group of townsmen class cleavages began to develop, but class never transcended race or *volk* as a focus of allegiance.

The South African writer Nadine Gordimer presented in her novel, *A World of Strangers*, a striking account of the social structure of Johannesburg. The hero of the story is an Englishman who comes to work in the city and makes friends among whites and among Africans. But whites and Africans, although constituting the 'world' of Johannesburg are strangers outside of prescribed relationships and, when the hero inadvertently gets his social lines crossed and white friend meets black friend, disastrous social episodes ensue. The groups 'cannot separate and cannot fuse'.

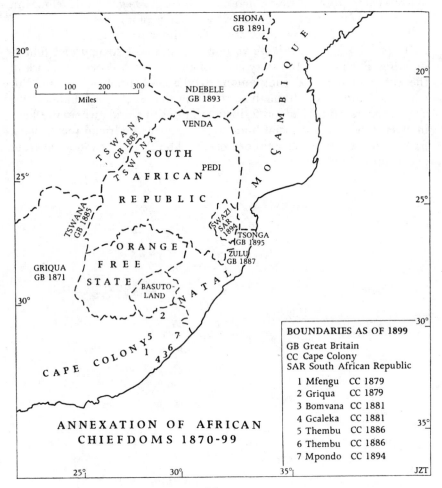

MAP 5.

V

THE SUBJECTION OF THE AFRICAN CHIEFDOMS, 1870–1898[1]

IN 1870 there were still numerous political units in South Africa. Some contained relatively homogeneous populations, others contained plural societies. Allowing for both these differentials, the units were of five distinct types. First, there was a large number of independent African chiefdoms, ranging from the Xhosa chiefdoms along the eastern frontier of the Cape Colony to the Venda chiefdoms in the northern Transvaal. Secondly, there was the southern Sotho Kingdom, annexed by Great Britain in 1868. Thirdly, there were still several small autonomous communities that were partly San, partly Khoikhoi, partly Coloured, and partly African, notably the so-called Griqua chiefdoms led by Nicholas Waterboer and Adam Kok. Fourthly, the South African Republic and the Orange Free State were Afrikaner republics, whose independence Great Britain had formally recognized in 1852 and 1854. Finally, the Cape of Good Hope and Natal were British colonies with representative parliamentary institutions. The first two types of units contained relatively homogeneous African societies; the last two contained plural societies dominated by white minorities.

The boundaries between most of these political units were indeterminate in 1870. The British colonies had official boundaries, the Afrikaner republics had delimited their common frontier, and the African chiefdoms also recognized the principle of territorial limits; but white and African claims did not always coincide and there were many

---

[1] This chapter is an interim report on a comparatively neglected aspect of South African history. We need to know much more about the complex process by which African chiefdoms become incorporated in white-controlled polities in the late nineteenth century—above all, about the diverse ways in which traditional African institutions were modified by interaction with institutions of Western provenance. Only when monographs, based on field research as well as documents, have been written on several individual cases, by scholars with some anthropological as well as historical training, shall we be in a position to reach definitive conclusions about the process as a whole.

The late Dr. C. F. Goodfellow was to have written this chapter and the next. He corresponded about them with me but after his death no manuscript was found among his papers. The structure of the two chapters is a modified version of what was worked out by Dr. Goodfellow in consultation with me and others.

I am indebted to Professor Monica Wilson, Professor and Mrs. John S. Galbraith, Professor Leo Kuper, Dr. T. R. H. Davenport, and Mr. Richard Elphick and other members of my 1968 seminar at the University of California, Los Angeles, for comments on this chapter.

disputed frontier zones, where communities overlapped and rival governments competed for jurisdiction and allegiance.

In the African chiefdoms, the events of the previous decades had evoked a desire to prevent further encroachments by white people. Chiefs kept in touch with one another, as they had always done, by an extensive use of messengers, and they sometimes tried to act in concert to defend their territories. But combinations were impeded by many factors. There was no sense of racial identity among Africans. They knew ties of kinship, of political affiliation, and of cultural affinity such as language; but racialism was not an African concept. (It would develop later, after prolonged mingling of Africans from different chiefdoms and linguistic groups in the mining and manufacturing towns, and bitter experience of colour bars devised by white men.) There were major cultural differences between Nguni and Sotho and deep historic rivalries between chiefdom and chiefdom, and between different segments of the same chiefdom. Moreover, by 1870 all chiefdoms were being subjected to pressures from one or more of the agents of white expansion—missionaries, traders, farmers, and government agents. Such agents had transformed the chiefdoms in varying degrees by 1870. In extreme cases, as with the southern Nguni and the southern Tswana, where missionaries had been working for many years, significant groups of educated, Christian Africans had rejected many of the traditional norms and customs and were rivalling the traditional political élites. It must also be noted that it was physically impossible for all of the African chiefdoms to co-operate effectively, because they were separated into several distinct clusters by wedges of white settlement. The Natal colonists divided the Zulu from the southern Nguni; and the republican Afrikaners kept the Pedi, the Venda, the Tswana, and the southern Sotho apart from one another. For these reasons, there never was a concerted African resistance to white expansion in South Africa. Each chief and each councillor responded to an external pressure in the light of his peculiar local circumstances and his personal disposition. In many cases he tried to turn the pressure to his own advantage, using white people as instruments of economic development or as allies against African enemies. Only rarely did he try to set up an absolute barrier against white intrusion.

The republican, colonial, and British governments, on the other hand, all saw a fundamental dichotomy between the white and the other— especially the African—inhabitants of South Africa. They refrained from using Africans as allies in their wars against white enemies in South Africa and they tried to prevent guns from passing into the hands of Africans. Moreover, virtually all white South Africans had a particularly strong sense of white racial identity, transcending all other distinctions that they made between human groups. They considered that it was in their common interest to subdue and control the African chief-doms. They hoped that some of the African land would then be thrown open to white settlement and that the energies of the African peoples would be made available to them as labourers.

Nevertheless, history had created a cleavage between white South Africans. Having been isolated from Europe for several generations and having adopted a distinctive rural mode of life and developed a new language, Afrikaners were conscious of being a separate people, rooted exclusively in South Africa; while the British community, newer to the country and replenished by fresh recruits from Great Britain, tended to despise Afrikaners and to look to London for protection against them as well as against Africans. Furthermore, the Afrikaners were themselves divided. They had no tradition of common political responsibility and since the Great Trek they had lived under different political systems and acquired different loyalties. In the Cape Colony and Natal, many of them had made an accommodation with English culture and British overrule; in the republics, the dominant sentiment was uncompromising aversion to British authority. Finally, the republics were themselves too fissi-parous, too weak, and economically too backward to command the allegiance of the colonial Afrikaners.

The only Power that had the resources to impose some sort of order on the South African scene was Great Britain. The British navy con-trolled the seas. Nearly all the external trade of South Africa was carried in British ships to and from the colonial ports of Cape Town, Port Elizabeth, and Durban; and its passage through the colonies, the republics, and the African chiefdoms was conducted mainly by British traders. Missionaries as well as traders operated among the most remote African chiefdoms, and most of them, too, were of British origin. That is to say, the informal British Empire of commerce and evangelization extended far beyond the frontiers of the South African colonies.

The majority of the British traders and missionaries, and their sup-porting agencies in the colonies and in Great Britain, wanted British administration to be extended throughout South Africa. Traders and import merchants and their financial backers looked to British control to produce stabler conditions and thus greater profits. Missionaries and missionary societies knew that many chiefs opposed the work of evan-gelization and they also considered that Great Britain should protect the African peoples from the rapacity of white farmers. In addition, many of the colonial officials saw the extension of British authority as the only means of curbing the strife between white and black, which not only disturbed the interior but also threatened the security of the colonial frontiers and the peace of the colonies.

Throughout the 1860s, British governments had continued to be averse to territorial expansion in general, and particularly averse to expansion in South Africa, where earlier annexations had incurred the hostility of Afrikaner Voortrekkers and led to costly involvements in their quarrels with Africans. To politicians and officials in London, South Africa seemed like a bottomless pit, which had absorbed continuous streams of taxpayers' money, without giving any appreciable return. It was only in the most exceptional circumstances that territorial expansion seemed justified; and even then permission was only given grudgingly and half-heartedly and on the strict understanding that the inhabitants of an annexed territory should pay for the costs of their administration. The annexations of the 1840s had extended the range of overt British political engagement, without advancing the pacification of South Africa; and the prospects arising from the annexation of Basutoland seemed no different. Mid-Victorian England lacked the incentives to impose its will upon South Africa as a whole.

That is not to say there was no vestige of a long-term South African policy in London. By 1870, two distinct systems of control had developed in the British Empire, in two very different social situations. Despotism, tempered by paternalism, was being applied in India, where society was almost wholly alien; and control of their local affairs had been delegated to colonial communities in Canada, Australia, and New Zealand, where white settlers predominated. The difficulty was that in several parts of the British Empire—such as the West Indies and South Africa—the social situations did not correspond with either the Indian or the Canadian model. In South Africa, the coexistence of the Afrikaner community and the British community reproduced some of the ingredients of Canadian society; but the great numerical superiority of the indigenous Africans suggested an Indian analogy. In practice London tended, hesitatingly and with many compromises and afterthoughts, to regard South Africa as a variant of the Canadian model and to apply to it the prescriptions of Lord Durham and Lord Elgin. The Cape Colony had been given parliamentary institutions in 1853, Natal in 1856; and in 1870 the Cape was on the verge of responsible cabinet government. It was hoped that the Cape Colony would become the instrument of order and integration throughout South Africa, assuming control of the African chiefdoms, forming some sort of union with the republics, and leaving Great Britain with the responsibility and the benefits of controlling the external relations of South Africa as a whole—her trade, defence, and diplomacy. In 1870 this policy had not been tested and its implications had not been fully appreciated; but it was the policy which would dominate British official thinking about South Africa until the 1890s.

Unfortunately for the British Government, the situation in South

Africa did not correspond with the requirements of British policy. The Cape Colony was not fitted to play the crucial role in which it was cast by Britain. In spite of the fact that the colony contained more white people than the rest of South Africa, they never numbered more than half a million in the nineteenth century and they were thinly spread over a vast area. The centrifugal forces that had produced the Eastern Separatist movement in the 1860s continued to operate. Trade rivalries between Cape Town, Port Elizabeth, and East London were intensified with the growth of the interior market after the discoveries of diamonds and gold. Cape politicians were sensitive about British attempts to influence their policy. Moreover, although an Afrikaner political organization was not consolidated until 1883 and none of its members ever became prime minister, all Cape cabinets had to pay attention to the interests and the attitudes of the Afrikaner voters, who were a majority of the electorate. Cape governments were also chronically short of money and competent personnel. In the Transkei, they gradually built up an efficient administrative cadre; but in attempting to rule Basutoland they over-reached themselves and made disastrous errors. As for Natal, its small and isolated white commmunity relied heavily on British military protection and was never in a position to exert a significant influence beyond its borders. It was not until 1893 that Natal acquired responsible government and after it had done so its politicians remained pre-occupied with the parish pump.

Nor did the republics conform to the picture as it was seen in Britain. Responsible to electorates composed primarily of scattered Afrikaner farmers, the governments of the republics were as anxious as any ex-colonial people in the twentieth century to translate their formal grant of independence into absolute political and economic autonomy, and they were extremely suspicious of interference by their former metropolitan rulers. In the Transvaal, especially, the central objective of state policy was to achieve and preserve complete independence from Britain. The activities of missionaries who obstructed the expansion of the republic and sought British protection for their chiefs, of traders who maintained the trade routes to the colonies, of speculators who got possession of large blocks of land and held them without improvement, and, ultimately, of *uitlanders* who invoked British support for their claims for local political power, kept suspicions alive and increased the determination to resist. At no time did the bulk of the Afrikaners in either republic desire to enter into a federal union which would have involved the loss of their independence. To have done so would have been to betray their Voortrekker heritage, which was their guide and inspiration.

During the 1880s a third factor emerged. Ever since 1806, European governments had left Britain as the unchallenged dominant power in

South Africa. In the 1880s, however, the pressures that led to the partition of tropical Africa among the European Powers spilled over into southern Africa. Germany proclaimed a protectorate over South West Africa, German agents negotiated with African chiefs along the unannexed portions of the south-east African coast, and the German Government encouraged the government of the South African Republic to defy Britain.

Consequently, none of the assumptions underlying British policy proved valid. The colonies were too weak to become agents of order and integration throughout South Africa. The republics were too firmly attached to their independence. And Britain's immunity from foreign European intervention in South Africa came to an end.

The result was that throughout the last thirty years of the nineteenth century the different South African communities continued to jostle one another in the numerous frontier zones between the political units and anarchy was endemic in many areas. But two distinct processes were taking place. One was the subjection of the African chiefdoms to white control; the other, the establishment of British supremacy, not only over African chiefdoms, but also over the Afrikaner republics.

In the first half of the period, the former process was dominant and the latter was secondary. The freedom of action of all the chiefdoms was reduced still further by white pressures, and many of them were incorporated in the republics, the colonies, or the dependent British Empire. Great Britain also annexed the Transvaal in 1877, but granted it a qualified independence again in 1881.

In the second half of the period, the remaining chiefdoms were subjected and the tensions between Great Britain and the Afrikaner republics grew to a crescendo, culminating in a devastating war. When the republics had submitted to *force majeure* in May 1902, the Union Jack flew from the Cape to the Limpopo and beyond.

These two processes were of course intimately related to one another. The outcome of clashes in one part of South Africa affected decisions elsewhere. For example, the check sustained by President Burgers's commandos at the hands of Sekhukhune's Pedi in 1876 was a factor leading to the British decision to annex the Transvaal; the elimination of the Zulu army, which had been a threat to the Transvaalers, in the war of 1879 encouraged them to rise in rebellion in 1880; and the preoccupation of the British forces with the Transvaal rebellion in turn encouraged the southern Sotho to persist in their defiance of the Government of the Cape Colony.

In this book the two themes are treated separately: the subjection of the African chiefdoms in this chapter, the relations between Great Britain and the Afrikaner republics in the next. The chronological sequence of the main events is set out in the appendix at the end of this chapter.

The subjection of the indigenous inhabitants of South Africa to white control was not, of course, an exclusively local phenomenon. It was part of a world-wide process that had started in the fifteenth century and was reaching its climax at the end of the nineteenth century, when the technological gap between the West and the societies of Africa and South-East Asia was greater than it had ever been before, and the peoples of Europe and of European descent were more confident than ever that it was their destiny to rule alien people and bring them 'the blessings of Christianity and Civilization'.

Nevertheless, in South Africa the process had distinctive local characteristics. Already by 1870, when there were still very few white people in tropical Africa, a white community was numerous and strongly entrenched in South Africa and all the South African chiefdoms had been brought within the range of white influences; and after 1870 the diamond- and gold-mining industries created a great increase in white power and in the demand for African labour.

Chiefdoms were undermined from within and overwhelmed from without. Resident missionaries were a revolutionary influence, because they condemned African customs and institutions and taught the social norms of nineteenth-century Europe as though they crystallized a moral code of universal validity. Resident traders meshed the chiefdoms more tightly into the network of British commerce and created a demand for European manufactures and the money with which to buy them. White farmers infiltrated inside the frontiers of African chiefdoms, often starting by asking permission from a chief or headman, but usually ending by claiming proprietary rights over farms. Recruiters sought labourers for railway construction and for the diamond- and gold-mines. Speculators solicited all manner of industrial and mining concessions from chiefs. Nearly all of these missionaries, traders, farmers, labour-recruiters, and concession-hunters believed that their interests would be served by the extension of white political authority over the African territories.

The extension of white authority was not a monolithic process. To construe it simply in racial or economic terms is to do violence to the truth. The British, the colonial, and the republican governments vacillated between co-operation and rivalry with one another; and none of them was uniformly and continuously expansionist. Furthermore, although the local missionaries, farmers, traders, speculators, and administrators were generally expansionist, they were so for different reasons and their goals were not compatible. The simplest case was Afrikaner expansion from the central high veld. This was conducted on traditional lines by small groups of farmers encroaching upon the territories of the Zulu, the Swazi, the Pedi, the Venda, and the Tswana. The farmers were encouraged by Transvaal officials and they knew that if they got into difficulties they would by supported by Transvaal commandos. On the other hand, British and colonial expansion was promoted by a wider range of agents and took more varied forms, ranging from sudden violent warfare (as against the Zulu in 1879) to subordination by diplomacy (as with the Mpondo and the Tswana chiefdoms).

Nor was the African response to white expansion monolithic. African rulers made alliances with white governments for protection against their African enemies and they also took advantage of divisions among the whites. When a choice was available, they usually preferred a colonial alliance to a republican, and a British alliance to a colonial, for they considered that the republics had the greatest and Great Britain the least interest in exploiting and disrupting them. Different African rulers also reacted in different ways. Some, such as Kgama of the Ngwato, tried to make an accommodation with the new forces, welcoming missionaries and traders and seeking British protection. Others, like Cetshwayo, tried to preserve the traditional order and to defend their territories against all comers. There were similar differences between rival segments of chiefdoms. One stood for the conservative and the other for the modernizing forces, or each sought an accommodation with a different white government. Thus, rivalries among white agencies and white governments became enmeshed with rivalries among African groups and African governments.

Nevertheless, by the end of the nineteenth century all the African chiefdoms had been subjected to white control. In many cases there was bloodshed before the new order was entrenched. The southern Nguni, who had already borne the brunt of white expansion since the late eighteenth century, fought again in the 1870s before they were finally subjected. The Zulu were peremptorily conquered by Great Britain in 1879. The Pedi and the Venda defied both the Afrikaner and the British governments of the Transvaal for many years before they were completely subdued. On the other hand, the Mpondo, the Swazi, and most of the Tswana chiefdoms submitted to white authorities without a fight in the face of strong pressure and after they had been surrounded (or nearly surrounded) by white-controlled territories. Only in one case did an African polity gain an important political objective by physical resistance to a white government. After defying their Cape colonial rulers, the southern Sotho were taken back under the wing of Britain (with the unforeseen consequence that in 1966 their descendants became formally independent again).

When fighting did take place, fire-power was the decisive factor.

Although many Africans managed to obtain fire-arms from traders, especially in Griqualand West in the 1870s, most of them were obsolete models such as British and continental European arms manufacturers were dumping in many parts of Africa in the late nineteenth century; and Africans rarely had adequate supplies of ammunition. Moreover, scarcely any African chiefdom modified its military institutions to make effective use of fire-arms. The southern Sotho came nearest to doing this; more typically, Cetshwayo's Zulu went to war in 1879 with the military organization and tactics of the time of Shaka. White forces, on the other hand, were always equipped with comparatively up-to-date weapons and superior ammunition supplies. Afrikaner commandos consisted of expert mounted riflemen; and British troops, though much less efficient under South African conditions, were also trained and organized to the use of fire-arms.

1. *The West Griqua: Diamond Field Politics*[1]

The diamond discoveries precipitated a political drama which formed an apt prelude to the subjugation of the remaining African chiefdoms to white control.

The land that was to become Griqualand West was an arid frontier zone, sparsely populated by a few thousand people who recognized several different political authorities. One of these authorities was the West Griqua chiefdom centred on Griquatown. Since 1834, when Sir Benjamin D'Urban, Governor of the Cape Colony, had made a treaty with Chief Andries Waterboer, giving him a salary and recognizing him as an ally, the West Griqua chiefdom had declined. Nicholas Waterboer was a weaker man than his father, whom he succeeded in 1853. The land dried up, the big game were destroyed, diseases attacked their livestock, and the Griqua were demoralized by 'Cape smoke' (cheap brandy) peddled by traders from the Colony. In 1870 they numbered less than a thousand poor and listless people, nearly all of whom lived to the west of the Vaal River.[2]

The other inhabitants included several bands of Khoikhoi scattered throughout the area and groups of Tswana mainly in the north; while in the east there were some Afrikaner farmers, citizens of the Orange

---

[1] The principal secondary accounts of the diamond fields dispute are in W. B. Campbell, 'The South African Frontier, 1865-1885: a Study in Expansion', *AYB*, xxii (1959), i; C. W. de Kiewiet, *British Colonial Policy and the South African Republics, 1848-1872*; J. J. Oberholster, 'Die Anneksasie van Griekwaland-Wes', *AYB*, viii (1945); G. M. Theal, *History of South Africa from 1795 to 1872*, iv; and J. A. I. Agar-Hamilton, *The Road to the North: South Africa, 1852-1886*. Contemporary documents and accounts include D. Arnot and F. Orpen, *The Land Question of Griqualand West*; A. F. Lindley, *Adamantia: the Truth about the South African Diamond Fields*; and the official record of *Evidence Taken at Bloemhof . . .*, 1871.

[2] J. S. Marais, *The Cape Coloured People, 1652-1937*, pp. 41-50.

Free State, with their African and Coloured dependants. A number of missionaries and traders, most of whom were British subjects, worked in the area from time to time and others passed through it to avoid the republican authorities on their way from the Cape Colony to the comparatively prosperous Tswana chiefdoms further north.

Before diamonds were discovered, there were several claimants to political sovereignty in the area. The Orange Free State claimed all the land east of the Vaal River as part of its inheritance from the Orange River Sovereignty, and it also claimed that the so-called Campbell Lands west of the Vaal River had been included in the land it had purchased from the East Griqua chief Adam Kok in 1861. The South African Republic claimed that its territory included all the land on the northern side of the Vaal River, at least as far west as its junction with the Harts. The most sweeping claim of all was made by David Arnot, an able Coloured lawyer from the Cape Colony, on behalf of his client Nicholas Waterboer. Arnot based his case on treaties made by the Waterboers and on the assertion that Cornelius Kok of the Campbell Lands had been a subject of the Waterboers. According to Arnot, the West Griqua state was bounded by the Orange River from Kheis to Ramah (in terms of the 1834 treaty with D'Urban) and by lines from Ramah to Platberg-on-Vaal (in terms of an 1838 treaty with Adam Kok, establishing a boundary between the two Griqua states), from Kheis to Boetsap (by an 1842 treaty with Mahura, a Thlaping chief), and from Boetsap to Platberg (by a proclamation issued by Waterboer in 1863 and subsequently endorsed by Mahura).

Arnot tried to gain support for this case from the colonial government; but although Richard Southey, the Cape Colonial Secretary, was as anxious as Arnot to block the westward expansion of the Republics, he could do nothing about it. If diamonds had not been found there, it is possible that Britain would not have intervened and that the entire area would have been incorporated in the Republics.

In 1869 the first diamond rush in South Africa took place. Its focus was the alluvial diggings, most of which were on the north side of the Vaal River, above its junction with the Harts, in the area claimed by the South African Republic. President M. W. Pretorius reacted by putting pressure on the local Tswana and Khoikhoi chiefs to acknowledge the sovereignty of the Transvaal; but when the *Volksraad* rashly granted a diamond-mining monopoly to a single company, the diggers formed local committees and defied the republican Government. Although Pretorius then hastily cancelled the monopoly and tried to woo the diggers with assurances of local self-government, they had been permanently estranged.

The second and major diamond rush took place in 1870 and 1871 to the dry diggings. These were south-east of the Vaal River, in the area which the Orange Free State Government had always regarded as falling within its territory. President J. H. Brand instructed a *landdrost* to assume authority over the dry diggings and he issued regulations to resolve disputes between the diggers and the companies which had bought the diamondiferous farms and recognizing the diggers' committees as subordinate local authorities.

Sir Philip Wodehouse left South Africa in May 1870. For seven months after there was an Acting Governor, Lieutenant-General Charles Hay, who had had very little political experience. This placed exceptional power in the hands of Richard Southey, the Cape Colonial Secretary. Southey was an expansionist. He believed that Britain should assume responsibility for law and order throughout South Africa, to curb the Afrikaner republics, protect the African chiefdoms, promote British commerce, and preserve British paramountcy. Southey asked Arnot to send him an elaborate statement of Waterboer's territorial claims and to persuade Waterboer to request British protection. He also put pressure on colonial newspaper editors and arranged for petitions to be signed by colonial merchants in favour of the annexation of the diamond fields. With these documents, Southey pressed the case for annexation upon Hay in Cape Town and upon the Colonial Office in London. Consequently the evidence at the disposal of his superiors made it seem that the Afrikaner republics were destroying a Coloured state and might, if unrestrained, break out of the net of British paramountcy. Hay responded by sending a Cape magistrate to the diggings, under the obsolescent Cape of Good Hope Punishment Act, 1836; while in London the British Colonial Secretary instructed the new Governor, Sir Henry Barkly, that after he reached South Africa he should annex the territory claimed for Waterboer, provided that the diggers and the indigenous peoples wanted it and the Cape Colonial Parliament would assume the cost and the responsibility for administering it.

On his arrival in South Africa, Barkly brushed aside Brand's attempts to demonstrate the validity of the Free State claims to the dry diggings and sent troops to the Orange River as a demonstration in support of the Cape magistrate; but his plans suffered a set-back when the Cape Parliament failed to give a firm commitment to incorporate Waterboer's territory. Meanwhile, one aspect of the territorial dispute was under arbitration. President Brand had refused to submit the Free State claims to arbitration by a British officer, but President Pretorius had allowed the Transvaal claims to be adjudicated by R. W. Keate, the Lieutenant-Governor of Natal. In the subsequent proceedings, Keate concluded that Waterboer's territory extended as far north-east as Platberg-on-Vaal. Vindicating one of the main geographical points in Arnot's claims for Waterboer, this decision made Arnot's entire case seem credible; and soon after it was announced Barkly decided to ignore that part of his instructions which required a commitment by the Cape Colony. In October 1871 he annexed 'Griqualand West' as a Crown Colony, with the boundaries set out by Arnot (see Vol. I, pp. 331–3).

The annexation of Griqualand West was a striking example of the capacity of determined individuals to enlarge the British Empire. Arnot, a private person with a Coloured man's grievance against Afrikaners who would not accept him as an equal, and an opportunistic eye to personal advantage, concocted a paper case that inflated a small, diffuse, and almost moribund polity into a sovereign state and claimed boundaries for that state that far exceeded the realities of occupation and authority. Southey, who knew better, accepted Arnot's case at its face value and manipulated the occasion provided by Wodehouse's departure to give London the impression that the indigenous people, the diggers, the missionaries, and the merchants were all clamouring for British intervention. The Colonial Secretary, Lord Kimberley, and the officials in the Colonial Office responded as Southey wished. Moved partly by economic and humanitarian considerations, but mainly by a sense that their imprecise concept of British paramountcy in South Africa was being challenged, they authorized annexation—but only on conditions compatible with their current policy of creating law and order in South Africa through the agency of a self-governing Cape Colony. Governor Barkly went a step further. Even though in 1871 the Cape Parliament would neither accept responsible government nor give an unequivocal commitment to assume responsibility for the territory, he annexed Griqualand West to the Crown in the hope that the other pieces would fall into place.

The electrifying effects of the annexation upon the Afrikaner people throughout South Africa and upon relations between Britain and the republics will be considered later. Here, it is sufficient to deal with the aftermath of annexation in Griqualand West itself. In 1875 the Government set up a Land Court to unravel the tissue of conflicting private claims to land in Griqualand West. Confronted with overwhelming evidence, the court decided that in most of the territory south-east of the Vaal River, including the dry diggings, titles based upon grants made by Waterboer were invalid. The British Government recognized that this decision destroyed the case for Waterboer's sovereignty in the Kimberley area and awarded £90,000 compensation to the Orange Free State.

Meanwhile, the British officials had been coerced by the diggers to consent to a *de facto* if not a *de jure* colour-bar in the diamond industry, restricting licences to mine and to deal in diamonds to white people.[1]

---

[1] S. T. van der Horst, *Native Labour in South Africa*, pp. 72–4.

The Griqua, and also the Khoikhoi and the Tswana inhabitants of the territory, soon became dissatisfied with the new order and in 1877 and 1878 they committed sporadic acts of violence. Volunteer forces suppressed these 'rebellions', causing a heavy loss of life.

In 1880 Griqualand West was incorporated in the Cape Colony. Although the Griqua were then allotted farms, locations, and village *erven*, they were soon persuaded to sell their land to white people for cash or liquor. By the end of the century, the people in whose name the territory had been annexed had ceased to exist as an organized community. The survivors worked for white men.[1]

Thus the south-westward expansion of the Afrikaner republics was checked, the road to the north was kept open for British missionaries and traders, and the diamond fields were brought within the British Empire and made the responsibility of a self-governing colony.

2. The Southern Nguni: The Politics of Divide and Rule[2]

By the 1870s the southern Nguni, alone among the Bantu-speaking peoples of South Africa, had had a full century of continuous contact with white people. They had suffered a series of defeats in which, time after time, their huts had been burnt, their cattle captured, their fields devastated. Successive blocks of land had been taken from them and turned into farms. Whole communities had been expelled from their homes and shunted about the country. The cattle-killing of 1857 had been a shattering blow to their moral fibre as well as their material welfare. Poverty was becoming endemic among the southern Nguni and the only way they had to alleviate it was by going out to work for white people.[3]

On either side of the Kei river there was a deep frontier zone, extending from about the Fish to the Mthatha, where whites and Africans had fought and co-operated for a hundred years. The Kei itself was the line where British sovereignty officially ceased. But it was not a line of division between black and white societies. Many Africans remained in the Ciskei and there were white residents east of the river. Nor was it a line of division between distinctive Nguni peoples. The Mfengu, remnants of Nguni tribes which Shaka had disrupted in Natal, were scattered in many localities on both sides of the river. Xhosa, too,

---

[1] Marais, p. 50.

[2] Campbell, op. cit.; C. W. de Kiewiet, *The Imperial Factor in South Africa*, chs. 7, 8; [John X. Merriman], *Selections from the Correspondence of John X. Merriman*, P. Lewsen (ed.), vol. i. *1870–90*, ch. 2; P. A. Molteno, *The Life and Times of Sir John Charles Molteno*, ii, chs. 25–9; G. M. Theal, *1795–1872*, iv, ch. 65; and *History of South Africa from 1873 to 1884*, i, chs. 2–7.

[3] See Vol. I, Ch. VI, and Vol. II, Ch. II, of this *History*. In the light of Professor Wilson's full chapter on the southern Nguni in the first volume of this work, I deal with them very briefly here.

lived on both sides of the river and they, also, were fragmented. The major Xhosa divisions were the Gcaleka and the Rarabe, which had split in the eighteenth century. In the early nineteenth century the Rarabe, in turn, had divided into Ngqika and Ndlambe segments and the wars that began in 1834, 1847, and 1850 and the cattle-killing of 1857 had caused further scattering and further subdividing. The Thembu, another great branch of the southern Nguni, were also scattered and divided.

Nor did the Kei River mark an abrupt termination of white political authority. For many decades Transkeian chiefs had turned to missionaries and traders, as well as to their African councillors, for advice. They knew from long experience that the rulers of the Cape Colony were capable of bringing overwhelming force to bear against them. Consequently, in their quarrels among themselves the weaker parties were prone to look for white support. This was particularly true of the Mfengu, who were protégés of the Cape Government. It was also true of the Thembu, who knew themselves to be weaker than the Xhosa. Moreover, in earlier years Britain had exercised jurisdiction east of the Kei and since British Kaffraria had been incorporated in the Cape Colony in 1865, the Cape Government had appointed officials to reside beyond the river among the Thembu, the Mfengu, and the Gcaleka-Xhosa, even though the river was the formal boundary. In spite of the fact that they had no powers, except over British subjects, that could be enforced in colonial courts, these men exerted great influence. They exercised judicial functions and some of them actually raised taxes from the people.

The culmination of the process of the subordination of the southern Nguni was delayed by divided counsels within the Cape Colony and between the colonial and the imperial governments. Some colonists were still imbued with the militaristic approach which had formerly permeated British official thinking about the frontier. According to them, the obligation of the government was to defend the colony from attack, and no more. Among the farmers in the frontier zone, however, defence considerations were confused with other purposes. Some coveted land across the Kei River which they had been on the verge of acquiring after the cattle-killing of 1857. Others wanted systematically to exploit the labour potential of the Transkeian peoples. In either case, annexation seemed to be desirable. Traders, missionaries, and frontier officials also favoured the extension of British or colonial control over the Transkei, but for additional or different reasons. They wished to pave the way for the more thorough dissemination of the Western values and the Western material techniques in which they all believed.

The expansionist forces began to triumph in the late 1870s, when a series of disturbances revealed the dangers of relying upon agents without legal powers to pacify the frontier communities. In 1875 Gange-lizwe, the Thembu paramount chief, was at odds with the Gcaleka-Xhosa and he asked for British protection. He had ill-treated one of his wives, who was a daughter of the Gcaleka paramount, Sarili (Kreli). Then in 1877 a drinking quarrel between Gcaleka-Xhosa and Mfengu drew in others until, in the early months of 1878, imperial as well as colonial troops, with Mfengu and Thembu allies under white officers, were engaged in crushing the Gcaleka-Xhosa and the Ngqika-Xhosa. As a result of these events, the Cape Parliament passed resolutions for the annexation of the territories between the Kei and the Mthatha. Only Fingoland and Idutywa had actually been annexed (1879), when the Zulu War and the southern Sotho rebellion caused a temporary reaction in the Cape Colony. The Scanlen ministry actually tried to persuade the British Government to assume control over the Transkei as well as Basutoland; but Britain declined and in 1885 the Cape Colony incorporated the remaining territories south of the Mthatha river.

Thus, a century after they had first begun to interact with Afrikaner farmers in the Fish River area, the southern Nguni were finally con-quered. In the process they had lost most of the land they had once occupied south of the Kei River; but, tempered by the southern Sotho re-bellion (below, pp. 268–70), the Cape politicians refrained from trying to appropriate land between the Kei and the Mthatha for white settlement.

The prestige of the southern Nguni chiefs had been seriously affected by the series of military defeats and the lamentable consequences of the cattle-killing. As a result, the colonial magistrates were able rather rapidly to become the effective administrators of their districts.[1] Having borne the brunt of white pressures and modern influences for so long, by the end of the nineteenth century the Mfengu and the southern Nguni were beginning to adapt to their role as conquered people. The Ciskeian and Transkeian reserves were studded with shops and mission churches and schools, and the people were beginning to make the long and diffi-cult transition from tribesmen to peasant farmers and migrant labourers, and, in some cases, to townsmen (Chaps. II and IV).

3. The Natal Nguni: Defiance and Reaction[2]

The context of race relations in Natal was very different from that in the Cape. In the 1870s, Natal was a colonial wedge between

[1] See [Sir Walter Stanford], *The Reminiscences of Sir Walter Stanford*, J. W. Macquarrie (ed.), *VRS*, 1958, 1962, which is an autobiographical account by one of the most distinguished of the Cape colonial administrators.

[2] E. H. Brookes and C. de B. Webb, *A History of Natal*, ch. 12; De Kiewiet, *Imperial Factor*, pp. 30–40; W. Rees (ed.), *Colenso Letters from Natal*; R. Russell, *Natal: The Land and its Story*; Theal, *1873–1884*, i, ch. 10.

two independent African states—the Mpondo and the Zulu; and inside the colony Africans outnumbered white people by about fifteen to one. For nearly a quarter of a century there had been domestic peace, as a result of the arrangements that had been made by Theophilus Shepstone (Vol. I, Ch. VIII). Under these arrangements, most of the Africans lived in 'locations' (reserves) under the authority of chiefs; and provided they paid their hut taxes, went out to work in sufficient numbers, and were respectful to white people, the Government was content. The essential human matrix was the trust that Shepstone had inspired in the chiefs, who looked to him as their patron and remained the real administrators of their people.

However, there were some chiefs with whom Shepstone never did establish effective relationships. Such a chief was Langalibalele (Langalibaletse), of the Natal section of the Hlubi. He and his followers had fled from Mpande's Zulu kingdom in the 1840s and been located by the Natal Government close under the Drakensberg, around the headwaters of the Bushman's River. There, being exceptionally isolated, they had been subject to even less interference than most other Natal Africans. Langalibalele had a great reputation among the Nguni and Sotho peoples as a rainmaker, which had made him the object of missionary criticism; but the Government had ignored him for many years.

In 1872, alarmed by the introduction of fire-arms into Natal by men returning from the diamond fields, the Government ordered the chiefs to see to the registration of all arms held by their people. Langalibalele ignored these instructions. When a messenger was sent to tell him to appear in Pietermaritzburg, Langalibalele abused him, recalling that in 1858 a fellow chief, Matyana, had been summoned to a 'peaceful meeting' by John Shepstone, brother of 'Somtseu', only to be confronted with a gun and arrested.[1]

Langalibalele's defiance was an unwonted challenge to the authority of the Government, which decided to make an example of him and thus to intimidate other chiefs and reassure the white population. Sir Benjamin Pine, the Governor, led a force of two hundred British troops, three hundred white volunteers, and about six thousand Africans to Langalibalele's location. The chief fled across the mountains to Basutoland with his cattle and most of his men of fighting age, but on the way his rearguard came to blows with a scouting party, killing three volunteers and two Africans. Pine then ordered the destruction of Langalibalele's chiefdom and of the adjacent Putili-Ngwane chiefdom, which was believed to have been concerting with Langalibalele. Their stock was seized, their land confiscated, and their people were distributed among white farmers. Langalibalele and his men were captured by

[1] Brookes and Webb, op. cit., p. 114.

Cape Mounted Police in the Leribe district of Basutoland. Molapo, son of Moshweshwe, betrayed him for a share of his cattle.[1] Pine then set up a special court to try Langalibalele and his councillors. Pine himself—the man who had led the expedition against the main prisoner and ordered the destruction of his chiefdom—presided over the court, which sentenced Langalibalele to banishment. Finally, Pine persuaded Sir John Molteno, Prime Minister of the Cape Colony, to have his parliament pass an Act for the confinement of Langalibalele on Robben Island, and there Langalibalele was sent. As a result of this display of force, Pine hoped that Langalibalele would have no imitators.

These proceedings had the full support of Theophilus Shepstone and the Natal colonists, who displayed an almost pathological desire for indiscriminate vengeance when they heard of the death of the three volunteers. However, Bishop Colenso courageously exposed the excesses which had been committed by the troops and the illegality of the proceedings of the special court. Caught between two fires, Lord Carnarvon, the Secretary of State, compromised. Pine was recalled; Langalibalele was removed from Robben Island to a farm in the Cape peninsula. Carnarvon also promised that reforms would be made in the administration of Africans in Natal; but in fact no substantial changes took place. The African population of Natal was quiescent for another generation, under the tutelage of successive members of the Shepstone dynasty, until in 1906 there was another act of defiance and another violent reaction (p. 345). White supremacy had been upheld in the Colony of Natal.

4. The Zulu: Military Conquest and Aftermath[2]

In the 1870s the Zulu kingdom was by far the most powerful African state south of the Limpopo. Cetshwayo, who succeeded his father, Mpande, in 1872, was an able ruler. He was not given to the capricious behaviour of his uncles, Shaka and Dingane, and he was firmer and more intelligent than his father. He consulted his councillors before coming to a decision, he was popular, and the kingdom was more closely united than it had ever been. Nevertheless, he had become heir to Mpande as a result of a great and bloody victory over his half-brother, Mbulazi, and there were relatives alive who were potential rebels.

Cetshwayo revitalized the army, which had become soft under Mpande. As in Shaka's day, conscription was enforced on all the young

[1] G. Tylden, *The Rise of the Basuto*, pp. 122–5.
[2] There is a considerable literature on the Zulu war, notably C. T. Binns, *The Last Zulu King*; Brookes and Webb, op. cit., chs. 10, 13–15, 18; R. Coupland, *Zulu Battle Piece: Isandhlwana*; De Kiewiet, *Imperial Factor*, pp. 207–47; J. Y. Gibson, *The Story of the Zulus*; D. R. Morris, *The Washing of the Spears*; Russell, op. cit.; Theal, *1873–1884*, i, chs. 13, 14; ii, ch. 15.

men, who lived in regimental barracks under strict discipline and were forbidden to marry until the king released them, a regiment at a time, at about the age of forty. The warriors were confident and assertive. They were too young to have experienced the defeats of 1838 and 1840 and they wished to wash their spears in blood to celebrate the accession of Cetshwayo.

The Zulu kingdom had fewer white residents than any comparable area further south. There were perhaps a dozen Norwegian missionaries and about as many traders; but converts were few and the volume of trade was small. Consequently, although both missionaries and traders regarded Cetshwayo's regime as inimical to their interests, they had few African followers and were not a threat to his authority. There was also a renegade Scot, John Dunn, who had ingratiated himself with Cetshwayo and become a district chief in the south of the kingdom, amply provided with wives, followers, and cattle. Cetshwayo used him as an intermediary with the Natal Government and as a gun-runner.

The traditional enemies of the Zulu were the Transvaal Afrikaners. It was their fathers who had defeated Dingane and it was they who were infiltrating into the north-western part of the kingdom in the area east of the Blood River, where there were no natural boundaries, and claiming it as their own. With Natal, on the other hand, the Tugela and Buffalo rivers formed a definite boundary line and there was comparatively little friction. Cetshwayo followed his father in basing his foreign policy upon the Natal alliance, even to the extent of an outward show of subordination. He invited Theophilus Shepstone to come and 'crown' him in 1873 and while Shepstone was there Cetshwayo allowed him to announce that there were to be new laws, prohibiting the indiscriminate shedding of blood. However, Shepstone had no means of interfering in the actual administration of the kingdom and Cetshwayo continued to regard the Natal alliance as a valuable safeguard against Transvaal aggression.

During the mid 1870s Transvaal pressure upon the disputed territory increased and yet the Transvaal was showing signs of palpable weakness in its failure to conquer Sekhukhune's Pedi (p. 282), who were not nearly as numerous as the Zulu. Morale in the Zulu army was good and the younger warriors clamoured for action against the Afrikaner intruders. When Shepstone entered the Transvaal in January 1877, Cetshwayo offered to help by having his army wash its spears in Afrikaner blood; but Shepstone restrained him. Then, suddenly, the entire basis of Cetshwayo's foreign policy was destroyed. Shepstone's annexation of the Transvaal (April 1877) transformed it from an Afrikaner republic into a British colony. Formerly, Shepstone had espoused the Zulu cause in the boundary dispute. Now he endorsed the Transvaal claims and as it became evident that his Transvaal regime depended on the support of the Afrikaner population, he decided to try to win that support by tackling Cetshwayo. Consequently, the foundations of Cetshwayo's security collapsed.

A diplomatic and military noose gradually tightened around the Zulu kingdom. Sir Bartle Frere, the High Commissioner, had been sent to South Africa to carry out Carnarvon's federation policy and Shepstone was able to convince him that the Zulu kingdom was a major obstacle. If the kingdom were overthrown, Shepstone argued, the Transvaal Afrikaners would be satisfied that their Government had a sound view of race relations and the strength to enforce its decisions, and they would be willing to federate with the British colonies. At the same time, the greatest menace to European civilization in South Africa would have been removed. Frere, who had had no previous experience of South Africa, accepted these arguments; and he and Shepstone sought to persuade the Colonial Secretary that there could be no stability in South Africa so long as there was an independent Zulu kingdom, with an army which they represented as menacing and a ruler they called tyrannical.

When Shepstone first revealed his thoughts, Lord Carnarvon told him to keep the peace at all costs. Frere and Shepstone had further cause for restraint. The Lieutenant-Governor of Natal had appointed a Commission to investigate the boundary dispute between the Zulu kingdom and the Transvaal colony and, after taking evidence from both sides, the Commission reported that the Transvaal claims to land east of the Blood River were without legal substance (June 1878). This report confirmed Sir Henry Bulwer, Lieutenant-Governor of Natal, in his belief that there was no reason to abandon the pacific policy towards Cetshwayo. On the other hand, there were incidents on the Natal–Zulu frontier, including a sortie across the Buffalo by some young Zulu warriors, who seized some Zulu women who had fled there from chief Sirayo; and, alarmed by rumours of war, the missionaries evacuated Zululand.

Frere exploited these events. He also delayed sending the full report of the Boundary Commission to London until he had received military reinforcements, until the senior military officer (General Thesiger, soon to become Lord Chelmsford) had worked out an invasion plan, and until he had softened up Carnarvon's successor, Sir Michael Hicks Beach, with frequent reiterations of his anti-Zulu refrain. Then, before London had had time to digest the Commission report, Frere presented Cetshwayo with an ultimatum, which included the demand that the Zulu army should be disbanded within thirty days. No self-respecting ruler could comply with such a demand. If Cetshwayo had tried to do so, one of his relatives would assuredly have ousted him with the support of the majority of the regiments. Consequently Chelmsford's invasion plan went into force on 11 January 1879.

Before the ultimatum expired, the Zulu army, about thirty thousand strong, gathered at Cetshwayo's capital, Ulundi, to be doctored for war. The officers had no detailed plans. Cetshwayo sided with those who were for mass attacks upon the enemy rather than guerrilla warfare, but he gave strict orders that the impis were on no account to invade Natal. Chelmsford's forces—about seven thousand British regulars and as many Natal African levies, with perhaps a thousand colonial volunteers—invaded the kingdom from three points, expecting a comfortable sweep to Ulundi. The Zulu army concentrated against the central column and on 22 January 1879 took most of it unawares at Isandhlwana, where the British army lost sixteen hundred men in its greatest disaster since the Crimean War. Chelmsford had ignored the warning of no less a person than Paul Kruger that the Zulu were not to be trifled with. In particular, Kruger had recommended that the British should always carry out reconnaissance in depth and should always entrench their camps; and Chelmsford had done neither of these things. However, after British reinforcements arrived the war gradually drew to its inexorable conclusion. John Dunn had defected from Cetshwayo with his followers at the very beginning and Hamu, Cetshwayo's cousin,[1] did so soon afterwards; but the decisive factor was fire-power. Many of the Zulu had guns of sorts, but they never made good use of them. In their training they had concentrated on hand-to-hand fighting with the short stabbing spear, as in the days of Shaka, and in trying to get to close quarters they suffered very severe losses. When Ulundi went up in flames on 4 July the Zulu army had ceased to exist.

By that time, Sir Garnet Wolseley had taken office as Governor of Natal and the Transvaal and High Commissioner in South East Africa. Since Isandhlwana had temporarily put a stop to the British Government's willingness to increase its South African responsibilities, Wolseley's instructions were that Zululand was not to be annexed. His problem was therefore to make a peace settlement that would prevent a revival of the Zulu kingdom and to do this without cost to Britain. The solution he adopted was a clever one. He banished Cetshwayo to Cape Town. He divided Zululand into thirteen separate territories under thirteen different chiefs. These chiefs included descendants of Zwide and Dingiswayo; Hamu, Cetshwayo's cousin who had deserted to the British in the war; Zibhebhu, who was a descendant of a brother of Shaka's father Senganzakhona and who had quarrelled with Cetshwayo; and the inimitable John Dunn. Cetshwayo's loyal councillors were placed under

---

[1] Hamu was Cetshwayo's cousin in terms of Zulu law and custom; in biological terms he was Cetshwayo's half-brother.

Zibhebhu. Each of the thirteen chiefs was made to undertake not to create an army and to accept the arbitration of the British Resident. But the British Resident, like similar officers in the Transkeian Territories before they were annexed, had no legal or physical means to enforce a decision.

This settlement has been condemned by all historians who have remarked upon it; but they have failed to emphasize its Machiavellian quality. No more astute device could have been found for setting Zulu against Zulu and thus consummating the military victory without further cost or responsibility. Wolseley had improved upon the classic imperial formula. 'Divide and Refrain from Ruling' was a shrewd technique in an area where imperial interests were merely negative.

The military defeat and Wolseley's settlement initiated a process of national disintegration. Scarcely any of the chiefs appointed by Wolseley were men of standing in their territories. In some cases they were challenged by rivals, such as a pretender who claimed to be genealogically senior to the appointed chief of Dingiswayo's lineage. There were also sharp disputes between the appointed chiefs; and white adventurers added fuel to the flames, attaching themselves to chiefs and aspirant chiefs as advisers and gun-runners.

It was not long before there were appeals for the restoration of Cetshwayo, whose cause was supported by Bishop Colenso and several British newspapers. In 1882, Cetshwayo was allowed to visit England, where he was lionized by a sentimental public and given presents by Queen Victoria, but although he was allowed to return home in 1883, Zibhebhu's territory in the north was excluded from his control and so were the territories along the Natal border in the south. These latter became known as the Zulu Reserve and they were brought under closer British surveillance, though still not annexed. Moreover, even within his attenuated kingdom Cetshwayo was made to undertake not to raise an army.

Civil war followed between Cetshwayo and Zibhebhu. Cetshwayo was at a disadvantage because his authority had lapsed during his exile. Zibhebhu soon got the upper hand and Ulundi was destroyed for the second time. Cetshwayo fled and he died in 1884. His surviving councillors treated his eldest son, Dinuzulu—who was a boy of fifteen—as his heir and they turned for support to the Afrikaner farmers who had been infiltrating into the northern part of Zululand during the previous two decades. The farmers recognized Dinuzulu as paramount chief and helped him triumph over Zibhebhu. In return, they proclaimed a 'New Republic' over a large area of north-western Zululand and claimed that the rest of the country, except for the Zulu Reserve adjacent to Natal, was subject to their protection.

Britain reacted against this extension of Afrikaner power into Zulu-land. After Afrikaners from the New Republic had pursued a Zulu chief into the Reserve and shot him there, there were negotiations and in 1886 Britain recognized the New Republic, but with reduced boundaries, and the government of the New Republic dropped its claim to a protectorate over Dinuzulu. In 1887 the New Republic was incorporated into the Transvaal and Britain annexed the rest of Zululand, divided it into districts, and appointed magistrates.

Dinuzulu and his councillors tried to prevent the magistrates from taking powers out of the hands of the chiefs, but it was too late. Dinuzulu was arrested, convicted of treason, and exiled to St. Helena; and when he was allowed to return it was only as a local headman ('government induna') in the Usutu district. By that time (1897), Zululand, and also Tongaland, had been incorporated in Natal, which had been granted responsible government. For many years, Natal farmers and speculators had coveted Zulu territory and the most conspicuous result of the transfer of Zululand to Natal was the appointment of a Land Commission, which delimited a number of locations for the Zulu and threw open the rest of the country to white settlement (1902-4).

The Zulu had been subjected in four stages. First, the kingdom was conquered and its army was broken up. Secondly, the country was split into thirteen separate units. Thirdly, white magistrates supplanted the chiefs as the most powerful men in their districts. And fourthly, the land was partitioned, leaving only about a third of the former kingdom in Zulu hands. Before the war, Theophilus Shepstone had expressed the hope that Cetshwayo's warriors would be 'changed to labourers working for wages'.[1] That process had begun by the end of the nineteenth century.

The British public was told that the Zulu war was a war to liberate the Zulu people from a tyrannical ruler and South Africa from a menace to 'Christianity and Civilization'. According to the historian George McCall Theal, 'The question was simply whether civilisation or barbarism was to prevail in the country.'[2] In fact, British forces destroyed

[1] De Kiewiet, *Imperial Factor*, p. 220.
[2] Theal, *1873-1884*, i. 305. Even C. W. De Kiewiet, the most imaginative and sensitive of the historians who wrote about the Zulu War in the 1930s, was blind to the political realities in African states. Of Cetshwayo's rejection of the British ultimatum, he wrote: 'Among savages with no government save the intermittent one of councils the party of action and violence must prevail' (*Imperial Factor*, p. 231). In fact, Cetshwayo, undone by Shepstone's volte-face and Frere's peremptory demands, had no option but to resist. There are of course numerous examples of African rulers restraining 'the party of action and violence': Mosh-weshwe, the southern Sotho king, always preferred diplomacy to warfare; and—to give one specific example—in 1891 Lobengula, the Ndebele king, prevented his regiments from attacking the Pioneer Column on its way to Mashonaland, even though his younger warriors were spoiling for a fight.

the Zulu kingdom because men on the spot managed to foment a crisis and then to persuade the British Government that the kingdom stood in the way of British interests.

5. *The Southern Sotho: The Politics of Resistance*[1]

In 1869 Great Britain had annexed the Southern Sotho kingdom at the request of the ageing King Moshweshwe to save it from complete dismemberment by the victorious Orange Free State (Vol. I, Ch. IX). In accordance with its policy of delegating its South African responsibilities to self-governing British Colonies, the British Government transferred Basutoland to the Cape Colony in 1871; but the Cape Colonial Government so completely mismanaged the Sotho that it became involved in a war that it could not win and it begged Great Britain to resume responsibility for Basutoland. Britain did so in 1884 and thereby set a precedent that was followed in the case of the Tswana and (later) the Swazi, with the result that these three territories were never included in the Union of South Africa and they became beneficiaries of the decolonization process after the Second World War. Consequently, the triangular relationship between the southern Sotho and the Governments of the Cape Colony and Great Britain in the years after 1869 was of crucial and enduring importance for all of southern Africa.

By the end of their long war with the Orange Free State, the southern Sotho had been reduced to poverty and brought to the brink of starvation; but they revived remarkably quickly. At home, the use of the plough became general and they produced a surplus of grain which they sold in the Orange Free State and Griqualand West. Many of them went out to work on Free State farms, on railway construction, and on the diamond fields, and with their wages they were able to buy guns from white traders, especially in Griqualand West. By the late 1870s, the southern Sotho were comparatively prosperous, well armed, and self-confident.

The Cape Colonial Government approached its new commitment in the light of its experience in the Ciskei and the Transkei, where it checked combinations among Africans by playing off chief against chief and curbed the powers of the chiefs by encouraging the magistrates to become the real rulers of their districts. The political situation among the southern Sotho seemed to provide ample scope for the policy of divide and rule. There had been strong fissiparous tendencies during the years

---

[1] E. H. Brookes, *The History of Native Policy in South Africa, from 1830 to the present day*; De Kiewiet, *Imperial Factor*; Lord Hailey, *Native Administration in the British African Territories*, Part V, *The High Commission Territories: Basutoland, Bechuanaland Protectorate and Swaziland*; G. Lagden, *The Basutos*; [Merriman], op. cit., vol. i; E. Smith, *The Mabilles of Basutoland*; Theal, *1795–1872*, iv; and *1873–1884*, ii; Tylden, op. cit.; J. Widdicombe, *In the Lesuto*.

of the war with the Free State and the decline of Moshweshwe; and after Moshweshwe's death in 1870, Letsie, his acknowledged heir, had little authority over his full brothers, Molapo and Masopha, his senior son Lerotholi, and the chiefs of the allied Taung and Phuthi peoples, Moletsane and Moorosi, each of whom had his own followers and his own territorial base. Nevertheless, the bonds between the Sotho chiefs and their people were still strong—unlike among the southern Nguni, where the prestige of the chiefs had suffered from nearly a century of military defeats. In seeking British protection against the Free State, the Sotho chiefs had not been prepared to tolerate any diminution of their authority over their own people.

Initially, the Cape Government was realistically cautious. Colonel Griffith, the 'Governor's Agent', did not have enough resources to challenge the powers of the chiefs, and the Molteno ministry did not press him to do so. It was Sir Bartle Frere, the Governor who dismissed Molteno in 1878, and Gordon Sprigg who then succeeded Molteno as Prime Minister, who are to be credited with the main responsibility for the collapse of Cape authority among the Sotho. Both Frere and Sprigg were understandably alarmed at the spread of fire-arms among Africans, and they construed the military posture of the Zulu, the continued resistance of the Pedi, the rising of the Xhosa, and the independent bearing of the Sotho as presaging a concerted movement to reject white authority. In 1879 imperial troops took decisive steps against the Zulu and the Pedi. In the area of Cape Colonial responsibility, Frere and Sprigg agreed that it was essential to disarm all Africans; but what they failed to do was to cut their coat according to their cloth.

In 1878 the Sprigg ministry steered through the Cape Parliament a Peace Preservation Bill, which gave the executive the right to issue proclamations ordering colonial Africans to hand in their arms. There was an immediate reaction in the south of Basutoland. Moorosi, the Phuthi chief, occupied a mountain which he had fortified with stone walls in the manner of Moshweshwe. In 1879 he defied the magistrate of Quthing and the Government decided to make an example of him. But although the colonial forces were assisted by Letsie, it took them six months of baffling operations before they managed to storm Moorosi's mountain and kill Moorosi. This they achieved in November 1879.

By that time Sprigg had convened a *pitso* and announced to the Sotho that they were to be disarmed, their hut tax was to be increased, and Moorosi's district was to be thrown open to white settlement. Sprigg was ignorant and foolish in the timing, the manner, and the substance of this declaration, which united the majority of the southern Sotho; and in the sequel he was also stubborn. Although Letsie petitioned

against disarmament and Colonel Griffith and the French missionaries advised against it, the proclamation was issued in April 1880.
Fighting began in September. Letsie, Lerotholi, Masopha, and Joel
(son of the recently deceased Molapo), who between them commanded
the allegiance of most of the Sotho, were sufficiently of one mind to
oppose the proclamation; and only Jonathan (Joel's rival for the succession to Molapo) and some of the sons of Moshweshwe's junior houses
sided with the government. Lerotholi was the leader of the resistance.
His strength was estimated at 23,000 armed and mounted men and he
deployed them more skilfully than Cetshwayo had done. Avoiding
large-scale engagements, he adopted guerrilla tactics, harassing the
colonial forces and their supply lines in all parts of the country. The
colonial forces were unequal to the tasks demanded of them by their
politicians. An unhappy amalgam of white, Coloured, and African
police, volunteers, and conscripts, they were for the most part poorly
armed, poorly trained, and poorly led, and they became greatly over-
extended when the resistance spread to East Griqualand and the Transkei, where not only the communities of Sotho origin but also the
Mpondomisi, some of the Thembu, and even the Griqua rose in rebellion.

The British Government did not provide the Colony with military
assistance. On the eve of the war, successive Secretaries of State had
warned the Cape that there would be no imperial aid if the Sotho
resisted the proclamation; and in the event there were no imperial troops
to spare once the Afrikaner inhabitants of the Transvaal had risen in
rebellion in December 1880. By April 1881 the resistance in East Griqualand and the Transkei had been crushed, but the Sotho continued to
hold their own, even though they were running short of food. Both sides
then accepted the arbitration of Sir Hercules Robinson, the newly
arrived High Commissioner. In his award, Robinson tried to save the
face of the Cape Colony by declaring that the Sotho were to register
and license their guns and pay compensation; but it was apparent to
everyone that the Sotho had triumphed, for the Cape Government had
withdrawn its troops and lacked the means to make the people register
their guns. On the other hand, the Sotho emerged from the Gun War
more divided than ever, for the old jealousies between the members of
Moshweshwe's family persisted and were compounded by a new cleavage
between those who had sided with the Government and those who had
fought against it.

The Cape ministry of Thomas Scanlen, which came into power in
May 1881, was faced with the consequences of its predecessor's rashness.
Its only remedy was to try to exploit the jealousies between the chiefs.
As John X. Merriman, a cabinet minister, elegantly expressed it in a

letter to the Prime Minister:[1] 'When we have split the chiefs up, we can throw our friends over and work with the *people* as against the chiefs, but this will take more time. The great thing is to excite a quarrel among the heads, and there are all the elements in the place, which only want a skilful hand to combine them.' On the other hand, J. M. Orpen, the new Governor's Agent, who sympathized with the Sotho and had been in touch with Moshweshwe and his family for many years, tried to gain the confidence of Letsie and Lerotholi and help them unite their people. But where coercion had failed, it was extremely difficult to create confidence. Joel and Jonathan continued their feud. Masopha, in possession of Thaba Bosiu, ignored everyone. *In extremis*, the Government employed Colonel Charles Gordon, fresh from his triumphs in the Tai-Ping rebellion in China, in the hope that he might perform some undefined political conjuring trick; but Gordon only made matters worse by working behind Orpen's back and then resigning in a temper. The Government then decided to withdraw. It repealed the Peace Preservation Act and implored Britain to resume responsibility for the Sotho. Indeed, so pessimistic had Scanlen and Merriman become that they tried to persuade Britain to take over the Transkei as well as Lesotho, leaving the Colony without burdens it seemed too weak to carry.

The Gladstone ministry declined to take the Transkei; but it did reluctantly agree to resume the responsibility for Basutoland, on condition that the Cape would contribute towards the expected financial deficit and the chiefs desired it. The chiefs were not unanimous. Masopha threatened to defy any magistrate who tried to give him orders; but since Letsie, Lerotholi, and most of the other chiefs declared that they wished to remain British subjects under the direct authority of the Queen, British rule was formally restored in 1884.

Saddled with a commitment it had never sought, the British Government's policy for Basutoland was essentially negative. Provided that it paid its way and did not disturb the peace of South Africa, the local administrators were given a free hand. It was Colonel Marshall Clarke, Resident Commissioner from 1884 to 1894, who established precedents that were followed for over half a century. He allied himself with the paramountcy of Letsie (d. 1891) and his successor Lerotholi (d. 1905) and encouraged them to unite all the inhabitants of the country behind them, so that British influence grew with the power of the paramount and in partnership with him. The last serious challenge from within the royal family came from Masopha, who defied the Government from Thaba Bosiu until he was subdued by Lerotholi shortly before his death in 1899. The powers of the paramount were also fastened on the many non-Kwena elements in the Sotho population by the placing of loyal

[1] [Merriman], i. 109. Likewise, pp. 108 and 111.

members of the royal family over their chiefs, so that the 'Sons of Mosh-weshwe' came to occupy most of the senior chiefly offices in the country. Moshweshwe's prohibition of white settlement was rigorously main-tained. All the land was regarded as the property of the nation and even traders occupied their sites on sufferance. Thus Letsie and Lerotholi, in partnership with Clarke and his successors, continued the process of nation-building that Moshweshwe had begun.

The colonial equilibrium was not achieved without cost to the Sotho. One weakness was a decline in popular participation in government, which had been so conspicuous a feature in traditional Sotho polities (Vol. I, Ch. IV). The *pitso* changed from a decision-making institution into an institution where chiefs announced decisions that had already been made by them in consultation with the British officials. Moreover, since the officials were loath to interfere, chiefs were able to abuse their powers, for example, in the allocation of arable land. Another weakness was that, although the British presence protected the Sotho from poli-tical interference by the colonies and republics, it did not give them economic autonomy. Within the boundaries that had been set in 1869, Basutoland was too small and too deficient in natural resources to sus-tain its population. Dependent for funds on local taxation, the admini-stration did little to remedy this situation and the people relied on the wages earned by those of them who went out of Basutoland to work in the colonies and republics. Thus the Sotho lived in two worlds. They had homes in a traditional rural society, ruled by their chiefs in partnership with British officials; but their major source of income was in a plural society dominated by white people.

6. *The Tswana: The Politics of Partition*[1]

The struggle that developed north of Griqualand West after Britain had annexed it in 1871 was concerned not so much with power over the Tswana peoples as with control of their territories, which contained the road that ran northwards from Kuruman through the principal Tswana settlements to the far interior, between the Transvaal high veld and the Kalahari desert. If Britain controlled the territories, missionaries and traders would have secure access to the far interior; if the Trans-vaal could control them, it would block the road, eliminate British

[1] Agar-Hamilton, op. cit.; Campbell, ch. 14; Hailey, ch. 2; W. J. Leyds, *The Transvaal Surrounded*; J. Mackenzie, *Austral Africa*; S. M. Molema, *The Bantu, Past and Present*; J. A. Mouton, 'Generaal Piet Joubert en sy aandeel in die Transvaalse Geskiedenis', *AYB*, 1957, i, ch. 10; A. Sillery, *The Bechuanaland Protectorate*, and *Sechele: the Story of an African chief*; Theal, *1873–1884*, ii, ch. 21; D. M. Schreuder, 'The Second Gladstone Administration and the Transvaal, 1880–85: an analysis of policy', unpublished D.Phil. dissertation, Oxford Uni-versity, 1968.

influence from its western border, and increase its own security. The Tswana were pawns in this competition between white people.

The capacity of the Tswana to withstand pressures was severely limited by their own internal divisions. Rivalries between chiefdoms persisted and often led to fighting, notably between the Kwena and the Kgafela-Kgatla and between the Tshidi-Rolong and the Ratlou-Rolong. There were also many debilitating dynastic quarrels within the chiefdoms. Consequently, interactions between rival white authorities and divided Tswana communities produced a series of cross-alliances. Some chiefdoms and segments of chiefdoms co-operated with Transvaal farmers and officials, and others with British missionaries, traders, and officials; and the outcome was the partition of the land and its inhabitants between the Transvaal, the Cape Colony, and Great Britain.

During the 1870s there was anarchy in the area west of the Transvaal and south of the Molopo River, where many small groups jostled for land and water. Most of the inhabitants were Tswana of the Tlhaping or Rolong branches, who had suffered severely from the invasions of the previous half century. Their morale was low and they had split into numerous petty chiefdoms, none of which had more than about fifteen thousand adherents. There were also several small bands of Khoikhoi and Coloured people; British military deserters and unsuccessful miners were drifting in from Griqualand West; and Transvaal farmers were continuing to occupy land in the eastern part of the area, ignoring the line laid down in the Keate Award.

In 1878 the disturbances among the Tlhaping in Griqualand West spread northwards, as a result of which a British military force came to Kuruman to restore order. It remained in the area for three years. John Mackenzie, an L.M.S. missionary at Kuruman, Colonel William Owen Lanyon, the Administrator of Griqualand West, and Sir Bartle Frere, the High Commissioner, all recommended that British authority should be formally proclaimed up to the Molopo River; but this was not done and the troops were withdrawn in 1881, as part of the general contraction of British responsibilities. The result was a return to anarchy and a great intensification of pressure from the Transvaal.

The Pretoria Convention of 1881 defined a western boundary for the Transvaal that fell far short of the road to the north. Nevertheless, it included in the Transvaal African and Coloured communities who were connected with communities on the other side of the border. The Convention also reserved control of relations between the Transvaal and the independent African chiefs to the British Resident at Pretoria.

The expansion that then took place was ostensibly a private affair. Afrikaner farmers from the Transvaal occupied lands beyond the Convention boundary, made agreements with Coloured and African chiefs, and became embroiled in their quarrels. At the same time, British people from Griqualand West became advisers of the other parties to the disputes, in the hope of winning land and loot. In this way internal quarrels among the Tswana and the Coloured peoples became intensified. In the south, Transvaalers co-operated with a Coloured leader, Taaibosch Massouw, who was at odds with a Tlhaping chief, Mankurwane; and further north, Transvaalers sided with the Ratlou-Rolong chief Moswete against his Tshidi-Rolong enemy Montshiwa. In both cases Transvaal aid proved decisive and in 1882 the Transvaalers proclaimed two independent republics—Stellaland, under Gerrit J. van Niekerk, with its centre at Vryburg, and Goshen, under Gey van Pittius, around a farm called Rooi Grond. These little states blocked the road to the north and were obviously destined to be incorporated in the Transvaal if Britain did not intervene.

When the Transvaal delegates went to London in 1883 to negotiate a new agreement, although the British Government was willing to relax its controls over their domestic affairs, Sir Hercules Robinson persuaded Lord Derby, the Colonial Secretary, to set a limit to Transvaal expansion to the west. In the London Convention of 1884 the south-western boundary of the Transvaal was moved slightly further into Tlhaping and Rolong territory, but not so far as the road to the north; and the Transvaal Government undertook to respect the boundaries, to prevent it subjects from encroaching beyond them, and to refrain from concluding treaties with African chiefs beyond the boundaries without British approval.

The London Convention did not end the matter. It still remained for Great Britain or the Cape Colony to create some sort of order where the Pretoria Government had been denied the right to do so; but this was delayed because of lack of co-operation between London and Cape Town. Initially, the British Government appointed John Mackenzie as Deputy Commissioner for the territory, but the status of the area was still vague and Mackenzie was not given sufficient resources to make an impression on van Pittius. In the circumstances, Mackenzie did well. He persuaded Mankurwane and Montshiwa to accept British protection and came to terms with a faction of the white people at Vryburg; but his mission was then sabotaged by Cecil Rhodes, who was at that time a member of the Cape Parliament and who wanted colonial, not British, authority to prevail in Bechuanaland. However, succeeding Mackenzie as Deputy Commissioner, Rhodes was no more successful in controlling the wild men of Goshen; and eventually President Kruger, who was impatient at the continued anarchy beyond his western border, issued a proclamation taking Goshen under Transvaal protection (September 1884).

Kruger's action provoked counteraction from London. Germany had proclaimed a protectorate over the coast of South West Africa in the previous month, so that Bechuanaland was no longer merely a trade route of problematical value, but a link between the previously isolated Transvaal and an African foothold of a major European power. That was why the British Government dispatched an expedition of five thousand men under Major-General Sir Charles Warren, with instructions to remove freebooters, restore order, respect African claims, and hold Bechuanaland pending further orders. Warren's force quickly over-awed the people of Stellaland and Goshen without bloodshed and the Tlhaping and Rolong who lived west of the Transvaal and south of the Molopo readily accepted British protection. Later in 1885 the area south of the Molopo was annexed as the Crown Colony of British Bechuana-land and ten years later it was incorporated in the Cape Colony.

North of the Molopo, the Tswana chiefs had not been subjected to such intense pressures as those to the south. Nevertheless, most of them had been attacked by Transvaalers at one time or another and the Ngwato also lived in fear of their Ndebele neighbours to the north-east. Moreover, L.M.S. missionaries had converted Chief Sechele of the Kwena and Chief Kgama of the Ngwato, and missionaries and traders had conditioned most of the Tswana chiefs to look to Britain for protection against Afrikaner expansion. Consequently, Warren had little difficulty in obtaining the submission of the three principal chiefs along the road to the north—Sechele, Kgama, and Gaseitsiwe of the Ngwa-ketse. In accepting British protection, each of these chiefs made in-ordinate territorial claims and explained that they had no desire to be closely controlled by British officials. As they saw it, British overrule was to protect them from their enemies—African as well as white—and help them to extend their authority, without affecting their powers over their own subjects.

During the 1890s the boundary of Bechuanaland Protectorate was extended northwards beyond latitude 22° to take in the rest of what is now Botswana, including the important Tawana chiefdom in the Okavango swamps. For a time it seemed likely that the entire Protec-torate would be transferred to the British South Africa Company. Provision was made for transfer in the Company's charter and in 1895 the lands of the Lete and the Tshidi-Rolong were actually transferred, as was a strip through the country for the Rhodesian railway; but the Kwena, Ngwaketse, and Ngwato chiefs, suspicious of the Company after it had crushed the (Ndebele) Matabele in the war of 1893, went to London to oppose transfer. Their request that they should stay under direct British control was granted and after the Jameson Raid the Lete and Rolong transfers were rescinded. Except for the railway strip and the Gaberones, Lobatsi, Tuli, Ghanzi, and Tati blocks of land, which the chiefs alienated to the British Government or to private companies for white settlement, all the habitable parts of the Protectorate remained in Tswana hands.

The British officials worked in co-operation with the chiefs in the Bechuanaland Protectorate, as in Basutoland. Although the officials intervened to settle boundary disputes between Tswana and also (and sometimes less wisely) in their dynastic quarrels, the Tswana chiefs retained considerable powers over their subjects under British protection, unlike the chiefs in areas under the control of white South Africans.

7. The Swazi: Concession Politics[1]

The subjugation of the Swazi is an example of a process that was more common in tropical Africa than in South Africa in the late nineteenth century. It was, as the Swazi say, the 'documents that killed us'.[2] First, the kingdom was demoralized by concessions, the full significance of which was incomprehensible to the king and councillors who put their marks to them; and then the kingdom was disposed of by treaties between the Transvaal and British governments, without regard to the Swazi.

Swazi foreign policy in the reign of Mswati (1840–68) and his successor Ludvonga (1868–74) was based on the premise that the Zulu, who had tried to destroy the kingdom in the time of Shaka and Dingane and continued to raid it thereafter, were the most serious menace. White people were treated as potential allies against the Zulu. Mswati asked Theophilus Shepstone to use his influence with Mpande to stop Zulu raids and entered into cordial relations with his Afrikaner neighbours in the Transvaal. He persuaded some Transvaal farmers to settle along the Pongola River as a buffer between his people and the Zulu; he allowed the Swazi borders to be defined by Transvaal boundary commissions even though that meant a series of contractions; and he even admitted a vague Transvaal overlordship.

In the early part of his reign, Mbandzeni (1874–89) continued Mswati's policy. He sent regiments to help both the Afrikaner and the British governments of the Transvaal to subdue the Pedi and in 1875 he probably put his mark to a treaty admitting that his people were 'subjects' of the Transvaal, while retaining full control of the administration of his kingdom. By 1881, however, Mbandzeni was becoming

[1] N. G. Garson, 'The Swaziland Question and a Road to the Sea (1887–1895)', *AYB*, 1957, ii; Hailey, op. cit.; H. Kuper, *An African Aristocracy: Rank among the Swazi*, Part I.

[2] H. Kuper, p. 24. Concessions were of course extracted from other rulers in South Africa, notably from the Tswana chiefs in the frontier zone in the western Transvaal; but Swaziland is the extreme South African case of a state that was undermined mainly by this method.

anxious about the effects of Afrikaner pressure and a clause was inserted in the Pretoria Convention, and repeated in the London Convention of 1884, under which both the British and Transvaal governments recognized the independence of the Swazi within defined boundaries.

The great concession era was the last five years of Mbandzeni's reign. The infiltration of Afrikaner stock-farmers, especially for winter grazing, became more intensive and there was also an overspill from the Barberton goldfields of prospectors and adventurers, most of them of British or colonial origin, who hoped that Swaziland might be found to possess gold, diamonds, or other valuable natural resources. These diverse types of white people pestered Mbandzeni and his councillors with gifts ranging from champagne to greyhounds, and promises of more to come, if he would only sign their documents. Mbandzeni was no simpleton; but he and his councillors had no means of grasping the full implications of the documents that were thrust at them. The concepts underlying many of the documents—such as the absolute alienation of land—were beyond the range of their experience and, since they had never welcomed missionaries at court, they had no comparatively disinterested white people to turn to for advice. Consequently, Mbandzeni got into the habit of placing his mark on documents submitted to him and enjoying the proceeds. By the end of his reign, he had crossed away almost the entire resources of the kingdom, actual and potential: the land, the minerals, and the rights to create and operate industries, customs duties, licences, railways, telegraphs, and postal services. Some of these rights were granted twice, thrice, even four times over to different concession-aires; and in 1889 they were capped by a super-concession which gave the holder the right to collect all the king's private revenues, including his concession revenues, for an income of £12,000 a year.

By 1889 there was a clear threat to the Swazi kingdom. The British Government had no direct interest in it, nor were the British conces-sionaires able to bring strong pressures to bear in London; but the Transvaal Government was determined to control the territory. Ever since the Great Trek, Afrikaner leaders in the Transvaal had hoped to gain access to the sea. By 1889 expansion to the west had been shut off by the British and the only part of the east coast that was not under British or Portuguese control was the gap between Zululand and Mozambique. The Swazi kingdom lay on the route to that gap and after the New Republic had been incorporated in the Transvaal (1887) the kingdom was almost surrounded by Transvaal territory. Further-more, many Transvaal citizens, including office-holders like Piet Joubert, the commandant-general, had acquired personal interests in Swaziland.

As the danger of Transvaal control mounted, Mbandzeni had asked for British protection and when that was refused he had appointed Offy Shepstone (Theophilus Shepstone junior) to advise him in his dealings with white people (1887). But Offy Shepstone was not a disinterested adviser and he used his appointment to feather his own nest.

After Mbandzeni's death, the noose tightened rapidly. The kingdom itself became more vulnerable because the heir chosen by the Swazi council was a minor. But the crucial factor was that the British colonial secretaries and high commissioners decided that Swazi independence was to be sacrificed, notwithstanding the clauses in the Pretoria and London Conventions. The events culminating in the subjugation of the kingdom are therefore to be seen in the context of Anglo-Transvaal diplomacy (below, p. 311–12).

In 1890 British negotiators offered the Transvaal control of Swaziland and the territories down to the sea, provided the Transvaal would enter into a customs union with the colonies; but this condition President Kruger and the *Volksraad* would not accept, fearing that it would result in the loss of Transvaal independence. The two governments then agreed to set up a joint administration (the first Swaziland Convention, 1890) and for the next few years Swaziland was controlled by a 'Joint Government' consisting of Transvaal and British representatives and Offy Shepstone as the representative of the Swazi regent and council. In fact, Transvaal influence became dominant. By the end of 1891 the Transvaal Government had spent £100,000 to buy from the original holders nearly all the concessions that were of political significance, including the super-concession mentioned above,[1] and it had also taken the egregious Offy Shepstone onto its payroll; while a court set up by the Joint Government had decided that most of the concessions were valid. In 1893 and 1894 there were further negotiations between Britain and the Transvaal, culminating in an agreement which made Swaziland a 'political dependency' of the Transvaal (the third Swaziland Convention, 1894).[2] The Swazi regent and council sent a deputation to London to protest and to ask for British protection; but early in 1895 the Transvaal assumed control of Swaziland without meeting any physical opposition.[3]

As it turned out, the period of Afrikaner domination of the Swazi was brief. After the South African War, the British Government separated

[1] Garson, p. 349, has a table summarizing these transactions.

[2] Note Hailey's commentary on this Convention (pp. 367–8): 'The Swazi have since that time always emphasized the fact that they were not parties to this Convention. But in the practice regulating these matters, the recognition accorded to a change of national status has more frequently depended on the decisions taken by exterior powers than on the wishes expressed by the inhabitants of the country concerned.'

[3] The wider hopes of the Transvaal were dashed. In 1895 Britain proclaimed a protectorate over Tongaland and the territories between Swaziland and Tongaland, consisting of three small chiefdoms, were incorporated in British Zululand.

Swaziland from the Transvaal and ruled it in much the same way as Basutoland, so that there was a revival of the power and the prestige of the traditional Swazi authorities. The great and enduring difference between the two territories was that in the one all the land was regarded as belonging to the Sotho nation, but in Swaziland, after a commission had tried to sort out the conflicting claims, white people were recognized as the legal owners of nearly two-thirds of the land.

8. The Mpondo and the East Griqua: The Politics of Intimidation[1]

In the early nineteenth century the Mpondo chiefdom, south of the Mtamvuna River, was the largest chiefdom in that area to survive the depredations of Shaka's impis. During those disturbances, it absorbed many refugees from the north; and three smaller chiefdoms—the Bhaca, the Xesibe, and the Mpondomise—looked to it for protection. When the Zulu menace disappeared, the Mpondo tried to establish control over these three chiefdoms, but they claimed to be independent. During the rest of the century the peace was frequently broken by raids and counter-raids between the Mpondo and the Bhaca, the Xesibe, and the Mpondomise.

The Mpondo chief Faku made a treaty with Britain in 1844. Britain recognized him as the ruler of the entire territory extending from the Mzimkhulu to the Mthatha rivers, and from the Indian Ocean to the Drakensberg. In fact, the Mpondo occupied part of the coastal sector; the Bhaca, the Xesibe, and the Mpondomise lived further inland; and between them and the Drakensberg there was an area which became known as Nomansland, where the only inhabitants were bands of San hunters and a few small Nguni and Sotho communities, over whom Faku had no control at all. In 1861 Faku placed Nomansland at the disposal of the Cape Governor, who arranged for Adam Kok to bring down his Griqua from the Orange Free State, where they had fallen on hard times since the withdrawal of British rule. Some three thousand Griqua arrived in 1863 to found a new East Griqualand. They divided part of the territory into farms and exercised some control over the Nguni and Sotho people who also settled there.

The Mpondo kingdom experienced the tensions which were endemic in the structure of all Nguni political units. The royal lineage was

---

[1] Campbell, chs. 7-8; W. Dower, *The Early Annals of Kokstad and Griqualand East*; S. J. Halford, *The Griquas of Griqualand*; M. Hunter, *Reaction to Conquest*; Marais, pp. 59-73; [Stanford] ii, chs. 25-40; Theal, *1795-1872*, iv, ch. 64 and *1873-1884*, i, chs. 7-9. I have also used an unpublished seminar paper, 'Aspects of Mpondo History in the Nineteenth Century', by G. Harinck.

grouped into two sections—the 'great house' and the 'right-hand-house' —and this division pervaded the entire state. Traditionally, when tensions between the two sections became too serious to be contained within a single polity, the senior member of the 'right-hand-house' left the territory of the chiefdom and founded a new chiefdom of similar structure in a new territory. Such a process began among the Mpondo under Faku, who allowed his son of the 'right-hand-house', Ndamase, to found a new unit west of the Mzimvubu River. When Faku died in 1868, he was succeeded by Mqikela, the senior son of his 'great wife'; and Ndamase and his successors assumed the rights of independent rulers. The Mpondo state was split in two.

Mqikela's difficulties were accentuated by the growth of white power and influence in Griqualand East. In 1872 a Cape colonial commission found that conditions on the borders between the Griqua and the Mpondo were anarchic, and virtually all the African chiefs in the area, including the Bhaca, Xesibe, and Mpondomise chiefs, asked for British protection. In 1873 the colonial government appointed a magistrate to East Griqualand and in the following years he extended his authority until, in 1879, Griqualand East was annexed to the Cape Colony. This growing involvement led the colonial government and its local representatives to espouse the cause of the Bhaca, the Xesibe, and the Mpondomise in their quarrels with the Mpondo. Moreover, white farmers settled in East Griqualand, where they began to buy out the Griqua landholdings; and they, as well as the traders, the missionaries, and the administrators, became advocates of intervention in Mpondo affairs.

During the 1870s, the High Commissioner tried to persuade Mqikela to sell Port St. Johns, at the mouth of the Mzimvubu River, which was the only non-annexed natural harbour on the south-east African coast. Failing in this, he did business with Nqiliso, son of Ndamase, who sold Britain Port St. Johns in return for recognition of his claim to be an independent chief (1878). The Cape Government then made a series of demands on Mqikela. It wanted him to recognize the transfer of Port St. Johns; to allow a road to be built from it to East Griqualand; to permit the main road through the Transkei from the Cape to Natal to pass through his territory; to stop his people from violating the East Griqualand border; to acknowledge the independence of the Xesibe and the Bhaca; and to hand over 'rebels' who had fled to Mpondo country during the wars.

Mqikela himself was a weak ruler. His affairs were conducted mainly by his chief councillor, Mhlangaso, who was a nephew of the 'right-hand-house' and tried to keep the chiefdom together and independent. Mhlangaso offset Cape pressures by dealing with Natal traders and the Natal government, and also with a group of German concession-hunters, who were interested in making Mpondo country a point of entry for German trade and political influence in South Africa.

The noose then tightened around the Mpondo in two stages. In 1885 Britain proclaimed a protectorate over the entire coastline to forestall German intervention; and the next year the Cape colonial government armed the Bhaca and the Xesibe, the Mpondo's most inveterate enemies, and sent Walter Stanford, the chief magistrate of the Transkei, to demand concessions. Under a threat of war, Mqikela and Mhlangaso signed a treaty acknowledging the independence of the Xesibe and Cape control of Port St. Johns and the Transkei road.

Soon afterwards Mqikela died. His 'great wife' had no children, and the councillors selected Sigcawu, of the oldest of the supporting houses of the 'great-house', to succeed him. At first the young chief retained Mhlangaso as a senior councillor, but then they fell out. If land had been available, Mhlangaso would probably have split the chiefdom, as Ndamase had previously done; but by that time the Eastern Mpondo were hemmed in on all sides. Consequently, Mhlangaso took up arms and tried to oust Sigcawu, and when that had failed he remained at large near the Natal border, intriguing with Natal whites.

Cecil Rhodes was responsible for the final stage in the subjection of the Mpondo. By 1894 the Eastern and Western Mpondo chiefdoms seemed, from Groote Schuur, to be anachronisms, weak in themselves, but dangerous as potential points of entry into South Africa by foreign rivals. Moreover, the civil war in the eastern chiefdom seemed likely to embroil the Cape Colony with Natal, while it also provided a pretext for intervention 'to keep the peace'. Accordingly, as Prime Minister of the Cape Colony Rhodes instructed Major Henry Elliott, chief magistrate of Thembuland, to annex both the Mpondo chiefdoms. Walter Stanford, who accompanied Elliott, recorded how Sigcawu was handled:[1]

It was quite within his power, Major Eliott said, to have brought an army into the country with him but such action he felt might have frustrated the desire he had for Sigcawu and his people to submit themselves peaceably to Government. The wish of the Government was that not a single life should be sacrificed or one head of cattle lost to the Pondos in connection with this matter. The issue rested with Sigcawu. The Government wanted peaceable annexation of Pondoland but if necessary they would not shrink from war. Sigcawu was hemmed in on three sides and behind him was the deep sea.

After discussing it with his councillors, Sigcawu submitted; and so did Chief Nqiliso of the Western Mpondo.

[1] [Stanford], ii. 152.

When Rhodes himself visited the territory soon afterwards, Sigcawu asked him for an increase in the salary he had been awarded, and that he should be recognized, under the Cape Government, as the supreme Chief of a united Mpondo people. However, as had happened earlier to the Xhosa and the Thembu, the Cape Government divided Mpondo country into several magisterial districts, and each magistrate opened his court to litigants and began to levy taxes. Sigcawu at first tried to obstruct the magistrates, as other chiefs had formerly done further west. Rhodes then had him arrested under *ad hoc* legislation hastily enacted by the Cape Parliament and he would probably have been exiled had not the Supreme Court upheld his appeal. By the end of the century the Mpondo, like the Xhosa and the Thembu and the other southern Nguni, had been firmly subordinated to the colonial magistrates.

In his account of these proceedings, the historian, George McCall Theal, writes:[1] '. . . in the nature of things a petty barbarous government could not be permitted to do whatever it pleased, even within the limits of its own territory, in opposition to the interests of a powerful civilized neighbour.' This is a most revealing statement of the doctrine that might is right—especially when it is white. In the 1840s it had served British imperial interests to recognize an Mpondo treaty state and use it as a buffer between Natal and the Cape Colony and between the high veld Voortrekkers and the sea. By the 1890s the Mpondo no longer served that purpose. Through their weakness and their internal political divisions, they constituted a potential threat to British supremacy in South Africa. They were therefore subjected.

9. *Mopping up in the Transvaal*

In the Transvaal some African chiefs continued to resist white control until almost the end of the nineteenth century. The most effective resistance was offered by the Pedi or northern Sotho chiefdom and the Venda chiefdoms. These chiefdoms occupied rugged country in the eastern and northern Transvaal and, when threatened, they retreated to mountain strongholds which they had fortified with stone-works. Many of their warriors had fire-arms, bought after working on the diamond mines in Griqualand West.

The Transvaal Governments (including the British regime of 1877–81) claimed jurisdiction throughout the territory between the Vaal and the Limpopo river westwards towards the Kalahari and eastwards into the low veld. Clashes occurred as white farmers intruded into chiefdoms which had not been subjected. Africans would harry the farmers to prevent them from becoming established. The local officials would

---

[1] Theal, *1873–1884*, i. 175.

then appeal to Pretoria and, if it seemed expedient, the *Volksraad* would instruct the commandant-general to raise commandos from several districts and discipline the recalcitrant chief. Piet Joubert, who held the office of commandant-general for many years, sometimes in combination with the office of Superintendent of Natives, became very skilled in dealing with African resistance.[1] He exploited internal divisions in the chiefdoms. He made good use of rivalries between chiefdoms, employing Swazi levies against the Pedi, Pedi against Mabhogo's people, and Tsonga and Swazi against the Venda. He also devised ways of coping with difficult terrain—besieging mountain fortresses, destroying African crops, cutting off their water supplies, and dynamiting their caves.

In the 1870s, the Pedi chiefdom under Sekhukhune was the most powerful African state in the eastern Transvaal. A counterpart of Moshweshwe's southern Sotho kingdom, it had become the rallying point for the survivors of the northern Sotho chiefdoms that had been disrupted by Mzilikazi and Shoshangane. Sekhukhune, who succeeded his father Sekwati in 1861, was determined to keep his independence and to continue to extend his authority over the northern Sotho.

By 1876 the Afrikaners in the Lydenburg district were alarmed at Sekhukhune's strength and disturbed by Pedi raids on their cattle. President Burgers then invaded Pedi country with a force of Afrikaner commandos and Swazi allies; but, after some initial successes, the force failed ignominiously before Sekhukhune's stronghold in the Lulu mountains, and the commandos disintegrated. At that stage Sekhukhune seemed invincible; but the tide soon turned. Early in 1877 Burgers organized a mercenary force which built forts at strong points and made it difficult for the Pedi to come down from their mountains to plant and reap their crops, as a result of which Sekhukhune made a show of submission. However, after the British annexation of the Transvaal, he acted independently again. Until the Zulu war was over, the British could do little about him, but then in November 1879 a mixed force, led by British regulars, stormed Sekhukhune's stronghold. Sekhukhune was taken captive to Pretoria and the British appointed his half-brother and rival, Mampuru, paramount chief of the Pedi. In 1881, at the time of the Pretoria Convention, Sekhukhune was released from captivity; but within a year Mampuru had had him killed.

The Transvaal Government then consolidated its hold over the Pedi by further intervention in dynastic politics. First, it appointed regents for Sekhukhune's child heir and imprisoned members of the royal family who protested. Then in 1896 General Joubert divided the Pedi country into two parts, under different chiefs, and when members of the royal family hired a lawyer to contest his decision, they were flogged. By the

[1] Mouton, op. cit.

end of the century the Pedi were divided: some acknowledged the young Sekhukhune II, others a son of Mampuru, and others a son of one of the former regents. The Pedi had been subjected by a combination of military force and political manipulation.[1]

After having Sekhukhune killed in 1882, Mampuru fled southwards to the protection of a chief whom the Afrikaners called Njabel. His father, Mabhogo, had built up a considerable following from Nguni and Sotho survivors of the Difaqane and 'Njabel' was continuing to expand the chiefdom and to defy the authority of the Transvaal Government. When he refused to hand Mampuru over, Joubert attacked with a force of two thousand Afrikaners, who were assisted by many Pedi who wished to avenge the death of Sekhukhune. After an eight months' siege, 'Njabel' and Mampuru surrendered and the chiefdom of 'Njabel' was utterly disrupted. The people were divided into small groups and 'apprenticed' to Afrikaner farmers.[2]

The Venda chiefdoms in the Soutpansberg had managed temporarily to reverse the tide of Afrikaner settlement in the 1860s (Vol. I, Ch. IX). During the 1880s Afrikaners reoccupied the area and in the 1890s Joubert led a series of expeditions against the Venda and associated chiefs, snuffing out their strongholds one by one. The final resistance came from Makhado and his son Mphephu, who tried to persuade other chiefs to join them in refusing to pay taxes to the republican officials and, when the idea of a grand alliance had failed, fought alone against heavy odds. Joubert drove wedges between Mphephu and the other Soutpansberg chiefs and in 1898 he mustered a force of nearly four thousand Afrikaners, with Swazi and Tsonga allies, and stormed Mphephu's stronghold, swept his people out of the mountains, and drove Mphephu himself across the Limpopo into Shona country. Thus, the last of the traditional chiefdoms of South Africa was conquered just a year before the white people fell out among themselves.[3]

---

[1] On the Pedi, see S. P. Engelbrecht, *Thomas François Burgers*, ch. 11; D. R. Hunt, 'An Account of the Bapedi', *Bantu Studies*, 5 (1931), 275–326; Theal, *1873–1884*, i, chs. 11–12, ii, chs. 18, 20; C. J. Uys, *In the Era of Shepstone*, ch. 7; T. S. van Rooyen, 'Die Verhoudinge tussen die Boere, Engelse en Naturelle in die Geskiedenis van die Oos-Transvaal tot 1882', *AYB*, 1951, i; G. P. J. Trümpelmann, 'Maléo en Sekoekoeni', *VRS*, 1957.

[2] On the conquest of Mabhogo's people, see Mouton, ch. 8; Theal, *1873–1884*, ii, ch. 20; and R. H. Massie, *The Native Tribes of the Transvaal*, pp. 86–7. From time to time the republican authorities ordered the destruction of other conquered communities by dividing them into small groups and distributing them as apprentices among Afrikaner farmers, e.g. David Massouw's Korana, who were dealt with thus in 1885 (Mouton, p. 146), and the people of 'Malaboch' in 1894 (ibid., p. 153).

[3] There is a great need for a historical account of the Venda, whose history is extremely interesting. What exists is particularly inadequate. See Mouton, ch. 15; J. I. Rademeyer, 'Die Oorlog teen Magato', *Historiese Studies*, 2 (1944), 79–122; H. A. Stayt, *The Bavenda*; N. J. van Warmelo, (ed.), *Contributions towards Venda History, Religion and Tribal Ritual*; R. Wessman, *The Bawenda of the Spelonken*.

The consequences of political subjection were not uniform for the African peoples of South Africa. Most chiefdoms survived as territorially based corporate entities under white over-rule, but the proportions of their ancestral lands that they still occupied varied very greatly. In the Transvaal and the Orange Free State, where white settlement had followed the destructive wars of the *Difaqane* (Vol. I, Ch. IX), some African communities had lost all their land and their surviving descendants were attached to other chiefdoms or lived in small, dispersed groups on farms owned by white men.

The administrative systems imposed by the white regimes created a second set of variables. In the Bechuanaland Protectorate and Basutoland, British officials found it expedient to treat chiefs as junior partners in a joint administrative enterprise and allowed them to continue to perform many of their customary functions. In the self-governing colonies and the republics, on the other hand, the local white rulers were primarily concerned to prevent the revival of the military power of the chiefdoms and to that end, as soon as they felt able to do so, they by-passed and weakened the chiefs.

Thirdly, the intensity of the impact of Western cultural and economic influences varied immensely from region to region. By the end of the nineteenth century, mission stations and schools, traders' stores, and labour-recruiting agents were numerous in the Ciskei, the Transkei, and Basutoland, but sparser in the other African areas, especially in the South African Republic, where the Government allowed only a few selected missionaries to operate.

These variables meant that Africans had a wide range of life experiences. Nevertheless, as has been shown in previous chapters, though the rate of change varied immensely, the direction of change was similar throughout South Africa. Political subordination was merely an aspect of a more comprehensive process of change. The African peoples of South Africa were being transformed from self-sufficient and autonomous chiefdoms into interlocking and dependent communities of peasants, living on attenuated tribal lands, and wage labourers, working in areas owned by white people. Moreover, by the end of the nineteenth century, the prototype of the typical black South African of the twentieth century had emerged: the African who was born and reared in a 'Native Reserve' or 'Bantu Area', who spent the middle years of his life working intermittently for white employers in 'White Areas', and who, when he was no longer employable, was constrained by economic necessity or by law to return to his 'Reserve' and to stay there until he died.

CHRONOLOGICAL TABLE TO
ILLUSTRATE CHAPTERS V AND VI

1861   Sekhukhune succeeds Sekwati as paramount chief of the Pedi.

1868   Death of Faku and recognition by Great Britain of the division of the Mpondo chiefdom.

1869   Great Britain annexes Basutoland at request of Moshweshwe. Diamond rush to alluvial diggings in Vaal-Harts area.

1870   Death of Moshweshwe: Letsie succeeds as paramount chief of Basutoland.

1870–1 Diamond rush to the dry diggings; foundation of Kimberley.

1871   Basutoland incorporated in the Cape Colony. Great Britain annexes Griqualand West.

1872   Cetshwayo succeeds Mpande as King of the Zulu. Cape Colony acquires responsible government.

1873   Rebellion of Hlubi chief Langalibalele in Natal.

1874   Mbandzeni succeeds Ludvonga as King of the Swazi.

1876   Sekhukhune's Pedi ward off attack by SAR commandos.

1877   Great Britain annexes the Transvaal.

1877–8 Rebellion of Griqua, Tswana, and Khoikhoi in Griqualand West. War between Xhosa and British and Cape Colonial forces.

1878   Chief Nqiliso of the western Mpondo sells Port St. Johns to Great Britain.

1879   January   British forces invade Zululand; Isandhlwana. Phuthi chief Moorosi rebels against the Cape Colony.
       August   Cape Colony annexes Fingoland, Idutywa, and Griqualand East.
       September Wolseley dictates peace terms to the Zulu.
       November   British forces defeat the Pedi and depose Sekhukhune.

1880   July   Letsie's southern Sotho rebel against the Cape Colony.
       October   Griqualand West incorporated in the Cape Colony.
       December   Transvaal Afrikaners rebel against Great Britain.

1881   Pretoria Convention: Transvaal Afrikaners obtain limited independence.

1882   Transvaal Afrikaners proclaim Stellaland and Goshen as independent republics.

1883   Cetshwayo returns to Zululand; civil war follows.

1884   Beginning of the great concession era in the Swazi kingdom.
    February   London Convention: SAR gains greater independence.
    March   Great Britain resumes control of Basutoland.
    August   Germany proclaims protectorate over South West Africa.
        SAR farmers proclaim the New Republic.
    September SAR annexes Goshen.
    December British military expedition reaches Cape Town en route to Bechuanaland.

1885   Great Britain annexes British Bechuanaland south of the Molopo.
Great Britain proclaims protectorates over Bechuanaland north of the Molopo and over the coastline between the Cape Colony and Natal.
Cape Colony annexes remaining territories west of the Mthatha.

1886   Great Britain recognizes the New Republic.
Sigcawu succeeds Mqikela as paramount chief of eastern Mpondo; his authority is challenged by Mhlangaso.

1887   Great Britain annexes Zululand.
SAR incorporates the New Republic.

1890   B.S.A. Co. settlers occupy Mashonaland.
First Swaziland Convention: Great Britain and SAR impose joint administration.

1893   Natal acquires responsible government.
Ndebele (Matabele) War.

1894   Cape Colony annexes Pondoland.

1895   SAR annexes Swaziland.
Great Britain annexes territories between Swaziland and the sea.
Cape Colony incorporates British Bechuanaland.
Jameson Raid.

1896–7 Shona and Ndebele rebel against the B.S.A. Co.

1897   Natal incorporates Zululand.

1898   SAR subject the Venda.

1899   Outbreak of the South African War.

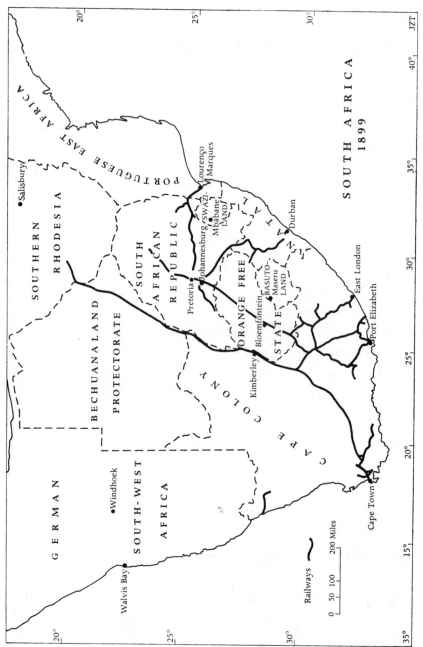

MAP. 6

VI

GREAT BRITAIN AND THE AFRIKANER REPUBLICS, 1870-1899[1]

IT has been the practice of some historians to view British policy in South Africa in the late nineteenth century in isolation from other aspects of British policy and without regard to the context of British decision-making. In particular, there is a tradition according to which Britain continually strove to suppress the liberties of the Afrikaner republics for reasons of territorial and economic avarice. The truth is far more complex. Between 1870 and 1895 British policy-makers blew hot and cold towards the Afrikaner republics. The most dramatic interference in that period—the annexation of the Transvaal in April 1877— was intended to be a step towards withdrawal from responsibility for the internal affairs of South Africa. It was only at the end of the century that a combination of personal, political, and psychological factors resulted in the violent suppression of both republics.[2]

The process of decision-making in metropolitan London was always complex. Cabinets were dependent on the accumulated knowledge of the permanent officials in the Colonial Office. They were also sensitive to a volatile 'public opinion', as expressed at the hustings and in Parliament, the press, and the London clubs, and to various pressure-groups with specific interests in South Africa, such as the missionary organizations and anti-slavery associations, commercial and shipping houses, and, eventually, diamond- and gold-mining corporations. Nevertheless, the holders of two offices were capable, individually, and more particularly, jointly, of involving the British Government in serious commitments in South Africa: the Colonial Secretary and the High Commissioner.[3]

---

[1] I am grateful to Dr. T. R. H. Davenport, Professor John S. Galbraith, and Professor Monica Wilson for comments on the draft of this chapter.

[2] The following general works on British imperial policy in the late nineteenth century are of special importance: *CHBE*, vol. iii, *The Empire Commonwealth, 1870–1919*, eds. E. A. Benians, J. R. M. Butler, P. N. S. Mansergh, and E. A. Walker; W. K. Hancock, *Survey of British Commonwealth Affairs*; P. Gifford and W. R. Louis (eds.), *Britain and Germany in Africa: Imperial Rivalry and Colonial Rule*; R. Koebner and H. D. Schmidt, *Imperialism: The Story and Significance of a Political Word, 1840–1960*; R. I. Lovell, *The Struggle for South Africa, 1875–99: a Study in Economic Imperialism*; R. Robinson and J. Gallagher, *Africa and the Victorians*; A. P. Thornton, *The Imperial Idea and its Enemies*, and *Doctrines of Imperialism*; R. W. Winks (ed.), *The Historiography of the British Empire-Commonwealth: Trends, Interpretations, and Resources*.

[3] The Secretaries of State for the Colonies who held office between 1870 and 1900 were: Earl Granville (Dec. 1868), Earl of Kimberley (July 1870), Earl of Carnarvon (Feb. 1874),

The very remoteness of South Africa from England and the exotic quality of its problems meant that most prime ministers and other members of the cabinet were poorly informed about South Africa. Consequently, at the London end the Colonial Secretary was given a great deal of latitude and he in turn gave a wide discretion to the High Commissioner in South Africa. Most Colonial Secretaries and High Commissioners were content to hold office rather than to initiate policies and most of the decisions that they made were merely *reactions* to South African events. But there were two colonial secretaries and two high commissioners who had strong imperialist convictions and used the powers of their offices to try to safeguard British interests in South Africa for future generations—Lord Carnarvon and Sir Bartle Frere in the 1870s and Joseph Chamberlain and Sir Alfred (Lord) Milner at the turn of the century. At other times British policy was negative, unco-ordinated, and unimaginative; but when these men were in office it was positive, co-ordinated, and inspired by a grandiose imperialist vision.

Virtually all late nineteenth-century British cabinet ministers and permanent officials believed that Britain should at least hold the Cape peninsula, because of its commercial and strategic importance on the sea route between Europe and Asia. The opening of the Suez canal in 1869 did not shake that conviction, for there could be no assurance that Britain would be able to dominate the canal in time of war. Beyond that, there were two basic policy questions. How far northwards and eastwards from the Cape peninsula did Britain have an interest in exerting supremacy? And how was British supremacy to be exerted where Britain did have an interest?

In answer to the first question, there were some who considered that the Cape peninsula was Britain's only real territorial concern in southern Africa and that provided the peninsula was strongly fortified it did not much matter who ruled the rest of the subcontinent. Gladstone and the Treasury officials were inclined towards this view, because, had it been adopted, it would have saved the British taxpayer a great deal of money. But the majority considered that the only way to hold the Cape peninsula securely was by controlling a considerable amount

Sir Michael Hicks Beach (Feb. 1878), Earl of Kimberley (Apr. 1880), Earl of Derby (Dec. 1882), Col. Frederick Stanley (June 1885), Earl Granville (Feb. 1886), Earl Stanhope (Aug. 1886), Sir Henry Holland (Lord Knutsford) (Jan. 1887), Marquess of Ripon (Aug. 1892), and Joseph Chamberlain (June 1895). The High Commissioners for South Africa and Governors of the Cape Colony were: Sir Philip Wodehouse (Jan. 1862), Sir Henry Barkly (Dec. 1870), Sir Bartle Frere (Mar. 1877), Sir Hercules Robinson (Jan. 1881), Sir Henry Loch (Dec. 1889), Sir Hercules Robinson (Lord Rosmead) (May 1895), and Sir Alfred Milner (May 1897). Between June 1879 and August 1881 there were separate High Commissioners for South-East Africa—Sir Garnet Wolseley (June 1879) and Sir George Colley (July 1880).

of contiguous territory;[1] and, having adopted that line of thought, they found additional reasons to vindicate extensive British territorial commitments in southern Africa. History, they believed, had imposed on the British Government an obligation to safeguard the interests of the British communities in the Cape Colony and Natal (and, later, the Transvaal), or to protect the African peoples from oppression by Afrikaners and British South Africans. The fact that these arguments were not completely compatible with one another did not seriously diminish their appeal. The growth of the diamond-mining industry in Griqualand West and the gold-mining industry in the Transvaal strengthened the previously tenuous economic arguments for territorial supremacy; and finally, towards the end of the century, the emergence of a powerfully armed Transvaal Republic and its flirtation with Imperial Germany aroused strategic anxieties, for if an independent Afrikaner republic became the strongest state in southern Africa it might eventually wrest control of the Cape peninsula from Britain.

The question as to how British supremacy was to be exerted resolved itself into two subsidiary questions. One concerned the ultimate political goal for South Africa; the other, the methods by which that goal was to be reached. Throughout the period under review, there was widespread agreement among British cabinet ministers and permanent officials as to the ultimate goal. The British colonies and Afrikaner republics, from the Cape to the Limpopo and perhaps beyond, were to be joined in a self-governing, white-controlled, federal Dominion under the British Crown, following the precedent of Canada which had been federated in 1867. It was assumed that such a Dominion would be strong enough, without British military or financial aid, to keep internal law and order and to absorb any African chiefdoms that had previously remained independent; that the British navy would protect it from foreign aggression; that British entrepreneurs would dominate its foreign trade; and that the British Government would control its foreign relations and, perhaps, have some final say in its treatment of its African inhabitants.

However, there were wide differences as to the methods by which that goal was to be reached. One way was to make the Cape Colony a self-governing colony, in accordance with the trend of the time in other British colonies of settlement, and then to leave it to the Cape to engross the other political units in South Africa. But this method did not work. The Cape Colony was too weak and its white inhabitants were too divided for it to become a reliable instrument of such a policy.

[1] This was similar to the process that led Lord Salisbury to believe that Britain should dominate the entire Nile valley and East Africa for the purpose of ensuring control over the Suez canal. See Robinson and Gallagher, op. cit.

Though the colony was granted responsible government in 1872, its first cabinet reacted against British attempts to coax it to play the desired role; and when Cecil Rhodes, as Prime Minister of the Cape Colony, did try to promote a South Africa federation, he resorted to actions which compromised the federal cause. The other way was by direct British action; and this was attempted in the 1870s by Lord Carnarvon and Sir Bartle Frere and at the turn of the century by Joseph Chamberlain and Sir Alfred Milner.

1. *Lord Carnarvon's Federation Scheme*[1]

After the Conventions of 1852 and 1854 had put the seal on the Voortrekkers' independence, the first senior British office-holder to espouse a policy of reuniting all the white communities in South Africa in some form of political union was Sir George Grey, governor of the Cape Colony; but in doing so he was defying the Colonial Secretary and he was recalled (Vol. I, pp. 432–3). The first colonial secretary to espouse such a policy was Lord Kimberley, who held the office from 1870 to 1874 as a member of Gladstone's Liberal cabinet. His reasons were primarily economic—the reduction of British expenditures in South Africa. The methods he envisaged were local South African initiatives, assisted by Britain and culminating in an Act of the British Parliament. However, there was not the slightest prospect that the governments of the Afrikaner republics would have voluntarily formed a union with the colonies under the British Crown, for that would have entailed the surrender of the independence the Vootrekkers had striven for; and their suspicions of Britain were rekindled at that very time by the annexation of the diamond fields. Many Free Staters and Transvaalers considered that they had been defrauded and some Afrikaners in the Cape Colony agreed with them. Consequently, although the Cape Parliament accepted responsible government in 1872 (Vol. I, pp. 330–3), it declined to assume the responsibility for Griqualand West and Britain continued to incur the full odium for the administration of that territory. The resultant of the political forces in South Africa was clearly centrifugal.[2]

In spite of his brief endorsement of the empire in his Crystal Palace speech in 1872, Benjamin Disraeli, Conservative Prime Minister from 1874 to 1880, was not himself much interested in colonies, and he gave a very free hand to Lord Carnarvon, his Colonial Secretary.[3] Carnarvon was an avowed imperialist.[4] He never recorded any very precise ideas about

---

[1] C. F. Goodfellow, *Great Britain and South African Confederation (1870–1881)*.
[2] Ibid., chs. 2–3.   [3] R. Blake, *Disraeli*, p. 665.
[4] A. H. Hardinge, *The Life of Henry Howard Molyneux Herbert, fourth Earl of Carnarvon*.

the structure of the empire, but he regarded it as his task, for the future power and security of Great Britain, to check the fissiparous tendencies in the colonies of settlement and, in particular, to unite South Africa under the Crown, as Canada had been united when he had been Colonial Secretary in 1867. The new Dominion was to extend at least as far north as the Limpopo, if not to the Zambesi or beyond. In 1876 he recorded the hope that Britain would dominate most of the African continent, warning others away with 'a sort of Munro [*sic*] doctrine'.[1] The role of the African inhabitants in the South African Dominion was to be subordinate: the white people were to have a monopoly of the local political institutions, but the British Government was to exercise some sort of control over legislation affecting Africans.[2] If local South African initiatives would not suffice to achieve this goal, then Carnarvon was prepared to make the British Government the instrument of South African unity.

As a preliminary step, Carnarvon sent the historian James Anthony Froude, who had written articles in support of imperial unity, on a mission to South Africa, ostensibly as a private traveller. Touring the republics as well as the colonies, Froude was impressed by Afrikaners and by their complaints about the annexation of Griqualand West. He advised Carnarvon that, provided the republics were conciliated and it was made clear that white people would be able to do as they wished towards Africans, the colonies and republics could be joined in a self-governing Dominion, except for the Cape peninsula, which Britain could control directly. In May 1875 Carnarvon sent a dispatch to the High Commissioner, Sir Henry Barkly, proposing that a conference of representatives of the white communities be held in South Africa to discuss native questions, the control of the arms trade, and, perhaps, confederation, and suggesting the names of the individuals who might represent the colonies at the conference.[3]

By that time, Carnarvon had decided to take a strong line with Natal, where the Langalibalele affair (pp. 260–1) had aroused the spectre of a general African rising. In February 1875 he appointed Sir Garnet Wolseley as special commissioner, with instructions to gain control of native policy for the British Government and, if necessary, to have the constitution amended by creating an official majority in the legislature. Carnarvon hoped this would prevent Natal from being a source of disturbance and ensure that its government co-operated with the confederation policy. Wining and dining Natal society, Wolseley persuaded

---

[1] Goodfellow, p. 117.

[2] As shown, for example, in Carnarvon's handling of the abortive South Africa Act, 1877; ibid., pp. 118–24, 129–34, 138–14.

[3] Ibid., ch. 4.

the legislature to increase its official members almost to the point where they became a majority.[1]

Elsewhere, Carnarvon's plan misfired. The confederation dispatch had an unfavourable reception in the Cape Colony. The ministry of John Molteno—the first under responsible government—reacted against what it construed as imperial interference. In particular, the naming of Cape representatives for the proposed conference gave umbrage because Carnarvon had included John Paterson, the leader of the Eastern Separatist movement, which Molteno had been trying to scotch (Vol. I, pp. 324–7). Accordingly, Molteno placed the dispatch before the Cape Parliament with a hostile minute and Parliament did nothing about it. Soon afterwards, Froude returned to South Africa, expecting to attend the confederation conference as the representative of the Imperial Government; when he discovered what had happened he indulged in a speech-making tour to whip up public support in the Cape Colony for federation, in the hope that, if Molteno remained unco-operative, Parliament would withdraw its support from him and turn to Paterson. But when the Cape Parliament reassembled in November 1875, the attack on Molteno fizzled out.[2]

For a short time Carnarvon seems to have been under the impression that the Transvaal would co-operate with his confederation policy. This was because in May 1875 he discussed his confederation dispatch with T. F. Burgers, the Transvaal President, in London and came to the conclusion that Burgers endorsed confederation.[3] In fact, Carnarvon should not have drawn such a conclusion from any remarks of Burgers. It would have been politically disastrous for Burgers to support any policy that would have made the Transvaal a part of the British Empire; and when he reported the discussion to his Acting-President, P. J. Joubert, Burgers made it clear that, while he was willing for the Transvaal to be represented at the proposed conference, he hoped to use it as a means for getting British approval for frontier adjustments and had no intention of supporting confederation.[4]

Formerly a *predikant* of the Dutch Reformed Church in the Cape Colony, Burgers had been elected President of the Transvaal in 1872, when there was a demand for a more sophisticated leader than M. W. Pretorius, under whom Transvaal expansion had been checked by the Keate Award. Burgers had high ambitions. He wanted to modernize the Transvaal and to connect it by rail with Delagoa Bay, and thus to free it from the British commercial stranglehold. His efforts were crippled

---

[1] Brookes and Webb, pp. 117–20.

[2] W. H. Dunn, *James Anthony Froude, a biography*, vol. i; Goodfellow, pp. 73–8, 83–90; [Merriman] i, 21–5; Molteno, i, chs. 13–15; ii, ch. 1; W. E. G. Solomon, *Saul Solomon: 'The Member for Cape Town'*, ch. 16.

[3] Goodfellow, pp. 66–7.   [4] Engelbrecht, pp. 125–8.

by three factors: poverty, which made the Republic dependent on loans and unable to employ efficient personnel; the hostility of the British traders and of many of the white immigrants at Lydenburg, where gold began to be mined in 1873; and the opposition of conservative Afrikaners, who disliked his liberal theological views and suspected his reforms, such as his attempts to create a modern educational system. Nevertheless, Burgers went to Europe in 1875 and, after visiting England, he toured the Continent, where he floated a railway loan and bought railway material from a Brussels firm.[1] These events drove a fateful wedge of distrust between Carnarvon and Burgers. The Colonial Secretary believed that the President had deceived him; and the President considered that it was British pressure that caused his loan to be undersubscribed, so that no progress could be made with the railway.

Rebuffed by the Government of the Cape Colony and deceived (as he thought) by the President of the Transvaal, Carnarvon revised his tactics. The conference would be held in London, not in South Africa; and first of all J. H. Brand, the President of the Orange Free State, whose reaction to the confederation dispatch had been cold, was to be conciliated by a settlement of the Griqualand West question. Brand went to London in May 1876 and negotiated from strength, because by that time the Griqualand West Land Court had upset the basis of Waterboer's claims to the area, including Kimberley, that the Orange Free State had regarded as its own (p. 256). Skilfully refraining from making any commitments on other issues, Brand accepted £90,000 compensation.[2] A London conference of a sort met in August; but it proved to be a damp squib. Brand was present, so was Theophilus Shepstone for Natal, and J. A. Froude attended for Griqualand West; but neither the Cape Colony nor the Transvaal was represented. The conference discussed various aspects of 'the native problem', passed ten vague and non-binding resolutions on the subject, and dispersed. Brand had seen to it that confederation was never discussed, while John Molteno, though in London, had refused to attend. Furthermore, in separate discussions and correspondence with Carnarvon, Molteno said that he would not sponsor the federal relationship that Carnarvon desired between the Cape Colony and Griqualand West as a first step towards his wider federation. Molteno was now willing for the Cape Colony to *incorporate* Griqualand West, but the time was not ripe for a more extensive union. When that time came, he considered that the Cape Colony, not the Imperial Government, should take the initiative and incorporate the other South African territories.[3]

[1] Ibid.

[2] Even though Griqualand West was an administrative nightmare and political control did not carry with it ownership of the mine, this was a curious sum to pay in compensation for a territory containing the richest diamond mine in the world.

[3] De Kiewiet, *Imperial Factor*, pp. 85–92; Goodfellow, ch. 6; Molteno, ii, chs. 19–20.

By the time the London conference had ended, Carnarvon was preparing a more dramatic method of achieving his ends. The rival claims of Portugal and Britain to Delagoa Bay had been submitted for arbitration to the President of France and in 1875 Marshal Macmahon gave his award in favour of Portugal. Macmahon's decision, combined with Burger's attempts to construct a railway to the bay, aroused the fear that if things were allowed to drift, the republics would slip out of the British commercial network, block the route from the Cape to central Africa, and ultimately dominate the destinies of South Africa. Carnarvon determined to nip this prospect in the bud while the Transvaal was still weak and at the same time promote his confederation policy from a new angle, by bringing the Transvaal within the British Empire. Pretexts were at hand to assuage the British public. There were the long-standing missionary charges that the Transvaalers practised slavery (Vol. I, pp. 435–7,); the British and colonial traders and bankers were concerned about the security of their investments in the Transvaal; and in September 1876 exaggerated reports reached London from Barkly about the Pedi victory over the Transvaal commandos led by President Burgers (p. 282 above). Carnarvon discussed the situation with Sir Garnet Wolseley, on whose advice he entrusted Theophilus Shepstone with the task of annexing the Transvaal. Shepstone's commission spoke of the need for obtaining popular consent, but he was privately told that the country was to be annexed in any case.[1] Shepstone entered the Transvaal with a small police escort in January 1877, settled down in Pretoria, and played a skilful waiting game. In a series of interviews with leading Transvaalers, individually and in small groups, Shepstone aroused their fears of the Zulu, whom he claimed to be able to control, he demanded that the *Volksraad* make financial and administrative reforms and when it had done so he declared that they were not good enough, and above all, he exploited their factionalism and their dislike of President Burgers. Finally the *Volksraad* adjourned, and so demoralized were the Transvaalers that on 12 April 1877 Shepstone proclaimed the Transvaal a British Colony and nobody lifted a finger in opposition.[2]

The annexation of the Transvaal was accompanied by two other moves. One was the passage through the British Parliament of the South Africa Act, 1877—a permissive Act which provided the machinery and the basic conditions by which the South African states might be joined together in a union under the Crown.[3] The other was the appointment of Sir Bartle Frere as High Commissioner and Governor of the Cape

[1] Goodfellow, pp. 115–16.
[2] De Kiewiet, ch. 5; Engelbrecht, chs. 11–16; Goodfellow, pp. 112–18, 124–8; S. J. P. Kruger, *The Memoirs of Paul Kruger*, ch. 6; Uys, chs. 6–12; van Jaarsveld, *Awakening*, ch. 6.
[3] Goodfellow, pp. 118–24, 129–34, 138–41.

Colony in succession to Barkly.[1] Frere, who had already had a distinguished career in India, was an imperialist after Carnarvon's own heart, and he was given the bait of a promise of the governor-generalship of the South African Dominion, if he could bring it into being. With both Natal and the Transvaal reduced to the status of Crown Colonies, with Frere's presence at the Cape, and with the South Africa Act in the statute-book, Carnarvon hoped that he was at last on the threshold of success. In fact, the prospects of confederation were as bleak as ever in January 1878, when Carnarvon suddenly resigned from the cabinet, in disagreement with Disraeli's determination to use force if necessary to prevent Russia from seizing the Straits and Constantinople, as the fruit of her victory over Turkey. Nevertheless, Frere, with the support of Carnarvon's successor, Sir Michael Hicks Beach, maintained the policy of British initiatives aimed at promoting federation; but nearly every one of Frere's major decisions, like those of Carnarvon, made the goal more unattainable.[2]

Frere never managed to establish a sound working relationship with the Molteno ministry in the Cape Colony. His experience, his temperament, and his style were very different from those of John Molteno. Frere had never previously held office in a colony of settlement and he had no understanding of the forces of colonial nationalism. To him, the interests of the empire were necessarily paramount over those of a colony—even a self-governing colony—whereas Molteno's entire public life was devoted to achieving and upholding responsible government. Frere wanted quick results and was willing to take short cuts, whereas Molteno believed that only time and restraint were needed to heal the scars among white South Africans. In a period when relationships between Great Britain and the self-governing colonies were still fluid and experimental, there were many occasions for quarrels between two such office-holders with such divergent views. As events in New Zealand had already shown, no question of imperial-colonial relations was fraught with greater difficulty than the question of the control of colonial forces in a local war in which they were engaged alongside imperial troops. In the war on the Cape eastern frontier in 1877–8, there was friction from the very beginning. Ultimately, the Prime Minister tried to assert control over the colonial forces by making them operationally independent of the British commanding officer. This led to confusion and in February 1878 Frere summarily dismissed Molteno. The dismissal, though strictly legal, was clearly contrary to the spirit of colonial self-government; but Frere was partially vindicated by the successful prosecution of the war and by the fact that his nominee, Gordon Sprigg, was able

[1] J. Martineau, *The Life and Correspondence of Sir Bartle Frere.*
[2] Goodfellow, pp. 144–52.

to form a government and, when Parliament met, to obtain a majority.[1] But the Sprigg cabinet was composed of men with poorer judgement than Molteno's and with Frere's encouragement it blundered into an attempt to disarm its African subjects, leading firstly to a six months' campaign against Moorosi in 1879 and then, in 1880–1, to a long and unsuccessful war against the southern Sotho (pp. 268–9). By the time that war was over, Frere had been recalled and the policy of confederation was dead.

Neither Carnarvon nor Shepstone had made realistic plans for the administration of the Transvaal. In his annexation proclamation of 12 April 1877, Shepstone undertook that 'the transvaal will remain a separate Government, with its own laws and legislature',[2] but he ruled the territory as a strict Crown Colony. This might have been tolerated for a while, if the administration had been imaginative and resourceful; but Shepstone initiated no significant reforms, his staff was small and poorly trained, and the only financial aid provided by the Imperial Government was a grant of £100,000 which Shepstone rapidly disbursed to persons who had claims against the State. When the British Treasury discovered that Shepstone's accounts were chaotic, an official was sent to Pretoria to eliminate irregularities and to see that expenditure did not exceed income.[3] Shepstone and Frere made one major bid to win the support of the Afrikaner population of the Transvaal and that was by precipitating the Zulu War; but the destruction of a British regiment at Isandhlwana in January 1879 merely exposed the ineptness of British military officers (pp. 262–4). Consequently, the initiative in the Transvaal passed from Shepstone to the Afrikaners.

Though there was no physical opposition to the annexation of the Transvaal, at its final session the Executive Council of the Republic instructed Paul Kruger, who had emerged as a principal representative of the conservative Afrikaners, and E. P. J. Jorissen, a Hollander whom President Burgers had imported to establish the educational system, to go to England to protest. Supplied by Shepstone with an inaccurate account of the state of public opinion among white Transvaalers, Carnarvon declined to discuss the deputation's request for a referendum on the annexation. On their return, Kruger and Jorissen reported to a well-attended meeting and it was decided to produce evidence of the attitude to the annexation by the customary Voortrekker method of signed petitions; and later in 1878 Kruger and Piet Joubert went to London, with papers purporting to show that 6,591 Transvaalers

[1] De Kiewiet, pp. 125–33, 165–74; [Merriman] i, ch. 2; Molteno, ii, chs. 25–31; Solomon, ch 18.
[2] G. W. Eybers (ed.), *Select Constitutional Documents Illustrating South African History*, p. 452.
[3] De Kiewiet, pp. 136–47.

opposed the annexation and only 587 were in favour of it; but Hicks Beach, who had to succeeded Carnarvon at the Colonial Office, declined to reopen the question.[1]

During 1879 the relations between ruler and subject deteriorated further. Shepstone was succeeded as Administrator by Sir Owen Lanyon under whom, as Dr. C. W. de Kiewiet has said, the government of the Transvaal became a 'timorous despotism',[2] remote from the people, obsessed with making ends meet by enforcing the tax laws, and dependent on small military garrisons stationed in the main towns. Meanwhile, the natural leaders of the Transvaal Afrikaners built up the morale which had been at so low an ebb in 1877 and prepared their people for armed resistance. In January 1879 Kruger and Joubert reported on their London mission to a large public meeting which took a resolution to work for independence, and in December a public meeting at Wonderfontein resolved to boycott British traders and all the official institutions. A rising might have been attempted in 1880, had not Gladstone's speeches in the British general election given hope for a change of policy: but when it became clear that the Gladstone ministry, under pressure from the officials in South Africa and the Colonial Office, had decided to retain the Transvaal, and that the British forces in Natal had been drastically reduced, the Transvaalers prepared for war. The outbreak was touched off when an armed party seized a wagon, which had been attached by order of the Potchefstroom magistrate because the owner, Piet Bezuidenhout, had refused to pay his taxes. Five thousand men met at Paardekraal in December 1880; and the *Volksraad* reconvened and gave executive powers to a triumvirate consisting of Paul Kruger, Piet Joubert, and ex-President M. W. Pretorius. To the last moment Lanyon refused to believe that a serious rising was imminent.[3]

Commandos quickly cut off the garrisons in the Transvaal, totalling three thousand British soldiers and armed volunteers, and a force of some two thousand Afrikaners occupied Laing's Nek, controlling the road through the Drakensberg from Natal, where there were 1,200 British soldiers. General Sir George Colley, High Commissioner for South-East Africa since the departure of Sir Garnet Wolseley, proceeded to make a series of military blunders, comparable with those that had led to Isandhlwana only two years before. He tried to storm the entrenchments at Laing's Nek and was repulsed; he was defeated again

---

[1] I. D. Bosman, 'Oorheersing en vrywording (1877–1884)', in A. J. H. van der Walt *et al.*, *Geskiedenis van Suid-Afrika*, i. 410–39; de Kiewiet, pp. 121–3, 210–13; Goodfellow, pp. 141–4; J. F. van Oordt, *Paul Kruger en de opkomst der Zuid-Afrikaansche Republiek*; D. M. Schreuder, op. cit.; van Jaarsveld, *Awakening*, ch. 7.

[2] De Kiewiet, p. 145.

[3] Bosman, op. cit.; De Kiewiet, pp. 247–63, 269–76; D. W. Krüger, *Paul Kruger*, vol. i; van Jaarsveld, *Awakening*, ch. 7; S. J. P. Kruger, chs. 7–8.

at Ingogo; and then, before waiting for the reinforcements that were on their way, he occupied Majuba mountain overlooking the Transvaal entrenchments in a brilliant night march, only to neglect to secure his position, so that Afrikaners were able to reach the summit in broad daylight and virtually to annihilate the British force, killing, wounding, or capturing 280 British soldiers. Colley himself fell in the holocaust (27 February 1881).[1]

Majuba was a wholly unnecessary military disaster for Britain. By the time it was fought the two Governments were in contact, through the mediation of President Brand of the Orange Free State. Afterwards, the Gladstone Government resisted the popular clamour for revenge and peace was signed in Pretoria by the triumvirate and British commissioners in August 1881.[2] Under the Convention of Pretoria, the Transvaal acquired 'complete self-government, subject to the Suzerainty of Her Majesty'. 'Suzerainty' was a term without modern precedent or any precise meaning; but the Convention also defined the boundaries of the Transvaal, gave a 'British Resident' powers over the African population, and entitled Britain to move troops through the country in time of war and to control its external relations.[3]

That was the end of the forward movement that had been inspired by Carnarvon and maintained by Frere. In Britain, the military disasters at Isandhlwana and Majuba created a reaction comparable with that which had followed Sir Harry Smith's forward movement in the 1850s. British policy swung back to financial caution and for the next fourteen years Britain would react to events in South Africa rather than attempt to mould South Africa into a united and loyal Dominion. In South Africa, the political interventions of Froude, the dismissal of the Molteno ministry by Frere, and the transformation of the Natal legislature by Wolseley raised doubts about the value of representative and responsible colonial institutions; the annexations of Griqualand West and the Transvaal indicated that Britain was liable to impose its will on weak states; their maladministration discredited British rule; the battles of Isandhlwana and Majuba revealed the incompetence of British military commanders; and the Convention of Pretoria showed that determined resistance could cause Britain to yield. These events also stimulated the emergence inside South Africa of an integrative force with goals directly opposite to those of Carnarvon and Frere.

---

[1] O. Ransford, *The Battle of Majuba Hill: the first Boer War.*
[2] De Kiewiet, pp. 278–88; S. J. P. Kruger, ch. 8; Ransford, pp. 125–33.
[3] Eybers, pp. 455–63.

2. *Afrikaner Nationalism, 'Colonialism', and Republicanism*

Before the 1870s, the Afrikaner people lacked a national consciousness. Since the Great Trek they had been thinly spread over a vast sub-
continent, divided among four different states and three different
churches, and devoid of common institutions or loyalties. They also
differed from one another in culture, for example in their language.
Some, especially those who lived in the anglicizing atmosphere of Cape
Town, were speaking English in their homes; others, including most of
the clergy of the Dutch Reformed Churches, clung tenaciously to Dutch
and looked down on Afrikaans as a country patois; while the bulk of the
Afrikaner people could neither understand English nor express themselves accurately in Dutch, and yet their own language had no literature. Nevertheless, among Afrikaners, as among the subject peoples of the
Austrian Empire, there were many of the pre-conditions for a nationalist
movement. The Afrikaners had a common historical background—most
of them were descended from the thousand free burghers who had been
enumerated in the Cape Colony in 1691, and virtually all of them from
the seventeen thousand of 1795. Many were aware of having kinsmen
in different parts of South Africa. There were also similarities in their
social situations and attitudes. They themselves regarded Coloured
people and Africans as inferiors, but they were conscious of being looked
down upon, in turn, by white people of British origin.

It was the events of the 1870s that began to evoke among Afrikaners
that combination of group insecurity and group pride that constitutes
a sense of nationality. By successively intervening in the Orange Free
State, the Cape Colony, and the Transvaal, Carnarvon and Frere
aroused widespread anxieties; while Colley's defeat at Majuba followed
by the British withdrawal from the Transvaal gave all Afrikaners a thrill
of achievement. At the same time, a group of Afrikaner intellectuals at
Paarl showed how the frustrations of individuals could be canalized into
group grievances against a common 'enemy' and also gave the ordinary
Afrikaner grounds for respecting his own culture.

S. J. du Toit, a *predikant* of the Nederduits Gereformeerde Kerk, was
the leader of a group of Afrikaner intellectuals who lived at Paarl and
had avoided being caught up in the anglicizing influences emanating
from Cape Town. Between 1875 and 1877 he and his friends founded
the Genootskap van Regte Afrikaners (Society of True Afrikaners) and
the newspaper *Die Afrikaanse Patriot*, and published *Die Geskiedenis van
ons Land in die Taal van ons Volk* (The History of our Country in the
Language of our People). The *Patriot* and the *Geskiedenis* were seminal.
Their central concept, set out simply and repetitively in the *Patriot* and
by historical example in the *Geskiedenis*, was that the Afrikaners were

a distinct people or nation, occupying a distinct fatherland, South
Africa, speaking a God-given language, Afrikaans, and endowed by God
with the destiny to rule South Africa and civilize its heathen peoples.
This was an appeal that was capable of striking a responsive chord in
the hearts of rural Afrikaners throughout South Africa. Nevertheless,
the circulation of the Paarl publications was small and they might have
been buried in oblivion had not the *Patriot* taken a uniquely strong line
on the Transvaal question. Whereas the Dutch papers of Cape Town
were equivocal at the time of the annexation and later wrote cautiously
about opposition to British misrule, the *Patriot* condemned the annexation from the first and in 1880 it came out for physical resistance, with
the result that it enjoyed a boom when the war had been fought and
won by the Transvaalers. Thanks to the men of Paarl, the Afrikaans
language was for the first time being printed with pride—and it was
being used, simply but forcefully, to disseminate a nationalist mystique.[1]

In 1879 du Toit also launched a political organization, the *Afrikaner
Bond*, which quickly struck roots in the central and eastern districts of
the Cape Colony. After the war, it became established, too, in the
republics. Du Toit himself was appointed superintendent-general of
education in the Transvaal and by May 1883 there were forty-three
branches of the *Bond*, extending from Cape Town to the Soutpansberg
(twenty-three in the Colony and ten in each of the republics).[2]

In the Cape Colony, however, du Toit's was not the only political
organization, nor the only political ideal, seeking the allegiance of
Afrikaners. The *Afrikaner Bond* was challenged by Jan Hofmeyr, a man
of caution and moderation who lived in Cape Town and edited a Dutch
newspaper, the *Zuid Afrikaan*. Hofmeyr made his first foray into politics
in 1878, when he organized opposition to an excise tax on brandy that
had been sponsored by the Sprigg ministry. Hofmeyr's *Boeren Bescherm-
ings Vereniging* (Farmers' Protection Association) soon grew from an
association of brandy producers into a general farmers' association and
it began to participate in parliamentary elections and campaign for the
recognition of Dutch as an official language.[3]

By 1883 there was intense competition for control of the Afrikaner
political movement in the Cape Colony. The differences between the
two leaders were accentuated by the publication of du Toit's draft of
a programme of principles, according to which South Africa was to be

---

[1] T. R. H. Davenport, *The Afrikaner Bond: The History of a South African Political Party
(1880–1911)*; J. D. du Toit, *Ds. S. J. du Toit in Weg en Werk*; G. S. and P. J. Nienaber, *Die
Geskiedenis van die Afrikaanse Beweging*; E. C. Pienaar, *Die Triomf van Afrikaans*; van Jaarsveld,
Die Afrikaner en sy Geskiedenis and *Awakening*.

[2] Map in Davenport, pp. xii–xiii.

[3] J. H. Hofmeyr, in collaboration with F. W. Reitz, *The Life of Jan Hendrik Hofmeyr (Onze
Jan)*.

united, independent, and controlled by Afrikaners. Whereas du Toit's nation was to be narrowly Afrikaner, Hofmeyr's was to include any white people who were truly South African; whereas du Toit had no confidence in the parliamentary system, Hofmeyr was for working within the existing colonial institutions; and whereas du Toit's *Bond* was pan-Afrikaner in scope, Hofmeyr wished to limit the political organization to the Cape Colony. It was Hofmeyr who prevailed, partly because he outmanœuvred the unskilful du Toit, but more especially because, though colonial Afrikaners may sometimes have been entranced by du Toit's emotional mystique, when it came to practical politics they were pragmatic and reformist rather than idealist or revolutionary.

Hofmeyr got his foot inside the *Bond* in 1882, when he founded a branch in Cape Town. Negotiations then took place, culminating in a congress at Richmond in May 1883, when representatives of the *B.B.V.* and the *Bond* agreed that the two organizations should be amalgamated.[1]

On two points, the original constitution of the amalgamated *Bond*[2] accorded with Hofmeyr's wishes. It stated that the *Bond* 'recognizes no nationality of any kind, save that of the Afrikaner', but included among Afrikaners 'all . . . of whatever descent, who aim at the welfare of South Africa'.[3] It also declared that the object of the *Bond* was 'the formation of a South African nationality by the fostering of true patriotism, as preparation for its final destiny: A United South Africa', but it made no reference to the elimination of British authority.

On the third point at issue, du Toit's views temporarily prevailed. The *Bond* constitution said that each South African republic and colony was a 'province' of the *Bond* and it created a central committee, consisting of two delegates from each province. But this was a pyrrhic victory. President Brand and President Kruger opposed the *Bond* in their republics. Since the initiative in launching the *Bond* in the Free State was taken by Chief Justice F. W. Reitz and in the Transvaal by Commandant-General Piet Joubert, the Presidents suspected that it might become a rival to their own authority; and since the *Bond* did not reject British supremacy they feared that it would infringe republican independence. Consequently, although the central committee met once, in 1886, it achieved little and the republican branches of the *Bond* gradually petered out.[4]

The lasting contribution of S. J. du Toit and the men of Paarl to Afrikaner nationalism was cultural rather than political. They showed

[1] Davenport, ch. 4; Hofmeyr, ch. 13.

[2] The constitution of the *Bond* is set out in Hofmeyr, pp. 649–52.

[3] In practice, Africans, Asians, and Coloured men were denied membership of the *Bond* and very few English-speaking white men joined it.

[4] Davenport, ch. 6.

that the Afrikaans language was capable of becoming a literary as well as an oral medium of communication. They also provided the nucleus of an enduring nationalist mythology; but they failed to create a pan-Afrikaner political movement. In the last quarter of the nineteenth century, as previously, Afrikaner political activity was channelled into the separate institutions of the different colonies and republics and the political decisions that Afrikaners made were determined by local interests and forces rather than by a concept of a transcendent Afrikaner nation. However, the purple patches in the writings of the men of Paarl were to play a significant role in the catastrophic denouement of Anglo-Afrikaner relations in the nineteenth century, because they impressed the British official mind with the conviction that there was a conspiracy for Afrikaner domination of South Africa. There was irony in this, because long before the outbreak of the South African War S. J. du Toit had broken with Kruger and become a fervent supporter of Cecil Rhodes.

In the Cape Colony the *Bond* flourished as a sort of political party under the leadership of Jan Hofmeyr.[1] From 1884 onwards it always had at least forty per cent of the seats in both Houses of Parliament and until 1898 it was the only organized party in the colony.[2] Nevertheless, the *Bond* never had a majority in the House of Assembly and, although individual *Bond*smen sat in cabinets, no *Bond*sman was ever Prime Minister. Hofmeyr himself was a member of the Scanlen cabinet that was formed in May 1881, but he resigned six months later, when his ministerial role seemed likely to lose him the confidence of Afrikaners, and he never joined another ministry. Instead, he marshalled the support of the *Bond* behind a government so long as it complied with his wishes and broke that government when it ceased to respond, or when a more profitable combination became available. In this way, the *Bond* exercised great influence over policy without having the final responsibility for ruling and taking the consequences of errors.[3]

In declining office, Hofmeyr declared that his health was bad, that his party lacked the talents to form an efficient administration, and that if it did form a government there might be an accentuation of 'racial' antagonisms between Afrikaners and British colonists.[4] The underlying reasons were probably psychological. Hofmeyr himself was a negotiator rather than an administrator, a conciliator rather than a partisan.

[1] Hofmeyr was treasurer of the *Bond* from 1883 to 1888 and chairman of its *Commissie van Toezicht op Elekties* (Committee of Supervision over Elections) from 1889 until his death in 1909; but even though he was never chairman of the *Bond*, he was always recognized as the leader. [2] Davenport, p. 309.

[3] Ibid., ch. 14; Hofmeyr, pp. 215 ff.; R. Kilpin, *The Old Cape House*, and *The Romance of a Colonial Parliament*; J. L. McCracken, *The Cape Parliament 1854–1910*.

[4] Davenport, pp. 306–10.

Consequently, he used the power of the *Bond* to obtain concessions for the colonial Afrikaner community. By 1884, the brandy excise was repealed and the Dutch language was being used in Parliament and the Law Courts, it was a compulsory subject in the civil service examinations, and it was the medium of instruction in some elementary schools. In 1887, the franchise qualifications were changed to make it difficult for 'tribal' Africans to obtain the franchise (p. 338). The result of these reforms was, as Hofmeyr had hoped, a gradual easing of the tensions between Afrikaners and British colonists and a growth of Afrikaner self-respect.

Hofmeyr found no difficulty in accepting the imperial connection, provided the British Government refrained from interfering in the internal affairs of the colony. Indeed in 1887, as a Cape representative at the colonial conference in London, he proposed that a tax be levied on foreign imports into Great Britain and the colonies and used for the support of the British navy. His attitude towards the Transvaal and the Orange Free State was a natural extension of his domestic policy. The immediate objective was to build up mutual confidence. Sooner or later, he believed, South Africa would and should be united, but whether as a British Dominion or an independent republic was a question best left for future decision.

In the early 1880s, Hofmeyr and the *Bond* tended to assume that there was a geographical demarcation between colonial and republican spheres of interest. They wanted the Cape to try to hold on to Basutoland and to incorporate the Transkei, but to leave the Tswana chiefdoms to be absorbed by the Transvaal. It gradually became apparent, however, that the interests of the Cape Colony were in many respects divergent from those of the republics. *Bond*smen were concerned that the Transvaal Government imposed duties on primary produce entering the Transvaal from the Cape Colony, that it placed men from the Netherlands in key administrative positions, and that it cultivated the friendship of Germany. Consequently, by the late 1880s Afrikaner as well as British Colonists were anxious to uphold the interests of the Cape Colony over against the other South African states. This was what made it possible for Cecil Rhodes to become Prime Minister, with *Bond* support, in 1890.[1]

The son of an English clergyman, Rhodes migrated to Natal for health reasons in 1870, at the age of seventeen.[2] He soon moved to the diamond fields where, as operations became deeper, he amalgamated

---

[1] Ibid., ch. 7; Hofmeyr, part iii.

[2] Sir T. E. Fuller, *The Right Honourable Cecil John Rhodes*; F. Gross, *Rhodes of Africa*; J. G. Lockhart and C. M. Woodhouse, *Rhodes*; J. G. McDonald, *Rhodes: a Life*; Sir L. Michell, *The Life of the Rt. Hon. Cecil John Rhodes*; S. G. Millin, *Rhodes*; W. Plomer, *Cecil Rhodes*; B. Williams, *Cecil Rhodes*. Most of these biographies are sycophantic. The work by Gross is critical, but impressionistic. A mature study is needed.

the claims of individuals and then of syndicates, and introduced mining engineers and machinery. Step by step he extended his control, until by 1891 his De Beers Consolidated Mines had a virtual monopoly of both the producing and the marketing sides of the industry. He also founded Consolidated Gold Fields, one of the strongest gold-mining corporations on the Witwatersrand.

Rhodes was not deeply interested in wealth as such: he was interested in power. During the 1870s he commuted between Kimberley and Oxford, where he eventually took a degree; and in the complementary environments of the South African veld and the Oxford lecture halls he formulated designs which, though hazy in detail, were simple and bold in outline. Mankind, he was sure, needed the leadership of the nations that seemed to him to be advanced and progressive—that is to say, Great Britain, in partnership with her colonies of settlement and alliance with the other Teutonic powers, Germany and the United States of America.[1] His own role was to promote the expansion of the British Empire in Africa, from its base in the Cape Colony, along the road to the north through the Tswana chiefdoms, the territories of the Ndebele and the Shona, and the East African highlands, to meet a southward thrust up the Nile Valley from Cairo. There was nothing exceptional in these projects, for social Darwinism and Anglo-Saxon racism were the main ingredients in the political fantasies of many Englishmen of the ruling classes in the Victorian Age; but Rhodes had exceptional means of promoting them. First, there were his riches, which he did not scruple to use to enlist support. Secondly, though his published speeches seem banal to the modern reader,[2] he was a persuasive talker and a skilful negotiator. Thus, he was able to win the confidence and co-operation of a remarkable variety of people.

The most significant of his conquests was Jan Hofmeyr. Rhodes became a member of the Cape Colonial Parliament in 1881 and after 1884, when General Warren brushed him aside in Bechuanaland (pp. 273-4), he determined that the northward expansion should take place under the aegis, not of the British Government, but of the colonial. It therefore became vital for him to secure the support of the *Afrikaner Bond* and in 1886 he began to cultivate the acquaintance of its leader. As acquaintance ripened into friendship, they found that their political attitudes had a great deal in common. They agreed that the British Government should not be permitted to interfere in the internal affairs of South Africa. They agreed that the future of South Africa depended on the

---

[1] Rhodes devoted a great deal of attention to his will, which in its final form set up Rhodes scholarships at Oxford for young men from the British Empire, Germany, and the United States.

[2] Vindex, *Cecil Rhodes: his Political Life and Speeches 1881-1900.*

co-operation of Boer and Briton. They agreed in regarding the African tribesmen as 'barbarous' people who should be prevented from obtaining a foothold in the political systems of the colonies and republics. In general terms, too, they agreed that South African union, and British imperial co-operation for trade and defence, were both desirable objectives; but they never jointly came to grips with the problem of reconciling these objectives with the fact that the Transvaal and the Orange Free State were determined to maintain their independence.

At first, Hofmeyr was reluctant to endorse Rhodes's plans for northward expansion, because they seemed to intrude upon the preserves of the Transvaal; but by 1890 Hofmeyr had come to regard the Transvaal Government as a major obstacle to harmony in South Africa; and when the Sprigg ministry was defeated in the House of Assembly, Rhodes was able to form a government that included members of the *Bond* and had the blessing of Hofmeyr. Thus was born a political alliance, based on the assumption that Rhodes as Prime Minister would promote the interests of the colonial Afrikaners and Hofmeyr as leader of the *Bond* would support Rhodes's plans for expansion beyond the Limpopo— a policy of colonial autonomy and expansion that became known as 'colonialism'.[1]

Meanwhile the republican constitution was restored in the Transvaal and Paul Kruger became President.[2] Kruger was born in the north-eastern Cape Colony in 1825 and as a child he took part in the Great Trek. Joining Potgieter's party, his family settled in the Transvaal, where the young Kruger became a conspicuous leader of commandos in their incessant clashes with Africans. He was a force for stability in the civil war of the 1860s, but in 1876 he turned against the modernizing President Burgers and then, during the British occupation, he became the inspiration of the resistance movement. When the Majuba campaign was over he was the natural leader of the conservative *burgers*, who elected him President for four successive terms (1883, 1888, 1893, 1898). On each occasion he was opposed by Piet Joubert, who came near to ousting him only in the 1893 election. Kruger ruled the country personally. Though he eulogized the *burgers* and the *Volksraad*, he made full use of his constitutional right to take part in debates and the *Volksraad* usually followed his advice. When thwarted, he could speak with frightening passion and in the last resort he would use the threat of resignation, which usually brought compliance with his demands. Policy was made

[1] Davenport, ch. 8; Hofmeyr, ch. 22. It is interesting that the word 'colonialism' was used with a different meaning from the one it was to acquire in the middle of the twentieth century.

[2] M. Juta, *The Pace of the Ox: the Life of Paul Kruger*; D. W. Krüger, op. cit.; S. J. P. Kruger, op. cit.; M. Nathan, *Paul Kruger: his Life and Times*; F. P. Smit, *Die Staatsopvattinge van Paul Kruger*; van Oordt, op. cit.

not only in formal sessions of the executive council but also in informal discussions at his home, where entry was open to all citizens, but a small group of friends and relatives constituted a permanent core of advisers. He placed Hollanders and Afrikaners from the Cape Colony in charge of the main administrative departments and one Hollander, Dr. W. J. Leyds, became State Secretary and a member of his inner circle.[1] He owed his success not only to his formidable personality and his strong hold over his people, but also to his steadfast pursuit of clearcut political objectives, which the *burgers* understood and supported. The Republic was to be made strong and independent, and it was to be kept under the control of its Afrikaner population.[2] Europeans—and especially British officials—often underrated him, because they were misled by his peasant appearance and manners and his extreme fundamentalism.[3]

Kruger's first major task as President was to try to remove the legal shackles that had been imposed on the Republic by the Pretoria Convention. In this, he was helped by crises in Ireland and Egypt, both of which the Gladstone cabinet regarded as being of infinitely greater concern to the British national interest than South Africa. Indeed, the cabinet saw no harm in appeasing the Afrikaner Republics, provided they were confined to the interior of South Africa. Consequently, after some haggling the Pretoria Convention was superseded by a new agreement in 1884. The London Convention made no reference to British suzerainty, restored the name South African Republic, and ended the attempt to maintain British control over the Republic's treatment of its African subjects; but it also denied the Republic the right to expand beyond its defined boundaries to the east or the west, or to conclude treaties with any state other than the Orange Free State without British approval.[4]

The discovery of the Witwatersrand main reef in 1886 was quickly followed by an influx of large numbers of white people from other parts of South Africa and from Britain and continental Europe to the new mining town of Johannesburg. These *uitlanders* seemed likely sooner or later to outnumber the Afrikaner population of the Republic.[5] Most of

---

[1] On the Hollanders in the South African Republic, see E. J. P. Jorissen, *Transvaalsche Herinneringen, 1876–1896*; P. J. van Winter, *Onder Krugers Hollanders*.

[2] In addition to the works cited in the previous two footnotes, see J. S. du Plessis, 'Die Ontstaan en Ontwikkeling van die Amp van die Staatspresident in die Zuid-Afrikaansche Republiek (1858–1902)', *AYB*, 1955, i.

[3] 'For instance both Kruger and Joubert are firmly convinced that the sun goes round the earth and nothing will shake this conviction.' Merriman to Mrs. A. Merriman, 7 Oct. 1887, in [Merriman] i. 271.

[4] The London Convention is in Eybers, pp. 469–74. See also D. M. Schreuder, op. cit.; and D. P. Faure, *My Life and Times*.

[5] No census was taken of the entire white population of the South African Republic and most diverse estimates were made of the relative numbers of *burgers* and *uitlanders*. In his review of the evidence, Professor Marais concludes that 'in January 1899 (a) there were probably more Boers (men, women, and children) than Uitlanders; (b) there may have been more

them were English-speaking people and English became the *lingua franca* of the gold-mining industry. But the *uitlanders* were a diverse, atomistic community. They included some of the human flotsam and jetsam that accumulated around all the great gold strikes of the nineteenth century, from California to Western Australia; a solid core of skilled artisans; a considerable number of engineers, lawyers, and other professional men; and entrepreneurs of all sorts and conditions, the most successful of whom dominated the great gold-mining corporations and became known as the 'magnates'. Capitalism itself presented a disunited front in the South African Republic. The magnates were of different national and class origins and sympathies. They were responsible to boards located in different European capital cities. And although most of them were able to co-operate for specific purposes where they had a common interest, such as the recruiting and control of African labourers, they were fiercely competitive in other respects, and those whose mines operated comparatively near the surface had different problems and desired different sorts of mining legislation from those who were working at deep levels.[1]

To the Kruger regime, the gold-mining industry was both an asset and a liability. It was an asset because for the first time it enabled the Transvaal to rise out of its chronic penury. It was a liability because the *uitlander* community was a potential Trojan Horse. The cultural gulf between the urban, individualistic, and materialistic *uitlander* community and the rural, socially integrated, and Calvinistic *burger* community was deep and the problem of an accommodation extremely difficult. The *burgers* recalled that the British element in the Transvaal had played a significant role in the events leading to the annexation of the Republic in 1877 and their suspicions of the political implications of the growth of Johannesburg were confirmed by the arrogant behaviour of many *uitlanders*. Consequently, the *Volksraad* took steps to ensure that the *uitlanders* should not be able to get control of the State. In 1890 it limited the *uitlander* franchise for presidential and *Volksraad* elections to those who, besides being naturalized citizens, had lived in the Republic for fourteen years. At the same time it created a 'Second *Volksraad*' for which naturalized citizens could vote two years after their arrival—but this body could deal only with specified matters relating to Johannesburg and the mining industry and its bills could become law only with the approval of the *Volksraad* proper, which remained the sovereign legislature.[2]

Uitlander than Boer male adults owing to the fact that adult males formed a relatively large proportion of the Uitlander population.' J. S. Marais, *The Fall of Kruger's Republic*, p. 3.

[1] On the *uitlanders*, see G. Blainey, 'Lost Causes of the Jameson Raid', *Economic History Review*, xviii, 2 (1965), 350–66; J. P. Fitzpatrick, *The Transvaal from Within*; J. H. Hammond, *The Autobiography of John Hays Hammond*; W. P. Morrell, *The Gold Rushes*.

[2] Eybers, pp. 488–98. On the franchise question, see the works cited above and also P. R.

Interactions between the Afrikaner population and the *uitlanders* continually caused friction. There was much administrative inefficiency, for the lower levels of the administration were manned by local Afrikaners, who were appointed with little regard to qualification and often as a result of nepotism. There was, too, considerable corruption at almost every level in the administration. The quality and cost of many goods and services used by the mining community were affected by the Government's policy of selling or granting concessions—that is to say, monopoly rights. The water supply of Johannesburg was operated by a concessionaire and was notoriously bad and expensive; and so were the manufacture of spirits and dynamite. The dynamite concession, first held by a German then by a French company, eventually passed to Nobels, and the price of this commodity, essential in gold-mining, was always inordinately high. The concession to build and operate trunk railway lines was given on very favourable terms to a Dutch company, and construction was slow and rates were high.[1] Since the Government also imposed customs duties on colonial produce, and on overseas goods over and above the duties levied by the colonial governments at the ports of entry, the cost of living for *uitlanders*, who relied very largely on colonial and overseas produce, seemed to be excessive. There were also other irritants, such as the lack of State support for English-medium schools.[2] However, notwithstanding the administrative inefficiency and corruption, the concessions, the high living costs, and the other irritants that arose from the fact that the Witwatersrand lay in a previously backward and undeveloped country, the *uitlanders* were not an oppressed community and there was no spontaneous, widespread discontent among them. They had come freely to the Witwatersrand, where most of them made a better living than previously. Except for a normal proportion of malcontents, they would have taken the inconveniences in their stride, had it not been for factors extraneous to the local situation. Indeed, few of them cared to identify themselves permanently with the Transvaal by becoming *burgers*, and fewer still were really concerned about the franchise.[3]

The Republican Government had three main external objectives: territorial expansion; commercial autonomy; and diplomatic support. Territorial expansion to the west was cut off before the discovery of the Witwatersrand gold reef by the incorporation of Bechuanaland in the

Botha, *Die Staatkundige Ontwikkeling van die Suid-Afrikaanse Republiek onder Kruger en Leyds*; J. H. Breytenbach, *Die Tweede Vryheidsoorlog*, i; M. Hugo, 'Die Stemregvraagstuk in die Zuid-Afrikaansche Republiek', *AYB*, 1947; G. D. Scholtz, *Die Oorsake van die Tweede Vryheidsoorlog, 1899–1902*.   [1] Marais, ch. 2; van Winter.

[2] J. Ploeger, 'Onderwys en Onderwysbeleid in die Suid-Afrikaanse Republiek onder Ds. S. J. du Toit en Dr. N. Mansvelt (1881–1900)', *AYB*, 1952, i.

[3] J. van der Poel, *The Jameson Raid*, pp. 6–7.

British Empire (pp. 273–4). The classic direction of the Afrikaner *trekboer* movement was to the north and ever since they had driven Mzilikazi across the Limpopo in 1838 the Transvaalers had considered that they had a special relationship with him and his successor, Lobengula. In 1887 Lobengula put his mark to a treaty presented by Pieter Grobler, an agent of the Transvaal Government, stating that Lobengula was an ally of the Republic and would admit a republican consul and allow him to exercise jurisdiction over Transvaal subjects. Grobler's treaty seemed to clear the way for Transvaal penetration and ultimate control of the lands across the Limpopo. But this development was checked by Cecil Rhodes, with the assistance of British officials. In 1888, at Rhodes's instigation, the High Commissioner sent John Moffat, son of the missionary who had befriended Mzilikazi, to obtain Lobengula's mark to another treaty, which gave the High Commissioner control over his treaty-making and concession-granting powers; and in the same year Charles Rudd, acting on Rhodes's behalf, obtained from Lobengula an exclusive concession over metals and minerals in his dominions and the right to exclude competitors. Rhodes then persuaded the British Government to issue a Royal Charter of Incorporation for his British South Africa Company, authorizing it to make treaties, to engage in mining and other economic activities, and to maintain a police force, subject to certain controls by the British Government, in an area vaguely and incompletely defined to the north of Bechuanaland and the South African Republic. In 1890 British South Africa Company pioneers occupied 'Mashonaland' and in the following year the still undefined territories of the Charter were taken under British protection. Thus Kruger was cut off from expansion to the north.[1]

Kruger did not strenuously oppose the British occupation of what was to become known as Rhodesia, because he was much more concerned with expansion to the east which, besides providing fresh land for his *burgers*, might have led to the sea and independent communication with the outside world. After 1887, when Britain annexed Zululand, the only portion of the south-east African coastline that was not under European control was the area known as Tongaland, including Kosi Bay, which was for a while thought to be a possible harbour. If the Republic was to reach Tongaland, it had to absorb the intervening territories, which included the Swazi kingdom, whose independence had been guaranteed by Britain and the Republic in the London Convention of 1884. Consequently, in 1889 Kruger let the British Government know that he would not oppose Rhodes's plans for the north if Britain would give him a free hand in the east. In March 1890, High Commissioner Sir Henry Loch,

---

[1] L. H. Gann, *A History of Southern Rhodesia: Early Days to 1934*; P. Mason, *The Birth of a Dilemma: The Conquest and Settlement of Rhodesia.*

accompanied by Cecil Rhodes, met Kruger at Blignaut's Pont and offered him a strip for a railway to Kosi Bay, provided that the Transvaal would enter into a customs union with the South African colonies as well as abandon its claims to the north. Kruger's Executive Council rejected this offer. Loch then appointed Jan Hofmeyr as his representative to negotiate with Kruger, as Hofmeyr was by that time committed to Rhodes's northern plans and deeply anxious that the Transvaal should enter into a South African customs union. The outcome was a convention signed in July 1890, which eventually led to the incorporation of Swaziland in the South African Republic in 1895 (p. 277); but the Transvaal would have nothing to do with a customs union and failed to get its seaport. The British Government closed the last gap in 1895 when it annexed Tongaland and the chiefdoms of Zambane and Mbegisa. Thus Kruger's republic was hemmed in, 'as it were in a kraal'.[1]

But even if the Republic could not actually engross additional territory, there was the hope that it might break out of the British commercial stranglehold by channelling its foreign trade through Delagoa Bay. This was the primary purpose of Kruger's railway and customs policies.[2] In 1885, on the eve of the discovery of the Witwatersrand gold reef, Kruger was constrained to offer the Cape Colony a customs agreement, but the Cape Government of Upington missed the opportunity. Later, Kruger repulsed all the efforts that were made by high commissioners and colonial governments to draw the Transvaal into a general South African customs union. Instead, he imposed a tariff on Cape produce and tried to delay the completion of the railway lines to the Transvaal from the colonial ports until the Delagoa Bay line was finished. In the event, the Cape line reached Johannesburg in 1892 and enjoyed a brief monopoly; but the Delagoa Bay line reached the Rand in 1894, followed by the Natal line in 1895. The Transvaal Government's ability to manipulate the rates over the Transvaal sections of the several lines and thus to ensure that the bulk of the Transvaal's external trade used the eastern line was limited only by its carrying capacity and the capacity of the harbour facilities at Delagoa Bay. Rhodes tried hard to counteract this by purchasing Delagoa Bay from Portugal, but without success.[3] Consequently, by the mid 1890s, although Kruger lacked political control over a port, he had a route to the sea which avoided British territory and the prospect of channelling the bulk of his foreign trade along it. This was at least a partial fulfilment of a major Voortrekker objective (Vol. I, pp. 357, 409); and to Rhodes it was a matter of grave concern.

[1] Garson, op. cit.; Hofmeyr, ch. 23; D. W. Krüger, ii, ch. 6.

[2] D. J. Coetzee, *Spoorwegontwikkeling in die Suid-Afrikaanse Republiek, 1872–1899*; J. van der Poel, *Railway and Customs Policies in South Africa, 1885–1910*; van Winter, op. cit.

[3] R. J. Hammond, *Portugal and Africa, 1815–1910: A Study in Uneconomic Imperialism*; P. R. Warhurst, *Anglo-Portuguese Relations in South-Central Africa, 1890–1900*.

Diplomatic factors accentuated Rhodes's concern. Kruger had always hoped that he might call in Britain's European rivals to offset British hegemony in South Africa. Before 1886 European governments did not take the pretensions of the Transvaal very seriously; but thereafter, as European capital became invested in the gold-mining industry and continental Europeans joined the *uitlander* community, the situation changed. In particular, among the *uitlanders* there were several thousand Germans, who supported the Kruger Government and its desire for a German alliance. W. J. Leyds, who became State Secretary of the Republic in 1889, exploited this factor and in the mid 1890s the German Government assisted the Republic. German diplomats encouraged Portugal to hold on to Delagoa Bay. The German Foreign Minister warned the British Foreign Secretary that Germany stood for the *status quo* in South Africa and opposed a commercial union between the Republics and the colonies, because that would lead to a British trade monopoly and would be tantamount to a British protectorate over the Republics. In fact, Germany lacked the naval strength to oppose Britain in South Africa and the German Government was merely exploiting the South African situation, as it had been exploiting the Egyptian situation, for the purpose of coercing Britain into association with the Triple Alliance. South Africa was but a pawn in German diplomacy, which was directed towards European power politics. But the British Government could not be quite sure that this was so; and Rhodes and Kruger were not in a position to comprehend the unreliability of German support for the Transvaal.[1]

3. *Collision Course*

Between 1895 and 1899 two attempts were made to curb the power and the autonomy of the Transvaal and bring it back within the British sphere of influence. The first was a plot to supplant the Kruger regime with one that would co-operate with Great Britain and the British South African colonies. The second was direct imperial pressure, which was increased until in October 1899 the Transvaal and its ally, the Orange Free State, declared war upon Great Britain.

By 1895 Rhodes was both optimistic and frustrated.[2] He was optimistic because many things had gone well for him. He had acquired

[1] H. E. W. Backeberg, 'Die Betrekkinge tussen die Suid-Afrikaanse Republiek en Duitsland tot na die Jameson-inval (1852–1896)', *AYB*, 1949, i; R. W. Bixler, *Anglo-German Imperialism in South Africa, 1880–1900*; J. Butler, 'The German Factor in Anglo-Transvaal Relations', and W. R. Louis, 'Great Britain and German Expansion in Africa, 1884–1919', in Gifford and Louis, op. cit.; Warhurst, op. cit.

[2] On the Jameson Raid, see G. Blainey, op. cit.; J. Butler, *The Liberal Party and the Jameson Raid*; E. Drus, 'A report on the papers of Joseph Chamberlain relating to the Jameson Raid and the Inquiry', *Bulletin of the Institute of Historical Research*, xxv (1952); H. M. Hole, *The*

virtually complete control of both the mining and the marketing sides
of the diamond industry and a large share of the gold-mining industry.
His hold over the *Bond* and the Cape Parliament seemed assured, even
though in 1893 he had had to form a new government after the resignation of three of his most capable ministers—John X. Merriman, J. W.
Sauer, and James Rose Innes. His opportunism had paid off in Rhodesia,
where the settlers were firmly entrenched and the first resistance of the
Ndebele had been crushed (1893). On the other hand, he was frustrated
by his failure to entice the South African Republic into a railway and
customs union with the British colonies, which was to have been a first
step towards some form of political union under the Crown. Instead,
the trend was in the opposite direction. Nourished by gold, the Transvaal was becoming the strongest state in southern Africa and it was
using its strength to break free from British control. In these circumstances, it was the gambler in Rhodes that came to the fore. During 1895
he decided to deploy his multifarious resources to arrest the growth of
Transvaal autonomy. His objective—a British South African Dominion
—was the same as Carnarvon's had been. His method—a *coup* in the
Transvaal—was very similar. But times had changed since Carnarvon's
day. It would be much more difficult to oust Kruger than it had been
to eliminate Burgers. The plot that Rhodes concocted hinged on two
conditions. There was to be an *uitlander* revolution on the Witwatersrand;
and the British Government was then to intervene—to sustain the
revolution and enforce a settlement.

In 1892 some of the *uitlanders* had founded the Transvaal National
Union, which held public meetings, bombarded the Government with
petitions for reform, and entered into relations with Kruger's Afrikaner
opposition. In 1895 Rhodes threw the resources of Consolidated Gold
Fields into this movement and some of the other deep-level mining
magnates, notably those of the Wernher-Beit group, also supported it. But
although there was widespread and public talk of revolution, there was
no true revolutionary spirit among the *uitlanders* and no firm leadership.
Many *uitlanders*, including outcrop mining magnates like J. B. Robinson
and Barney Barnato, stood aloof from the movement. Others supported
it as a device to frighten the Government into granting reforms, or to
replace Kruger with some Afrikaner who they hoped would be more
pliable, such as Piet Joubert or Lucas Meyer. The leaders themselves,
who included Lionel Phillips, J. P. Fitzpatrick, and George Farrar,

Jameson Raid; M. G. Holli, 'Joseph Chamberlain and the Jameson Raid: a bibliographical
survey', *Journal of British Studies*, May 1964; Marais, op. cit., chs. 2–4; E. Pakenham, *Jameson's
Raid*; van der Poel, *Jameson Raid*; R. H. Wilde, 'Joseph Chamberlain and the South African
Republic, 1895–1899; a Study in the Formulation of Imperial Policy', *AYB*, 1956, i; and the
biographies of Cecil Rhodes and Paul Kruger (above) and L. S. Jameson and Joseph Chamberlain (below).

were wealthy men, incapable of revolutionary ardour. Though they accumulated a number of fire-arms, their military plans were fuzzy and organization virtually non-existent. Moreover, they never agreed among themselves as to what form of government should replace the Kruger regime. Some were for a reformed republic; only a few wanted to turn the Transvaal into a British Colony.

By the 1890s, the scramble for Africa was far advanced. The days were past when British power, prestige, and prosperity, and British domination of the markets of the undeveloped as well as the developed parts of the globe, could be assured by private enterprise with minimal official backing. Using protectionist tariffs, Germany, other western European countries, and the United States had become formidable industrial rivals. The significance of Africa to Europeans—actual, potential, and imaginary—had changed with the development of steam transport and the heightening of tensions among the European powers. Since Britain had occupied Egypt in 1882, Britain, France, Germany, King Leopold of Belgium and others had been laying claim to the bulk of the African continent, each fearing that if it stood aside, the others would nevertheless proceed and monopolize the trade and the resources of the areas they incorporated in their empires.[1]

British newspapers gave their readers racy and partisan accounts of the events of the scramble; professors and prelates endowed them with a moral purpose; fiction writers made heroes of empire-builders.[2] Some of this attention was devoted to South Africa. Articles featured the growth of the gold-mining industry, the grievances of the *uitlanders*, and their revolutionary chatter. Readers were given the impression that Kruger's Government was oppressing their kinsmen and was an anachronistic obstacle to British expansion.

The leaders of both the main political parties remained committed to the goal of federation of the South African colonies and republics that had been pursued without success for a generation. Their differences concerned emphasis and method. The Liberal Party, which had been responsible for evacuating the Transvaal in 1881 and which included radicals like Morley as well as imperialists like Rosebery, was not likely to resort to force against the Kruger regime. That was shown in 1894, when Sir Henry Loch, the High Commissioner, who had gained an exaggerated impression of the strength and the purpose of the *uitlanders*, proposed that the British Government should help them to carry out a *coup*; but Lord Ripon, the Liberal Colonial Secretary, would have

---

[1] The voluminous historiography of the scramble for Africa is illustrated in R. F. Betts, ed., *The 'Scramble' for Africa: Causes and Dimensions of Empire*. On the British participation in the 'Scramble', see Robinson and Gallagher, op. cit., and R. W. Winks (ed.), *British Imperialism: Gold, God, Glory.*

[2] Thornton, *Imperial Idea*, ch. 2, discusses 'The Imperial Idea at its Zenith'.

none of it.[1] In June 1895, however, the Unionists came into power and Lord Salisbury, the Prime Minister, gave great latitude in the formulation of colonial policy to a most exceptional Colonial Secretary, Joseph Chamberlain.[2]

Chamberlain had started his political career as a radical Liberal, but in 1886 he had led a secession from the Liberal Party because, as an avowed imperialist, he could not support Gladstone's policy of Home Rule for Ireland. He was the most vigorous member of Salisbury's cabinet and, coming from the ranks of the urban industrialists, he was a man whom the aristocratic Salisbury neither understood nor controlled. His appointment marked a return to Carnarvon's proclivity for intervening in South Africa to advance towards the bipartisan goal of federation under the Crown, but with a determination and persistence that were new.[3]

The first evidence of this came soon after Chamberlain had taken office. The Netherlands Railway Company, which owned and operated the Transvaal sections of the lines from Durban and the Cape ports, as well as the entire line from Delagoa Bay, was in a position to determine the distribution of traffic among them by imposing differential tariffs and a tariff war quickly flared up with the Cape Colony. In 1895 the Cape Government tried to circumvent the Transvaal tariff by arranging for the transport of goods from the Vaal River to the Witwatersrand by ox-wagon. Kruger retaliated by closing the Vaal drifts to ox-wagon traffic. Chamberlain then arranged with the Cape Colonial Government for a joint military expedition if necessary and he sent Kruger a strong protest; whereupon Kruger reopened the drifts (October 1895).

By that time Rhodes's plans were far advanced. Since early August, his agent, Dr. Rutherfoord Harris, had been in London, trying to persuade Chamberlain to hand over to the British South Africa Company a strip of land in the Bechuanaland Protectorate along the Transvaal border, ostensibly for the construction of a railway line from the Cape Colony to Rhodesia; and in November Chamberlain authorized the cession. In the course of these negotiations Chamberlain became aware, not only that there was an *uitlander* plot against the Transvaal Government (which was common knowledge), but also that Rhodes was the chief instigator of the plot and that he needed the Bechuanaland strip because he intended to launch a military expedition from it, under the command of his friend and lieutenant, Dr. Leander Starr Jameson, to assist the *uitlanders*. Likewise, in October 1895 Rhodes himself explained his plans to Graham Bower, the Imperial Secretary in Cape Town, and

[1] Butler, *Jameson Raid*, pp. 31–4.
[2] J. A. S. Grenville, *Lord Salisbury and Foreign Policy: The Close of the Nineteenth Century*.
[3] J. L. Garvin, *The Life of Joseph Chamberlain*.

Sir Hercules Robinson, the High Commissioner. In November, Robinson reported to Chamberlain what he expected to happen. The *uitlanders* would proclaim a provisional government; he himself would go to Pretoria to arbitrate; a Constituent Assembly would be elected by male adult suffrage; and the Transvaal would become a liberalized and anglicized republic and would enter into a customs and railway union with the colonies. Chamberlain replied that he agreed, except that Robinson was to ensure that the Transvaal became a British Colony. In December, when President Cleveland delivered a message to Congress that threatened to precipitate a serious Anglo-American crisis over the boundary dispute between Venezuela and British Guiana, Chamberlain had Rhodes informed that he should resolve the Transvaal question at once, or delay it for some years; and he arranged for military reinforcements to be sent to South Africa. But although Chamberlain helped the plot along in these ways, he did not control it. He left it to Rhodes to create the Witwatersrand uprising and use Jameson's force.

The denouement was Gilbertian. As the time set for the Rand revolution approached, the members of the *uitlander* Reform Committee became divided and confused. They quarrelled about the rival merits of the *vierkleur* and the Union Jack. Many of them held back because they distrusted Rhodes and suspected that he was using them for purposes he had not revealed. By 27 December it was evident that there would be no revolution. Informed of this, both Chamberlain and Rhodes realized that they would be in serious political trouble if Jameson invaded the Transvaal without the pretext of a Rand revolution. Accordingly, Chamberlain had cables sent to Rhodes, threatening to revoke the Charter of the British South Africa Company if Jameson moved; and Rhodes had a telegram sent telling Jameson to stay where he was. But Jameson was an impetuous man, with an adolescent sense of the heroic.[1] Hoping to goad the Reform Committee into action, he invaded the Republic with a motley force of about five hundred company police from Pitsani in the Bechuanaland railway strip on 29 December 1895. The Reform Committee did then assume control of Johannesburg, but it also entered into negotiations with Kruger. On 2 January 1896, Jameson surrendered to republican commandos near Krugersdorp. Robinson then went to Pretoria, not to preside over the incorporation of the Transvaal into the British Empire, but to call upon the Reform Committee, too, to capitulate. From the points of view of Rhodes, Chamberlain, and the Reform Committee, the worst had happened— a compromising fiasco; from the point of view of Kruger, the best—the tortoise had stuck out its head and he had chopped it off.

The members of the Reform Committee were tried for high treason

[1] I. Colvin, *The Life of Jameson.*

by a Transvaal court. The four leaders—Lionel Phillips, John Hays Hammond, George Farrar, and Frank Rhodes (brother of Cecil Rhodes) —were sentenced to death, but Kruger commuted the sentences into fines of £25,000 each. Sixty others were fined smaller sums. Kruger handed the members of the invading force over to the British Government for trial and Jameson and five officers were convicted under the Foreign Enlistment Act of 1870 and sentenced to up to fifteen months' imprisonment without hard labour. Rhodes himself accepted responsibility for the plot and resigned from the prime ministership of the Cape Colony; but he retained his parliamentary seat and he contrived to preserve the Charter of the British South Africa Company by blackmailing Joseph Chamberlain with a threat to expose his complicity in the Raid. Chamberlain avoided exposure. Although, yielding to pressure, he had the House of Commons appoint a committee of inquiry, he himself was a member of that committee and he had little difficulty in preventing it from probing his conduct too deeply, with the result that the report of the committee castigated Rhodes and Jameson but exonerated Chamberlain and the officials of the Colonial Office. Thus the Chartered Company kept control of Rhodesia and Chamberlain and the British Government emerged officially unscathed.[1]

The Raid accentuated the polarizing tendencies in white society in South Africa. Many British South Africans felt humiliated and Afrikaners recoiled in the conviction that no Englishman was to be trusted. During 1896, British South Africans founded a South African League, with separate organizations in the Cape Colony, Natal, and the Transvaal, to uphold British supremacy and the League was soon urging the British Government to intervene directly in the Transvaal.

Kruger's handling of the Raid earned him the respect of Afrikaners everywhere and vindicated his leadership of the Transvaal burghers, who gave him an immense majority in the presidential election of 1898. Confronted with the agitation of the South African League, he imported large stocks of arms from Europe and took steps to curb the political activities of *uitlanders*, increasing the size of the police force on the Witwatersrand, suppressing newspapers that abused his regime, and limiting the holding of public meetings. He also subordinated the judiciary. The Constitution of the Republic, which had been drafted in the 1850s for a simple agrarian state, was full of ambiguities. In 1897, to the astonishment not only of Kruger but also of many lawyers, Chief Justice J. G. Kotze gave a judgement to the effect that laws that had been

[1] Chamberlain's complicity in the Raid was widely suspected at the time, but it was not clearly demonstrated until his own papers and those of Sir Graham Bower, the imperial secretary in Cape Town in 1895, had become available to historians. These papers have been used by the authors of recent works on the Raid, including J. Butler, E. Drus, J. S. Marais, and J. van der Poel.

enacted by the *Volksraad* as simple resolutions were not valid, because there were clauses in the Constitution requiring specific procedures, including a three-quarters majority and a time delay. Since the majority of the laws of the Republic had been passed as resolutions, Kotze's judgement threatened virtually the entire legal system. The *Volksraad* reacted by denying the judiciary the right to test the validity of resolutions of the *Volksraad* and empowering the President to dismiss any judge who refused to take an oath 'not to arrogate to myself any so-called right of testing'. Sir Henry de Villiers, Chief Justice of the Cape Colony, mediated an agreement, in terms of which Kruger was to introduce a new Constitution and Kotze, meanwhile, was not to apply the testing right. In 1898, however, Kotze announced that, since no new Constitution had been adopted, he regarded the agreement as defunct; whereupon Kruger dismissed him.[1]

The Raid also led to a tightening of the alliance between the two Afrikaner republics. When Jameson invaded the Transvaal, President M. T. Steyn sent an Orange Free State commando to the Vaal river under a treaty of 1889, which bound each republic to assist the other if its independence was threatened. In 1897, a new treaty reaffirmed the obligation of mutual assistance and also provided for the establishment of an advisory council, which was to make recommendations for the creation of a federal union between the two republics.[2]

In the Cape Colony, the Raid destroyed the basis of Anglo-Afrikaner political co-operation—Rhodes's alliance with the *Bond*. The white electorate split on a racial basis; except that a few Afrikaners remained loyal to Rhodes (some of them financially corrupted) and a few who were not Afrikaners, including experienced and talented parliamentarians like W. P. Schreiner and John X. Merriman, co-operated with the *Bond* for the purpose of limiting Rhodes's influence and stopping British interference in the internal affairs of South Africa. In 1898 a bitterly contested election resulted in a narrow victory for the *Bond* and its allies and in October Schreiner formed a government.[3]

While the dust from Jameson's Raid was settling in South Africa, power in the British cabinet was passing from the Prime Minister to the

---

[1] On the South African Republic on the eve of the war, see W. K. Hancock, *Smuts: The Sanguine Years 1870–1919*; and G. D. Scholtz, op. cit. On the judicial crisis, see J. G. Kotze, *Biographical Memoirs and Reminiscences*; L. M. Thompson, 'Constitutionalism in the South African Republics', *Butterworths South African Law Review*, 1954; and works cited in previous footnotes.

[2] On the Orange Free State on the eve of the war, see J. G. Fraser, *Episodes in my life*; and A. Kieser, *President Steyn en die Krisisjare, 1896–1899*.

[3] On the Cape Colony on the eve of the war, see Davenport; J. H. Hofmeyr; and J. L. McCracken; also C. Headlam (ed.), *The Milner Papers (South Africa) 1897–1899*; [Merriman] ii, iii; and E. A. Walker, *Lord de Villiers and his Times: South Africa 1842–1914*, and W. P. Schreiner: a South African.

Colonial Secretary. Lord Salisbury was a conservative in the aristocratic tradition. Cynical about the moods of the British public, he
strove to keep Britain free from entanglements in the European alliance
system and to confine the use of force to those areas which were most
essential to the national interest as he saw it—India, Egypt, and the
upper Nile.[1] But by 1898 Salisbury was ailing and the dominant member
of the cabinet was the brash and forceful Joseph Chamberlain, who was
susceptible to the popular racialism and jingoism of the time and willing
to take risks to uphold British interests wherever they seemed to be
threatened. More than any of his nineteenth-century predecessors in
high office in Britain, he was prepared to extend the role of the State, at
home and abroad. Where British interests could be sustained by private
enterprise, without the British Government having to make substantial
financial contributions or assume direct administrative responsibilities,
Chamberlain was content; but where private enterprise seemed incapable of sustaining British interests, he considered that the Government should intervene.[2] For example, the Royal Niger Company having
proved unequal to the task of consolidating British power in the face of
French expansion, Chamberlain commissioned a West African Frontier
Force under the command of Frederick Lugard, who prevented the
French from gaining access to the navigable lower Niger in 1897.[3] He
applied the same principle in South Africa. The Jameson Raid having
shown that Rhodes, with only covert official support, was incapable of
checking the growth of Afrikaner power, Chamberlain decided that the
British Government should do so by direct and overt action.

Chamberlain did not quickly come to the conclusion that war was an
appropriate way to consolidate British supremacy in South Africa, for
he realized that to place British supremacy on an enduring basis it was
essential to obtain the voluntary co-operation of Afrikaners. But Chamberlain made three errors of judgement which cumulatively led to war.
First, he greatly exaggerated the extent of the threat to British interests
in South Africa. Misled by jingo rhetoric from the South African League,
he came to believe that there was a pan-Afrikaner conspiracy to gain
control of the entire region and eliminate British influence. In fact
there was no such conspiracy. The Transvaal Government itself began
a process of reform when the young and able Jan Christiaan Smuts was
appointed State Attorney in May 1898.[4] Given time and the absence of
external threats to its survival, it was capable of accommodating the
uitlanders. Moreover, the Government of the Orange Free State and the
Bond party in the Cape Colony were distinct and moderating forces,

    [1] Grenville, pp. 127–8.   [2] Garvin, iii; Grenville, loc. cit.
    [3] J. E. Flint, *Sir George Goldie and the Making of Nigeria*; M. Perham, *Lugard: The Years of
Adventure*.   [4] Hancock, ch. 5.

and each of them had a great interest in preserving the peace. Secondly, Chamberlain assumed that if the British Government applied diplomatic pressure systematically and relentlessly upon the Kruger regime, it would yield rather than go to war with Britain. In this, he seriously underestimated the confidence of the Transvaalers in their capacity to defend their country. They recalled that Britain had relinquished control over the Transvaal under pressure in 1881. They despised a military command that had succumbed to the defeats at Majuba and Isandhlwana. They expected help not only from the Orange Free State but also from Afrikaners in the Cape Colony and Natal. Some of them even clung to the hope that Britain's European rivals would provide effective support. Above all, they had an overwhelming belief in their right to maintain their independence. Thirdly, Chamberlain selected as High Commissioner in succession to Sir Hercules Robinson a man who contributed to his first two errors of judgement and who had no compunction in leading Britain into war; and he failed to restrain that proconsul from doing so.

Chamberlain chose Sir Alfred Milner for the South African appointment because of his proven administrative ability and his outspoken advocacy of British imperialism.[1] Experience under Lord Cromer in Egypt had confirmed Milner in his inclination to equate civilization with good government and his chauvinistic assumption that the 'British race' had unique imperial gifts and a moral right to rule other peoples, whether Asians, Africans, or Afrikaners. In a period when other industrial nations were expanding and challenging Britain's economic leadership, he deemed it essential that the 'British race' should consolidate its resources. The centrifugal forces in the British Empire had to be checked, especially in South Africa, 'the weakest link in the imperial chain'. In all this, Milner's views were close to those of Chamberlain. Where he differed was in his authoritarianism and his tendency to reduce complex issues to simple antitheses. Lacking parliamentary experience, Milner had little respect for democratic processes and was prone to brush aside criticisms of his policies. In South Africa, he became committed to the South African League's partisan interpretation of the issues. A man was to be judged by the touchstone of loyalty. If a man was loyal, he would work to restore and extend British supremacy; otherwise he would thwart it. There were no intermediate positions in Milner's eyes. He failed to appreciate the positions of the Schreiner Government in the Cape Colony, the Steyn Government in the Orange Free State, and the reformers in the Transvaal administration, all of whom were fundamentally

---

[1] Headlam, op. cit.; V. Halpérin, *Lord Milner and the Empire: The Evolution of British Imperialism*; Lord Milner, *The Nation and the Empire: Being a Collection of Speeches and Addresses*; Eric Stokes, 'Milnerism', *Historical Journal*, v. (1962), 47–60.

well-disposed towards Britain and anxious to preserve the peace, provided only that the British Government refrained from threatening the integrity of the Transvaal State. Moreover, Milner had a stronger will than Chamberlain. Consequently, the Colonial Secretary and the High Commissioner jointly carried Britain into a war with the Afrikaner republics. Milner inflated the jingo forces and blocked the moderating forces inside South Africa and presented Chamberlain with arguments for intervention; and Chamberlain, thus equipped, allowed diplomatic pressures to pass from brinkmanship to military commitment and then persuaded the British cabinet that war was necessary.

The diplomacy leading to the outbreak of war has been ably described by Professor J. S. Marais and need not be dealt with in detail here.[1] It was the re-election of Kruger as President of the South African Republic early in 1898, followed by the dismissal of Chief Justice Kotze, that made Milner decide to take the initiative. In March 1898, replying to an address of welcome from the Graaff-Reinet branch of the *Afrikaner Bond*, he raised the loyalty issue and advised the *Bond* to insist that the Transvaal Government reform itself. Later that year Milner went to England to lobby Chamberlain and other politicians of both parties and thereafter he worked to precipitate a conflict.

The quasi-legal basis for British intervention was the claim that Britain had suzerainty over the South African Republic. Suzerainty had indeed been included in the preamble to the Pretoria Convention of 1881; but it was not mentioned in the London Convention and Chamberlain's claim that it still existed because it had not expressly been withdrawn was contrary to the facts. Indeed, while he was conducting the 1884 negotiations Lord Derby, the then Colonial Secretary, had himself crossed out the entire preamble from his working copy of the 1881 document.[2] When the Transvaal repudiated the claim of suzerainty in an 1898 dispatch, Chamberlain did not retract; but thereafter he fell back on two propositions that were political rather than legal in character—that Britain was the paramount power with special rights and interests throughout South Africa, and that Britain had a duty to protect its citizens from oppression by the Transvaal Government. British demands were then concentrated on the treatment of the *uitlanders* and, especially, their admission to the franchise.

When he returned to South Africa early in 1899, Milner encouraged the South African League to step up its demands for reform.[3] The league

---

[1] *The Fall of Kruger's Republic.* See G. H. L. Le May, *British Supremacy in South Africa, 1899–1907,* and works cited in previous footnotes.　　[2] Schreuder, pp. 293–4.

[3] The weakness in the interesting analysis of Robinson and Gallagher is that it takes the South African League too much at its face value. The vigour of the league was not spontaneous, but was a consequence of encouragement and direction by Chamberlain and Milner. See Marais, *passim.*

responded vigorously on the Witwatersrand, producing a petition with over 21,000 signatures calling for British intervention. Meanwhile, the Transvaal Government tried to settle the *uitlander* problem by direct negotiations with the leaders of the mining industry; but one of those leaders, Percy Fitzpatrick, who was in touch with Milner and the Colonial Office, sabotaged the negotiations by giving premature publicity to the demands of the mining representatives. In May, having previously forwarded the *uitlander* petition and written a series of dispatches endorsing it, Milner sent Chamberlain a telegram for publication, declaring that 'The case of intervention is overwhelming' because 'The spectacle of thousands of British subjects kept permanently in the position of helots . . . calling vainly to Her Majesty's Government for redress, does steadily undermine the influence and reputation of Great Britain and the respect for the British Government within the Queen's Dominions.'[1]

The Cape Colonial Government tried desperately to ward off a conflict. Schreiner proposed that the differences should be discussed by a conference of representatives of the South African Colonies and Republics. Milner blocked this proposal. Instead, at the end of May he himself met Kruger in Bloemfontein. He excluded Schreiner from the conference, refused to discuss anything except the *uitlander* franchise, and demanded that Kruger should give the vote to all *uitlanders* who had lived in the republic for five years. When Kruger was not willing to go so far, Milner abruptly broke off the talks. Thereafter, the Cape Government continued to try to mediate and the Transvaal Government made a series of further proposals. In August, Smuts said the Transvaal Government would grant the demands that Milner had made in Bloemfontein, provided the British Government would drop its claim to suzerainty and refrain from further interference in the internal affairs of the Republic contrary to the London Convention. Chamberlain rejected these conditions.

By that time it was evident that no European power would attempt to help the Transvaal. The Kaiser had aroused expectations of German support in January 1896, when he sent Kruger a telegram congratulating him on the capture of Jameson's men; but in August 1898 Germany left Britain a free hand in South Africa when an Anglo-German agreement provided for the partition of Angola and Mozambique between Britain and Germany if, as was then expected, Portugal's financial difficulties made it impossible for her to retain them—and southern Mozambique, including Delagoa Bay, fell within the British sphere.[2] In 1898, also, the

[1] Ibid., p. 267; Headlam, i. 349–53.

[2] Grenville, ch. 8; Warhurst, ch. 5. See also Bixler; Butler, 'German Factor'; Hammond; and Louis.

Fashoda crisis had ended with France yielding to Britain on the upper Nile, an area which both powers regarded as strategically important, with the result that France was in no position to challenge Britain in South Africa, where she had no interests or ambitions. Consequently, Chamberlain was able to persuade the British cabinet to face the prospect of war with equanimity, though not with enthusiasm. In September, Chamberlain prepared for the cabinet a memorandum which echoed Milner's views: 'What is at stake', he declared, 'is the position of Britain in South Africa—and with it the estimate formed of our power and influence in our Colonies and throughout the world.'[1] Military reinforcements were then sent to South Africa and Chamberlain drafted an ultimatum. But by that time Presidents Kruger and Steyn and their advisers were convinced that Britain was determined to destroy the independence of the South African Republic. Accordingly, wishing to strike before the reinforcements arrived, Kruger issued his own ultimatum, which expired on 11 October 1899 Thus Britain went to war to establish British supremacy throughout South Africa: the Republics, to preserve their independence.[2]

[1] Cited by Le May, p. 25.

[2] Of the various theories that have been advanced to account for the South African War, the most original was that of J. A. Hobson, in *The War in South Africa: its causes and effects* and *Imperialism: A Study*. His argument, that the war was brought about by the mining magnates and their financial allies for increased profits, was a forerunner of Lenin's economic interpretation of imperialism (*Imperialism: the Highest Stage of Capitalism*). Subsequent research has not vindicated Hobson. For extracts from the explanations of Hobson and others, see T. C. Caldwell, *The Anglo-Boer War: Why was it Fought? Who was Responsible?*; also Winks, op. cit. My conclusions are in substantial agreement with those of Professors Le May and Marais.

VII

THE COMPROMISE OF UNION[1]

1. *The High Tide of Imperialism*

THE South African War was known at the time as the Boer War or the Second War of Freedom (*Tweede Vryheidsoorlog*), depending on one's point of view.[2] The British Government and people entered into the war comparatively light-heartedly, because the British Empire and the Afrikaner Republics seemed so unevenly matched. The Royal Navy had absolute control of South African waters and the isolation of the republics was reinforced by a secret Anglo-Portuguese Declaration of 14 October 1899, reaffirming the seventeenth-century treaties of alliance and forbidding the passage of arms through Lourenço Marques.[3] Moreover, although the republican government tried hard to get external aid and although European and American opinion was strongly pro-Boer, no foreign government lifted a finger in the Afrikaner cause.[4] It has been estimated that about 88,000 men fought on the republican side at some stage in the war—73,000 Transvaal and Orange Free State burghers, 13,000 colonial 'rebels', and 2,000 foreign volunteers; and that nearly 450,000 men in uniform served the British cause— 256,000 British regulars, 109,000 British volunteers, 53,000 South African colonists, and 31,000 from Canada, Australia, and New Zealand.[5]

[1] I am most grateful to Mrs. Claire Pirone who has typed the manuscripts of all my chapters in both volumes of this *History* with skill and intelligence; also to Professor John S. Galbraith, Professor Monica Wilson, and Miss Jocelyn Murray who noted some errors in this chapter.

[2] For the vast literature on the South African War, see C. F. J. Muller, F. A. van Jaarsveld, and Theo van Wijk, *A Select Bibliography of South African History*, pp. 65–70. The following is a brief selection: (*a*) Eyewitness accounts: W. S. Churchill, *London to Ladysmith via Pretoria*; C. R. de Wet, *Three Years' War*; J. D. Kestell, *Through Shot and Flame: the Adventures and Experiences of J. D. Kestell, Chaplain to President Steyn and General Christian de Wet*; D. Reitz, *Commando: a Boer Journal of the Boer War*; and W. K. Hancock and J. van der Poel, *Selections from the Smuts Papers*, 'Memoirs of the Boer War' (i. 537–663). (*b*) Secondary works: L. S. Amery, (ed), *The Times History of the War in South Africa*, 7 vols.; W. K. Hancock, *Smuts*, i, chs. 5–10; E. Holt, *The Boer War*; D. W. Krüger, *Paul Kruger*, ii, ch. 11; Rayne Kruger, *Good-bye Dolly Gray: the Story of the Boer War*; Le May, op. cit.; L. Marquard (ed.), *Letters from a Boer Parsonage*; F. M. Maurice and M. H. Grant, *History of the War in South Africa, 1899–1902*, compiled by direction of His Majesty's Government; W. B. Pemberton, *Battles of the Boer War*.

[3] R. J. Hammond, p. 257; Warhurst, p. 149. Nevertheless, the republics received considerable supplies by the Delagoa Bay route until the British occupied the Transvaal section of the railway line in Sept. 1900.

[4] J. S. Galbraith, 'The Pamphlet Campaign on the Boer War', *Journal of Modern History*, xxiv, 2 (1952), 111–26; W. J. Leyds, *Correspondentie, 1899–1902*; G. D. Scholtz, *Europa*.

[5] Holt, p. 293.

The British Government respected one significant taboo. Whereas the fighting men of India had played a part in many British campaigns in tropical Africa, none was used in the South African War. By tacit agreement both sides also refrained from involving the African peoples of South Africa in their fighting, except as unarmed servants and scouts and, on the British side, as guards. Bitterly though the war was fought, it was a 'white man's war'. Neither side had the slightest intention of doing anything to weaken white control over the African population; and, except in a few cases, Africans did not make use of the opportunities they were given for attacking Afrikaners and their property.

The isolation and numerical weakness of the republicans were offset by other factors. Most of the burghers had been bred to the horse and the rifle and had spent many months of their lives on commando service against Africans (pp. 281–3). Expert horsemen, superb marksmen, they also had in the German Mauser rifle, which the Transvaal Government had imported in large quantities since the Jameson Raid, a weapon that was superior to the British Lee-Enfield. They knew their own terrain intimately. They had the interior lines and, initially, no supply problem, for they could live off the country; while large numbers of British troops were tied down in communication and commissariat services. Moreover, the loose, democratic commando organization was admirably suited to the needs of a people in arms and once the cautious, older men had been relieved of their commands (for example, Piet Joubert was succeeded by Louis Botha as Commandant-General of the South African Republic early in 1900), the republics had resourceful and imaginative leadership. On the other hand, the British army, with its parade-ground training, its textbook orthodoxy, its rigid social separation between officers and men, and its poor horsemanship and marksmanship, found it as difficult to adapt to novel conditions in enemy territory as it had over a century earlier in the American War of Independence. As in that war, too, there was a vast disparity in morale. The Republican burgher was convinced of the justice of his cause and in many cases believed in a very simple and direct sense that an all-powerful God was on his side; whereas the British Tommy had only the sketchiest idea of what the war was about and what he did know gave him no incentive to sacrifice. Consequently, though isolated and inferior in numbers and equipment, the Afrikaner republics were able to hold the British Empire at bay for two and a half years thanks to their mobility, their marksmanship, their experience, and their morale; and in so doing they dealt a substantial blow to the jingo element in British imperialism.[1]

The fighting fell into three phases of unequal duration. At the outset, the republics took the offensive. Their main forces struck south-eastward,

[1] Thornton, *Imperial Idea*, ch. 3, 'The Impact of War'.

occupying the northern districts of Natal, besieging Ladysmith, and repelling a series of counter-attacks. Commandos also invaded the Cape midlands, where they gained recruits from among the Afrikaner colonists, and others moved westwards to cut off British communications along the railway from the Cape to Rhodesia and besieged British garrisons in Kimberley and Mafeking. In December 1899 Afrikaners defeated British attacks on all three fronts—at Colenso, Stormberg, and Magersfontein. Nevertheless, by the end of the year all three republican advances had lost their impetus. This was crucial in Natal, where Joubert had rejected advice to strike onwards to the coast and the port of Durban before the British built up their strength. Instead, he concentrated on holding what he had got in the first thrust and conducting a leisurely siege of Ladysmith.

· In the second phase, starting early in 1900 the British, commanded by Lord Roberts of Kandahar with Lord Kitchener of Khartoum as his Chief of Staff,[1] relieved the besieged towns, turned back the republican advances, captured four thousand men at Paardeberg under General Piet Cronje, occupied Bloemfontein, Johannesburg, and Pretoria, drove the aged President Kruger into exile via Lourenço Marques, and gained control of the entire railway network, including the Delagoa Bay line—the republics' last link with the outside world. In December 1900, having proclaimed the annexation of both republics under the names Transvaal and Orange River Colony and believing that the war was over except for mopping-up operations, Roberts returned to England, to be fêted as a national hero.

But Roberts had miscalculated. The republics had by no means given up the struggle. Long before Roberts left South Africa, they had resorted to guerrilla warfare under Louis Botha, J. H. de la Rey, C. R. de Wet, and other leaders. They regrouped their forces in small, mobile commandos. Most commandos operated in their home areas—living off the country, seizing British supplies, cutting the railway tracks, annihilating small British units, eroding the fringes of larger columns, and almost invariably inflicting many more casualties than they suffered. Other commandos, including one under J. C. Smuts, the former Cambridge undergraduate and Transvaal State Attorney, penetrated deep into the Cape Colony where they, too, were nourished and aided by kinsfolk. President Steyn of the Orange Free State and Acting-President Schalk Burger of the South African Republic also remained at large and mobile, eluding all attempts at capture. Although the British had defeated the republican armies and occupied their towns and railway communications, they had not won the war. They were confronted with a nation in arms.[2]

---

[1] D. James, *Lord Roberts*; P. Magnus, *Kitchener*.
[2] Reitz's *Commando* is the classic account of the Boer resistance. Smuts's 'Memoirs' also are very revealing.

Lord Kitchener devised plans to crush this resistance. To make sure that captured burghers would not fight again, he deported them to prison camps in St. Helena, Bermuda, Ceylon, and India. To stop the commandos from obtaining food, shelter, and remounts from the civilian population, he burnt farm buildings, destroyed stock, and rounded up the women and children from the countryside and placed them in what were called concentration camps. There, they suffered an appalling mortality from dysentery, measles, enteric fever, and other diseases, partly because the camps were administered by inferior military personnel and partly because the rural Afrikaners lacked knowledge of the hygienic requirements for communal life. By October 1901 the death rate in the camps had soared to 344 per thousand per annum. The camps were then transferred to civilian administration and the death rate began to drop, reaching twenty per thousand per annum by the end of the war; but by that time about 25,000 women and children had died in the camps.[1] Kitchener also built blockhouses at intervals of a mile and a half along the railway lines and elsewhere across the country. Each blockhouse was manned by seven soldiers and three or four African watchmen-cum-servants, and linked with its neighbours on either side by barbed wire fences and telephones. A series of systematic sweeps or drives were made within the perimeters of these fenced areas. Meanwhile, Johannesburg became the nucleus of a pacified and protected zone. The mines began to produce gold again and Afrikaners who surrendered voluntarily in response to an intensive campaign of threats and promises resumed farming operations. Some burghers even served the British forces as 'National Scouts', to hasten the end of what they realized was becoming a hopeless struggle. Consequently, the fighting capacity of the republics was gradually eroded. By May 1902 their field strength had declined from a peak of over fifty thousand to about twenty-two thousand men, most of whom were undernourished, ill clad, fatigued, and dispirited. There was no general collapse, however. Botha, de la Rey, de Wet, and many other commando leaders remained at large in the republics, as did Smuts in the Cape Colony, and they continued to make effective raids on supply columns as well as to elude their pursuers.

The first serious peace feelers took place in February and March 1901, when the governments of the two republics met at Middelburg to consider a proposal put to them by Kitchener. They rejected it, because it involved acceptance of British rule. President Steyn in particular was adamant in holding out for independence. In April 1902 the republican

---

[1] On the concentration camps, see A. C. Martin, *The Concentration Camps, 1900–1902: Facts, Figures and Fables*; and J. C. Otto, *Die Konsentrasiekampe*; also, Le May, ch. 4; and G. B. Pyrah, *Imperial Policy and South Africa, 1902–10*, Appendix 2.

governments met again, at Klerksdorp, and agreed to negotiate with Kitchener. They themselves proposed a settlement under which they would have retained their independence, with an *uitlander* vote and a commercial union with the colonies. The British Government, strengthened by a khaki election that had given the Unionists 402 seats in the House of Commons in October 1900, was determined that the annexations should stand. It rejected the Afrikaner proposal and countered with a modified version of the Middelburg offer. The republican governments then declared that they were not entitled to consent to the loss of independence without the approval of their fighting men. Accordingly a conference of sixty representatives of the commandos was convened, under a British safe-conduct, to consider the British terms. This remarkable gathering met in May 1902 at Vereeniging. As each representative reported on the military situation in his area, it became clear that the composite picture was extremely bleak. Their governments then made a last attempt to obtain a settlement on the basis of independence, with the Witwatersrand detached from the South African Republic, but Kitchener rejected this proposal. Then, using the Middelburg offer as a basis, Kitchener and Milner, in cable consultation with London, thrashed out a draft agreement with the republican governments. The agreement was then debated by the fighting men at Vereeniging and on 31 May they voted fifty-four to six for acceptance. That night what became known as the Peace of Vereeniging was signed in Pretoria by Kitchener and Milner and members of the governments of the South African Republic and the Orange Free State, which thereby ceased to exist as independent states.[1]

The burghers were to surrender their arms and recognize the authority of King Edward VII. There was to be a general amnesty, with a few exceptions. A commission was to be appointed in each district to assist in the resettlement of the inhabitants. There were also three articles that were of major political significance, because they were crucially related to Milner's post-war plans.

Milner and Chamberlain had led Britain into war to establish British supremacy throughout South Africa. This was like trying to square the circle. By resorting to war, and then allowing the military commanders to do what they considered necessary to win the war, they had opted for coercion as the means of attaining the objective. But how was military victory to be translated into enduring British supremacy in a country where white people were outnumbered by Africans, and white people

[1] De Wet, pp. 371–506; Kestell, op. cit.; J. D. Kestell and D. E. van Velden, *The Peace Negotiations Between the Governments of the South African Republic and the Orange Free State, and the Representatives of the British Government* . . . ; Headlam (ed.), *The Milner Papers*, ii, ch. 9; Hancock and van der Poel (eds.), *The Smuts Papers*, i. 511–34. The text of the Peace of Vereeniging is in Eybers, pp. 345–7.

of British descent by Afrikaners against whom the war had been waged, in an age when both British parties were committed to the doctrine that established white communities in the British Empire should run their own affairs?

In January 1900 Chamberlain had told Milner that he proposed to appoint a commission to report on the future of South Africa. Milner had fiercely and successfully resisted this proposal. He wished to control the formulation and administration of the post-war settlement himself. He knew what he wanted and how he would set about achieving it. 'The *ultimate* end', he wrote to Fitzpatrick in November 1899, 'is a self-governing white Community, supported by *well-treated* and *justly governed* black labour from Cape Town to Zambesi.'[1] But meanwhile the white South African community had to be made loyal to the British Empire. To achieve that, he reasoned in December 1900, involved two processes. First, the Afrikaners must be outnumbered by white people of British descent. When the war was over, there was bound to be a massive British immigration to the Witwatersrand gold-fields. That could be left to take care of itself; but the Government should assist British immigrants to establish themselves in the countryside, as a leaven to the rural Afrikaners. Secondly, the Afrikaners themselves must be denationalized. Since their nationalism was a function of their isolation and backwardness, it would be eradicated by modernization—a liberal educational system, efficient administration, and economic development. Meanwhile, the former republics should be ruled as Crown colonies—and the Cape Colony too, if its Parliament and Government proved recalcitrant —until the Afrikaners had been swamped and denationalized. Then self-government could be granted and all of South Africa could be safely joined together in a federal Dominion, its loyalty assured by its British political majority and the denationalization of the Afrikaners.[2]

In the correspondence and the negotiations that culminated in the Treaty of Vereeniging, Milner intervened decisively for the sake of this programme. Whereas Kitchener and Chamberlain would have been willing to concede the Boers' request for the recognition of Dutch as an official language alongside English, Milner whittled it down to what became article 5 of the Treaty:

> 5. The Dutch language will be taught in public schools in the Transvaal and the Orange River Colony where the parents of the children desire it, and will be allowed in Courts of Law where necessary for the better and more effectual administration of justice.

Whereas Kitchener supported the Boers' request that the Treaty should mention a specific date by which self-government would be granted to

---

[1] *Milner Papers*, ii. 35–6. Italics in the original.   [2] Ibid., pp. 242–4.

the former republics, Milner, supported on this point by Chamberlain, ensured that article 7 included no time-table for constitutional development:

> 7. Military administration in the Transvaal and Orange River Colony will at the earliest possible date be succeeded by civil government, and, as soon as circumstances permit, representative institutions, leading up to self-government, will be introduced.

And whereas Kitchener and Chamberlain had believed that Coloured people and Africans should have some say in politics when parliamentary institutions were created in the new colonies, Milner had the Treaty make no mention of Coloured people and expressly exclude all Africans from participation in politics until *after* power had been transmitted to the local white community:

> 8. The question of granting the franchise to natives will not be decided until after the introduction of self-government.

That is to say, throughout the treaty-making process Milner paved the way for his denationalization programme, and the one significant concession he made to Afrikaner sentiment was at the expense of Africans and Coloured people.[1]

Milner had moved to Johannesburg in August 1901, while the war was still in progress. Combining the offices of High Commissioner for South Africa and Governor of the Transvaal and the Orange River Colony, he ruled the former republics as Crown colonies until he left South Africa in April 1905. From London, he had the almost invariable support of Joseph Chamberlain and his successor at the Colonial Office, Alfred Lyttelton; locally, he appointed young Oxford graduates— 'Milner's kindergarten'—to the key administrative positions. When the war was over, he had the Afrikaner people resettled on their land from the commandos, the concentration camps, and the prisoner-of-war camps and provided with assistance for rebuilding their homes and resuming farming operations. He amalgamated the Transvaal and Orange River Colony railway systems and expanded them. He created a customs union, including all the British colonies and protectorates south of the Zambesi.

However, as British war expenditures and post-war grants ceased, the war-time boom gave way to an economic recession. This was a matter of grave concern to Milner. He had assumed that under British rule the gold-mining industry would rapidly surpass its pre-war levels of employment, production, and profits and become a mainspring for general South African economic development and modernization. In fact, the

[1] L. M. Thompson, *The Unification of South Africa, 1902–1910*, pp. 10–12.

industry did not regain its pre-war scale until 1904 and during 1903 many of the British and colonial soldiers who had taken their discharge in South Africa began to drift away. A major problem for the mining companies was a shortage of cheap labour. Even though Milner negotiated a *modus vivendi* with Portugal for the resumption of labour recruiting in Mozambique, it took some time to build up the recruiting system to its former level. To remedy this shortfall, Milner gave effect to a mining directors' proposal that labourers should be imported from China, on short-term contracts terminating in compulsory repatriation. Chinese labourers began to arrive in June 1904. By the end of 1905 they formed nearly a third of the total mine labour force and the industry was entering a period of rapid growth.

Nevertheless, in the time allowed to him Milner failed to achieve the conditions which he had believed to be essential before it would be safe to establish responsible government in the former republics. The Afrikaner people were not swamped by white people of British descent. There was no mass British immigration to the towns and fewer than three thousand British settlers—men, women, and children—were established on the land under his subsidized scheme. Consequently, the basic political demography of South Africa remained substantially unaltered. In 1911, Afrikaners continued to form well over fifty per cent of the white population of South Africa. As before the war, they were much more numerous than people of British descent in the Orange River Colony and the Cape Colony and about as numerous in the Transvaal. Only in Natal was there a clear British majority in the white population.

Nor were the Afrikaners denationalized. The pre-war diplomacy that Milner and Chamberlain directed, the events of the war that they unleashed, and the reconstruction that they controlled had the reverse of the effect that they had intended. In making an assessment of Afrikaner nationalism similar to the assessment that Lord Durham had made of French-Canadian nationalism in the 1830s, Milner ignored the evidence that was available in his time to suggest that Durham had been wrong. Though the Afrikaner nationalist movement, like the French-Canadian, had developed among an isolated and non-industrialized people, isolation and economic backwardness were not essential conditions for its survival. What it did thrive upon was external pressure. The first clear manifestation of Afrikaner national sentiment had occurred in response to the pressures exerted by Lord Carnarvon and Sir Bartle Frere (pp. 301–4). The abortive *coup*, the coercive diplomacy, the military conquest, and the bureaucratic reconstruction of the decade of Unionist rule at the turn of the century gave it a second, more powerful, and more lasting stimulus. Though they were defeated and impoverished, the Transvaal and Free State Afrikaners retained an indelible conviction that their cause had been just. Moreover, the majority of the colonial Afrikaners had identified themselves with the republican cause and over ten thousand of them had risked the penalties for treason by joining or assisting the commandos. Consequently, the Afrikaner people emerged from the war proud of the republics' resistance to overwhelming odds and more determined than ever to retain their corporate identity. Far from destroying Afrikaner nationalism, Milner and Chamberlain were the greatest recruiting agents it ever had.[1]

2. The Transfer of Power[2]

At the beginning of 1905, imperialism seemed triumphant, both in Britain and in South Africa. The Unionists had a large parliamentary majority in Westminster, Milner and his staff ruled the former republics as Crown colonies, and Jameson's Progressive Party, assisted by the temporary disfranchisement of the rebels, was in power in Cape Town. In fact, imperialism was on the brink of a steep decline.

In its hold on the British public, the new imperialism of Chamberlain and Milner reached its zenith in 1900—the year of 'mafficking', the march to Pretoria, and the khaki election, when the Government's version of the origins of the war still seemed credible and the British role in the war glamorous. By 1902, however, many British people were finding it difficult to escape the conclusion that their country was behaving like a bully in its bloody, expensive, and inglorious attempt to round up scattered bands of impoverished guerrillas; and when the war was over the reaction continued. The Unionist party itself experienced serious strains, especially after Joseph Chamberlain resigned from the cabinet in 1903 to advocate tariff reform, for the purpose of knitting the Empire together as an economic bloc, but at the cost of abandoning the free trade principles that had prevailed in England since the middle of the nineteenth century. The result was that the Unionists lost a series of by-elections and in December 1905 they were succeeded by a Liberal ministry under Sir Henry Campbell-Bannerman, who immediately obtained a dissolution of Parliament and won a large majority in a general election. Not that the Liberals spoke with one voice. In the early stages of

[1] Thompson, pp. 12–17. See also Le May, ch. 7; Pyrah; Stokes, op. cit.; and *The Milner Papers*, ii. For accounts favourable to Milner, see E. Crankshaw, *The Forsaken Idea: A Study of Viscount Milner*; Halpérin, op. cit.; W. B. Worsfold, *The Reconstruction of the New Colonies under Lord Milner*; and J. E. Wrench, *Alfred Lord Milner: the man of no illusions, 1854–1925*.

[2] R. Hyam, 'Smuts and the Decision of the Liberal Government to grant Reponsible Government to the Transvaal, January and February 1906', *Historical Journal*, viii. 3 (1965), 380–98; Le May, ch. 8; P. N. S. Mansergh, *South Africa 1906–1961: the Price of Magnanimity*; Pyrah, pp. 161–81; *Smuts Papers*, ii. 205–327; J. A. Spender, *The Life of the Right Hon. Sir Henry Campbell-Bannerman*; Thompson, pp. 17–30.

the war they had been deeply divided, with outright imperialists like Lord
Rosebery on the one flank and radical pro-Boers like Lloyd George on
the other. But Campbell-Bannerman gradually restored some cohesion,
by conceding the imperialists' demands that the party should not try to
revoke the annexations of the republics and by endorsing the pro-Boer
abhorrence of Kitchener's farm-burnings and concentration camps,
which he called 'methods of barbarism'.

Campbell-Bannerman's South African policy was an updated version of the policy that had been pursued by most British governments,
especially Liberal governments, since the middle of the nineteenth
century. The objective, as ever, was a united, self-governing, pro-British
South Africa. That objective, Campbell-Bannerman believed, could
only be attained with the co-operation of the Afrikaner people. The
coercive policy of the Unionists had been profoundly damaging to
British interests because it had alienated Afrikaners. It was vitally
necessary to reverse that process—to make amends to the Afrikaners by
trusting them and giving them a share in the government of the former
republics. Though there was an element of risk attached to that course,
the alternative of continued forceful suppression of Afrikaners seemed
impossible: the British people would not tolerate it and the increasing
tensions in the European state system made it essential to stabilize
South Africa at once. Moreover, there were indications that a bold
gamble might pay off. In the Cape Colony, Afrikaners and Britons had
co-operated most successfully in the early 1890s until Rhodes had betrayed the alliance, and since then first Schreiner and then Merriman
had built a new Anglo-Afrikaner coalition. In the Transvaal itself the
young men who had emerged from the war as the new Afrikaner
leaders seemed themselves to be conciliatory. As a matter of policy,
therefore, Campbell-Bannerman and his cabinet decided to make a bid
for Afrikaner cooperation by granting self-government to the former
republics on terms that would promote co-operation between the local
Afrikaner and British communities.

By the time the Liberal Party came into power, the Afrikaner inhabitants of the former republics were beginning to recover from the effects
of the war. *Predikants* were using their great influence to hold them together and keep them true not only to their Calvinist religion, but also
to their culture—healing the rifts between *bittereinders* (bitter-enders),
hensoppers (hands-uppers), and National Scouts, and founding Christian
National schools to give the people an alternative to Milner's public
schools, where English was the sole medium of instruction. Journalists
and poets were writing in the Afrikaans language in an emphatically
nationalist spirit. Moreover, starting in the Transvaal and spreading to
the Orange River Colony, the most distinguished generals of the

guerrilla war were transforming themselves into politicians—convening meetings to criticize the Milner regime in general and its decision to import Chinese labour in particular. In January 1905 Louis Botha announced the formation of a political movement—*Het Volk* (The People)—which stood for full self-government for both the Transvaal and the Orange River Colony and quickly gained the support of the vast majority of the Transvaal Afrikaners.

On the other hand, the British community in the Transvaal was divided. Milner's obsession with 'race' had led him to make a profound miscalculation about the political motivation and behaviour of South Africans of British origin. He had failed to realize that, when it came to the pinch, whatever British sentiments they may have had would in most cases be subordinated to their economic interests, which were widely divergent. In his haste to revive and expand the gold-mining industry, Milner allied himself so closely with the deep-level gold-mining interest that he alienated many other British Transvaalers, including artisans with populist leanings, professional and business men who were not dependent on the deep-level gold-mining corporations, and executives of the diamond mines and the outcrop gold mines. Consequently, the Progressives who endorsed Milner's programme were led by George Farrar and Sir Percy Fitzpatrick, both of whom were senior executives of deep-level gold-mining corporations; while the Responsibles (later called Nationals), led by professional men such as Richard Solomon, declared for responsible government, and there were even some diamond-mining and outcrop gold-mining executives like J. B. Robinson who gave financial and press support to *Het Volk*.[1]

The brain behind *Het Volk* was that of J. C. Smuts. Early in 1906 he went to London to lobby members of the new Government for responsible government on conditions that would prevent power from passing into the hands of the mining magnates. His appeal coincided with the predilections of the Prime Minister—and of Winston Churchill, who was holding his first executive post of Under-Secretary of State for the Colonies under Lord Elgin. The cabinet decided to give the Transvaal responsible government and it sent a committee, headed by Sir Joseph West Ridgeway, to South Africa to try to get the Transvaal parties to agree upon an electoral system. After long discussions with all the interested white parties, the committee recommended a compromise between the proposals of *Het Volk* and those of the Progressives,[2] and

[1] See the important article by D. J. N. Denoon, ' "Capitalist Influence" and the Transvaal Government during the Crown Colony period, 1900–1906', *Historical Journal*, 11, ii (1968), 301–31; also the same author's 'The Transvaal Labour Crisis, 1901–1906', *Journal of African History*, 8, iii (1967), 481–94.

[2] The report of the West Ridgeway Committee has only recently been made available to historians. It was used by Professor G. H. Le May, op. cit.

its recommendations were embodied in Letters Patent issued in December 1906.[1]

The Transvaal Constitution was a version of the well-established model of colonial responsible government. There was a bicameral legislature, consisting of a Legislative Council and a Legislative Assembly. In the first instance, the fifteen members of the Legislative Council were nominated by the governor, but after five years they were to have been appointed by the governor-in-council—i.e. by the governor acting on the advice of the cabinet. The electorate comprised the white male adult population. In the first Assembly, there were thirty-four seats for the Witwatersrand, six for Pretoria, and twenty-nine for the rest of the colony. A commission divided each of these three regions into the appropriate number of single-member constituencies, each containing approximately the same number of voters, but with a latitude of fifteen per cent either way, and the Constitution obliged the commission to give 'due consideration' to existing boundaries, community or diversity of interest, means of communication, and physical features. Subsequently, a new voters' roll was to be compiled every four years and a new commission was to be appointed every four years, firstly, to divide the seats between the Witwatersrand, Pretoria, and the rest of the country in proportion to their numbers of registered voters, and secondly, to divide each of the three regions into single-member constituencies in accordance with the same rules that had been laid down for the first commission. English was the official language of parliament, but Dutch could be used in debate and parliamentary papers were published in both languages. Bills amending the Constitution, or placing restrictions on non-white people only, or providing for the importation of indentured labourers from outside South Africa, were to be reserved by the governor for consideration by the King (i.e. the British Government); and no more licences were to be issued for the importation of indentured labourers under the 1904 ordinance.

In making their recommendations for the division of the seats in the first Assembly, the West Ridgeway committee had hoped that it would be impossible for either *Het Volk* or the Progressives to obtain a clear majority. Botha, Smuts, and their colleagues did not expect to win a majority and they made an electoral compact with the Nationals. However, *Het Volk* won thirty-seven of the sixty-nine seats in the election and in March 1907 Louis Botha formed a government, consisting of four members of *Het Volk* and two Nationals.

The West Ridgeway committee had also been instructed to report on an electoral system for the Orange River Colony and Letters Patent providing a Constitution for that colony were issued in June 1907. That

[1] Cd. 3250 (1906). See also N. G. Garson, 'Het Volk', *Historical Journal*, 9, i (1966).

Constitution was similar to the Transvaal one, with a two-fold primary division of the seats in the Assembly between the rural areas, and the towns and villages.[1] When the general election was held in November 1907, the *Orangia Unie*—the Orange River Colony equivalent of *Het Volk*—won thirty of the thirty-eight seats and Abraham Fischer became Prime Minister.

Thus, for the second time in a generation, the swing of the pendulum in British politics produced a radical political change in the interior of South Africa. In 1881 a British Liberal administration had restored a qualified independence to the Transvaal only four years after it had been annexed under the Conservatives: in 1907, only five years after Britain under the Unionists had completed the conquest of the Afrikaner republics at a cost of twenty-two thousand men, two hundred million pounds, and universal obloquy, Britain under the Liberals gave them responsible government. Arthur Balfour, leader of the Opposition, denounced the change as 'the most reckless experiment'.[2] It was, indeed, a remarkable step. The history of colonies with responsible government had already shown that in vesting power in a local cabinet, responsible to a local legislature, Britain relinquished her capacity to control a colony. In 1838 Lord Durham had envisaged colonial self-government as a division of powers between a dominant imperial government and a subordinate local government, but by 1907 the balance had shifted decisively. Self-governing colonies controlled their public lands, formulated their tariff policies, initiated changes in their constitutions, and decided whether or not to send military aid to Britain in time of war. The right of the imperial government to disallow colonial laws had become obsolete by disuse, and even the reservation of classes of bills specifically mentioned in colonial constitutions rarely resulted in the thwarting of the will of a colonial legislature. Power over its internal affairs was transferred to the colony, leaving Britain with a declining influence—and with legal controls that were impressive in form but feeble in substance.

Radical in one respect, the changes effected in 1907 were reactionary in another. Previously, when creating parliamentary institutions in South Africa, British governments had refrained from making race a criterion for participation in the political system. In the Cape Colony under the 1853 Constitution and in Natal under the 1856 Constitution, male adult British subjects, irrespective of race, had been entitled to be registered as voters, if they possessed prescribed economic qualifications.[3] At the outset, however, the electorates were almost entirely white in both colonies and subsequently the original British intentions were overridden in different degrees by the parliaments of the two colonies.

[1] Cd. 3526 (1907).   [2] Pyrah, p. 181.   [3] Vol. i, pp. 322–3, 386.

In the Cape Colony, while retaining the colour-blind form of the electoral laws, the colonial Parliament amended them with the purpose and effect of checking the increase in the number of African and Coloured voters, by introducing an educational test, and by raising the economic qualifications and defining them so that land occupied under traditional African tenure should not constitute a qualification.[1] In Natal, the colonial Parliament passed laws excluding virtually all Africans and Asians from the franchise.[2] The result was that in 1909 white people formed twenty-three per cent of the population and had eighty-five per cent of the votes in the Cape Colony, and white people formed eight per cent of the population and had ninety-nine per cent of the votes in Natal.[3] These precedents suggested that once Britain transferred political power to a white minority in a colony, that minority would take steps to maintain its position of dominance.

In the Afrikaner republics, participation in the political process had always been a white monopoly. During the second half of the nineteenth century, there had been frequent allegations in the British press that Africans, Asians, and Coloured people were ill-treated in the republics, and Milner and Chamberlain made charges of ill-treatment part of their case for British intervention in 1899.[4] Nevertheless, as explained above (p. 331), the Peace of Vereeniging provided that 'natives' should be excluded from the franchise when self-government was granted to the Transvaal and the Orange River Colony. Moreover, in the reconstruction period Milner did scarcely anything to raise the status or improve the lot of the non-white inhabitants of the colonies.

In the years following the South African War, British Liberals were perplexed about this problem. Those who were most concerned for the welfare of the African and Asian subjects of the Crown were also apt to be the most emphatic pro-Boers, for it was revulsion from the excesses of imperialism that operated in both cases. Although they respected the argument that the imperial government had an obligation to hold the balance between white settlers and indigenous peoples in colonial societies, in 1907 it seemed to most of them that the events of the previous decade had created a still greater obligation to make amends to the Afrikaners. They realized that if they tried to provide votes for Africans, or Asians, or Coloured people, both the British and the Afrikaner communities would be outraged and the attempt at appeasement would fail. Consequently, they persuaded themselves that they were bound by the Peace of Vereeniging to launch the former republics into

[1] Davenport, pp. 118–23, 147–8; Eybers, pp. 73–4; J. H. Hofmeyr, *Hofmeyr*, pp. 309–11, 429–37; J. Rose Innes, *Autobiography*, pp. 74–5, 95–6; McCracken, ch. 6.
[2] Brookes and Webb, 76–7, 182; Eybers, pp. 194–7, 215.
[3] Thompson, pp. 110–11.   [4] Marais, pp. 258–62.

responsible government with electorates that were exclusively white (although that treaty contained nothing that need have prevented them from including Asian and Coloured men) and that the white electorates could then be relied on to treat their unenfranchised subjects with increasing liberality (in spite of the precedents to the contrary). So it was that the period of imperial rule did not shake the rigid caste-like structure of society in the former republics and Campbell-Bannerman's Liberal Government took no steps to redistribute power within them before relinquishing imperial control.[1] This was to be crucial for all South Africa.

The swing of the political pendulum was completed in February 1908, when Jameson resigned as Prime Minister of the Cape Colony. His successor was John X. Merriman,[2] an experienced politician, whose South African Party depended on the support of the Afrikaner *Bond*, but also included a few English-speaking people like Merriman himself, who had been profoundly alienated by the excesses of British imperialism. Only in Natal, with its British electoral majority, were politicians sympathetic to imperialism still in the saddle.

3. *The Policy of Conciliation*

By the end of the nineteenth century, a process of social and economic change was taking place within the Afrikaner community. As a result of the closing of the frontiers of white settlement and the growth of the market economy, many families were being reduced to landlessness and becoming either *bywoners* (clients of landowners, with squatting rights) or unskilled urban workers. At the same time, more capable men were exploiting the opportunities presented by the growth of urban markets to become progressive, capitalist farmers and a few, after higher education in the Cape Colony and in Britain or the Netherlands, were practising as lawyers or journalists. Thus, diversification was taking place within a previously egalitarian Afrikaner community. The war accentuated these tendencies. When it was over, many former burghers of the republics failed to become re-established as independent farmers. Moreover, with the removal of the last survivors of the Voortrekker generation (epitomized by the death of Paul Kruger in Switzerland in 1904), leadership was passing to a new type of man: the war hero, who was usually a progressive farmer and, in some cases, also a qualified lawyer. Politics in South Africa was to be dominated by this class until the middle of the twentieth century.

Louis Botha was in many ways typical of the new leaders.[3] Born in

[1] Pyrah, ch. 4.

[2] Sir P. Laurence, *The Life of John Xavier Merriman*; [Merriman] *Correspondence*.

[3] The best biography of Botha is F. V. Engelenburg's *General Louis Botha*. See also Earl Buxton, *General Botha*.

1862 of Voortrekker parents, he had scarcely any formal education and was never interested in literary culture. Striking out on his own in his youth, he took part in the development of the New Republic and became a progressive farmer, accumulating land and importing breeding stock. After serving as field-cornet and native commissioner in the Vryheid district, in 1898 he was elected to the *Volksraad* of the South African Republic, where he tended to side with those who wished to come to terms with the *uitlanders* and incorporate those of them who desired citizenship into the ruling class. Nevertheless, the outbreak of the war found him utterly loyal to the republican cause. Rapidly promoted General, he urged that the whole of Natal should be overrun by the commandos before British reinforcements arrived, but the aged Commandant-General restrained him and by the time he succeeded Joubert the commandos were retreating everywhere and the British army was in Bloemfontein. After the fall of Pretoria, Botha was one of those who planned the guerrilla war and conducted it successfully, but in the negotiations at Pretoria and Vereeniging he was a realist and used his influence for peace.

Unlike Botha, Jan Smuts was an intellectual.[1] Born near Riebeeck West, fifty miles north-east of Cape Town, in 1870, he had a brilliant student career at Stellenbosch and Cambridge and in 1895 he settled in Cape Town, writing articles for local newspapers while he waited for briefs. Initially, he supported the Anglo-Afrikaner political alliance led by Cecil Rhodes, but to him, as to many other colonial Afrikaners, the Jameson Raid was a traumatic experience. In 1897 he moved to the South African Republic where, early in 1898, Kruger appointed him State Attorney. In that office, he tackled the problems of corruption and incompetence in the administration and at the same time helped the President and the State Secretary cope with British diplomatic pressure. Like Botha, he threw himself heart and soul into the war effort. After the fall of Pretoria, he learnt the craft of guerrilla warfare from J. H. de la Rey and he then led the most successful of all the commando invasions of the Cape Colony; but in May 1902 he, like Botha, bowed to the facts and exhorted the representatives of the commandos to accept the peace terms rather than to continue a struggle that had become suicidal.

After the war, these two dissimilar men drew together in friendship and political partnership. Their talents were complementary. Botha was gregarious, capable of talking to Afrikaner farmers in their own idiom; Smuts was more introverted but, with the cosmopolitan interests

---

[1] W. K. Hancock's biography is authoritative: *Smuts: the Sanguine Years, 1870–1919*, and *Smuts: the Fields of Force, 1919–1950*; see also *Smuts Papers*; and H. C. Armstrong, *Grey Steel: J. C. Smuts, a Study in Arrogance*; F. S. Crafford, *Jan Smuts: a Biography*; S. G. Millin, *General Smuts*; and J. C. Smuts (junior), *Jan Christian Smuts*.

of the intellectual, he had contacts in pro-Boer and pacifist circles in England. Botha was a simple, persuasive talker; Smuts was more effective on paper. The bonds between them were mutual respect and a similar response to the political situation in post-war South Africa. As the strengths and weaknesses of the Milner regime became apparent, they began criticizing it and building up a political following and in 1904 they founded *Het Volk*.

The word they used to describe their policy was 'conciliation'. By this they meant that the forces of conflict in South Africa were to be mitigated by the realization that each corporate group was part of a larger entity. Conciliation was to be applied at four distinct levels. First, the Afrikaners were to be reconciled to one another. *Bittereinders* were to readmit *hensoppers* and National Scouts to their society; brother was to forgive brother for making different decisions in the stress of war. Secondly, Afrikaners were to be reconciled with Transvaalers of British descent, for their fates were bound up together and their welfare would depend on their capacity to co-operate. Afrikaners were to understand that it was not the typical *uitlander* who had been responsible for the war, but mining magnates and British officials; and British Transvaalers were to respect the burghers for their attempt to preserve their independence. Thirdly, the regional disputes in South Africa were to be overcome by joining the four colonies together into an indissoluble union based on the principles of conciliation. Finally, a solution was to be found to the problem of relations between Great Britain and South Africa by securing scope for South African national fulfilment within a liberalized Empire. At each of these levels, the imperatives were the same: bury the hatchet; promote the common interest; and build the future on trust and confidence.[1]

By 1908, the conciliation policy seemed to be bearing fruit at all levels. Transvaal Afrikaners were united in *Het Volk*; *Het Volk* was co-operating with the Nationals and surprising the Progressives with its moderation; Botha and Smuts were establishing cordial relations with political leaders in the other three colonies; and the decision of Campbell-Bannerman's Government to give the two former republics self-government on terms satisfactory to *Het Volk* and the *Orangia Unie* was a fine augury for harmonious relations between Britain and South Africa. The action of the Liberal Government was, indeed, a remarkable vindication of the conciliation policy. It had a life-long effect on Botha and Smuts, giving them confidence in the British people and the British imperial system and convincing them that conciliation was politically rewarding as well as morally sound.[2] With their expanding majority in the Transvaal

---

[1] Engelenburg, ch. 14; N. G. Garson, 'Het Volk'; Hancock, i, chs. 11–12; Thompson, pp. 30–3.

[2] Engelenburg, ch. 15; Hancock, i. 215–17; Le May, p. 185; Thompson, p. 32.

Parliament, with the gold-mines expanding rapidly, and with the four self-governing colonies on the same constitutional footing as each other, Botha and Smuts saw an opportunity to apply their ideas on a larger scale.

Although the conciliation policy was in the ascendant by 1908, it was open to attack from two sides. On the one hand, some Afrikaners regarded it as dangerous. These were mainly religious people, steeped in the doctrine propounded by *predikants* that Afrikanerdom was an organic unit with a divine mission. It seemed to them that the first task of Afrikaner politicians who attained positions of power after the war was to protect Afrikaner material and cultural interests. Otherwise, they feared that Afrikanerdom would be overwhelmed by British financial strength and English culture. Only when Afrikanerdom had become strong and self-confident would it be safe to co-operate with Britain and British South Africans. In the Transvaal, these critics of conciliation included A. D. W. Wolmarans, an old associate of Paul Kruger, and C. F. Beyers, a young war hero; but Botha and Smuts kept a firm hold over the *Het Volk* organization and the attacks of Wolmarans and Beyers did not constitute a serious immediate threat to their leadership. In the Orange River Colony conditions were different. There, Afrikaners had so great an electoral majority that the *Orangia Unie* did not need to win over English-speaking voters. The two most influential men in the colony were M. T. Steyn,[1] the ex-President, who had avoided having to sign the Peace of Vereeniging by resigning from the presidency on account of ill health, and J. B. M. Hertzog,[2] a lawyer and war hero, who was Minister of Education. Both Steyn and Hertzog were critical of the conciliation policy and, when Smuts steered an education Act through the Transvaal Parliament that stopped short of placing the Dutch language on a footing of equality with English in the schools, and Botha attended the 1907 colonial conference in London and made speeches extolling the British Empire, they began to suspect that Botha and Smuts had become disloyal to the Afrikaner cause.

On the other hand, though the conciliation policy was dangerously radical from the point of view of conservative Afrikaners, it was reactionary from the standpoint of the majority of the inhabitants of South Africa. The South African nation envisaged by Botha and Smuts was a white nation; the British Empire they were prepared to co-operate with was a white-controlled Empire. In their attitude to Africans, Asians, and Coloured people, they were typical Afrikaners. In the early twentieth century, when social Darwinism pervaded the culture of the western world, Afrikaner race attitudes were not fundamentally different

---

[1] N. J. van der Merwe, *Marthinus Theunis Steyn: 'n Lewensbeskrywing.*
[2] C. M. van den Heever, *General J. B. M. Hertzog.*

from the attitudes that prevailed in Europe and the United States. There was certainly no great gulf between the position of Smuts and the position of Milner. For both, social equality across the colour line was unthinkable; equality of cultural attainment was impossible, except in rare individual cases; and political equality in a plural society like South Africa was undesirable, because Africans could not use political power wisely, and it would be suicidal for any white politician to espouse it. In reasoning thus, Milner and Smuts were dismissing the experience of the Cape Colony. As a Cape Colonial by birth and upbringing, Smuts was familiar with the Cape experience; and John X. Merriman reminded him of it in 1906. Merriman criticized Smuts's recommendation that the new Transvaal Constitution should include a political colour bar. To ignore the majority of the population, he wrote, was wrong in principle and would lead to a serious division in South Africa between the Cape Colony and the rest. It would be wiser to apply a modified version of the Cape Colonial system—to have a high, uniform, colour-blind franchise, which would not endanger white supremacy because the vast majority of those who qualified would be white men, but would nevertheless provide a safety-valve. To this, Smuts gave the paternalist rejoinder: '. . . it ought to be the policy of all parties to do justice to the Natives and to take all wise and prudent measures for their civilization and improvement. But I don't believe in politics for them.'[1]

There was a decisive difference between the two classes of people who were estranged by the conciliation policy. Afrikaners were able to work within the political apparatus provided by the colonial constitutions to safeguard their material and cultural group interests; but, except in the Cape Colony, Africans, Asians, and Coloured men had no legal means of exerting power within the system—and even there their power was very meagre.

4. The Making of the Union

By the time the swing of the political pendulum was completed by the formation of Merriman's *Bond*-supported ministry in the Cape Colony in February 1908, plans were being made for the unification of the four self-governing colonies. Indeed, there was a sense of urgency.

One reason for this feeling was economic: the existing system of trade relations in southern Africa was on the verge of collapse.[2] The system was governed in part by the Anglo-Portuguese *modus vivendi* which Milner had signed in 1901. In return for the grant to the gold-mining companies of the right to recruit African labourers in Mozambique, Milner

[1] *Smuts Papers*, ii. 242.
[2] R. J. Hammond, ch. 11; Thompson, pp. 52–60; J. van der Poel, *Railway and Customs Policies in South Africa, 1885–1910*, chs. 7–8.

had agreed that the railway freight rates between Lourenço Marques
and Johannesburg should be lower than those between the British
colonial ports and Johannesburg, by as much as they had been before
the war, and that the customs duties on goods entering the Transvaal
from Lourenço Marques should not be higher than those on goods
entering the Transvaal from the British colonial ports. The trade system
was also governed by railway and customs agreements that had been
made between the four British colonies under Milner's leadership in
1903, when the Transvaal and Orange River Colony were Crown
colonies. In 1908 this system was in a state of collapse, because of the
divergent interests of the four British colonies. Natal and the Cape
Colony, severely hit by the post-war recession and largely dependent on
railway and customs receipts for revenue, wished to raise the rates and
tariffs. The Transvaal and the Orange River Colony, less severely hit
by the recession and less dependent on rates and tariffs for revenue,
wished to lower the rates and tariffs in the interests of consumers of
imported goods. These basic conflicts of interest were complicated by
competition for the Witwatersrand trade between Lourenço Marques,
Durban, and the Cape colonial ports. Lourenço Marques appropriated an
ever-increasing share of the trade, basically because it was the closest
port to the Witwatersrand; and no Transvaal government dared break
the *modus vivendi*, because that would have resulted in the immediate
stoppage of the supply of Mozambique labourers to the gold-mining
industry. Furthermore, as each of several new railway connections was
opened, the flow of trade between the ports and the interior was changed.
Consequently, there was a series of crises. In 1906 the customs and railway agreements were patched up, but no party was satisfied—least of
all the Transvaal.

Soon after the Botha Government came into power, it gave notice
that the Transvaal intended to withdraw from the customs union—
notice that was due to expire on 1 July 1908. The events of the past few
years had shown that there was no way of regulating the customs tariff
and the railway rates to the satisfaction of all the colonies. The high
tariff need of the coastal colonies clashed with the low tariff need of the
Transvaal. The coastal colonies' appetite for the Transvaal trade clashed
with the Transvaal's interest in the Delagoa Bay route. Recent events
had also shown that the Transvaal held the whip hand. Thanks to her
possession of the one great industry in all South Africa, the coastal
colonies had become dependent upon her; and thanks to the position of
Delagoa Bay, she could afford to be independent of them. Economic
factors therefore pointed to two possibilities. Either the four colonies
could go their separate ways, in which case the Transvaal (in association, no doubt, with the Orange River Colony) would be able to prosper

by setting up a customs barrier against Natal and the Cape and concentrating her trade through Delagoa Bay, and the coastal colonies would be hard put to make ends meet; or the four colonies could join in a political union and thus bury the causes of their disputes. But one thing was clear: the half-way house of a customs union, buttressed by railway agreements, between independent administrations, had been tried and found wanting.[1]

Events in Natal were another factor that led many white South Africans to believe that some form of political union was urgently necessary. In spite of the fact that the South African War took place so soon after the last African chiefdoms had been incorporated in the Afrikaner republics and the British Empire, Africans made no major attempt to regain their independence during the war. In the Transvaal, Pedi and Tswana tribesmen attacked Afrikaners from time to time, but these were sporadic and unco-ordinated actions.[2] For the most part, Africans respected the instructions given them by both sides that they were to refrain from intervening in 'the white man's quarrel'. Nevertheless, in the eastern half of South Africa the white communities still felt insecure. Although all the chiefdoms were formally subject to white overrule, most of them were very lightly controlled. The white administrators were few and far between and had to rely on influence rather than force to exert authority.

Faced with the problems of depression finance, in 1905 the Natal Parliament enacted a poll tax of £1 a head. Early in the following year, when they began to collect the tax, the magistrates of the Umgeni and Greytown districts were defied and Bambata, a former chief whom the Government had deposed, crossed the Tugela and rallied several thousand Zulu to his side. The Natal militia quickly suppressed the rebellion, with a loss of thirty white men and some three thousand Africans. In 1907, having come to the conclusion that Dinuzulu, son of Cetshwayo and the head of the Zulu royal house, had been behind the rebellion and was plotting further resistance, the Natal Government re-mobilized the militia and arrested Dinuzulu; and in 1908 it placed him on trial on twenty-three counts of treason before a special court.[3]

By that time a government commission had revealed that the Natal Africans had substantial grievances. Many of them did not have enough land to live on and were the victims of financial extortions at the hands of private individuals. Moreover, since the retirement of Theophilus Shepstone the officials had lost contact with the chiefs so that there had

---

[1] The above paragraph is from Thompson, pp. 59–60.
[2] E.g. R. Kruger, pp. 417, 423–4; and *Smuts Papers*, i. 597–9.
[3] J. Stuart, *A History of the Zulu Rebellion, 1906, and of Dinuzulu's Arrest, Trial, and Expatriation.* A new work on the rebellion by Dr. Shula Marks will soon be published.

been no constitutional means for the redress of grievances.[1] Later, when Dinuzulu's trial was at last completed in March 1909, the presiding judge concluded that there was no evidence that he had fomented the 1906 rebellion or subsequently conspired to raise a further rebellion.[2]

These events had widespread repercussions. They undermined the confidence of the British community in Natal in its capacity to stand on its own feet and prepared it to consent to a political union with the other colonies, even at the risk of being ruled by Afrikaners. They caused politicians in the other colonies to fear the consequences if Natal was left to its own devices. They also alienated Natal from the British government and people. In particular, the decision of the Natal Government to suspend Dinuzulu's salary as a headman from the date of his arrest—which deprived him of the means to pay for his defence—was construed as mean and arbitrary conduct.[3]

The movement that led to the unification of South Africa had two distinct sources. One was imperialist, the other anti-imperialist. When Milner left South Africa in April 1905, most of the young men he had recruited remained behind to administer the former republics under Milner's successor, Lord Selborne, until power was transferred to the Botha and Fischer cabinets in 1907. These men, and Selborne himself, were more or less deeply imbued with Milner's imperialist philosophy, but they lacked his dogmatism and his narrowness of vision. After the change of government in Britain, they became anxious about the future of South Africa. This was not simply because they regretted Campbell-Bannerman's decision to give self-government to the Transvaal so soon after the war. They also feared that vested interests would be built up around the autonomy of each South African colony, that intercolonial economic disputes would continue, and that the High Commissioner would inexorably become involved as arbitrator, with the result that there would be a further revulsion against the imperial connection and a further weakening of British influence in South Africa. On the other hand, if the South African colonies were united, the intercolonial conflicts would disappear and the country might become prosperous enough to attract immigrants from Britain on a large scale. To Selborne and the members of the Kindergarten, therefore, unification was desirable not only because it would be beneficial to South Africans, but also because it seemed to be the one remaining way of achieving the most important of Milner's political objectives in South Africa—a British electoral majority.

Nevertheless, Selborne and his colleagues knew very well that they had to move extremely warily in the situation created by the defeat of the Unionists and the promise of self-government. Anything tainted

---

[1] *Natal Native Affairs Commission, 1906–1907, Report* and *Evidence.*
[2] Cd. 4585 (1909).   [3] Thompson, pp. 41–9.

with imperial interference would be suspect to Afrikaners. Accordingly, they tried to encourage South Africans to unite, without revealing their own motives. After preliminary discussions within the Kindergarten group and with some of their Progressive friends, Lionel Curtis resigned from his post as Assistant Colonial Secretary of the Transvaal in October 1906 and prepared a memorandum in which he set out the arguments for union in a way that was calculated to attract white South Africans of all backgrounds. Afrikaners and South Africans of British descent, the memorandum contended, were racially compatible and destined to fuse with one another. Even after the Transvaal and the Orange River Colony attained self-government, South Africans would still not have control of their own affairs if the colonies remained disunited, because their economic rivalries would continue to produce intercolonial clashes and the imperial government would be obliged to intervene. Union was also desirable so that a uniform 'native policy' could be devised and applied. Only then would white South Africans be secure against African uprisings and only then would the labour potential of the African population be rationally distributed. A united South Africa would be a strong and prosperous state and in due course it would extend its authority over the territories to its north.[1]

After Curtis's draft had been discussed and amended by the other members of the Kindergarten and by Selborne, it was arranged with Jameson, in his role of Prime Minister of the Cape Colony, that the Government of the Cape Colony should formally invite the High Commissioner to review the relations between the South African colonies. Then, in January 1907, Selborne sent copies of the memorandum, over his own signature, to all the South African governments and in July 1907 the memorandum was published.[2]

Unification was not merely the imperialists' prescription for South Africa. It had always been a declared objective of the Afrikaner *Bond* in the Cape Colony and many republican Afrikaners, too, had looked forward to the day when the South African states would be united. Before the war, however, it had always been beyond the bounds of practical politics, because the republicans could not contemplate surrendering their independence and the colonials saw no reason or method to reject the British connection. The war removed that difficulty. Anti-imperialists in all four colonies could look to unification as the means of consolidating the white South African communities and eliminating imperial interference. The depression, the economic disputes between the colonies, and the Natal rebellion strengthened their desire for union.

[1] Ibid., pp. 61–70.
[2] Cd. 3564 (1907); republished in B. Williams (ed.), *The Selborne Memorandum: a Review of the Mutual Relations of the British South African Colonies in 1907*.

However, as the Kindergarten campaign developed, they became anxious lest the country should be rushed into union on British and Progressive Party terms. Accordingly, Merriman poured cold water on the Selborne memorandum when it was published in July 1907 and restrained some of his more sanguine colleagues from giving it precipitate support, while Smuts and Botha declined to be drawn into too close an association with the popular movement for unification that Curtis and his colleagues were trying to launch in conjunction with mining magnates like Sir Abe Bailey. Eight months later, however, the situation had changed. The Orange River Colony as well as the Transvaal had become self-governing and Merriman had supplanted Jameson as Prime Minister of the Cape Colony, giving anti-imperialists control of three of the four self-governing colonies. Unification might now be achieved under anti-imperialist auspices. By that time, too, Botha and Smuts were beginning to encounter isolationist sentiment in the Transvaal *platteland*, where conservative Afrikaners were arguing that the Transvaal should go its own way and turn its back on the impoverished coastal colonies. Smuts therefore suggested—and the Cape and Orange River Colony leaders agreed—that in May 1908, when representatives of the colonies were due to meet to consider the Transvaal's notice to quit the customs union, they should initiate a process of unification.[1]

From then onwards the role of the Kindergarten was secondary. Curtis and his colleagues collected factual information which was published in *The Government of South Africa*;[2] they founded bipartisan Closer Union Societies up and down the country and launched a monthly journal, *The State*, to publicize the cause of union; and Smuts employed one of them, R. H. Brand, as his constitutional assistant—but it was South African politicians who controlled the process of unification.

The intercolonial conference of May 1908 patched up the railway and customs agreements again and recommended to the parliaments of the four self-governing colonies that they should appoint delegates to a National Convention, to prepare a draft constitution for a united South Africa. In the Convention, there were thirty delegates with voting rights —twelve from the Cape Colony, eight from the Transvaal, and five each from Natal and the Orange River Colony. Fifteen were members of the anti-imperialist ruling parties of the Cape Colony, the Transvaal, and the Orange River Colony; the parties in opposition to them had eight seats, Natal had five, and there were two Cape Colonial independents. Fourteen were Afrikaners, sixteen of British origin. They represented a full spectrum of white South African leaders, ranging from M. T. Steyn, the ex-President of the Orange Free State who came out of

---

[1] Thompson, pp. 70–82.
[2] Published anonymously in 2 vols., Cape Town, 1908.

retirement for the occasion, to L. S. Jameson, the Raider; and from Louis Botha, Jan Smuts, J. H. de la Rey, C. R. de Wet, and J. B. M. Hertzog, who had fought with the commandos during the war, to Sir George Farrar and Sir Percy Fitzpatrick, who were mining magnates.

The Convention sat behind closed doors in Durban and Cape Town, under the chairmanship of Sir Henry de Villiers, Chief Justice of the Cape Colony, between October 1908 and February 1909, when the delegates unanimously signed a report, including a draft constitution. This report was then debated by the colonial parliaments. In May 1909 the Convention reassembled in Bloemfontein to consider amendments that had been recommended by the parliaments of the Cape Colony and Natal and the delegates agreed unanimously upon an amended draft constitution. The amended draft was then approved unanimously by the parliaments of the Transvaal and the Orange River Colony and with only two dissentients by the parliament of the Cape Colony. In Natal, it was submitted to a referendum of the voters, when three-quarters of the votes cast were in favour. The four colonial governments then sent delegates to London to confer with Lord Crewe, the Colonial Secretary, after which the British Government introduced into Parliament a South Africa Bill, which was substantially the same as the draft adopted in South Africa, with verbal amendments that had been accepted by the colonial delegates. This Bill was enacted by Parliament without alteration. Finally, on 31 May 1910, exactly eight years after the Peace of Vereeniging, the four colonies became the constituent provinces of the Union of South Africa and Louis Botha formed a government.[1]

This was a notable victory for Botha and Smuts and their policy of conciliation. By the time the Convention first met, Smuts had devised a constitutional scheme that took account of the chief political forces that had to be reckoned with, circulated copies of his scheme to key delegates, amended it to make it acceptable to the delegates of the ruling parties in the Orange River Colony and the Cape Colony, and even made sure that, with one further change, it would be supported by the entire Transvaal delegation, Progressive and *Het Volk* alike. In the Convention, Smuts tactfully refrained from thrusting his own scheme forward, but the constitution that was hammered out point by point, and section by section, was in most respects similar to that which Smuts had prepared. Moreover, throughout the Convention, except for one moment of near collapse in Bloemfontein, the Transvaal delegates put aside their party differences and acted as a united team, setting an infectious example of Anglo-Afrikaner co-operation, so that both inside and outside the Convention people talked of a Convention spirit, and delegates with backgrounds as diverse as those of Botha and Jameson,

[1] Thompson, op. cit.

or Fitzpatrick and de la Rey, came to speak of a true peace between Boer and Briton.

5. *The Conditions of Union*

The conditions on which the four colonies joined together were the result of conflicts of regional and racial interests and ideologies. Five main issues were involved. Should power be concentrated in the new central government and (within the central government) in a cabinet responsible to Parliament, or should power be divided between the centre and the regions and (within the centre) between wholly distinct legislative and executive bodies? Who should have the right to take part in political elections and hold political offices? What electoral system should be adopted? What provisions, if any, should be made to protect Afrikaner culture? And what should be done about Basutoland, Bechuanaland Protectorate, Swaziland, the Rhodesias, and other possible recruits to a united South Africa? The decisions of the National Convention on these issues, determining the distribution of power and the ways in which it might lawfully be exercised, were to have enduring effects on the subsequent history of South Africa.[1]

Before any sort of combination became practical politics, most white South Africans had tended to assume that, if a combination was made, it would be federal in form, following the American, Canadian, and Australian precedents. But Merriman was a convinced unificationist from the first and, partly under his influence, Smuts moved closer and closer to a unitary position as he worked on his preparations for the Convention. Merriman and Smuts believed that federalism was an unnecessarily expensive form of government and they disliked the prospect that it might lead, as in the United States, to the appropriation of political functions by a non-elective body, the judiciary; whereas they considered that under union the central government would be able to act more promptly and effectively in an emergency and Afrikaners and British South Africans would more rapidly fuse into a single white nation.[2]

Opposition to unification was centred in Natal. The 'garden colony', with its British electoral majority, held aloof from the main currents of

---

[1] The chief publications dealing with the work of the National Convention are: (*a*) Contemporary sources: R. H. Brand, *The Union of South Africa*; G. R. Hofmeyr (ed.), *Minutes of Proceedings with Annexures (selected) of the South African National Convention . . .* ; [F. S. Malan], *Die Konvensie-dagboek van sy edelagbare François Stephanus Malan, 1908–1909*, J. F. Preller (ed.) VRS 1951; *Smuts Papers*, ii. 331–638; Sir E. H. Walton, *The Inner History of the National Convention of South Africa*; (*b*) Later works: the biographies of Smuts (Hancock, i. ch. 13), and the president of the Convention (E. A. Walker, *Lord de Villiers and His Times: South Africa 1842–1914*, chs. 24–6); and Thompson, op. cit.   [2] Thompson, pp. 101–9.

South African politics. Most of the colonists feared Afrikaner domination and would have liked to have been able to keep Natal separate from the other colonies. By 1908, however, that did not seem possible. Still in the grip of the post-war economic depression, Natal was particularly heavily dependent on the Witwatersrand trade, which might have been denied her altogether if the other colonies had united without her. Moreover, the 1906 rebellion and the Dinuzulu scare had created a demand for military support. Consequently, the Natal delegates went to the National Convention with a draft constitution for a loose federation, which would have given the white people of Natal financial relief and physical security, without depriving them of control over their internal affairs; and they were anxious that at the very least there should be effective safeguards for Natal's individuality, even if the constitution was basically unitary in form.[1]

This was the first substantial issue dealt with by the Convention. Merriman moved a resolution, which he had worked out with Smuts, to make each self-governing colony a province of a legislative union. Steyn supported the resolution, thereby removing any possibility that the two smallest colonies might stand together for states' rights, and the resolution was adopted with minor amendments. Later, the Convention created for each province an elected provincial council with power to make ordinances on several specified subjects—but except for school education these subjects were devoid of political significance. Moreover, all provincial ordinances were to require the endorsement of the central government before they became law, the head of the provincial government was to be appointed by the central Government, and Parliament was empowered to change the provincial constitutions without the consent of the provinces. Indeed, the constitution as adopted was more completely unitary than Smuts had anticipated in any of his pre-Convention plans. There were no true federal checks upon the power of the central Parliament.[2]

There were, however, a few sops to Natal opinion in the decisions concerning the structure of parliament. Many Convention delegates would have liked to have created a unicameral parliament, with the seats allotted without regard to the claims of Natal for special representation; but to appease Natal a second chamber—the Senate—was

[1] Ibid., pp. 165–71. Among other South Africans who expressed a preference for a federal form of union were W. P. Schreiner, who declined to be a member of the Convention because he was committed to defending Dinuzulu from the charges brought against him by the Natal Government, and his sister, Olive Schreiner, the author. See E. A. Walker, *W. P. Schreiner: A South African*, and Olive Schreiner, *Closer Union: A Letter on the South African Union and the Principles of Government.*

[2] Thompson, pp. 186–92, 248–60; Brookes and Webb, ch. 24; [F. S. Malan] pp. 22–39; Walton, ch. 3.

created, with eight members elected by the provincial councillors and the members of the House of Assembly for each province, and eight nominated by the Governor-General-in-Council (i.e. the central Government). Nevertheless, the Senate was made the weaker of the two parliamentary chambers, as was already the case with the House of Lords in England. It could neither originate nor amend money Bills (though it could reject them) and in the event of a disagreement between the two Houses the Governor-General could convene a joint sitting of both Houses, when the Bill would pass if it received a majority of the votes of the members present—in which case the Senate, with only forty members, would be likely to be overwhelmed by the House of Assembly, with an original membership of a hundred and twenty-one.[1] Natal, and also the Orange Free State, was also given some preferential treatment in the composition of the House of Assembly. The two smaller provinces were each to have at least seventeen members in the House until, under a complicated formula, the total membership reached a hundred and fifty, when the seats were to be distributed among the provinces in proportion to the numbers of their white male adult inhabitants.[2]

Closely linked with their preference for a unitary constitution was the belief of Smuts and Merriman in the British system of parliamentary supremacy. That is to say, they wanted the executive branch of government to be responsible to the legislative branch and they wanted the constitution to be flexible, so that the legislature would be able to pass laws on any subject, including laws amending the constitution itself, by bare majorities in both Houses. The South African precedents were not uniform on these questions. In both the Afrikaner republics, the president had been elected directly by the people and had not been responsible to the *Volksraad*; and, in addition, in the Orange Free State the constitution had guaranteed specific rights against amendment by the legislature and the constitution itself had only been amendable by a three-quarters majority in two successive annual sessions of the *Volksraad*. On the other hand, in each of the four colonies that were uniting the formal head of the executive was a governor representing the King, but the governor had to act on the advice of his cabinet, consisting of ministers who were members of and responsible to the colonial Parliament; a colonial Parliament enacted all types of legislation by the bare majority procedure; and the only legal limitations on its powers were imperial controls (such as the reservation of Bills on particular topics), which represented what was left of British supremacy over the colonies.[3]

Smuts and Merriman were more successful in getting their way on

---

[1] Thompson, pp. 203–12.   [2] Ibid., pp. 226–35.

[3] Ibid., pp. 97–101. The only South African who put the case for a rigid constitution and judicial interpretation was J. G. Kotzé, the former Chief Justice of the South African Republic.

these questions than they dared to hope before the Convention met. The constitution as adopted provided for the British cabinet system, with a governor-general as the formal head of the executive. It also gave parliament 'full power to make laws for the peace, order, and good government of the Union' and empowered Parliament to amend or repeal any section of the constitution by a law passed in the ordinary way by bare majorities in both Houses, with a few exceptions that are noted below. Thus, Natal was worsted on federalism and also on its desire for general constitutional rigidity. The British system of parliamentary supremacy was to prevail in South Africa.[1]

These recommendations of the Convention were bitterly attacked in the Natal press and Parliament and the Natal delegates went to the Bloemfontein session of the Convention with a sheaf of federal amendments, only to be outvoted by the other delegates for the second time. In the referendum campaign that followed, opponents of the constitution took an essentially racial attitude, predicting that union on the terms offered would lead to Afrikaner domination; but the delegates responded by pointing to the economic facts and the Natal electorate approved of union under the draft constitution by 11,121 votes to 3,701.[2]

Until the Convention met, there seemed to be a danger that the movement towards South African unity would collapse because of the differences among the franchise qualifications in the four colonies. How could the qualified, non-racial franchise of the Cape Colony be reconciled with the racial but otherwise unqualified franchise of the Transvaal and the Orange River Colony? White people in Natal as well as the inland colonies feared that if anything like the Cape franchise were adopted, white supremacy would be threatened; and since there were no non-white voters to consider in the Transvaal and the Orange River Colony and scarcely any in Natal, the delegates of those colonies were able to adopt an extreme view in the Convention. In the Cape Colony, on the other hand, the Coloured and African voters were numerous enough to affect the outcome of elections in many constituencies, with the result that the political parties competed for their votes and the legislature and executive acted with comparative restraint in dealing with their communities. Indeed, virtually all Cape politicians professed to approve of the principle of a non-racial franchise; and during the 1907–8 election the leaders of both the political parties in the Cape Colony gave assurances that they would not sacrifice the principle of 'equal rights for all civilized men', even for union. No doubt this was largely because the Cape franchise had proved to be innocuous from the white point of view

[1] Ibid., pp. 198–202, 204, 279–84.   [2] Ibid., pp. 193–6, 311–13, 348–62, 375–9.

during half a century of operation, but there were a few white politicians who sincerely believed that under a political colour-bar the non-white communities would not be justly treated.[1]

Pressures for a liberal solution were also exerted by African and Coloured organizations, by British liberals, and by the British Government. The Coloured community's African Political Organization, which had branches in the inland colonies as well as in the Cape Colony, petitioned the Convention for the grant of political rights to all 'fully civilised' people.[2] A Witwatersrand group of Africans, calling themselves the Transvaal National Natives Union, presented a similar petition.[3] J. A. Hobson, the English economist, and several Liberal parliamentary backbenchers wrote to try to persuade Smuts and Merriman to give African and Coloured men a share of power; and in May 1908 Colonel J. E. B. Seeley, the Colonial Under-Secretary, gave the House of Commons the assurance that the British Government was committed to providing Africans with some special representation to safeguard their rights.[4]

On the other hand, the Africans in the Cape Colony were comparatively quiescent before the Convention met, in spite of the fact that they were the only African community in South Africa with an effective say in the existing political system. Both the leading Bantu newspapers of the Colony—J. T. Jabavu's *Imvo* which supported the South African Party and A. K. Soga's *Izwi La Bantu* which supported the Progressives —expressed some apprehensions about the union movement, but nevertheless advised their readers to trust the Cape delegates to look after their interests in the Convention. This was partly, no doubt, a direct response to the declarations that had been made by the white leaders of both the political parties; but it was also because the Africans who participated in the colonial political system and controlled the Bantu newspapers were for the most part drawn from the new class of ministers of religion, teachers, clerks, small traders, and farmers with individual tenure. All of them derived benefits and prestige from their status as voters, had an interest in consolidating their position as an educated class, distinct from the 'tribal' masses, and feared to jeopardize their position by showing distrust of the white political leadership.[5]

Merriman and Smuts had given careful thought to this problem in preparing for the Convention. Early in 1908, Merriman wrote to Smuts to say that the difficulty might be overcome by allowing the different

[1] Thompson, pp. 109–16. There are mines of relevant information in *South African Native Affairs Commission, 1903–5, Report and Appendices*, and in *Natal Native Affairs Commission, Report and Evidence*. See also McCracken, ch. 6.　　　[2] Thompson, p. 214.

[3] Ibid., p. 215.　　　　　　　　　　　　[4] Ibid., pp. 121–3; *Smuts Papers*, ii. 437–8.

[5] Thompson, pp. 214–15. See also S. Trapido, 'African Divisional Politics in the Cape Colony, 1884–1910', *JAH*, 9, 1 (1968), 79–98.

colonial franchise laws to continue to operate in each province after union, and protecting the established rights of the Cape African and Coloured communities against hasty amendment by the Union Parliament.[1]

When the subject was first debated in the Convention, most of the delegates favoured some solution that could be applied uniformly throughout the union, though they differed as to what that solution should be. Colonel W. E. M. Stanford, a former Transkei administrator, supported by other Cape delegates, proposed a uniform, non-racial franchise; Sir Percy Fitzpatrick wanted universal suffrage for white men and votes for those African, Coloured, and Asian men who could pass a test of 'civilization'; and F. R. Moor, Prime Minister of Natal, supported by Louis Botha and other northern delegates, wanted an absolute political colour bar; while Merriman moved a resolution for the continuation of the existing colonial franchise laws, with safeguards for the non-white communities in the Cape Province. After a long and heated debate, the problem was referred to a committee.[2]

The committee had before it, besides the recommendations that had been made in debate, important information concerning the attitude of the British Government. Sir Henry de Villiers, as president of the Convention, was anxious that the delegates should succeed not only in agreeing among themselves upon a constitution for a united South Africa, but also in producing a scheme that would be acceptable to the British Parliament, which alone had the legal competence to give legal effect to it. To this end, he played his cards very skilfully. First, he invited Lord Selborne, as High Commissioner, to make his views known to the Convention. Selborne's reply proposed a scheme for the registration as voters of African, Coloured, and Asian men who could obtain a certificate of 'civilization' from a judge, and warned the Convention that the British Government's attitude to the incorporation of Basutoland, Bechuanaland Protectorate, and Swaziland in the proposed union would be affected by the decision on the franchise. In answer to a further inquiry from de Villiers, Selborne wrote that if the Convention could not agree upon a uniform franchise, he was confident that the British Government would be 'wholly sympathetic' with a solution along the lines proposed by Merriman. Selborne also declared that he did not think the British Government would object to a provision making non-white people ineligible for membership of parliament, if the constitution was otherwise acceptable. Taking this letter as a green light for imperial endorsement, the committee and the Convention acted upon Merriman's plan. The draft constitution provided for the maintenance

[1] Ibid., pp. 120–6; *Smuts Papers*, ii.
[2] Thompson, pp. 215–20; [F. S. Malan], pp. 40–59; Walton, pp. 118–44.

of the existing franchise laws in each province of the Union until they were altered by the Union parliament, and for the protection of the non-white peoples of the Cape Province from disfranchisement on racial grounds by the requirement that any such Bill should be passed by both Houses of Parliament sitting together and at the third reading be agreed to by not less than two-thirds of the total membership of both Houses. The draft constitution included two related provisions—one to appease the liberals and the other to appease the northern delegates. Four of the eight nominated senators were to be 'selected on the ground mainly of their thorough acquaintance, by reason of their official experience or otherwise, with the reasonable wants and wishes of the Coloured races in South Africa'; but every Member of Parliament was to be of 'European descent'.[1]

When the draft constitution was published, these decisions were criticized from both sides. In the parliamentary debates in the northern colonies, there were severe attacks on the continuation of the non-white franchise in the Cape Province, several speakers revealing a strong desire to expunge it at the earliest possible moment.[2] On the other hand, W. P. Schreiner, the former Prime Minister of the Cape Colony, who had not been a member of the Convention, described the draft constitution as 'illiberal and short-sighted in its conception of the people of South Africa'.[3] African journalists and clergy denounced the franchise provisions and the exclusion of non-whites from Parliament and they convened a 'Native Convention', which met in Bloemfontein in March 1909 and passed resolutions declaring that the Imperial Government was 'bound by both fundamental and specific obligations towards the Native and Coloured races of South Africa to extend to them the same measure of equitable justice as is extended to those of European descent'.[4] The Coloured community reacted vigorously. After holding meetings in sixty places, the A.P.O. convened a conference in Cape Town, where the delegates protested against the exclusion of non-Europeans from Parliament and the insecurity of the Cape franchise, and asked that the franchise be extended to all 'qualified persons' in the northern provinces.[5] The Bloemfontein session of the National Convention had before it these resolutions and also a letter signed by clergy of all the leading Protestant Churches in South Africa, except the Dutch Reformed Churches, deploring a political colour bar. Nevertheless, the Convention ignored these appeals and made no changes in the relevant sections of the draft constitution.[6]

Thwarted in South Africa, the A.P.O. and the Native Convention

---

[1] Thompson, pp. 220–6; Walker, de Villiers, ch. 25
[2] Thompson, pp. 329, 332–4, 358.   [3] Ibid., pp. 315–16.
[4] Ibid., pp. 325–6.   [5] Ibid., pp. 326–7.   [6] Ibid., p. 375.

organized a deputation to London. The deputation was led by Schreiner and included Dr. Abdurahman, the president of the A.P.O., J. T. Jabavu, the editor of *Imvo*, and the Revd. W. Rubusana. They took with them an appeal to the British Government and Parliament signed by twenty-two prominent white inhabitants of the Cape Colony. Schreiner and his colleagues did their best, arguing their case in an interview with Lord Crewe, the Colonial Secretary, at meetings with members of Parliament and of the Anti-Slavery and Aborigines Protection Society, and in statements and letters to the press. The *Manchester Guardian* supported them; and so did a number of influential people, notably Sir Charles Dilke, M.P., G. P. Gooch, M.P., W. T. Stead, and Sir Harry Johnston. Nevertheless, the leaders of both parties welcomed the South Africa Bill as the best possible sequel to the grant of responsible government to the former republics. Though many members of Parliament would have preferred that the constitution should not have contained a political colour bar, most of them reasoned that it was politically impracticable to attempt to alter the unanimous recommendations of the National Convention and the nearly unanimous wishes of the parliaments of four self-governing colonies. Furthermore, the official delegates of the colonies did what they could to discredit Schreiner, insisted that they were not authorized to consider amendments of substance to the draft constitution, and declared that any British attempts at interference would do more harm than good to the non-white peoples of South Africa, whereas, they argued, if there was no interference, white South Africans could be trusted to promote the real interests of their fellow countrymen. The result was that Lord Crewe made no attempt to modify the relevant provisions, and the members of both front benches defended them in both Houses of Parliament.[1] In the House of Lords, no amendment was carried to a division. In the House of Commons, although some Liberal backbenchers, Irish Nationalists, and Labour members fought the colour bar to the end, no amendment received more than fifty-seven votes. The dominant mood was expressed by H. H. Asquith, the Prime Minister, who declared that 'Any control or interference from outside . . . is in the very worst interests of the natives themselves. . . . I anticipate that, as one of the incidental advantages which the Union of South Africa is going to bring about, it will prove to be a harbinger of a native policy more consistent, and . . . more enlightened than that which has been pursued by some communities in the past.'[2] Nevertheless in his last speech on the Bill he added: 'While we part from this measure without any . . . amendment . . . I am sure our fellow subjects will not take it in bad part if we respectfully and very

[1] Ibid., pp. 402–32; Walker, *Schreiner*.
[2] *Parl. Deb.*, 5th Ser., Commons, ix, col. 1010.

earnestly beg them at the same time that they, in the exercise of their undoubted and unfettered freedom, should find it possible sooner or later, and sooner rather than later, to modify the provisions.'[1] In this way the British Government and Parliament finally washed their hands of responsibility for the political rights of Africans, Asians, and Coloured people.

The controversy that gave most concern to the Convention and came closest to wrecking the entire unification movement did not concern the political role of the subordinate communities, but the distribution of power within the dominant, white community. This was inevitable. In the three colonies where political parties existed, the principal political division was the same: parties that were predominantly rural and Afrikaner versus parties that were predominantly urban and British. Any constitution for a united South Africa would therefore establish the ground rules for later phases in an existing political struggle. The South African Party, the *Orangia Unie*, and *Het Volk* would benefit if the rules were like those that had always prevailed in the Cape Colony. There, the constitutional ordinance of 1853 had divided the colony into constituencies based on administrative divisions, in such a way as to allot more voters to a House of Assembly seat in the urban than the rural constituencies. Although additional seats had been created from time to time by legislation, the initial advantage to the rural voters had never been eliminated. In 1909 the main urban constituencies of the Cape peninsula, Port Elizabeth, East London, and Kimberley contained forty-three per cent of the electorate and returned only twenty-four per cent of the members of the House of Assembly. As they looked ahead to the aftermath of union, including the prospects of further British immigration to the towns and the incorporation of Rhodesia as a fifth province, the South African Party delegates to the Convention regarded it as essential that they should preserve the traditional rural advantage in the Cape Province and apply it also to the other provinces. In this contest, they had natural allies in the *Orangia Unie* delegation. They also had allies among the Natal delegates, since the electoral system of Natal was like that of the Cape Colony. In 1908 Durban and Pietermaritzburg had thirty-eight per cent of the voters and returned only nineteen per cent of the members of the Natal Legislative Assembly, with the result that rural politicians dominated the political system in Natal and although they were of British descent they tended to ally themselves with the rural interest on this issue.[2]

If the *Het Volk* delegation had supported the S.A.P., the O.U., and the Natal delegates, they would collectively have had a large majority in the Convention; but this did not happen. The Progressive and *Het*

---

[1] *Parl. Deb.*, 5th Ser., Commons, ix, col. 1657.   [2] Thompson, pp. 126–31.

Volk leaders had debated the question at great length before the West Ridgeway committee in 1906, with the result that the Transvaal Constitution had created an electoral system that went a long way towards meeting the Progressive demand for 'Equal Rights' (pp. 335-6). As they prepared for the Convention, the Progressive delegates insisted that Equal Rights should also be included in any constitution for a united South Africa. By Equal Rights they meant, firstly, that each Member of Parliament should represent, as nearly as possible, the same number of voters (not white inhabitants, because the British population of South Africa still included a far higher proportion of adult men than the Afrikaner population); and secondly, that the constituencies should be freshly delimited at regular intervals by impartial commissions (to take account of the expected immigration of English-speaking people). In making these demands, the Progressives were supported by Curtis and the other members of the Kindergarten, and also by Lord Selborne who, as we have seen (p. 346), was hoping that union would stimulate British immigration. Smuts and Botha yielded to this pressure. The Transvaal election of 1907 had shown them that, even where rural Afrikaners and urban British people were as evenly matched as they then were in the Transvaal, a moderate Afrikaner party was capable of winning elections without the assistance of loaded constituencies. They therefore concluded that to accept the Progressive demand for Equal Rights was not too high a price to pay for the bipartisan support that would be a striking demonstration of their conciliation policy. Accordingly, the Transvaal delegation went to the Convention as a united team, pledged to give effect to Equal Rights. On Smuts's advice, they were also committed to proportional representation, with the single transferable vote—a system which British enthusiasts had persuaded Smuts would help to moderate the tensions between the two sections of the white population.[1]

After heated exchanges, the Convention in its first report adopted the Transvaal scheme, but with qualifications. Electoral divisions were to return three or more members to the House of Assembly by proportional representation—except in special cases of sparsely populated areas where divisions might return fewer members. After every quinquennial census, a judicial commission was to delimit the divisions on the voters' basis— but the commission was to be permitted to depart from equality by up to fifteen per cent either way from the average (as in the Transvaal Constitution), and in so doing it was to give consideration not only to the four factors mentioned in the Transvaal Constitution (p. 336), but also to a fifth factor, 'sparsity or density of population'.[2]

[1] Ibid., pp. 131-4; Sir P. Fitzpatrick, *South African Memories*; *Smuts Papers*, ii.
[2] Thompson, pp. 235-42.

When this report was published in February 1909, the electoral provisions met with a barrage of criticism from Afrikaners in the Cape Colony. Politicians did sums and concluded that the S.A.P. would not win a majority of the Cape Province seats on the terms set out in the draft constitution.[1] When the Cape Parliament met, Merriman yielded to the pressure from below and supported a resolution demanding that all rural divisions should have fifteen per cent fewer and all urban divisions fifteen per cent more voters than the average.[2] These manœuvres provoked violent reaction in the English South African press and Lord Selborne himself wrote to tell Botha that if the Equal Rights provisions were mutilated, 'there is no sacrifice or effort which I would not . . . make to prevent the consummation of . . . Union . . .'.[3]

The Bloemfontein session of the National Convention was a stormy one. The S.A.P. and O.U. delegates made concerted efforts to carry the Cape amendments. The Progressives held private consultations with Selborne. The solidarity of the Transvaal delegation collapsed. For a time, it looked as though the Convention would disintegrate in anger. Eventually, however, the Convention accepted a compromise based on a proposal of Sir Henry de Villiers. Proportional representation was abandoned; the electoral divisions were to return one member each to the House of Assembly. The rest of the scheme that the Convention had previously agreed upon was not touched, but Bills passed by the South African Parliament to amend any part of the electoral system were to be reserved for the royal pleasure (i.e. for decision by the British Government).[4]

Sir Percy Fitzpatrick and his Progressive colleagues regarded these decisions as a victory. They considered that their essential demands had been met and they did not regret the dropping of proportional representation, which had not originally figured in their platform but had been added to it by Smuts as a result of lobbying by the English Proportional Representation Society.[5] That was also the view in Britain, where both the major parties welcomed the Bill as a 'token of reconciliation', 'the most wonderful issue' out of the discord of the past, and the Liberal Party claimed it as a major political achievement.[6]

From the Progressive point of view, the electoral system that was thus embodied in the South African Constitution was certainly a great advance on the methods that had prevailed in the South African Republic before the war and that had continued to prevail in the Cape Colony down to the time of union. But Fitzpatrick and the other Progressive and Unionist members of the Convention had failed to foresee the consequences of the concessions they had made in allowing a differential

---

[1] Thompson, pp. 315–25. [2] Ibid., pp. 336–48. [3] Ibid., pp. 362–5.
[4] Ibid., pp. 365–72. [5] Ibid., pp. 372–4. [6] Ibid., pp. 416–32.

of up to thirty per cent in the number of voters to a division, with 'sparsity or density of population' as one of the criteria for applying the differential. In practice, this criterion was to be given great weight by all delimitation commissions, to the immense advantage of the party representing the rural voters. In all elections, this was to be a significant factor; in elections where the numerical strengths of the predominantly urban party and the predominantly rural party were approximately equal, it was to be crucial—as in 1948, when it enabled Dr. D. F. Malan to form a government.

While Progressive support for unification depended mainly on the electoral system, the support of the *Orangia Unie* delegates depended on the Convention's decision on the language question. J. B. M. Hertzog feared that the Afrikaner people would indeed be denationalized, as Milner had intended, if the modern industrial sector of the economy continued to expand under the control of English-speaking people, unless special steps were taken to protect Afrikaner culture; and he discerned the crucial importance of language to the survival of a distinctive national group in a plural society. Early in 1908 he piloted through the Orange River Colony Parliament a bill to place the Dutch and English languages on exactly the same footing in the public schools of the colony, by making the home language of the pupil the medium of instruction up to standard IV, and both English and Dutch the media of instruction thereafter, each in exactly half of the curriculum. This Act was denounced by the English-medium press throughout South Africa, which described Hertzog as the incarnation of narrow, exclusive, anti-British nationalism; and he in turn concluded that his fears were amply justified. Consequently, Hertzog decided that he could only support union if the Constitution provided absolute security for the survival of Dutch, by giving it equal treatment with English in Parliament and in the civil service, the law courts, and the public schools through-the country. In this, he had the support of his *Orangia Unie* colleagues, including the immensely prestigious ex-President Steyn, and some of the Afrikaner delegates from the other colonies.[1]

Hertzog's diagnosis of the intentions of the English-speaking delegates was correct. Men like Jameson and Fitzpatrick associated Dutch—and especially Afrikaans—with cultural backwardness, and hoped and assumed that in the course of time English would oust it from South Africa. Even Merriman believed that this would happen; while neither Botha nor Smuts was associated with the Afrikaner cultural movement and neither of them was sensitive to the intensity of feeling of Hertzog and his colleagues. Consequently, the Transvaalers arrived at the

[1] Ibid., pp. 34–6, 135–8; van den Heever, op. cit.; van der Merwe, ii.

Convention assuming that Hertzog should be satisfied with a brief resolution declaring that both English and Dutch would be official languages
of the Union and usable in Parliament and the law courts; while Hertzog
arrived with a long and detailed resolution, designed to make it compulsory for all civil servants to know both languages, and he declined
to play an active part in the Convention until this question had been
settled. Accordingly, the question came up for discussion during the
first week of the Convention. Hertzog and Steyn made impassioned and
moving speeches for the fullest recognition of Dutch. To their surprise,
the English-speaking delegates responded in a conciliatory manner, and
after informal discussions Hertzog's resolution was unanimously adopted
in an abbreviated form, but still containing the key phrase that, besides
being declared to be official languages, 'English and Dutch . . . shall be
treated on a footing of equality, and possess and enjoy freedom, rights
and privileges. . . .' Later, when the Convention decided to make the
voting rights of the non-white communities in the Cape Province alter-
able only by a two-thirds majority of both Houses of Parliament, Hertzog persuaded the Convention that the same protection should be given
to the language section. With these decisions, Hertzog and his colleagues
were content. Although they had not gone so far as Hertzog had hoped,
they seemed to provide an adequate legal basis for the preservation of
the Dutch language, and with it Afrikaner culture, in the face of the
anglicizing forces emanating from the towns.[1]

Even though the four self-governing colonies were the only founder
members of the Union, it was generally assumed at the time, by white
politicians in South Africa as well as in Britain, that when the Union
had solved its teething problems it would, as a matter of course, absorb
the other British territories in southern Africa and indeed in central
Africa. These territories fell into two main groups: Southern Rhodesia,
North-Eastern Rhodesia, and North-Western Rhodesia, which were
administered by the British South Africa Company under its royal
charter; and Basutoland, Bechuanaland Protectorate, and Swaziland,
which were administered by the High Commissioner for South Africa.

Southern Rhodesia was considered to be nearly ripe for incorporation;
but before they committed themselves the settlers—a predominantly
British community of twelve thousand people—wanted to build up their
numerical strength under the shelter of the Company and to satisfy
themselves that the Union was not going to fall under Afrikaner domination. Three Southern Rhodesian delegates—two nominated by the
Company and one elected by the settlers—attended the Convention, with

[1] Van den Heever, pp. 267–9; [F. S. Malan], pp. 24–5, 38–47; van der Merwe, ii. 227–9;
Walton, pp. 97–108; Thompson, pp. 192–8.

the right to speak but not to vote; and the Constitution included a provision empowering the King to issue an order-in-council incorporating the territories administered by the Company in the Union, on receipt of requests from both South African Houses of Parliament.[1]

The future of the High Commission Territories was not so easily settled. Smuts and most of the other members of the Convention hoped that they would be included in the Union from the beginning, but the British Government would not permit this. It recognized that it had special obligations to the African inhabitants of those territories, in consequence of the circumstances under which they had been incorporated in the British Empire; and it knew that the leading chiefs did not desire to be placed under the control of white South Africans. On the other hand, the British Government expected that it would eventually become impracticable to continue to administer them from London. Accordingly, Lord Selborne suggested to the Convention that the Constitution should empower the British Government to transfer the territories to the Union at some unspecified later date, subject to conditions to be set out in the Constitution for the protection of the African inhabitants. This suggestion was adopted. A section of the Constitution empowered the King to issue an order-in-council transferring the territories to the Union, which would then rule the territories subject to conditions laid down in the schedule to the Constitution. This schedule spelt out the ways in which the British Government hoped to safeguard the interests of the African inhabitants after their incorporation in the Union—for example, by prohibiting the alienation of African land. The drafting of the schedule gave rise to sharp disputes between the British Government and the Convention and, later, between the British Government and the South African delegates who went to London in 1909. However, its contents never went into operation and they ceased to have legal significance after the Union became a sovereign state as a result of the enactment of the Statute of Westminster (1931) and the Status of the Union Act (1934).[2]

6. Conclusion

In 1910 British policy-makers at last attained their primary goal in South Africa. The South Africa Act united the territories occupied by white people in a British Dominion under a government which could fairly claim to represent both the white communities and which was led by men who were sincerely committed to a policy of Anglo-Afrikaner

---

[1] L. H. Gann, *A History of Southern Rhodesia*, pp. 208–18; J. P. R. Wallis, *One Man's Hand: The Story of Sir Charles Coghlan and the Liberation of Southern Rhodesia*; Thompson, pp. 150–1, 269–71.

[2] Lord Hailey, *Native Administration*, Part V; R. P. Stevens, *Lesotho, Botswana, and Swaziland*; Thompson, pp. 124–6, 271–9, 407–14.

conciliation and co-operation with the other members of the British Empire. H. H. Asquith and Lord Crewe presided over the creative withdrawal that had eluded a long line of predecessors, stretching back to Sir George Grey (Vol. I, pp. 432–3). Crewe expressed the cabinet's satisfaction in the House of Lords. The unification of South Africa, he said, would place the self-governing British Dominions in something like their final form: 'There is the great American group, the great Pacific group, and the great African group. There may be some re-arrangement and some modification, but it is, I think, reasonable to say that for many years to come, longer than the life of any of us here, these three great divisions will form the main self-governing parts of the British Empire outside these islands.'[1]

On the other hand, as Asquith was aware when he made his final speech on the South Africa Bill in the House of Commons (pp. 357–8), in attaining the primary goal of its South African policy, Britain had sacrificed the secondary goal. That goal had been set out by Lord Stanley, Colonial Secretary, in 1842, when he had instructed Sir George Napier that in annexing Natal it was 'absolutely essential . . . That there shall not be in the eye of the law any distinction of colour, origin, race, or creed; but that the protection of the law, in letter and in substance, shall be extended impartially to all alike.'[2] Any final assessment of the achievement of an imperial power must depend largely upon the sort of society it left behind when it withdrew. In withdrawing from South Africa, Great Britain left behind a caste-like society, dominated by its white minority. The price of unity and conciliation was the institutionalization of white supremacy.[3]

The remaining chapters of this book show how political forces have operated within the framework that was devised by the National Convention and given legal efficacy by the British Parliament. There have been three related processes: the struggle among the white people of South Africa for control of the machinery of government by winning elections (Chapter VIII); diverse attempts by the non-white peoples of South Africa to obtain a share in the control of the machinery of government, with a view to changing the racial structure of society (Chapter IX); and the elimination of the last vestiges of British imperial authority over South Africa and the warding off of new external challenges to the system of white supremacy (Chapter X).

[1] *Parl. Deb.*, 5th Ser., Lords, ii, col. 767.   [2] Vol. i, p. 372.

[3] Since 1910 the constitutional history of South Africa has been evolutionary. Even the change to a republic in 1961 did not mark a break in continuity. The new constitution was merely the South Africa Act of 1909 as amended from time to time by the South African Parliament, and revised to replace the Governor-General by an elected President as the formal head of state, when all extant laws not specifically repealed or amended by the new constitution remained in force. See H. R. Hahlo and E. Kahn, *The Union of South Africa: The Development of its Laws and Constitution*, and E. Kahn, *The New Constitution: being a supplement to South Africa, the Development of its Laws and Constitution*.

VIII

AFRIKANER NATIONALISM

1. *Introduction*

FROM their earliest days the Afrikaner[1] people have felt themselves threatened, from inside their borders and from without, to a degree few other nations or groups have experienced or believed. At times the threat to their national identity or to their distinct and separate existence was real and serious, at others it was long-range and tenuous; often it was more illusory than real. But it was always a factor, even when it was manufactured by a leadership aware of the efficacy of danger as a rallying and unifying political call. Hence the almost paranoiac persistence with which some enemy or threat or peril appears in the story of Afrikaner nationalism.

The fear of domination or absorption or being, in the country's idiom, 'ploughed under', came, originally, from the presence in their midst or on their insecure frontier, of the numerically superior and usually undeveloped indigenous races, which were all non-white. Subsequently the fear was directed at the British Government and the settlers who had migrated to South Africa from 1820 onwards. And finally, again, at the African, Coloured, and Asian peoples as well as their white fellow countrymen who spoke English. In the case of the English-speakers it was a fear that the Afrikaner people would be absorbed by or have to merge their identity with the rest of the white peoples and so form a broadly based South African nation (as distinct from an Afrikaner nation with appendages) with its own more inclusive nationalism and speaking two languages. The idea that Coloured, still less African or Asian people, should form one nation with the Afrikaner was never entertained.[2]

All this helped to influence Afrikanerdom's[3] character and philosophy

---

[1] Afrikaner: A white inhabitant of South Africa whose home language is Afrikaans. The official Afrikaans dictionary, *Woordeboek van die Afrikaanse Taal* (Pretoria, 1950) defines 'Afrikaner' thus: 'One who is Afrikaans by descent or birth; one who belongs to the Afrikaans-speaking population group.' So far as is known, the word was first used on 6 Mar. 1707, when Hendrik Bibault declared at Stellenbosch: 'Ik ben een Africaander.'

[2] In 1965, Afrikaners constituted just under 60 per cent of the white population of South Africa; most of the remainder spoke English. In the 1960 census about 2 per cent gave their home language as both English and Afrikaans.

[3] Afrikanerdom in this chapter—and in much South African writing—is frequently referred to as personified. This is how Afrikaners regard it; they put it above the individual and deliberately accord it a personality.

decisively.[1] The will to survive against odds called for faith, courage, and determination, but it also produced a spirit of defensiveness and something of an inferiority complex which manifested itself in various ways. Isolated for generations from the main stream of Western thought and action, and surrounded and outnumbered by underdeveloped and often backward peoples of different colour and culture, the Afrikaner had already realized in the eighteenth century that to retain his separate identity he would have to remain aloof from other races, especially non-whites. If to do this effectively and avoid being submerged or absorbed entailed the domination of other groups, so it had to be.

It came about, therefore, that the numerically small and widely dispersed Afrikaner people, descendants of Dutch, French, and German immigrants, with a later sprinkling of British, gradually developed a group consciousness which, by the end of the nineteenth century, had grown into a national cohesion with its own distinctive philosophy and way of life.[2]

It was the war between Britain and the Transvaal in 1880–1 that finally gave form and content to the nationalism latent in the Afrikaner people[3] although the growth of nationalism in Europe during the latter part of the nineteenth century undoubtedly left its mark on Afrikaner thinking. In the same way the nationalism in Europe after 1918, and in Africa after 1945, made an impact on Afrikaner nationalism and contributed to its character as part of a world-wide phenomenon. Undoubtedly, however, the elation and pride which flowed from the victory in the battle of Majuba in the 'First War of Independence' did much to stimulate that Afrikaner consciousness which had already found expression in the formation of the *Afrikaner Bond* in the Cape by the Revd. S. J. du Toit in 1879, and made the people still more aware of their separate identity and their potential strength.[4]

---

[1] 'In essence Afrikaans nationalism was a question of the heart. As a result of British politics in South Africa, a nationalism developed that showed signs of a feeling of injustice and frustration. There was a feeling of inferiority, of having been insulted, of having been looked down upon, and of having had honour and dignity offended.'—F. A. van Jaarsveld, *The Awakening of Afrikaner Nationalism*, p. 221.

[2] By the 1960s the following kind of sometimes unintelligible mysticism was occasionally used to explain the genesis of Afrikaner Nationalism and justify its existence: 'The invisible flame which burns but does not consume, the invisible national flame which inspired the Afrikaner to political-republican independence in his own country, forms a part of this Western nationalism. It became visible as the Afrikaner's own presentation of reality in his own language and image of the world; as an Afrikaans mode of social intercourse and co-existence . . .'. P. J. Meyer, in *Die Republiek van Suid-Afrika*, ed. F. A. van Jaarsveld and G. D. Scholtz, p. 289. (All quotations from Afrikaans sources in this chapter have been translated into English.)

[3] 'As far as the coming into being and continued existence of the Afrikaner nation is concerned, the struggle of the Free Burghers (in Simon van der Stel's time) ranks equally with the Great Trek and the First War of Freedom.'—G. D. Scholtz, in *Die Republiek van Suid-Afrika*, p. 26.   [4] Van Jaarsveld, *Awakening*, p. 10.

From the outset, Afrikaners had difficulty in deciding what their attitude to their English-speaking fellow citizens should be, a difficulty which was to continue plaguing them down the years. Du Toit began by believing in an exclusive Afrikaner unity. But J. H. ('Onze Jan') Hofmeyr, a co-founder of the *Bond*, had other ideas: he made the organization his instrument for achieving linguistic and cultural equality between the two sections of the European population.[1] He went further, and used it to achieve a partnership between the two groups in the same way that James Barry Munnik Hertzog, the father of modern Afrikaner nationalism, tried to do half a century later.[2] These two conceptions of nationhood, a 'pure' Afrikaner unity on the one hand, and a broadly based white South African unity on the other, were to vie with one another with periodic intensity in the years ahead: after the Anglo-Boer War in the Botha–Smuts era, before and during the Second World War in the Hertzog period, and finally after South Africa had become a republic in 1961.

The Afrikaner consciousness which took root in the last quarter of the nineteenth century was stimulated in the Cape Colony, and particularly in the two Afrikaner Republics, by the folly of the Jameson Raid (inevitably identified with Rhodes and British imperialism). The misery of the concentration camps and Kitchener's farm-burning policy in the Anglo-Boer War, together with the way in which these came to be exploited in later years, added to the emotion, as did the attempt of Milner to anglicize the people of the Orange River Colony and Transvaal during the period of reconstruction following the war.[3]

To a degree, therefore, modern Afrikaner nationalism was a reaction and a response to British imperial policy of the late nineteenth and early twentieth centuries. The Anglo-Boer War, in fact, probably did more to unite Afrikanerdom and infuse it with purpose and determination than any other single factor before or after. 'The war gave to Afrikaners throughout South Africa common victims to mourn, common injuries upon which to brood, a common cause in the restoration of republicanism and, in the tragic figure of Kruger, dead in exile, a martyr around whom myths could be woven.'[4]

If the disappearance of the two Boer republics was not to mean also the disappearance of the Afrikaner people as a distinct and separate nation with its own history, traditions, religion, philosophy, language, and culture, then what had been lost in the 'Second War of Independence'

---

[1] W. H. Hancock: *Are there South Africans?*, p. 14.　　　　[2] Ibid., p. 16.

[3] 'President Steyn said that the war, with its common suffering, losses, sacrifices and heroism had awakened the feeling of brotherhood among Afrikaners and produced the political ideal of a re-established republicanism.'—M. C. E. van Schoor, in *Die Republiek van Suid-Afrika*, p. 145.

[4] G. H. L. le May, *British Supremacy in South Africa*, p. 213.

had to be regained and reconstructed. The war had failed to deprive the Free Staters and Transvaalers of their sense of nationhood and their feeling of racial integrity. At the same time it had restored the bond between the Boers of the Cape and the Boers of the ex-republics—a bond which time and distance had tended to weaken.[1]

The establishment of some two hundred Christian-National Education schools in the Transvaal and Orange River Colony out of funds collected from the people was proof, if any were needed, that the Afrikaners had no intention of abandoning their traditions and their language, no matter how determinedly Milner tried to undermine them.

In the ex-republics as much as in the Cape Colony, therefore, the flame of Afrikaner nationalism continued to burn throughout the period of British reconstruction leading to Union. In the Cape the majority of the Afrikaners in the *Afrikaner Bond* believed that their patriotism could find expression within the Empire, while Botha and Smuts, in *Het Volk* party in the Transvaal, continued to advocate conciliation and co-operation with the English-speaking section—a policy to which they had committed themselves after the war. In the Free State, however, Hertzog, while prepared to work with the former enemy and its allies, was very much on the defensive, and he and his party, the *Orangia Unie*, were not prepared for the sake of co-operation to surrender any Afrikaner principle.

So, although at Union there was no concerted or unified Afrikaner nationalist movement as such, it was there in embryo. Talk of Afrikaner *volkseenheid* (unity), which had grown more frequent on the eve of the Anglo-Boer War[2] grew after defeat into a sense of common destiny inspired by the realization that Afrikaner interests overlapped as never before.[3] Hertzog was looked upon as the unofficial national spokesman of Afrikaner separatism, but as the most prominent Free Stater after Steyn, he nevertheless became a member of Botha's first Union Cabinet. This was a coalition administration and consisted of representatives of the South African Party in the Cape, and the *Orangia Unie* and *Het Volk* parties which, in 1911, were to amalgamate to form the South African Party. Opposed to it was the largely English-speaking Unionist Party as well as the Labourites, also mostly English-speaking. Botha claimed to stand midway between Hertzog (who lost no time in making plain his discomfort in his new surroundings) and the Unionists. In fact Botha would gladly have excluded Hertzog from his cabinet if he could have done so without antagonizing the Free State. As it was, Hertzog was very quickly to become an embarrassment to the

---

[1] After the Boer War, President Steyn did much to propagate the ideal of a united Afrikanerdom and a united republican South Africa among Cape Afrikaners. Van Schoor, p. 145.
[2] T. R. H. Davenport, *The Afrikaner Bond*, p. 251.   [3] Ibid., p. 251.

Government. His fervent advocacy of strict equality of treatment for the Dutch and English languages in education, which he had preached and practised in the Free State as part of his two-stream policy for the two language groups[1] and now wanted carried out in the country as a whole, needlessly alarmed and angered the English-speaking community. By separating the Afrikaner and the English-speaking peoples, Hertzog hoped to prevent the anglicization or absorption of his own people by the rest. The idea was that the two 'streams 'should run parallel in the national life, that the one should not be inferior to the other, and that the two languages should receive equal treatment. Apart from this, Hertzog began to pay increasing attention to the constitutional issue, attacking the Unionists for their advocacy of a larger South African contribution to the maintenance of the Royal Navy, and taunting his own party because it would not state unequivocally its attitude to the Union's status as an independent State. His campaign reached its climax at De Wildt, a small railway halt in the Transvaal, on 7 December 1912, when he gave form and substance to his idea of Afrikaner nationalism in more specific and challenging terms than before.[2] In a speech which was to become historic as marking the birth of the National Party[3] of today, he reminded his audience of a previous statement that 'South Africa must be governed by the Afrikaner' (a term in which he included all whites who accepted South Africa as their fatherland, no matter what language they spoke).[4] 'The time has come when South Africa can no longer be ruled by non-Afrikaners, by people who do not have the right love for South Africa. The leader of the Opposition Unionist Party (Sir Thomas Smartt) says he is an imperialist first and then an Afrikaner. . . . Imperialism is only acceptable to me as far as it is of service to South Africa. When it comes into conflict with the interests of South Africa, I am a decided opponent of it. I am prepared to let my future career as a politician rest on this. . . . I am not one of those who always talks of conciliation and loyalty, because those are idle words which deceive no one', he said in an obvious reference to the Botha–Smuts policy.[5]

Here was the kernel of the thinking of Hertzog's followers who were

[1] Ibid., p. 300.   [2] Van Schoor, p. 148.

[3] 'National Party' is the official name. Because they believe that this is contrary to common usage, and therefore misleading in this context, many South Africans prefer to call it the 'Nationalist Party'.

[4] As leader of the National Party, Hertzog did not succeed in persuading English-speaking South Africans that they were included in his conception of 'Afrikaner': they continued to hold aloof and the National Party's membership was overwhelmingly Afrikaans-speaking. It was only when he became leader of the United Party in the early 1930s that Hertzog's more embracing conception of 'Afrikaner' came to be accepted a little more generally. The current understanding of the term in South Africa is that it applies exclusively to Afrikaans-speakers.

[5] C. M. van den Heever, *Generaal J. B. M. Hertzog*, p. 313; and van Schoor, p. 149.

to form the National Party: a policy of South Africa first, the pitting of South African nationalism against British imperialism, and the two-stream philosophy of Hertzog himself. The Botha Cabinet could not survive the De Wildt speech, so Botha resigned in order to get rid of Hertzog, who himself had refused to modify his views or leave the cabinet. Botha's tactics angered Hertzog,[1] who thereupon launched a campaign preaching his doctrine, attacking Botha as a protagonist of imperialism and the surrender of the rights of the Afrikaans-speaking people, and condemning 'foreign fortune-seekers' who sought to exploit South Africa for their own selfish ends—a reference to mine-owners and overseas capitalists generally. He condemned, too, the Botha–Smuts policy of conciliation and advocated a 'South African Nationalism' which alone would produce a 'true unity of hearts' among the different population groups.[2] In spite of the gap between the two men's views, attempts were made to bring Botha and Hertzog together again, but these finally failed at a party congress at the end of 1913. Six weeks later, from 7 to 9 January 1914, at a conference in Bloemfontein, it was formally decided to establish the National Party. Its programme of principles stressed the need to develop a 'powerful conception' of 'national self-sufficiency' and declared emphatically 'that the interests of the Union came before those of any other country'.[3]

Afrikaner nationalism thus for the first time became a co-ordinated, country-wide movement and vehicle of the strivings and aspirations of a people who wanted to retain their separate identity and their independence. From the outset the party was identified with an Afrikaner nation and much of its success in later years must be ascribed to its skill in persuading Afrikaners, and particularly non-Nationalist Afrikaners, that '*die party is die volk en die volk is die party*'[4] or as Dr. Verwoerd was to assert almost without challenge during his premiership, 'The National Party was never and is not an ordinary party. It is a nation on the move.'[5] This identification was perhaps the chief magnet which finally drew and kept the overwhelming majority of Afrikaners together after generations of schism and squabble.

There was another factor which, from the outset, played a continuing role in holding the Afrikaner people together and shaping their political philosophy, namely, the Calvinism preached and practised by the Dutch Reformed Churches,[6] of which 90 per cent of Afrikaners are adherents.

---

[1] Van den Heever, p. 316.   [2] Van Schoor, p. 149.   [3] Ibid., p. 153.
[4] 'The party is the nation and the nation is the party.'
[5] Brochure issued by Transvaal National Party on its 50th birthday, 8 Sept. 1964.
[6] There are three branches of the Dutch Reformed Church: the *Nederduitse Gereformeerde Kerk*, with (in 1966) approximately 1,300,000 members; the *Nederduitse Hervormde Kerk van Afrika*, with 185,000; and the *Gereformeerde Kerk*, with 100,000. Of the white inhabitants of South Africa, about 45 per cent belong to the Dutch Reformed Church.

Calvin divided the human race broadly into the elect and the rest. Afrikaner leaders, however, interpreted his doctrine to refer not to individuals alone but to nations, and they applied this formula specifically to their own people. In time this led to a sort of neo-Calvinist philosophy which the politicians exploited to prove the necessity of maintaining national or racial identity as well as to justify divisions between nations and races. 'We believe that the only road is that which fulfils the demands of our Calvinist creed', said Mr. W. A. Maree, leader of the National Party in Natal, in 1966.[1] God had put the Afrikaner people in southern Africa with a purpose. 'God saved the Afrikaner people at Blood River and allowed them to carry on to where they are today', said Professor F. J. M. Potgieter, of the Divinity Faculty at Stellenbosch University.[2]

Nationalist Afrikaner writing down the years reflects the Calvinistic belief that the State is divinely ordained and created, that it can exist independently of the citizen, over whom it has exclusive powers, and that rulers are finally responsible to God, whose agents they are and in whose name they act. This neo-Calvinism was clearly tailored to fit Nationalist Afrikaner prejudices.[3] In the nineteenth century du Toit, the *Afrikaner Bond* founder, expressed his belief in a mystical or supernatural creation of the Afrikaner nation when he wrote of God having 'brought together' members of various nationalities in South Africa and 'given' them a language.[4] God's hand was always clearly 'visible' in the history of the nation, which had a task, or mission, or calling. This was presented, initially, as the opening up of the interior of the country for Christianity and civilization. But God's will also was that the Afrikaner people would once and for all live free from British authority.[5]

In the preamble to the Constitution of the Republic of South Africa, the role of God in the creation of the State is acknowledged in these words: 'In humble submission to Almighty God, who controls the destinies of nations and the history of peoples, who gathered our forebears together from many lands and who gave them this their own, who has guided them from generation to generation; who has wondrously delivered them from the dangers that beset them.' In the Republic of South Africa Constitution Act, 1961, itself, God is credited with having given South Africa, 'this their own' land, to a specific people, and with having protected the people from threats and perils. And the

---

[1] *South African Press Association file*, 16 Dec. 1966.   [2] Ibid.

[3] (*a*) 'Their religion, setting them apart from the unelected pagans about them, bred in them a sense of special destiny as a people.'—C. W. de Kiewiet, *A History of South Africa*, p. 23; (*b*) 'The identification of God's aims with those of the people and the people's with those of God is a very dangerous phenomenon in South Africa.'—Dr. G. C. Oosthuizen, *Delayed Action*, p. 112.

[4] Van Jaarsveld, *Awakening*, p. 223.   [5] Ibid., p. 224.

constitution of the powerful and influential secret society, the *Afrikaner Broederbond*, states that the *Bond* 'is born of the deep conviction that the Afrikaner nation was put in this land by God and is destined to continue its existence as a nation with its own nature and calling'.[1]

The authoritarianism of Afrikaner neo-Calvinism is also reflected from time to time in the history of Afrikaner nationalism. To take one example, a Draft Republican Constitution drawn up and published by a number of Afrikaner nationalist organizations in 1942, provided for a 'Christian-National state, based on the word of God', with a State President 'directly and only responsible to God over and against the people and altogether independent of any vote in Parliament'.[2]

Just as Calvinism sought in Geneva to renew society by penetrating life at every depth, public as well as private, so the Dutch Reformed Church strove hard to make itself and its own brand of Calvinism felt in the life of the Afrikaner people. Although there was never any formal or official relationship between church and party, the Dutch Reformed Church became in a very real sense the National Party at prayer.[3] During the Rebellion of 1914—the armed uprising of some Afrikaners against the Government's decision to go to war against Germany on England's side, and with the object of regaining independence for the two former republics—congregations were split on political lines and separate provision was made for worship for followers of one or the other party. In the same year the first move was made to divide the Students' Christian

---

[1] *Report of the Commission of Inquiry into Secret Organizations*, 1965.

[2] *Die Transvaler*, 23 Jan. 1942.

[3] 'The concern of churches in and outside South Africa about what seems like a spiritual alliance between the Nederduitse Gereformeerde Kerk (N.G.K.) and the National Party with its ideology of apartheid has found expression in something like a final appeal phrased in the form of a question by the Moderature of the Netherlands Hervormde Kerk, namely, whether it should still continue to regard the N.G.K. as a church. However this attitude which has revealed itself in the Netherlands Hervormde Kerk may be judged, one thing is certain and that is that the N.G.K. will urgently have to establish for itself that the price it will have to pay for the questionable praise it is receiving and the kudos it may enjoy as the bulwark of ideals of the Afrikaner people, is too high. No church can afford it. . . . The salvation of the [Afrikaner] people is not, however, synonymous with the policy of apartheid, with the politics of the National Party, with the self-maintenance of the Afrikaner amidst the "dangers" which "threaten" his identity, the white colour of his skin, his language, his culture, his economy, his political predominance; and the selfless service which the N.G.K. owes the people is not a slavish subservience to a sectionalist, party political, white Afrikaner ideal. . . . In the present political situation in South Africa it (serving as the bulwark of the ideals of the Afrikaner people) has only one meaning: it is the bulwark of a particular political party. It is the servant of a foreign master. And an element which is at present predominant in the N.G.K. lends substance to this claim upon it. The N.G.K. is embroiled in a titanic struggle for the retention of its identity as Church of Christ. Its essential being is at stake: it is being tempted to substitute another master for its own Lord.'—From a leading article of 15 Dec. 1966, in *Pro Veritate*, a Christian monthly and mouthpiece of the Christian Institute of Southern Africa, edited by a former minister of the Nederduitse Gereformeerde Kerk. The Founder-Director of the Institute (1963) was the Revd. C. F. Beyers Naude, a former moderator of the N.G.K. in the Southern Transvaal.

Association into two bodies, one for English and the other for Afrikaans-speaking youth—a split which finally came about forty-one years later, when the movement was broken up into four separate compartments: Afrikaans, English, Coloured, and African. Again, when the National Party opposed South Africa's entry into the Second World War, individual ministers openly sided with the party and in some cases even refused to perform a marriage ceremony for men in uniform. Some ministers, however, volunteered for service in the armed forces and were attached as padres on the same basis as other denominations. In 1944, when the National Party was in the midst of its struggle to control the trade-union movement in the Transvaal, a group of Dutch Reformed churchmen were openly active and fifteen of them issued a pamphlet 'White South Africa, Save Yourself', in which the 'pure race'[1] theory of the National Party was underwritten and 'foreign', that is non-Nationalist, influences in the trade-union movement condemned. Finally, in 1950 a specially convened national conference of Dutch Reformed Churches approved the policy of separate living areas for different population groups, known as 'territorial apartheid', and urged the Government to put it into force—a proposition which the Prime Minister rejected as impracticable.[2] Throughout the early years of Nationalist rule in the 1950s, individual ministers in the Church sought to find scriptural justification for the National Party's race policies and practices.

While important elements in the Church have always kept aloof from party politics, Nationalist politicians have consistently exploited the Afrikaner's religious sentiments and associations for party political purposes. This has been done principally by equating Nation, Church, and Party. One of the party's frankest chroniclers writes: 'Without hesitation it can be said that it is principally due to the Church that the Afrikaner nation has not gone under. . . . With the dilution of this philosophy it [the Afrikaner nation] must inevitably disappear . . . that is the great difference between the Afrikaner nation and other nations.'[3]

Nationalist politicians have not only appealed to the strongly religious streak in the Afrikaner's make-up, but equally persistently to his pride of nation and race. In developing the instinct of self-preservation and

[1] South Africans use the word 'race' to describe both physical and cultural differences between peoples. A 'race', therefore, is not only a group of persons of common descent or origin: it also includes questions of outlook and attitude, of emotional values, of *mores*. Different language groups, such as Afrikaans and English, or Nguni and Sotho, are popularly spoken of as *races*, but physical differences are taken as the most important. The legal definition of race turns on physical difference or cultural characteristics which are thought to be associated with physical differences.

[2] *Hansard*, 12 April 1950, cols. 4141-2.

[3] G. D. Scholtz, *Het Die Afrikaanse Volk 'n Toekoms?*, pp. 80-1.

underlining the idea of the Afrikaner people as a separate and distinct national entity, the leaders often played on the emotions of fear and prejudice. For the first quarter of the twentieth century the enemy was British imperialism and its 'agents' in South Africa. Afrikaner Nationalism's opponents and the English-speaking population in general were accused of putting Britain before South Africa and of being inferior patriots with at best a divided loyalty. Then, for the 1929 election, the 'Black menace' was introduced as a potent ally, and for two decades at least 'British Imperialism' and 'Black menace' were to run in harness as potent election winners.[1]

The 1948 election victory of Afrikaner Nationalism was due primarily to its promise to secure the safety of the white man by a policy of apartheid or race separation in which white domination was implicit. The appeal was still initially to the Afrikaner, but it soon came to be broadened to include all white men, who were adjured to stand together and fight for survival against the torrent of Blackness which threatened from inside and out. This intensified emphasis on white survival inside South Africa coincided with the post-war revolution in Africa and the rush to independence of dependent peoples, which in turn increased outside pressure on South Africa to modify its colour policies and abandon apartheid. All these factors combined to introduce a new and more potent dimension into the politics of fear. Henceforth, according to the Nationalist policy-makers, the fight was to be not only for the survival of Afrikanerdom but for that of the white man, now pitted against the evil forces of communism and liberalism which a 'sickly West' had unloosed on the world. The Afro-Asian peoples, that is, people of colour again, as well as liberals everywhere, particularly in America and Britain, became the enemies against whom the white man had to be warned.[2]

---

[1] By 1968 the National Party had been in power for twenty years.

[2] In a leading article on 15 Dec. 1966, *Die Transvaler*, the official organ of the National Party in the Transvaal, edited by one of the party's historians, G. D. Scholtz, wrote: 'This struggle [for the self-maintenance of the Afrikaner nation] continues today. A numerically small nation has for more than a century been busy with a struggle for self-maintenance. . . . In the first place the struggle is against the same obtrusive barbarism which the Voortrekkers faced 128 years ago. Today still the Afrikaans nation of 2,000,000 must wage a political and spiritual struggle to maintain itself against barbarism. In the second place, there is a struggle against other whites. In the past this struggle was primarily against whites who were not of South Africa, but who used the fatherland of the Afrikaans nation from strategic and economic considerations to further the interests of another country. One need only refer here to the imperialism of the 19th century. The protagonists of this ideology wanted to see the Afrikaans nation disappear. . . . Today the Afrikaans nation still faces a dual onslaught . . . there is still always the onslaught of the barbarism of Africa. . . . In the place of British imperialism there has now come the British-American liberalism. Whatever the difference between the supporters of imperialism and of liberalism, on one specific subject they are in complete agreement. This is that the Afrikaans nation must disappear. . . . Between the liberalism and the barbarism there exists at the moment an intimate bond. . . . This struggle will be of a protracted nature.'

Afrikaner leaders realized, however, that if world pressure was to be resisted, some change in domestic tactics was necessary in order to strengthen the home front and at the same time to alter the world's image of South Africa's race policy. As a result modifications were brought about in the policy and the implementation of apartheid, on which Afrikaner Nationalism had ridden to almost unchallenged authority and power in the white community by the middle 1960s. By this time, too, it was obvious that Afrikaners could wield the power in the white camp as long as they remained united and thus retained a numerical superiority. They could afford, therefore, to bring in 'outsiders' without having to make concessions or water down their own racial convictions in any important way. As a result, the emphasis in the Nationalist appeal moved to attracting English-speaking support, provided this involved no surrender or dilution of Nationalist principle.

This policy bore some fruit, and by 1965 a Nationalist newspaper claimed a 'breakthrough' to the English-speaking voter. 'Nationalism no longer belongs only to the Afrikaans-speaking, and this assurance that other language groups accept the Nationalist Party conditions for co-operation, creates for the first time since 1910 the genuine basis for white unity growth. It is not now a case of a compromise between irre-- concilable policy directions, but a bringing together of people who agree on the cardinal problem of colour. The foundation-stone of a new South African nation has been laid'.[1] According to another commentator, the path had now been prepared for political grouping according to conviction rather than (white race) origins.[2]

In the line-up of white versus black nationalism, implicit in the apartheid doctrine, all recruits to the white side were welcome. The threat from inside and outside South Africa had become far greater than any that 'the English' and other enemies of yesteryear had posed. Now, in the eyes of Nationalism, the 'enemy' included everyone prepared to share political power with the non-white peoples. All were lumped together and condemned either as 'liberalists' or 'communists',[3] or simply 'enemies of the people'. This is how the emphasis came to be put less on the threat to the Afrikaner than on that to the white man. So it came about, in the mid 1960s, that Afrikaner Nationalism was preparing to move a few degrees nearer to the Hertzog ideal of white political unity and a single white South African nation. But by this time the base would be that of Afrikaner Nationalism in which the Afrikaner would be the dominant partner, and not of South Africanism of the later

---

[1] *Dagbreek*, 28 Mar. 1965.   [2] W. van Heerden, ibid.

[3] In Nationalist terminology 'liberalist' was a shade worse than 'liberal' and 'communist' was a statutory term embracing all who in any way might advance the aims and objects of communism without necessarily having to subscribe to Marxism or even be a party supporter. See *Suppression of Communism Act* (No. 44 of 1950) and amendments.

Hertzog kind, in which the roles and ideals of the two language groups would be more clearly equal. The wheel was coming full circle after sixty years—but it was revolving on a different axis.

In this situation of embattlement, moreover, apartheid itself had to be modified in an attempt to find some accommodation with the African majority inside South Africa. The emphasis shifted from physical or territorial segregation to political segregation in which attention came to be focused on the Bantustans, the reserved African homelands, and the political rights and 'separate freedom' accorded people there. Some Afrikaner Nationalist leaders at least admitted that it was impossible to deny to the non-white peoples what they and their predecessors had demanded for their own people: the right of self-determination. They hoped, through the Bantustan policy, to meet some of the criticism that Africans were denied any political voice, by providing for self-determination for them in their own areas. The more thoughtful realized, however, without openly admitting as much, that the party was left with the heart of the colour problem: how to meet the political aspirations of Africans in white areas and how to evolve a system of effective consultation which would satisfy the non-whites and lead to government by consent, all without surrendering white political power. Afrikaner policy-makers believed that once the party agreed to share political power with the non-whites, its own days and the days of the white man in general were numbered. Here was the dilemma the party faced in the second half of the 1960s: could it for ever avoid sharing political power? Was it possible to keep off collision course indefinitely? The more astute Afrikaner leaders were anxious to avoid a head-on clash between Afrikaner and African nationalism, which the party's own policy of separation down the years had done so much to make inevitable if not to foster. They feared that there could be only one outcome. This was why they tried so desperately to find a by-pass.

The pages that follow will attempt to tell in the broadest outline the story of Afrikaner Nationalism's triumphs and tragedies, its failures and achievements, the good it has done for South Africa as well as the hurt. The story would be incomplete without underlining the paradox of a proud, courageous, and individualistic people, friendly, warm-hearted, and generous, which claimed for themselves personal and group freedom which they were loath to extend to others because they feared that if they did so, they would disappear as a separate nation; of a people who never tired of proclaiming their attachment to democracy yet were quite prepared to resort to authoritarian and undemocratic measures to defend what they demanded for themselves but denied others. Time alone will tell whether, in their bid for self-preservation, Afrikaner leaders went too far in demanding exclusive political power and so missed the opportunity of achieving an accommodation with those they feared most, non-white peoples with whom they shared South Africa. Similarly, it remains to be seen whether, in elevating race pride and purity to the level of a religion, and in failing to make its nationalism inclusive rather than exclusive, the Afrikaner leaders down the years may not have helped to fashion the weapons which could one day be used against their people. Did the Afrikaners, so fond of quoting Biblical precept, ignore the two injunctions that some other South Africans thought necessary for their salvation: 'What shall it profit a man, if he gain the whole world, and lose his own soul?' and 'Whosoever will save his life shall lose it'?

2. *Struggle for Unity*

From its earliest days Afrikaner Nationalism tended to have a personalized political philosophy. Just as Paul Kruger in the Transvaal, M. T. Steyn in the Free State, and J. H. Hofmeyr in the Cape, came to represent the Afrikaner people's political aspirations in the closing stages of the nineteenth century, so, after the achievement of Union in 1910, Hertzog became the embodiment of a nation's aspirations. His personality as much as his principles determined his following and gave form to his party's policy and expectations. What Hertzog decreed was accepted unquestioningly and the Orange Free State became the seedbed of Afrikaner Nationalism. When Hertzog was supplanted by D. F. Malan, the political centre of gravity moved to the Cape Province, and the ideology of the former Dutch Reformed Church minister, who left the pulpit to become a newspaper editor and politician, influenced the philosophy of Afrikanerdom in important ways, not least in the emphasis given to the semi-mystical and the religious, and the appeal to return to the tried and trusted paths of the past. It was Malan, moreover, who revived the republican ambitions of Afrikaner Nationalists—the yearning to return to the status of the two Boer republics before the Anglo-Boer War—even though neither his own nor the Cape Province's republican convictions were ever as ardent as those of men in the ex-republics. Malan's major contribution to his party, however, was to give to the Afrikaner people a greater degree of unity than they ever before possessed—to bring together those who, in Nationalism's eyes, belonged together.

By the end of the Second World War the country's economic centre of gravity had shifted decisively to the Transvaal, and it was natural that in the early 1950s political power moved northwards with Malan's successors, J. G. Strydom and H. F. Verwoerd. Nationalism, in consequence, came to reflect more of that province's frontier traditions and its leaders' uncompromising approach. Where Malan still had some scruples about how to deprive the Cape Coloured people of their common roll franchise rights, Strydom, the 'little Kruger', who saw in republicanism a shield to protect and preserve the white man as well as a political goal, justified his violation of the spirit of the Constitution by arguing that the white man's existence was at stake and that the end justified the means.[1]

A weakness of the personality cult was its proneness to produce schism, a spectre and fear which has haunted Afrikanerdom throughout its history. When Hertzog established the National Party he had the support of only a minority of Afrikaners: and although his appeal was to both language groups, 'to all who love South Africa', his backing came almost exclusively from the Afrikaans-speaking population. The majority of Afrikaners continued to stand by the two Boer leaders, Botha and Smuts, and their policy of seeking an accommodation with the English-speaking section.

(The 1914 Rebellion[2] and its aftermath, including such incidents as the excution of Jopie Fourie, an army officer who defected to the rebels and was court martialled and sentenced to death, drove the wedge deeper than ever into the Afrikaner people. In the Cape almost as much as in the Free State and the Transvaal, Afrikaners were divided into rebels and anti-rebels, with scores of thousands not specifically committed. But it was to the National Party that the rebel leaders, De Wet, Beyers, and Kemp, were committed because they wanted no part in 'England's wars' and saw in the world war an opportunity of regaining the independence lost twelve years earlier. And there is no doubt that the uprising helped Hertzog's cause by focusing attention on his struggle for sovereign independence.

At the first general election which it contested in 1915, the National Party won 27 seats and attracted over 78,000 votes compared with 92,000 who supported the majority South African Party. 'The success which the party achieved', wrote an official chronicler fifty years later, 'must be ascribed to the realisation of the Afrikaans-speaking people that they had a task to perform, ideals to achieve and principles to give expression to. . . . The National Party, with principles which spoke from the heart of the people, was on the road to victory.'[3]

Even when the National Party emerged from the election of 1920 as the strongest single party (it won 44 seats as against the South African

---

[1] G. Coetzee, *Hans Strydom*, p. 55.

[2] In this armed protest against South Africa's decision to invade German South West Africa, about 7,000 Free Staters and 3,000 Transvaalers participated. It lasted only a few months before being put down, primarily because leaders like Hertzog did not give it overt support. Van Schoor, p. 153.

[3] M. P. A. Malan, *Die Nasionale Party van Suid Afrika*, p. 44.

Party's 41, the Unionists' 25, and Labour's 21), the longed-for unity of
Afrikanerdom remained a fairly distant ideal. Attempts to unite the
National and South African parties failed, and three years later Hertzog
thought it expedient to enter into an election pact with the predominantly English-speaking Labour Party led by F. Creswell. He hoped, in
this way, to break into the urban areas, where his support was meagre,
and appeal, through the Labour Party, to the white workers, whom the
Nationalists undertook to protect against competition from black labour.
Hertzog must have realized that the Labour Party could never become
a truly socialist party as long as it based its policy on the support of
a white élite labour force and excluded all non-white workers. In fact,
as has been pointed out, the Nationalist–Labour Pact was a 'marriage
of convenience: essentially it was a white man's front against the Africans,
created for the purpose of raising white wages and ensuring jobs for
"poor whites", the overwhelming majority of whom were Afrikaners'.[1]

An overall majority of eighteen for this coalition at the general election
of 1924 gave Afrikaner Nationalism its first taste of power since Union.
Hertzog had come a long way and already had the backing of a majority
of Afrikaners. But Afrikanerdom remained disunited as tens of thousands
of Afrikaners continued to stand by Smuts and his policy of co-operation
with English-speaking South Africans. In 1929 the National Party won
an outright Parliamentary majority on its own—78 seats to the 70
obtained by its opponents combined—and Hertzog began to think that
the stage had been reached when his two-stream policy of parallel
development for the two language groups on a basis of equality could
be implemented on his own terms. In 1930, therefore, he was able to tell
the Free State National Party conference: 'The time has come for us
South Africans, Afrikaners or English, to recognise the fact that as long
as we remain separate and try to reach our goals along different roads,
we must expect that most of what we as a nation wish to attain will not
be achieved. After what has been accomplished at the Imperial conferences of 1926 and 1930, there remains no reason whatsoever why, in
the field of politics and statecraft, Afrikaans and English South Africans
should not feel and act in the spirit of a consolidated South African
nation.'[2] His convictions were strengthened by his anxiety to gain
sufficient support for the colour legislation he had long been contem-
plating, but for which he required a far larger parliamentary majority
than any which he, as National Party leader, could hope to command
in the foreseeable future. Moreover, the economic needs of the day
began to weigh heavily with him. Economic nationalism, the concomi-
tant of the sovereign independence which the National Party was so
anxious to emphasize in those early days of power, aggravated South

[1] W. H. Vatcher, *White Laager*, p. 49.   [2] *The Friend*, 4 Dec. 1930.

Africa's plight. By keeping the country on the gold standard long after common sense had dictated that she should follow Britain off gold, the party caused needless economic hurt. Hertzog saw the need to tackle this crisis on the broadest front. He realized, too, that the economic blizzard could force him and his party out of office, and he was determined to prevent this. On the constitutional issue, moreover, Hertzog believed that South Africa had made such progress that nothing could be lost by more broadly based co-operation with English-speaking South Africans, who, for reasons of sentiment, had been opposed to co-operation with the Nationalists.

That Hertzog's desire to bring about a broader white unity, a South African rather than an exclusive Afrikaner nationalism, was sincere, was borne out by the history of the next six years. The coalition agreement which he entered into with Smuts early in 1933, and which in the following year led to the fusion of the two parties and the formation of the United South African National Party with Hertzog and Smuts as leaders, was to split Afrikanerdom wide open once again. Any sort of co-operation with 'the enemy' of old was anathema to many of the diehards in the ranks of Afrikaner Nationalism. The association with Smuts and his 'Khakis',[1] they argued, was artificial and dangerous, and the Afrikaner would have to sacrifice too much for uncertain ends: he would be outwitted by the 'slim [crafty] Smuts'. According to E. G. Jansen, 'the opponents of fusion did not trust General Smuts to maintain Nationalist principles or the national direction'[2] particularly since many of his followers were in favour of the imperialist direction. General Hertzog taunted these opponents with being afraid to make themselves felt or to maintain their principles in a new party. His view was that the constitutional struggle had ended with the Statute of Westminster and that the struggle for language equality had been decided with the South African Party's acceptance of language equality as a principle of co-operation. There was, therefore, no longer any need for the existence of two separate parties.

His view was widely shared among the rank and file and three of the four provincial National Parties voted in favour of fusion with the South African Party. Only the Cape, under Malan's leadership, opposed it. It was inevitable, therefore, that the National Party would continue or be revived in one form or another. Malan and his followers, however, did not break with Hertzog immediately: they took part, as members of the National Party, in the 1933 election, fought on an electoral standstill agreement between the parties, and then went into opposition.

[1] A Hindu term, used by Afrikaners for British soldiers in the Boer War which came to be applied to their English-speaking opponents by Nationalists. It was a term of contempt.
[2] Van der Walt, Wiid, and Geyer, *Die Geskiedenis van Suid Afrika*, i. 661.

As a result a bitter struggle began between them and the Fusionists for control of branches, constituency committees, and provincial executives of the old National Party. With the help of the *Broederbond*[1] Dr. Malan and his followers emerged with the lion's share. They also obtained control of the influential Afrikaans Press with the exception of Hertzog's own paper in the Transvaal.

Hertzog blamed the *Afrikaner Broederbond* for Malan's decision to oppose Fusion and publicly denounced the movement. In a speech to his constituents he declared that after Malan had become a member of the *Bond* he had changed from being a supporter of unity between Afrikaans- and English-speaking South Africans, to become a protagonist of Afrikaner domination.[2]

Those Afrikaners who opposed fusion argued that it was essential to retain the right of secession from the British Commonwealth and of neutrality in 'England's wars'. It would, they maintained, be impossible to achieve this if they belonged to a party in which English-speakers had an equal voice. Furthermore, they did nothing to hide their almost traditional distrust and dislike of 'the English', meaning, usually, English-speaking South Africans opposed to the strivings of Afrikaner Nationalism. More important, however, was the determination of the militant Afrikaner leader to resist 'absorption' by other non-Afrikaner elements or integration in a broader South Africanism and to enhance the exclusiveness of the National Party. This ideal could best be achieved, they felt, by refusing to amalgamate with 'outsiders' or to water down in any way the principles of exclusive Afrikaner Nationalism. Only thus, it was believed, would the Afrikaner nation retain its separate identity and remain in being.

Because the *Afrikaner Broederbond's* documents are secret, outsiders do not know to what degree the *Bond* was responsible for this more militant and exclusive approach. But non-Nationalist Afrikaners were convinced that the early 1930s marked a watershed in Nationalist Afrikanerdom's history and that from this stage on, more than ever before, the *Bond* leadership was determined to rule South Africa according to its own separatist principles.[3] It is significant that in the years that followed Malan's break with Hertzog and in which the National Party was re-established in all four provinces[4] there began the mobilization of Afrikaner resources in every sphere of life on a scale, and with a co-ordinated intensity, which could not have taken place without some

[1] J. P. Cope, *South Africa*, p. 112.
[2] For the full text of Hertzog's speech on the *Broederbond* on 7 Nov. 1935, see Vatcher, p. 243.
[3] Only Afrikaans-speaking whites may be members of the *Broederbond*.
[4] Initially it was known as the Purified National Party. From 1940 to 1951 it was called the Reunited National or People's Party. It then reverted to the name National Party.

central directing and guiding agency like the *Broederbond*. And in every instance the mobilized forces were harnessed, directly or sometimes indirectly, in the service of the National Party.

One of the results was that by 1938 the National Party increased its strength in Parliament from 20 to 27 seats, winning 247,000 votes in the general election of that year. In other words, it was once again growing and attracting increasing Afrikaner support after the events of 1933–4. The outbreak of the Second World War, however, was to give yet another twist to Afrikaner Nationalism and incidentally bring the party face to face with the gravest threat to its existence it had ever experienced from Afrikaners themselves.

When South Africa had to decide whether or not to declare war on Germany in 1939, Hertzog urged neutrality and Smuts involvement. Hertzog's attitude was in large measure the product of his fierce South Africanism and his life-long opposition to South Africa's participation in 'England's wars'. Partly, too, it was a result of his own failure to appreciate the real nature and objectives of the Third Reich and the Nazi threat, as well as the sympathy of some of his younger advisers, like Pirow, for Hitler, and their antipathy to Britain. Moreover, he saw in the outbreak of the war an opportunity for the Afrikaner people to test the reality of South Africa's sovereign independence. He argued that the Afrikaner had in the past been asked to make sentimental concessions, and he thought or hoped the bulk of the English-speaking people would now make a great concession to Afrikaner sentiment. If they did this it would not only destroy the 'purified' Nationalist movement, but it would also hasten the political merging of the two language streams into the broad river of South Africanism. He felt that there were powerful reasons for not plunging a deeply divided state into war, but believed that South Africa could nevertheless honour her obligations to Britain and the Commonwealth, which would have the use of the naval base at Simonstown and all the facilities of South Africa's ports and docks. If South Africa were drawn into the war later, it would be on the side of the Allies. In the words of a contemporary observer, 'Hertzog was misled about the causes of the war, but his understanding of its ultimate political consequences for South Africa was greater than was realised in his day.'[1]

It was not to be: Smuts insisted that South Africa should show her hand without delay and he narrowly won the day. Parliament decided on an immediate declaration of war on Germany by 80 votes to 67, and Hertzog, having been refused a dissolution by the Governor-General, Sir Patrick Duncan, resigned. An immediate result was that Hertzog and Malan were thrown together again, having found common ground

[1] Cope, pp. 114–15.

on the neutrality issue, and the goal of Afrikaner unity once more hove in sight. At a vast open-air meeting at the site of the Voortrekker Monument outside Pretoria, 70,000 people 'raised their hands and promised never again to break away from one another'.[1] The irony of this gathering was that, when the foundation stone of this Afrikaner shrine was laid in 1938, Hertzog, although Prime Minister and probably the greatest Afrikaner of them all, was not asked to perform this ceremony on the grounds that he was a 'controversial politician'. The real reason was that he was at the time *persona non grata* because he had 'strayed' from the Afrikaner path and joined forces with 'the English' and with anti-Nationalist Afrikaners.

Within fifteen months the solemn undertaking given at the Voortrekker Monument had turned to ashes and Afrikaner unity again became a distant ideal. Old suspicions and antagonisms between the followers of Hertzog and Malan ran deep, and although an agreement to co-operate was arrived at in January 1940, neither side was really satisfied or happy. Hertzog remained lukewarm about republicanism, whereas Malan's followers grew more clamorous and insistent on immediate action, especially when they felt—or hoped—that Germany would win the war and South Africa could become a republic. A vast rally, convened without Hertzog's knowledge, in the shadow of the Boer War Women's Monument in Bloemfontein, passed a resolution emphasizing that the time had come to declare a free, independent republic; that the republic had to be founded 'in the religion, history and traditions of the Boer nation', and that it was to embody the traditions of Christian-Nationalism. Hertzog refused to have anything to do with the campaign, and relations between him and Malan worsened.

In the end the break came, but not on republicanism. It was on the issue of South Africanism, on the attitude of Afrikaner people to the English-speaking section, that the split took place after months of hesitant co-operation and tortuous negotiation over esoteric points of policy and procedure. Hertzog was suspicious of the motives of his new associates and erstwhile opponents. Therefore he wanted the clause in the programme of principles in the National Party-to-be dealing with the English-speaking section to be formulated as follows: 'The party aims at the development of South African national unity based on the equal rights of the Afrikaans- and English-speaking populations, coupled with the recognition and appreciation of one another's heritage.'[2]

His opponents, on the other hand, insisted on something a little more circumscribed: 'The party aims at the nurturing of a powerful

---

[1] M. P. A. Malan, p. 189.   [2] Ibid., p. 199.

appreciation of natural independence as well as the promotion of a strong feeling of national unity, based on a common and undivided dedication to South Africa and its interests, and the recognition of the equal language and cultural rights of both sections of the white population.'[1]

Hertzog was convinced that his opponents were not prepared to give equal political rights to the English-speaking section. Here he based his judgement as much on the spirit of the congress proceedings and proposals as on the resolution's wording. And when he realized that the majority of delegates were against him on this point, he walked out of the congress—and out of political life—with these significant words: 'We remain Afrikaners. Let us do nothing which is unworthy of the volk or which will lead to its downfall. In time all will come right again.'[2]

To Hertzog this was a moment of infinite hurt, bitterness, and disappointment. The break with Smuts the previous September had, apart from other things, put an end to his work and ideal of deliberate nation-building. He became aware then that he was not to see the realization of his great dream: the political merging of the two streams of national life, Afrikaans and English, in a new and broader nationalism which would be truly South African. This was to have been the culmination of his life's work, which had started with his struggle to ensure equal treatment for the Afrikaner in all spheres of life. It was he who had lifted the Afrikaner from inferiority and inequality to the position where, by 1924 already, 'he could hold his head high in South Africa and treat with the Englishman for the first time on a basis of equality'.[3] Now in his last years, the chosen representatives of those same people had rejected his counsel and his ideals—the people on whose behalf he had, in the uncompromising days of 1931, refused an honorary degree from his old university, Stellenbosch, because he regarded some of the other prospective recipients to be 'enemies of the Afrikaner'.[4] It was a tragic end to a great and selfless career.

The theory of Hertzogism did not go out of public life altogether with its originator's departure. It continued to be propagated by his friend and disciple, N. C. Havenga, who, in 1941, formed the Afrikaner Party specifically to keep Hertzogism alive. The Party's principles were those enunciated by Hertzog at the last Free State National Party congress which he attended. Although its electoral support was meagre—it did not win a single seat at the 1943 election and polled only 14,759 votes in the 24 constituencies it contested—it remained in being because of the potency of Hertzog's memory and the determination of his devoted followers to keep his ideals of moderation alive.

[1] M. P. A. Malan, p. 200.   [2] Die Vaderland, 7 Nov. 1940.
[3] Roberts and Trollip, The South African Opposition, p. 10.
[4] Recounted in Die Burger, Cape Town, of 3 Jan. 1967.

In 1947 Malan, 'the man of national unity' as he came to be known, entered into an electoral agreement with the Afrikaner Party, primarily in an effort to unite Afrikanerdom before the election of the following year, and allocated to Havenga and his followers a number of reasonably safe Nationalist seats. Of these the Afrikaner Party won nine. This gave it the balance of power in a House of 147, of which 70 were members of the United and Labour Parties, 65 were Nationalists and three representatives of the Africans. Havenga's inclusion in the Malan Cabinet gave him a measure of bargaining power which he used, albeit hesitantly and usually behind the scenes, to curb Nationalist action on those issues on which Hertzog had felt strongly: Afrikaner-English-speaking relations, the strict observance of constitutionalism, the Coloured vote, and republicanism. He also opposed a move to abolish what was left of African representation in the House of Assembly. These were essentially delaying tactics, however: they had no lasting influence on Nationalist policy. At Malan's prompting, Havenga agreed to a merger of the Afrikaner and National Parties in 1951, and that was the beginning of the end of Hertzogism. When Malan retired as leader of the National Party in 1954 his own preference for a successor was Havenga. But the National Party caucus thought differently. It had no time for the 'moderation' of Hertzog's erstwhile lieutenant: the result of the 1953 election had given it confidence to press on with issues like republicanism and the abolition of the common franchise of the Coloured people, and it did not want any delaying action by Havenga. So it chose the Transvaal leader and republican crusader, Strydom, to succeed Malan. This was a humiliation Havenga could not bear and, like his leader fourteen years earlier, he resigned from Parliament and disappeared from public life after half a century of service.

When the Free State National Party congress in November 1940 opted for the exclusive, non-Hertzog path, it set the course which Afrikaner Nationalism was to follow for the next decade at least. But the party's troubles were by no means over with the departure of Hertzog from the scene. Apart from the nuisance value of those Hertzogites who remained loyal to their former leader, there remained the para-military and authoritarian *Ossewabrandwag* movement, formed largely on National-Socialist lines. Offshoot of a nation-wide symbolic ox-wagon trek to commemorate the centenary of the Great Trek, the organization, founded in 1938, gained ground rapidly when its leadership was taken over by a former Secretary for Justice and Administrator of the Free State, Dr. J. F. J. van Rensburg. In time it came to challenge the authority of the National Party—and even to usurp some of its functions.

The *Ossewabrandwag* movement captured the imagination of the

Afrikaner people at a significant moment in their history when division and political defeat had brought them to a state of deep depression. It offered an alternative to the squabbles of party politicians and promised a unity which would bridge political differences and which had thus far proved all too elusive. Its semi-military organization appealed to the interest which uniforms, honorific titles, and pageantry had for some Afrikaners, and took the mind back to the heroic struggle of the Boer republics at the turn of the century.[1] And to a minority, the more naïve, it seemed to offer a possible road back to political power—and to a republic independent and free of the Commonwealth link. The organization of groups of Afrikaners in commando-like bodies resulted from the direct influence on *Ossewabrandwag* leaders of Hitlerism and what it stood for. Many of its members—estimated at 2,000 by ex-members of the organization in later years—were interned for anti-war activities and actions inimical to the interests of the State. One of them was the subsequent Nationalist Prime Minister, Mr. B. J. Vorster, who was an *Ossewabrandwag* 'general'. In 1948 Mr. Vorster was rejected by the National Party as a possible parliamentary candidate because of his war-time outspokenness.

As the *Ossewabrandwag* grew—at one stage it claimed to have 250,000 members—it became more sure of itself and soon began to worry the Nationalist leaders, who saw their positions of leadership being usurped. Negotiations were therefore opened to sort out the respective fields of activity for the two movements. This ended in an agreement which, however, the two sides interpreted differently. The Nationalists maintained that they were the political front of Afrikanerdom and that the *Ossewabrandwag* should confine itself to the cultural and organizational spheres. The *Ossewabrandwag* disagreed: it wanted to span all Afrikaner activity. For months the dispute dragged on. At the same time, another anti-democratic organization, Mr. Oswald Pirow's New Order, modelled on National-Socialist lines, was also harrying the party and being accused of interfering in the political sphere.

It was, like all civil 'wars', a bitter and unrelenting fight, for the prize was the 'soul'[2] of Afrikanerdom as well as its immediate control. In fighting the *Ossewabrandwag*, Malan emphasized the identity of his party with the Afrikaner nation.

We are not a party political organization in the ordinary sense of the term [he argued]. We are far more than that. As the *Herenigde Nasionale of Volksparty* we embody the two basic conceptions without which no Afrikaner nation would have been possible. The one is the National idea and the other is the idea of restored Afrikaner unity ... we occupy a central position in our

[1] See also Roberts and Trollip, p. 74.

[2] 'Soul' is a favourite and frequently used word in the literature of Afrikaner Nationalism—another example of the extent to which the conception of Afrikanerdom has been personalized.

Afrikaner national life. If we split, then our nation splits in all directions. On the other hand, if we stand together then our whole nation closes its ranks in every other sphere. . . . We can make our nation or break it.[1]

A little ironically, Malan and his followers in effect found themselves defending the system of Parliamentary democracy for which some members had never had much enthusiasm, and which they had derided, in the early days of the war, as being inspired by British-Jewish-Capitalist-Imperialist-Masonic influences. In its opposition to South Africa's participation in the war, the National Party had laid itself open to the charge not only of supporting Nazi Germany, but of itself drifting towards National-Socialism. The suspicion of non-Nationalists was further aroused when the *Ossewabrandwag* took the initiative in publishing the Draft Republican Constitution (see p. 372) which provided for a strangely mixed authoritarian, parliamentary, corporative structure, and in which English was to be 'a second or supplementary language'. At least one leading Nationalist newspaper (*Die Transvaler*, edited at the time by Dr. Verwoerd, later to become Prime Minister) welcomed the draft 'as an indication of the general direction which the party has already adopted'.[2]

However, in the end Malan out-manœuvred the *Ossewabrandwag*, and as the hopes of a German victory receded, the anti-authoritarian element in the National Party began to get the whip hand and lead it back closer to the path of parliamentary democracy—the path which had originally taken it to power. Once the *Ossewabrandwag*'s influence had been neutralized—Malan achieved this by persuading the Afrikaners that it preached an unacceptable ideology and that its aims were not the same as those of the National Party and therefore not in the interests of the *volk*—there remained the mopping up of some bitter-end Hertzogites before he continued the consolidation of Afrikanerdom.

Malan's rallying cry became: 'Bring together all who, from inner conviction, belong together.' It was to prove a potent and in the end an irresistible slogan after the disunity and frustration of the pre-war and war years. The electoral pact with the Afrikaner Party and the subsequent amalgamation of the two parties on Nationalist principles was an important milestone. And although scores of thousands of Afrikaners in all provinces continued to support Smuts and his United Party, the election of 1948 was to show that approximately two thirds of the Afrikaners had been shepherded back into Afrikaner Nationalism's kraal. The Nationalist groups won 79 seats against the combined opposition's 71, although polling 100,000 fewer votes. For the first time since the early 1930s Afrikaner Nationalism was in power without extraneous aid and it could rule alone. The consolidation of the forces of Afrikaner

---

[1] D. F. Malan, *Glo in u Volk*, p. 38.   [2] *Die Transvaler*, 13 Jan. 1942.

Nationalism was taken further at the elections of 1953, 1958, 1961, and 1966 until Malan's ideal of bringing together all who, out of inner conviction, belonged together, had all but been realized.

There remained outside the Afrikaner laager, however, a small hard core of Afrikaners, perhaps between fifteen and twenty per cent, who refused to throw in their lot with Afrikaner Nationalism. They distrusted its attitude to English-speaking South Africans, rejected the stridency of its 'baasskap' ('bossism') philosophy vis-à-vis the non-white peoples, deplored its equivocation with regard to the rule of law, and remained loyal to the Botha–Smuts tradition of a broadly based white South Africanism. Their influence in the non-Nationalist parties, the United and Progressive in particular, was out of proportion to their numerical strength. Because of their political awareness they tended to oppose Afrikaner Nationalism more vigorously and effectively than their English-speaking compatriots. They regarded themselves as South Africans first and as Afrikaners second. They were dismissed by the Nationalists either as detribalized Afrikaners or as traitors to their people.

In spite of the unity and consolidation of Afrikaner forces, there continued, in the late 1960s, to be stresses and strains which showed that the destiny of Afrikaner Nationalism had not been finally decided. History, geography, and economics had all left their mark on the Afrikaner people and contributed to their character. In the south, where Afrikaners lived a less exposed life than their northern compatriots and where the benign influence of Europe had been more direct and continuous, rank-and-file Nationalism tended to be less inflexible and softer, more disposed to reach some accommodation with other white groups without radically altering the framework of political life. From the Dutch Reformed Church Theological College in Stellenbosch and from the Victoria College (later to become the University of Stellenbosch), for instance, young men had gone to many parts of South Africa and exercised considerable influence on the society in which they practised their professions. Compared with the more inflexible attitudes of the 1930s and onwards, this influence made for moderation and tolerance, and nowhere was this more evident than in the matter of language. English was the official language at the Cape until Union, Dutch was used in the pulpit and on ceremonial occasions, and while Afrikaans was spoken, it was not yet a written language. English thus became the language of business and Parliament, the medium of instruction in education, and the language in which educated men and women corresponded and conversed. With the growth of Afrikaner nationalism this attitude towards English, and towards the use of Afrikaans, was bound to change.[1]

[1] See also L. Marquard, ed., *Letters from a Boer Parsonage*, p. 13.

Moreover, for three-quarters of a century the Cape had had African and Coloured men with certain property and (after 1892) educational qualifications on a common electoral roll and Cape Afrikaners therefore tended to take a more tolerant view of the political threat of non-whites. For the large Coloured community the Cape Afrikaner had a measure of sympathy and fellow-feeling which changed, however, in the mid thirties and then usually under pressure from other Provinces. It was this that gave the Cape wing of the National Party the reputation of being more liberal and accommodating than its counterparts in the northern provinces. In the Transvaal, in particular, the Afrikaner Nationalists were brashly racist.[1] Apart from what they inherited of the uncompromising Kruger tradition, men like Tielman Roos (before he mellowed after a period as an Appeal Court judge), Jan Kemp, and J. G. Strydom were far more intolerant and inflexible than the leadership in the Cape, for over thirty-five years in the hands of D. F. Malan.

It was in the north, moreover, that the first large-scale contact between white and black in industrial surroundings took place. Here, for the first time, the white worker, as distinct from the landowner, saw the threat of competition for jobs and began the agitation for the kind of protection he received from the Nationalist-Labour government from 1924 onwards. Afrikaners, like Africans, had begun their large-scale migration to the towns and cities, the mines and factories, during the great depression and great drought of the early 1930s. They became urbanized in large numbers and found the transition from a land-owning rural employer background to an urban wage-earner situation difficult and painful. Inevitably this had an influence on their outlook. From being easy-going, slow-moving, friendly, tolerant men on the land, they tended to take on the characteristics and philosophy of the urban worker without the comforts and easy living of country life. They began to take their new approach to life into the National Party, which itself came to reflect some of the harsher, relentless, isolationist, and authoritarian philosophy of the 'new' Afrikaner for whom life in the cities was often grim and earnest.

[1] In 1941, for instance, Jews were excluded from membership of the National Party in the Transvaal—a bar which was removed from the party's constitution in 1951. Before and during the Second World War anti-Semitism was fairly rife among members of the National Party and one of its leading members, E. H. Louw, a subsequent Minister of Foreign Affairs, in 1939 introduced a private member's bill to stop Jewish immigration. It failed. When the party came to power in 1948, the Government displayed a sympathetic attitude to Israel and Dr. Malan was one of the first Prime Ministers of any country to visit the new State. Afrikaner-Jewish relations became strained again in 1957, when South African Jews were blamed for not dissociating themselves from or condemning Israel's critical attitude to apartheid in United Nations forums. The Jews were told, by Nationalist newspapers, to explain their loyalties. (Afrikaans newspapers, Oct.–Nov. 1967.)

Periodically, then, this dichotomy between the south and the north revealed itself within the body of Afrikanerdom—in literature, in the theatre, in business, in education, even in sport. Usually the tensions were smoothed over for the sake of unity, but not for long. Broadly speaking, it was a struggle between tolerance and intolerance, between the liberal conservatives and the reactionaries, the limited democracy school of thought against the semi-authoritarians, the protagonists of separate freedoms for the non-white peoples against the inflexible 'baas-skappers' (dominators). Time, however, tended to blur this distinction.

Up till the late 1960s one of the unresolved dilemmas of Afrikaner nationalism was whether the movement could afford to remain bogged down in nineteenth-century concepts of race and politics or whether (and how) it should move ahead into the later part of the twentieth century.

In the years following the death of Dr. Verwoerd (1966), the struggle between the two tendencies in the party, represented by the 'verligtes' (enlightened) on the one hand, and the 'verkramptes' (reactionaries) on the other, came to the surface in the cultural and religious as well as political spheres. The need to find some modus vivendi with Black Africa, the need to form a united white front against militant African national-ism from beyond the Zambesi, and the economic facts of life in South Africa which called for growing African participation in the semi-skilled and skilled labour categories—all this strengthened the case of the en-lightened group. This element advocated an outgoing foreign policy and some relaxation of policy in respect of the colour bar in sport, not domestically but in the international sphere where South African participation was involved.

The tide, therefore, appeared to be flowing in favour of the more enlightened element in the National Party in the late 1960s, although external pressures on South Africa, in aggravating the defensive philo-sophy of the laager, helped to strengthen the hand of the 'verkramptes'. Moreover, in the Dutch Reformed Church the reactionaries remained firmly in the saddle and set their face against any flexibility of policy. Party and Church appeared for the time to be less monolithic, but the effect of this on the outcome of the struggle to decide in which direction Afrikanerdom should move as the final quarter of the twentieth century approached remained uncertain.

3. *The Drive to Sovereign Independence*

Afrikaner Nationalism's attitude to the issue of sovereign indepen-dence for South Africa falls into two distinct periods: the drive to attain Dominion status and then independence for South Africa within the

Commonwealth of Nations, with which the founder of the party came to be satisfied, and the subsequent struggle for republican independence, within the Commonwealth if necessary, but preferably outside it.

Hertzog's 'South Africa first' motto was the logical precursor of the drive for sovereign independence. Although as a strict constitutionalist he could not support the armed revolt of some of his Free State and Transvaal compatriots against South Africa's decision to go to war with Germany in 1914, he was vigorously opposed to 'fighting England's wars', and the Rebellion strengthened his determination to attain a status where South Africa should be the sole arbiter in this and other foreign policy matters. In 1919 he led a 'freedom deputation' to Paris to plead for 'complete independence for South Africa', and if that was unattainable, the return of the independence of the two ex-republics and the right of the Cape and Natal to determine their own future. This fitted clearly into this pattern of sovereign independence.[1] A direct outcome of this abortive mission was a recommendation by the Federal Council of the National Party to the four provincial congresses to recast the programme of principles of the party in such a way that the independence ideal was clearly formulated. The party now became committed to fighting by constitutional means for the extension of the rights and freedoms of the country 'until sovereign independence is attained and the Union becomes in all respects the equal of Britain'.[2]

In spite of some agitation within Nationalist ranks for secession from Britain after the First World War, Hertzog resisted it. In 1923, when he entered into the election agreement with the Labour Party, then largely supported and led by English-speakers, he gave a categorical assurance that he would take no steps to secede from the Commonwealth. But he drove on towards complete self-determination for South Africa and when the Imperial Conference of 1926, largely as a result of his insistence, but strongly backed by Canada, adopted the Balfour Declaration recognizing the autonomy of members of the Commonwealth and their equality with one another, he felt his ideal of a sovereign independent South Africa had come close to attainment.[3] But according to E. G. Jansen, a leading Nationalist of the day and a subsequent Governor-General of the Union, the outcome was not acceptable to all Nationalists.[4] Many clearly hated the reference to the Dominions being united by a 'common allegiance to the Crown'; they disliked the Crown and looked

---

[1] Van der Walt et al. i. 653. [2] Ibid. i. 654.

[3] In 1927, Hertzog persuaded his followers to change the constitutional clause in their party's constitution to read as follows: 'The National Party accepts the declaration of the Imperial Conference of 1926, and agrees that it amounts to the attainment of sovereign independence and of the power to exercise our State functions according to our own wishes.' —D. W. Krüger, The Age of the Generals, p. 152.

[4] Jansen's chapter in Van der Walt et al. i. 658.

upon the idea of owing allegiance to it as un-Afrikaans. Some young intellectuals in the party also rebelled: they thought Hertzog had not taken them any further along the independence road than Smuts's status position of 1919.[1] The extent to which this half-satisfaction with the Balfour Declaration and its lineal successor, the Statute of Westminster, was real, became obvious once Dr. Malan took over the National Party leadership in 1934.

As early as 1917 the Federal Council of the Party noted in its annual report that the republican feeling was being 'immeasurably strengthened' by the war policy of the Government,[2] and issued a comprehensive statement which came to be regarded as the republican credo of the National Party. While recognizing the existence of republican sentiment and welcoming this as 'wholly explicable and justifiable', the statement also acknowledged the necessity of bringing these feelings 'under proper discipline' and leading them in the right channels 'for the welfare of South Africa'.[3] This was clearly an attempt to satisfy non-republicans as much as republicans. Although the Free State and Transvaal parties decided in 1920 to allow republican propaganda to be made by their members, it was only in 1930, when a group of impatient young parliamentarians established the *Republikeinse Bond* as a pressure group, that the issue began to assume more than theoretical importance.

Hertzog, however, had remained lukewarm about republicanism,[4] and at the 1930 congress of the Free State National Party he expressed himself vigorously against it as a plank in the party platform and condemned those propagating it. For some time this settled the issue, although elements in the party kept on propagating the ideal. Therefore, as soon as Malan and his followers broke with Hertzog over Fusion, the 'new' National Party revived the issue. So, in the debates on the 1934 Status of the Union Act, which gave final confirmation to the independent status of South Africa within the Commonwealth, the leaders of the Free State and Transvaal National Parties both came out vigorously in favour of a republic. In 1935 the Federal Council of the party, under strong Transvaal and Free State pressure, unequivocally adopted republicanism as the most desirable form of government for South Africa, even though there was some disagreement on the vigour with which this aim should be pursued.[5] The party felt that only in

---

[1] D. W. Krüger, loc. cit.   [2] M. P. A. Malan, p. 48.   [3] Van Schoor, pp. 156–7.

[4] 'He was [in 1919] in favour of a republic if it would contribute to the solidarity of the Afrikaans- and English-speaking sections. . . . He could never in later years, be described as a republican.'—Van Schoor, p. 155.

[5] Dr. Verwoerd wrote in 1966 that Dr. Malan had remonstrated with him in 1937–8 because he was advocating republicanism too fervently in his newspaper. He added that he refused to listen. It is possible that this claim was part of the myth-making process in which Nationalist leaders indulged in an attempt to claim credit for bringing about a republic. See van Jaarsveld and Scholtz, p. 5.

republicanism could the Afrikaner's political destiny be fulfilled and South Africa's full independence brought home to the world. On the negative side, however, the old antipathy to Britain and things British, including, in many cases, English-speaking South Africans, was a powerful motivating force and a potent political weapon. Britain had taken away the independence of the ex-republics, and the restoration of republican freedom became an idealistic beacon and goal.

From then until it finally came to power in 1948, the National Party, particularly under pressure from elements in the Free State and Transvaal, where the republican sentiment had always been stronger than in the Cape or Natal, laid increasing emphasis on the need to attain a republic quickly. During the Second World War in particular it stressed the need to break with Britain. In the 1948 election, however, when its war-time isolationism came under heavy fire and it was anxious not to drive away English-speaking support, the party soft-pedalled the issue a little and concentrated instead on colour and the threat to the white man's position of dominance. Having once won, it felt freer to open the stops again, however much non-republicans may have helped to bring it to power. In 1949, when the Commonwealth Prime Ministers' conference granted India the right to retain its Commonwealth membership although it had become a republic, Dr. Malan had insisted that all the Commonwealth countries had an equal right with Britain to say whether republican India would remain in the Commonwealth. The National Party thereupon decided on a change of tactics in an effort to allay the suspicions of those South Africans who feared that republicanism meant the severance of all ties with the Commonwealth. Under the Transvaaler, J. G. Strydom, who throughout his career was a passionate advocate of republicanism, the party announced that it would regard the fact of becoming a republic and breaking with the Commonwealth as two quite separate and distinct steps: the second would not automatically or even necessarily follow on the first.

In the event two steps became unnecessary. Greatly daring, in the eyes of many South Africans, Verwoerd took the issue to the country in October 1960, and won a mandate for the establishment of a republic by 850,458 votes to 775,878 votes. Six months later he went to the Commonwealth Prime Ministers' conference in London and in an unexpected move, withdrew his application for South Africa's continued membership in the face of what he regarded as attempts to interfere in the domestic affairs of South Africa by some of the other member-nations who were sharply critical of the apartheid doctrine, and looked upon it both as a threat to the Commonwealth's existence and as being in conflict with its philosophy.

Although this withdrawal had not been planned and shocked some Nationalist opinion almost as much as it did the strong pro-Commonwealth feeling among non-Nationalists, the complete break suited most Nationalists.[1] This was their promised land: a free and independent republic divorced from Britain and from the Commonwealth. The last shot had finally been fired in the Boer War: the enemy of 1899 had been pushed aside and vanquished, the humiliating Treaty of Vereeniging had finally been torn up, and the freedom of the Transvaal and Free State Republics restored and extended not only to the two former colonies of the Cape and Natal, but also, in a sense, to South West Africa, over which the Nationalists had shown so much pro-German concern in 1914. The wheel had indeed come full circle. Nor was it any longer necessary to fly the Union Jack alongside the country's official flag (which had been part of the 1928 flag settlement achieved by Hertzog), for in 1957 the Strydom Government had legislated for only one official flag to be flown on all occasions and had announced that the national anthem was to be *Die Stem van Suid Afrika* (The Voice of South Africa), which would be sung alone on State occasions without 'God Save the Queen'.

It was a measure of the degree to which Afrikaner Nationalism's ideas had come to be accepted as representing South African opinion that neither the flag nor the anthem decisions caused more than a ripple of concern. Thirty years previously either would have sent the country into paroxysms of excitement and anger. It was also a measure of the extent to which South Africans had progressed to nationhood in spite of, as well as because of, the way in which Afrikaner Nationalist leaders had forced the pace. After the Second World War, and under the influence of Malan, the demand for a return to a Kruger-type republic with an executive Chief of State had been dropped and the emphasis placed primarily on the effect of republicanism on South Africa's relations with the rest of the world and on the need for the country to decide its own destinies. Furthermore, because enthusiasm for the Commonwealth idea was beginning to wane among white South Africans who looked without relish at the growing number of non-white members in the Commonwealth, the idea of a republic was less abhorrent to non-Nationalists than it had been thirty years previously.

At the same time the internal colour problem had become all-important by 1960, and constitutional matters tended to become irrelevant in the face of more pressing issues. Moreover, by adopting a step-by-step technique and so conditioning public opinion, the National Party had played its cards shrewdly and in the end achieved its ideal with less

[1] Dr. Verwoerd wrote in 1966 that he had been spiritually prepared for the break when it came. Van Jaarsveld and Scholtz, p. 7.

rancour than its most ardent protagonists would have dared to hope for even five years previously.

4. Broederbond *and Separatism*

In the political shadows there operated, particularly after the early 1930s, a secret organization, the *Afrikaner Broederbond*, whose precise role in, and influence on, Afrikaner Nationalism it was never possible to determine with accuracy, but which were always considerable and sometimes decisive.

The *Bond*'s own version, strictly for public consumption, was that it was a national and not a political organization. In a limited sense this was true, and it is even possible that its founders did not intend it to be anything more than a 'service' organization. In time, however, and inevitably in view of what it sought for Afrikanerdom, its activities spilled over into the political sphere, and exercised an important if not overriding influence on politics. P. J. Meyer, a one-time chairman of the *Broederbond*, wrote in 1966: 'The main purpose of this cultural movement was to purify Afrikaans nationalism of all elements by which it could destroy itself and to build it on a Christian-Protestant basis, with (as yardstick) the legal principles of the Holy Writ, the guidelines of our Christian national tradition and the demands of the time in which we live, in all spheres of life to full independence and maturity.'[1]

A one-man commission of inquiry into secret organizations, appointed in 1964 by the Government—at the instigation of its opponents— accepted the *Broederbond*'s version of its activities. The *Bond*, it said, was an organization 'in which Afrikaners could find each other in the midst of great confusion and disunity and be able to work together for the survival of the Afrikaner people in South Africa and the promotion of its interests'.[2] The report found that although it 'studies, discusses and takes a stand on matters such as, for example, education, separate development etc., which also fall within the political field, and although it is not unimportant for the realization of its aims which political party is in power, it does not arrogate to itself the function of a political party by attempting to capture governmental power for itself in order to realize its fixed aims. The Bond is a service organization intended to serve the Afrikaner, and its field of operations is the sphere of work of the Afrikaner people as a separate historical, Protestant-Christian language and cultural community'.[3]

The *Bond*'s activities, the report continued, 'are determined by the

---

[1] Ibid., p. 305.
[2] *Report of the Commission of Inquiry into Secret Organizations*, 1965, p. 3.
[3] Ibid., p. 4.

needs of the Afrikaner people at that particular moment. So, for example, the principal function of the Bond during the initial period of existence was the unification of Afrikaner and Afrikaner as members of the same language and cultural community.'[1] The report came to the conclusion that 'the Bond's achievements, within the relatively short space of its existence, are indeed impressive, especially in certain fields such as, for example, the bringing together or unification of Afrikaners, the Afrikaans language, Afrikaans culture and traditions, the Afrikaners' share in the national economy and the commercial world, and the promotion of good relations between the whites and non-white groups of South Africa'.[2]

Opponents and critics of the *Bond*—and they included two Afrikaans-speaking Prime Ministers of South Africa, Hertzog and Smuts, as well as other Afrikaners—have a different version of the *Bond* and its aims and activities. Smuts said in Parliament in 1945, in justification of his Government's action in banning public servants from being members of the *Bond* or from participating in its proceedings, that he regarded the Bond as a dangerous political organization which was operating in secret in order, *inter alia*, to promote the interests of one section of the population at the expense of those of the other, and which was attempting to capture key positions in the country with a view to exerting an influence on the national policy.[3] To this the one-man commission of 1965 replied that while the *Bond* did promote Afrikaner interests, it did not do so at the expense of the interests of any other section of the population.

The first full-scale public assault on the *Broederbond* came from Hertzog in 1935 in a speech to his constituents at Smithfield. He blamed it for opposing the Fusion of the National and South African Parties and denounced the movement as a 'grave menace to the rest and peace of our social community, even where it operates in the economic-cultural sphere'.[4] The organization, he maintained, was striving 'by way of domination on the part of the Afrikaans-speaking section to put their foot on the neck of English-speaking South Africa'. Hertzog added: 'I know of few towns and villages in the Free State where the Broederbond has not established for itself a nest of five, six, or more Broeders to serve as a focal point for Bond propaganda, and I also know that there is hardly a single nest on which there is not at least one teacher sitting as a hatcher.'[4]

The most revealing statement, however, came in a private circular quoted by Hertzog and issued on 16 January 1934, by the chairman of the *Broederbond*, Professor J. C. van Rooy, of Potchefstroom University,

---

[1] *Report of the Commission of Inquiry into Secret Organizations*, 1965, p. 5
[2] Ibid., p. 5.   [3] *Hansard*, 21 Mar. 1945, cols. 3878–87.
[4] *The Friend*, 8 Nov. 1935.

and the secretary, Mr. I. M. Lombard, which read, *inter alia*: 'Let us focus our attention on the fact that the primary consideration is whether Afrikanerdom will reach its ultimate destiny of baasskap [domination] in South Africa. Brothers, our solution for South Africa's ills is that the Afrikaner Broederbond shall rule South Africa.'[1]

To this statement there was never an adequate reply. Without necessarily accepting that the *Bond* was 'a kind of Gestapo',[2] there were many South Africans who agreed with Smuts that at some stages in its career the *Bond* had been 'a dangerous, cunning, political Fascist organisation',[3] whose object was to perpetuate Afrikaner rule and to achieve dominance for Nationalist Afrikaners in every possible sphere.

Membership was confined to white males over 25 years of age, who 'must be Afrikaans-speaking, belong to the Protestant faith and be professing members of one of the three Afrikaans churches, not be Free-masons, have a clean character and firm principles [this also applying to their Afrikanership], and accept South Africa as their only father-land'.[4] In 1964 there were 6,768 members divided into 473 divisions (cells, opponents of the *Bond* call them). Three recent Prime Ministers of South Africa were generally assumed to be members of the *Bond* (Dr. Malan, Mr. Strydom, and Dr. Verwoerd).

Opponents of the *Bond* believed that it acted as Afrikanerdom's brains trust and principal co-ordinating agency, planning tactics as well as broad strategy. Its influence, they believed, varied from time to time, depending on the needs of the day and the receptivity of the politi-cians. The overlap in membership of the National Party leadership and the inner core of the *Broederbond* was obvious, particularly after Hertzog's departure from the scene.

The *Broederbond*'s influence in religious and cultural circles was con-siderable if not decisive, and it was also credited with inspiring and vigorously implementing the strongly separatist movement which mani-fested itself from the early 1930s onwards. It is difficult to say just what influence the *Bond* exercised on the powerful Dutch Reformed Church, but one revealing incident might be quoted. In January 1967 a lay delegate to the synod of the *Gereformeerde Kerk* in Potchefstroom tried unsuccessfully to persuade the synod to record its opposition to attempts by the *Broederbond* to 'dictate' to church members. Quoting a 'strictly confidential' circular of 1 August 1962, the delegate maintained in his petition that it was clear that the *Broederbond* sought to tell members how to act at church meetings. He asked the synod to point out to its

---

[1] Ibid.
[2] Smuts was accused of having labelled it as such in Parliament: *Hansard*, 21 Mar. 1945, col. 3878 ff.   [3] Ibid.
[4] *Report of Commission of Inquiry into Secret Organizations*, p. 5.

members the dangers of belonging to the *Bond* and 'to warn them that membership of the Bond was incompatible with membership of the Gereformeerde Kerk'. Because the petition did not conform to the correct procedure, the synod refused to discuss it.[1] In its early days particularly, *Bond* membership contained many teachers and ministers of religion, as General Hertzog said in his Smithfield speech. These people in turn, as was only natural, exercised a dominant influence in the affairs of such bodies as the *Federasie van Afrikaanse Kultuurverenigings* (*F.A.K.*), the Federation of Afrikaans Cultural Organizations, which became Afrikanerdom's principal co-ordinating agency in the social, literary, artistic and economic fields, and which undoubtedly played a vital role in the history of Afrikaner nationalism.[2]

The *F.A.K.* was established in 1929 on *Broederbond* initiative, and there were several periods when the two bodies shared their senior executive officer, Dr. P. Koornhof, who subsequently became a member of Parliament. By 1937 the *F.A.K.* had over 300 affiliated organizations, one-third of them language and cultural associations, and two-thirds made up of church councils and other church organizations, charitable groups, student and youth groups, scientific study circles, and educational organizations.

In two fields, in particular, the *F.A.K.* was to exercise an influence which was positive and creative and which undoubtedly impinged on the political sphere: in stimulating interest and pride in Afrikaans literature and art, and in encouraging and assisting the Afrikaner to enter more fully than in the past into the industrial and business life of the country. In a third field, the educational, its influence was vital, while its encouragement of such parallel but sectional movements as the Voortrekkers (counterpart of the Girl Guides and Boy Scouts) and *Noodhulpliga* (counterpart of the St. John Ambulance Association or of the Red Cross) had positive value while contributing to Afrikaner separatism in fields where united endeavour would have contributed to a broader South Africanism embracing both white language groups. In 1967, the national leader of the Voortrekker movement was to claim publicly that 'without the Voortrekker movement the National Party would not have come to power in 1948, nor would South Africa have become a republic in 1961'.[3]

Education was always a concern of Afrikaner leaders, who saw in it a primary field of work in their attempts to build a nation and to prevent the de-Afrikanerization of the young.

[1] *Die Beeld* (Johannesburg) 22 Jan. 1967.
[2] '. . . in 1929 the Federation of Afrikaans Cultural Associations came into being, as a result of which the Afrikaans language started permeating all spheres of life and parts of our country as the important structural principle of Afrikaans nationalism.'—Meyer, in van Jaarsveld and Scholtz, p. 305. [3] *Die Transvaler*, 6 Nov. 1967.

Afrikaans schools, Afrikaans teachers' training colleges, Afrikaans universities and other educational institutions were essential to lead the Afrikaans child through his mother tongue into the cultural life of his own people, an introduction through which the Afrikaans national spirit was formed to achieve its highest prestige potential. In these educational institutions the flame of Afrikaans nationalism, as the bearer also of Afrikaans republican independence, constantly burned high and brightly.[1]

It was not until 1939, however, that the *F.A.K.* organized a Christian-National Education conference from which was born the Institute for Christian-National Education.[2] Like the National Party, the Institute insisted on mother-tongue instruction. In consequence, wherever the party came to power it separated the children of the two language groups by encouraging the establishment of single-medium as opposed to either dual- or parallel-medium schools, denied parents the right to choose in which language their children should be educated, and insisted on compulsory mother-tongue instruction. The Institute urged, and the party accepted in general terms, that the education of Afrikaner children should be both Christian and national. Christian was defined as a view of life 'based on Holy Scripture and formulated in the articles of faith of our three Afrikaans churches', while national meant 'love for everything that is our own, with special reference to our country, our language, our history and our culture'. In their original programme the sponsors of Christian National Education put forward extreme fundamentalist doctrines which included the condemnation of the theory of evolution and support for that of predestination. They insisted, too, that history and geography were to be taught as divinely determined. Teachers who were not prepared to subscribe to these doctrines would not be appointed.[3] However, this was going too far even for many Nationalists, and the more extreme demands were later quietly dropped.

The reply of Afrikaner leaders to the charge that they segregated the white children of the two language groups and so produced a dichotomy in the white community, was that every people has a distinctive life of its own which education should not only recognize but intensify. Separation for the purpose of implementing mother-tongue instruction was therefore no disservice, they maintained. Opponents of Afrikaner Nationalism and of Christian-National education, on the other hand, pointed out that it would not be possible to build a truly South African nation, with two languages and cultures but common aims and objectives, as long as the children of the two language groups were forcibly separated

---

[1] Meyer, p. 306.
[2] The Christian National Education of the 1950s was unlike that of the post-Boer War period: it was chauvinistic and narrowly based and far more impregnated with political ideology than the venture of fifty years before. See L. Marquard, *People and Policies of South Africa*, pp. 209–13.   [3] Ibid., p. 210.

at school. In 1967, an official mouthpiece of the National Party, *Die Transvaler*, was able to write: 'Without the application of the system of Christian-national education the political history of South Africa over the last thirty or forty years would have been entirely different.'[1]

In the economic sphere the *F.A.K.* did its most significant and valuable work immediately before and after the Second World War. First, in 1938, there was launched the *Reddingsdaadbond*, a movement intended to save Afrikaners from penury, lift them up economically and guide them into fields of opportunity in the rapidly growing towns and cities. In the following year, the First Peoples' Economic Congress was held, described as 'the greatest single catalyst in the economic independence process of the Afrikaner'.[2] Out of this was born the *Ekonomiese Instituut* (Economic Institute), a service organization to help Afrikaners entering industry and commerce as entrepreneurs, an objective which was to attain spectacular results in the decade following the war. The idea of mobilizing Afrikaner capital and purchasing power succeeded brilliantly in the expanding economy of the time, and by the 1960s the Afrikaner, who in any event dominated the agricultural scene, had established for himself a niche in such sectors of the country's economic life as secondary industry and life insurance, with a toehold in commerce, mining, and finance.

The leaders of Afrikanerdom realized that political power was of limited value without economic power, and the economic movement was in part at least designed to secure such power. By the second half of the 1960s the movement had succeeded beyond the expectations even of its own sponsors, and had, incidentally, contributed considerably to the economic development of the country and the raising of the living standards of non-Afrikaners as well as Afrikaners. Banks, insurance companies, and building societies had been established and were controlled by Afrikaners, while a foothold had been obtained in gold- and coal-mining. Afrikaners, who had long dominated the agricultural industry, had become entrepreneurs in various segments of secondary industry. As a predictable and desired by-product, Afrikaner Nationalism had been given further powerful underpinning to equip it for the task of governing South Africa as the senior and dominant white partner.

In the trade-union sphere, also, the planners and policy-makers of Afrikaner Nationalism had not been inactive. Early in the 1930s a campaign had been launched to capture the key organization in the country, the South African Mineworkers' Union, a numerically powerful body of white workers, and to infiltrate such bodies as the Garment

---

[1] *Die Transvaler*, 7 Nov. 1967.

[2] E. P. du Plessis, *'n Volk Staan Op*, pp. 97–133. This book is enlightening in that it shows how often Afrikaner economic undertakings were the result of patriotic urges.

Workers' Union. Here, too, success was beyond expectations, but not without struggle. The trade-union movement was split ideologically as well as racially with important sections openly espousing the philosophy of Afrikaner Nationalism, and all divided on lines of colour. The *Blanke Werkers Beskermingsbond* (White Workers' Protection Association) openly backed racial separation in employment and job reservation, and refused to have anything to do with any trade union which sought to welcome workers of all races. It was militantly pro-Nationalist. At the national economic conference in 1939 the chairman of the *Reddingsdaadbond*, Dr. N. Diederichs, a subsequent Nationalist Cabinet Minister, explained that one of the movement's objects was to make the Afrikaner worker part and parcel of the national life and to prevent Afrikaner workers developing as a class distinct from other classes in the Afrikaner national life. Dr. T. E. Donges, another of Nationalism's planners and the Republic of South Africa's first President-elect, explained that foreign influences would have to be removed from the trade unions and the Afrikaner worker kept within the church and his national and cultural heritage.[1]

In addition to the agencies and organizations already listed, and an old-established association for the advancement of science and an academy of arts, Nationalist planners brought into being a separate university students' organization, the *Afrikaanse Studentebond*, counterpart of the older and non-sectional National Union of South African Students; and a separate body for the study of race relations, the *Suid-Afrikaanse Buro vir Rasseaangeleenthede* (counterpart of the long-established non-racial South African Institute of Race Relations), formed to underwrite apartheid and open to white members only. For the establishment and growth of separate Afrikaans-medium universities, Afrikanerdom's guiding spirits were also able to take credit. There were five such institutions at the end of 1967, all contributing to the economic and scientific development of South Africa, as well as to its literary and artistic progress.

By the time South Africa became a republic, the dichotomy of white South Africa as between the two language groups was all but complete —thanks to *Broederbond*-Afrikaner Nationalist drive and inspiration. Once separation had been achieved and unity and loyalty to the group could be maintained, Afrikaner political control was more or less assured. In the attainment of all this, the Afrikaans newspapers played a vital part. From the outset Hertzog realized that Afrikaans would be the main instrument of Afrikaner survival and nation-building; and throughout the last half-century the language was in fact so used. 'The coming into being, growth and development of the Afrikaans language is the other side of the establishment, growth and development of the Afrikaner nationalism in which the republican constitutional ideal is rooted. The

[1] A. Hepple, *South Africa*, p. 236.

maintenance and development of Afrikaans was at the same time the maintenance of an own nationalism as the striving to self-sufficiency in all spheres of life.'[1] Without the Afrikaans language there would have been no Afrikaner nation and certainly no Afrikaner Nationalist movement. Culture and art were also inspanned in the drive to make the Afrikaners proud of themselves as a group or a nation or 'race' as they put it. Dr. H. J. Terblanche, chairman of the Society for the Maintenance of Afrikaans, expressed the idea in these words: 'Afrikaans, the language which God gave us, is our greatest and most precious possession. If our language disappears, our nation will without doubt also disappear.'[2]

Early in its existence, the National Party saw the necessity of establishing its own Press. When *Die Burger*, the first daily newspaper, with Dutch as its medium, began in Cape Town, it was edited by Dr. D. F. Malan. In Bloemfontein and Johannesburg, too, it was potential politicians who became the editors of the party organs: Dr. Verwoerd, who became Prime Minister, and Dr. A. J. R. van Rhyn, who was in the Malan Cabinet. These and other newspapers subsequently established were official party organs and made their appeal as such. They became the rallying point and focus of Afrikaner Nationalism, and it is inconceivable that the party would have succeeded without their daily, dedicated, and often skilful support.

5. *Race and Colour*

Basic to any evaluation of Afrikaner nationalism is an understanding of its race policies, for it was on these that it finally rose to commanding power. In South Africa race is always equated with skin pigmentation and to people of different colours specific characteristics are often attached by whites. So, for instance, Africans (blacks) are said to be slow, lazy, and smelly; Coloureds (brown) are said to be rowdy and cheerful; South African Indians are said to be crafty. Parliament has from time to time defined the different population groups. The Population Registration Act of 1950, for instance, which sought to compartmentalize the population of South Africa and to specify their rights and privileges, defined a Coloured person (one of mixed descent) as a 'person who is not a white person or a native'. A 'native person' is one who is 'in fact or is generally accepted as a member of any aboriginal race or tribe of Africa', that is, a black person. A 'white person' is one 'who in appearance obviously is or who is generally accepted as a white person, but does not include a person who, although in appearance obviously a white person, is generally accepted as a Coloured person'. In 1956 the Act was amended by the addition of a clause stating that

[1] Meyer, p. 294. [2] Dr. H. J. Terblanche, *Die Burger* (Cape Town), 3 Jan. 1967.

a 'person who in appearance obviously is a member of an aboriginal race or tribe of Africa shall for the purposes of this Act be presumed to be a native unless it is proved that he is not in fact and is not generally accepted as such a member'. In 1962 a further amendment laid down that a white person means a person who (a) in appearance obviously is a white person and who is not generally accepted as a Coloured person: or (b) is generally accepted as a white person and is not in appearance obviously not a white person, but does not include any person who for the purposes of his classification under this Act, freely and voluntarily admits that he is by descent a native or a Coloured person unless it is proved that the admission is not based on fact'.

Afrikaner Nationalists talk of blood as being either 'pure' or 'mixed'. 'Race purity', therefore, means 'purity of blood'. Language and traditions are said to be 'in the blood'. This contributed to the theory of Afrikaners being a 'pure race' and a 'race apart' in South Africa, and explained their tardiness in acknowledging that their English-speaking compatriots were as loyal and patriotic South Africans as they themselves. It was here that the idea of non-Afrikaners being second-class citizens took root in fringe Nationalist thinking and mythology. The confusion in popular usage is reflected in the multiplicity of definitions of race in different laws, and the failure of an official committee appointed to define categories to achieve acceptable definitions.

The separatist approach for the white community which was implicit in the early stages of Hertzog's two-stream policy, made it inevitable, indeed natural, that when the National Party came to formulating its colour principles for public consumption, separation would be their basis. Yet in 1914 'the Native question' was mentioned only in passing, even though Hertzog had begun to preach a form of race segregation in 1913, and had in fact been working on draft legislationto submit to the cabinet when he broke with Botha the year before.

When the Nationalists came to power in 1924, the colour issue began to assume an urgency in South African politics that had been lacking before and which it was not to lose again. By 1925 Hertzog was saying that the African franchise in the Cape had become a danger 'to the whole country'. He reckoned that in twelve of the fifty-one constituencies, the African vote had played a 'very special' role.[1] This influence would grow, he predicted, and in time lead to a demand for the extension of the African vote to the other provinces—something which Nationalism would not tolerate because, it was argued, it would mean the eventual swamping of the white voters. Here, then, was the writing on the wall for common-roll representation for Africans in the central legislature. In 1926, therefore, Hertzog submitted four Bills to

[1] M. P. A. Malan, pp. 108–9.

Parliament: the Representation of Natives Bill, the Native Council Bill, the Native Land Bill, and the Coloured Persons' Rights Bill. The under-lying purpose of this proposed legislation was to 'clearly establish the principle that the government of the country must be in white hands and strongly safe-guarded against any encroachment or weakening by non-whites'.[1] In a speech that came to be known as Nationalism's Black Manifesto, Hertzog in 1929 officially committed the National Party to keeping South Africa a 'white man's land'—a phrase that was to echo down the years as the central article of faith in the Afrikaner Nationalist creed and the most compelling inducement to the white voter to support the National Party. In the doctrine of 'franchise equality' which he tried to pin on to Smuts without much factual justification, Hertzog saw 'the end of the White man in South Africa. . . . Unless the Native vote in the Cape is separated from that of the whites, the Native vote will be the cause of the greatest tragedy in the history of South Africa.'[2] He made little headway with his legislative proposals in the years following his 1929 election victory, but kept on preparing public opinion for a break with the common franchise roll tradition of the Cape and for a system of communal representation for Africans which would guarantee political power to the white man.

After Fusion, in 1933, he was able to embark on translating his theories into legislative fact. The upshot was that in 1936 the Africans in the Cape were deprived of their common roll franchise, and as compensa-tion given the right to elect three whites to Parliament and two to the Cape Provincial Council. Africans throughout the country were given the right, through an electoral college system, to elect four white senators. A Natives' Representative Council was set up consisting of twelve elected and four nominated Africans, together with five Euro-pean officials, with the Secretary for Native Affairs as chairman. The council was an advisory body only, but for a time it was regarded by many whites and some Africans at least as a useful sounding-board and platform for African opinion. In addition, legislative provision was made for the purchase of just over 15,000,000 acres of additional land for exclusive African occupancy. By 1967, 12,000,000 acres had been acquired, giving the Africans 34,000,000 out of the 37,500,000 acres promised. (The total acreage of South Africa is 302,000,000.)

As far as Hertzog was concerned, this constituted the basis of segrega-tion and would probably have been the end of the corrosion of non-white political rights. But elements in his party who were opposed to African representation in Parliament also wanted the removal of the Coloured voters of the Cape from the common roll, something for which some Nationalists had first agitated as far back as 1922. So when Malan took

---

[1] Hepple, p. 108.   [2] *The Friend*, 19 Apr. 1927.

over the leadership of the party, the demand for the political separation of the Coloureds became a plank in his platform—a demand which Hertzog came to stigmatize as 'falsity and infidelity'[1] and a betrayal of the trust of the Coloured in the word of the white man.

Dr. Malan bided his time and when he came to power in 1948, he met the demand in his party for action on African political rights by abolishing the Natives' Representative Council, claiming that it had become a forum for anti-white agitation, and scrapping legislation providing communal representation for the Indians in Parliament and the Natal Provincial Council, and in 1951 he introduced the Separate Representation of Voters Act. This removed the Coloureds of the Cape from the common roll on which they had voted since 1853, and provided, instead, that they should elect four white representatives in Parliament and two in the Cape Provincial Council. When the Appeal Court declared the legislation *ultra vires* the South Africa Act (which provided that all non-white franchise changes were to be subject to a two-thirds majority of both Houses in joint session), the country was plunged into a constitutional crisis which kept it in turmoil for years.

The Government was not to be thwarted, however. It enacted the High Court of Parliament Act which set up a 'court' consisting of members of Parliament and senators to which the right of appeal would lie from the Appellate Division of the Supreme Court. This 'court' actually sat and 'reinstated' the separate roll. But the Appeal Court found the High Court invalid and the *status quo* was restored. So the matter was postponed till a 'fresh mandate' was given at the 1953 general election. Even then, the Government, at a combined session, could muster only 129 instead of the 138 votes required for a two-thirds majority. It was therefore left to the next Prime Minister, the more determined and inplacable J. G. Strydom, to settle the issue. He did this in two stages. Firstly, he enlarged the Appeal Court from five to eleven members and provided for a full quorum in all cases where legislation was in dispute. (Strydom explained that when the validity of legislation was questioned in future, the Appeal Court bench would not consist solely of judges whose views were irretrievably bound to one or other particular approach.[2] His Minister of Justice, Mr. C. R. Swart, subsequently the first President of the Republic of South Africa, added that Parliament was to be made 'completely sovereign so that it could pass laws as it wishes'.)[3] Secondly, he increased the size of the Senate from forty-eight to eighty-nine members and changed the basis of election in such a way that the National Party had 77 representatives and the combined opposition only twelve. This 'packed' Senate, condemned by opponents

---

[1] *Cape Times*, 5 Apr. 1938.   [2] *Hansard*, 1955, col. 4714.   [3] Ibid., col. 4690.

of Nationalism as a cynical piece of political jerrymandering, was justified by the claim that it was the 'will of the people', and that the electorate had instructed the Government to remove the Coloured voters of the Cape from the white man's roll. 'The voice of the people has been and is for it [the party] the highest political authority', wrote the party's Federal Council secretary, Senator M. P. A. Malan, years later. 'That is why it fought till it won.'[1] So, in February 1956, the Cape Coloured voters were finally removed from the common roll and South Africa took another stride away from the Western conception of shared government and government by consent. In reply to charges that political cynicism and opportunism had reached their zenith, the Nationalists said that South Africa had to be made safe for the white man, and that in any case the Coloured vote had been abused and exploited by whites without any advantage accruing to the Coloured people and that they would be far better off on a separate roll.[2]

But this was only one of the multitude of pieces the National Party was devising to fit into its complicated race jigsaw in which there was to be the maximum amount of separation of people of different colour. A party commission, under the chairmanship of Mr. P. O. Sauer, M.P., had produced a report in time for the 1948 general election[3] which put into currency the word 'apartheid' (inadequately translated as 'separateness'), and gave the party an emotional concept whose magic was to work domestically but bring obloquy on South Africa abroad as a symbol of repression and discrimination and white domination.

The introduction to the Sauer Report[4] emphasized that there were two directions in which colour policy could go: the policy of equality, which aimed at giving equal rights to all civilized and developed people, irrespective of race or colour, within the same constitutional framework, and the granting of the vote to all non-whites as they became capable of making use of democratic rights; and the policy of apartheid, which had grown out of the experience of the established white population of the country, 'and is based on the Christian principle of right and justice'. This aimed at the maintenance and protection of the white population 'as a pure white race', the maintenance and protection of the indigenous race groups 'as separate national communities', with possibilities of developing in their own areas to 'self-protecting

[1] M. P. A. Malan, p. 268.

[2] This was the theme of all Nationalist newspaper comment at the time. See *Die Burger* (Cape Town), *Die Transvaler* (Johannesburg), and *Die Volksblad* (Bloemfontein).

[3] The Sauer commission consisted of Mr. P. O. Sauer, M.P. (a subsequent cabinet minister), Dr. E. G. Jansen (a subsequent Governor-General), Mr. J. J. Serfontein, M.P. (a subsequent cabinet minister), Dr. G. B. A. Gerdener, a theologian, and Mr. M. de W. Nel, M.P. (a subsequent cabinet minister).

[4] It was published in all party newspapers, at greatest length in *Die Burger*, 29 and 30 Mar. 1948, from which the quotations in this section are taken.

national unities and the development of national pride, self-respect and mutual respect *vis-à-vis* the different races of the country'.

While equality would lead to 'national suicide of the white race', the report continued, the policy of apartheid would protect and make safe each race's character and future, with full opportunities for development and self-maintenance in its own area. One race would not be a threat to the other.

While seeking the well-being of white and non-white, the party felt this could be best achieved 'by the maintenance and protection of the white race, and accepts this as the fundamental basis of its policy'. It therefore undertook to protect the white race properly and effectively 'against any policy, philosophy or attack which might endanger or undermine its continued existence'. At the same time it rejected any policy of suppressing or exploiting the non-whites by the whites. 'National policy must be so designed that it will advance the ideal of ultimate complete separation on a natural basis.'

As far as the African population was concerned the report emphasized that the reserved areas should become their 'true fatherland'. 'The party realizes the danger of the flood of Africans moving to the cities and undertakes to protect the white character of our cities and to provide in a forceful and effective way for the safety of individuals and property and the peaceful life of the inhabitants.'

In the towns, all Africans would be put in separate residential areas. 'The native in our urban areas must be regarded as a "visitor" who will never be entitled to any political rights or to equal social rights with the whites . . .' The number of detribalized Africans had to be frozen by a strict system of influx control.

The report expressed its opposition to the organization of Africans in trade unions and favoured a system whereby the State would look after their interests in the role of guardian. In addition, a national system of labour control should be instituted.

Education for Africans had to be on a 'firm Christian-National basis, and must take account of the needs and level of development of the mass of natives. It must build character and anchor the native to his national characteristics.' The African would ultimately have to be responsible for the expenditure on and control of his own education under white supervision. He would also be guided to establish his own social, health, and welfare services in the reserves.

The Sauer Commission went on to deal with political representation for Africans. Apart from three senators nominated for their knowledge of the needs and desires of the African peoples, there would be four white senators elected by African councils. The representation of Africans in the House of Assembly and Cape Provincial Council would be abolished, and the seven senators would not be allowed to vote on issues of confidence, declarations of war, or the political rights of non-whites. A form of local government, more or less on the basis of the Bunga (Transkei) sytem would be instituted, and the Natives' Representative Council would be abolished. There would also be urban councils, 'which, however, will never be able to develop into independent bodies'. 'Under this system the native will ultimately be able to find expression for his political aspirations in the reserves instead of having political rights in the white areas.'

For the Coloureds the report suggested substituting their common roll franchise (with the whites) with three white representatives in each of the Cape Provincial Council and Parliament. These representatives were to have limited voting powers and would be elected by a Coloureds' Representative Council, which in turn would be chosen by Coloured voters. In addition, a system of regional Coloured councils with local jurisdiction was recommended in place of the existing local government franchise rights.

As far as the country's 500,000 Indian inhabitants were concerned, the Sauer report said: 'the party regards the Indians as a strange and foreign element which is not assimilable . . . they must be treated as an immigrant community'. It went on to recommend the repatriation of as many Indians as possible in co-operation with India 'and/or other countries'. No further Indian immigrants would be allowed into the country. There would be apartheid between whites and Indians and between Indians and other non-white groups. The Asiatic Land Tenure and Indian Representation Act of 1946 was to be 'reviewed immediately': Indians would be given no representation in the law-making processes of the country; they would be settled in separate areas and not allowed to live or own property in white areas; whites would not be allowed to live in Indian areas, or to trade there or own property. Opportunities for Indians to trade outside their own areas would be 'drastically curtailed', and Indian traders would gradually be moved out of African areas.

In its subsequent election manifesto,[1] which incorporated the essence of the Sauer report, the National Party declared that its colour policy was founded on the two fundamental principles of apartheid and guardianship. This, said the party's leader, Dr. Malan,[1] did not mean suppression of the non-whites, but the elimination of race friction by the recognition of their right of existence and their freedom of development. Other Nationalist comment on the Sauer report stressed that the alternative to apartheid was equality, and equality would mean the downfall of Western civilization and its standard-bearers (the whites) in South Africa.[2]

[1] *Die Burger*, 21 Apr. 1948.   [2] Ibid., 29 Mar. 1948.

It was left to a Government commission on the socio-economic development of the Reserves (the Tomlinson Commission) ten years later to fill in many of the spaces left blank by the Sauer Commission. Professor Tomlinson and his associates found that the reserved African areas would, if fully developed over the next forty years, be able to support a population of about ten million, which, at the time, would be about half the total African population of South Africa.[1] (Practical experience in the decade following the publication of the Tomlinson report was to show how wildly optimistic even this reckoning was.)

The Sauer report, therefore, provided an accommodating and flexible framework into which the National Party almost immediately began to pour a torrent of legislation which was to bring about radical changes in the relationships between the race groups and also set the pattern for South Africa's race development for many years to come.

The Prohibition of Mixed Marriages Act, for example, was designed to stop the few marriages (less than one hundred a year) between white and non-white, while the Immorality Act extended to all non-white people the prohibition already applying to sexual intercourse between white and African.

The Population Registration Act[2] brought into being a national register in which every individual's race was classified, and set up a Race Classification Board to adjudicate in cases of doubt. Critics of the Government believed that the national register was primarily designed to draw a line between white and Coloured and to prevent the crossing of the colour line into the white camp by Coloureds. Nationalists, on the other hand, looked upon the act as vital to the implementation of apartheid by clearly defining who was who, and therefore entitled to what.

Then came the Abolition of Passes and Co-ordination of Documents Act, which co-ordinated the pass laws and made them easier to implement and administer. It was compulsory for African men—and eventually for women—to carry a 'reference book' or identity card containing details of the holder and where he worked as well as the employer's name and signature. It was now possible to make sure that no African could obtain employment unless he possessed a reference book. Moreover, no worker could leave one job for another without a discharge signature from his previous employer. It consequently became more feasible to check the movements of individual Africans. The legislation relaxed restrictions on the movements of Africans in minor ways, but facilitated refinements of the control exercised over the influx of Africans to urban areas. This was the primary purpose: to stop the flow to the urban areas and to restrict the population of Africans in urban areas

[1] Commission for the Socio-Economic Development of the Bantu Areas within the Union of South Africa (Government Printer, U.G. 61/1955).   [2] See also above, pp. 402–3.

by expelling those thought to be surplus to the requirements of the area
or who were for one reason or another deemed (by an official) to be
undesirable. The machinery was harsh and although often ineffective,
produced bitterness and hardship by depriving people of the right to
sell their labour in the best market and also, in many cases, by keeping
families separated for years on end. The effect was to aggravate and
extend the system of migratory labour whereby the wage-earning father
would live in one area and his family elsewhere. The Nationalists justified
this severely criticized system by maintaining that the African worker was
in the 'white areas' on sufferance or simply as a visitor, and therefore had no
rights in those areas. The inhumanity of such a system did not escape the
Government's critics, although the policy undoubtedly had the support
of countless whites who were not Nationalists and who saw little wrong
with such direction and compulsion applied to the non-white peoples.

The Group Areas Act was the weapon the Nationalist Government
used mainly to bring about physical separation of the races where this
did not already exist. Intended, in the first place, to bring about residential segregation, particularly in urban areas, the Act was gradually
amended and extended so that the authorities could, for example, prevent non-whites from using 'white' sports facilities like club houses,
or from attending cinemas, entertainments, or other public functions
with whites. Variously described as 'the kernel of the apartheid policy'
(Dr. Malan),[1] and 'the cornerstone of positive apartheid' (Dr. Donges),[2]
the Act was constantly being modified in an attempt to make it workable.
It made possible, after a while, the movement of whole communities,
like groups of Indians in Durban and Johannesburg, of Coloureds in Cape
Town and Johannesburg, and of Africans in Johannesburg and Durban
or wherever they were deemed to constitute a 'black spot' in a 'white'
area. It was also effectively used as an instrument for slum clearance,
and in many cases compelled local authorities to provide non-white
housing on a scale they might otherwise not have done. The number of
whites compulsorily moved under the Act was infinitesimal compared
to the number of non-whites.

To these basic measures must be added the Bantu Education Act,
designed to give Africans an education in line with their needs and
opportunities as a separate community and bitterly opposed by Africans
because of the suspicion that its real purpose was to equip them only for
a subsidiary role in life. There followed the Extension of University
Education Act, which created separate higher education facilities for
Africans, Coloureds, and Indians, and closed the 'white' universities to
non-whites except on permit in cases where a particular course or degree
was not available at a non-white institution. The Separate Amenities

[1] *Hansard*, 31 May 1950, cols. 7722–30.   [2] Ibid., 29 May 1950, cols. 7434–50.

Act, again, laid down that amenities (such as railway waiting-rooms) may be separate but not necessarily equal to those of whites, while the amended Industrial Conciliation Act (1965) provided for and encouraged the formation of separate trade unions for different races, even within the same trade. The industrial conciliation law made no change in the status of Africans, who, since 1924, had not been recognized as workers for the purposes of the Act. Because of this dichotomy, provision had to be made for job reservation in order to avoid wage undercutting of white by non-white workers. The ideological nature of this legislation was emphasized by the Minister of Labour when he noted in 1954 that both the statutory colour bar and the conventional colour bar were in conflict with economic laws. 'The question, however, is this: what is our first consideration? Is it to maintain the economic laws or is it to ensure the continued existence of the European race in this country?' He had no hesitation in answering in favour of race.[1]

The Bantu Authorities Act of 1951, which provided for local self-government for Africans at the tribal level, was hailed by party spokesmen as the principal instrument of 'positive apartheid'. Eight years later came an elaboration of this Act in the form of the Promotion of Bantu Self-Government Act. This envisaged the advancement of self-government for Africans in their reserved areas to something approaching provincial status. It was intended, too, as compensation for terminating African communal representation in Parliament and the Cape Provincial Council, as well as for the abolition, in 1949, of the Natives' Representative Council (see p. 405). The Prime Minister, Dr. Malan, justified his actions in these words: 'We have the choice of either giving the whites their own territory and the Bantu theirs, or of giving everybody one state and seeing the Bantu govern.'[2]

Faced with the problem of political rights for Africans in so-called white areas, the Government in 1961, in the Urban Councils Act, provided for the establishment of councils of Africans in urban areas on the basis of their national units, to maintain association with the reserves and with authorities which were largely tribal. The point of this link was that Africans should cease to pursue a place in white democracy and be helped to fall back on the tribal paths of government.[3] But the idea of giving Africans living in white areas a vote for governments in far-off tribal areas, which had no jurisdiction in the urban areas and no power to improve or change the urban society in which urban Africans lived and worked, made little appeal to black or white.

It was still necessary, in the Government's eyes, to clamp down on the political and semi-political activities of the non-white peoples in the so-called white areas. More particularly it aimed at preventing

[1] Ibid., 1954, col. 5854.   [2] Ibid., 1959, col. 6513.   [3] Hepple, p. 116.

co-operation between white and non-white on any political level. To achieve this it was prepared to go to extraordinary lengths which its opponents condemned as undemocratic and often vicious in their harshness. Its main legislative instruments were the Suppression of Communism Act, which not only proscribed the Communist Party but gave the Government powers to act against other organizations and individuals deemed by the Minister of Justice to be communist, and the Unlawful Organizations Act. This measure made it possible to proscribe organizations deemed to prejudice the safety of the State even if they were not communist. And from the Minister's decision there was no appeal to the courts. This made it possible for the Government to ban bodies such as the African National Congress, the Pan-Africanist Congress, and the multi-racial Congress of Democrats.

The Suppression of Communism Act included a definition of communism which was wide enough to enable action to be taken against well-nigh anyone who thought radically, and was in fact used to immobilize and in some instances deprive of their livelihood, trade-union officials and others active in workers' organizations or in politics generally.[1] The Act defined communism as the doctrine of Marxist socialism as expounded by Lenin or Trotsky, the Comintern or the Cominform, or 'any related form of that doctrine expounded or advocated in the Union for the promotion of the fundamental principles of that doctrine', or a 'doctrine which aims at bringing about any political industrial, social or economic change within the Union by the promotion of disturbances or disorder, by unlawful acts or omissions or by means which include the promotion of disturbance or disorder, or such acts or omissions or threat'.

Taken together, the Suppression of Communism Act and the Unlawful Organizations Act constituted a powerful legislative weapon against radical political activity. Backed by an Act providing the severest penalties for breaking laws in order to protest against laws, the Criminal Law Amendment Act, the Government was able to break the passive resistance campaign (1952–3) against unjust laws and to make the trade-union movement ultra-cautious by the simple process of 'naming' individuals who were thereafter not allowed to carry on their occupations or professions. The Suppression of Communism Act also enabled the Government to clamp down on organs of opinion which it 'deemed' to be advancing the objects of communism. It did this in the case of *New Age* (formerly *Guardian*) and *Torch*, and used administrative measures to harass other minority-view journals such as the Liberal organ *Contact*, which were outspokenly anti-Nationalist and gave expression to non-white as well as radical white views.

[1] By the end of 1955, no fewer than fifty-six key officials had been removed from office in this way.

This and similar legislation designed to suppress political activity by non-whites or by multi-racial bodies had the effect, after a while, of driving most non-white and inter-racial political activity underground, and some people resorted to violence. Many of them were caught and punished. The legislation also had the effect of bringing to the front a leadership which almost inevitably was more radical and less amenable to co-operation than its predecessors. The place of Chief Albert Luthuli, Nobel Prize winner, for instance, came to be taken by men who did not believe in co-operation between white and non-white and who looked to violence rather than evolutionary change to achieve their objective of a society which the non-whites would dominate. By the mid 1960s, the Government had virtually put a stop to African political activity and almost every recognized or accepted leader of the previous decade had been driven out of politics, being either in gaol or a refugee. But this did not happen before there had been two major security trials and an uncounted number of cases involving subversion, actual or planned, in the course of which scores of individuals were sentenced to imprisonment for what the Western world regards as political crimes.[1] Legislative provision was also made in the General Law Amendment Act, 1964, for the detention in solitary confinement for periods up to ninety days for questioning, of people suspected of being in possession of information about subversion. Scores of men and women were so detained. Some were subsequently charged, some gave evidence for the State, others refused, and some were released without any further action being taken against them. The ninety-day provision was suspended in 1966, but was in effect overtaken by powers under the Criminal Procedure Act No. 96, of 1965, to detain witnesses for up to one hundred and eighty days in cases involving security and certain other offences.

Sabotage, of which there had been sporadic outbreaks in preceding years, had already been made a capital offence in the General Law Amendment Act of 1962, while in further amendments (1963 and 1964) provision was made for placing under house arrest those whose political activities were regarded as 'inimical' to the interests of the State; for the extension—subject to annual Parliamentary review—of sentences of people imprisoned for security crimes; trial without preparatory examination; sentences ranging from five years' imprisonment to death for receiving sabotage training outside the country; and detention of suspect mail.[2] The Public Safety Act of 1953 had already given the

---

[1] Between January 1963 and December 1965, nearly two hundred political trials took place, involving over 2,000 accused, mostly Africans. Forty-nine were sentenced to death, fifteen to life imprisonment, and about 1,300 to imprisonment amounting to about 8,000 years.—Hepple, p. 172.

[2] Ibid., p. 168.

Government power to declare a state of emergency and rule by decree without Parliament.

As a result of this legislation groups and individuals intent on radical opposition to the Nationalist Government found political activity hazardous, if not impossible. To begin with action was concentrated mainly on radical left-wing organizations and persons; but the focus of attention moved rightwards; and in the mid 1960s it was liberalism as such that was under fire. The national chairman of the Liberal Party, Mr. Peter Brown, was gagged and his movements were restricted under the Suppression of Communism Act, although in Western terms he would have been classified as an old-style liberal. Passport control was used as a political weapon against many others, including Mr. Alan Paton, president of the Liberal Party. In 1965, when the Progressive Party won the two seats allocated to the Coloured people in the Cape Provincial council, the Government promised legislation to prevent whites from taking any part in non-white politics, although it was not clear how this was to be achieved as long as whites were to represent Coloureds in a white legislature. The intention was that politically white and non-white were to be kept apart and power concentrated in white hands. The preamble to the 1966 Prevention of Improper Interference Bill, which sought to bring about this further separation between white and non-white, reflected Nationalist philosophy in these words:

Whereas the traditional way of life of the Republic of South Africa requires that every population group shall develop independently within its own group, but with mutual co-operation and assistance; and whereas every population group has an inalienable right to live and to strive according to its own traditional way of life, as being the only foundation for ensuring lasting peace and good order; and whereas the whites as the guardians of the other population groups accept their mission to lead the non-white population groups to self-realisation and to safeguard them against political exploitation by others as the sole guarantee for the continued existence of both their own and the other population groups: . . .

This Bill was in 1967 sent to a Joint Select Committee of Parliament.

Apartheid, however, had its positive side as well, and it was the achievement of Dr. Verwoerd, the Prime Minister who was struck down by an assassin in his bench in the House of Assembly in 1966, that he gave to the theory a philosophic basis and content.[1] Early in his premiership he envisaged the ultimate emergence of some sort of commonwealth of states in South Africa. He told Parliament: 'If it is within the power of

[1] 'Long before he became Prime Minister he had . ... begun to mould the instinctive but shapeless philosophy of apartheid into a coherent and intellectually respectable canon. His theory of separate freedoms was his most important contribution to Afrikaner Nationalism, oppressed as it was with an uneasy sense of guilt before the accusing eyes of the world. It was able to hold up its head again.'—Leading article in *The Star* (Johannesburg), 8 Sept. 1966.

the Bantu and if the territories in which he now lives can develop to full independence, it will develop that way. . . . My belief is that the development of South Africa on the basis of this Bill will create so much friendship, so much gratitude, so many mutual interests in the process of the propulsive development that there will no longer be hostile Bantu states, but that there will arise what I call a Commonwealth, founded on common interests and linked together by common interests.'[1] Not much was heard about the commonwealth idea during the following years, but at the time of his death Verwoerd was working towards an accommodation with neighbouring African territories. He became the first South African Prime Minister to meet the head of an African State on a basis of equality, when he and Chief Leabua Jonathan, of Lesotho, conferred in Pretoria in September 1966. He went out of his way to stress his anxiety to live on terms of friendship with all well-disposed African states. He envisaged the day when the so-called 'Bantu Homelands' inside South Africa would attain their independence and coexist peacefully with white South Africa.[2] All the Africans' political desires, he said, could be met in the Homelands. He believed that neither white nor non-white would find happiness or complete fulfilment in integration and that the only hope lay in a system of maximum separation. Integration, he said, had never worked anywhere. It was under his inspiration that there developed the idea of 'separate freedoms' for white and non-white, an idea vigorously propagated by the National Party mouthpiece in the Cape, but less fervently in the rest of the country. The difficulty was that while the pure theory of separation had its attractions for non-white as well as white, it remained, in the eyes of its opponents, largely impracticable. Moreover, its implementation would inevitably result in hardship and discrimination.[3]

It was in the Transkei, an area reserved for African occupation in the eastern Cape Province, and inhabited by 1,500,000 Xhosa people, that the theory of 'separate freedom' was first applied. As an exercise in self-government on a relatively unsophisticated level it was an experiment with interesting possibilities. Although all the 'Homeland's' laws were subject to final approval by the South African Government, it did give the African people there experience in running their own domestic affairs—foreign policy, defence, the police and security, customs, posts, currency, and immigration were among the powers reserved for the South African Government in Pretoria—and might have led to greater

---

[1] *Hansard*, 20 May 1959, cols. 6214–41.

[2] Ibid. See also *Verwoerd aan die Woord*, a collection of Verwoerd's speeches from 1948 to 1962.

[3] '. . . he [Dr. Verwoerd] failed completely to sell his theory of separate freedoms to the world—the facts looked too damningly against it. He rode apartheid too hard in all its pettiness to lend verisimilitude to his larger image.'—*The Star*, 8 Sept. 1966.

economic development of the territory were it not for the limitations on 'white' capital and entrepreneurs to participate. Instead a Bantu Development Corporation was set up to help Africans launch their own business and industrial undertakings. This left the territory woefully short of development capital and technical knowledge and skill.

This experiment in self-government was in time to be extended to seven other 'national units' in different parts of South Africa. The difficulty was that these were not, like the Transkei, compact and separate regions, but a number of widely scattered and fragmented areas, separated by 'white' areas. How they were to be consolidated into single viable economic units was not clear.

The charge against the separate freedom policy was that in the white man's territory, comprising 87 per cent of the country's land surface and containing seven-twelfths of the total African population, the African had no political rights worth mentioning and no voice whatever in the central legislature. In other words, over most of the country and certainly where it mattered most, the white man was in absolute and undisputed control with no suggestion of sharing political power with the Africans he ruled. This was the position in spite of the fact that the role of the African in the economic life of the country continued to grow in importance.[1]

6. *The Anti-Nationalist Forces*

It was fortunate for Afrikaner Nationalism that during a vital phase of its existence when it was fighting for parliamentary power and for Afrikaner unity, the political forces ranged against it were led by one who was essentially an internationalist. Although an Afrikaner himself, Smuts had down the years become more interested in world and British Commonwealth than in national affairs. After his experience and his achievements in the First World War, his membership of the Imperial War Cabinet, and his role in drafting the Covenant of the League of Nations, it was perhaps not surprising that many South Africans, particularly Afrikaners, were persuaded that Smuts's concern was more with the world outside South Africa than with domestic affairs. The great esteem in which he was held by the British people during the closing stages of the First World War, combined with his barely concealed impatience with the trivialities of domestic politics, made him an easy, if unfair target for those, like Hertzog, who condemned him as 'the handyman of the Empire', the South African prepared to put Britain and her Empire before his own country. While Hertzog went around preaching

[1] According to the South African *Monthly Bulletin of Statistics* for October 1966, 539,000 out of a total labour force of 601,000 in mining were Africans, 320,000 out of 549,000 in manufacturing were non-whites, and 164,000 out of 236,000 in construction were non-whites.

his doctrine of sovereign independence for South Africa, Smuts was satisfied with and proud of his country's status as a member of the Commonwealth of Nations. He saw no conflict in being at once a good South African and a staunch Commonwealth man. His opponents thought differently.

Furthermore, while Afrikaans was his mother tongue, Smuts's enthusiasm for the language and the literature that the Afrikaners started producing in the 1880s was never sufficiently fervent to prevent his detractors from accusing him of being uninterested and unconcerned about the things of the spirit of his own people.

All this made Afrikaner Nationalism's task easier when it came to persuading the electorate that its party was the National Party of true patriots which could always be trusted to safeguard and advance South Africa's highest interests. Smuts and his associates were dismissed and reviled as 'English jingoes', and it is indisputable that some of the men round Smuts in Afrikaner Nationalism's formative years were this and little more. In fact, the jingoism of many English-speaking South Africans in the first quarter of the twentieth century had much to do with the success of Afrikaner Nationalism in its formative years. The result was that the most effective opposition to the intolerance and white separatism of Afrikaner Nationalism often came from Afrikaners. It was Afrikaners who fought most successfully against the isolationism and racialism which were inherent in Afrikaner Nationalism, and who strove for a more broadly based South Africanism than that of the Nationalists. They wanted their patriotism to include those English-speakers who felt as they did on national issues and who also believed in real equality between the two white language groups.

In later years, it was these Afrikaners who fought the racial intolerance, arrogance, and chauvinism of the neo-Nationalism of the post-Hertzog era with conviction and dedication, often at great personal sacrifice to themselves and their careers and professions, for a tightly organized Afrikanerdom did not hesitate to impose sanctions on those who refused to conform. It was these non-Nationalist Afrikaners who, in the days of the Second World War, saw South Africa's destiny linked with that of Britain and the United States and not with Hitler's Germany, and who unhesitatingly backed the Union's war effort. J. H. Hofmeyr and F. S. Malan were Afrikaners whose liberal patriotism it was difficult to match among English-speaking South Africans.

The English-speaking opposition to Afrikaner Nationalism was often ineffective, shortsighted, and unwise. The reasons lay in its failure to understand the nature and purpose of Nationalism's philosophy and in the absence of a positive purposeful creed of its own. In the realm of colour, the English-speaking community not only often showed that it was unaware of the real nature and needs of a plural society, but was in some ways as susceptible to the virus of racialism as its Afrikaner counterpart. This paralysed its opposition to Afrikaner Nationalism's extreme segregationist plans even when these were believed to be inimical to the country's interests.

The English-speaking section failed to propagate the idea of political integration as the counterpart of economic integration because this would have meant the advocacy of a form of political partnership between white and non-white, a suggestion from which the majority shrank. It was far easier—and far more comfortable—to accept the *status quo* with its built-in advantages for white-skinned citizens—the policy of '*baasskap*' —than to advocate change, which would have meant the abolition of the colour bar and equality of opportunity for all groups of the population, that is, a common society. Even a group as forward-looking as the Progressive Party, with its preponderance of English-speaking members, shrank from the idea of a franchise which was not heavily weighted in favour of the whites.

Moreover, by dragging their feet on issues like bilingualism, the right of self-determination and sovereign independence, the flag and the anthem, by a lukewarmness and worse to the Afrikaans language and its literature, its art and music—in brief, by an air of superiority and a lack of interest in the Afrikaner and his life and work, the English-speaking community lost the support of many non-Nationalist Afrikaners and played into the hands of Afrikaner nationalism by laying themselves open to the charge of being sectional, second-class citizens and lukewarm patriots crippled by a dual loyalty (to South Africa and to Britain). Often this was untrue and unjust; but too often it was a valid indictment. A certain casualness on the part of many English-speaking South Africans suited those only too ready to pose as super-patriots and contributed greatly to the growth and aggressiveness of Afrikaner Nationalism.

In the political sphere the strident jingoism of many of its opponents played into the hands of the National Party, which claimed to be the only genuinely South African party. This was true of elements in the Unionist Party, the first vehicle of English-speaking South Africans after Union, and more so of its lineal successors a generation later, the Dominion and Federal Parties. English-speaking jingoes who posed as mouthpieces of the moderate English-speaking South African, gave to the opponents of Afrikaner Nationalism a stigma which the more reasonable anti-Nationalists found difficult to avoid or counter.

Partly because of the failure of the parliamentary Opposition to make any real impact on a frustrated electorate, the fight against Afrikaner Nationalism in the period following the Second World War was characterized by extra-parliamentary activity on a scale the country had seldom previously experienced. Two anti-Nationalist movements in particular captured the public imagination, the War Veterans' Torch Commando, which at the height of its power in 1952–3, had an effective membership of close on 250,000 men and women; and the Women's Defence of the Constitution League (popularly known as the Black Sash because of its habit of wearing black sashes during silent public demonstrations). The Sash, although numerically far smaller, remained in being longer than the Torch Commando as a movement of conscience and protest against the violation of the spirit of the South African Constitution.[1]

The formation of the Torch Commando was a response to the Government's plans to remove the Cape Coloured people from the common voters' roll. It came into being almost spontaneously on a wave of popular revulsion against what anti-Nationalists felt to be the Government's unconcern for constitutional law and procedure. It organized meetings throughout the country and launched a 'steel commando' drive on Cape Town from all corners of the land which captured public imagination and for a time frightened the Government. For the 1953 general election it formed a United Democratic Front with the United and Labour Parties, and for a time it looked as though the Nationalists were on the defensive. Afrikaners played a considerable part in the Torch Commando's affairs. But political inexperience and ineptitude, and some injudicious speech-making by over-enthusiastic Torchmen enabled the Government to accuse the movement—and all associated with it—of planning armed rebellion. Moreover, the United Party and the Commando had difficulty in agreeing on election tactics; and finally the Commando itself ran into difficulties over the problem which ultimately reduced most anti-Nationalist movements to impotence: the question of the relationship between white and non-white in the community, and of the role, if any, which the non-whites could or should play in predominantly white ventures, whether political or not.

When, therefore, the Nationalists won the 1953 election with an increased majority—and again the electorate had voted 'white'—the Torch Commando, already weakened by the dissension over goals and tactics which so often paralysed progressive movements in South Africa, had little to hold it together and died. Once again the Nationalist stratagem of frightening the white electorate with talk of non-white domination and of smearing its most dangerous opponents as 'revolutionary' or 'liberal' or 'communist' or simply 'unpatriotic', had worked.

The Black Sash movement, founded to challenge the Government's— and the country's—conscience over the packing of the Appeal Court

[1] The Black Sash was still a force in the late 1960s.

and the Senate in order to take the Coloureds off the common electoral roll, operated on a smaller scale and depended on silent protest in public places to make its impact. For a while it annoyed the National-ists, whose ridicule failed to silence a movement of conscience which stimulated into political awareness many who were a-political and would otherwise have remained unaware of the political issues in dispute. It, too, had difficulty on the issue of non-white membership, but sur-vived as a small, vigorous, compact group which enlarged the scope of its activities by undertaking practical work of assistance to non-whites in need of guidance and counsel in problems of everyday living. It con-tinued, too, to protest against what it regarded as unjust laws and administrative acts. In this way, it managed to play a significant role in keeping meaningful dissent alive.

In both the Torch Commando and the Black Sash movement, as in bodies like the Education League, formed to fight Christian-National Education, English- and Afrikaans-speaking South Africans worked together to oppose what they regarded as the excesses of Afrikaner Nationalism. Nevertheless, it remained one of the most disputed ques-tions of South African political life why the English-speaking community, which had contributed so signally to the development of the country in a variety of spheres, have seldom if ever since Union produced politicians of equal stature to their Afrikaans-speaking compatriots. In spite of the contribution they made earlier to the establishment of a free Press, an independent and incorruptible judiciary, parliamentary democracy, a civil service of impartiality and integrity, the English-speaking section's role in the political sphere was usually a secondary one. A notable exception to this rule was to be found in the Cape Colony of the late 1800s and early 1900s, when the political scene there was dominated by men such as W. P. Schreiner, John X. Merriman, James Rose Innes, Cecil Rhodes, Starr Jameson, and Thomas Smartt. And in Natal, the overwhelmingly English-speaking province, the political leadership was always in English hands, but only occasionally in those of more than ordinary ability.

Part of the explanation for the failure of the English-speaking section to play its full part was to be found in the numerical relationship be-tween the two language groups; and early in South Africa's modern history, when Merriman was overlooked as the Union's first Prime Minister, it became an unwritten convention that the leader of a party which appealed to both language groups had to be an Afrikaner be-cause Afrikaners would vote for an 'Englishman' with reluctance.

But that was hardly the whole explanation. It had been said in criticism—and in defence—of the English-speaking South African that he was so busy either making money for himself or developing the country economically and staffing the professions, that he had no time for politics, which he left to the Afrikaner, who had been left behind in the economic race and therefore had more incentive to try to improve his lot through political action. The cynics said the English-speaker simply let the Afrikaner do his 'dirty' work for him. Whatever the explanation—and it probably included the fact that the average English-speaker never felt passionately enough about anything political for long enough to take effective action—it certainly made Afrikaner National-ism's task of winning and retaining political power easier.

Yet when all this and more had been said about the English-speaking South African's record in the political sphere—and his role in stimu-lating political opponents to emulate his best qualities should not be forgotten—it remained true that for half a century the English-speaking electorate opposed Afrikaner Nationalism, not always wisely or effec-tively, but at times, as during the constitutional crisis of the 1950s, with spirit and determination and in the highest traditions of Parliamentary democracy. The old Unionist Party, the South African Party, and the United Party all had a hard core of English-speaking support, just as did the Labour Party before and even after the Second World War. And all radical movements, parliamentary and extra-parliamentary, which had seen clearly the long-term dangers of unbridled Afrikaner Nationalism, almost always had English-speakers as the driving force. This was true of the Progressive Party which, although Afrikaner-led, consisted in its for-mative years mostly of urban English-speakers who opposed the separatist society of Afrikaner Nationalism with a philosophy of franchise on merit. It was also true of the non-racial Liberal Party as well as of parties further to the Left, all of which had strong English-speaking support.

Among those who opposed Afrikaner Nationalism and supported more radical causes, Jewish people were prominent. Although some supported the Nationalists, the majority believed in a more broadly based approach which was less sectional or intolerant. Their influence in progressive political movements was stronger than their numbers seemed to warrant and was often exercised at the risk of attracting racial rather than political criticism from their opponents.

The English-speaking South African failed politically where the vast majority of white men in Africa failed: in not realizing in time that, in spite of Afrikaner Nationalism's assertions to the contrary, the best hope for white and non-white alike lay in a society genuinely shared on a basis of merit and achievement. As it was, a substantial proportion of those who did realize this were English-speakers who remained true to Western liberal traditions of democracy and who stood for a free and open society. The alternative to a shared society in South Africa was the race separation which Afrikaner Nationalism was striving to attain.

Many English-speakers remained sceptical of the practicability or justice of this doctrine but lacked the will to face the implications of a common society. As a result, in the mid 1930s, there was a tendency to climb on to the Afrikaner Nationalist bandwagon when the tide of African Nationalism elsewhere in Africa began to lap the borders of the Republic and an Afrikaner Government sought safety in an increasingly heavily armed laager.

Was there a political role left for the English-speaking South African who refused to identify himself with the Afrikaner Nationalist and his theory of race separation and white domination in a racially mixed society? Destined to be members of a politically impotent minority, some became confirmed believers in the Nationalist doctrine of white supremacy. Others succumbed to the temptation to withdraw into the comfortable circle of their own interests and affairs, thereby abdicating all political responsibility. Many remained in the United Party in the belief that they were upholding their traditional values.

But an articulate and courageous minority was aware that it had to keep the flame of the liberal Western tradition burning so as to be ready to help light the way into the future for all the peoples and races of South Africa should the current experiment of racial exclusiveness and domination prove to have been unworkable. These people —with the brave support of some Afrikaans-speaking South Africans— took their stand on the dignity of man and did what they could to work for the open society which, they were convinced, would ultimately replace the walled-in ethnic communities heading, they feared, for conflict. In doing so these English-speaking South Africans believed that in refusing to betray their heritage of Western civilization they were being true to their own world background, as well as to their local historical role.[1] Their case, they believed, was based on humanity and on the logic and imperatives of the South African situation.

SUMMARY OF ELECTION RESULTS
SINCE 1938

No. of seats held by each party after general election

1938

United Party	111
National Party	27
Dominion Party	8
Labour Party	4

[1] See Anthony Delius in the *Cape Times*, 30 Sept. 1963.

1943

United Party	89
National Party	43
Labour Party	9
Dominion Party	7
Independents	2

1948

National Party	70
United Party	65
Afrikaner Party	9
Labour Party	6

1953

National Party	94
United Party	57
Labour Party	4

1958

National Party	103
United Party	53

1961

National Party	105
United Party	49
National Union	1
Progressive Party	1

1966

National Party	126
United Party	39
Progressive Party	1

IX

AFRICAN NATIONALISM IN SOUTH AFRICA, 1910–1964[1]

NATIONALISM is not easily defined in the context of South African society, which binds together, in a political unit, diverse racial and ethnic groups. In the broad sense of South African nationalism, it would have about the same meaning as when applied to many of the independent states of Africa, as, for example, Kenya or Uganda. It would refer to a consciousness of unity and a stability of integration still to be achieved. The African National Congress, in its campaigns in the 1950s, declared its commitment to this broad ideal of an inclusive South African nationalism; and it was precisely this conception of an inclusive nationalism, which the South African Government, under National Party rule, rejected.

In the South African context, the term nationalism is generally qualified by reference to the group which is the carrier of the nationalism in question. The term 'white' or 'European' nationalism is not used, though all white groups participate in the system of political domination over other racial groups; presumably the political bonds and sentiments of unity between white groups would be described as racism. So, too, 'non-white' nationalism is hardly a meaningful concept, and is not used in relation to movements of 'non-white' political unity in South Africa. Consciousness of identity among English-speaking South Africans was fused with sentiments of loyalty to Britain, and this impeded the growth of a purely local English nationalism, though there was some expression of English nationalism in the coastal regions of Natal, both before and after the Second World War. There has been no development of a specifically Indian or Coloured nationalism; presumably both groups lack the sentiments of unity, the territorial base, and the numbers

[1] I should like to express my grateful thanks to the African Studies Center of the University of California for its help, to Sheridan Johns for many stimulating discussions and generous help, to Gwendolen Carter for generously making available to me her magnificent collection of South African documents and affording me such excellent facilities for work at Northwestern University, to Hans Panofsky for his consistent helpfulness, to Anthony Ngubo for his analysis of some of the materials he sought out relating to the early history of African nationalism, to Leonard Thompson for access to his library and his knowledge of South African history, to Edna Bonacich for her help in the final work on this chapter, and her suggestions for the concluding section, and to Hilda Kuper, Monica Wilson, and Leonard Thompson for their comments on an earlier version of this chapter.

necessary for a politically effective movement of nationalism. Only Africans and Afrikaners are generally regarded as carriers of nationalism by students of South African society.

While nationalism is used to describe both African and Afrikaner nationalism, these two nationalisms derive from very different social bases. The primary basis for Afrikaner nationalism is the bond of a common language and culture. But national consciousness is not automatically given by language and culture. As has been shown in Chapter VIII, Afrikaner national consciousness developed during the last decades of the nineteenth century, in the course of conflict with the British Imperial power, and by a process of historical interpretation and ideological formulation.[1] Positively, it was defined by reference to language, culture, shared historical experience, a strong sense of kinship, claims to a common territory, and belief in a divine mission, and negatively by opposition to the English and rejection of Africans.

The development of nationalism among Zulu or Xhosa, based on common language, culture, and territory, would correspond to concepts of nationalism in Europe, or among the Afrikaner people. But from an African point of view, and indeed by common convention, outside Afrikaner nationalist circles, this consciousness, which the policy of apartheid sought to foster, would be described as tribalism.[2] The concept of nationalism is reserved for movements of national consciousness and organization among all the African peoples of South Africa. Its basis is thus a perception of a common racial identity, a shared historical experience of subordination, and a common civic status in South African society. There is neither a common traditional language nor common traditional culture, and the common territory is that established by the incorporation of the various African groups into the Union of South Africa.

The broad conception of a racially based African nationalism is used in this chapter. The occasion for its development was the establishment of the Union of South Africa in 1910, and this is the starting-point of the present narrative, though with retrospective comment. The chapter describes the history of African nationalism mainly as it developed within the Union, since this was the centre of African nationalism in the south, and movements of African nationalism developed late in the

---

[1] For a discussion of the growth of Afrikaner national consciousness, see F. A. van Jaarsveld, *The Afrikaner's Interpretation of South African History*, particularly pp. 33–45 and 54–7; and L. M. Thompson, 'South Africa' in R. W. Winks (ed.), *The Historiography of the British Empire-Commonwealth*, 225–6, and 232–3, and 'Afrikaner Nationalist Historiography and the Policy of Apartheid', *JAH*, 3 (1962), 125–41.

[2] See the comments of P. L. van den Berghe on the confusing use of the term 'tribalism', in *Africa—Social Problems of Change and Conflict*, p. 440. In the same volume, P. Mercier, writing 'On the Meaning of Tribalism in Black Africa', distinguishes 'tribal nationalisms' from 'territorial nationalisms' (p. 495).

history of the High Commission Territories and under different political conditions.

African nationalism is here conceived as a general reaction to incorporation within the Union of South Africa of a diversity of African peoples. Its growth is expressed in a consciousness of common interests and political identity among the different African societies, and in political organization reflecting that consciousness. Its goals in regard to other groups vary from the desire for interracial co-operation and an ultimately broadly inclusive South African nationalism, as in the policies of the African National Congress, to the more exclusive relations envisaged in the political programme of the Pan-Africanist Congress. African nationalism must be seen in the context of the relations between the different racial, ethnic, and tribal groups in South Africa, because it is essentially a product, and expression, of group relations. This chapter is accordingly a political history of African nationalism in the context of the relations between these different groups in South Africa.

Retrospect

By the end of the nineteenth century, armed conflict between African chiefdoms and Europeans had virtually ceased. With the annexation of Pondoland in 1894, formal incorporation of Africans into the colonies of the Cape and Natal, and into the South African and Orange Free State Republics, was complete. It had proceeded simultaneously with conquest. Racial conflict was increasingly transformed from warfare between autonomous political units into political struggles between dominant and subordinate strata of the same political unit. The rising led by the minor Zulu chief, Bambata, in 1906, against the imposition of a poll tax in Natal, was the last of the chiefdom-based armed conflicts prior to the establishment of the Union of South Africa, and it was quickly suppressed.

At the time of Union, conditions did not favour the growth of African nationalism. The colonies and republics which were then incorporated as the provinces of the Cape, Natal, Transvaal, and Orange Free State, had followed different policies, which created different social situations for Africans, who were already diversified in language and custom. Moreover, industrialization and urbanization had not yet advanced to a stage at which large numbers of Africans from different societies would be brought into enduring contact under the same living and working conditions, and there were few other developments which might have promoted association between them.

In the *Cape* were concentrated Xhosa and Coloureds, and there were also large numbers of whites. Of a total population in the Cape of over two and a half million, about 59 per cent were African, 23 per cent white, and 18 per cent Coloured (including an Asian population of about 0·3 per cent).[1] African settlements were largely confined to the Transkei, as a result of the Kaffir Wars (as they are conventionally called) or the Wars of Dispossession (as they are being called by African writers). At the time of Union, the inhabitants of the Transkei, the largest area of continuous African settlement in South Africa, were almost entirely African.[2] Small African reserves interspersed with white settlements in the Ciskei, and mission reserves and urban locations, doubtless provided more opportunity for contact with persons of different race than the purely African areas of the Transkei. While land tenure was largely communal, there was some development of individual tenure in the reserves; Africans also acquired small holdings of land outside the reserves, the law imposing no restriction upon such acquisition.[3]

The political status of Africans in the Cape was quite distinctive, as compared with the position in the other territories. Under the Constitution, by which representative government was granted to the Cape in 1853, no discrimination was made between subjects of different colour, in eligibility either for the franchise or for election. Every male British subject over the age of twenty-one, who had occupied for twelve months property to the value of £25 or was in receipt of annual earnings of £50 or annual earnings of £25 plus board and lodging was entitled to vote. The Secretary of State to the British Government stated the principle governing these franchise provisions, as follows: 'It is the earnest desire of Her Majesty's Government that all her subjects at the Cape without distinction of class or colour should be united by one bond of loyalty and a common interest and we believe that the exercise of political rights enjoyed by all alike will prove one of the best methods of attaining this object.'[4]

The effect of the qualified franchise was to encourage the formation of a political élite among Africans. In principle and *de jure*, the franchise was not discriminatory; in practice, given inequality in the distribution of income and property among the racial groups, it enfranchised whites and disenfranchised the great majority of non-whites. With white settlers in control, after the granting of responsible government in 1872,

---

[1] Figures for population in the different provinces are derived from returns for the 1911 Census in *Union Statistics for Fifty Years*, pp. A–3 to A–5, and *Official Yearbook of the Union of South Africa*, no. 1/1917, ch. III. See also L. M. Thompson, *The Unification of South Africa, 1902–1910*, p. 486.

[2] About 97·5 per cent. *Official Yearbook of the Union of South Africa*, no. 1/1917, p. 159. See above, pp. 51–3, 60–1, for discussion of land tenure in the reserves.

[3] *Report of the South African Native Affairs Commission, 1903–5* (hereafter *1903–5 Report*), pp. 14–18.

[4] J. S. Marais, *The Cape Coloured People, 1652–1937*, pp. 214–15.

the franchise qualification could be readily amended so as to regulate the influx of voters. This power was exercised in 1887, under the Registration Act, when rights in tribally owned property were excluded from the property qualification for the franchise, and in 1892, under the Franchise and Ballot Act, which raised the property qualification to a value of £75, expunged the £25 salary qualification, and imposed a simple educational test, i.e. signing one's name, and writing one's address and occupation. These Acts set an early precedent for the progressive diminution of African political rights in the Union by constitutional measures. At the same time, they helped to maintain the élite status of African voters in the Cape, setting them apart from the great mass of unenfranchised Africans, and also creating political interests among Africans in the Cape distinct from those of Africans in other parts of the Union.

Political activity of the enfranchised was channelled, in part, toward a relationship auxiliary to white political parties. This tendency was expressed in the political leadership of John Tengo Jabavu, editor of the first African political newspaper, *Imvo Zabantsundu*, founded in 1884 and published weekly in Kingwilliamstown, and in the establishment in the same year in the Kingwilliamstown constituency of a Native Electoral Association which supported the independent and liberal candidate, James Rose Innes.[1] A more specifically African orientation was expressed in *Imbumba Yama Afrika*, formed in the Eastern Cape in 1882, and described by Forman as the seed of the African National Congress.[2]

The other major non-white group in the Cape, the Coloured, may be viewed in many respects as intermediate between Africans and whites. Patterson suggests that it was the arrival of Africans which prevented the amalgamation of Coloureds and whites.[3] Sections of the Coloured people assisted both groups; they served whites as interpreters and soldiers, but they also allied themselves with Xhosa in the frontier wars.[4] In the electoral contests, they followed the leadership of whites, mostly supporting, according to Roux, the Afrikaner Bond in the rural districts of the Western Province, and Independents in Cape Town.[5] It was only in 1902 that they established a Coloured political organization in Cape Town under the name of the African Political Organization, with branches in the Cape, Transvaal, and Orange Free State.[6] Its formation was stimulated by discrimination against Coloured people in

---

[1] J. Rose Innes, *Autobiography*, p. 52; E. Roux, *Time Longer than Rope*, p. 56; L. Forman, *Chapters in the History of the March to Freedom*, pp. 9 ff.

[2] Ibid., p. 9. See also L. Kuper, *An African Bourgeoisie*, p. 193.

[3] S. Patterson, *Colour and Culture in South Africa*, p. 5.

[4] M. Wilson, Vol. I, Ch. VI, pp. 246-9. See also Marais, pp. 213-14.

[5] Roux, p. 55.

[6] Thompson, *Unification of South Africa*, p. 214; Marais, pp. 275-6.

the Republics.[1] Forman writes that the organization, though predominantly Coloured, included many African members, and that it was the first political organization of non-Europeans from all parts of South Africa.[2] Africans and Coloureds do not seem to have entered into effective political relations prior to Union,[3] nor indeed in the period after Union.

In *Natal* (including Zululand) were concentrated the Zulu. It was also the main area of settlement for Indians, who arrived first under indenture in 1860, and later also as 'passenger' or 'free' Indians. Africans constituted almost 80 per cent of the population of nearly 1,200,000 at the time of the 1911 Census, and Indians about 11 per cent; there were relatively small numbers of whites (about 8 per cent) and very few Coloureds (less than 1 per cent). African settlement was dispersed, following the dismemberment of the Zulu kingdom, the distribution of Zulu in reserves in Zululand and Natal, and their fragmentation under a system of indirect rule.[4] Large numbers were also living as tenants on the land of white farmers, and there were mission stations adjacent to the reserves, and some landownership by individual Africans, or syndicates of Africans, the law placing no restriction upon their acquiring land outside certain areas.[5]

The political system, though modelled on that of the Cape Colony, effectively disenfranchised Africans. The declared policy of the British on the annexation of Natal was that there should not be in the eye of the law any distinction or disqualification whatever founded upon mere distinction of colour, origin, language, or creed,[6] and under the Charter of Natal, in 1856, the franchise was granted to males over the age of twenty-one, owning immovable property to the value of £50 or renting such property to the yearly value of £10; there was no disqualification of Africans either as voters or as members of the Legislative Council.[7] Africans were, however, subject to their own customary laws,[8] and thereby legally separate from other sections of the population. By Law 11 of

---

[1] Marais, loc. cit.   [2] Forman, pp. 13–14.

[3] See Roux, p. 66, on the rejection by Jabavu of the possibility of a united front with Coloured people.

[4] See M. Palmer, *The History of the Indians in Natal*, pp. 12–13, for comments on indirect rule in Natal, Nigeria, and Tanganyika.

[5] See *1903–5 Report*, pp. 18–21; The South African Native Races Committee (eds.), *The South African Natives, Their Progress and Present Condition*, ch. 2; E. Roux, 'Land and Agriculture in the Native Reserves', and A. M. Keppel-Jones, 'Land and Agriculture Outside the Reserves', in E. Hellmann (ed.), *Handbook on Race Relations in South Africa*, chs. VII and VIII, for discussion of African land tenure and distribution of African settlement. Thompson, *Unification of South Africa*, at p. 490, tabulates figures for distribution of African settlement in about 1913.   [6] W. M. Macmillan, *Bantu, Boer, and Briton*, p. 214.

[7] E. H. Brookes and C. de B. Webb, *A History of Natal*, p. 75.

[8] These were finally codified in Law 19 of 1891. See E. H. Brookes, *The History of Native Policy in South Africa from 1830 to the Present Day*, pp. 191–2.

1862, as amended by Law 28 of 1865, provision was made for the exemption of Africans from Native customary law, on petition to the Governor, furnishing proof, *inter alia*, of the ability to read and write.[1] The effect was to create within the African population an educated élite of the exempted, many of whom served in roles auxiliary to white administrators, educators, and missionaries.[2] By Law 11 of 1865, all unexempted Africans were disenfranchised; the franchise was available only to certain categories of the exempted, under such onerous conditions that in 1909 Natal had only six African voters.[3] Here again was a precedent for the constitutional diminution of African political rights.

Indians in Natal, in association with Indians in the Transvaal, and under the leadership of Mohandas Gandhi, pioneered militant forms of constitutional political struggle. The white settlers of Natal, having brought over indentured Indians, as a more reliable source of cheap, regular labour than African peasants in Natal and Zululand, soon began to agitate against Indians, as they settled in Natal on expiry of their indentures;[4] according to the report of the Wragg Commission in 1887, a majority of white colonists were sharply opposed to the presence of the free Indian as a rival and competitor either in agricultural or commercial pursuits.[5] The hostility of whites was further aroused by the immigration into Natal of passenger Indians.

The granting of responsible government to Natal in 1893 was followed by a series of discriminatory laws, imposing a tax on Indians, who, on expiry of the period of indenture, neither renewed their indentures, nor returned to India; denying Indians the right to acquire the franchise, though retaining the franchise for those already registered; providing arbitrary powers for the refusal of trading licences; and seeking to restrict Indian immigration.[6] Gandhi had immediately responded to white settler agitation against Indians by founding the Natal Indian Congress in 1894, the concept of Congress being taken over from the Congress in India.[7] He launched the first civil disobedience campaign in the Transvaal during the period 1906–8 and a second campaign in Natal in 1908. Resistance continued, and in 1913 a further campaign was directed

---

[1] See E. H. Brookes, *The History of Native Policy in South Africa from 1830 to the Present Day*, p. 58.

[2] See L. Kuper, *An African Bourgeoisie*, op. cit., pp. 144–5. Brookes writes that Natal Africans did not avail themselves largely of the privilege of exemption, no applications having been received prior to 1876 (*The History of Native Policy in South Africa*, op. cit., 59).

[3] L. M. Thompson, *Politics in the Republic of South Africa*, p. 27, and Brookes and Webb, op. cit., pp. 76–7.

[4] M. Palmer, op. cit., ch. 3. See also Hilda Kuper, *Indian People in Natal*, ch. 1.

[5] As quoted by M. Palmer, op. cit., p. 46.   [6] Ibid., ch. 4.

[7] M. K. Gandhi, *The Story of My Experiments with Truth*, p. 149. See also M. K. Gandhi, *Satyagraha in South Africa*; and H. S. L. Polak, 'Early Years', in H. S. L. Polak *et al.*, *Mahatma Gandhi*, for an account of Gandhi's campaigns in South Africa.

against a decision of the Supreme Court, invalidating marriages cele-
brated according to Indian religious rites, and against the tax on the
ex-indentured; this took the form of a defiance of the law prohibiting
movement of Indians between Natal and the Transvaal.[1] There appears
to have been no political co-operation between Indians and Africans at
this stage.

The relatively small population of the *Orange Free State*, a little over
half a million, consisted of about 62 per cent Africans, mainly Tswana,
33 per cent whites, largely Afrikaans-speaking, and 5 per cent Coloured.
There were also one hundred and seven Asiatics, whose entry into the
territory was prohibited save for certain specified purposes.[2] There
were two reserves, Witzies Hoek and Thaba Nchu, of negligible dimensions, on which lived small numbers of Africans, the great majority
being dispersed on the farms of white landowners.[3] Africans were debarred from acquiring ownership of land, though rights to farms owned
by Africans in the district of Thaba Nchu were guaranteed;[4] and they
were excluded from the franchise.

In the *Transvaal* were concentrated Tswana, southern Sotho, and Pedi
peoples; there were also many Africans of Shangaan and Nguni groups.[5]
Population was growing rapidly by migration of both Africans and
whites from the rural areas, and by immigration of Europeans, to the
goldfields of the Witwatersrand. At the time of the 1911 Census, Africans
constituted about 72 per cent of the population of almost one and three-
quarter million, whites 25 per cent, both Afrikaans- and English-
speaking, Coloureds 2 per cent and Asians less than 1 per cent. Shortly
after Union, about one fourth of the Transvaal African population
was in the towns, almost one half on farms owned by whites, and the
remainder on small reserves, mission stations, and Crown land; there
was some private ownership of land by Africans.[6]

Africans were denied the franchise, as were also Coloureds and Indians. Outside the reserves, Africans were obliged to carry passes, and
it was the extension of the system of compulsory registration to Asiatics
which provoked the first civil disobedience campaign in South Africa.
Gandhi and other Indians served a term of imprisonment for refusal to
comply with the law, and 2,000 registration certificates were publicly
burnt in 1908 by way of protest. Indians in the Transvaal and in Natal

---

[1] See accounts by Gandhi, Polak, and Palmer.
[2] Palmer, p. 55; *Official Year Book of the Union*, no. 1/1917, p. 190.
[3] Macmillan, *Bantu, Boer, and Briton*, p. 353; *1903–5 Report*, pp. 21–2.
[4] Ibid.; A. M. Keppel-Jones, in Hellman, p. 192.
[5] *1903–5 Report*, pp. 6–7. See also *The Native Tribes of the Transvaal* (London, H.M.S.O., 1905).
[6] Thompson, *Unification of South Africa*, p. 490. See also maps in the *1903–5 Report* showing
land reserved for and/or occupied by Africans, Annexures A, B, C, and D. In the South
African Republic, Africans could not acquire ownership of land; a Supreme Court decision

acted together in further campaigns of civil disobedience, with a measure of success, the Smuts–Gandhi agreement of 1914 providing relief from some of the discriminatory laws defied by the passive resisters.[1]

These varied conditions of life imposed on Africans, prior to Union, a regional form of political organization. Some impression of its nature may be gained from evidence given to the South African Native Affairs Commission, 1903–5, and from petitions submitted to the British Government. In the evidence to the Native Affairs Commission, reference was made to two organizations in the Cape, a Vigilance Association in the Transkei for the purpose of teaching Africans a little more politics, agriculture, and farming,[2] and a Cape Native Congress, recruited mainly from residents in the urban locations.[3] In Natal, there was the Natal Native Congress, formed immediately before or during the Anglo-Boer War to present grievances, complaints, or requests to the Government of the Colony and to educate Africans in laws affecting them; its members were 'the Christian and civilized', but the organization sought to represent all sections of the African population; meetings were held annually with some fifty to one hundred representatives from all parts of the colony.[4]

Petitions to the British Government provide further evidence of political organization. The executive of the South African Native Congress, an organization working chiefly in the Cape Colony,[5] submitted in 1903 a statement to the Secretary of State for the Colonies, dealing with questions 'affecting the Natives and Coloured People Resident in British South Africa' and commenting on the difference in the administration of Boers and Africans, an amnesty granted to the former, confiscation of lands to the latter.[6] *Imvo Zabantsundu* (25 April 1905) printed a petition from members of the Native United Political Association of the Transvaal Colony and of the Natives of that Colony, addressed to King Edward VII, and complaining of the tendency toward 'class' legislation during the past two years in the Transvaal Colony to the detriment of the status and position of natives of the Transvaal. A letter addressed to the Commissioner for Native Affairs, Johannesburg, advising that the petition was being circulated for signature, was signed on behalf of the Basuto Committee, the Native Congress (Transvaal), and the Transvaal Native Vigilance Association.[7] There was also a petition to

in 1905, however, enabled Africans to receive transfer direct and to own their lands personally. Brookes, *History of Native Policy*, p. 359.

[1] Palmer, pp. 65–75.   [2] See Para. 14,088.   [3] Para. 14,202.

[4] Paras. 33,325, 25,538, 26,428, 32,252, 32,257, 32,077, and 32,072. The phrase 'the Christian and civilized' was used in the question put to the witness, and assented to by him (para. 32,254).   [5] *The Aborigines' Friend*, June 1906, p. 591.

[6] *Questions Affecting the Natives and Coloured People Resident in British South Africa* (East London, Office of *Izwi Labantu*, 1903(?)).

[7] *Imvo*, 18 Apr. 1905. Z. K. Matthews in 'Late S. M. Makgatho ... Great teacher-politician' refers to the African Political Union as one of the earliest political organizations among

King Edward VII from the Orange River Colony Native Congress, raising the issue of representation for His Majesty's native subjects.[1]

Processes of change were, however, already creating conditions more favourable to African political movements which would transcend both regional and societal divisions among Africans. The differences in cultures and structures of these African societies were perhaps not in themselves formidable obstacles to intersocietal relationships. Monica Wilson writes that there was some movement between Nguni, Sotho, Venda, and Tsonga groups, each absorbing remnants of the other, and that despite detailed differences, there was great similarity in intellectual systems, and in the framework of conceptions of kinship, ancestors, the role of the chief, and the rule of law.[2] There were, however, difficulties of communication between members of different language groups, such as the Sotho- and Nguni-speaking peoples, but perhaps the main obstacles to intergroup relations were subjective attitudes of tribal patriotism and disdain for, or suspicion of, or past conflict with, other groups, rather than any objective incompatibility in culture, and the lack of contact in social situations providing opportunity for the pursuit of common interests. This opportunity for a broad African nationalism was beginning to arise out of urbanization, industrialization, Western education, and conversion to Christianity.

The result of these processes was a restructuring of African societies, and the emergence in particular of two strata significant for African nationalism, the educated Christians and the urban proletariat. Educated Christians, who were attracted to Western culture, became the main carriers of African nationalism, initiating the movement and shaping its ideology. African nationalism, that is to say, was the political expression of a stratum intermediate between traditional African and Western European societies: somewhat detached from, and sometimes suspected by, the former; and used, as an auxiliary élite of clerks, interpreters, teachers, evangelists, and pastors, but also excluded, by the latter. Much of the ambivalence of African nationalism in South Africa derives from this social situation.

Prior to Union, there was already a stratum of educated Christian Africans. Some impression of the occupations they followed is conveyed by evidence submitted to the South African Native Affairs Commission in respect of the 3,448 African students who passed through the Lovedale Missionary Institution from its opening in 1841 until December 1896.[3]

Africans in the Transvaal, later replaced by the Transvaal African Congress (*Imvo*, 28 Oct. 1961). See *Imvo*, 11 Jan., 13 Feb., 11 Mar., 1 May, and 3 July 1906, and 19 Mar. 1907, for further references to political activity in this period.

[1] *Files of the Aborigines' Rights and Protection Society* (Rhodes House Library, Oxford), June 1906.

[2] Vol. I, Ch. IV, p. 182.　　　　　[3] Vol. v, Annexure 8, pp. 18–19 of Annexures.

Over seven hundred were in professional occupations, mostly teachers but including also eight law agents, two law clerks, one physician, and two editors or journalists; almost one hundred were clerks and interpreters, about one hundred and seventy artisans, and over six hundred labourers and farmers. There were other good missionary schools in addition to Lovedale, such as Healdtown and Clarkebury in the Cape, and Adams and St. Augustine's in Natal, but only a negligible proportion of African school children attended school even in the Cape, where education for Africans was most advanced; and there were hardly any facilities for higher school education.[1] Some Africans were able to attend schools and universities overseas. D. D. T. Jabavu writes that 'it was once computed by the Cape Education Department that between ninety and a hundred Native young men had gone to America from Cape Colony alone for education during the period of the ten years 1898–1908'.[2] The Natal Native Affairs Commission of 1906–7 found that at least a hundred and fifty Africans from South Africa had gone to America for study.[3]

Conversion to Christianity provided a religious basis for the association of Africans of different societies which was not present in the rituals and beliefs associated with the ancestral spirits. The potentially unifying influence of Christianity, as a basis for African nationalism, was, however, greatly reduced by a variety of factors. Membership of Christian congregations must have been largely tribal for many years, by reason of the concentration of tribal groups in different rural areas, and of problems of language in the urban areas. Moreover, denominationalism could be highly fragmenting and exclusive, analogous to tribalism;[4] and Christianity was introduced to Africans in a great variety of denominations. In the census of 1911, over one quarter of the African population was returned as Christian (about 11 per cent of all Africans as Methodist, 4·2 per cent in Anglican churches, 3·6 per cent Lutheran, 2·4 per cent Congregational, 1·8 per cent in Dutch Reformed Churches, 1·7 per cent Presbyterian, and the balance in a variety of denominations). And finally the Christian missions brought Africans and whites together in new structures of relationship, and under dedication to a universal ethic, conditions which might be expected to counteract tendencies toward the expression of an exclusive nationalism.

There was, however, in the development of Ethiopianism an expression of racially exclusive, and potentially nationalist, sentiment. Ethio-

---

[1] See also Annexure 8, vol. i, pp. 66–74; *The South African Natives*, pp. 136–91; and P. A. W. Cook, 'Non-European Education', in Hellmann, pp. 348–55.

[2] *The Life of John Tengo Jabavu*, p. 70.

[3] Cited by B. G. M. Sundkler, *Bantu Prophets in South Africa*, p. 43.

[4] See by way of illustrative example John L. Dube's dismissal of Roman Catholicism, *A Talk Upon My Native Land*, pp. 43–4; and comments on denominationalism in L. Kuper, op. cit., pp. 193–4.

pianism had two aspects, a general though vague political ideology, combining Pan-African and black solidarity, and a religious organizational form of African (or Negro) autonomy. Its inspiration was West Indian and American Negro, and it developed in the United States of America during the nineteenth century. John L. Dube, who studied at Oberlin College, U.S.A., and later became first president of the South African Native National Congress, expressed very clearly, in a paper published in 1892, his own acceptance of the Ethiopian call to Africa.[1] He was also influenced by Booker T. Washington's programme for educational self-help to establish Ohlange Institute in Natal.[2] P. Ka Isaka Seme, who inspired the founding of Congress, was similarly attracted by Ethiopian sentiment as shown in his speech on 'The Regeneration of Africa', delivered at Columbia University in 1906.[3] There was a curious proposal by Joseph Booth, an English missionary, to African intellectuals in Natal in 1896 that they establish an Ethiopian-type movement, a precursor in fact of Marcus Garvey's Universal Negro Improvement Association. Booth proposed an African Christian Union which would combine religious faith, economic self-help, demands for equality with Europeans by Christian and lawful methods and an unswerving policy of Africa for the Africans. But his attempt foundered on African distrust for whites.[4]

At the level of religious organization, there had been several tribal churches which preceded the establishment of the first Ethiopian Church in South Africa in 1892, by the Revd. M. M. Mokone, a Wesleyan minister. Following the formal incorporation of the Ethiopian Church into the African Methodist Episcopal Church, a Negro Church in the U.S.A., Bishop Turner of the A.M.E. visited South Africa in 1898 and ordained sixty-five ministers, thereby giving great impetus to religious Ethiopianism.[5] The specific rejection of white domination in the assertion of African religious autonomy would seem likely to stimulate African nationalism. But there was an even greater tendency to fragmentation in the independent churches than in the mission churches, and presumably also an ambivalence, since Ethiopianism combined emancipation

[1] *A Talk Upon My Native Land*, p. 46.
[2] G. Shepperson, 'Notes on Negro American Influences on the Emergence of African Nationalism', *JAH* 1 (2), (1960), p. 310.
[3] W. H. Ferris, *The African Abroad*, vol. i, pp. 436–9.
[4] G. Shepperson and T. Price, *Independent African*, pp. 74–6, 202. Later in 1913, when Booth established the British Christian Union, he was somewhat more successful, gaining support from John L. Dube, first President-General of Congress, and Solomon T. Plaatje, Secretary-General. See also Roux, *Time Longer than Rope*, pp. 84–6.
[5] See F. B. Bridgman, 'The Ethiopian Movement and Other Independent Factions Characterized by a National Spirit', *The Christian Express*, vol. 33, no. 397 (Oct. 1903), 150–3, and no. 398 (Nov. 1903), 166–8; Sundkler, *Bantu Prophets*, ch. II. Bridgman gives the numbers ordained as sixty ministers and deacons; Sundkler cites sixty-five ministers.

from mission authority with acceptance of religious ideas introduced by the missionaries. In the years immediately preceding Union and particularly at the time of the Bambata rebellion, there was much alarm among white settlers over the political role of the Ethiopian churches, but little evidence of any direct involvement of these churches in African political movements.

A militant movement of African nationalism was dependent upon the readiness of the stratum of educated Christian Africans to lead the masses in action, and upon the growth of a large urban African pro-letariat. Neither of these conditions was realized for many years. There was a sentiment among educated Christian Africans that they constituted a special category, distinct from the broad masses of their people. It is impossible to estimate the extent to which this sentiment was held, though illustrative documentation is readily available; but the type of employment open to educated Africans, and in the Cape Colony also the political arrangements, must have encouraged movement toward the dominant white élite and away from the African masses. In any event, there were relatively few African workers in the towns for the educated to lead and these workers could hardly be described as urbanized. However, the Kimberley diamond-mines and the Witwaters-rand gold-mines were already attracting workers from different African groups, and at the time of the 1911 Census there were over one hundred thousand Africans in Johannesburg and about half a million in all the urban areas (that is, over one-third of the total urban population).[1]

1910–1936: Political Exclusion and Social and Economic Interdependence

In the decades immediately after Union, successive governments laid the political and administrative basis for the routine subjugation of Africans, and a militant Afrikaner nationalist movement mobilized both for the seizure of power from English-speaking whites, and for a more complete domination over Africans. During the same period, there was increasing contact between members of different racial groups, and an extension and growth of interracial relationships in the developing economy and society of South Africa. This combination of political domination and economic interdependence, of exclusion and partici-pation, has remained characteristic of South African race relations and given them the dialectical quality of increasing political repression with increasing interrelationship; it has also affected African political move-ments with ambivalence.

[1] *Official Yearbook of the Union of South Africa, 1910–1916*, pp. 156, 161, and 165.

In inter-African relationships, there was the beginning of a self-conscious movement of African nationalism with the founding of the South African Native National Congress in 1912. Urbanization and industrialization provided more favourable conditions for contact, but stimulated a brief period of militant trade unionism rather than a more vigorous expression of African nationalism. Indeed, Congress was almost defunct at the close of this period, when the passage of the Representation of Natives Act and the Native Land and Trust Act in 1936, revived political activity, encouraging both African nationalism and a movement for political unity between Africans, Indians, and Coloureds.

The period 1910–36 is often interpreted as a period in which African political action was haltered by trust in the benevolent intentions of white men, and the belief that acquisition of Western culture would be rewarded by the extension of political rights. This interpretation seems most improbable. It postulates extreme *naïveté* in circumstances which could not have failed to impress upon conquered Africans, by direct experience, a realistic perception of white domination as it affected political rights, access to land, and opportunities for employment.

In the political sphere the South Africa Act not only deliberately retained the effective disenfranchisement of Africans in three of the territories, but it rendered the Cape franchise explicitly vulnerable by providing procedures for its abrogation. The value of the Cape African franchise was further reduced by the great increase in white voters as a result of Union, and by loss of the right to direct representation in Parliament. After Union, there was a consistent trend for reduction of African political rights: in the proposed abolition of the African franchise in the Cape by the Pact Government of the National and Labour Parties in 1926; in the introduction of universal adult franchise for white men and women in 1930 and 1931; and in the removal of Cape African voters from the common roll, and the limitation of African parliamentary representation to three elected white members for the Cape and four elected white senators for the Union as a whole, under the Representation of Natives Act, 1936.

Settlement on the land followed much the same pattern as the political dispensations. By the Wars of Dispossession, white settlers appropriated most of the land, thus reducing the pastoral Africans to economic dependence. The Natives Land Act of 1913 maintained, in the allocation of scheduled areas for African reserves, this grossly unequal division of land; it further reduced the legal status of Africans by denying them the right to purchase land outside the scheduled areas from persons other than Africans, save in the Cape Province or by special dispensation of the Governor-General in the Transvaal and Orange Free State; and it caused the exodus of many Africans from the farms of white owners under conditions of extreme hardship, as a result of regulations against labour tenancy. Though the Government recognized the inadequacy of the allocation of land for Africans, and the Native Land and Trust Act of 1936 made provision for the release of further land, the total allocation for Africans will amount to only 13·7 per cent of the land area of South Africa.[1]

The land wars, as de Kiewiet observed, were also labour wars. Africans lost free access to land, but were permitted to draw sustenance from it as labourers, herdsmen, tenants, or renters.[2] Land laws largely ratified the conquests of the nineteenth century, displaced many Africans from their traditional societies, and transformed them *inter alia* into a landless and exploitable proletariat. Labour laws and regulations followed a consistent pattern of discrimination between whites and Africans in opportunities for employment, conditions of work, and recognition as workers.

Prior to Union there were already in force in the four territories Masters and Servants laws which attached criminal liability to the breach of certain contracts of work,[3] and in the republics the colour bar was established as policy.[4] After Union, as has been shown, regulations under the Mines and Works Act of 1911, and later under the Mines and Works Amendment Act of 1926, and the provisions and administration of the Apprenticeship Act of 1922, effectively excluded Africans from many skilled occupations. At the same time there was wide discrepancy between rates of pay for skilled (largely white) occupations and unskilled (mostly African, but also Indian and Coloured). The Civilized Labour policy of the Pact Government discriminated in favour of the impoverished whites who had been moving into the towns since the beginning of the twentieth century, and it has remained a persistent feature of the wage structure.

Pass laws were enforced in the northern provinces prior to Union, and the Natives (Urban Areas) Act of 1923, the Native Administration Act of 1927, and the Native Service Contract Act of 1932 continued this system of control, conferring extensive powers for the regulation of movement, residence, and employment.[5] The Native Labour Regulation Act of 1911 made breaches of contract by African labourers on mines and works a criminal offence, and African strikers might be prosecuted either under this Act or under the Masters and Servants laws. Organiza-

[1] Thompson, *Politics in the Republic of South Africa*, p. 40.

[2] C. W. de Kiewiet, *A History of South Africa, Social and Economic*, p. 180.

[3] S. T. van der Horst, 'Labour', in Hellmann, p. 145, and generally pp. 144-57; M. Horrell, *Racialism and the Trade Unions*, pp. 1-3.

[4] De Kiewiet, p. 228.

[5] E. Kahn, 'The Pass Laws', in Hellmann, pp. 275-91, and especially pp. 283-6; van der Horst, loc. cit.

tion of African workers was further discouraged by the provisions of the Industrial Conciliation Act of 1924, which excluded from the definition of employee persons whose contracts of service were regulated by pass laws, or who were recruited by labour agents.[1]

The actions of the British Government, to whom Africans turned for relief from these repressive laws in the years immediately preceding and following Union, were also unambiguously discouraging. The Treaty of Vereeniging did not stipulate that Africans should be enfranchised, but left the issue for decision until after the grant of self-government.[2] Africans were not consulted on the terms of Union, which contracted the political rights of a population already largely disenfranchised. The South African Native Convention that met in 1909 to protest against the terms of the draft constitution had no official status and its resolutions carried no weight. Equally ineffective were the representations made in England by a deputation under the leadership of W. P. Schreiner, white independent member of the Cape Parliament, with J. T. Jabavu and Revd. W. Rubusana, as delegates of the South African Native Convention, and Dr. Abdurahman and others, as delegates of the (Coloured people's) African Political Organization.[3] In 1914, representations to the Colonial Secretary and the British House of Commons against the provisions of the Natives Land Act of 1913, made by a deputation from the South African Native National Congress, again failed to influence policy.[4] A memorial from Congress to King George V at the end of the First World War cited the African contribution of workers in the campaigns in South West Africa, German East Africa, and France, and the loss of 615 men when the S.S. *Mendi* sank; and it reminded His Majesty that the war had been fought to liberate oppressed peoples, and to grant to every nation the right to determine its sovereign destiny. But the Congress deputation was not heard at Versailles; and it was informed by the British Colonial Office that the Government could not interfere in the internal affairs of the Union of South Africa. Even this avenue of representation to the British Government was closed by the attainment of independent status under the Statute of Westminster in 1931.

It is difficult to see what room there could be for illusion, more particularly as to the policies of the Union Government. In the Northern Provinces, relations between the races must always have discouraged faith in the good intentions of the whites, and even in the Cape Colony there had been manipulation of the African franchise prior to Union, and diminution of their political rights on entry into the Union, which

[1] Van der Horst, pp. 144–8; de Kiewiet, pp. 271–6; Horrell, pp. 2–3.
[2] Thompson, *Unification of South Africa*, pp. 11–12.
[3] Ibid., chs. VI and VII, and esp. pp. 326, 385, and 431–2; *Izwi Labantu*, 16 Apr. 1909.
[4] M. Benson, *The African Patriots*, pp. 33–7; Roux, *Time Longer Than Rope*, p. 110.

exposed Cape Africans to the hostile policies of the northern provinces. But there is no need to speculate about the probable influence of objective conditions on the subjective reactions of African leaders, since there is much evidence of a bitter and realistic appraisal of white policies in the decades immediately before and after Union. The following references represent a somewhat arbitrary selection from the available evidence.

H. Selby Msimang, one of the early Congress leaders, wrote that the Treaty of Vereeniging of 1902 was regarded as a shameless betrayal of Africans, who had greatly assisted the prosecution of the war against the republican forces, and that the movement toward Union heightened the tension, born of fear that united European power over Africans would mean, if not open slavery, then something like economic strangulation.[1] Thompson records that nearly all politically conscious non-Europeans in South Africa were bitterly disappointed in the draft constitution for Union, and that when Stanford, Independent member of the Cape Parliament, toured the Transkei, he found tribal Africans concerned about the exclusion of non-Europeans from Parliament; urban Africans were deeply resentful.[2] In letters to *The Times* in England, Dr. Abdurahman quoted remarks by Botha, Smuts, and Dr. Krause to show that there was a likelihood that the Union Parliament would use its powers to obliterate the Cape non-white franchise, and J. T. Jabavu wrote that imperial sanction of the colour-bar provisions of the draft Act might become a precedent for legislation by the Union Parliament 'against all native advance'.[3]

The Natives Land Act, striking at the very basis of African life, provoked strong reactions. Congress, in a petition dated 14 February 1914, declared that it was evident that the aim of the law was to compel service by taking away the means of independence and self-improvement.[4] Plaatje documented the oppressive operation of the Act in a vigorous indictment of white policies.[5] The 'explosive development' of African independent churches was a reaction, according to Sundkler, to the Natives Land Act, one of the great crises of the century in African eyes. He writes that 'from 1913, the burning desire of the African for land and security produced the apocalyptic patterns of the Zionist or Messianic myths, whose warp and woof are provided by native land policy and Christian, or at least Old Testament, material'.[6] Membership in the Bantu Separatist Churches was not shown in the Census before

---

[1] '50 Years on the Road to Liberty', *Contact*, 2 Apr. 1960, p. 9.
[2] Thompson, *Unification of South Africa*, p. 325.
[3] Ibid., p. 406. [4] *The Cape Argus*, 14 Feb. 1914.
[5] S. T. Plaatje, *Native Life in South Africa*.
[6] Sundkler, p. 330. See also M. Hunter, *Reaction to Conquest* (2nd edn.), pp. 560–72, and her comments on the Israelites and the Wellington Movement.

1936; at that date, over one million Africans, about one-sixth of the African population, were returned as members of separatist churches.[1]

When African leaders resumed political activity, which they had suspended during the war from sentiments of loyalty, Meshach Pelem, in his presidential review of South African race relations at the convention of the newly inaugurated Bantu Union of the Cape Province, denounced the ignominious surrender of African rights to the Afrikander party by the British, whereby they taught the people of South Africa the new doctrine that 'white' was supremacy and 'black' was slavery; he described the constitutional protection for the Cape vote as a farce, merely set up to deceive the British authorities and people; and he declared that British principles of government were being superseded by the old, crude, savage ideas and methods of the defunct republics of the Transvaal and Free State. The Revd. Zaccheus R. Mahabane, in his presidential address on 'The Colour Bar' to the Cape Province Native Congress in May 1920, denounced as political oppression, slavery, and persecution of the worst type, the denial of their natural and inalienable rights to the original and permanent inhabitants;[2] and in 1927 he declared that the immediate effect of Dominion status for the Union was that those sections of the population who were represented neither in Government nor Parliament had been handed over by the Imperial Conference to the merciless mercy of the ruling races of 'this land of Colour-bars'.[3] The operation of these colour bars, by which the Pact and preceding Governments laid the basis for apartheid, was analysed with political sophistication, in the light of later developments, by such leaders as Professor D. D. T. Jabavu[4] and Dr. A. B. Xuma.[5]

In the context of these reactions, the view that Africans relied on petition, deputation, and humble submission in innocent trust of their white rulers is untenable. The contrary view, that there was complete mistrust and total rejection, is equally untenable. Instead, both the objective situation and the subjective reactions must be seen as composed of varied tendencies, some social processes and attitudes drawing persons together in interracial relationships of interdependence and co-operation, and others separating them in mutual hostility and disdain.

In the economy there was substantial separation between the subsistence and exchange sectors, and between the wage and occupational structures of African and white employment, but the war had stimulated

---

[1] *Union Statistics for Fifty Years*, p. A–29. This includes Zionist and Ethiopian churches. For discussion of the distinction between Ethiopian churches maintaining the dogma of the parent churches and the syncretistic Zionist churches, see Sundkler, pp. 53–9.

[2] *The Good Fight*, p. 7.

[3] Presidential address to the African National Congress, January 1927; ibid., p. 40.

[4] *The Black Problem*; '*Native Disabilities*' in South Africa; *The Segregation Fallacy*.

[5] A. B. Xuma, *Reconstituting the Union of South Africa or A More Rational Union Policy*.

private manufacturing industry,[1] and increasing interdependence in an industrializing society. The Native Affairs Act of 1920, the Natives (Urban Areas) Act of 1923, and the Native Administration Act of 1927 laid the basis for the separation of whites and Africans, but the 1936 Census showed that there were over half a million more Africans outside the native areas than inside them.[2]

In religion, if the growth of independent churches is some measure of the rejection of whites, then the retention by Ethiopian churches of the doctrines of mission churches reflects ambivalence, and the movement of African converts into mission churches expresses some affirmation and acceptance of the white men who had introduced Christianity to Africans. Growth of membership in the mission churches was even more remarkable than the growth of independent churches. In the 1936 Census, about one-third of the total African population was returned as affiliated to other than independent African churches, and the membership of the Methodist, Lutheran, Catholic, and Presbyterian churches was predominantly African.[3]

In formal organizations, if the general pattern was one of segregation, there was also interracial association in the Joint Councils of Africans and Europeans, which started in 1921; in the Communist Party, founded in the same year; in the European-Bantu Conferences, first held in 1923; in the South African Institute of Race Relations, and a variety of welfare organizations;[4] and in university education, with the establishment of the South African Native College at Fort Hare in 1916, and the admission of non-European students to the Universities of the Witwatersrand and of Cape Town. Particularly the participation in mission churches and voluntary associations is an indication of some mutual trust between Africans and whites.

Differences in race attitudes and ambivalence in race relations are likely to find expression in different adaptations to South African society,[5] and in different ideologies of nationalism. Presumably rejection of whites would tend to be associated with an exclusive form of nationalism, and acceptance, with a form of nationalism corresponding more to a South African, than a specifically African, nationalism. These two forms of nationalism were the basis of the major political divisions in the African nationalist movements in the 1950s, and they were probably present at the inception of Congress.

[1] Van der Horst, in Hellmann, pp. 116–21.
[2] De Kiewiet, pp. 236–42.
[3] *Union Statistics for Fifty Years*, A–29.
[4] Q. Whyte, 'Inter-racial Co-operation', in Hellmann, pp. 651–68.
[5] See, for example, the distinction between School and Red Xhosa in P. Mayer, *Townsmen or Tribesmen*, pp. 3–4 and 20–41, and discussion by M. Wilson, Vol. I, p. 265, and Vol. II, pp. 74–6.

Ngubane distinguishes three schools of African reaction to Union.[1] The first, represented by the philosophy of J. T. Jabavu, sought to base political action on bonds of unity transcending race. The second emphasized Cetshwayo's doctrine of racial solidarity, that salvation for Africans lay in creating a black united front. Ngubane mentions differences within this school. Dr. P. Ka I. Seme, who initiated the movement for Congress, wanted a new united people whose solidarity would bring about the extension of the area of liberty. Dr. J. L. Dube, who supported Seme, also emphasized racial solidarity, but he wanted to restore to Africans what was their own, expressing his political philosophy in the phrase *'lapho ake ema khona amanzi ayophinde eme futhi'* (where there was once a pool, water will collect again).[2] The third school, represented by Bambata's supporters, believed that Africans must regain their freedom on the battlefield where they had lost it. Thus both Jabavu and Seme stood for an integrated interracial society, to be achieved by different political means, however, whereas Dube inclined toward an Africanist ideology.

The political philosophy of Jabavu falls outside the context of African nationalism, and the Bambata school was not a force within African nationalism until about the late 1950s. In effect the African nationalist movement was represented in ideology by the second school and in political organization, for the most part, by the South African Native National Congress (or African National Congress, as it was renamed in 1923 to express the desirability of including all Bantu organizations, and all peoples of African descent domiciled within the Union and in other parts of Africa).[3] Seme conceived of Congress as an organization which would overcome the divisions of tribalism and forge a united African nation. 'The demon of racialism, the aberrations of the Xosa-Fingo feud, the animosity that exists between the Zulus and the Tongaas, between the Basutos and every other Native must be buried and forgotten; it has shed among us sufficient blood! We are one people. These divisions, these jealousies, are the cause of all our woes and of all our backwardness and ignorance today.'[4]

Congress was established at a meeting of representatives of provincial associations and vigilance committees, chiefs, delegates, and other leading men in the High Commission Territories and the provinces. Participating associations were invited to form as affiliated bodies 'a Federation of one Pan-African Association' under the name of the South African Native National Congress, with two Houses, an Upper House

---

[1] J. K. Ngubane, *An African Explains Apartheid*, pp. 69–73.
[2] Ibid., p. 71.
[3] See the Bill of Rights passed by the South African Native National Congress (*The Friend*, 29 May 1923).   [4] *Imvo*, 'Native Union', 24 Oct. 1911.

of Chiefs, and a Lower House of Commoners. The objectives[1] were to form a national association; to discourage or eliminate racialism and tribal feuds, jealousy, and petty quarrels by economic combination, education, goodwill, and other means; to represent and educate African opinion; to work for removal of the Colour bar, and to promote representation in Parliament and other public bodies, under control of Congress. The means for attainment of these ends included resolutions, protests, propaganda, deputations, passive action or continued movement, united action, and, when the time was ripe, the election of candidates to all legislative and administrative bodies. The term passive action is not clear but may refer to the technique of passive resistance.

Activities of Congress took the forms of petitions and deputations to the South African Government and overseas, passive resistance, and participation in the developing labour movements and in the preliminary stages of organization for non-European unity.

The deputations overseas in 1914 and 1919 were financed by contributions from Africans in the hope of relief from the hardships of the Natives Land Act, and, after the war, in the expectation that African loyalty would be recognized 'in some spectacular form or another'.[2] Disappointment must have been all the more intense. The failure of the 1919 deputation caused 'colossal frustration', manifested by 'upheavals throughout the country'.[3] The consequences were, however, not entirely negative. These deputations were significant as part of a continuous pattern of relationship of Africans and the African nationalist movement to outside movements and powers. The paper delivered by J. T. Jabavu to the Universal Races Conference in London in 1911;[4] the speeches by members of the Congress deputation to many branches of the Brotherhood Movement and of the Anti-Slavery and Aborigines Protection Society in England, and the contacts with members of the British press and Parliament;[5] the attendances by Plaatje at the Pan-African Congress in Paris,[6] by John L. Dube at the Pan-African Congress in England,[7] by Congress President-General Z. R. Mahabane, with Dube, at the International Missionary Conference in Belgium,[8] and by Congress President-General Gumede at the conference of the League Against Imperialism in Belgium in 1927;[9] all these were part of the international context of South African race relations and of African

---

[1] Inter alia, see constitution as approved by the Executive Committee in Aug. 1918, and discussion by G. M. Carter, The Politics of Inequality, p. 366.

[2] H. Selby Msimang, '50 Years on the Road to Liberty', p. 12.

[3] Idem., 'S.A.'s Freedom Struggle in Focus', Contact, vol. 3, no. 15, 30 July 1960, p. 7.

[4] 'Native Races of South Africa', in G. Spiller (ed.), Papers on Interracial Problems Communicated to the First Universal Races Congress, held at the University of London, July 26–29, 1911, pp. 336–41.   [5] Plaatje, chs. XVI–XVIII.

[6] Benson, p. 49.   [7] Skota, p. 145.   [8] Benson, p. 61.   [9] Loc. cit.

nationalism in South Africa. And in 1935, interest in international relations was greatly aroused among broad masses of the African population by the Italian invasion of Abyssinia.

Passive resistance in the form of civil disobedience, had been effectively established in South Africa by Gandhi under conditions of repression which rendered it a seemingly appropriate mode of political action, and Africans early used the same technique as in Gandhi's campaign against registration certificates.[1] The first action, in 1913, by African women in Bloemfontein against the extension of the pass laws to women by municipalities in the Orange Free State, spread to other towns and continued for some years,[2] with, apparently, some minor successes.[3] In 1919, according to the account given by Makgatho, in his presidential address to Congress, the Johannesburg and other Rand branches had decided to throw away their passes, and by courting arrest, to secure the Government's attention to African grievances; thousands of men and women were arrested, driven like cattle, trampled by mounted police, and shot at by white volunteers. He referred to some men and women being in their graves as a result of this refusal to buy any more passes; he commented that more help had been received from Europeans than from Africans in the Cape, who enjoyed the franchise, and he thanked the small band of Englishmen in and out of Parliament, and friends and sympathizers of the missionary associations, who had stood by Africans throughout the dark days under the pitiless yoke of the Natives Land Act and the 'no-pass' agitation.[4] The charge by the mounted police had been directed against Africans peacefully gathered outside the courthouse where the first trial of resisters was being held after a campaign in which resisters had not only surrendered their own passes, but had also collected passes from other Africans.[5] In 1930, the Communist party proposed a mass burning of passes on Dingaan's Day (16 December); there was an effective response only in Durban, where police invaded the demonstration, shot the organizer, and in the ensuing conflict killed or mortally wounded three more Africans and seriously wounded twenty.[6]

---

[1] In my book *Passive Resistance in South Africa*, I wrote (on p. 9) that passive resistance ceased as a method of struggle in South Africa from the beginning of the First World War, when Mahatma Gandhi returned to India, until the end of the Second World War. This is quite mistaken, as the present chapter shows.   [2] Roux, *Time Longer than Rope*, p. 117.

[3] Benson, p. 48. Accounts given by Roux, loc. cit., Ngubane, p. 81, and Benson are in somewhat different terms. Kahn, in Hellmann, writes that African women were rewarded with fines and imprisonment, and that 'it was only in 1917, after the African Political Organization (a body representing the Coloured who were under similar disabilities as the Natives) had taken up the matter, that as an administrative measure the police in the Free State did not impose the pass laws on Native women' (p. 281).

[4] *Minutes of the Eighth Annual Conference of the South African Native National Congress*, Queenstown, 6 May 1919.   [5] Benson, pp. 44–6; Roux, pp. 117–21.   [6] Ibid., ch. XX.

There appear to have been no other passive resistance movements in this period. Neither the refusal of the Israelites to vacate the Bulhoek commonage in 1921, nor the refusal of the Bondelswart tribe in South West Africa in 1922 to pay a dog tax, are to be classified as passive resistance, since they both lacked the commitment to non-violence. A number of campaigns, however, were projected but not launched, as at the third non-European Conference (1931) which resolved to urge upon Government steps toward the total abolition of the pass system since it was regarded as a badge of slavery, failing which Conference would set aside a day not later than during 1934, on which all Africans should destroy their passes.[1]

The results of African passive resistance were almost entirely negative, in contrast to the resistance campaigns of Indians in South Africa which achieved some concessions. The difference between them lay in the fact that the people of India, and the Governments in India and Britain, were concerned to secure proper consideration of Indian grievances, but there was no such intervention by the British Government on behalf of Africans. Moreover, Indians were a small minority in South Africa, and General Smuts, in his negotiations with Gandhi, might feel inclined to display some of the accomplishments of the philosopher-statesman. He showed no such inclination toward the campaigns of the African majority, suppressing them with extreme brutality.

The resistance movements were part of a general ferment, associated with industrialization in the years after the war. White workers were particularly volatile. They included British workmen, from a highly industrialized society, men with craft skills, experience of trade unions, and some exposure to socialist doctrine, and Afrikaner workmen, moving into the towns from their rural impoverishment, relatively unskilled and highly vulnerable to competition from Africans. Both sections interpreted their interests and those of African workers as antagonistic, an interpretation encouraged by the structure of South African society, and they sought, by militant action, to secure their positions against competition. Even before Union, in 1907, there had been a strike by white miners on the Witwatersrand against policies which, *inter alia*, extended the field of skilled work for Africans.[2] This was also the issue in the 1922 strike of white miners on the Witwatersrand,[3] which was suppressed with much bloodshed, under conditions that gained from the electorate the necessary support to return to power, in 1924, the Pact Government, a government even more racially repressive than preceding governments.

---

[1] *Minutes of the Third Conference*, held in Bloemfontein on 5, 6, 7 Jan. 1931. See also *Imvo* 3 Feb. 1931.

[2] Roux, p. 145.   [3] See generally Roux, ch. XIV.

Most African workers had been raised in a subsistence economy; they were migrant workers or still in the early stages of establishment as an urban proletariat, and without experience of industrial and trade-union organization. They were nevertheless responsive to the idea of workers' organizations, and Congress participated to some extent in the working-class movements of this period. In 1918, the Transvaal branch of Congress organized protest meetings in support of sanitary workers who had been convicted under the Masters and Servants Laws for strike action;[1] and in 1920, Congress gave some slight support in the strike of 40,000 African miners on the Witwatersrand, but not the organization which might have made the strike more effective.[2] Selby Msimang and other members of Congress were active in the organization of workers and in campaigns to improve conditions. But the participation of Congress as such was only marginal, perhaps by reason of class differences between the leaders of Congress and the workers, or by reason of a conception that trade-union organization was not appropriate action for a political association.[3] In consequence, the lead was taken by the Industrial and Commercial Workers Union of Africa and the Communist Party of South Africa.

The Industrial and Commercial Workers Union was established at the first national conference of African Trade Unions, held in Bloemfontein in 1920, under the sponsorship of Selby Msimang and Clements Kadalie. There were represented the Industrial and Commercial Union, which had been formed in Cape Town in 1919 by Kadalie in association with a white socialist, and included both African and Coloured workers; the Native Labour Union of Port Elizabeth; delegates from the Orange Free State and a representative of the Women's League of the Congress. Becoming centralized under the domination of Kadalie,[4] and with a large membership at the height of its power in 1928,[5] the ICU constituted a potentially powerful political movement. But it lost ground rapidly as a result of failures in organization, rivalries between leaders resulting in a series of secessions, tensions between the communists and the more conservative leaders, and the repressive powers assumed by the Government under the Native Administration Act of 1927, and later under the Riotous Assemblies Amendment Act of 1930; by this time, however, the ICU had ceased to be a significant force, though retaining some vitality in Durban and East London.

The Communist Party, after the accession of the Pact Government, began to establish itself as a predominantly African organization.

---

[1] S. W. Johns III, 'Workers' Challenge to White South Africa: Labor Unrest and the Establishment of the ICU', paper presented to the African Studies Association, Oct. 1966, p. 6. [2] Roux, p. 132, and Benson, pp. 49–50.
[3] See discussion by Johns, p. 8. [4] Johns, pp. 9–12, and p. 25.
[5] Roux (p. 167) suggests almost a quarter-million strong.

It formed a number of African trade unions, and these were organized into a Non-European Trade Union Federation, which in 1928 claimed a membership of 10,000 on the Rand.[1] In *The Communist International*, membership of the Communist Party was given as about 1,750, of whom 1,600 were 'natives or coloured'.[2] Members of the party were active in the ICU, as well as in Congress. James Gumede, Congress President-General, returned in 1928 from a visit to the Soviet Union, an enthusiastic supporter of the communists.[3] His radicalism, and that of the communists within Congress, provoked a reaction, and in 1930 Seme was elected President-General, initiating a period of extreme decline in the affairs of Congress. Repression by the Government and change of policy within the Communist Party, as well as party purges of membership, brought the Communist Party similarly into a decline.[4]

The change of communist policy in 1928, when the party adopted the slogan of a 'Native Republic', illuminates the problem of reconciling, on a non-racist basis, African nationalism and the claims of Africans as a majority, with the rights of Coloureds, Indians, and whites. The new policy was directed to the establishment of an independent native South African republic as a stage toward a workers' and peasants' republic, with full, equal rights for all races. The argument that this policy did not protect whites was rejected as nothing else than a cover for the unwillingness to accept 'the correct principle that South Africa belongs to the native population'.[5]

The decline of Congress following its rejection of communist leadership was almost complete. Members of the national executive complained of the stultifying effects of factionalism in some of the provinces, and of disorganization in Congress and all other kindred organizations of the African peoples, amounting to a state of chaos and confusion in the case of Congress.[6] Seme expressed his deep despair that everyone had failed—Congress, his critics, other African organizations, chiefs, parents, all African leaders—and that nothing short of a miracle could save the African people from a state of degeneration and ruin; and he complained of personal fights (*ubutakati*) and of quarrelsome and self-seeking leadership.[7]

Certainly failures in organization, such as the leadership of Seme himself, rivalries and schisms in the Cape and Natal, and assertions

---

[1] Roux, pp. 207–9.   [2] Vol. 6, no. 2, 15 Dec. 1928, p. 53.
[3] Roux, p. 211.
[4] Ibid., pp. 256–9. See generally, chs. XIV–XXI, for an account of African labour movements and of Communist party activity during this period.
[5] *The Communist International*, vol. 6, no. 2, 15 Dec. 1928, p. 54.
[6] *Umteteli wa Bantu*, 23 July 1932.
[7] P. Ka I. Seme, 'The African National Congress—Is it dead?', *Imvo*, 1932 (?) or see 'Mr. Seme's Memorandum', *Umteteli wa Bantu*, 23 July 1932.

of provincial autonomy, all contributed to the decline of Congress. But there were also deeper causes in the general political and social situation. Pressures from the African people were ineffective against governments which persistently rejected deputations, forcibly checked demonstrations, suppressed militant leaders, transformed chiefs into government servants, and systematically extended domination. Among Africans there was not yet the social basis for a mass movement uniting provinces, peasants, and townsmen; the failure of campaigns and other political action had been discouraging; and Africans were suffering great hardship under the Civilized Labour policy and during the economic depressions of 1929–32. For whatever reasons, Congress was not in a position to offer leadership, and initiative both in the movement for non-European unity and for resistance to the Representation of Natives Act in 1936 passed from Congress.

There were marked differences in the social situation of Indians, Coloureds, and Africans. In the case of Indians, the link with India continued to be significant. The reactions of the Government of India to the discriminatory provisions of the Areas Reservation Bill (1925) for segregation and registration of Indians, and its participation in a Round Table Conference of the two governments, resulted in the Cape Town Agreement in 1927. The Government of India thereby assented to arrangements for the voluntary repatriation of Indians, and the South African Government acknowledged an obligation to improve educational and other facilities for those Indians who would become part of the permanent population.[1] Against this background, it was possible for Xuma, who later became President-General of the African National Congress, to state in a paper on 'Bridging the Gap Between White and Black in South Africa' that Indians did not fall within the purview of the discussion, because according to Sastri (first Indian Agent-General), Indians could not make common cause with Africans without alienating the right of intervention on their behalf by the Government of India.[2] External relations gave Indians a distinctive status within South African society.

In the same paper, Xuma dismissed the case of the Coloured man, on the ground that the missionaries had fought and secured some of the rights for the Hottentot until the Coloured man was in principle accepted as a white man politically, industrially, economically, and educationally. By this argument, Xuma raised the slightly intermediate status of Coloureds to equality with whites, and ignored the wide range of discrimination against Coloureds, and the strong and persistent

[1] Brookes and Webb, pp. 288–9.
[2] Paper read before the Conference of European and Bantu Christian Student Associations held at Fort Hare, 27 June to 3 July 1930.

tendency within Afrikaner nationalism to reduce non-Europeans to a common subordination. Coloureds were also adversely affected in employment by the Civilized Labour policy, and in political rights by the extension of universal adult franchise to whites, and by provisions for challenging registration of non-European voters.[1] At the same time, there were marked differences in the social and political situation of Coloureds arising from the internal structure of South African society, which held them back from political co-operation with Africans and Indians.

Notwithstanding these differences, the initiative for the convening of the Non-European Conferences was taken by Dr. Abdurahman, President of the African (i.e. Coloured) People's Organization. The first conference met in 1927 and included representatives from both the African National Congress and the South African Indian Congress, which had been formed in 1920. While the constitution of the Indian Congress prevented the representatives from committing their Congress in any way, it did not prevent their demonstrating, by attendance, sympathy with the movement.[2] At the third conference in January 1931 delegates resolved to establish a central body of the constituent associations of Bantu, Coloured, and Indian organizations.

The chairman of the Non-European Conference, Professor D. D. T. Jabavu, took an active lead in the campaign against the Representation of Natives Bill and the Native Trust and Land Bill, and in the convening of an All-African National Convention, widely representative of African leaders and organizations, in Bloemfontein location, on 15–18 December 1935, the year of the celebration of the Silver Jubilee of Union. Indian and Coloured delegates also participated in the Convention. The demonstration of widespread rejection of the Bills in meetings of Africans held throughout the country, and of massive support for the All-African Convention, and the representations made by a deputation from the Convention, were of no effect. When the All-African Convention met again in June 1936 the Bills were already laws. For Africans, these laws constituted a crisis comparable to those of the constitution of Union and of the Natives Land Act. Their significance for the course of race relations, and for African nationalism, was not that Africans were thereby disillusioned and moved to militant action, but rather that the laws raised formidable barriers to co-operative political action between Africans and whites. In the words of Selby Msimang, then General Secretary of the All-African Convention, Africans had no alternative but to accept the position created by the Native Bills that they were not part

[1] Marais, ch. IX.
[2] See Statement by Revd. Lawrence for Indian Congress, *Minutes of the First Non-European Conference*, Kimberley, 23, 24, 25 June 1927, p. 10.

of the South African community, that European interests were not bound together with African, and that there was no longer any community of interest between Europeans and Africans.[1]

3. 1937–1947: Transition

These years, between the passing of the Representation of Natives Act and the return to power of the Afrikaner nationalists, marked the transition to a modern industrial economy, and laid the basis for the political struggles in the era of African decolonization. As shown in Chapter I of this volume, abandonment of the gold standard in 1932 and demand for locally manufactured goods during the Second World War greatly stimulated economic growth, particularly in private manufacturing industry, and Africans participated increasingly in the modern exchange economy. They moved into the towns and into the main centres of industrial employment, where they found also a milieu for intergroup contact. In 1946, there were almost two and a half million Africans economically active in the modern sector of the economy.[2] The percentage of Africans in towns rose from 18·4 in 1936 to 23·7 in 1946, an increase of over half a million persons; the numbers employed in industrial occupations grew from about 270,000 in 1936 to 457,000 in 1946; and there was some growth in the numbers of Africans engaged in professional, clerical, and other white-collar occupations.[3] While these economic changes provided a more favourable basis for African nationalism, they also enlarged the areas of interracial interdependence, and afforded greater opportunity for interracial association. There was increasing contradiction between the rigid political separation and the changing social and economic patterns of association, and hence stimulus for quite varied and conflicting patterns of race relations.

Africans were immediately obliged to decide whether they would co-operate with the Government in carrying out the provisions of the Representation of Natives Act. The ensuing controversy among African politicians, and also among Coloured and Indian politicians, crystallized the opposition between political ideologies of co-operation and of non-co-operation, the latter becoming, by accident perhaps rather than necessity, the declared policy of a movement for Non-European Unity.

A different form of this problem, namely, the appropriate group basis for co-operative political action, confronted Indians and Coloureds. The alternative policies were expressed in political movements of a conservative or accommodating nature, oriented toward whites, and

[1] H. Selby Msimang, The Crisis.
[2] D. Hobart Houghton, The South African Economy, p. 155.
[3] Union Statistics for Fifty Years, pp. A–10 and A–33.

in more radical movements of co-operation with Africans, the great majority of Indians and Coloureds, however, remaining politically inert. For Africans, the alternatives were political association with other racial groups, or a racially exclusive form of struggle. Within Congress the dominant policy became one of interracial political action, but there also developed an exclusive form of nationalism, organized as a Congress Youth League, and committed to the political philosophy of Africanism. Political action and attitudes of Africans were greatly influenced by the political attitudes of South African whites. The Second World War stimulated contradictory ideological tendencies within the white groups, one trend being toward interracial co-operation and liberalism, the other toward extreme racism, particularly among the Afrikaners and the Natal English.

It was not immediately clear that the political ideology which inspired the Representation of Natives Act would largely exclude effective political co-operation between Africans and whites. The Act provided some means, though mainly symbolic, for relating Africans to Parliament through the election of four white senators for the Union as a whole, and three white members of Parliament for the Cape; and it brought together, in common political action, both Africans and whites, the latter mainly liberal in outlook, but including some communists. It also established the Natives Representative Council as an advisory body to report on legislation affecting African interests. Like the African Advisory Boards in local government, and the 'Native Conferences' of African chiefs and leaders under the Native Affairs Act of 1920, the Council was essentially an 'intercalary' structure, inserted between the dominant white group and the subordinate African masses, and designed for consultation with, and more effective government of, Africans. But there was always the possibility that Africans might be able to use these structures to advance the interests of their own people, and that consultation might change progressively to participation.

In retrospect, the hope that co-operation under the Representation of Natives Act might contribute to African political advancement seems unrealistic. At the time, however, there were no doubt many considerations, apart from the compulsions of limited choice, to persuade African leaders to explore the possibilities of co-operation through consultative councils. The relations between groups within societies are not often so polarized as to exclude all hope by subordinate groups of progressive change. In South Africa, during this period, there was not only growing interdependence between the races in the economy, where, no doubt, many Africans participated by necessity, but also growing interdependence in fields of voluntary endeavour; and it seemed at times that the Second World War might act as a catalyst of progressive change, rather than, as actually happened, contribute to increased and more totalitarian repression.

Some indication of increasing voluntary co-operation between Africans and whites is given by the growth of African membership in the mission churches. Membership in the Christian denominations, excluding the independent Bantu churches, rose from under two and a quarter million in 1936 to over three and a quarter million in 1946; and in each of the main denominations there was an increase in the proportion of Africans relative both to the total African population and to the total membership of all races within the denomination.[1] The Joint Councils of Europeans and Africans, established to promote interracial co-operation, and to investigate, and make representations on, matters affecting the welfare of Africans, offered a field for joint endeavour, functioning rather like small local welfare agencies, under the aegis of the South African Institute of Race Relations. In the welfare field, there was some small extension of services to Africans, and some establishment of agencies with interracial membership, dedicated to African welfare.[2] Education was overwhelmingly elementary, in schools controlled by missions, but there were some African university students in contact with students of other races, under conditions which influenced the political ideologies, and subsequent political roles, of both the African and non-African students. The African Democratic Party, founded in 1943, provided a new political party of co-operative interracial action, but proved ephemeral.

Experience in the First World War must have discouraged any anticipation that loyalty would receive recognition in the form of political or other rights, and African leaders were little inclined to trust the good intentions of the Government. The joint executive committees of the All-African Convention and of Congress recorded their conviction that the territorial integrity of the Union of South Africa could only be effectively defended if all sections of the population were included in the defence system of the country on equal terms, and that the removal of such grievances as the pass laws and low wages would go far to counteract subversive propaganda among Africans. Congress, though loyally sympathetic to the British Commonwealth of Nations, was not willing to renounce demands for democratic rights, and the right to form trade unions, asserting that these were inseparable from the world-wide struggle for freedom and social justice.[3]

Initially, it did seem that the Government might begin to reverse

[1] Based on *Union Statistics for Fifty Years*, p. A–29; Whyte, in Hellman, pp. 656 ff.
[2] Ibid., pp. 651–68.
[3] *Minutes of the Annual Conference of the African National Congress*, Bloemfontein, 15–17 Dec. 1940.

its policy of segregation, revise pass laws and recognize African trade unions; and the war itself was seemingly being waged against precisely those principles of extreme racialism and oppression which were represented by the Nazis, but embodied also in the structure of South African rule. The Atlantic Charter was a charter also for the African people in South Africa, and the Government's representative at the sixth session of the Natives Representative Council in December 1942 had indicated 'that the Freedoms vouchsafed to the peoples of the world in the Atlantic Charter were indicated for the African people as well'.[1] The application of the Charter to South African society was made explicit in 'The Atlantic Charter from the African's Point of View' and in the 'Bill of Rights', drawn by a committee of African leaders, mostly professional men, and adopted by the African National Congress in December 1943. But there was no naïve assumption that the claims would be granted for the mere asking; on the contrary, the President-General described them as a challenge to the African people to organize and unite under the mass liberation movement of the African National Congress.[2]

It soon became clear that there was little likelihood of the South African Government initiating change toward a democratic society. A manifesto adopted in August 1943, for submission to the All-African Convention by its executive committee, declared that as soon as the enemy was thrown out of Africa, promises to abolish the pass laws and recognize trade unions ceased altogether, but that even before this it had become obvious that they were empty promises never to be fulfilled;[3] and a letter from the Prime Minister, dated 20 September 1944, disputed the Congress's interpretation of the Atlantic Charter. Representations by Africans inside South Africa were quite ineffective; their representations outside the country were, however, beginning to be significant. They had maintained their traditional links with organizations overseas, and the African National Congress was represented at the Pan-African Congresses in Manchester, in 1945, and in Dakar, in 1947.[4] But it was the attack on the South African Government at the United Nations, led by the delegation of the newly independent Indian Government, with assistance, by lobbying, from representatives of the African and Indian Congresses,[5] which introduced a new phase of international involvement in South African race relations.

Meanwhile race conflicts followed their customary course in South Africa. There were disturbances in 1942 following a wage dispute between African workers and the Pretoria municipality, and in 1944,

---

[1] *Africans' Claims in South Africa* (Johannesburg, African National Congress, 1945), p. 1.
[2] Ibid., Preface by Dr. A. B. Xuma.
[3] Special session of Executive, Bloemfontein, 27–8 August 1943. See I. B. Tabata, *The All African Convention*, ch. 7, and especially p. 69.
[4] Benson, pp. 117, 146.   [5] Ibid., pp. 138–9.

in Johannesburg, when an African was knocked down and killed by a tram-car.[1] The failure of municipalities to provide housing for many of the workers drawn into industrial employment led to a great spawning of shanty-towns.[2] Wages were so depressed that a proposed increase of one penny in the bus fare between Alexandra Township and Johannesburg precipitated a boycott of the bus transport services, most of the workers walking many miles to their places of employment.[3] There were sixty illegal strikes between the introduction of War Measure 145 of 1942, which prohibited strikes by Africans pending awards by arbitrators, and the end of 1944.[4] On the gold-mines, which set the standard for depressed African wages, some 50,000 African miners came out on strike in 1946 under the leadership of the African Mineworkers Union, which the leaders of the Transvaal African National Congress had initiated in 1941.[5] The brutal manner in which this strike was broken, the failure of the Government to consult with the Natives Representative Council which was in session at the time of the strike, and general frustration with the ineffectiveness of the consultative procedures, led the members to move the adjournment of the Council and the abolition of all discriminatory laws. Events were moving African leaders toward a boycott of the Representation of Natives Act, toward non-co-operation, and toward an increasing rejection of the possiblity of evolutionary change. Since the evolutionary procedures were associated with white liberals, relations with them were particularly affected, though the liberals were a quite negligible minority, with far less power to influence events than the African leaders themselves.

The boycott of the Natives Representative Council may have had some symbolic significance for Africans as a rejection of dependent political status.[6] Certainly African leaders had become more militant; and Congress was growing in strength and assurance, following reorganization under Xuma's leadership. There was a more secure social basis for African nationalism, with the intermingling of peoples of different groups under the common conditions of industrial life. In churches and sports associations, in trade unions, in the Natives Representative Council, Joint Councils, and the Institute of Race Relations, men of different regions and groups had been brought together in the pursuit of common interests.[7] The virtual loss of the franchise in the Cape had reduced the Cape African voters to much the same depressed political

---

[1] Roux, pp. 313–16. [2] Ibid., p. 323.
[3] Ibid., ch. XXV.
[4] M. Horrell, *South African Trade Unionism*, p. 69.
[5] Roux, ch. XXVI; Benson, p. 125.
[6] See Revd. Z. R. Mahabane, *The Good Fight*, for his address to the Conference of the Non-European Unity Movement, Dec. 1946, p. 62.
[7] J. K. Ngubane, *Should the Natives Representative Council be Abolished?*, pp. 15–16.

status as Africans in other provinces.[1] Afrikaner nationalism had shown an affinity for totalitarian forms of racial oppression by a movement within it toward national socialism, and by the founding of Nazi-type organizations.[2] With Afrikaner nationalism exceedingly inflamed, first by the Voortrekker centenary celebrations and later by hopes of a Nazi victory, the threat of perpetual and extreme subordination for Africans was abundantly explicit.

Under these conditions, if consultation within the parliamentary framework had failed, as seemed the case, then it was to be expected that political action would tend to move into extra-parliamentary channels; and if there were few effective organizations within which Africans and whites could take common political action, and if the extreme differences in political status made co-operation difficult and suspect, then it was to be expected that Africans would be more ready to explore the possibilities of political co-operation with Indians and Coloureds.

On their side, Indians and Coloureds were also encouraged to seek political co-operation with Africans, as a result of the social changes within South African society. Industrialization increasingly provided a common work milieu for large numbers of Africans, Coloureds, and Indians; and education and urban contact facilitated the exchange of ideas and the development of common purposes. There was the same challenge for Indians and Coloureds, as for Africans, in the ideological conflicts of the war, and the same threat from Afrikaner nationalism. Indeed, Afrikaner nationalism might seem more threatening to Indians, whom the nationalists regarded as alien and unassimilable, directing against them a most fierce racism; and Coloureds had good reason to fear rejection by a people to whom they were so close in culture and ancestry. In fact, even before the National Party came into power in 1948, there were changes toward a *gleichschaltung* of non-Europeans.

In 1943, the Government established a Coloured Advisory Council (originally a Coloured Affairs Department) to develop closer contact with the Coloured community and to gain first-hand information of its special needs and purposes.[3] The effect was to polarize political opinion into two organizations, the Coloured People's National Union, committed to co-operation with the Government, and the National Anti-C.A.D. (C.A.C.) Committee, a federation of Coloured organizations rejecting co-operation with the Government and participation in the

---

[1] See Revd. J. A. Calata's comment on the aloofness of the Cape African Congress, and his appeal to Cape Africans, now that they had lost their franchise, to rally round Congress and join their brethren in the North to plan salvation (Presidential address, Conference of Cape African National Congress, 4 July 1938).

[2] B. Bunting, *The Rise of the South African Reich*, ch. 6.

[3] Patterson, pp. 42–3. See also R. M. de Villiers, 'Politics', in Hellmann, ch. XXI, pp. 524–7.

Council, which was seen as an expression and instrument of segregation, but seeking political co-operation with Africans and Indians in a unity movement against racial discrimination. In December 1943 the Anti-C.A.C. Committee met with the All-African Convention to found the Non-European Unity Movement on a programme of non-collaboration with the oppressors, refusal to work the instruments of oppression, and commitment to a principled struggle for the realization of a ten-point programme of democratic rights.[1] In principle the Unity Movement was not anti-white; in practice, its propaganda was directed bitterly against whites under the stereotype of *herrenvolk*.

For Indians, in the *gleichschaltung* with Africans, there was no ambiguity in the implications of the new laws. Virulent agitation in the early years of the war, directed against Indians by the English people of Natal and based on what was described as Indian 'penetration' of European areas, led to the passage of interim restrictive legislation in 1943, and to the Asiatic Land Tenure and Indian Representation Act in 1946. This was designed to maintain extensive segregation of Indians in both the ownership and occupation of land. By way of compensation, Indians were offered a form of communal representation, modelled on that of Africans, save that in the Natal Provincial Council the two representatives of the Indian community might themselves be Indian. In Durban, Indians immediately responded with a passive resistance movment taking the symbolic form of occupation of unused land, and nearly two thousand Indians went to prison; and they rejected the communal representation, which was abolished by the National Party Government in 1949.

In the course of the struggle against segregation, there was a polarization of political attitudes between radicals and moderates in the Indian community, as in the Coloured. In 1945, an Anti-Segregation Council, opposed to co-operation with Europeans in implementing segregation, and favouring a united front with Africans and Coloureds, had gained sufficient support to take over the leadership of the Natal Indian Congress.[2] The moderates, representing mainly the interests of merchants, withdrew to form the Natal Indian Organization, oriented and accommodating toward Europeans, but rejecting compulsory segregation and subordinate status. With the rise of a more radical leadership in the Transvaal Indian Congress, as well as in the Natal Indian Congress, there was a firm ideological basis for joint political action with the African National Congress. Dr. Yusuf Dadoo, President of the Transvaal Indian Congress and a member of the Communist Party, served under

[1] T. Karis, 'South Africa' in G. M. Carter, *Five African States*, p. 546; Tabata, pp. 77–81.
[2] I have largely followed Palmer, ch. VII, and H. Kuper, *Indian People in Natal*, ch. III, in this account of political changes within the Indian community.

Dr. Xuma in the anti-pass campaign of 1944,[1] and in March 1947 the Presidents of the African National Congress, and of the Transvaal and Natal Indian Congresses signed an agreement to work for franchise and other rights.[2]

Thus in both the Indian and Coloured communities there were movements for political co-operation with Africans, but they bore the stamp of very different political ideologies. Ngubane writes that the main centres of these movements were Durban and Cape Town, Indians being concentrated in the former, and Coloureds in the latter, and that the most enthusiastic supporters in Durban were mainly the communists, and in Cape Town the Trotskyists. He suggests that the communists favoured multi-racial groupings as the basis of co-operation, while the Trotskyists argued that unity should rest on the basis of co-operating individuals; hence the Unity Movement became increasingly a non-racial organization.[3]

At this stage, when conditions favoured interracial co-operation between Africans, Indians, and Coloureds, and when the African National Congress was moving toward political alliances with non-African organizations, there arose within Congress itself a more exclusive form of African nationalism under the leadership of the African National Congress Youth League.[4] Resolved on militant action for national liberation and critical of past policy, but nevertheless loyal, the Youth League was established under the authority of a resolution of Congress in 1943, at about the same time that the Anti-C.A.C. Committee and the All-African Convention were founding the Unity Movement.

In its international perspective, the Youth League was Pan-Africanist, asserting the inalienable right of the African to Africa, which was his continent and motherland, and seeking to galvanize Africans throughout the continent into one homogeneous nation. Each nation had its own peculiar contribution to make toward human progress; each had its own divine destiny, and that of Africans was to make Africa free among the nations of the earth.

In its South African ideology, the Youth League emphasized the exclusive basis of African solidarity, as a race and a nation. It argued that since white South Africans viewed South African race problems through the perspective of race, it was imperative that Africans should do the same. Rejecting interpretations of African oppression in terms

---

[1] Benson, p. 115; de Villiers, in Hellmann, p. 517.   [2] Ibid, p. 140.

[3] Ngubane, *Should the Natives Representative Council be Abolished?*, pp. 95–6.

[4] The account of Youth League policy is constructed from the following sources: Congress Youth League Manifesto, Mar. 1944; letter dated 16 Mar, 1945 from Youth League (Transvaal) to the Secretary, Progressive Youth Council, Johannesburg; Basic Policy of Congress Youth League; A. M. Lembede, 'Some Basic Principles of African Nationalism', *Inyaniso*, Feb. 1945, n. 4; and Ngubane, pp. 96–8.

of social class, which would have provided a basis for interracial solidarity, the Youth League declared that Africans were oppressed as a nation, and under different conditions from those which applied to Indians and Coloureds. It described itself as opposed to any form of racism and of discrimination against minorities, and stated it was willing to co-operate with other non-European groups on common issues, but, it declared the only force which could achieve freedom was that of African nationalism organized in a national liberation movement led by Africans themselves; Africans could co-operate with others only as an organized, self-conscious unit, that is to say, when they themselves had achieved uinty. As to relations with Europeans, Africans would be wasting their time and deflecting their forces if they looked to them for inspiration or help in their political struggle.

4. *1948–1964: Counter-revolution*

The implementation of apartheid which dominated political action and race relations after 1948 was in the nature of a counter-revolution by whites. This does not imply that Africans attempted a revolution, though it was threatened, or that the counter-revolution was a reaction to the threatened revolution: on the contrary, it was planned in advance. The term refers rather to the increasing mobilization and use of force against opposition, the continuous erosion of the rule of law and the assumption of extraordinary powers, justified as the defence of the traditional way of life against international communism; and it refers also to attempts to reverse, by legislation and penal sanctions, those processes which were drawing the peoples of South Africa away from plural division toward a common society.

The counter-revolution was directed to the control of social change, in the interests of white domination, by monopoly of the constitutional means of change; the equating of the attempt to bring about change by illegal means with communism, under heavy penal sanctions; the eradication, again under penal sanction, of many interracial relationships on the basis of equality, and the general reduction of interracial contacts, though not in industry and commerce; the fragmentation of Africans by policies designed to strengthen tribal organization and solidarity; the raising of barriers to association between Africans, Coloureds, and Indians; indoctrination in the ideology of apartheid; and the perfecting of the instruments of repression.[1] Whatever its ultimate consequences, the counter-revolution was effectively carried out in its initial phases.

The structure of parliamentary rule assured an almost complete monopoly of constitutional power, which the National Party nevertheless

---

[1] Kuper, *Passive Resistance in South Africa*, ch. II, and *An African Bourgeoisie*, chs. IV and V.

proceeded to strengthen by systematic removal of non-white affairs from politics to administration. Removal from politics was substantially effected by the abolition of all elected parliamentary representation for Africans, the withdrawal of Indian rights to representation, though these had never been exercised, and the reduction of Coloured representation to symbolic status on the basis of a communal (or segregated) 'voters' roll. Centralized administrative control was extended by enlarging the functions of the Bantu Affairs Department, and by establishing separate departments for Coloured Affairs and for Indian Affairs, a Coloured Representative Council, and a consultative Indian Council.[1] These steps ensured maximum control over change by parliamentary means, while attempts to bring about change by extra-parliamentary means were increasingly interpreted as the crime of communism under the Suppression of Communism Act of 1950, which created also the offence of statutory communism, constituted by doctrines or schemes for bringing about political, industrial, social, or economic changes through disorder or unlawful acts or omissions.

Further powers to regulate race relations in conformity with the apartheid model were granted by a systematic series of laws governing almost the entire range of human relations, from marriage to association in schools or voluntary welfare associations. The Group Areas Act (1950) for segregation in ownership and occupation, in residence and in trade; the Bantu Education Act (1953) and the Extension of University Education Act (1959), for segregation of scholars; the Native Laws Amendment Act (1957)[2] and regulations under the Group Areas Act for control of interracial association, raised formidable barriers against social relationships between persons of different race.

The segregation of Africans, Coloureds, and Indians, in separate residential areas, schools, universities, and the segregation of their affairs in different departments of state, is likely to fragment interracial opposition to white domination. Social conditions become less favourable to African solidarity by segregation into language groups in urban residential areas, schools, and universities, and into separate Bantu authority structures in the reserves. There must also be some erosion of sentiments of African nationalism as a result of the Government's efforts to inculcate values compatible with apartheid policy by extensive propaganda, the use of traditional languages in schools, and the teaching of tribal history and tradition. Positive inducements in the form of restricted opportunities in trade and government service, and in promises of self-government, the elaborate structure of indirect rule in the Tran-

[1] Thompson, *Politics in the Republic of South Africa*, pp. 86–7.
[2] See M. Horrell, *Survey of Race Relations*, *1952–3*, p. 66; *1957–8*, pp. 195–9; *1958–9*, pp. 266–8; and *1956–7*, especially pp. 54–60.

skei, representing a first model of the promised land, also fragment African solidarity.

African political movements after 1948 can be understood only in the context of the apartheid counter-revolution, and as a reaction against it, though at first the African National Congress seemed to take the initiative in the political struggle. At its annual conference in 1949, Congress adopted a militant 'Programme of Action', planned by the Youth League and designed to secure freedom from white domination and to gain direct representation on all governing bodies, by such means as the boycott of 'differential political institutions', strikes, civil disobedience, and non-co-operation.[1] Three major demonstrations were held in 1950; a Freedom of Speech Convention, opened in Johannesburg by the new President-General of Congress, Dr. J. S. Moroka; May Day or Freedom Day demonstrations against discrimination, under communist sponsorship and with interracial participation; and, again with interracial support, on 26 June, a National Day of Protest against the Bills for Group Areas and Suppression of Communism, and a National Day of Mourning for Africans who had lost their lives in the struggle for liberation. In 1951, Coloureds formed the Franchise Action Council to oppose the Separate Representation of Voters Bill, and organized an effective strike in Port Elizabeth and the Cape Peninsula, with some support from Africans and Indians.[2]

The broadening of the struggle and mounting apartheid legislation provided a favourable setting for interracial action. A conference of the national executives of the African and Indian Congresses, with representatives of the Franchise Action Council, appointed a Joint Planning Council to co-ordinate the efforts of the national organizations of the African, Indian, and Coloured peoples in a mass campaign for repeal of the laws relating to passes, group areas, separate representation, and Bantu Authorities, and for the withdrawal of the so-called 'rural rehabilitation scheme'. Concluding that in the given historical conditions of South African society, the appropriate forms of struggle were the defiance of unjust laws, and industrial action, the Council declared itself in favour of defiance in the initial phases of the struggle; and on 26 June 1952 the Congresses launched a civil disobedience campaign.

The political alliance of Africans and Indians had been severely tested in a destructive race riot by Africans against Indians in Durban (January 1949) and by the ambivalent attitudes of some of the African Congress leaders in Durban, as well as by the demands of a mass meeting of Africans in Durban for a boycott of Indian stores and ultimate

---

[1] G. M. Carter, *African Concepts of Nationalism in South Africa*, pp. 9–10; E. Feit, *South Africa, The Dynamics of the African National Congress*, ch. I.

[2] This account follows Kuper, *Passive Resistance in South Africa*, p. 98 ff.

transfer of Indian trade and transport services in African areas;[1] but co-operation between the leaders of the two Congresses was in fact strengthened by the crisis. Nevertheless the very different social situations of the racial groups raised difficulties in the way of their co-operation; and in the Defiance Campaign, different targets had to be selected for each of the racial groups—pass laws for Africans, provincial barriers and segregation for Indians, and segregation for Coloureds. In consequence, membership in each volunteer corps of resisters was limited to members of a particular racial group, racially mixed units being permitted only where the law or regulation applied in common to all groups.

Regional participation varied greatly for reasons which are not clear. In the Western Cape (the main area of Coloured settlement), in Natal (with its concentration of Indian settlement), and in the Free State, relatively few resisters defied the laws. The great majority, that is to say about two-thirds of the 8,557 resisters, were in the eastern Cape, an area relatively homogeneous in African composition. By contrast, less than one-fourth came from the Transvaal, in which there was, at the time of the 1951 census, the main concentration (40 per cent) of the African population of the Union and great heterogeneity in societal origins. Many explanations are advanced for the greater strength of resistance in the eastern Cape: the longer period of contact with Europeans; the extent of conversion to Christianity; the strength of trade unions; the relatively more liberal policies in the past and hence the sharper reactions to the deprivations of apartheid; political training acquired in the exercise of a limited franchise; and efficient organization. The more homogeneous character of the African population may also have been a factor.[2]

Resistance reached its zenith in October 1952, and then rapidly declined, following violent conflicts in the eastern Cape, the Witwatersrand, and Kimberley, and Government counteraction against the campaign. The Courts punished the rank and file severely for such routine offences as the failure to carry a pass, and convicted, under suspended sentence, most of the national leaders and many provincial leaders for offences against the Suppression of Communism Act. The Government banned leaders by authority of this Act and of the Riotous Assemblies Act, and assumed further repressive powers under two new laws, the Public Safety Act, which provided for the declaration of states of emergency, and the Criminal Law Amendment Act, which was specifically directed against civil disobedience.

The compaign thus had the negative consequence of increasing the repressive powers of the State and of liquidating many African and

---

[1] Kuper, *An African Bourgeoisie*, pp, 301–2.
[2] Kuper, *Passive Resistance in South Africa*, p. 124.

Indian leaders. But it attracted international attention and condemnation of apartheid policy: it stimulated a symbolic participation by white resisters, and the founding of two political parties, a radical Congress of Democrats, representing the unit of whites in a Congress alliance of racial organizations, and the South African Liberal Party, a multiracial political party, largely under white leadership; and it raised the membership of the African National Congress to a reputed one hundred thousand, the majority being in the eastern Cape.

The increased number of members might have been the basis for a militant movement of African nationalism, under the new President-General, Chief Albert Luthuli. The Defiance Campaign was, however, interracial in organization and objectives, guided by a political ideology of inclusive South African nationalism, and not by a specifically African nationalism; and the next major campaign, resulting in the Congress of the People, in 1955, achieved an even higher level of interracial political co-operation. Its success contrasted sharply with two abortive, and somewhat confused, campaigns of the African National Congress conducted at about this time. The first was against the implementation of the Bantu Education Act, but African opinion was divided on the desirability of a boycott and non-co-operation. The second campaign, against the removal of Africans from the western areas of Johannesburg—this being part of the Government's general policy of confining Africans to peripheral segregated areas, and of eliminating African freehold rights to property[1]—was overwhelmed by the Government's resolute use of force.

The Congress of the People was sponsored by the African National Congress, the South African Indian Congress, the South African Congress of Democrats, the South African Coloured People's Organization (founded in 1953), and the South African Congress of Trade Unions (established in 1955 and representing about 30,000 workers, mainly African, Coloured, or Indian, but including some whites).[2] It was thus interracial in sponsorship, though the white and Coloured organizations had few members. Meetings organized throughout the country collected grievances and appointed delegates to the Congress, which took the form of a mass convention at which delegates adopted a Freedom Charter.

The Freedom Charter was the charter of a democratic South African nationalism. It proclaimed 'that South Africa belongs to all who live in it, Black and White', thus implicitly denying the conception of 'Africa for the Africans'. It sought not the rule of the African majority, but 'a democratic state, based on the will of all the people', in which the people would govern. It thus sought not a transfer of power to

---

[1] There has been some reinstatement of the right to acquire freehold in designated areas. Horrell, *Survey, 1961–2*, pp. 149–50.

[2] Horrell, *South African Trade Unionism*, pp. 22–3, for an account of the formation of SACTU.

Africans, but a sharing of power, as earlier in 'The Atlantic Charter from the African's Point of View', which explicitly rejected claims for sovereign rights in favour of full citizenship rights and direct participation in councils of state;[1] and it combined a bill of rights with such socialist aims[2] as the transfer of the mineral wealth beneath the soil, the banks and monopoly industry to the ownership of the people as a whole.

The Charter acted as a catalyst, provoking reaction by both Afrikaner and African nationalists. From the perspective of Government apartheid policy, the Charter movement was subversive by reason both of its democratic objectives and its affirmation of interracial co-operation, and the Government responded by raids against the Congresses, political bans and the mass arrest of 156 leaders on charges of treason. From an Africanist perspective (that is to say, from the perspective of an exclusive African nationalism, emphasizing the primacy of African rights on the African continent), the interracial ideology of the Charter, the interracial composition of the alliance, and the influence of non-African leadership were a betrayal of African nationalism, and the Africanists seceded from the African National Congress in 1958 to form the Pan-Africanist Congress in the following year. From some African perspectives, the vague socialism of the Charter was too radical a commitment, or at any rate, inexpedient.[3]

At about this time, there was an increasing impatience in African political circles with non-violent methods of struggle. There were risings among the peasants in some of the reserves. The Government was seeking to impose its Bantustan policies, and to indoctrinate Africans with tribal nationalism and reverence for tribal tradition. Thus almost all the political ideologies now found expression—the insurrections of peasants and movements toward revolutionary violence, as in the ideology of Bambata; the tribal nationalism of Bantustans under Government pressure; the interracialism or inclusive South African nationalism of the African National Congress; and the exclusive African nationalism of the Pan-Africanist Congress.

The peasant risings in the period 1957–62 were a reaction to poverty, deprivation, and tension, heightened by the application of the Bantu Authorities Act, the deposition of chiefs, the imposition of rural rehabilitation schemes, the restriction on movement into the towns, and the requirement that women carry passes. Precipitating factors varied in the different reserves, in the Hurutshe Reserve and in Sekhukhuneland in the Transvaal, in Zululand and in eastern Pondoland.[4] The disturbances in Zululand were part of a broader movement of protest in

---

[1] Horrell, *South African Trade Unionism*, p. 5.
[2] See Carter, *African Concepts*, p. 12.   [3] Feit, ch. III.
[4] For an account of these risings, see G. Mbeki, *South Africa: the Peasants' Revolt*, ch. 9.

Natal, initiated by women who proceeded to picket the municipal African beerhalls of Durban. These demonstrations erupted into destructive riots, following the violent intervention of the police in the great shanty-town of Cato Manor and the destructive reaction of African men. In Zululand, the movement also took the form of demonstrations led by women, who destroyed the cattle-dipping tanks they were obliged to maintain without reward.[1] Here, too, there was some involvement of the men, so that for a short time, it seemed that there might be a great rising of the Zulu people against the Government. In eastern Pondoland the risings began to assume the dimensions of a mass revolt, with strong support among the peasants and organization and discipline through committees and people's courts. All these risings were suppressed with much brutality, particularly in Pondoland, where the Government used military force, Sten guns and armoured cars against the peasants[2] and carried out mass arrests under emergency regulations proclaimed for the Transkei.

The peasant revolt in Pondoland recalls the Bambata rebellion and it included also a widespread refusal to pay taxes, but it became linked with the broader struggle for national liberation. For the African nationalist movement, the revolt was significant in extending the struggle to the rural areas, and increasing its power and flexibility.[3] For the Government, the revolt had the added significance that it challenged the Bantu Authorities system in the Transkei, the only reserve in which the movement from territorial authority to 'self-government' could be readily accomplished in the immediate future.[4]

The conferring of 'self-government' on the Transkei under the Transkei Constitution Act of 1963 raised many problems for African national leaders. 'Self-government' was clearly a system of indirect rule, which vested very limited powers in a legislature dominated by chiefs, whose responsibility was to the Government of South Africa and not to the voters of the Transkei.[5] The possibility of independence, based on a viable economy, was entirely remote. It was difficult to see how Bantustans and Bantu Authorities might be used to advance the national movement. Seemingly, they could only fragment African solidarity. They appealed to tribal, not national, sentiment, and to a spirit of wearied disillusionment with the struggle for integration.[6] They attracted to government service men who might otherwise have been available for the national movement, thereby creating conflict between

---

[1] Kuper, *An African Bourgeoisie*, ch. 2.   [2] Mbeki, p. 117 ff.   [3] Ibid.

[4] See C. R. Hill, *Bantustans—The Fragmentation of South Africa*, for an account of Bantu Authorities and Bantustans; and M. Wilson, above, pp. 89–92.

[5] Mbeki, p. 136.

[6] See Carter, *Separate Development: The Challenge of the Transkei*, pp. 9–12, and *African Concepts*, pp. 16–17, for some documentation of statements by African leaders over the years relating to acceptance of an equitable separation as a last resort.

the collaborators and non-collaborators. In the Transkei this conflict merged in the opposition between a policy of racial exclusiveness, represented by the party of the Chief Minister with the support of many of the chiefs, and a policy of racial inclusiveness or of non-racialism represented by the opposition, with considerable popular support. Once again, African political ideologies showed this tendency to polarize, away from, and toward, the other races in South African society.

The commitment to an interracial programme of action was strengthened by the Congress of the People. Its ideology of interracial cooperation was consistent with many of the social and economic changes in South African society, resulting from industrial and urban growth, the increasing numbers of educated persons of all races, and the sharing of a common culture.

Industry and commerce had greatly expanded, and in 1960 about five and a quarter million persons were engaged in the modern sector of the economy, Africans representing 65 per cent of the economically active population. The economy was becoming integrated, though this process was by no means complete, since large numbers of Africans were still involved in subsistence agriculture and migrant labour, and there was an excessive disparity between the wages of skilled and unskilled labour.[1] While many unskilled African workers earned below the level necessary for adequate survival in poverty, employment and real wages in manufacturing industry had risen appreciably; there was continued diversification of African occupations, with increasing numbers engaged as traders, professionals, clerical workers, artisans, and semi-skilled factory workers.[2] The urban growth accompanying industrialization had redistributed population from less than 25 per cent in the towns immediately after Union to almost 47 per cent in 1960. Whites and Asians were highly urbanized (83 per cent), and Coloureds appreciably so (68 per cent) but the percentage of Africans in urban areas had also risen, even under the policy of apartheid, from less than 24 per cent in 1946 to 32 per cent in 1960.[3] Racial and tribal apartheid was being applied in education, but there were already, in 1961, about 2,200 African university graduates, who shared with the highly educated of other races many of the elements of a common educational experience. There was probably growing African ambivalence toward, and expressed rejection of, Christianity, but African membership in the established mission denominations continued to increase, even in the Dutch

[1] Houghton, *The South African Economy*, pp. 205–7. See also P. L. van den Berghe, *South Africa, A Study in Conflict*, for analysis of the relations between economic change and political repression.

[2] Ibid., p. 224; Kuper, *An African Bourgeoisie*, Parts II and III.

[3] *Population Census*, 6 Sept. 1960, vol. i, Geographical Distribution of the Population (Pretoria, 1963), p. 8.

Reformed Churches, in seeming disregard of their support for apartheid.[1] Some of the churches of English-speaking Christians, and especially the Methodist Churches, were responding to the changing conditions by policies designed to reduce racial discrimination and segregation. The Progressive Party was founded in 1959 as an interracial political party. Increasingly people of different races were coming together in recreation and social relations and voluntary work. The great range of laws passed to separate the races and the severity of their sanctions provide a measure of the strength of the forces bringing the races together in complex networks of interrelationship.

The Congress Alliance promoted its interracial objectives, externally by seeking international support in the East and the West and maintaining increasingly extensive relations with governments and political movements outside of South Africa. Messages of support from other countries became a regular part of the proceedings at annual conferences and demonstrations of the Congresses. Internally, the Congress Alliance sought to advance its policies, with the assistance of auxiliary organizations, in a series of campaigns. The South African Congress of Trade Unions, the interracial organization founded in reaction to the exclusion of African trade unions from the South African Trade Union Council in 1954,[2] became a regular unit of the Congress Alliance, initiating campaigns for a basic wage of £1 per day. The Federation of South African Women, also interracial in membership, mobilized women in two demonstrations at Government headquarters in Pretoria, the first in 1955, against unjust laws, and the second, in 1956, against the pass laws, with twenty thousand women present.[3] These were part of a larger movement against the carrying of passes by women. A variety of sports associations, though not members of the Congress movement, nevertheless contributed to the political objectives of interracial co-operation by bringing together African, Indian, and Coloured sports associations in a movement for the desegregation of sport, representations being made to the international sports tribunals to sanction desegregation by withdrawal of recognition from the South African associations under white control.[4]

The problem for the Congress Alliance was to mobilize politically the great mass of the non-white peoples, particularly the African masses, since the Coloureds were still largely insulated against political co-operation with Africans, and Indians were too limited both in numbers

---

[1] The 1960 Census showed an increase in Africans returned as members of the Dutch Reformed Churches to about 557,000 as compared with 267,000 in 1946. For changes in religious affiliation, see Table I in Appendix.

[2] Bunting, p. 275.

[3] H. Joseph, *Tomorrow's Sun*, ch. 3.

[4] Kuper, *An African Bourgeoisie*, pp. 50–1 and ch. 22.

and in active political involvement, to constitute an effective force against white domination. The methods used were the economic boycott, which was effectively exploited in a small way, and the 'stay-at-home', a symbolic demonstration of strength and a training in the withholding of labour, preparatory to a general strike. The problem for the Government was to prevent the Congresses developing an effective organization and acquiring or demonstrating mass support. Overwhelmingly preponderant strength lay with the Government, and it used the powers it already commanded, and added further powers of exile and arrest without trial, to suppress the campaigns, which were announced well in advance and conducted openly, but never achieved sufficient support to compel political change, even when relatively successful as in 1957.[1] In 1960 the Government proclaimed a state of emergency, arresting many political leaders for long periods without trial, and it declared the African National Congress and the Pan-Africanist Congress unlawful organizations.

The last campaign, a three-day 'stay-at-home' to coincide with the proclamation of the Republic in May 1961, provoked massive anticipatory counteraction by the Government and failed in its objectives. It closed an era of non-violent resistance, and introduced a brief period of sabotage by the organization Umkonto we Sizwe (Spear of the Nation) until the arrest of important leaders in 1963, and their sentence to life imprisonment in the 'Rivonia' trial in 1964. The movement was interracial in membership, and an offshoot from the African National Congress, but apparently not a part of that organization. According to the Congress leader, Nelson Mandela, the decision to use sabotage was determined by the desire to spare life, and to find a form of violent action which would not needlessly embitter race relations, though the intention was to move to guerrilla warfare if sabotage failed to bring about political change.[2] The Rivonia trial marks the end of the period of interracial political action by the Congress Alliance.

The Congress of the People had, however, also stimulated a reaction against interracial co-operation in the form of a political movement of exclusive African nationalism. This exclusive nationalism had seemingly always been present within the African National Congress, but it was not formulated as an effective political ideology until the advent of the A.N.C. Youth League and the Pan-Africanist Congress. Disagreement over the Freedom Charter, rejection of interracial political alliance, dissatisfaction with Congress leadership and campaigns, and a variety

---

[1] For accounts of these campaigns from different political perspectives, see Benson, Bunting, and Feit.

[2] N. Mandela, *No Easy Walk to Freedom*, pp. 171-7. There was also for a brief period an African Resistance Movement, mostly white in membership, revolutionary in objectives, and expressing interracial solidarity.

of internal conflicts finally resulted in the founding of the Pan-Africanist Congress.

The Pan-Africanist Congress claimed that it was returning to the original nationalism of the African National Congress. It charged that in the Congress Alliance, the African National Congress had abandoned the nationalist tradition for a policy of multi-racialism. This policy was represented as a perpetuation of racial differences, with protected rights for racial minorities; and it was contrasted with the Pan-Africanist policy of non-racialism, which was represented as based on conceptions of the individual as the bearer of political rights, and not the racial group. In fact, the ideology of the Pan-Africanist Congress emphasized racial exclusiveness, asserting that Africans were oppressed, not as a class, but as a nation, under distinctive material and political conditions, which imposed the need for a specifically African liberatory movement. The African masses were said to be the key to the struggle and they could only be organized under the banner of African nationalism in an all-African organization where Africans would by themselves formulate policies and decide on methods of struggle, without interference from groups of minorities which arrogantly appropriated to themselves the right to plan for Africans.[1] The political goal was to be government of the Africans, for the Africans, by the Africans, but persons from other racial groups would not be excluded from the Africanist democracy, if they owed their only loyalty to Africa and if they accepted the rule of the African majority. The Congress was committed to a policy of Pan-Africanism and seemed to incline toward a form of socialism.

There was in this ideology an assertion of racial and national exclusiveness, but with some ambivalence, expressed in the espousal of non-racialism. The emphasis on African rule represented a revolutionary change from earlier African policies directed toward a sharing, rather than a transfer or seizure of, power. It expressed the new possibilities of African dominance with the rapid decolonization of the African continent, and a new confidence in Africa's changing role in world affairs, following the independence of Ghana in 1957, and the Conference of Independent African States and the All-Africa Peoples' Conference in 1958. The Pan-Africanists were not committed to non-violence, and indeed projected an image of themselves as resolute and courageous men, who would take whatever steps were necessary for African liberation. In the commitment to exclusive and militant African nationalism or Africanism, in the rejection of multi-racialism, in the goal of African majority rule, and in the readiness for violent revolutionary struggle, the Pan-Africanist Congress was seemingly quite opposed to the policies of the

---

[1] Kuper, *An African Bourgeoisie*, ch. 23.

African National Congress, but there was in fact, within the latter organization, a responsiveness to Africanism within South Africa, and to Pan-Africanism on the African continent.

In this context, it is somewhat surprising that the first and only South African campaign of the Pan-Africanist Congress, in 1960, was modelled on the campaign for the Defiance of Unjust Laws in 1952, and indeed on Gandhi's campaign in 1907. The result was predictable. The movement was deprived of its leaders who resolutely defied the pass laws and offered themselves for arrest, and the Pan-Africanist Congress was proscribed as an illegal organization, and driven underground in South Africa, though it surfaced elsewhere on the African continent and overseas. The massacre at Sharpeville on 21 March 1960, when the police fired on unarmed demonstrators against the pass laws, and a demonstration in Cape Town on 30 March, when 30,000 Africans marched to the centre of Cape Town, near the Houses of Parliament, gave the Pan-Africanist Congress a national, and indeed international, significance. But the Pan-Africanist Congress had ceased to be an effective political organization in South Africa itself. It was apparently connected in some way with Poqo, a terrorist organization, which was quickly suppressed by the Government. Thus by 1964, both the Congress Alliance and the Pan-Africanist Congress had been suppressed inside South Africa, and there was little evidence of independent African political action.

5. Review

Two main conclusions emerge from this account of African nationalism in South Africa. The first is that its main political expression has been subsidiary to a broader movement of an inclusive, interracial South African nationalism. The more exclusive, specific form of African nationalism attained only momentary political organization and action. The second conclusion is that African nationalism at no time became a major force in the political life of the country, with sufficient strength to challenge the structure of white domination. Certainly the great repressive power exercised by all South African Governments effectively curbed the rise of African nationalism, but explanation must also be sought at deeper levels in the nature of South African society, and in the characteristics of its African peoples and leaders.

The dominant facts of South African society are its interracial composition and development. There are large numbers of whites, Coloureds, and Indians, who have all contributed to the growth of the country, and are bound together by innumerable ties of interdependence in its industrialized economy. Few sectors or groups could be detached without serious disruption of the society. Moreover, the urban forms, the industrial skills, the educational system, and many of the religious beliefs were largely introduced from western Europe, so that the contribution of whites is deeply embedded, together with the contributions of other racial groups, in the foundations of the society. The present cohesion of the different racial and ethnic groups derives in part from this interweaving of roles, interests, and contributions. It is not simply the result of the exercise of naked force.

The effect of the interracial core of the society, of industrial development and economic interdependence, and of white dominance and influence, has been to draw Africans, Indians and Coloureds towards the whites and towards the common sectors of the society. It is expressed in a dualism in the political movements of Coloureds—accommodation, on the one hand, to whites with detachment from the subordinate Africans, and commitment, on the other hand, to Non-European Unity with non-co-operation toward the ruling whites. The dominant tendency among Coloureds generally is, however, one of accommodation, in consequence also of their intermediate status in the structure of the society. Among Indians, there is the dualism of accommodation to whites in the policies of the South African Indian Organization, and probably in the attitudes of most Indians, and of interracial political action in the policies of the South African Indian Congress. The dualism naturally inhibits effective action based on Non-European Unity.

African political movements are more varied, since Africans derive from originally distinct political units, and since their combined numbers may promise an ultimate domination. But among Africans, too, political action has generally taken the form of accommodation to whites, or organization for a democratic interracial society, as in the African National Congress. This is not only a consequence of the pull of the interracial core of the society. There is also, among large numbers of Africans, a positive affirmation of many of the values and achievements of Western society, and a desire for many of the qualities of a Western way of life. It is significant that African political movements have been almost entirely free of nativistic elements.

Quite apart from the general interracial character of South African society, and the attraction of a Western way of life, there are no doubt many other circumstances which prevented Africans from taking effective action for national liberation. African political life seems to have been basically conservative. At any rate, there was a recoil from radicalism in critical periods of African political development, as in the reaction against the Communist Party in the Industrial and Commercial Workers Union in 1926, and in the African National Congress under the presidency of Gumede. So, too, the exclusive nationalism and anticommunism of the Pan-Africanist Congress were a reaction against the radical interracialism of the Congress Alliance and against communist influence within it; and the opposition between these sharply contrasted policies might have had the effect in time of a conservative equilibrium, if the two organizations had not been proscribed by the Government.

Of much greater significance than any conservative political tendency is the heritage of sectional and regional differences. African political leaders and writers tend to deny that tribal loyalties are a divisive element in African nationalism, and they often equate discussion of tribalism with support of apartheid. But given the original constitution of Africans into separate political units, with varied cultures and languages, and the regional differences in the territories prior to Union; given some persistence of tribal tradition, in the reserves, after Union; and given some discontinuity between rural subsistence and the modern exchange economy, and between the Western-educated élites and the peasants in the reserves; it would indeed be surprising if African solidarity were not appreciably fragmented by sectional loyalties. Moreover, under apartheid, these sectional loyalites receive political reinforcement.

The movement of the High Commission Territories to independence may also have the effect of reinforcing sectional loyalties. There have always been close political relations between Africans in the High Commission Territories and Africans in the Union, as a result of geographical proximity, the arbitrary nature of territorial boundaries, the poverty of the territories which compelled many Africans to seek employment in the Union, and poor facilities for higher education, which encouraged study in the Union's high schools and universities, and thus promoted contact between members of an educated élite across territorial boundaries.[1] Even the political separation of the countries was not entirely divisive, since for many years both the British and South African Governments contemplated that the High Commission Territories would be incorporated in the Union of South Africa.

In the political relations between Africans in the Union and Africans from the High Commission Territories, the Union influence was inevitably dominant, since its populous industrial cities were the centres of African political and trade union movements, and its universities trained many of the political leaders and shaped their political ideologies. Africans from the High Commission Territories, and also from other African territories, shared in the exploration of political ideologies in the universities; and they served in trade unions, the African National

---

[1] See J. Halpern, *Basutoland, Bechuanaland, and Swaziland, South Africa's Hostages* for a discussion of the educational facilities in the High Commission Territories, particularly pages 204-14, 307-14, and 410-17. South African schools and universities were almost entirely closed to Africans from the High Commission Territories during the 1950s.

Congress Youth League, the African National Congress, the Pan-Africanist Congress, and other South African political movements.[1] The Congresses sought a broadly based African unity; hence they drew no distinction in the political role of Africans from different territories, and they raised no obstacle to their participation.

As a result of this active participation in Union politics by Africans from the Territories, and as a result also of the active involvement in the politics of the three Territories by refugees from the Union, national movements in the High Commission Territories came strongly under the influence of African political movements in the Union. Ideological perspectives and forms of organizations were imported from the Union into the very different contexts of peasant societies, under British rule, with relatively homogeneous African populations apart from Botswana, and negligible numbers of whites apart from Swaziland. The Basutoland African Congress (later the Basutoland Congress Party) was founded in 1952 under the inspiration of the African National Congress, though it subsequently moved toward the Pan-Africanist Congress; the Bechuanaland People's Party, organized in 1960 on lines similar to those of the African National Congress, seemingly expressed factional conflict in different ideological tendencies, favouring either the African National Congress or the Pan-Africanist Congress; and the Swaziland Democratic Party, formed in 1962, and later merged in the Imbokodvo National Movement, adopted in 1964 the Freedom Charter framed by the African National Congress and other members of the Congress Alliance.[2]

Political activity in the High Commission Territories was, however, by no means the simple product of South African political movements. There were political conflicts over the powers of traditional rulers, problems of succession, national rights to land and incorporation into the Union of South Africa. Some of the modern movements came under other influences, such as the Swaziland Progressive Party (1960), which was an outgrowth of the Swaziland Progressive Association established by the British Resident Commissioner in 1929,[3] and the Ngwane National Liberatory Congress (1963), which was oriented toward Ghana and Pan-Africanism. Moreover, during the movement by Lesotho and Botswana toward national independence in 1966, and by Swaziland toward self-government in 1967, much of the political activity was a

[1] Halpern gives biographies of Ntsu Mokhele, first president of the Basutoland African Congress (pp. 140–2), Motsamai Mpho, secretary-general of the Bechuanaland People's Party (pp. 288–90), John June Nquku, founder of the Swaziland Progressive Party, Dr. Ambrose Pesheya Zwane, leader of the Ngwane National Liberatory Congress, and Dr. Allen Nxumalo, leader of the former Swaziland Democratic Party (pp. 348–55).

[2] Ibid., pp. 142–61, 286, 355; E. S. Munger, *Bechuanaland—Pan-African Outpost or Bantu Homeland*, p. 23.   [3] Ibid., p. 347.

direct response to specific territorial interests in the role of traditional authorities, in problems of economic development and of economic dependence on the Republic, and in foreign and international relations. The political movements in the Territories increasingly detached themselves from the influence of African political movements in the Republic and began to respond to the new political situation of national independence.

In some respects, the independence of the neighbouring states seems likely to weaken African political movements within the Republic. There are many southern Sotho, Tswana, and Swazi living in the Republic. Some are citizens of Lesotho, Botswana, or Swaziland but work in the Republic, and others are subjects of the Republic, who still identify or maintain kinship or other ties with residents in the Territories. Inevitably their political activity is diverted in some measure from African movements in the Republic to involvement in the politics of the new nation states. Moreover, as has been shown above, African nationalism is fragmented by sectional loyalties.

In other respects, energy, support, and influence may flow back from the new nation states. If the Republic, Lesotho, Botswana, and Swaziland are viewed as a broad system of race relations, then the independence of the African states automatically changes that system, and reduces the extreme disparity in political power between Africans and whites. Moreover, the new nations, notwithstanding their economic dependence, may be expected to exert some pressure for the improvement of the status of their nationals, and of Africans generally, in the Republic. But the ruling parties in the three states (the Basuto National Party, the Bechuanaland Democratic Party, and the Imbokodvo National Movement) are conservative politically, in consequence perhaps of their need to relate both to the traditional authorities in their own territories and to the National Party Government in the Republic; and they are all committed to policies of non-racialism and of interracial co-operation. Hence their immediate influence on African politics in the Republic seems likely to favour conservative policies and interracial ideologies, rather than exclusive or militant African nationalist movements.

Support for these exclusive and militant forms of African nationalism now comes from African states to the north, which fall outside the economic dominion of the Republic. Following the suppression of the Congress Alliance and the Pan-Africanist Congress, there is little evidence of African nationalist activity inside the Republic. African nationalist movements have moved across the borders into the international arena. African leaders, during the 1950s, had established relations with political movements and leaders in other countries, and these relations, against the background of international conflict, are now the basis of African nationalism. They will no doubt shape its future course, as this is affected also by internal changes in South African society, consequent upon economic development in the Republic and political independence in the former High Commission Territories.

TABLE I

Religious Affiliations of Africans

	Number		
	1911	1936	1960†
Dutch Reformed	71,422	154,180	556,898
Anglican	170,704	407,528	748,135
Presbyterian	68,211	108,094	204,585
Congregational	95,706	57,054	135,167
Methodist	451,746	795,369	1,313,129
Lutheran	144,244	307,387	539,213
Roman Catholic	24,058	232,905	760,607
Apostolic		13,003	304,583
Other Christian	27,615	62,691	507,567
Bantu Churches		1,089,479	2,188,303
Islam	1,896	1,440	
Other and Unspecified	1,301	37,959	3,649,602
No Religion	2,962,103	3,329,600	
Total	4,019,006	6,596,689	10,907,789

	Distribution over Denominations (%)		
	1911	1936	1960†
Dutch Reformed	1·8	2·3	5·1
Anglican	4·2	6·2	6·9
Presbyterian	1·7	1·6	1·9
Congregational	2·4	0·8	1·2
Methodist	11·2	12·1	12·0
Lutheran	3·6	4·7	4·9
Roman Catholic	0·6	3·5	7·0
Apostolic		0·2	2·8
Other Christian	0·7	1·0	4·6
Bantu Churches		16·5	20·1
Islam	0·1		
Other and Unspecified		0·6	33·5
No Religion	73·7	50·5	
Total	100·0	100·0	100·0

† Figures taken from *Population Census, 1960, Sample Tabulation*, No. 6, pp. 2, 16, 25, 29. The rest are taken from *Union Statistics for Fifty Years*, pp. A–26—A–29.

TABLE I (*cont.*)

	Distribution within Denominations (%)		
	1911†	1936	1960‡
Dutch Reformed		10·9	23·9
Anglican		44·4	53·0
Presbyterian		55·0	63·3
Congregational		36·8	46·7
Methodist		78·0	77·1
Lutheran		78·3	83·4
Roman Catholic		63·6	70·2
Apostolic		22·8	63·1
Other Christian		35·5	61·8
Bantu Churches		100·0	100·0
Islam		1·8	
Other and Unspecified		59·9	96·4
No Religion		68·8	

† These percentages cannot be calculated because figures for religious affiliation of Coloureds and Asians are not available for 1911.

‡ Figures taken from *Population Census, 1960, Sample Tabulation*, No. 6, pp. 2, 16, 25, 29. The rest are taken from *Union Statistics for Fifty Years*, pp. A–26—A–29.

X

SOUTH AFRICA AND THE MODERN WORLD[1]

1. *Introduction*

THE pattern of South Africa's foreign relations as it has developed over the last five decades reflects the connection between domestic issues and the pursuit of external objectives. Historically speaking, these can be defined as follows: (*a*) the search for status in the British Empire and Commonwealth; (*b*) the maintenance of friendly relations with other African territories; (*c*) the incorporation of the three High Commission territories, Basutoland, Bechuanaland, and Swaziland. In addition, there is South Africa's changing role in international organization. South African participation in the League of Nations and the United Nations has mirrored the aspirations of her leaders and the obstacles encountered.

The maxim 'foreign policy begins at home' is peculiarly appropriate for a State in which the traditional conflict between English and Afrikaner for mastery over the domestic political system has been inextricably involved with the issue of South Africa's status in international society. Throughout the interwar period the Imperial connection was the one external issue of real significance in domestic political debate. It was overlaid with ideological overtones for the protagonists who recognized its importance as a weapon in the domestic struggle. Yet although Nationalist aspirations for a republic, no less than Smuts's vision of the Commonwealth, were each in large part conditioned by the exigencies of local politics, both doctrines reflected divergent views about the desirability of isolation from the mainstream of international life and the opposite value of co-operation with a group of like-minded states.

Given the domination of this particular theme in the formulation and conduct of foreign policy, it is not surprising that relatively little attention was focused elsewhere. The 'special relationship' with Britain—its advantages and drawbacks and the degree to which it could and should be changed or abrogated—was defined by policy-makers and opposition alike as the primary national interest to which all other aspirations in

[1] The author is grateful to the Royal Institute of International Affairs, the Institute of Race Relations, the editors of the *Journal of Commonwealth Political Studies*, and the Leicester University Press for permission to utilize material which first appeared under their auspices.

the external field were subordinate. As Bruce Miller has perceptively remarked: 'South African history . . . is very much a matter of constant tension, not only *about* Britain, but also *with* Britain.'[1] This emerges very clearly in the debate between Britain and South Africa over the future of the three High Commission Territories, the existence of which as enclaves in the heartland of South Africa was a constant affront to Afrikaner Nationalist susceptibilities. The rest of Africa remained a closed book to the vast majority of white South Africans, while the League of Nations—sitting in distant Geneva—seemed an essentially Europe-centred organization, despite the sporadic criticisms levelled at the Union by the Mandates Commission over the administration of South West Africa.

Moreover, in strategic terms South Africa was protected by her geographical isolation from the main centres of world conflict. Situated at the tip of a relatively underdeveloped continent, the Union had always relied on the protection of the Royal Navy against the threat of an external attack by sea.[2] To the North her borders were protected by the buffer territories of Southern Rhodesia and Bechuanaland, while reasonably close economic and diplomatic relations existed with the Portuguese administration in Mozambique. The end of the First World War brought South Africa control of the mandated territory of South West Africa, and the elimination of German power, if not of German aspirations, in the southern part of the continent. Consequently, in the period between the two world wars, the maintenance of a large defence force was unnecessary. Indeed, before the Second World War the main role of the Union defence force was the limited one of helping settler communities in British Africa in the event of African revolt.[3]

This situation changed radically after the Second World War. From 1948 onwards the elevation of apartheid into a symbol of survival for Afrikaner nationalism made domestic policy a crucial factor in governing South Africa's relations with the outside world. It is true that racial segregation has a long history in South Africa, but in the pre-war years external criticism of this policy was neither widespread nor sustained. Large parts of Asia and Africa were still Imperial domain and South Africa and the colonial powers had at least this feature in common, that they deemed themselves solely responsible for the welfare and security of their non-white subject people. It was the coincidence of the rise of new independent Asian and African states, pledged to end racial discrimination within and without their borders, and the elevation of

[1] J. D. B. Miller, *Britain and the Old Dominions*, p. 94.
[2] Strategically, the Union ports, in particular the naval base at Simonstown, were extremely valuable to Commonwealth shipping on those occasions when the Mediterranean route was dangerous to follow.
[3] E. A. Walker, *Htstory of Southern Africa*, p. 685.

apartheid by the Nationalist Government into an all-embracing political and social theory, and its implementation as a policy of large-scale social engineering, that forged the bond between foreign and domestic policies in the post-war world. It would not be an exaggeration to say that South Africa thus found herself in a 'cold war' situation, and indeed the ideological overtones to the dispute took on, for both sides, all the attributes of a moral crusade.

The militant anti-Communism of the Nationalist Government made its leaders sensitive to the need for alliances.[1] However, the very foundations of Nationalist domestic policy made the search for allies extremely difficult. It is significant that South Africa, unlike Australia, Canada, New Zealand, and Pakistan, had no share in the various regional defence pacts established in the post-war period. Admittedly there was in 1951 an attempt to institute a regional defence treaty for South and East Africa, when representatives of South Africa, the United Kingdom, Belgium, Ethiopia, France, Italy, Portugal, and Southern Rhodesia met at Nairobi. These discussions broke down when it became apparent that the South African Government would not be a party to any military arrangements entailing the use of arms by Africans. In the changed circumstances of the 1960s, it was impossible for the Western Powers to consider any alliance with South Africa, for to do so would be to provoke the bitter hostility of the independent African states. The Simonstown base and the sea route round the Cape were still important factors in British foreign policy, as the 1956 Suez crisis made clear. Their usefulness, however, would not have been extended by more precise definition of alliance. Indeed, the Anglo-South African Naval Agreement of June 1955 created no political obligations for either party. As W. C. B. Tunstall commented: 'It is simply concerned with naval co-operation between the parties and the use of South African bases, under conditions both of peace and war. Neither party gives any guarantee to the other in terms of a defensive alliance.'[2]

Thus South Africa was bound to be ruled out as an acceptable party in any military pact designed to protect, for example, the western half of the Indian Ocean, for India could have been expected to raise the most profound objections to an arrangement of this kind. The Central African Federation had a negative value as a buffer state in the 1950s and early 1960s, but the majority of its white inhabitants were then chary of close military ties with South Africa for these were bound to have political implications.

[1] See J. D. B. Miller, *The Commonwealth and the World*, p. 196.
[2] W. C. B. Tunstall, *The Commonwealth and Regional Defence*, p. 51.

2. *The Search for Status*

The importance of domestic factors is amply demonstrated in the long debate over South Africa's status as a member of the British Commonwealth. Improved status within the Imperial association in particular, and within international society in general, was a perennial concern for South African leaders of all major parties from 1910 onwards. Yet it was one which paradoxically served to divide the white majority into two antagonistic factions.

Traditionally, English-speaking South Africans resented the exclusive nature of Afrikaner nationalism, especially its insistence that white unity was only possible on the assumption that non-Afrikaners accepted the values of Afrikanerdom and recognized its special claim to embody the '*Volkswil*'. For the Afrikaner Nationalist, the English-speaking group was regarded as having 'a special relationship' with Britain, conflicting with any loyalty its members owed to the South African State. Their traditional attachment to the symbols of this relationship—the crown and the Union Jack—their loyalty to the Commonwealth ideal, and their cultural and educational links with Britain, all suggested to the Afrikaner that his English-speaking counterpart was divided in his allegiance. This attitude was reinforced by a conviction that this group constituted a British 'presence' in South Africa, acting as a constant reminder of the role that British imperialism had played in the Afrikaner's history.

The politics of the first forty years of the Union were, therefore, dominated by a struggle for power between the two white minorities, in which the Afrikaner Nationalist enjoyed an inestimable advantage over his English adversary. For the former, the conflict could be interpreted in terms of an ideology emphasizing two related themes: the struggle to achieve national self-determination, and the positive and peculiar contribution that Afrikaners alleged that they alone could make to the solution of the 'native problem'. The achievement of the second aspiration was dependent on the first, for only when a Nationalist Party was firmly established as the government of South Africa could the necessary measures be taken to safeguard the Afrikaner heritage against the challenges posed by a large and restless non-white majority. Self-determination would, by itself, constitute a barren and short-lived victory, if nothing substantial was done to halt the insidious process of racial integration which had followed South Africa's industrial expansion in the decades before and after Union in 1910.

Thus precisely because Nationalist policy was ideological in content, its protagonists appeared to have a comprehensive answer for South Africa's problems, appropriate not only for the relatively narrow issue of English-Afrikaner relations, but also in the wider context of the determination to withstand any threat to white dominance from non-white sources of pressure.[1] Afrikaner resentment against the English-speaking community's lack of sympathy was not mollified by the tendency of the latter to accept the leadership of 'moderate' Afrikaners like J. C. Smuts and J. H. Hofmeyr, branded by extreme Nationalists as deserters from the Nationalist cause. They were condemned as prepared to sacrifice 'real' Afrikaner interests on the altar of a spurious South African nationhood, ostensibly designed to unite both white groups, but in practice nothing more than a cunning ideological device to keep political power by deceiving enough Afrikaners into giving their support to what was in reality the English-speaking interest.

Yet Smuts was as much involved as Hertzog and subsequent Nationalist leaders in the struggle to give the Union a status compensating for the defeat of 1902 and the subsequent period under British rule. Smuts too must be bracketed with Hertzog and Mackenzie King in their successful attempts to transform Empire into Commonwealth. Nationalist leaders like Malan were equally adamant about the need to enhance South Africa's status, but they went further than Smuts, and looked to the creation of a republic outside the Commonwealth as the final fulfilment of the Afrikaner struggle to be free of the Imperial connection. Indeed, for the Afrikaner Nationalist, the struggle to give South Africa equality of status was an extension into the realm of external affairs of the domestic struggle to gain recognition of the Afrikaner's equality with his English-speaking countrymen in the political, economic, and cultural life of the nation. The influential domestic factor was the Afrikaner group, split between the two camps of the party of Botha and Smuts and the Nationalist minority.

By contrast with the newly independent Commonwealth states of today, foreign policy did not figure prominently in the calculations of the leaders of the newly created Union of South Africa. External relations were confined to those with Britain, who in turn maintained her prerogative of directing an Imperial foreign policy. Botha and Smuts concentrated on interpreting the Imperial link to supporters and opponents alike, in the hope that Boer and Briton would be consolidated into one people and that the bitter memories of the past, and in particular of the Anglo-Boer war, would be eradicated. Depending for electoral support on members of both language groups, Smuts could never afford to antagonize either. This in large part explains his particular conception of the Commonwealth and South Africa's place in it.

[1] Two quotations will illustrate this change in the internal balance of power. 'All South African politics is a quarrel between Afrikaners on what attitude they shall take to the English.' (Smuts speaking before the war.) 'All politics now is a struggle among the English to decide what attitude they shall take to the Afrikaner.' *Die Burger*, Feb. 1961. Quoted in M. Broughton, *The Press and Politics in South Africa*, p. 91.

To understand the importance of the Nationalist victory in 1948 in South Africa's search for status, something must be said about the personal contribution that Smuts made to this great debate. With Botha in 1914 he made sure of South Africa's participation in the First World War and as Prime Minister he followed the same course in 1939. As Professor Eric Walker remarked:

> . . . what other prudent course was open to a small and isolated crowned republic [sic] which possessed the Cape Peninsula, so often taken, coveted and retaken . . . the half-way house between Europe and the East, and now also the gateway to the treasure house of the Witwatersrand? The Union must look round for a protector in a world in which small states commonly fared worse than great, and where should it look but to the power, which as Hertzog generously acknowledged, had done more for it than any other power had done or would do?[1]

On each occasion, Smuts was faced with considerable opposition from Afrikaner Nationalist opponents, whose republican cause gathered strength from the fact of the Union's alliance with Britain. He was given a seat in the Imperial War Cabinet in 1916 and he played an active part in the allied defeat of the Central Powers. His conception of South Africa's national interest was very different from those of his opponents at home. The Boer republics of the second half of the nineteenth century had been isolationist in outlook; their very existence was due in part to the desire of the Boer to escape colonial rule by Britain, and, by implication, contact with the outside world. Fiercely independent and Calvinistic in outlook, the Boers in the old republics cherished an ideal of a pastoral community untainted by the industrial revolution which was rapidly transforming Europe and the United States. Despite the discovery of gold in the later 1880s and the consequent industrial development of the Witwatersrand area, the old outlook persisted and found expression in the extreme republican wing of the National Party organized in 1914. Deriving its political inspiration from continental rather than Anglo-Saxon sources, and backed by a vigorous Calvinistic creed, the new party stressed the injuries and humiliations of the past, promising a future where the Afrikaner *volk* would be supreme and free of external commitments. Smuts was bitterly attacked for his Imperial sympathies; these were exploited by Nationalist leaders like Dr. Malan to entrench and consolidate sentiment hostile to Britain and the Imperial link. Given this particular conception of status, it is not surprising that to many republicans both world wars seemed remote and of little consequence to the Union.

One can readily understand the bitter Afrikaner resentment of Smuts's

[1] Walker, op. cit., p. 691.

performance on the international stage. To him South Africa was part of a greater whole, the British Empire, the constituent members of which all shared a common interest when danger threatened a part of that whole. He saw both wars as more than just local European affairs, and the policies of Germany and her allies as constituting a direct threat to the British Empire and by implication, South Africa. He saw the twin dangers threatening Britain—the possibility of the continent being dominated by one strong power and the corresponding threat of German naval expansion to British communications. On these communications depended the safety of the link between member states. He expressed this point of view in a speech in London on 15 May 1917 and at the same time defined a broad concept of Commonwealth:

It is not only Europe we have to consider, but also the future of the great Commonwealth to which we all belong. This Commonwealth is peculiarly constituted. It is scattered over the whole world. It is not a compact territory, and it is dependent for its very existence on world wide communications —communications which must be maintained or this Empire goes to pieces. . . . you do not want to standardize the nations of the British Empire; you want to develop them toward greater, fuller nationality. These communities, the offspring of the Mother Country, or territories like my own, which have been annexed after the vicissitudes of war, must not be moulded on any one pattern . . . this British Commonwealth of Nations does not stand for standardization or denationalization, but for the fuller, richer, and more various life of all the nations comprised in it.[1]

Here he was stating a political principle which subsequently became widely acceptable as the basis of the Commonwealth ideal. If the Imperial connection was to have any significance for his own countrymen, both English and Afrikaner, his particular conception of that link was the only one possible.

He rejected the idea of Imperial federation out of hand; he thought it totally unsuitable for so diverse a group of states and in any case unacceptable to many of his own countrymen. The Commonwealth concept offered him the only means of reconciling South Africans of both national groups to each other and to continued association with the mother country and the member states. Smuts's definition of the Commonwealth idea clearly owes much to the tangled domestic situation of his own country. Association on these terms he regarded as vital in a world where events in Europe had in the past and might well in the future have profound effects on the security of states like the Union, however distant from Britain.

For many Afrikaners and English-speaking South Africans, the quarrel over their country's status in the Commonwealth appeared settled with

[1] J. C. Smuts, *Jan Christian Smuts*, p. 190.

Hertzog's acceptance of the Balfour Declaration in 1926 and his sub-sequent co-operation with Smuts in amending the South Africa Act and incorporating the substance of the 1931 Statute of Westminster into the Status of the Union Act of 1934. In terms of this legislation South Africa was deemed to be 'a sovereign independent state' with its government recognized as the sole authority in both domestic and foreign affairs. It was significant, however, that in the 1934 correspondence between the two leaders which preceded the fusion of their parties into a single United Party, both agreed to differ on the contentious issues of the divisibility of the Crown and the rights of neutrality and secession. Nor was this disagreement included in the Articles of Fusion; indeed the price of getting any agreement was the twin defections of Dr. Malan and his supporters from Hertzog's following, and Colonel Stallard and a group of obdurate English-speaking M.P.s from the South African Party. Thus for contemporaries the real significance of the settlement of the status issue was measured in domestic terms: an embryonic South African nationhood had at last been created which both Smuts and Hertzog profoundly believed would flower over time into full maturity. At this stage their differences over the principle of neutrality seemed theoretical; the harsh test of decision in the event of a major conflict involving the Commonwealth and by implication South Africa seemed a remote contingency. The next five years were to dispel this optimistic mood, however, and the outbreak of war in 1939 finally ended the political co-operation of the two ex-Boer generals.

Looking back on Smuts's career, one must acknowledge the extra-ordinary degree to which Smuts himself dominated the external relations of South Africa with the outside world. He was after all the representative of a relatively insignificant State. Yet he gave South Africa a status in the international society out of all proportion to her size and population: in the eyes of many outside, South Africa was identified with the person of Smuts.

In this respect he bears comparison with President Wilson, for both tended to view their specific national interests in broad international terms. Each saw his respective country as part of a wider association of states (for Smuts at least, the League was in one sense an amplification of the Commonwealth idea), mutually determined to promote peaceful change and outlaw war as an instrument of policy. Their idealism, however, was not shared by sections of their own countrymen and both had the bitter experience of seeing their policies repudiated by opponents at home.

Thus up to 1945 discussion about South Africa's external relations was on the whole confined to evolving a status acceptable to both white national groups within the country, but it was the interaction of foreign and domestic politics which set limits to the debate on status. In other words, it was the Commonwealth connection which was at stake and the area of disagreement was scarcely ever widened to cover relationships with states and people outside the Commonwealth. When events outside the Commonwealth were discussed, these were usually seen in the light of their effect on relations between the United Kingdom and South Africa. Even the growing strength of Germany and the possibility of a second world war were often discussed in the context of South Africa's commitment to the Commonwealth, for the twin issues of secession from the Commonwealth and neutrality in any world conflict were closely interwoven.

The end of the 1914–18 war found South Africa subject to increased stresses, with the Afrikaner as eager as any Czech or Pole to plead his case for self-determination. Similarly, the Second World War so stimulated the growth of Afrikaner nationalism that at its end the National Party, a united force at last, found itself sole heir to the republican tradition and dedicated to fighting Smuts and the United Party instead of resigned to perpetual wrangling with splinter groups on minute issues of principle and personality.[1]

At the same time international society was changing rapidly. Western Europe, weakened by six years of intensive warfare, was dependent upon the United States for military and economic assistance. The dropping of the first atom bomb on Japan in 1945 presaged a revolution in strategy and military technology, to which no power, large or small, and however geographically isolated, could afford to remain indifferent. But more important to South Africa's external position than even these immense alterations to the pattern of international society was the colonial revolution then beginning in Asia and Africa. The granting of independence to India, Pakistan, Burma, and Ceylon in the immediate post-war period not only necessitated a rapid revision of traditional concepts of the Commonwealth, but added a new dimension to the foreign policies of all states within that association. There were few powers which could afford the luxury of a policy of isolation, least of all South Africa, situated as it was at the tip of a predominantly black continent.

The Nationalist victory in 1948 put an end to Smuts's career as a politician, and his death in 1950 brought an end to an era in imperial thought. The new concept of a multi-racial Commonwealth was foreign to his way of thinking. Indeed, he was extremely doubtful about the wisdom of the Attlee government's decision to extend independence to the four major Asian colonies. This he described as 'an awful mistake'.[2] Although

[1] See M. Roberts and A. Trollip, *The South African Opposition 1939–45.*
[2] Smuts, op. cit., p. 507.

his prestige abroad had mitigated some of the criticism inspired by his domestic policies, he had not found foreign policy an easy task in the post-war world.

Professor Julius Lewin has rightly drawn attention to the curious divorce between political and economic power in South Africa, for it helps to explain the frustration of many English-speaking South Africans at the course of events after 1948.[1] Their discontent sharpened as the Government proceeded to sacrifice constitutional principle to the demands of ideological necessity,[2] and break link by link the ties that bound English-speaking South Africa to the Commonwealth. Nor was this attachment to the Commonwealth merely sentimental; breaking the link meant more, too, than the loss of Imperial preference. These two foci of discontent were connected, for the drive towards the establishment of a republic represented the culmination of twelve years of Nationalist rule during which the Constitution had been relentlessly undermined. The growth of organizations like the Torch Commando, the Federal Party, and the Defenders of the Constitution reflected the increasing concern of English-speaking South Africans with their future status under a republican constitution. Their language, the education of their children, their faith in constitutional government—all these seemed in jeopardy. This feeling was probably stronger in Natal than anywhere else in the Union, and it was here that the Federal Party, for example, gained most of its support. Indeed, it came into existence partly because its leaders regarded the United Party as ambivalent on the republican issue.[3]

It is doubtful, however, whether this opposition of English-speaking South African organizations substantially delayed the institution of a republic. Certainly the thirteen-year delay in fulfilling the 1948 election promise on this issue is interesting. The explanation lies in a combination of internal and external factors: the initial reluctance to follow the precedent set by the Asian member-states of a republic within the Commonwealth was probably due to the Government's belief that the domestic aspect of its policy required consolidation before embarking on this particular goal, and possibly because its leaders recognized that the declaration of a republic within the Commonwealth might have been construed by South Africa's critics as a preliminary move to departure from the association and still further erosion of the constitution. Throughout this period the Commonwealth connection was accepted

---

[1] Julius Lewin, *Politics and Law in South Africa*, p. 30.

[2] I refer here to the long-drawn-out struggle over the Separate Representation of Voters Bill and the constitutional crisis this provoked in the 1950s.

[3] This party proposed the establishment of a federal system in which the rights of an English-speaking province like Natal would be protected by a rigid constitution. It fought a number of seats against United Party nominees without success.

as a useful buffer against the hostility which domestic treatment of the non-whites was engendering. Yet Commonwealth support at the United Nations was embarrassing to the South African Government. In a sense South Africa's position was ambivalent for, while South Africa desperately needed what support it could get at the United Nations, many Nationalists, thinking nostalgically of the isolation of the old nineteenth-century republics, preferred to see South Africa with a republican constitution outside the Commonwealth. Nevertheless in the late 1950s little was heard of the republican proposal even from the extreme right wing of the party. Dr. Verwoerd, and no doubt the Department of External Affairs, were clearly aware of the advantages of continued Commonwealth membership in a world increasingly hostile to South Africa. Imperial preference, for example, was an obvious economic advantage for some South African products; the Commonwealth Relations Office kept South Africa informed of current international developments to an extent which would not have been possible were the latter ever to contract out of the association. It was clear to the leaders of the National Party that withdrawal would almost certainly have intensified criticism from non-white members.[1]

The 1960 Referendum was fought on the explicit assumption that South Africa would remain in the Commonwealth even if a majority declared itself in favour of a republican constitution. To this extent, then, the traditional Afrikaner Nationalist interpretation of the status question was profoundly modified by external pressures against which the Commonwealth was reluctantly seen as a shield of sorts. Certainly the status issue was settled in a way very few of the early Nationalist leaders would have predicted or for that matter welcomed. But status of the formal variety, so dear to Nationalist theorists, was at last achieved with the declaration of the Republic on 31 May 1961.

In fact, this delay in achieving republican status—the object of generations of Nationalist struggle and a basic source of ideological strength—and the way in which it eventually came about probably helped the Government in its subsequent relations with the English-speaking group. Nationalist leaders always stressed that white unity would only be possible when English-speaking Africans had at last come to recognize that they did not form 'part of a nation overseas', when their interests as part of a white minority predominated over any sentiment about their British ties.

This argument gained force from the circumstances surrounding South Africa's withdrawal from the Commonwealth. Dr. Verwoerd was able to demonstrate convincingly that the old Commonwealth of white dominions, linked to the mother country, existed no more. In its place

[1] Miller, *The Commonwealth and the World*, p. 204.

stood a multi-racial association of states, the majority of which were bitterly hostile to South African racial policies, and cared little, if anything, for the so-called rights of an English-speaking white minority. To remain a member of an association of this kind, in their view bent on destroying the white man's position, would be to expose South Africa as a whole to continued indignity and offer a ready-made platform for her enemies. As two authorities have argued: 'It was widely accepted [in South Africa] that Dr. Verwoerd's position on the matter in London had been forced upon him by the truculent attitude towards South Africa taken by the Asian and African Commonwealth members.'[1]

In his speech to the House of Assembly on 23 March 1961 the Prime Minister, Dr. Verwoerd, made it clear that he had withdrawn from the Commonwealth because: 'What they sought was not equality through co-existence and non-subordination in countries like South Africa, but the domination of superior numbers in the name of full equality and, therefore, eventual victory over the whites by forcing out or swallowing up the whites. It was there that we had to draw the line.'[2]

His emphasis on the danger of permitting this degree of interference in the domestic affairs of a member state and the consequences that would follow such interference undoubtedly struck a responsive chord in the thinking of many white South Africans, undermining the traditional hostility to Nationalist policies on domestic issues. Many, it is true, disagreed with the Bantustan programme; what they could not easily forgive was the outside world's apparent indifference to the material advantages enjoyed by Africans in the Republic as compared with other African states. It was this allegedly misinformed criticism which aroused their patriotism, and indirectly benefited the Government's position, while events elsewhere in Africa contributed to the solidarity of white opinion.

In effect, the formerly conflicting notions of national interest merged to produce a consensus of opinion of the importance of keeping the outside world at bay. To this extent, then, there was fundamental agreement on South Africa's national interest between the majority of both white groups and their leaders, however much they disagreed on domestic issues. It was this agreement which strengthened the confidence of the Government in its claim to speak and act in the external field on behalf of all white South Africans and, by the same token, complicated the task of the two main opposition parties in their attempts to form and offer alternative domestic and foreign policies.

[1] N. M. Stultz and J. Butler, 'The South African General Election of 1961', *Political Science Quarterly*, 78 (1963), 86–110.

[2] Quoted in N. Mansergh (ed.), *Documents and Speeches on Commonwealth Affairs, 1952–62*, p. 378.

It is significant that the republican issue did not figure largely in the parliamentary election of October 1961.[1] Both the United and the Progressive Parties stressed South Africa's growing isolation in international society, but this appeal made little headway against Dr. Verwoerd's insistence on the stark choice facing the electors: 'Your choice is more sharply defined than at any previous election, namely between a white republic, with non-white neighbours, and a multi-racial fatherland with, first a multi-racial and, later, a black-government.'[2] The implication was clear: isolation might have its dangers, but any concessions to the non-white majority with a view to appeasing external hostility were infinitely more dangerous to the white man's position. To argue that a United Party or Progressive victory would materially contribute to ending this isolation and restoring confidence in the South African economy showed a pathetic misunderstanding of the real object of Afro-Asian demands.[3] The electorate took the point and the National Party was returned to office with an increased majority, which suggested that many moderate Afrikaners and some English-speaking electors were deserting the United Party.

In defining their attitude to South Africa's external position during the 1960s, both the United and Progressive Parties had to be cautious. Both recognized implicitly that to formulate an alternative foreign policy, in a situation where the latter must inevitably be concerned to defend domestic policy, was to operate in a vacuum. In this respect these two parties were in a more difficult position than their counterparts in other states, where a viable distinction could be drawn between foreign and domestic policy in the electoral debate between Government and Opposition. Both parties therefore concentrated their energies on demanding radical changes on the domestic front as a logical priority to any improvement in South Africa's international position.[4] Logic was reinforced by tactical considerations based on an intuitive sense that in a situation where there existed a wide measure of agreement between parties on the importance of preserving the white man's position against

[1] Cf. L. Marquard, writing in 1959: 'It is doubtful whether the majority of voters would today support a republic; and if it did, the opposition would be so fierce and bitter that it would not be a stable republic.' *People and Policies of South Africa*, p. 161.

[2] *The Star* (Johannesburg), 16 Oct. 1961, quoted by Stultz and Butler, op. cit., p. 97.

[3] 'In this connection let me say to my hon. friends on the other side that on this occasion we were under fire because we happened to be the governing party, but with their policy, which is also a policy of discrimination in the eyes of the world, they would have found themselves inevitably in the same difficulty, if not now then a little later, unless they were dishonest or unless they accepted the policy of the absolute surrender of the white man.' (Extract from Dr. Verwoerd's speech on the 1961 Commonwealth Conference, quoted in Mansergh, op. cit., p. 387).

[4] Cf. the following statement contained in a Progressive Party pamphlet: 'It was the international dislike of our race policies that made us a pariah at the United Nations and resulted in our departure from the Commonwealth.'

internal and external pressures, Opposition politicians had to be wary in their use of South Africa's unpopularity abroad as a weapon for attacking the Government.

The United Party, for example, tried to draw a distinction between the importance of maintaining links with the Western powers and resisting the pressure of South Africa's Afro-Asian and Communist enemies. This distinction emerged clearly in an important speech delivered by the party leader, Sir de Villiers Graaff, to the Central Congress of the United Party in Bloemfontein on 19 November 1963: 'These nations of the Western world are not asking for one man, one vote, in spite of the efforts of Government propaganda, led by Mr. Eric Louw to make us believe that this is the minimum they will demand from us.' He emphasized that all South Africa's friends required was 'a moderation of policies' and argued that the United Party policy of race federation met the case exactly. He admitted that no policy, short of full universal franchise, could satisfy the second group, and emphasized that a United Party government would never concede this. 'The question, however, remains as to whether our proposals will give the countries of the Western world a case which they can defend in international forums.'[1]

The United Party's belief that 'responsible' elements in world opinion would accept its policy of race federation was an instance of how far external pressures forced this traditionally conservative party to rethink its attitude to the racial issue. Previously, the notion of 'white leadership with justice', involving presumably a more 'humane' implementation of existing discriminatory legislation, was represented as the maximum the party was prepared to concede to African nationalist aspirations. However, the platform for the 1961 election went further, including proposals to give legal and political equality to the Cape Coloured population, a promise of negotiation with the Indian community on their future status, and the establishment of a federation with representatives for each racial group in a central legislature, although in time direct African representation might be permitted.[2] The external influence should not, however, be exaggerated; a more potent one was probably the emergence in 1959 of the Progressive Party and its frank recognition that South Africa was a multi-racial society requiring a political structure which took this salient fact into account.

---

[1] In the same speech, he quoted the words of Mr. Peter Thomas, British Delegate in the General Assembly's Special Political Committee: 'Ought we not to give consideration to the possibilities of finding some bridge, some compromises, between the ultimate objectives of the South African government, as we have heard them stated in this Assembly, and the concept of a full multi-racial society, to which the vast majority of nations subscribed?' (See United Party broadsheet (Johannesburg, 1963).)

[2] This was offered as a tentative prospect and not given prominence in United Party propaganda.

This brief excursion into domestic party politics has relevance here because few whites in South Africa drew a sharp distinction between internal threats and the external pressures that menaced their position. A grudging confidence in the Government's ability to handle the domestic situation was easily translated into a belief that unyielding resistance to external demands was the only policy that guaranteed survival. Annual increases in defence expenditure evoked relatively little protest and there did not seem to be any widespread objection to the institution of compulsory military service. Given this climate of opinion, it is not surprising that the two Opposition parties had little to offer in the way of an alternative foreign policy. Indeed, at times Sir de Villiers Graaff used arguments not dissimilar from those of the Prime Minister in appealing for a greater understanding abroad of South Africa's problems.

The following extract is worth quoting in full for the revealing light that it sheds on the bipartisan approach to the problem of explaining South Africa's case to the outside world:

I think it is right that we should remind the countries of the west of a few matters. We are the largest white community in Africa; and with many thousands of non-Europeans who have learnt to share our civilization with us; we are far and away the largest westernized group on the continent of Africa; we are not a settler community. We are a permanent population that has as much right here as any other race or group. We have no other home and no other loyalties. We are white Africans just as there are white Americans; our population ratios are such that experience in other African states with settler communities cannot and certainly should not be applied here; our people have the highest standard of living of any state in Africa and that goes for our non-Europeans as well; we are the most highly industrialized state in Africa, and well able to meet our own needs in arms and ammunition for internal security; we reject one-man-one-vote absolutely but cannot understand why it should be asked of us, save by those who wish to destroy our civilization, and our standards.[1]

Thus in so far as South African foreign policy was concerned to defend domestic policies, opposition politicians had to avoid creating an impression of 'un-South African' behaviour—the consequence of accepting that the demands of the outside world had relevance for any solution to the country's problems. Opposition leaders, who repeatedly stated their objections to the Government's handling of external affairs, were nevertheless often forced to add the cautious rider that they would resist any attempt by the outside world to deny to South Africa her right to find her own solutions in her own time. This attitude reflected a

---

[1] In the speech by Sir de Villiers Graaff on 19 Nov. 1963. See p. 490, n. 1.

compound of electoral calculation and patriotic fervour essential for any appeal to a white opinion increasingly sensitive to overseas criticism.

3. *South Africa as an African Power*

A traditional aspiration of South African foreign policy, and one to which all political parties at least paid lip-service, was that of co-operation with other states on the continent in developing resources and raising standards of living. The peculiarly South African notion of 'white civilization' and the need to maintain it at all costs, were interpreted by the leaders of all major parties as having relevance beyond the Union's borders. As Professor W. M. Macmillan wrote, 'South Africans . . . express . . . at times almost a proprietary interest in the Africa beyond.'[1]

The presence of Southern Rhodesian observers at the National Convention in 1908 and the 1923 referendum in that territory on union with South Africa are concrete examples of the latter's interest in firm ties between the white communities scattered across the continent. Success in this venture, however, proved impossible. Afrikaner Nationalists, intent on dominating the political structure of the Union, saw the addition of several thousand British settlers as a threat to their own emerging culture. Rhodesians themselves, as their adverse vote in the 1923 referendum made clear, looked with considerable misgiving on the prospects of closer political ties with what appeared to be an alien anti-British group.

Despite this setback, South Africa was still seen as the leading state on the continent, and Smuts's writings on the future of Africa are an illuminating text on this theme.[2] But by 1935 the only prospect in view was the possible establishment of two or three federations between the Limpopo and the Sudan 'linked to the Union by a common native policy' and 'directly flowing from the common native policy, a common defence policy'.[3] Implicit in this view was an admission that the old dream, once shared by Rhodes and Smuts, of a *single* state covering this area, was finally shattered. It is true that the Second World War brought a degree of co-ordination in defence policy as South African and British troops fought side by side in Ethiopia and the Western Desert. As late as 1943 Smuts was probably still thinking in terms of a common native policy when he made his proposal for a regional grouping of British territories in close association with the Union as the senior partner. But this hope came to nothing.

[1] W. M. Macmillan, *Africa Beyond the Union*, Hoernlé Memorial Lecture (Johannesburg, 1949), p. 6.
[2] J. C. Smuts, *Africa and some World Problems*.
[3] Oswald Pirow quoted in Walker, op. cit., p. 685.

In the early years of Nationalist rule Dr. Malan, then Prime Minister, like his predecessor General Smuts, disagreed profoundly with the British policy of colonial emancipation in Asia and Africa. He argued that this policy constituted an open invitation to Communist infiltration, and his objection in 1952 to the admission to the Commonwealth of former British colonies must be seen in the twin context of South African anti-Communism and the fear that the Commonwealth would suffer dilution by the addition of non-white elements. To this end he suggested an 'African Charter', underwritten by South Africa and the colonial powers, and designed to contain any attempt at Communist aggression in Africa. Thus Dr. Malan saw South Africa's role as that of a European state in Africa whose interests were tied to those of the colonial powers; hence his dismay at the policy of decolonization which in his view threatened this alleged common interest.

The emergence of independent states on the continent of Africa was quite foreign to the experience of Nationalist leaders of Dr. Malan's generation, and the failure of their rearguard action to halt or at least slow down the process was implicitly recognized by Malan's successor, J. G. Strydom. He realized that protest would be fruitless and indeed ill advised from the point of view of future relations with the new states. In August 1955 he gave expression to this changing attitude, claiming that: 'The relationship between South African and non-White states in Africa, with their millions of inhabitants, should be one of mutual interested parties in Africa, without hostility toward one another— a relationship of peoples and governments who recognized and respected one another's right of existence.'[1] This plea for coexistence between white and black governments was later reinforced by an admission of the need for diplomatic exchanges, while in March 1957 Eric Louw, then Minister for External Affairs, explained that his policy was based on the premiss that South Africa 'must accept its future role in Africa as a vocation, and must in all respects play its full part as an African power'. This, he argued, would enable the Union to act as a 'permanent link between the Western Nations, on the one hand, and the populations of Africa south of the Sahara on the other'.[2] He admitted that the success of this policy would depend on the African states adopting a less prejudiced view of the apartheid policy, recognizing that it constituted no threat to their integrity. This would come in time, as the new states learned to take advantage of the contribution South Africa could make to their welfare in view of her position as the most highly industrialized

[1] Speech to Natal National Party Congress, Vryheid, 25 Aug. 1955 (S.A. Information Service, *Fact Paper no. 72*, 1959), p. 5.
[2] Address at Graduation Day Ceremony, Pretoria University, Mar. 1957 (State Information Office, *Fact Paper no. 33*), p. 9.

state on the continent, with considerable resources of specialized scientific and technical knowledge available for assisting their development. This emphasis on technological and economic co-operation was repeated on many occasions, and as late as 1959 Dr. Verwoerd, Strydom's successor as Prime Minister, was arguing that it might be an effective substitute for the diplomatic and political links which had failed to materialize by that date.

Throughout this period Government spokesmen made much of South Africa's role in four organizations connected with scientific and technical development in Africa on a multilateral basis: the Commission for Technical Co-operation in Africa south of the Sahara and its subordinate bodies, the Foundation for Mutual Assistance in Africa south of the Sahara, and the Scientific Council of Africa; and also the United Nations Economic Commission for Africa. Louw stressed that member states were 'learning to trust one another', but this was an empty claim at that stage as the majority on these bodies consisted of the colonial powers. When the balance swung in favour of newly independent states, South Africa found herself in hostile company and withdrew support from all four. Nevertheless the Nationalist Government continued to pay lip-service to the ideals of inter-African co-operation outlined in Louw's 1957 speech and it probably had very little choice in the matter, if it were not to admit publicly that it had no alternative but to 'face the future as a stranger, an alien in practical isolation'.[1]

Thus in the 1950s and early 1960s South Africa's domestic policies appeared to have damaged irretrievably the aspirations for coexistence entertained by her leaders, and this exclusion from the affairs of the continent went beyond a blank refusal to countenance South Africa's presence in regional organizations or the mutual extension of diplomatic privileges. It involved nothing less than an attempt to impose a physical and psychological isolation on South Africa, as the resolutions of successive conferences of the Organization for African Unity made abundantly clear. The Addis Ababa conference in 1963, for example, called for a ban on South African aircraft and shipping from the air space and the harbours of independent Africa; trade boycotts were imposed, and South Africa was forced to withdraw from the International Labour Organization, the Food and Agriculture Organization, the World Health Organization, and the Olympic Games.[2] Finally, the establishment of a National Liberation Committee designed to assist freedom movements in South Africa with finance and military training was an index of the radical African states' determination to end white rule in the Republic.

---

[1] *Fact Paper, no. 72*, op. cit.

[2] South Africa willingly withdrew from UNESCO as a mark of protest against that organization's decision to investigate racial questions on a scientific basis.

Yet despite all these difficulties, by 1966 the Government felt sufficiently confident of its internal and external position to begin the process of translating the aspiration to be an African power into reality, exerting its political and economic influence in the southern third of the continent and perhaps beyond. The first sign of this 'outward looking' foreign policy was a trade agreement signed between South Africa and Malawi in 1966, shortly followed by the decision to exchange diplomatic representations with Dr. Banda's government. In 1967 discussions with Lesotho were begun about possible South African support for the financing of the Ox-bow hydro-electric scheme.[1] The basic premiss underlying this new policy was clear—namely that a sharp distinction could be maintained between domestic and foreign policy, as independent Africa came to terms with a regime, the internal complexion of which had traditionally been an object of profound dislike and a stumbling block in the way of better relations. Furthermore, for South Africa's rulers, the task of domestic consolidation—an essential preliminary to a more positive external stance—was complete, and the Republic could embark on its new course sure in the knowledge that there would be few if any significant internal or external repercussions.

The reasons for this new-found confidence can be briefly stated: first of all, the Nationalist Party found itself in the enviable position of having little if anything to fear from the white opposition parties in the context of electoral politics. This was especially true in the area of foreign policy, for the Government's new initiatives received bipartisan support. Secondly, the long-cherished goal of a republic had been achieved with no obvious economic or strategic disadvantages, despite the dire prophecies of the Opposition leaders throughout the 1950s. Thus a major traditional problem of foreign policy appeared satisfactorily resolved and both policy-makers and the public could focus on new issues nearer home, which in any case carried fewer ideological overtones than the republican issue.

Thirdly, the Government had effectively blunted the nationalist aspirations of the non-white majority (see preceding chapter). Fourthly, the Government felt confident that it could cope with any attempt at insurgence whether internally organized or externally provoked, and to this end organized its defence system on a counter-insurgency basis. Fifthly, it had over the years succeeded in winning the support of the English-speaking section of the population on a fairly large scale and in particular had persuaded the latter to accept the Nationalist estimate of the measures required to maintain internal stability. Finally, the

[1] It is interesting to note the establishment of an air link in 1967 between South Africa and the Malagasy Republic and the efforts made to establish trade links with the Francophone states.

economy had prospered dramatically since 1960. Thus these factors taken together provided the confidence required to launch new initiatives in the field of foreign policy.

This confidence was also promoted by external developments. Down to 1968, the O.A.U. had failed to alter the balance of power in southern Africa either through unilateral action or by attempts to persuade the Great Powers to act through the agency of the United Nations. The frustration of the African states was connected indirectly with the *dètente* between the West and the Soviet Union and the slackening in the competition between the two super-Powers for the allegiance of the uncommitted neutralist states of the Third World. A further complication was the increasing instability of Africa as a whole, and this weakness in the domestic base of many African states was reflected in their decreasing ability to influence the Great Powers in the direction of radical pressures against the White South. In this context, the South African Government clearly counted on the assumption that a *status quo* conscious West would be very reluctant to intervene in an area which appeared politically stable and with which it was increasingly involved in terms of trade and investment.

Finally, the 1966 judgement of the World Court on the South West Africa dispute removed yet another element of uncertainty in South Africa's external position. For a brief moment in the 1960s it seemed possible that the U.N. would become actively involved in the dispute over South West Africa, which in terms of international law, and perhaps politics, appeared to be South Africa's Achilles heel. The judgement coincided with the advent to power of conservative, moderate African governments in the three former High Commission Territories, all firmly committed to coexistence with South Africa; these developments further strengthened the convictions of the Nationalist élite that it had little to fear from the outside world, least of all from independent Africa.

4. *South Africa and the High Commission Territories*

The South African desire to incorporate all three High Commission Territories has a long history, the early years of which have been covered in preceding chapters in this volume. During the debate on the South Africa Act, the responsible ministers in the British Government gave assurances that Parliament would have the fullest opportunity of discussing and, if so inclined, of disapproving any proposal for the transfer of the three Territories to South African jurisdiction; also the inhabitants of the Territories would be consulted and their wishes taken into account. These assurances were repeated and strongly emphasized at intervals during the next thirty years whenever the question arose.

That all three Territories remained heavily dependent on South Africa in economic terms was a strong argument supporting the Union's claim. A high proportion of their menfolk found employment in the mines and farms of South Africa and their remittances made a vital contribution to the local economies. (This dependence was especially striking in the case of Basutoland which annually 'exported' some 43 per cent of its adult male population to its richer neighbour, receiving an average in the post-war period of £500,000 in deferred payments for their labour.) Each Territory also received a fixed percentage of the total receipts accruing to the customs union which covered southern Africa as a whole and in addition shared a common banking, currency, and postal system with South Africa. The great bulk of the Territories' trade was done with the latter and it was therefore difficult to escape the conclusion that economic logic dictated that absorption by South Africa should be their ultimate political destiny.

It should, however, be stressed that the traditional aspiration of South African policy-makers for incorporation was based on more than the objective factors of geographical integrity and economic interdependence. Psychological factors played their role as well. The initial refusal of the British Government to yield control in the first decade of the century was regarded by the Afrikaner inhabitants of the two northern colonies as an adverse comment on their own racial policies. Secondly, they were, in later years, instinctively aware that—in theory at any rate—the British administration in each of the Territories was committed to a policy fundamentally opposed to their own and by implication regarded as politically and morally superior. At the same time, South African governments objected to a situation which effectively precluded them from applying a single uniform native policy to southern Africa as a whole.

Furthermore, in the four decades after 1910, the Territories were a symbol of the tangible presence of British authority 'in the heart of our country' and a constant reminder of the intrusive role of the Imperial factor against which Afrikaners had struggled throughout their history. The 'morbid interest' of the British Government in the welfare of the African was an element in this hostility and was associated with the wider struggle for status which characterized relations between Britain and the Union after 1910. Thus the deep-rooted desire to incorporate the Territories was an aspect of the nationalism which has permeated Afrikaner thinking throughout the century. Moreover, the existence of an Imperial enclave like Basutoland was a reminder that the Afrikaner struggle for national self-determination was necessarily incomplete so long as territorial boundaries did not correspond to their conception of geographical and, by implication, national integrity. These factors explain the growing hostility of many Afrikaner Nationalists in the 1930s to continued British refusals to meet their demands and suggest why the desire for incorporation was closely linked with the desire for a change in South Africa's 'status' within the British Empire and subsequently the Commonwealth.

The British response to the demand for incorporation was initially based on the assumption that in time South African policy with regard to the indigenous African population would change as the 'liberal' influence of the Cape Colony spread to the two northern provinces. When that happened—it was implicitly understood—British objections to handing the Territories over to South African jurisdiction would presumably wither away.[1]

By the mid 1930s, however, there was clearly little prospect of this happening, and public opinion in the United Kingdom had been aroused to an awareness of the economic condition of the Territories by the investigations of Sir Alan Pim on behalf of the British Government and the writings of scholars such as Margery Perham.[2] By this time, too, General Hertzog had succeeded in obtaining the status to which he felt South Africa was entitled in the international community, signified by the Balfour Declaration of 1926 and the constitutional recognition of this status in the Statute of Westminster of 1931 and the Status of the Union Act of 1934. Given South Africa's new constitutional position, it was believed that the safeguards of the Schedule were inoperative and Hertzog assumed that he was in a better position to negotiate transfer.

In 1934 Hertzog took a stronger line than previously, suggesting that if transfer were delayed difficulties would arise for the inhabitants of the Territories, especially with regard to their rights and privileges in the Union. Hertzog discussed the issue with Mr. J. H. Thomas, Dominions Secretary, during his visit to London in 1935. Thomas himself was apparently influenced by the arguments of those who felt that the Union's claims were strong; it is possible that he was impressed by the views of a number of prominent experts on African affairs who, in a deputation to him, argued that South Africa should be given the prospect of transfer by stages.[3] Thomas, too, recognized the need—emphasized by the Pim

---

[1] 'There had . . . been something almost pathetic in the faith shown by some members of the National Convention in the certainty of the survival of the franchise system of the Cape against any attacks that might come from the less liberal members of the new Union Parliament. It was impossible, one of them said, "To find a single instance when a great body of persons . . . , a whole race, has been disfranchised in democratic times." ' Lord Hailey, *Native Administration in the British African Territories*, Pt. V, *The High Commission Territories*, pp. 50–1.

[2] See the opposing views presented by Margery Perham and Lionel Curtis in their book, *The Protectorates and South Africa*, on the advisability of coming to terms with the Union on this issue.

[3] This deputation included Lord Lugard, Lord Lothian, and Lord Selborne. An opposing

Reports—for economic assistance to the Territories, and was therefore favourable to associating the Union in the work of development.

Thomas replied with an *aide-memoire* presented to Hertzog in May 1935, in which the pledges made to Parliament since 1909 were set down in detail in an appendix, and in which the British Government suggested (and obtained South African agreement to) a policy of close co-operation between the two countries involving on South Africa's part an expenditure of £35,000 in the High Commission Territories. Therefore, according to the *aide-memoire*, 'if transfer were to become a matter of practical politics, it could be effected with the full acquiescence of the populations concerned,' who could be shown evidence of the Union Government 'working in concert with local Administrations with a real and generous desire to develop and improve conditions . . .'.[1] The conflicting interpretations put on this arrangement by each side were a major theme in discussions on the future of the Territories up to 1939.[2]

From 1937 onwards there was sporadic discussion about the way in which South Africa proposed to administer the Territories should incorporation take place. In 1938 a Joint Advisory Conference was established to study possibilities of co-operation in the development of the Territories. But nothing came of this and in 1939 both governments agreed to drop the question of transfer for the time being. Indeed, throughout the 1930s it is fair to say that the disagreements between Britain and South Africa were symptomatic of a fundamental divergence between the two governments. For Britain, the promises made to Parliament about consultation were of paramount importance and this invariably governed their attitude to South African demands. For South Africa economic co-operation was 'a prelude during which the natives would be prepared for . . . inevitable incorporation in the Union'.[3] The provocation and threats of Hertzog's speech in June 1936, in which he hinted broadly at a possible closure of South African markets to the Territories and the loss of their privileges in the Union, was symptomatic of a new aggressiveness towards the Territories on the part of Afrikaner Nationalists, particularly in the more extreme Transvaal. Throughout this period the inhabitants of the Territories made their own opposition to incorporation abundantly clear. Their

view, which by implication suggested another reason for Thomas's willingness to compromise, was presented by Sir Herbert Stanley, who criticized the notion that the inhabitants should 'have to pay the price for the maintenance of cordial relations between the United Kingdom and the Union'. Lord Hailey, *The Republic of South Africa and the High Commission Territories*, pp. 71–2.

[1] *Basutoland, the Bechuanaland Protectorate, and Swaziland: History of Discussions with the Union of South Africa, 1909–39*, Cmd. 8707, pp. 53–7.

[2] For a more detailed analysis of these discussions, see J. E. Spence, 'British Policy towards the High Commission Territories', *Journal of Modern African Studies*, 2 (1964), 235–42.

[3] I. Edwards, *Protectorates or Native Reserves?* (Africa Bureau, London, n.d.), p. 17.

leaders, as much as those of Britain and South Africa, all had long memories of the past; it would never be easy, either then or in the future, as Hertzog himself put it, 'to stop the little child from crying'.

The fears of the inhabitants did not abate in the years after the Second World War and were strengthened by a number of ministerial statements in the South African Parliament after 1948. As early as 1949, for example, Dr. D. F. Malan raised the matter with British representatives at the Commonwealth Conference; he was critical of the British Government's attitude, and issued a warning that his Government was considering a petition to the British Parliament for the transfer of all three Territories to South African jurisdiction. The question was discussed publicly during the visit of Mr. Patrick Gordon Walker, then Secretary of State for Commonwealth Relations, to South Africa in February 1950. Dr Malan argued that the delay in effecting transfer implied a 'position of inferiority' for the Union as a Commonwealth state, on the grounds that no other member of the Commonwealth would tolerate being 'compelled to harbour territories, entirely dependent upon her economically and largely also for their defence, but belonging to and governed by another country'.[1] This emphasis upon Commonwealth status, coming from the leader of a party traditionally hostile to the Commonwealth connection, gave an ironic twist to the standard arguments for incorporation employed by South Africa in the preceding forty years. The South African Government re-emphasized its concern at the delay in 1951, 1954, and 1956; Gordon Walker and his successors at the C.R.O. stood firm, however, on the principle of consultation with the inhabitants of the Territories, implying that the British Government was very unwilling to enter into negotiation with the South African authorities.

The publication in 1954 of the Tomlinson Commission Report on Separate Development again focused attention on the Territories. All three were included in the proposal for seven Bantustans, although Dr. H. F. Verwoerd, then South African Minister for Native Affairs, denied that their inclusion was a basic requirement for the success of his policy. Five years later, in a speech in the House of Assembly, he dismissed the possibility of incorporation by South Africa as incompatible with the British policy of granting independence to African territories. This candid admission of reality had never been matched by any of Dr. Verwoerd's predecessors as Prime Minister, and it clearly revealed his inability at that time to conceive of full independence for the Bantustans and by implication for the High Commission Territories as part of that scheme.

Then, in September 1963, Dr. Verwoerd suggested that Britain and the High Commission Territories should co-operate with South Africa

[1] N. Mansergh (ed.), *Documents and Speeches on Commonwealth Affairs*, ii. 922.

in 'planning the orderly development of southern Africa including the three protectorates, with a view to the consolidation of White and Black areas':[1]

> We [he declared] would aim at making them democratic states in which the masses would not be dominated by a small group of authoritarians . . . [but in which] . . . the whole population [would be led to] democratic rule over its own country . . . we would steer away from the principle of multiracialism . . . Where Whites would be needed and must remain for some time in those areas and occupations, they would become voters in the Republic of South Africa, just as the Bechuanas, the Basutos or the Swazis will, when they work in the Republic, be voters in their respective homelands.[2]

Although he emphasized that incorporation was no longer his country's objective, he did challenge the British Government to allow him to explain to the Territories the advantages which would, in his view, follow from their administration as an integral part of the Bantustan scheme. This speech aroused considerable disquiet in Basutoland in particular, and rekindled fears among the inhabitants that incorporation was an idea still very much alive in the thinking of the South African Government.

Dr. Verwoerd's proposal must be seen in the wider context of the Republic's policy towards independent Africa. In August 1964 Dr. Verwoerd commented on the possibility of a multi-racial common market in southern Africa 'in which none of the member nations would have political control over any of the others, but in which all would co-operate to their mutual benefit'.[3] He referred more specifically to the High Commission Territories in a speech on 31 May 1966 in which he said, 'we have no wish, in spite of what some say, to exploit others. Our nearest neighbours . . . need have no fear . . . we will not interfere in the development of Basutoland, Swaziland, Bechuanaland, Malawi or any other state of Africa. . . .'[4]

With the granting of independence to Lesotho and Botswana in 1966, the South African Government was presented with the opportunity of translating its stated policy into reality. It could be argued that

[1] A. J. H. van der Walt, 'Dr. Verwoerd's African Policy', *Africa Institute Bulletin* (1966), 263.

[2] *The Road to Freedom for Basutoland, Bechuanaland, Swaziland* (Department of Information, *Fact Paper no. 107*, 1963), p. 14.

[3] Reported in *The Star* (Johannesburg), 29 Aug. 1964.

[4] Van der Walt, op. cit., p. 265. N.B. the following extract from a speech made in 1961: 'It is in another sense, namely that a nation that is strong, and that is big, and that is developed, can be a friend of others that are not so far advanced and need help. It can give service—not leadership, but service: co-operation, assistance, help. And the help that we can in particular give is knowledge: knowledge of how to handle certain practical problems. And it is particularly in countries where the circumstances correspond to your own that you can impart knowledge. . . . It is for this reason that we could actually be a greater friend and a better helper.' Ibid., p. 261.

whenever the Republic's leaders considered the shape of future developments in the Territories in the years before independence, their
preference lay in a continuation of British rule in each rather than in
having to face the uncertainties of the situation in which an African
government, possibly with Pan-African sympathies, was in control.
And in Basutoland the superior organization of the radical nationalist
Congress Party coupled with its overwhelming victory in the 1960
elections made this seem a very real possibility.

Particularly disturbing to Dr. Verwoerd and his ministers was the
increasing use of all three Territories as staging posts for the flight of
political refugees, from South African jurisdiction, and their potential
significance as bases for the launching of subversion and sabotage
against the Republic. There were, too, a number of instances in which
refugees had been kidnapped from all three Territories—the most
notorious being the abduction by South African police of Anderson
Ganyile from Basutoland—and many elements in white opinion in the
Republic had little hesitation in regarding the Territories as havens for
the training of saboteurs and terrorists. In 1965 the British Government
introduced in all three the Prevention of Violence Abroad Proclamation which made it a crime to plan, aid, instigate or incite acts of violence in any outside state and at the time same restricted the political
activities of refugees in each Territory. Nevertheless, the South African
Government might well have questioned whether independent African
governments would be quite so committed to maintaining the *status quo*
on the refugee question. The latter was already a troublesome issue in
the years before independence, and it was recognized that the new
governments of Lesotho and Botswana would require all their skills to
avoid the extremes of appeasement and provocation of the Republic.
Thus a distinction would have to be made between the danger that
would follow to each from an acceptance of the Republic's wishes on the
refugee issue and its opposite—namely, allowing subversive elements to
use the new states as bases for infiltration.

Yet another reason for wanting the maintenance of British control
was connected with growing pressure for economic and military sanctions against the Republic which manifested itself at the U.N. and elsewhere throughout this period. As the writer argued in another context:

. . . the ending of British rule in the Territories will mean less of a dilemma
for Britain in deciding whether to support proposals at the United Nations
for action against the Republic. The continued survival of the Territories as
independent states would then be the responsibility of the United Nations,
and specific British responsibilities for their welfare might no longer be a
factor deterring the United Kingdom.[1]

[1] J. E. Spence, *Republic Under Pressure: A Study of South African Foreign Policy*, p. 95.

These considerations provide a plausible reason for Dr. Verwoerd's offer, in September 1963, to explain to the Territories the role they might play in an enlarged Bantustan arrangement. The proposal could be interpreted as a last attempt to stave off independence and the difficulties this might bring in its wake to the Republic's leaders—not least, perhaps, in the contrast provided between the status of the Transkei Bantustan and an independent Lesotho adjacent to it.[1]

Once it became clear, however, that Basutoland's and Bechuanaland's advance to independence could not be reversed, the emphasis on 'guardianship'—explicit in the September 1963 speech—was dropped, to be replaced by the traditional arguments for coexistence with independent African states. In June 1964, for example, Dr. Verwoerd informed the Senate of the South African Parliament that despite the fact that:

the gradual process of independence in the Territories may cause difficulties (my italics) ... if this is their place of employment, if this is the source of their revenue, if our co-operation in connection with customs revenue, is in their interest, then any individual government that is established there must maintain friendship with its neighbour in the interests of its own people.[2]

The emphasis on the Territories' economic dependence on the Republic was significant; coexistence had as its price 'good' behaviour on the part of the new governments and a recognition on their part of their common vulnerability to South African pressures.

5. *South Africa and International Organization*

(a) *The League of Nations*

It is time to turn to the record of South African participation in international organization. Smuts's role at the Peace Conference of 1919 and his influence on the drafting of the Covenant are well-established signposts of his career. South Africa was not alone in regarding the Covenant primarily as a guarantee of the security of small states. When the national interest demanded, the South African Government was a firm supporter of strict adherence to the obligations of the Covenant, as in the case of

[1] N.B. the following quotation from Dr. Verwoerd's 1963 speech:
'We are often asked when the Transkei plan is going to be applied to other groups in South Africa, such as the Tswana, Sotho and Zulu groups. Close liaison with the Territories would create new opportunities more quickly for those Black areas at present under our control which are their neighbours and for which we are seeking further development and freedom. Were it possible for them to be joined to those High Commission Territories to which their people are ethnically linked, then the present difficulty of establishing one big Tswana area, or one large Sotho or Swazi area in South Africa would fall away.' *The Road to Freedom*, p. 15.

[2] Quoted by J. Halpern, *Basutoland, Bechuanaland and Swaziland—South Africa's Hostages*, p. 437.

sanctions against Italy in 1936. Indeed, with New Zealand, South Africa stood firm on this issue when other powers had retreated to a less demanding position. Moreover, the existence of the League with its provisions for collective security helped ease the relationship between Smuts and Hertzog on the vexed issue of South African participation in a war on Britain's side: the principle of 'one for all and all for one' meant in theory that the Union could ally herself with the majority in the League against any single offender against the Covenant without fear of any infringement of status. Nevertheless the apparent failure of the League in the late 1930s disillusioned many South Africans, while the by-passing of the League as war approached in 1939 made all the more likely the split between Hertzog and Smuts on the issue of war or neutrality.

However, the degree of public interest in the League throughout this period must not be exaggerated. Smuts, like Wilson, had believed in the restraining influence of public opinion in preventing international conflict. Yet the force of democratic public opinion was no more operative in the Dominions than it was in Europe in restraining the enemies of the League of Nations. Nowhere was this truer than in South Africa for much of the inter-war period; politicians and public alike shared a general lack of interest in overseas issues, leaving Smuts a lonely and isolated figure in his concern for the League of Nations and the conditions of international society generally.[1] To all intents and purposes South Africa's environment did not appear to have changed radically since 1919; certainly a substantial body of opinion was unaware of any change.

There was, however, one issue on which there was disagreement between South Africa and the League.[2] During the First World War, South West Africa had been captured from Germany, and South Africa had hopes for its annexation. At the conclusion of the war, however, President Wilson's opposition to the annexation of former enemy territories won the day: and the mandates system was devised. Under this system, laid out in Article 22 of that part of the Versailles Treaty which constituted the Covenant of the League of Nations, ex-enemy territories would be governed by individual states, which were in turn accountable to the League. The peoples in these ex-enemy territories who were 'not yet able to stand by themselves under the strenuous conditions of the modern world' were to be governed for their own 'well-being and development' and as 'a sacred trust of civilization'. (Art. 22 (1).)

[1] Smuts's views in this period are discussed at length in Sir Keith Hancock's *Smuts— The Fields of Force, 1919–1950*, pp. 267–87.

[2] In this context the author is grateful to Dr. Rosalyn Higgins for permission to use material contained in 'South Africa and the United Nations', an unpublished paper written for the Institute of Commonwealth Studies, London.

The mandated territories were divided into three groupings. The 'A' and 'B' groups were regarded as more advanced than the 'C' class mandates, of which South West Africa was one. In the case of the latter, Article 22 (6) provided that:

Owing to the sparseness of their population or their small size, or their remoteness from the centres of civilization, or their geographical contiguity to the territory of the Mandatory [they could] . . . be best administered under the laws of the Mandatory as integral portions of its territory, subject to . . . safeguards . . . in the interests of the indigenous population.

Two points were immediately apparent: South West Africa was designated a 'C' class mandate by virtue of its small population and its geographical proximity to South Africa, but hardly because of 'small size'; and South Africa as Mandatory was perfectly entitled to administer South West Africa as an integral part of its territory.[1] In other words, the provisions of Article 22 of the League Covenant did not—especially in so far as class 'C' mandates were concerned—prohibit white domination; but they did seek to prevent white exploitation.

His Britannic Majesty accepted the mandate of South West Africa on behalf of South Africa; and Germany signed the Treaty of Versailles, formally ceding its colonies to the Allies. The allotment of South West Africa to His Britannic Majesty (for and on behalf of South Africa) was not, it should be noted, made by the League Covenant itself, but by a decision of the Supreme War Council in May 1919. Subsequently, the League Council passed a resolution that it 'will take cognizance of the Mandatory Powers appointed to it in order to ascertain that they conform to the prescription of Article 22 of the Covenant'.

The draft mandate submitted by the British Government on 14 December 1920, was confirmed by the League Council with only minor textual alterations. The preamble to the mandate recited that the Union of South Africa 'had agreed to accept the Mandate (and) . . . to exercise it on behalf of the League of Nations in accordance with the following provisions . . .'.

Article 2 of the Mandate then provides:

The Mandatory shall have full power of administration and legislation over the territory subject to the present Mandate as an integral portion of the Union of South Africa, and may apply the laws of the Union of South Africa, to the territory, subject to such local modifications as circumstances may require. The Mandatory shall promote to the utmost the material and moral

[1] For excellent descriptions of the background to the mandate, see E. Landis, 'South West Africa in the International Court: Act II, Scene I', *Cornell Law Quarterly*, 44 (1964); and D. H. Johnson, 'The Legal Position of South West Africa', unpublished paper written (Nov. 1964) for the Institute of Commonwealth Studies, London.

wellbeing and the social progress of the inhabitants of the territory subject to the present Mandate.

In Article 6 the Mandatory ('His Britannic Majesty for and on behalf of the Government of the Union of South Africa') agreed to submit reports annually to the Council. Article 7 stipulated:

The consent of the Council of the League of Nations is required for any modification in the terms of the present Mandate. The Mandatory agrees that if any dispute whatever should arise between the Mandatory and any other Member of the League of Nations relating to the interpretation or the application of the provisions of the Mandate, such dispute if it cannot be settled by negotiation, shall be submitted to the Permanent Court of International Justice provided for by Article 14 of the Covenant of the League of Nations. The present Declaration shall be deposited in the archives of the League of Nations. . . .

These arrangements were clear enough and unexceptional, but the Minutes of the Permanent Mandates Commission provide evidence of considerable criticism of South African administration of the Territory and refute the claim made by the Union in 1946 and subsequent years at the United Nations that the Commission had been completely satisfied with South Africa's record. Recent research suggests that throughout the inter-war period, the Commission found itself at odds with the Union Government on the question of incorporation of the Territory.[1]

Although the issue of sovereignty was the chief cause of dispute between South Africa and the Commission, the latter was also critical of the quality of South Africa's administration of the Territory. In particular its members singled out the low level of African education, the introduction of the Native Reserve system, the extension of the Colour Bar Act of 1926 to the Territory, and the handling of the Bondelzwarts Revolt of 1922. The Commission's general dissatisfaction with South Africa's handling of the Territory emerges very clearly in a speech made by Commissioner Rappard in 1936: 'After watching developments for the last fourteen years, he could not find any evidence that progress had been made . . . of all the native populations with which the Commission had to deal, that of South West Africa seemed the most backward: its position was static and static on a deplorably low level.'[2]

(b) South Africa and the United Nations

Few independent African or Asian states were represented in the League of Nations, which in any case was more concerned with the maintenance of the *status quo* in the strict political sense than with fostering change in the social and economic conditions of its various member

---

[1] See e.g. S. Kavina, 'South West Africa—An International Problem', unpublished M.A. thesis, University of Edinburgh, 1967.

[2] *Minutes of the Permanent Mandates Commission*: 9th Session, 1926, p. 106.

states. After 1945 the new states emerging from colonial rule challenged the very assumptions on which white colonial rule had hitherto been based. These followed an unbending anti-colonialist line, deploring racial discrimination, bitterly resenting the imposition of a colour bar on non-whites, and sweeping aside all Union protest against illegal interference in domestic affairs as merely 'legal sophistry'. South African domestic policies were therefore bound to become an object of universal interest. Furthermore, in the General Assembly of the United Nations the principle of majority decisions more easily exposed South Africa to condemnatory resolutions than did the unanimity rule of the League Assembly.

In one respect at least a new dimension was added to South African policy after 1948. The mounting pressure of world opinion against its racial policies forced the Union into defending its domestic policies on the widest possible front. Thus for a small power its representation abroad became extensive; this was particularly true of the State Information Service which attempted to project abroad a favourable image of the efforts the Government was making to raise the social and economic level of the non-white population. Foreign policy became in large part concerned with the attempt to justify Government policy towards the non-white population, and South Africa's predominantly defensive stance at the United Nations was the concrete expression of this particular approach.

As a member of the United Nations, South Africa was exposed to the conflict between the two principles of self-determination and domestic jurisdiction. Many Afro-Asian states argued that 'respect for Human Rights overrides judicial limitations'. As the Pakistani delegate observed in 1952, 'It is better to be carried away by emotions than bogged down by legal sophistications.'[1] And as one observer commented in 1961, [the dispute] 'over S.W. Africa and the Union's racial policy are now so closely interwoven that they react one upon the other in ways which, if not easy to define, nevertheless inflame the atmosphere in which either is considered'.[2]

The price of South Africa's defensive posture at the U.N. was a steady deterioration in her stature in international society after the Second World War. Year by year the attacks on South Africa's policies increased in scope and hostility as the consensus of opinion against her widened to include nearly all the members of the organization. It is true that this antagonism varied in depth from the bitter anger of the African states to the verbally hostile attitude of the Western powers, whose commitment in practice to the *status quo* contributed to the sense of impotence

[1] M. Wight, *The Power Struggle within the United Nations* (Proceedings of the Institute of World Affairs, New York, 1956), p. 225.
[2] R. B. Ballinger, *South West Africa: The Case Against the Union* (SAIRR, 1961), p. 43.

and frustration of the anti-colonial group at the United Nations. Thus for much of the post-war period South Africa was in a peculiarly isolated position in the international system and what follows is an attempt to explore the implications of this isolation.

The decline in stature after 1945 was all the more ironic given the high expectations entertained about their country's role in world affairs by its wartime leadership. In 1940, for example, the Prime Minister, General J. C. Smuts, spoke hopefully of the time when the Union would take its 'rightful place as leader in pan-African development and in the shaping of future policies and events in this vast continent'.[1] He remembered no doubt the honourable role which South Africa had played in the League of Nations (of which he was so notable an architect), particularly in its unswerving support of sanctions against Italy in 1935. It was plausible to argue therefore that the provisions of the Charter of the new organization would help guarantee the security of small states, particularly those like South Africa which, despite considerable domestic opposition, had played a key role in the struggle to defeat the Axis powers and whose leader had enjoyed prestige among the allies out of all proportion to the real power of his country. The South African delegations to Dumbarton Oaks and San Francisco participated actively in the drafting of the Charter and Smuts himself made a major contribution to the writing of the Preamble. There was no disagreement over the formulation of the Charter articles on human rights, although a first hint of the conflict to come appeared in the discussion on the allocation of areas for trusteeship agreements, when a South African representative stated his country's intention of annexing South West Africa and was ruled out of order by the Chairman.

Smuts's aspirations were, however, rapidly disappointed. In 1946 at the first meeting of the General Assembly he heard his Government's Indian policy subjected to violent criticism by the Indian and Soviet delegations and on his return to South Africa he referred to the General Assembly as a compound of 'emotion, passion and ignorance'.[2] For the first time the vast majority of white South Africans became aware, however dimly, that the postwar world was going to offer a disquieting challenge to the traditional assumptions on which the structure of their society was based. Previously those assumptions had rarely, if ever, been the object of sustained criticism from an international society which had taken for granted the sanctity of a state's claim to handle its domestic affairs in any way it deemed appropriate. But with the growth of

[1] L. W. Holborn, *War and Peace Aims of the United Nations*, p. 341.

[2] Walker, op. cit., p. 762. The General Assembly voted 32 to 15 for a settlement of the dispute over the status of Indians in South Africa and by 36 to 0 rejected Smuts's request to incorporate South West Africa. (At this time only 14 of the 54 states represented in the organization were Afro-Asian.)

nationalism in the colonial possessions of the European powers and the subsequent emergence of a large number of new states in Asia and Africa—all of which were bitterly antagonistic to colonialism and racial discrimination—South Africa's domestic policies were bound to become an object of universal concern. This no doubt would still have been the case had Smuts's United Party remained in office in 1948; but the coming to power and the continuation in office of an Afrikaner Nationalist Party, inflexibly convinced of the rightness of its apartheid policies and ideologically determined to secure and maintain the white man's position, widened the gulf between South Africa and its critics abroad and accelerated the demands for radical change at the United Nations and elsewhere.

The establishment of the United Nations also added a new dimension to the struggle of the non-white nationalist movement within the Union. This was reflected in the ideology which gave intellectual coherence to its aspirations and in the tactics employed to realize those aspirations. Appeals to the outside world for support against an indifferent and repressive government at home were nothing new in the history of nationalist endeavour. Deputations had after all been sent to Britain in 1909 to protest against the constitution drawn up by the delegates to the National Convention and to Versailles in 1919 to state the African case to the peace-makers. But the hopes engendered by the Wilsonian declaration of brotherhood and democracy soon faded, and many colonial nationalists turned to organizations like the World League Against Colonial Oppression, which they described as a 'real League of Nations', representing 'many hundreds of millions of unorganized and oppressed people' in contrast to the 'league of governments' sitting in distant Geneva.[1]

In 1945, however, the Charter of the new organization with its emphasis on trusteeship, human rights, and racial equality seemed to presage a new dispensation of which African leaders were quick to take advantage.[2] In 1946 the African National Congress sent its President, Dr. Xuma, to lobby the delegates of the General Assembly, particularly those representing India and led by Sir Maharaj Singh, a former Indian High Commissioner to South Africa. And there is some evidence to suggest that, before he lost office, Smuts was embarrassed by these

[1] Note the words of an Asian delegate to the International Democratic Congress for Peace (1926): 'When the European people think of peace they think of it only in terms of Europe.' J. F. Triska and H. E. Koch, 'The African States at the United Nations', Review of Politics, 21 (1959), 1–23.

[2] In this context should be noted the fact that the African National Congress sent a delegation to the Manchester Pan African Congress of 1945 and in the same year adopted the Bill of Rights drawn up by the Committee of African Intellectuals. The language of this document reflected the ideals of the Atlantic Charter—a declaration which excited considerable interest among Africans in the Union.

protests of his fellow countrymen. In 1947, for example, he published his *New Deal for Natives*—perhaps a clumsy and certainly unsuccessful attempt to forestall objections in the Native Representative Council and at the same time permit himself an easy passage in defending his Government's policies at the United Nations.[1] It is clear, however, that Smuts gained nothing from these attempts to appease both local and international opinion and his white political opponents were quick to castigate him for his failure at the United Nations, the attacks of which probably contributed, if only marginally, to his defeat in the election of 1948. Nevertheless, despite its relatively moderate tone, the concern of the organization for the realization of non-white aspirations had been amply demonstrated and in the years to come the ideals of the Charter were to be used as an ideological weapon in the struggle of non-white political movements against apartheid.[2] At the same time their leaders directed a stream of petitions and delegations at the various organs of the United Nations which, as its Afro-Asian membership increased, were seen as instruments to promote radical political change in the South African political system.

Thus the existence of an international organization to which appeals could be made by the leaders of the disenfranchised majority forced the South African Government into the role of a defendant at the bar of 'world opinion' against the accusations of those who would equate its particular policies with the worst excesses of colonialism in general. Paradoxically, the defence offered for these policies (especially after the late 1950s) was based on the moral validity of the Bantustan concept as a South African variety of decolonization, i.e. the creation of six or seven 'self-governing' states based on the boundaries of the major ethnic groups. It was argued that this approach to self-determination was not dissimilar from that practised for example by the United Kingdom, especially in the three High Commission Territories where South African spokesmen claimed the parallel was particularly close.[3]

[1] An illuminating conversation occurred between Smuts and Xuma when they met in New York. To Smuts's question about his reasons for being at the U.N., Xuma replied, 'I came here to be near my Prime Minister. I have had to fly 10,000 miles to meet my Prime Minister. He talks *about* us but he won't talk *to* us.'

[2] Cf. the language of the Freedom Charter adopted by the Congress Alliance in 1956 which is a far cry from the tone of the debates of the Native Representative Council in the 1930s.

[3] 'The Act for the promotion of Bantu self-government provides the means for the different Bantu territories to progress along the road toward self-government, and eventually to form part of a South African Commonwealth, together with the Union of South Africa, which will during the intervening period act as the guardian of the emergent Bantu self-governing states. . . . It follows recent trends and developments in the African continent, and aims at progressively giving the Bantu control of his own homeland.' Statement by Mr. Eric Louw, South African Minister of External Affairs, at the 1959 Session of the General Assembly. (Quoted in H. H. Bierman (ed.), *The Case for South Africa: Speeches by Mr. E. H. Louw*, pp. 58,

For the African states, however, in so far as white minority rule had always represented an essential feature of colonialism, the practice of apartheid and the massive apparatus of legislation required to enforce it were a legitimate target of moral indignation that fitted easily into the framework of an anti-colonialist ideology.[1] The fact that there was no easily recognizable metropolitan power in the South African context, and that white and black were inextricably bound together by economic links of increasing complexity as industrial development had proceeded, might, for some, have dented the logic of the African claim to lump together South Africa and the ex-colonial powers of Europe; but this in no important practical sense affected the usefulness of the argument as a weapon in the struggle against the Republic. (The appeal of an ideology depends, after all, on the emotional response it inspires in its adherents rather than on neat academic distinctions; to be effective it must inevitably oversimplify and select those aspects of a situation which more readily lend themselves to single-cause explanations.) Thus for the Afro-Asian group at the United Nations, South Africa (with Portugal and Rhodesia) was the last remaining representative of an obsolete colonial tradition rather than a conflict-ridden plural society, the problems of which resembled more nearly those of similar societies elsewhere.

None the less, the South African defence of its policies tried to meet both these interpretations—presenting the evolution of Bantustans as a form of decolonization while at the same time rejecting the opposite principle of political and economic integration as a basis for a solution of the problems of a plural society. It cited in support of the policy the evidence of territorial partition in areas such as the Indian sub-continent, Ireland, and Palestine, and, in defending the Group Areas legislation, 'exposed' the failure of integrationist policies in Britain and the United States.[2] Neither justification was accepted by critics at the United Nations, who in the ideological debate appear to enjoy the best of both worlds. The Republic's policies could be branded as colonialist and its Government denied the one defence the European powers were able to

60.) 'Our policy is directly in line with the African revolution, which has as its main objective self-determination for all.' Dr. Hilgard Muller, South African Foreign Minister. (Quoted in *The Star* (Johannesburg), 9 Nov. 1963.)

[1] In a speech on Algiers Radio on 20 May 1963, Premier Ben Bella stated that Africans had no right to think of eating while their brothers were dying from oppression in South Africa and the Portuguese territories: 'So that the peoples still under colonial rule may be liberated, let us all agree to die a little.'

[2] 'The purpose of the Act is to prevent the growth of mixed areas and communities which often leads to slum conditions and to racial clashes. That is what is happening today in many American cities and also in certain London districts.' Speech to the Special Political Committee of the United Nations by Mr. Louw, 11 Nov. 1961. (Quoted in Bierman, op. cit., p. 113.)

offer—namely their evident willingness under nationalist pressures to forego control over their colonial dependencies. In particular, opponents of South Africa denied the South African claim that independence was contemplated for the Transkei.

(c) The Major Sources of Conflict between South Africa and the United Nations

White opinion in South Africa received its first severe jolt in 1946 when Smuts, speaking for the Union in the General Assembly, found his Indian policy the subject of bitter attack from both the Indian and Soviet delegations. In the inter-war period a series of compromises on the question of the status of the Indian minority had been reached. This was the result of bilateral negotiation between the two governments concerned rather than multilateral discussions in the forum of the League Assembly. Smuts was prepared to offer South African Indians a degree of political representation in the hope that the economic and social *status quo* could be maintained, but with the victory of the Nationalist Party in 1948 any hope of a negotiated settlement on a bilateral basis faded and Indian resentment, particularly of the Group Areas Act, mounted throughout the 1950s.[1]

This Act was designed to enforce complete social and residential segregation by dividing the urban areas of South Africa into separate racial zones. It particularly affected the Indian community, which had long held established property rights in many urban areas and now faced the loss of a livelihood earned from trading, and was an obvious cause of ill feeling and source of bitter criticism at the United Nations and elsewhere. In replying to this criticism the South African Government was unable to offer any positive arguments about its intention towards the Indian minority, and was forced to fall back on counterclaims of discrimination in India of the *tu quoque* variety. (This approach should be contrasted with the efforts made to convince outside opinion of the merits of the Bantustan plan for the African population.) In 1962, at the seventeenth session of the General Assembly, the item concerning the treatment of people of Indian and Pakistani origin, which up to then had been regularly discussed in the Assembly, was merged with the item entitled 'Race Conflict' under the heading of 'Policies of Apartheid' and this, together with the issue of South West Africa, constituted the major areas of violent disagreement between South Africa and the great majority of member states of the Organization.

This disagreement was reflected in the growing number of resolutions passed by the General Assembly, and, after 1960, by the Security Council condemning the policy of apartheid. Up to that date, however,

[1] India was the first state to impose economic sanctions against South Africa—as early as 1946.

these resolutions were largely verbal indictments and had virtually no impact on the Government's determination to pursue its chosen course. Nevertheless, their regular appearance on the agenda of the General Assembly established the claim of that body to discuss issues which, although technically domestic, were deemed to involve accepted human rights and became therefore the concern of the international community of states. The Sharpeville shootings of 1960, coinciding with an increase in the African membership of the United Nations, brought the conduct of South Africa to the attention of the Security Council, which passed a resolution (S/4300), with only Britain and France abstaining, stating that the Government's policies had 'led to international friction and if continued might endanger international peace and security'. The support of the United States for the resolution marked a dramatic change in its attitude to South Africa, and the British abstention was translated into a positive vote against South African policies in the General Assembly debate in April 1960 when a condemnatory resolution (1598 (XV)) received a massive majority of 96 to 1. The British vote was significant because it marked a departure, in fact if not in theory, from the traditional British emphasis on the sanctity of the principle of domestic jurisdiction. This resolution requested all states 'to consider taking such separate and collective action as is open to them, in conformity with the Charter of the United Nations, to bring about the abandonment of [the apartheid] policies'. This was the first occasion on which the General Assembly had given approval to a resolution asking for action against the Union, and it stands in sharp contrast to earlier expressions of condemnation and exhortation to the Nationalist Government to change its ways.

The next three years witnessed repeated attempts to persuade member states to take action against South Africa. In 1962 a resolution asking for economic and diplomatic sanctions was passed by 67 votes to 16 with 23 abstentions.[1] Although the resolution obtained a two-thirds majority, its application was not mandatory on member states, while Britain and the United States, the two powers most able to damage South Africa in the terms laid down by the resolution, voted with the minority.

The African states, fresh from their labours at Addis Ababa in May 1963, then succeeded in raising the apartheid question in the Security Council in the hope that a mandatory resolution under Chapter 7 of the Charter would be passed. The draft resolution, presented to the Council in August 1963 by Ghana, Morocco, and the Philippines,

---

[1] Res. 1761 (XVII), GA, 6 Nov. 1962. It included a request to member states to close their ports and airports to South African ships and aircraft and refuse the sale of arms. A special committee was also established to consider further action.

alleged that the situation in South Africa was 'endangering international peace and security' and in one paragraph called on member states to 'boycott all South Africa goods and to refrain from exporting to South Africa strategic materials of direct military value . . . and cease forthwith the sale and shipment of arms, ammunition of all types and military vehicles'. The United States objected to the assumption that the South African situation endangered international peace and refused to support any call for action under Article 39 of Chapter 7. Nevertheless it stated its intention of stopping the sale of American weapons to South Africa from 1 January 1964. Britain concurred with this but added the proviso that its own ban of arms exports would apply only to those which might be used for enforcing apartheid legislation and not to weapons for defence against external attack. These two powers, not being prepared to support that part of the resolution calling for economic sanctions, achieved a separate vote on that paragraph of the draft resolution, and —together with Brazil, China, Norway, and France—abstained. On 7 August 1964, when the resolution as a whole was put to the vote, only Britain and France abstained. The United States defended her decision to support the resolution as a whole on the grounds that any action taken would fall under Chapter 6 of the Charter and was not therefore mandatory.

South Africa's isolation received added confirmation from the resolution of the General Assembly in the autumn of 1963 pronouncing censure on its decision to hold a further treason trial. The voting on this occasion was 106 to 1 with no abstentions, and a second resolution of the General Assembly during a debate on South West Africa in November 1963 recommended the institution of an oil embargo against the Republic. (The Western powers, however, refused to support this.) On 4 December 1963 the Security Council unanimously adopted a Norwegian resolution asking for an arms embargo and proposing the establishment of a Group of Experts, charged with the responsibility of finding ways and means of 'resolving the present situation' in South Africa and of considering what part the United Nations might play in the achievement of that end.

This group, under the chairmanship of Alva Myrdal, published its report in April 1964 and recommended, *inter alia*, the following lines of action: (1) the creation of a fully representative national convention in the Republic as a first step towards devising a more democratic constitution; (2) the establishment of a United Nations South African Education and Training Programme designed to 'enable as many South Africans as possible to play a full part as quickly as possible in the political, economic and social advance of their country'; (3) an examination by the Security Council of the logistics of economic sanctions;

(4) the implementation of sanctions in the event of a refusal by the South African Government to give a satisfactory reply to the United Nations proposals arising out of the committee's recommendations.[1]

This brief survey of the United Nations discussion on the policy of apartheid shows how far majority opinion in the eighteen years of that Organization's existence shifted from merely verbal condemnation to resolutions demanding forceful measures involving economic, diplomatic, and military sanctions. The Western powers were step by step forced into abandoning their early support for South African counter-arguments based on Article 2 (7) of the Charter, and also their later rather contrived attempts to maintain a position compounded of verbal hostility and a reluctance to take any action that might upset the *status quo*. Admittedly neither the United States nor Britain was prepared to view the South African situation as a threat to international peace and security or to support collective measures under Chapter 7 of the Charter. But the decision to accept a ban on the sale of arms was, from an Afro-Asian point of view, a significant victory in the struggle against Western inertia—if only because it demonstrated that the Western powers could be pushed into taking active measures.

This point had relevance in any consideration of the South West African issue. Western objections to mandatory action against apartheid under Chapter 7 of the Charter were based, legally speaking and ignoring questions of national interest, on the premiss that the Republic's policies could not be construed as a threat to the peace and therefore any action under Chapter 7 would be illegal.

The dispute on the status of the territory has a long history going back to 1946 when South Africa requested the General Assembly to agree to annexation. This was refused, the Assembly proposing that South West Africa become a Trust Territory of the United Nations. Indeed, many states were of the opinion that Chapter 11 of the Charter made obligatory the transfer of previous mandates to the trusteeship system. For the next two years the Smuts Government undertook to administer it in terms of the original mandate and adhered to the Assembly's ruling against annexation. Pressure on South Africa to accept trusteeship status was maintained until 1950. In that year the International Court, asked for an advisory opinion by the General Assembly, stated that South Africa could not alter the status of the territory unilaterally and remained bound by the mandate, including Article 2 which obliged the mandatory power to 'promote to the utmost the material and moral well-being and the social progress of the inhabitants of the territory'. In addition, the Court advised that the United

[1] *A New Course in South Africa* (1964), p. 27.

Nations had the right to supervise the administration of the territory, provided this did not exceed the degree and kind of supervision exercised by the Mandates Commission.

South Africa disregarded this opinion (she was not legally bound to obey it), and the United Nations responded by establishing a committee of five to review the situation. The deadlock remained, however, and in 1953 a second committee—the Committee on South West Africa—reported that the South African Government was not prepared to consider any solution except a partition of the territory into a southern half annexed by the Union and a northern half administered as a Trust Territory. This proposal was rejected by an overwhelming majority of the General Assembly. In 1955 the Court gave an advisory opinion on the voting majority required in the Assembly for decisions on reports and petitions concerning South West Africa. In 1956 it advised that it would be in order for the Committee on South West Africa to grant oral hearings to petitions relating to the territory. In June 1960 Ethiopia and Liberia, as former members of the League, agreed on behalf of the African group at the United Nations to refer the question of South West Africa to the International Court. The complainants asked the Court among other things to declare that apartheid was practised in the territory; that this practice violated Articles 2 and 22 of the original mandate, and finally, that the South African Government should cease this practice forthwith. In December 1962, by 8 votes to 7, the Court ruled that it had jurisdiction to give a judgement on the merits of the case, and proceeded to an examination of the merits of the dispute during four years of protracted litigation between 1962 and 1966. The applicants repeated their requests, and during the course of the case they urged upon the Court an additional claim—namely, that apartheid was contrary to a now established norm of international law which prohibited racial discrimination.

Eventually the Court, in its highly surprising judgement of 18 July 1966, declared that Ethiopia and Liberia had failed to establish any legal right in respect of the claims which it had put before the Court, and that it could not therefore pronounce upon these claims one way or the other. This was so even in respect of those claims which merely sought confirmation, in this binding judgement, of what the Court had said previously in Advisory Opinions on the continued existence of the mandate, and rights and duties thereunder. The Court also said—in a statement that perplexed many lawyers as well as laymen—that this objection to the *locus standi* of the applicants was *not* reversing what the Court had already decided on the question of jurisdiction in 1962. The majority of judges seemed to be of the view that confirming that the applicants had status to bring the case in 1962, was a matter different from, and thus not inconsistent with, denying that they had status to receive an answer in 1966.[1]

The reaction of South Africa, inevitably, was to treat this judgement as a great victory, and to portray it as a vindication of her arguments and policies. The point that South Africa had only won because the Court *declined* to pronounce upon her policies was not an easy one to explain, and undoubtedly South Africa benefited thereby.

The pressure against South Africa in international organizations was not limited to the United Nations; it extended to virtually all of those Specialized Agencies which did not rely on a weighted voting system. Interestingly, however, the Western nations disassociated themselves from such pressure in the Agencies to a much greater degree than they felt able to in the United Nations itself. The reasons were three. In the first place, they were able to argue convincingly that technical bodies discussing health, food resources, or aviation were not the appropriate place to wage campaigns of this sort. Secondly, the Afro-Asian approach was to seek the expulsion or suspension of South Africa, and most Western nations contended that the Special Agencies should only have had recourse to such action for clear breach of their own rules; expulsion on grounds of racial discrimination should only have followed upon a guiding decision taken by the United Nations itself. Finally, the attempts to expel South Africa in certain cases forfeited the sympathy of the West, because they were carried out within the framework of Agencies whose constitutions did not allow for expulsion. The Afro-Asians thus had to resort to demands for alteration of the constitution, or to walk-outs. Both methods necessitated prolonged stoppages in the normal technical work of the agencies. The International Labour Organization and the World Health Organization were cases in point. None the less, the Afro-Asian countries were fairly successful in achieving their professed objective—the non-participation of South Africa in the Specialized Agencies—for South Africa on several occasions felt it prudent to withdraw before her expulsion could be demanded. Thus the Republic left the International Labour Organization in 1961 and the World Health Organization in 1965.

(d) The South African Defence and the Impact on Domestic Policies

The unique position in which South Africa found itself at the United Nations had important implications in the domestic arena. For an increasing majority of white South Africans, the annual debates on their country's domestic policies served as confirmation of the perverse inability of the outside world to understand and sympathize with their peculiar difficulties. The Government encouraged the view that the United

---

[1] See Higgins, op. cit., on which this analysis is based.

Nations was an institutionalized version of a world-wide conspiracy to traduce South Africa and set in motion forces designed to destroy 'white civilization'. The country's stance at the United Nations was presented as that of a small power gallantly upholding the principles of the Charter against those who would use it as an ideological weapon to win support for action against South Africa. The anti-colonial posture of the new states of Africa was interpreted as a subtle disguise cloaking the expansionist aims of their great power masters—the Soviet Union and China. This tendency to equate nationalism with communism, to picture South Africa as the pawn in the struggle between East and West for the support of the non-aligned powers, was a constant theme in parliamentary debates on foreign affairs. The following extract from a speech by the late Prime Minister, Dr. Verwoerd, is representative of this attitude:

In recent years a development has taken place at UN which was not foreseen—the addition of a large number of new states, particularly in Africa but also in Asia. That created a block of countries which were completely inexperienced even so far as their own government was concerned . . . both the western bloc and communist bloc seek the support of the Afro-Asian bloc . . . South Africa is landed in the position where both sides attack her . . . because in this way the friendship of the Afro-Asian countries can be sought . . . without any doubt the attacks against us are created by the struggle of communism for world domination and not so much in local factors.[1]

Moreover the organization was often presented as having lost sight of its original goals. In this context, Mr. Eric Louw, then Minister for External Affairs, remarked in 1957:

Because of the preponderant strength of the Bandung–Soviet bloc, I am not very optimistic about the future of the United Nations and I am not the only one to hold that view. . . . There is a widespread feeling . . . that the United Nations is going the way of the old League. It has wandered from its Charter and the United Nations will have to get back to the Charter, possibly a revised Charter. Our position is this. We fully appreciate the need for a world organization, but then it must be an effective organization. If it is not going to be effective, one wonders whether you must not get back to the old balance of power system of alliances where the Western countries will rely on NATO, rather than on the United Nations. That seems to me the way things are going. . . . I can assure hon. members that things are not right with the United Nations, something will have to be done to put things right. But while the United Nations continues to interfere in our domestic affairs, we will not find it possible to co-operate.[2]

In a speech a year later, Mr. Louw stressed South Africa's unique role as a small power and there emerged an unspoken assumption that

[1] *House of Assembly Debates*, 1961, vol. 107, col. 4173.
[2] Ibid., 1957, vol. 95, col. 7676.

the incorporation of South Africa in the Western defence system would solve many of the difficulties produced by isolation:

That sub-article 2 (7) was introduced especially for the protection of the smaller countries, and if it is to disappear now because it has been continually ignored, then I want to know what protection UNO is going to afford in the future to the smaller countries. The whole complexion of UNO has changed . . . by 1970 . . . 37 white Western countries will be members of UNO as against 59 Afro-Asian communistic and borderline states. . . . One might well ask oneself what the future of the United Nations is going to be in 1970 under that set-up.

It seems to me that what will happen then is that the Western Countries will have to form themselves into another group . . . alongside NATO . . . there will have to be a South Atlantic Treaty Organization as well, and that they will have to stand together . . . we shall be going back again to the old days before the League of Nations.[1]

Another line of attack pointed a contrast between South Africa's impeccable international behaviour and that of states prepared to allow a double-standard to motivate their voting in the General Assembly:

But it is not only the Bandung countries who pay lip-service to the Charter, Western nations are also guilty. They also appear to have a double standard of international morality . . . Western European and South American delegations which had voted against South Africa or were passively prepared to permit interference in our domestic affairs, actively lobbied to prevent an unfavourable vote for Britain and France on that very same issue, viz. of interference in their domestic affairs. It is clear that there is a double standard of international morality. A difference is made between the large states, and the smaller states.[2]

This assertion by Mr. Louw was linked with accusations of 'horse-trading' techniques to win majorities for particular resolutions, and at the same time a legalistic-moralistic element emerged in the criticism made of the 'self-interested' behaviour of member states and their failure to observe the Charter:

I cannot help but come to the conclusion that the reasons for the undoubted decline of the United Nations is the compelling motive of self-interest. Nations act like the individuals of which they are composed. . . . Self-interest has led to undesirable practices. Everybody knows that leaders of delegations indulge in a certain amount of 'horse-trading'. It is an established practice— you vote for me on this issue and I will vote for you on another.[3]

Ministerial speeches in the House of Assembly defending South Africa's stand at the United Nations were in content virtually indistinguishable

[1] Ibid., 1958, vol. 97, col. 5624.   [2] Ibid., 1957, vol. 95, col. 7608.
[3] Ibid., col. 7606.

from those made in the General Assembly by the Government's representatives. Up to 1958, South Africa's case emphasized the moral and legal correctness of the Government's external posture. Attempts to handle criticism of apartheid from a 'rectitude' base stressed the sanctity of Charter provisions such as Article 2 (7) and the rights of states to resist interference in matters of domestic concern.

In later years, however, the South African delegation at the United Nations attempted a more positive defence and the emphasis switched from argument couched exclusively in terms of 'legitimacy' to claims for a more sympathetic hearing based on the Government's plans to develop Bantustans within South Africa and its desire to co-operate with independent Africa through organizations such as the C.C.T.A., the C.S.A., and F.A.M.A.

At the 1959 session of the General Assembly, for example, Mr. Louw argued that separate development was more than just a pragmatic response to the decolonization proceeding elsewhere on the continent. Citing the statements made by General Smuts in the interwar period, the South African Foreign Minister argued that this policy was a traditional feature of his country's pattern of race relations and one which if fully implemented offered the most hopeful prospect for an accommodation between black and white, because it provided for the realization of each racial group's aspirations for self-determination.[1] This change in tactics, forced upon the Government by the swelling chorus of anti-colonial attacks as the number of African states increased in the General Assembly, brought few if any advantages. Those states still prepared to defend the regime at the United Nations were unwilling to offer, in justification of their reluctance to take punitive action against South Africa, arguments based on the merits of the separate development policy. (And indeed, as has been noted earlier, the Western powers were eventually pushed by Afro-Asian pressure into taking stands—admittedly largely verbal—severely critical of the Government's policy.)

Furthermore as the pressure for sanctions mounted in the 1960s, South Africa was increasingly forced back into adopting legal and moral arguments of the *tu quoque* variety. Mr. Louw in particular spared no effort to point to derelictions of human rights in the states of his chief accusers.[2]

---

[1] Bierman, op. cit., pp. 49–61. Nevertheless an emphasis on the strict 'legality' of the Charter remained prominent in ministerial statements, particularly in the context of domestic debate on foreign affairs, as the following quotation illustrates: 'I can say that South Africa strongly insists on the principle laid down in 1945 that the Charter cannot simply be amended by interpretation. The attitude of this government is that the Charter, like every other contract between parties, cannot be amended without the permission of all the parties to the contract. The Republic therefore rejects all efforts to amend the Charter by interpretation.' Dr. Hilgard Muller, Minister of Foreign Affairs, *H.A.D.*, 1965, vol. 15, col. 7694.

[2] See for example his statements to the Special Political Committee of the U.N. on 23 Oct., 11 Nov., and 28 Nov. 1961. Quoted in Bierman, op. cit., pp. 96–132.

In November 1962, moreover, in a speech to the General Assembly, he bitterly attacked those who pressed for punitive measures against his Government. He laid stress on the welfare programmes—health, education, and housing—provided by his Government for the non-white majority as compared with those available in 'the countries of most of the sponsors of this resolution'. He reiterated the dangers implicit in ignoring Article 2 (7) of the Charter, coupling them with a fierce denunciation of those who saw in South Africa's policies a 'danger to international peace and security'. He argued that 'there must be at least two parties if there is to be a threat to world peace', implying that the African states were responsible by their actions for the existence of any such threat.[1] In an earlier speech to the General Assembly, in September 1961, Mr. Louw drew a sharp distinction between the stability of South Africa and the 'unrest and turmoil in several other African countries'. In the same speech he stated that his Government would not contribute to United Nations expenses in the Congo, and at the same time he attacked the United Nations action taken against Katanga, on the grounds that the organization was using its powers in attempting 'to force a political arrangement on the people of Katanga where conditions had been relatively stable, both politically and economically'.[2]

The significance of these arguments, whether presented in the House of Assembly or the General Assembly at the United Nations, must be measured in terms of their domestic impact rather than any impression created abroad. South African delegates to the organization were not unique in recognizing that uncompromising stands on principle at the United Nations paid indirect dividends for a government's position at home.[3] For the vast majority of white South Africans the organization was a symbolic and constant reminder of the hostility directed at their Government's policies in the post-war period. The debates in the General Assembly and the ideological overtones of insult and recrimination were construed by the white electorate as evidence of

---

[1] Ibid., pp. 142–52.

[2] Ibid., p. 80. Cf. Dr. D. F. Malan (then Prime Minister) defending his Government's decision to send military support to the U.N. operation in Korea in 1951. He emphasized the need to support the organization's efforts to 'combat aggressive Communism', but at the same time rejected 'its tendency to take upon itself the task of righting the affairs of the world . . . [and] . . . the undoing of the white population in this country, namely the surrender of power into the hands of the non-European population'. In the same debate, Dr. E. Dönges, Minister of the Interior, supported his leader on the grounds that the U.N. was now getting back to the real object for which it had been created. H.A.D., 1951, vol. 74, cols. 184–6 and 523.

[3] 'But I would also say this, that it is unlikely that the South African government will put its representatives in the position of being insulted there, as happened during the last two sessions . . . the South African representative was jeered at by the Blacks in U.N. . . . but I want to say that insults hurled at the representative of a nation at an international conference are insults hurled also at the country he represents.' Dr. Hilgard Muller, H.A.D., 1965, vol. 5, col. 151.

a vicious, unrestrained, and emotionally immature attitude on the part of the Afro-Asian contingent, whose influence on the Western powers was seen as disproportionate to their 'real' weight as members of international society. The organization was pilloried as impotent, an 'irresponsible luxury, tolerable only because of its ineptitude and, perhaps, because its decline or demise is imminent'.[1]

Moreover white opinion in South Africa was encouraged to draw a sharp distinction between the ideological claims made by the African states at the United Nations and the performances of their governments in the domestic sphere where, it was alleged, violations of human rights, the development of one-party political systems, and the prevailing atmosphere of political and economic instability did not provide sound credentials for attacking the Republic's record. That these states' aspirations to liberate South Africa through the agency of the United Nations should be paid even lip-service by the Western powers was a source of profound dissatisfaction to many white South Africans and explicable only in terms which suggested that these powers were bent on appeasing the forces of anti-colonialism. Nor did the Government, in seeking to broaden the base of electoral support, hesitate to take advantage of this dissatisfaction. Its spokesmen dwelt at length on the contrast between the instability of the areas like the Congo, the failure of partnership in Central Africa, and the security, political and economic, enjoyed by South Africa's white minority.[2] Furthermore, the policies of the colonial powers were cited as evidence of a 'sickly liberalism' which failed to distinguish the real threat—namely, the spread of Communist influence in those areas where a failure of nerve on the part of European governments contrived to force their hurried and ignominious exit. By contrast the South African government's initiation of the Bantustan experiment was cited as a praiseworthy example of a controlled and evolutionary decolonization, based on the premise that adequate economic and political foundations were essential if the reserve areas were to stand on their own at some distant and unspecified point in the future. Indeed, there were times when South African leaders gave the impression of claiming

[1] R. B. Ballinger, *South Africa and the U.N.: Myth and Reality* (South African Institute of International Affairs, Johannesburg, 1963), p. 11. In one New Year message Dr. Verwoerd expressed himself as follows: 'It may be regrettable that the United Nations no longer embodies the hopes of mankind. Everyone must face the fact, however, that since young, duck-tailed nations practically took charge of determining the majority vote, the United Nations commands little respect. It is a platform for their display of juvenile aggressiveness and their inferiority complexes. . . . The grand adventure of the nations has become a sordid scramble for the microphone—the new toy of the exhibitionist and the agitator.'

[2] 'Not for us the sudden upheavals which created the chaos of the Congo, and the struggle of multi-racialism elsewhere, where each group seeks to dominate and lack of confidence in what may happen creates economic uncertainty.' Dr. Verwoerd, reported in the *Natal Mercury* (Durban), 1 June 1961, quoted in C. de B. Webb, 'Foreign Policy of the Union of South Africa', in J. E. Black and K. W. Thompson (eds.), *Foreign Policy in a World of Change*, p. 437.

universal applicability for the concept of separate development. They more than hinted that white South Africa had a peculiar responsibility to take up the burden of 'white civilization', which others elsewhere had let slip because of short-sighted considerations of expediency.[1]

Reading the record of debates on the apartheid and related issues, the unwary might be forgiven for thinking that the Republic's isolation within the Organization was an accurate mirror of the position in international society generally. In an ideological sense this was true: the Organization, in institutionalizing the hostility against South Africa, contributed in great degree to giving apartheid a universal connotation in the minds of politicians and their publics. The African and Asian states played the crucial role, forcing the Western powers into taking a position which, but for this pressure, might have remained one of relative indifference to the domestic affairs of a small power, traditionally prepared to offer support at times of crisis and one having ties of kinship, trade, and historical connections.

Nevertheless, Western support for Afro-Asian demands rarely moved beyond verbal denunciation, and the South African Government shrewdly calculated that the real challenge to its integrity came not from the United Nations (which could only be as effective as its most powerful members were prepared to allow it to be), but from the threat of internal uprising or wars of liberation mounted and supported beyond its borders. Unilateral relations with the Western powers were, therefore, much more important to the Republic than attempts to use the institutions of multilateral diplomacy to its own advantage. And if the price of tough, ruthless domestic policies (in part designed to preserve the external image of stability and prosperity and so impress its mentors abroad with the foolhardiness of upsetting the *status quo*) was expulsion or forced resignation from a variety of international organizations, then the price did not seem unreasonable in terms of calculations based on the options open to a small power, particularly one as peculiarly constituted as the Republic. This is not to argue that South Africa attached no importance to its membership of the United Nations.[2] Participation in the debates

---

[1] Speaking on foreign policy in 1964, Dr. Verwoerd, the Prime Minister claimed that '. . . present-day international politics prove that the world is sick, and that it is not up to South Africa to allow herself to be dragged into that sickbed. It is white South Africa's duty to ensure her survival, even though she is accused of being isolated under such a policy. . . . The tragedy of the present time is that in this crucial stage of present-day history, the white race is not playing the role which it is called upon to play and which only the white race is competent to fulfil. . . . Is not our role to stand for the one thing which means our own salvation here but with which it will also be possible to save the world, and with which Europe will be able to save itself, namely the preservation of the white man and his state?'

[2] Concerning South Africa's membership in the U.N., Dr. Verwoerd once likened it to her former membership in the Commonwealth, namely '. . . to withdraw at a certain stage when it is no longer possible to remain a member and at the same time look after South Africa's

had an obvious domestic pay-off, for it 'mobilized the supporters of apartheid',[1] while expulsion or resignation would have deprived the Republic of the last remaining forum in which the apartheid case could be defended. The advantages inherent in continued membership may have been only marginal, but they would not be lightly foregone in an uncertain world.[2]

6. Conclusion

This account of South Africa's foreign relations deals with the inter-action between three factors which dominate South Africa's role in the modern world: (a) domestic preoccupations; (b) Afrikaner nationalism and its influence on Commonwealth relations; and (c) the impact of changes in international society on a small state, where policies have become increasingly out of step with international ideological trends.

Inexorable limits are imposed on South Africa by her relative small-ness as a State in the international system.[3] Like all small powers, she has a limited range of options. Yet for much of the inter-war period she was able to capitalize on her geographical isolation from the centres of conflict, and to concentrate on domestic issues. The most important of these—the conflict between the two white language groups—impinged on foreign policy to the extent that the 'two demands, for equality between Afrikaners and British on the soil of South Africa, and equality of status between South Africa and Great Britain, were interwoven'.[4] Moreover, it could be argued that this absorption in the status issue was a 'luxury', permissible only in an environment which in the 1920s and

interests and retain her honour . . . South Africa is aware of the difficult circumstances prevailing there. She is also aware of the desire of the Western nations that she should remain a member. If, however, they want to keep her there they will have to consider her position, together with the other factors which weigh with them; in evolving her policy, South Africa will have to continue to place her interests first in making her decision one way or another as all countries do.' *H.A.D.*, 1964, vol. 9, col. 61.

[1] T. Hovet, *Africa in the United Nations*, p. 214. Note the following statement by a United Party spokesman on foreign affairs in the debate on the Korean War in 1951: 'I do not believe UNO is doomed. I believe it will be an appalling disaster if UNO is doomed . . . UNO is young and inexperienced, it will learn its limitations and proper functions by degrees.' *H.A.D.*, 1951, vol. 74, col. 488. This statement had an archaic ring about it in the context of South African attitudes to the organization which clearly hardened as the General Assembly increased its membership after 1956.

[2] No serious attempt was mounted in the U.N. to expel South Africa, though the Security Council was nominally asked by the Assembly to look into this matter. The African states were divided as to whether this was a desirable objective: quite obviously, expulsion would have done little, if anything, to promote a change in South African racial policies.

[3] It seems justifiable to regard South Africa as a small power if we accept the view that '. . . small powers are almost by definition "local" powers whose demands are restricted to their own and immediately adjacent areas, while great powers exert their influence over wide areas.' A. B. Fox, *The Power of Small States: Diplomacy in World War II*, p. 3.

[4] W. K. Hancock, *Survey of British Commonwealth Affairs*, i. p. 271.

early 1930s appeared secure and free from any hint of disturbance by more powerful and aggressive rivals.

Nor did this geographical remoteness imply political isolation, for as a Commonwealth member South Africa was linked with a group of states whose combined weight in international politics more than made up for their individual weakness. Indeed, General Hertzog himself admitted the reality and significance of the link with Britain particularly during the Italo-Ethiopian War when, in the expressive words of Sir Keith Hancock, 'the shelter behind which the old legalistic controversies had been debated seemed now to be collapsing'.[1]

Yet however serious the external threats which manifested themselves in the late 1930s, the Union was accepted as a legitimate member of the international system both by its fellow Commonwealth states and the rest of the world. The quality of its leadership, particularly that of J. C. Smuts and J. H. Hertzog, was admired for its contribution to the evolution of the Commonwealth and, in Smuts's case, for his intellectual appreciation of the problems that beset men and states in the twentieth century. Throughout the inter-war period, on matters of foreign policy outside the framework of Commonwealth relations, South Africa was essentially a supporter of the *status quo* and its attitude was shared by many European small power contemporaries at the League of Nations for which that Organization was both a symbol of security in a hostile world and a guarantee of the *status quo* against the aggressive designs of their more powerful neighbours.

And whatever the shortcomings of South Africa's foreign policy may have been in this period, the fact remains that in the two decades that followed the Balfour Declaration of 1926 it was always possible for the Government to operate a traditional foreign policy on the implicit assumption that its leaders exercised *legitimate* authority over the various national groups within South Africa and was therefore legally and morally qualified to speak on their behalf in the external arena. Thus no South African Government ever felt the need to defend its representative function, indeed its right to be in power at all, for there were few critics at the international level who questioned the political integrity of the South African State.

Yet this is precisely what happened after the Second World War as a new group of states—the products of Western decolonization—transformed both the physical and psychological boundaries of international society. Many of these states were small, but they differed substantially

---

[1] Cf. Hertzog's remarks in this particular context when he alluded to '. . . one of the bloodiest and cruelest periods the world has ever known . . . Yet we hear from the opposition that we should regard Great Britain as our enemy, as if we are not going to have enough enemies. And we must do this to a country which has handed us our freedom to use as we think fit!' Ibid., pp. 283–4.

from their predecessors of the inter-war period: these had been ideo-logically on the defensive and their commitment to the *status quo* was related to their need to defend the international system sanctified by the Versailles Treaty—of which they were the ultimate beneficiaries and in some cases the offspring. The new Afro-Asian states were by contrast dissatisfied, unwilling to accept a permanent division of international society between the powerful and the weak, the rich and the poor. Moreover their leaders were united in their hostility to what remained of the old colonial system (and here as we have noted, South Africa was firmly included) and bitterly committed to alter a *status quo* which allowed white minorities to deny black majorities the basic right of national self-determination. Their anti-colonialism had, in effect, the status of a revolutionary ideology and its impact, particularly at the United Nations, was profound.[1] In particular, in its capacity as an 'instrument of public diplomacy', the United Nations institutionalized with maxi-mum publicity the conflict between South Africa and its critics.[2] This process gave the Republic a unique status as a small power in twentieth-century international politics, denying to it the elementary advantage of a 'rectitude base' which an earlier generation had taken so easily for granted.[3] In terms of this ideology South Africa stood condemned and isolated, its domestic system constantly exposed to the moral indigna-tion of the African and Asian states for which the traditional distinction between the sanctity of domestic jurisdiction and the State's external obligations, together with the claim of the South African Government to speak for the majority within its borders, were both equally unaccept-able. Thus increasingly after 1948 South Africa's foreign policy was primarily concerned with defending domestic policy and by implication the very structure of South African society and the values underpinning it.

By the mid 1960s, with their country shunned as an alliance partner by the Western bloc, unable for ideological reasons (in particular, a deep-rooted anti-communism) to opt for neutrality on the Swedish or Irish models, and deprived of the small power's traditional first line of defence—moral self-justification—South African foreign policy-makers concentrated on two areas of interest. The first was the estab-lishment of closer links with the Western powers, on which it was hoped to impress an image of the Republic as a stable, rich, and secure society,

---

[1] Nearly a third of all roll-call votes in the General Assembly were concerned with African questions. Up to the 16th Session, out of 1,747 resolutions, 336 dealt with African issues in whole or in part and 260 exclusively; 30·8 per cent of the latter arose out of the domestic policies of the South African Government. Hovet, op. cit., p. 206.

[2] Ibid., p. 214.

[3] i.e. the capacity to appeal to world opinion as an innocent and peace-loving power in a world of squabbling and aggressive giants. Fox, op. cit., pp. 2–3.

a pillar of the international order, against which it would be folly to launch economic and military sanctions. Secondly, the South African Government began a self-conscious exercise of regional influence in the southern and central third of the continent, designed largely to ensure the continued existence of pliable governments, willing to deal firmly with any who might attempt to use their territories as launching pads for subversion against the Republic. Internally, South Africa appeared to have confounded those critics who had prophesied imminent disaster ever since the accession of the Nationalist party to office in 1948. Twenty years later the same party was still in power, sufficiently confident of its domestic base to begin the operation of a foreign policy more flexible and more in keeping with the economic and military strength of the richest state on the African continent. A new search for status had begun.

BIBLIOGRAPHY

OFFICIAL PUBLICATIONS

Basutoland, *Annual Reports* (London).
Basutoland, *Report (1945–6) of the Commission on Education in Basutoland* (Pretoria. G.P.—31540).
Basutoland, *Population Census*, 1956 (Maseru, 1958).
Bechuanaland Protectorate, *Annual Report*, 1964 (London).
Bechuanaland Protectorate, *Census*, 1964.
Cape of Good Hope, *Agricultural Miscellanea*. Extracts from Vols. I to V of the Agricultural Journal published by the Department of Agriculture (Cape Town, 1897).
Cape of Good Hope, *The Bloemhof Arbitration Bluebook*: Evidence taken at Bloemhof before The Commission appointed to investigate the claims ... to ... the diamond fields (1871).
Cape of Good Hope, *Blue Book of the Colony*, annual to 1885; thereafter, *Statistical Register of the Colony*, to 1910.
Cape of Good Hope, *Blue Book on Native Affairs*, G. 27—'74; G. 16—'76; G. 12—'77; G. 3—'84.
Cape of Good Hope, *Census of the Colony*, 1865, 1875, 1891, 1904.
Cape of Good Hope, *Report of the Commission on Native Laws and Customs, 1883* (G. 4—'83, 1883).
Cape of Good Hope, *South African Native Affairs Commission: Report, 1903–1905*, 6 vols. (Cape Town, 1905).
Cape of Good Hope, *Report of the Native Affairs Commission* (1910).
Cape of Good Hope, *Report from the Select Committee on Granting Lands in Freehold to Hottentots* (S.C. 11—'54).
Cape of Good Hope, *Report of the Select Committee appointed to take into consideration the subject of the introduction of Kafirs into the Colony* (A. 4—'59, 1859).
Cape of Good Hope, *Report of the Select Committee appointed by the Legislative Council to consider and report upon The Convict Department* (C. 3—'66, 1866).
Cape of Good Hope, *Report of the Select Committee on the Supply of the Labour Market* (A. 26—'79, 1879).
Cape of Good Hope, *Report of the Select Committee on Colonial Agriculture and Industries* (A. 1.—'83, 1883).
Cape of Good Hope, *Report of the Select Committee on the Pass Laws of the Colony* (A. 15—'83, 1883).
Cape of Good Hope, *Report of the Select Committee on the Improvement of the Wine Industry* (A. 6—'84, 1884).
Cape of Good Hope, *Report of the Select Committee on the Pass Laws* (A. 11—'86, 1886).
Cape of Good Hope, *Report of the Select Committee on Master and Servant Acts* (A. 3.—'89, 1889).
Cape of Good Hope, *Report of the Select Committee on the Labour Question* (A. 12—'90, 1890).
Cape of Good Hope, *Report of the Select Committee on the Labour Question* (C. 2—'92, 1892).
Cape of Good Hope, *Report of the Select Committee on Agricultural Schools* (A. 5—'94, 1894).

Cape of Good Hope, *Report of the Select Committee on Agricultural Distress* (A. 1—'98, 1898).

Cape of Good Hope, *Reports by Professor R. Koch upon his investigation into Rinderpest at Kimberley, December 1896 to March 1897* (G. 70—'97, 1897).

Cape of Good Hope, *Report of the Superintendent-General of Education for 1897* (G. 32—'98, 1898).

Great Britain: Parliamentary Papers. Cd. 3250: *Papers re Transvaal Constitution of 1906* (1906).

Great Britain: Parliamentary Papers. Cd. 3526: *Orange River Colony Letters Patent and Instructions for Governor, 5 June 1907* (1907).

Great Britain: Parliamentary Papers: Cd. 3564: *A review of the present mutual relations of the British South African Colonies, to which is appended a memorandum on South African Railway Unification and its effects on Railway Rates* (1907).

Great Britain: Parliamentary Papers: Cd. 4585: *Further Correspondence relating to the Trial of Dinuzulu and other Natives in Natal* (in continuation of [Cd. 4404] of 1908) (1909).

Great Britain: Parliamentary Papers: Cmd. 8707: *Basutoland, the Bechuanaland Protectorate, and Swaziland : History of Discussions with the Union of South Africa, 1909–39* (1952).

Great Britain: Parliamentary Papers. Hansard: House of Lords Debates, 5th ser. ii (1909).

Great Britain: Parliamentary Papers. Hansard: House of Commons Debates, 5th ser. ix (1909).

Johannesburg Municipality: *Minutes* (1903).

Natal, *Blue Book*, to 1892/3; thereafter *Statistical Year Book*, to 1910 (Pietermaritzburg).

Natal, *Blue Book on Native Affairs, 1904* (Pietermaritzburg, 1905).

Natal, *Census Reports*, 1891, 1904.

Natal, *Native Affairs Commission, 1906–1907*, Report and Evidence, 2 vols. (Pietermaritzburg, 1907).

Natal, *Reports of Resident Magistrates and Administrators of Native Law on Natives, 1880* (Pietermaritzburg, 1881).

Orange Free State, *Census*, 1880.

Republic of South Africa, *Report of the Commission appointed to Inquire into the Events on 20 to 22 November 1962, at Paarl* (Pretoria, 1963) (R.P. 51—1963).

Republic of South Africa, *Interim Report of the Commission of Enquiry into Agriculture* (Pretoria, 1969) (R.P. 61—1968).

Republic of South Africa, *Debates of the House of Assembly (Hansard)* (Cape Town).

Republic of South Africa, *Economic Development Programme for the Republic of South Africa, 1966–1971* (Pretoria, 1966).

Republic of South Africa, *Population Census, 6 September 1960*, Vol. 1. *Geographical Distribution of the Population* (Pretoria, 1963).

Republic of South Africa, *Statistical Year Book, 1964, 1965, 1966*.

Republic of South Africa, Department of Agricultural Economics and Marketing, *Annual Report of the Secretary, 1965–66* (1967) (R.P. 33—1967).

Republic of South Africa, Department of Agricultural Economics and Marketing, *Supplementary Data to the Abstract of Agricultural Statistics* (January 1969).

Republic of South Africa, Department of Agricultural Technical Services, *Agricultural Research*, 5 parts (1962).

Republic of South Africa, Department of Agricultural Technical Services, *Agriculture in the Economic Development of South Africa* (1963).

Republic of South Africa, Department of Agricultural Technical Services, *Annual Report, 1965–1966* (1967) (R.P. 36—1967).

Republic of South Africa, Department of Bantu Education, *Report of the Commission of Inquiry into the Teaching of the Official Language and the Use of the Mother Tongue as the Medium of Instruction in Transkeian Primary Schools* (R.P. 22—1963).

Republic of South Africa, Department of Bantu Education, *Bantu Education Journal* (November 1966).

Republic of South Africa, Department of Information, *Bantu* (September 1963).

Republic of South Africa, Department of Information, *Bantu on Farms* (n.d.).

Republic of South Africa, Department of Information, *Basutoland, Bechuanaland, Swaziland, The Road to Freedom for* (Fact Paper no. 107, 1963).

Republic of South Africa, *South African Reserve Bank Annual Report.*

Republic of South Africa, *South African Reserve Bank Quarterly Bulletin.*

South African Republic, *Groen Boeke van de Zuid-Afrikaansche Republiek*, 3 vols. (Pretoria, 1884–98).

South African Republic, *Uitslag van de Volkstelling verhouden in de Zuid-Afrikaansche Republiek den 1st April, 1890.*

Swaziland, *Annual Report*, 1963 (London).

Transvaal, *Report of the Transvaal Labour Commission* (Johannesburg, 1903).

Transvaal, *Report of the Commission concerning Pretoria Indigents* (Pretoria, 1905).

Transvaal, *Report of the Indigency Commission, 1906–1908* (T.G. 13—'08, Pretoria, 1908).

Transvaal, Native Affairs Department, *Laws and Regulations etc. specially relating to the Native Population of the Transvaal* (Pretoria, 1907).

Transvaal, Native Affairs Department, *Short History of the Native Tribes of the Transvaal* (Pretoria, 1905).

Transvaal, Province of, *Report of the Local Government Commission (1921)* (T.P. 1–1922, Pretoria, 1922) (Stallard Commission).

Union of South Africa, *Census of the Union*, 1911, 1921, 1936, 1946, 1951, 1960.

Union of South Africa, *Official Yearbook*, No. 1/1917 (1918).

Union of South Africa, Bureau of Census and Statistics, *Agricultural Census*, Nos. 1–37, 1918–1962/3.

Union of South Africa, Bureau of Census and Statistics, *Union Statistics for Fifty Years*, 1910–1960, Jubilee Issue (1960).

Union of South Africa, House of Assembly Debates.

Union of South Africa, Senate Debates.

Union of South Africa, *Native Affairs Commission Reports.*

Union of South Africa, *Verbatim Reports of the Natives Representative Council*, Annually 1937–1950 (except 1947, 1948).

Union of South Africa, *Report of the Economic Commission* (U.G. 12—'14, 1914).

Union of South Africa, *Report of the Tuberculosis Commission* (U.G. 34—'14, 1915).

Union of South Africa, *Report of the Natives Land Commission* (U.G. 19—'16) (Beaumont Commission).

Union of South Africa, *Report of the Native Affairs Commission, 'Israelites' at Bulhoek and Occurrences in May 1921* (A. 4—'21).

Union of South Africa, *Report of the Native Churches Commission* (1925) (U.G. 39—'25).

Union of South Africa, *Report of the Economic and Wage Commission* (1926) (U.G. 14—'26) (Clay Commission).

Union of South Africa, *Report of the Native Economic Commission 1930–2* (U.G. 22—'32).

Union of South Africa, *Report of the Commission to inquire into Co-operation and Agricultural Credit* (1934) (U.G. 16—'34).

Union of South Africa, *Report of the Police Commission of Inquiry, 1937* (U.G. 50—'37).

Union of South Africa, *Report of the Commission on the Cape Coloured Population of the Union* (1937) (U.G. 54—'37).

Union of South Africa, *Report of the Asiatic Land Laws Commission* (1939) (U.G. 16—'39).

Union of South Africa, *Third (Interim) Report of the Agricultural and Industrial Requirements Commission* (1941) (U.G. 40—'41) (Van Eck Report).

Union of South Africa, *Report of the Native Affairs Commission on Kaffir Beer* (1942–3).

Union of South Africa, *Report of the Indian Penetration Commission, 1943* (1st, U.G. 39—'41; 2nd, U.G. 21—'43).

Union of South Africa, *Report of the Judicial Commission of Enquiry into the Pretoria Municipal Riot of 28 December 1942* (1943).

Union of South Africa, *Report of the Witwatersrand Mine Native Wages Commission, 1943* (U.G. 21—'44).

Union of South Africa, *Interim Report of the Commission of Enquiry into matters affecting the Indian Population in the Province of Natal, 1945* (U.G. 22—'45).

Union of South Africa, *Report of the Commission to Enquire into the Disturbances of 30 August 1947 at Moroka Emergency Camp Johannesburg* (1947).

Union of South Africa, *Report of the Penal and Prison Reform Commission* (1947) (U.G. 47—'47).

Union of South Africa, *Report of the Native Laws Commission, 1946–8* (U.G. 28—'48) (Fagan Commission).

Union of South Africa, *Report of the Commission of Enquiry into the Disturbances in the Witzieshoek Native Reserve* (U.G. 26—'51).

Union of South Africa, *Report of the Commission on Native Education, 1949–51* (U.G. 53—'51).

Union of South Africa, *Report of the Commission for the Socio-Economic Development of the Bantu Areas within the Union of South Africa* (U.G. 61—'55) (Tomlinson Report).

Union of South Africa, *Government Decisions on the Recommendations of the Commission for the Socio-Economic Development of Bantu Areas within the Union of South Africa* (W.P.F.—'56).

Union of South Africa, *Report of the Commission of Inquiry into European Occupancy of Rural Areas* (1960) (Du Toit Commission).

Union of South Africa, *Minute addressed to the Honourable the Minister of Native Affairs by the Honourable Sir W. H. Beaumont, Chairman of the Natives Land Commission* (1916) (U.G. 25—'16).

Union of South Africa, *Report of the Housing Committee* (1920) (U.G. 4—'20).

Union of South Africa, *Final Report of the Drought Investigation Committee* (1923) (U.G. 49—'23).

Union of South Africa, *Report of the Select Committee on the Gold Standard* (S.C. 9—1932).

Union of South Africa, *Report of the Interdepartmental Committee on Native Education, 1935–36* (U.G. 29—'36).

Union of South Africa, *Report of the Native Farm Labour Committee 1937–39* (1939).

Union of South Africa, *Report of the Interdepartmental Committee on the Social, Health and Economic Conditions of the Urban Natives* (1942).

Union of South Africa, *Report of the Committee appointed by the Ministers of Justice and Native Affairs, July 1942, to investigate the position of crime on the Witwatersrand and in Pretoria* (1943).

Union of South Africa, *Report of the Social Security Committee* (1944) (U.G. 14—'44).

Union of South Africa, Department of Agriculture and Forestry, *Reconstruction of Agriculture* (1943–4).

Union of South Africa, Department of Agriculture, *Agro-Economic Survey of the Union* (Economic Series No. 34, 1948).

Union of South Africa, Department of Agriculture, *Handbook for Farmers in South Africa*, 3 vols. (1957).

Union of South Africa, Department of Agriculture, Division of Economics and Markets, *An Abstract of Agricultural Statistics* (1958).

Union of South Africa, Department of Agricultural Economics and Marketing, *Handbook of Agricultural Statistics, 1904–1950* (1960–1).
Union of South Africa, Department of the Prime Minister, *White Paper on Agricultural Policy* (W.P. 10—'46) (1946).
Union of South Africa, Board of Trade and Industries, Report 282: *Investigation into Manufacturing Industries in the Union of South Africa* (1945).
Union of South Africa, Social and Economic Planning Council Report No. 4, *The Future of Farming in South Africa* (1945) (U.G. 10—'45).
Union of South Africa, Social and Economic Planning Council Report No. 8, *Local Government Functions and Finances* (1945) (U.G. 40—'45).
Union of South Africa, Social and Economic Planning Council Report No. 9, *Native Reserves and their Place in the Economy of the Union of South Africa* (1946) (U.G. 32—'46).
Union of South Africa, Ciskeian Territories General Council, *Proceedings and Reports* (King William's Town, 1934–1956) (Ciskei Bunga Reports).
Union of South Africa, Transkeian Territories General Council, *Proceedings and Reports* (Umtata, 1903–1956) (Bunga Reports).
Union of South Africa, *Report on Native Location Surveys, Cape Town* (U.G. 42—'22).
Union of South Africa, *The Union of South Africa and the War* (G.P. 1948).
Union of South Africa, Weather Bureau, *Climate of South Africa* (W.B. 23 parts, 1960).
United Nations, *Economic Survey of Africa*, Vol. 1. (E/CN/14/370, Ethiopia).
United Nations, *Report of the Special Committee on the Policies of Apartheid* (New York, 1963).
United Nations, *A New Course in South Africa: Report of the Group of Experts established in pursuance of the Security Council resolution of 4 December 1963* (New York, 1964).

PRINTED BOOKS AND PAMPHLETS

Acocks, J. P. H. *Veld Types of South Africa* (Pretoria, 1953).
Agar-Hamilton, J. A. I. *The Road to the North, South Africa, 1852–1886* (London, 1937).
Albertyn, J. R. *Land en Stad* (Cape Town, 1959).
—— *My Eie Boeresitplekkie* (Pretoria, 1941).
—— *The Poor White Society* (Stellenbosch, 1932).
—— Du Toit, P., and Theron, H. S. *Kerk en Stad-Verslag van die Kommissie van Ondersoek van die Gefedereerde N.G. Kerke na Kerklike en Godsdienstige Toestande in die Nege Stede van die Unie van Suid Afrika* (Stellenbosch, 1947, 2nd edn. 1948).
Amery, L. S. (ed.). *The Times History of the War in South Africa*, 7 vols. (London, 1900–9).
Amphlett, G. T. *History of the Standard Bank of South Africa Ltd., 1852–1914* (Glasgow, 1914).
Anon. *Georg Schmidt en sy opvolgers, 1737–1937* (Herrnhut, Saxony, 1937).
Anon. *The Government of South Africa*, 2 vols. (Cape Town, 1908).
Armstrong, H. C. *Grey Steel: J. C. Smuts, a study in arrogance* (London, 1946).
Arndt, E. H. D. *Banking and Currency Development in South Africa, 1652–1927* (Cape Town, 1928).
Arnot, D., and Orpen, F. H. S. *The Land Question of Griqualand West: an inquiry into the various claims to land in that territory; together with a brief history of the Griqua nation* (Cape Town, 1875).
Astor, Viscount, and Seebohm Rowntree, B. *British Agriculture* (Harmondsworth, 1939).
Austin, D. *Britain and South Africa* (London, 1966).
Ayliff, J., and Whiteside, J. *History of the Abambo* (Butterworth, Cape Province, 1912).

BALLINGER, R. B. *South Africa and the UN: Myth and Reality* (Johannesburg, 1963).
—— *South-West Africa: The Case against the Union* (Johannesburg, 1961).
BARKER, A. *Giving and Receiving* (London, 1959).
BEET, G. *The Grand Old Days of the Diamond Fields* (Cape Town, 1932).
BEETHAM, T. A., and SALTER, N. (eds.). *The Future of South Africa: A Study of British Christians for the World Council of Churches* (London, 1965).
BENIANS, E. A., BUTLER, J. R. M., MANSERGH, P. N. S., and WALKER, E. A. (eds.). *The Cambridge History of the British Empire*, vol. iii, *The Empire–Commonwealth, 1870–1919* (Cambridge, 1959).
BENNETT, H. H. *Soil Erosion and Land Use in the Union of South Africa* (Pretoria, 1945).
BETTS, R. F. (ed.). *The 'Scramble' for Africa: Causes and Dimensions of Empire* (Boston, 1966).
BIEBUYCK, D. (ed.). *African Agrarian Systems* (London, 1963).
BIERMAN, H. H. (ed.). *The Case for South Africa: Speeches by E. H. Louw* (New York, 1963).
BINNS, C. T. *The Last Zulu King: The Life and Death of Cetshwayo* (London, 1963).
BIXLER, R. W. *Anglo-German Imperialism in South Africa, 1880–1900* (Baltimore, 1932).
BLACK, J. E., and THOMPSON, K. W. (eds.). *Foreign Policy in a World of Change* (New York, 1964).
BLAKE, R. *Disraeli* (New York, 1967).
BOSERUP, E. *The Conditions of Agricultural Growth* (London, 1965).
BOSMAN, G. *The Industrialization of South Africa* (Rotterdam, 1938).
BOSMAN, I. D. 'Oorheersing en vrywording (1877–1884)', in van der Walt, A. J. H., *et al.* (eds.), *Geskiedenis van Suid-Afrika*, 2 vols. (Cape Town, 1955).
BOTHA, P. R. *Die Staatkundige Ontwikkeling van die Suid-Afrikaanse Republiek onder Krüger en Leyds: Transvaal 1844–1899* (Amsterdam, 1926).
BRAND, R. H. *The Union of South Africa* (Oxford, 1909).
BREYTENBACH, J. H. *Die Tweede Vryheidsoorlog*, 2 vols. (Cape Town, 1948, 1949).
BROKENSHA, D. *Social Change at Larteh, Ghana* (Oxford, 1966).
BROOKES, E. H. *The History of Native Policy in South Africa from 1830 to the Present Day* (2nd edn., Pretoria, 1927).
—— *South Africa in a Changing World* (Cape Town, 1953).
—— *Things Old and New* (Johannesburg, 1961).
—— and MACAULAY, J. B. *Civil Liberty in South Africa* (Cape Town, 1958).
—— and WEBB, C. DE B. *A History of Natal* (Pietermaritzburg, 1965).
BROUGHTON, M. *The Press and Politics in South Africa* (Cape Town, 1961).
BURGER, J. (pseudonym of MARQUARD, L.). *The Black Man's Burden* (London, 1943).
BUTLER, J. (ed.). *Boston University Papers in African History, I* (Boston, 1964).
—— 'The German Factor in Anglo-Transvaal Relations', in Gifford, P. and Louis, W. R. (eds.), *Britain and Germany in Africa* (New Haven, Connecticut, 1967).
—— *The Liberal Party and the Jameson Raid* (Oxford, 1968).
BUTTERFIELD, H. *Christianity in European History* (London, 1951).
BUXTON, EARL. *General Botha* (London, 1924).
CALDWELL, T. C. *The Anglo-Boer War: why was it fought? who was responsible?* (Boston, 1965).
CALPIN, G. H. *There are no South Africans* (London, 1941).
—— *The South African Way of Life* (London, 1953).
CALVOCORESSI, P. *South Africa and World Opinion* (London, 1961).
CARNEGIE COMMISSION, Report of *The Poor White Problem in South Africa*, 5 vols. (Stellenbosch, 1932).
CARR, E. H. *What is History?* (London, 1961).
CARROLL, F. *South West Africa and the United Nations* (Lexington, U.S.A., 1967).

CARSTENS, W. P. *The Social Structure of a Cape Coloured Reserve* (Cape Town, 1966).

CARTER, G. M. *The Politics of Inequality: South Africa since 1948* (London, 1958).

—— (ed.). *Five African States* (London, 1964).

CHASE, J. C. *The Cape of Good Hope and the Eastern Province of Algoa Bay* (London, 1843; Facsimile Reprint, Cape Town, 1967).

Christian Handbook of South Africa, The (Lovedale, 1938).

CHURCHILL, W. S. *London to Ladysmith via Pretoria* (London, 1900).

COCKRAN, B. *International Relations and South Africa* (Johannesburg, 1963).

COETZEE, A. *Die Opkoms van die Afrikaanse Kultuurgedagte aan die Rand 1886–1936* (Johannesburg, 1937; Cape Town, 1938).

COETZEE, D. J. *Spoorwegontwikkeling in die Suid-Afrikaanse Republiek, 1872–1899* (Cape Town, 1940).

COETZEE, G. *Hans Strydom* (Cape Town, 1958).

COETZEE, J. H. *Verarming en Oorheersing* (Bloemfontein, 1942).

COLE, M. *South Africa* (London, 1961).

COLLINS, W. W. *Free Statia* (Cape Town, 1965).

COLVIN, I. *The Life of Jameson*, 2 vols. (London, 1922, 1923).

COOK, P. A. W. 'Non-European Education', in Hellmann, E. (ed.), *Handbook on Race Relations in South Africa* (Cape Town, 1949).

COPE, J. *South Africa* (London, 1965).

COUPLAND, R. *Zulu Battle Piece: Isandhlwana* (London, 1948).

COWEN, D. V. *The Foundations of Freedom* (Cape Town, 1961).

CRAFFORD, F. S. *Jan Smuts: a biography* (Cape Town, 1945 and 1946).

CRANKSHAW, E. *The Forsaken Idea: a study of Viscount Milner* (London, 1952).

CRONJE, G. and VENTER, J. D. *Die Patriargale Familie* (Cape Town, 1958).

DAVENPORT, T. R. H. *The Afrikaner Bond: the history of a South African political party (1880–1911)* (Cape Town, 1966).

DAVIS, J. A. and BAKER, J. K. (eds.). *Southern Africa in Transition* (New York, 1965).

DE BEER, Z. J. *Multi-racial South Africa* (London, 1961).

DE GRUCHY, J. *The Cost of Living of Urban Africans in Johannesburg, 1959* (Johannesburg, 1960).

DE JOUVENAL, B. *Sovereignty* (Cambridge, 1957).

DE KIEWIET, C. W. *British Colonial Policy and the South African Republics, 1848–1872* (London, 1929).

—— *A History of South Africa: Social and Economic* (London, 1941).

—— *The Imperial Factor in South Africa: a study in Politics and Economics* (Cambridge, 1937).

DE KOCK, M. H. *Selected Subjects in the Economic History of South Africa* (Cape Town, 1924).

DE TOCQUEVILLE, A. *De la Démocratie en Amérique* (Paris, reprint, 1951).

DE VILLIERS, R. M. 'Politics', in Hellmann, E. (ed.), *Handbook on Race Relations in South Africa* (Cape Town, 1949).

DE WET, C. R. *Three Years' War (October 1899–June 1902)* (London, 1902).

DENNIS, S. S., BEACH, H. P., and FAHS, C. H. (eds.). *The World Atlas of Christian Missions* (New York, 1911).

DICKIE-CLARK, H. F. *The Marginal Situation* (London, 1966).

DISON, L. R., and MOHAMED, I. *Group Areas and their Development* (Durban, 1960).

DOUGHTY, O. *Early Diamond Days* (London, 1963).

DOWER, W. *The Early Annals of Kokstad and Griqualand East* (Port Elizabeth, 1902).

DOXEY, G. V. *The High Commission Territories and the Republic of South Africa* (London, 1963).

—— *The Industrial Colour Bar in South Africa* (Cape Town, 1961).

Du Plessis, E. P. (ed.). *'n Volk Staan Op: Die Ekonomiese Volkskongres en Daarna* (Pretoria, 1964).

Du Plessis, J. *A History of Christian Missions in South Africa* (Cape Town, reprint, 1965).

Du Toit, J. D. *Ds. S. J. du Toit in Weg en Werk* (Paarl, 1917).

Du Toit, P. J. *The Farmer in South Africa* (Cape Town, n.d.).

Dunn, W. H. *James Anthony Froude, a biography*, vol. i (Oxford, 1961).

Education Panel, The, 1961. *Education and the South African Economy* (Johannesburg, 1966).

Edwards, I. *Protectorates or Native Reserves?* (London, n.d.).

Eicher, C. K., and Witt, L. W. (eds.). *Agriculture in Economic Development* (New York, 1964).

Ekonomiese Instituut van die F. A. K. *'n Volk Staan Op* (Cape Town, 1964).

Elton Mills, M. E., and Wilson, M. *Land Tenure* (Pietermaritzburg, 1952).

Engelbrecht, S. F. *Thomas Francois Burgers: a biography* (Pretoria, 1946).

Engelenburg, F. V. *General Louis Botha* (Pretoria, 1929).

Evans, M. S. *Black and White in South East Africa* (London, 1911).

Eybers, G. W. (ed.). *Select Constitutional Documents Illustrating South African History, 1795–1910* (London, 1918).

Fagan, H. A. *Our Responsibility: a Discussion of South Africa's Racial Problems* (Stellenbosch, 1960).

Farmers' Encyclopedia (Cape Town, 1967).

Faure, D. P. *My Life and Times* (Cape Town, 1907).

Federale Armsorgraad van die Gefedereerde N. G. K. *Die Stadwaartse Trek van die Afrikanernasie* (Johannesburg, 1947).

Fick, J. C. *The Abuse of the Soil, Veld and Water Resources of South Africa* (Cape Town, 1944).

Finberg, H. P. R. (ed.). *Approaches to History* (London, 1962).

Fisher, L. H. *The Harvest Labor Market in California* (Cambridge, Mass. 1953).

Fitzpatrick, Sir J. P. *South African Memories* (London, 1932).

—— *The Transvaal from Within: a private record of public affairs* (London, 1900).

Flint, J. E. *Sir George Goldie and the Making of Nigeria* (London, 1960).

Fox, A. B. *The Power of Small States Diplomacy in World War II* (Chicago, 1959).

Frankel, S. H. *Capital Investment in Africa* (London, 1938).

—— *Co-operation and Competition in the marketing of maize in South Africa* (London, 1926).

—— *The Railway Policy of South Africa* (Johannesburg, 1928).

Fraser, J. G. *Episodes in My Life* (Cape Town, 1922).

Freislich, R. *The Last Tribal War* (Cape Town, 1964).

Friedman, B., and others. *Looking Outwards: Three South African Viewpoints* (Johannesburg, 1961).

Fugard, A. *The Blood Knot* (Cape Town, 1963).

Fuller, Sir T. E. *The Right Honourable Cecil John Rhodes* (London, 1910).

Gann, L. H. *A History of Southern Rhodesia: Early Days to 1934* (London, 1965).

Garvin, J. L. *The Life of Joseph Chamberlain*, vols. i–iii (London, 1933–4).

Germond, R. C. *Chronicles of Basutoland* (Morija, 1967).

Gibson, J. Y. *The Story of the Zulus* (Pietermaritzburg, 1903).

Gifford, P., and Louis, W. R. (eds.). *Britain and Germany in Africa: Imperial Rivalry and Colonial Rule* (New Haven, Connecticut, 1967).

Glass, Y. *Industrial Man in Southern Africa* (Johannesburg, 1961).

Goldblatt, I. *The Mandated Territory in South West Africa in Relation to the United Nations* (Cape Town, 1961).

Goodfellow, C. F. *Great Britain and South African Confederation (1870–1881)* (Cape Town, 1966).

GOODFELLOW, D. M. *A Modern Economic History of South Africa* (London, 1931).

GORDON-BROWN, A. (ed.). *The Narrative of Private Buck Adams* (Van Riebeeck Society, Cape Town, 1941).

GOVAN, W. *Memorials of the Rev. James Laing* (Glasgow, 1875).

GRANT, G. C. *The Liquidation of Adams College* (Private circulation, n.d.).

GRENVILLE, J. A. S. *Lord Salisbury and Foreign Policy: the Close of the Nineteenth Century* (London, 1964).

GROSS, F. *Rhodes of Africa* (London, 1956).

GROSSKOPF, J. F. W. *Carnegie Report on the Poor White Problem*, vol. I, *Rural Impoverishment and Rural Exodus* (Stellenbosch, 1932).

HAHLO, H. R., and KAHN, E. *The Union of South Africa: The Development of its Laws and Constitution* (London, 1960).

HAHN, T. *Tsuni-‖Goam* (London, 1881).

HAILEY, LORD. *Native Administration in the British African Territories*, Part V, *The High Commission Territories: Basutoland, Bechuanaland Protectorate and Swaziland* (London, 1953).

—— *The Republic of South Africa and the High Commission Territories* (London, 1962).

HALFORD, S. J. *The Griquas of Griqualand* (Cape Town, 1949).

HALPÉRIN, V. *Lord Milner and the Empire: the Evolution of British Imperialism* (London, 1952).

HALPERN, J. *Basutoland, Bechuanaland and Swaziland, South Africa's Hostages* (London, 1965).

HAMMOND, J. H. *The Autobiography of John Hays Hammond*, 2 vols. (New York, 1935).

HAMMOND, R. J. *Portugal and Africa, 1815–1910: a study in uneconomic imperialism* (Stanford, 1966).

HANCOCK, W. K. *Smuts*, I. *The Sanguine Years, 1870–1919* (Cambridge, 1962); II. *The Fields of Force* (Cambridge, 1968).

—— *Are there South Africans?* (Johannesburg, 1966).

—— *Survey of British Commonwealth Affairs*, 2 vols. (London, 1937–42).

—— and VAN DER POEL, J. (eds.). *Selections from the Smuts Papers*, 4 vols. (Cambridge, 1966).

HARDINGE, A. H. *The Life of Henry Howard Molyneux Herbert, fourth Earl of Carnarvon*, 3 vols. (London, 1925).

HEADLAM, C. (ed.). *The Milner Papers*, 2 vols. (London, 1931, 1933).

HELLMANN, E. (ed.). *Handbook on Race Relations in South Africa* (Cape Town, 1949).

—— *Rooiyard—A Sociological Survey of an Urban Native Slum Yard* (Livingstone, 1948).

—— *Sellgoods* (Johannesburg, 1953).

—— *Soweto—Johannesburg's African City* (Johannesburg, 1968).

HENDERSON, W. P. M. *Durban—Fifty Years Municipal History* (Durban, 1904).

HEPPLE, A. *South Africa, a Political and Economic History* (London, 1966).

HOBART HOUGHTON, D. *Some Economic Problems of the Bantu in South Africa* (Johannesburg, 1938).

—— *Economic Development in a Plural Society* (Cape Town, 1960).

—— *The South African Economy* (Cape Town, 1964 and 1967).

—— and WALTON, E. M. *The Economy of a Native Reserve* (Pietermaritzburg, 1952).

HOBSBAWM, E. J. *The Age of Revolution* (London, 1962).

HOBSON, J. A. *Imperialism: a Study* (London, 1902).

—— *The War in South Africa: Its Causes and Effects* (London, 1900).

HOFMEYR, G. R. (ed.). *Minutes of Proceedings with Annexures (selected) of the South African Convention* (Cape Town, 1911).

HOFMEYR, J. H. *What of the Future?* (Johannesburg, 1948).

HOFMEYR, J. H. in collaboration with REITZ, F. W. *The Life of Jan Hendrik Hofmeyr (Onze Jan)* (Cape Town, 1913).

HOLBORN, D. W. *War and Peace Aims of the United Nations* (New York, 1952).

HOLE, H. M. *The Jameson Raid* (London, 1930).

HOLLEMAN, J. F. (ed.). *Experiment in Swaziland* (Cape Town, 1964).

HOLLOWAY, J. E. *Apartheid—A Challenge* (Johannesburg, 1964).

HOLT, E. *The Boer War* (London, 1958).

HOMANS, G. C. *English Villagers in the Thirteenth Century* (Cambridge, Mass., 1942).

—— *The Human Group* (London, 1951).

HORRELL, M. *African Education : Some Origins and Development until 1953* (Johannesburg, 1963).

—— *A Decade of Bantu Education* (Johannesburg, 1964).

—— *Group Areas in the Transvaal—the Emerging Pattern* (Johannesburg, 1966).

—— *Racialism and the Trade Unions* (Johannesburg, 1959).

—— *South African Trade Unionism* (Johannesburg, 1961).

—— *Survey of Race Relations in South Africa* (Johannesburg, 1956–69, published annually).

—— *Visit to Bantu Areas of the Northern Transvaal* (Johannesburg, 1965).

HORTON, J. W. *The First Seventy Years, 1895–1965* (Johannesburg, 1968).

HORWITZ, R. *The Political Economy of South Africa* (London, 1967).

HOVET, T. *Africa in the United Nations* (London, 1963).

HUNTER, G. (ed.). *Industrialization and Race Relations* (London, 1965).

HUNTER, M. (WILSON, M.) *Reaction to Conquest* (London, 1936 and 1961).

HURWITZ, N. *The Economics of Bantu Education in South Africa* (Johannesburg, 1964).

IMISHUE, R. W. *South West Africa, an International Problem* (London, 1965).

INTERNATIONAL COMMISSION OF JURISTS, *South Africa and the Rule of Law* (Geneva, 1960).

JABAVU, D. D. T. *An African Independent Church* (Lovedale, 1942).

—— *The Black Problem: Papers and Addresses on Various Native Problems* (Lovedale, 1920).

—— *The Findings of the All African Convention* (Lovedale, 1935).

—— *The Life of John Tengo Jabavu, Editor of 'Imvo Zabantsundu', 1884–1921* (Lovedale, 1922).

—— (ed.). *Minutes of the All African Convention* (Lovedale, 1936).

—— *Native Disabilities in South Africa* (Lovedale, 1932).

—— *The Segregation Fallacy and Other Papers* (Lovedale, 1928).

JABAVU, J. T. 'Native Races of South Africa', in G. Spiller (ed.), *Papers on Inter-racial Problems Communicated to the First Universal Races Congress, held at the University of London, 26–29 July 1911* (London, 1911).

JACKS, G. V., and WHYTE, R. O. *The Rape of the Earth: A World Survey of Soil Erosion* (London, 1939).

JAMES, D. *Lord Roberts* (London, 1954).

JONES, G. P., and POOL, A. G. *A Hundred Years of Economic Development in Great Britain: 1840–1940* (London, 1940).

JORDAN, A. C. *Ingqumbo Yeminyanya* (Lovedale, 1946).

JORISSEN, E. J. P. *Transvaalsche Herinneringen, 1876–1896* (Amsterdam, 1897).

JUTA, M. *The Pace of the Ox: the Life of Paul Kruger* (Cape Town, 1938).

KAHN, E. *The New Constitution: being a supplement to South Africa, the Development of its Laws and Constitution* (London, 1962).

—— 'The Pass Laws', in Hellmann, E. (ed.), *Handbook on Race Relations in South Africa* (Cape Town, 1949).

KARIS, T. 'South Africa', in Carter, G. (ed.), *Five African States* (London, 1964).

KAWA, R. T. *I-Bali lama Mfengu* (Lovedale, 1929).
KEET, B. B. *Whither South Africa?* (Stellenbosch, 1956).
KEPPEL-JONES, A. *Friends or Foes?* (Pietermaritzburg, 1950).
—— 'Land and Agriculture Outside the Reserves', in Hellmann, E. (ed.), *Handbook on Race Relations in South Africa* (Cape Town, 1949).
KESTELL, J. D. *Through Shot and Flame: The Adventures and Experiences of J. D. Kestell, Chaplain to President Steyn and General Christian de Wet* (London, 1903).
—— and VAN VELDEN, D. E. *The Peace Negotiations between the Governments of the South African Republic and the Orange Free State, and the Representatives of the British Government, which Terminated in the Peace Concluded at Vereeniging on the 31st May, 1902* (London, 1912).
KHAMA, TSHEKEDI. *Bechuanaland and South Africa* (London, 1955).
KIESER, A. *President Steyn en die Krisisjare, 1896–1899* (Cape Town, 1939).
KILPIN, R. *The Old Cape House, being Passages from the History of a Legislative Assembly* (Cape Town, 1918).
—— *The Romance of a Colonial Parliament* (London, 1938).
KOEBNER, R. and SCHMIDT, H. D. *Imperialism: The Story and Significance of a Political Word, 1840–1960* (Cambridge, 1964).
KOLB, P. *The Present State of the Cape of Good Hope*, 2 vols. (London, 1731).
KOÖPERATIEWE RAAD van die SUID-AFRIKAANSE LANDBOU-UNIE. *Inleiding tot die Koöperatiewese* (Pretoria, 1966).
KOTZE, J. G. *Biographical Memoirs and Reminiscences*, 2 vols. (Cape Town, 1934, 1947).
KRÜGER, B. *The Pear Tree Blossoms* (Genadendal, 1968).
KRÜGER, D. W. *The Age of the Generals* (Johannesburg, 1958).
—— *Paul Kruger*, 2 vols. (Johannesburg, 1961, 1963).
—— (ed.). *South African Parties and Policies 1910–1960* (Cape Town, 1960).
KRUGER, R. *Good-bye Dolly Gray: the Story of the Boer War* (London, 1959).
KRUGER, S. J. P. *The Memoirs of Paul Kruger, Four Times President of the South African Republic, Told by Himself* (London, 1902).
KUPER, H. *An African Aristocracy: Rank among the Swazi* (London, 1947).
—— *Indian People in Natal* (Pietermaritzburg, 1960).
—— *The Uniform of Colour* (Johannesburg, 1947).
—— in KUPER, L. *An African Bourgeoisie* (New Haven, Connecticut, 1965).
KUPER, L. *An African Bourgeoisie* (New Haven, Connecticut, 1965).
—— WATTS, H., and DAVIES, R. *Durban, A Study in Racial Ecology* (London, 1958).
LAGDEN, G. *The Basutos: the Mountaineers and their Country*, 2 vols. (London, 1909).
LANTERNARI, V. *The Religions of the Oppressed* (Chicago, 1960).
LAURENCE, Sir P. *The Life of John Xavier Merriman* (London, 1930).
LEA, A. *The Native Separatist Church Movement in South Africa* (Cape Town, n.d.).
LEGUM, C. and M. *South Africa—Crisis for the West* (London, 1964).
LEISS, A. C. (ed.). *Apartheid and United Nations Collective Measures: an Analysis* (New York, 1965).
LE MAY, G. H. L. *British Supremacy in South Africa 1899–1907* (Oxford, 1965).
LENIN, V. I. *Imperialism: the Highest Stage of Capitalism* (London, 1916).
LEWIN, J. *Politics and Law in South Africa* (London, 1963).
LEYDS, W. J. *Correspondentie, 1899–1902*, 9 vols. (The Hague, 1919–34).
—— *The Transvaal Surrounded: a Continuation of* 'The First Annexation of the Transvaal' (London, 1919).
LICHTENSTEIN, H. *Travels in Southern Africa, 1803–6*, 2 vols. (Cape Town, 1928–30).
LINDLEY, A. F. *Adamantia: the Truth about the South African Diamond Fields: or, a Vindication of the Right of the Orange Free State to that Territory* (London, 1873).
LIPSEY, R. G. *An Introduction to Positive Economics* (2nd edn., London, 1966).

Lockhart, J. G. and Woodhouse, C. M. *Rhodes* (London, 1963).

Lombard, J. A., and Stadler, J. J. *Die Ekonomiese Stelsel van Suid-Afrika* (Cape Town, 1967).

Long, B. K. *In Smuts' Camp* (London, 1945).

Louis, W. R. 'Great Britain and German Expansion in Africa, 1884–1919', in Gifford, P., and Louis, W. R. (eds.), *Britain and Germany in Africa* (New Haven, Connecticut, 1967).

Lovell, R. I. *The Struggle for South Africa, 1875–1899: a Study in Economic Imperialism* (New York, 1934).

McCracken, J. L. *The Cape Parliament, 1854–1910* (Oxford, 1967).

MacDonald, J. G. *Rhodes: a Life* (London, 1927).

McKay, V. *Africa in World Politics* (New York, 1963).

Mackenzie, J. *Austral Africa*, 2 vols. (London, 1887).

—— *Ten Years North of the Orange River: 1859–1869* (Edinburgh, 1871).

Mackintosh, C. W. *Coillard of the Zambezi* (London, 1901).

Macmillan, W. M. *Africa beyond the Union* (Johannesburg, 1949).

—— *Bantu, Boer, and Briton: the Making of the South African Native Problem* (Oxford, 1963).

—— *Cape Colour Question* (London, 1927).

—— *Complex South Africa* (London, 1930).

Magnus, P. *Kitchener: Portrait of an Imperialist* (London, 1958).

Malan, D. F. *De Achteruitgang van Ons Volk* (Cape Town, 1917).

—— *Afrikaner Volkseenheid en my Ervarings Op die Pad Daarheen* (Cape Town, 1959).

—— *Foreign Policy of the Union of South Africa* (Pretoria, 1948).

—— *Glo in u Volk!* (Cape Town, 1917).

Malan, F. S. *Die Konvensie-dagboek van sy edelagbare François Stephanus Malan, 1908–1909*. Edited by Preller, J. F. (Van Riebeeck Society, Cape Town, 1951).

Malan, M. P. A. *Die Nasionale Party van Suid Afrika, 1914–1964: Sy Stryd en Sy Prestasies* (Cape Town, 1964).

Malherbe, E. G. *Education and the Poor White* (Stellenbosch, 1932).

Mansergh, N. *The Commonwealth and the Nations: Studies in British Commonwealth Relations* (London, 1948).

—— (ed.). *Commonwealth Perspectives* (London, 1958).

—— (ed.). *Documents and Speeches on Commonwealth Affairs, 1952–62* (London, 1963).

—— *South Africa 1906–1961: the Price of Magnanimity* (London, 1962).

—— *Survey of British Commonwealth Affairs: Problems of Wartime Cooperation and post-war change, 1939–1952* (London, 1958).

Marais, J. S. *The Cape Coloured People, 1652–1937* (London, 1939; reprint Johannesburg, 1957).

—— *The Fall of Kruger's Republic* (Oxford, 1961).

Marquard, L. *People and Policies of South Africa* (Cape Town, 1960).

—— *South Africa's Colonial Policy* (Johannesburg, 1957).

—— *South Africa's International Boundaries* (Johannesburg, 1958).

—— *The Story of South Africa* (London, 1950).

—— (ed.). *Letters from a Boer Parsonage: Letters from Margaret Marquard during the Boer War* (Cape Town, 1967).

—— *The Native in South Africa* (2nd edn., Johannesburg, 1948).

Martin, A. C. *The Concentration Camps, 1900–1902: Facts, Figures and Fables* (Cape Town, 1957).

Martineau, J. *The Life and Correspondence of Sir Bartle Frere*, 2 vols. (London, 1895).

Marwede, H. H. T. and Mamabolo, G. G. *Shall Lobolo Live or Die?* (Cape Town, 1945).

MARWICK, B. A. *The Swazi* (Cambridge, 1940).

MASON, P. *The Birth of a Dilemma: The Conquest and Settlement of Rhodesia* (London, 1958).

MASSIE, R. H. *The Native Tribes of the Transvaal* (London, 1905).

MATTHEWS, J. W. *Incwadi Yami or Twenty Years Personal Experience in South Africa* (New York, 1887).

MAUD, J. P. R. *The Johannesburg Experiment* (Oxford, 1938).

MAURICE, F. M., and GRANT, M. H. *History of the War in South Africa, 1899–1902, compiled by direction of His Majesty's Government*, 8 vols. (London, 1906–1910).

MAYER, P. *Tribesmen or Townsmen* (Cape Town, 1961).

MERRIMAN, J. X. *Selections from the Correspondence of John X. Merriman*, Edited by Lewsen, P., 3 vols. (Van Riebeeck Society, Cape Town, 1960, 1963, 1966).

MEYER, P. J. *Trek Verder: Die Afrikaner in Afrika* (Cape Town, n.d.).

MICHELL, SIR L. *The Life of the Rt. Hon. Cecil John Rhodes, 1853–1902*, 2 vols. (London, 1910).

MILLAR, T. B. *The Commonwealth and the United Nations* (Sydney, 1967).

MILLER, J. D. B. *Britain and the Old Dominions* (London, 1966).

—— *The Commonwealth and the World* (London, 1958).

MILLIN, S. G. *General Smuts*, 2 vols. (London, 1936).

—— *Rhodes* (London, 1933).

MILNER, LORD. *The Nation and The Empire: being a collection of Speeches and Addresses* (London, 1913).

MOLEMA, S. M. *The Bantu, Past and Present* (Edinburgh, 1920).

—— *Montshiwa, 1814–96* (Cape Town, 1966).

MOLTENO, P. A. *The Life and Times of Sir John Charles Molteno*, 2 vols. (London, 1900).

MORRELL, W. P. *The Gold Rushes* (New York, 1941).

MORRIS, R. B. *The Washing of the Spears* (New York, 1964).

MULLER, C. F. J., VAN JAARSVELD, F. A. and VAN WIJK, T. *A Select Bibliography of South African History* (Pretoria, 1966).

MWELI SKOTA, T. D. *The African Yearly Register* (Johannesburg, n.d.).

NATHAN, M. *Paul Kruger: his Life and Times* (4th edn., Durban, 1944).

NDAMASE, V. POTO. *Ama-Mpondo Ibali ne-Ntlalo* (Lovedale, n.d.).

NEL, B. F. *Naturelle-opvoeding en -onderwys* (Bloemfontein, 1942).

NEUMARK, S. D. *Economic Influences on the South African Frontier, 1652–1836* (Stanford, California, 1956).

NIENABER, G. S. and P. J. *Die Geskiedenis van die Afrikaanse Beweging* (Pretoria, 1941).

NYEMBEZI, C. L. S. *A Review of Zulu Literature* (Pietermaritzburg, 1961).

OBERHOLSTER, J. J. *Die Anneksasie van Griekwaland-Wes* (Archives Year Book for South African History, 1945).

OOSTHUIZEN, G. C. *The Theology of a South African Messiah* (Leiden, 1967).

OTTO, J. C. *Die Konsentrasiekampe* (Cape Town, 1954).

PAKENHAM, E. *Jameson's Raid* (London, 1960).

PATON, A. *Cry the Beloved Country* (London, 1948).

—— *Hofmeyr* (Cape Town, 1964).

—— *The People Wept* (Durban, n.d.).

PATTERSON, S. *Colour and Culture in South Africa, A Study of the Status of the Cape Coloured People within the Social Structure of the Union of South Africa* (London, 1953).

—— *The Last Trek* (London, 1957).

PAUW, B. A. *Religion in a Tswana Chiefdom* (London, 1960).

—— *The Second Generation* (Cape Town, 1963).

PAUW, S. *Die Beroepsarbeid van die Afrikaner in die Stad* (Stellenbosch, 1946).

PELLS, E. G. *300 Years of Education in South Africa* (Cape Town, 1954).

PELZER, A. N. (ed.). *Verwoerd Aan die Woord: Toesprake 1948–1962* (Johannesburg, 1964).

PEMBERTON, W. B. *Battles of the Boer War* (London, 1964).

PERHAM, M. *Lugard: the Years of Adventure* (London, 1956).

—— and CURTIS, L. *The Protectorates and South Africa: the Question of their Transfer to the Union* (London, 1935).

PHILIP, J. *Researches in South Africa*, 2 vols. (London, 1828).

PHILLIPS, R. E. *The Bantu in the City* (Lovedale, 1938).

PIENAAR, E. C. *Die triomf van Afrikaans: historiese oorsig van die wording, ontwikkeling, skriftelike gebruik en geleidelike erkenning van ons taal* (Cape Town, 1943).

PIENAAR, S. W., and SCHOLTZ, J. J. J. *Glo in u Volk: Dr. D. F. Malan as Redenaar* (Cape Town, 1964).

PIM, H. *A Transkei Enquiry, 1933* (Lovedale).

PIROW, O. *J. B. M. Hertzog* (Cape Town, 1958).

PISTORIUS, P. V. *No Further Trek* (Johannesburg, 1957).

PITT-RIVERS, J. A. (ed.). *Mediterranean Countrymen* (Paris, 1963).

—— *The People of the Sierra* (London, 1954).

PLAATJE, S. T. *Native Life in South Africa* (2nd edn., London, n.d.).

PLANT, A. 'Economic Development, 1795–1921', *Cambridge History of the British Empire*, vol. VIII (Cambridge 1936; 2nd edn., 1963).

PLAYNE, S. (ed.). *Cape Colony* (London, 1910–11).

PLOMER, W. *Cecil Rhodes* (London, 1933).

PYRAH, G. B. *Imperial Policy and South Africa, 1902–10* (Oxford, 1955).

RABIE, J. *Die Evolusie van Nasionalisme* (Cape Town, 1960).

—— *Ons die Afgod* (Cape Town, 1958).

RANSFORD, O. *The Battle of Majuba Hill: the first Boer War* (London, 1967).

READER, D. H. *The Black Man's Portion* (Cape Town, 1961).

—— *Zulu Tribe in Transition* (Manchester, 1966).

REDFIELD, R. *Peasant Society and Culture* (Chicago, 1956).

REES, W. (ed.). *Colenso Letters from Natal* (Pietermaritzburg, 1958).

REITZ, D. *Commando: a Boer Journal of the Boer War* (2nd edn., London, 1931).

Report of Proceedings of National Conference on Report of the Commission on Native Education (Johannesburg, 1952).

RHOODIE, N. J., and VENTER, H. J. *Die Apartheidsgedagte* (Cape Town, 1960).

RICHARDS, A. I. *The Changing Structure of a Ganda Village, 1892–1952* (Kampala, 1966).

ROBERTS, M. *Labour in the Farm Economy* (Johannesburg, 1959).

—— and TROLLIP, A. *The South African Opposition 1939/45* (London, 1946).

ROBERTSON, H. M. *South Africa—Economic and Political Aspects* (Durham, 1957).

ROBINSON, R., and GALLAGHER, J., with DENNY, A. *Africa and the Victorians: the Official Mind of Imperialism* (London, 1961).

ROGERS, H. *Native Administration in the Union of South Africa* (Pretoria, 1949).

ROSE, E. B. *The Truth about the Transvaal* (London, 1902).

ROSE INNES, J. *James Rose Innes, Chief Justice of South Africa, 1914–1927: Autobiography*. Edited by B. A. Tindall (Cape Town, 1949).

ROSE INNES, R. W. *The Glen Grey Act and the Native Question* (Lovedale, 1903).

ROSS, J. C. *Soil Conservation in South Africa* (Pretoria, 1963).

ROSTOW, W. W. *Stages of Economic Growth* (Cambridge, 1960).

ROUX, E. 'Land and Agriculture in the Native Reserves', in Hellmann, E. (ed.), *Handbook on Race Relations in South Africa* (Cape Town, 1949).

—— *The Veld and the Future* (Cape Town, 1946).

RUBUSANA, W. B. *Zemk' inkomo Magwalandini* (London, 1906).

RUOPP, P. (ed.). *Approaches to Community Development* (The Hague, 1953).

RUSSELL, R. *Natal: the Land and its Story* (Pietermaritzburg, 1904).

SANDOR, *The Coming Struggle for South Africa* (London, 1963).

SCANLAN, D. G. (ed.). *Church, State and Education in Africa* (New York, 1966).

SCHAPERA, I. *Married Life in an African Tribe* (London, 1940).

—— *Migrant Labour and Tribal Life* (London, 1947).

—— *Native Land Tenure in the Bechuanaland Protectorate* (Lovedale, 1943).

SCHLEMMER, L. 'The Resettlement of the Indian Communities in Durban and some Economic, Social and Cultural Effects on the Indian Community', in *The Indian South African* (Durban, 1967).

SCHNELL, E. L. G. *For Men Must Work* (Cape Town, 1954).

SCHOLTZ, G. D. *Die Oorsake van die Tweede Vryheidsoorlog, 1899–1902*, 2 vols. (Johannesburg, 1947).

—— *Europa en die Tweede Vryheidsoorlog, 1899–1902* (2nd edn., Johannesburg, 1941).

—— *Het die Afrikaanse Volk 'n Toekoms?* (Johannesburg, 1953).

SCHREINER, O. *The Story of an African Farm* (London, 1883).

—— *Closer Union: a letter on the South African Union and the principles of government* (London, 1909).

SCHULTZ, T. W. *The Economic Organization of Agriculture* (New York, 1953).

SCHUMANN, C. G. W. *Structural Changes and Business Cycles in South Africa* (London, 1938).

SHEDDICK, V. *Land Tenure in Basutoland* (London, 1954).

SHEPHERD, R. H. W. *Lovedale and Literature for the Bantu* (Lovedale, 1945).

—— *Lovedale, South Africa* (Lovedale, n.d.).

SHEPPERSON, G. and PRICE, T. *Independent African: John Chilembwe and the Origins, Setting and Significance of the Nyasaland Native Rising of 1915* (Edinburgh, 1958).

SILLERY, A. *The Bechuanaland Protectorate* (London, 1952).

—— *Sechele: The Story of an African chief* (Oxford, 1954).

SMIT, F. P. *Die Staatsopvattings van Paul Kruger* (Pretoria, 1951).

SMIT, M. T. R. *The Romance of the Village Ugie* (Cape Town, 1964).

SMITH, E. *The Mabilles of Basutoland* (London, 1939).

SMITH, P. *The Beadle* (new edn., Cape Town, 1956).

SMUTS, J. C. *Africa and some World Problems* (London, 1930).

—— *The Basis of Trusteeship* (Johannesburg, 1942).

—— *Greater South Africa* (Johannesburg, 1940).

SMUTS, J. C. (jr.). *Jan Christian Smuts* (London, 1952).

SOLOMON, W. E. G. *Saul Solomon: 'The Member for Cape Town'* (Cape Town, 1948).

SOUTH AFRICAN AGRICULTURAL UNION, *Memorandum for Submission to the Commission of Enquiry into Agriculture* (May 1967).

—— *Report of the General Council for submission to the Annual Congress, October 1967* (Bloemfontein).

SOUTH AFRICAN INSTITUTE OF RACE RELATIONS. *African Farm Labour* (Johannesburg, 1959).

—— *Farm Labour in the Orange Free State* (Johannesburg, 1939).

—— *The Western Areas Removal Scheme* (Johannesburg, 1953).

SOUTH AFRICAN NATIVE RACES COMMITTEE (eds.). *The Natives of South Africa* (London, 1901).

—— *The South African Natives, their Progress and Present Condition* (London, 1909).

SOUTHERN, C. *Wyksdorp: A Study of a South African Village* (Communications from the School of African Studies, Cape Town, 1962).

SPENCE, J. E. *Lesotho—The Politics of Dependence* (London, 1968).

—— *Republic under Pressure: A Study of South African Foreign Policy* (London, 1965).

—— 'The Republic of South Africa and her Neighbours', in *Africa South of the Congo* (London, 1968).

SPENCE, J. E., and THOMAS, E. *South Africa's Defense* (Los Angeles, 1966).

SPENDER, J. A. *The Life of the Right Hon. Sir Henry Campbell-Bannerman*, 2 vols. (London, 1923).

SPOONER, F. P. *The South African Predicament* (London, 1960).

STANFORD, SIR W. *The Reminiscences of Sir Walter Stanford*, 2 vols. Edited by J. W. Macquarrie (Van Riebeeck Society, Cape Town, 1958, 1962).

STAYT, H. A. *The Bavenda* (London, 1931).

STEVENS, R. P. *Lesotho, Botswana and Swaziland: the former High Commission Territories in Southern Africa* (New York, 1967).

STEWART, J. *Lovedale Past and Present* (Lovedale, 1887).

STEYN, A. F. *Die Bantoe in die Stad—Die Bantoegesin* (Pretoria, 1966).

STUART, J. *A History of the Zulu Rebellion, 1906, and of Dinuzulu's Arrest, Trial, and Expatriation* (London, 1913).

SUID-AFRIKAANSE BURO VIR RAASE-AANGELEENTHEDE (SABRA). *Die Naturel in die Suid-Afrikaanse Landbou* (1954).

SUNDKLER, B. G. M. *Bantu Prophets in South Africa* (London, 1948, 1961, 1964).

THEAL, G. M. *History of South Africa from 1795 to 1872*, 5 vols. (4th edn., London, 1919).

—— *History of South Africa from 1873 to 1884*, 2 vols. (London, 1919).

THOM, H. B. *Die Geskiedenis van die Skaapboerdery in Suid-Afrika* (Amsterdam, 1936).

THOMAS, W. I., and ZNANIECKI, F. *The Polish Peasant in Europe and America* (New York, reprint, 1958).

THOMPSON, L. M. *Politics in the Republic of South Africa* (Boston, 1966).

—— 'South Africa', in R. W. Winks (ed.), *The Historiography of the British Empire–Commonwealth* (Durham, North Carolina, 1966).

—— *The Unification of South Africa, 1902–1910* (Oxford, 1960).

THORNTON, A. P. *Doctrines of Imperialism* (New York, 1965).

—— *The Imperial Idea and its Enemies: a Study in British Power* (London, 1959).

TRACY, M. *Agriculture in Western Europe* (New York, 1964).

TRANSVAAL AND ORANGE FREE STATE CHAMBER OF MINES. *Annual Report, 1964* (Johannesburg, 1965).

TREVELYAN, G. M. *British History in the nineteenth century and after, 1782–1919* (2nd edn., London, 1937).

TROLLOPE, A. *South Africa* (London, 1878).

TUNSTALL, W. C. B. *The Commonwealth and Regional Defence* (London, 1959).

TYLDEN, G. *The Rise of the Basuto* (Cape Town, 1950).

UNESCO. *Social Implications of Industrialization and Urbanization in Africa South of the Sahara* (London, 1956).

UNIVERSITY OF NATAL, DEPARTMENT OF ECONOMICS. *The African Factory Worker* (Cape Town, 1950).

UNIVERSITY OF NATAL, INSTITUTE FOR SOCIAL RESEARCH. *The Baumannville Community* (Cape Town, 1955).

UNIVERSITY OF SOUTH AFRICA, BUREAU OF MARKET RESEARCH. Report No. 3, *Income and Expenditure Patterns of Urban Bantu Households, Pretoria Survey*, 2 vols. (Pretoria, 1961).

—— Report No. 6, *Income and Expenditure Patterns of Urban Bantu Households, South-Western Townships Johannesburg* (Pretoria, 1963).

—— Report No. 8, *Income and Expenditure Patterns of Urban Bantu Households, Cape Town Survey* (Pretoria, 1964).

—— Report No. 9, *Income and Expenditure Patterns of Coloured Households, Cape Peninsula* (Pretoria, 1965).

—— Report No. 11, *Income and Expenditure Patterns of Urban Coloured Households, Durban Survey* (Pretoria, 1966).

UNIVERSITY OF SOUTH AFRICA, BUREAU OF MARKET RESEARCH, Report No. 13, *Income and Expenditure Patterns of Urban Bantu Households, Durban Survey* (Pretoria, 1966).
—— Report No. 14, *Comparative Income Patterns of Urban Bantu, Pretoria, 1960–1965* (Pretoria, 1966).
UYS, C. J. *In the Era of Shepstone : being a Study of British Expansion in South Africa (1842–1877)* (Lovedale, 1933).
VAN BILJON, F. J. *State Interference in South Africa* (London, 1938).
VAN DEN HEEVER, C. M. *Generaal J. B. M. Hertzog* (Johannesburg, 1943) (English translation, Johannesburg, 1946).
VAN DER HORST, S. T. *Native Labour in South Africa* (Cape Town, 1942).
—— *African Workers in Town* (Cape Town, 1964).
—— 'The Effect of Industrialization on Race Relations in South Africa', in Hunter, G. (ed.), *Industrialization and Race Relations* (London, 1965).
VAN DER MERWE, N. J. *Marthinus Theunis Steyn : 'n lewensbeskrywing*, 2 vols. (Cape Town, 1921).
VAN DER POEL, J. *The Jameson Raid* (Cape Town, 1951).
—— *Railway and Customs Policies in South Africa, 1885–1910* (London, 1933).
VAN DER WALT, A. J. H., WIID, J. A. and GEYER, A. L. (eds.). *Geskiedenis van Suid-Afrika*, 2 vols. (Cape Town, 1955). Revised edition edited in one volume by D. W. Krüger (Cape Town, 1965).
VAN JAARSVELD, F. A. *The Afrikaner's Interpretation of South African History* (Cape Town, 1964).
—— *The Awakening of Afrikaner Nationalism, 1868–1881*. Translated from Afrikaans by F. R. Metrowich (Cape Town, 1961).
—— *Die Afrikaner en sy Geskiedenis* (Cape Town, 1959).
—— *Lewende Verlede* (Johannesburg, 1961).
—— and SCHOLTZ, G. D. *Die Republiek van Suid-Afrika : Agtergrond, Onstaan en Toekoms* (Johannesburg, 1966).
VAN OORDT, J. F. *Paul Kruger en de Opkomst der Zuid-Afrikaansche Republiek* (Amsterdam, 1898).
VAN RENSBURG, H. *Their Paths Crossed Mine* (Johannesburg, 1956).
VAN ROOYEN, J. J. *Die Nasionale Party: Sy Opkoms en Oorwinning: Kaapland se Aandeel* (Cape Town, 1956).
VAN WALSEM, D. J. *The Elgin/Grabouw and Vyeboom Area* (Bureau for Economic Research, University of Stellenbosch, n.d.).
VAN WARMELO, N. J. (ed.). *Contributions towards Venda History, Religion and Tribal Ritual* (Pretoria, 1932).
VAN WINTER, P. J. *Onder Krugers Hollanders : Geschiedenis van de Nederlandsche Zuid-Afrikaansche Spoorweg-Maatschappij*, 2 vols. (Amsterdam, 1937, 1938).
VAN WYK, S. *Die Afrikaner in die Beroepslewe van die Stad* (Pretoria, 1968).
VAN WYK LOUW, N. P. *Liberale Nasionalisme* (Cape Town, 1958).
VATCHER, W. H. *White Laager* (London, 1965).
VILAKAZI, A. *Zulu Transformation* (Pietermaritzburg, 1962).
VINDEX. *Cecil Rhodes : his Political Life and Speeches, 1881–1900* (London, 1900).
WALKER, E. A. *A History of South Africa* (London, 1928, 3rd edn., 1957).
—— *Lord de Villiers and his Times : South Africa, 1842–1914* (London, 1925).
—— *W. P. Schreiner : a South African* (London, 1937).
WALKER, I. L., and WEINBREN, B. *2000 Casualties* (Johannesburg, 1961).
WALLIS, J. P. R. *One Man's Hand : the Story of Sir Charles Coghlan and the Liberation of Southern Rhodesia* (London, 1950).
WALTON, SIR E. H. *The Inner History of the National Convention of South Africa* (Cape Town, 1912).

WANGEMANN, H. T. *Maléo en Sekoekoeni*. Edited by G. P. J. Trümpelmann, translated by J. F. W. Grosskopf (Van Riebeeck Society, Cape Town, 1957).

WARHURST, P. R. *Anglo-Portuguese Relations in South-Central Africa, 1890–1900* (London, 1962).

WELLINGTON, J. H. *South West Africa and its Human Issues* (London, 1967).

—— *Southern Africa, A Geographical Study*, 2 vols. (Cambridge, 1955).

WELLS, J. *Stewart of Lovedale* (London, 1908).

WESSMAN, R. *The Bawenda of the Spelonken* (London, 1908).

WHETHAM, E. H., and CURRIE, J. I. *Readings in the Applied Economics of Africa*, 2 vols. (Cambridge, 1967).

WHYTE, Q. 'Interracial Cooperation', in Hellmann, E. (ed.), *Handbook on Race Relations in South Africa* (Cape Town, 1949).

WIDDICOMBE, J. *In the Lesuto* (London, 1895).

WIGHT, M. *The Power Struggle within the United Nations* (New York, 1956).

WILCOCKS, R. W. *The Poor White* (Stellenbosch, 1932).

WILLIAMS, B. *Cecil Rhodes* (London, 1921).

—— (ed.). *The Selborne Memorandum: a Review of the Mutual Relations of the British South African Colonies in 1907* (Oxford, 1925).

WILMOT, A. (ed.). *The Book of South African Industries* (Cape Town, 1892).

WILSON, F. *Labour in the South African Gold Mines, 1936–1969* (Cambridge, forthcoming).

WILSON, G. and M. *The Analysis of Social Change* (Cambridge, 1945).

WILSON, M., KAPLAN, S., MAKI, T., WALTON, E. M. *Social Structure* (Pietermaritzburg, 1952).

WILSON, M. and MAFEJE, A. *Langa* (Cape Town, 1963).

WINKS, R. W. (ed.). *British Imperialism: Gold, God, Glory* (New York, 1963).

—— *The Historiography of the British Empire–Commonwealth: Trends, Interpretations, and Resources* (Durham, North Carolina, 1966).

WOLF, E. R. *Peasants* (Englewood Cliffs, 1966).

WOODWARD, C. VANN. *Origins of the New South* (Baton Rouge, 1951).

WORSFOLD, W. B. *The Reconstruction of the New Colonies under Lord Milner*, 2 vols. (London, 1913).

WRENCH, J. E. *Alfred Lord Milner: the Man of no Illusions, 1854–1925* (London, 1958).

XUMA, A. B. *Reconstituting the Union of South Africa* (Lovedale, 1932).

YATES, P. L. *Food, Land and Manpower in Western Europe* (London, 1960).

ARTICLES

ANON, 'The South African Native's Point of View', *Round Table*, 19 (1928/9).

BACKEBERG, H. E. W. 'Die betrekkinge tussen die Suid-Afrikaanse Republiek en Duitsland tot na die Jameson-inval (1852–1896)', *Archives Year Book for South African History* (1949) i.

BERG, E. J. 'Backward sloping Labour Supply Functions in Dual Economies—the Africa Case', *Quarterly Journal of Economics* (August 1961).

BEYLEVELD, A. J. 'The development of production control in the wine industry', *Agrekon* (5. 1. 1966).

—— 'Ostrich Farming in South Africa', ibid. (6. 3. 1967).

BIESHEUVEL, S. 'Some Characteristics of the African Worker', *Journal of the South African Institute of Personnel Management*, 15. 5 (1962).

BLAINEY, G. 'Lost Causes of the Jameson Raid', *Economic History Review*, 2nd ser., 18 (1965), 350–66.

BOARD, C. 'The Rehabilitation Programme in Bantu Areas', *South African Journal of Economics*, 32 (1964).

BOTHA, M. C. 'Ons Stedelike Bantoebeleid teen die Agtergrond van ons Landbeleid', *Journal of Racial Affairs*, 15 (1964).

BRANDEL, M. 'Urban *Lobolo* Attitudes', *African Studies*, 17, 1 (1958).

BRIDGMAN, REV. F. B. 'The Ethiopian Movement and other Independent Factions Characterised by a National Spirit', a Paper read at the Natal Missionary Conference, *The Christian Express*, vol. 33, No. 397 (1 October 1903) and No. 398 (2 November 1903).

CAMPBELL, W. B. 'The South African Frontier, 1865–1885: a study in expansion', *Archives Year Book for South African History* (1959) i.

Christian Express, 1 October 1906 and 1 May 1967.

COBDEN, M. 'The Bloodiest Place on Earth', *Rand Daily Mail*, 18 February 1967.

COOPPAN, S., and NAIDOO, B. A. 'Indian Adjustments to Urbanization', *Race Relations Journal*, XXII, 2 (1955).

DALE, R. 'South Africa and the World Community', *World Politics*, XVIII (1966).

DAY, R. H. 'Technical Change and the Sharecropper', *The American Economic Review*, LVII, 3 (1967).

DENOON, D. J. N. ' "Capitalist influence" and the Transvaal Government during the Crown Colony period, 1900–1906', *Historical Journal*, xi, 2 (1968), 301–31.

—— 'The Transvaal Labour Crisis, 1901–6', *Journal of African History*, vii, 3 (1967), 481–94.

DRUS, E. 'A Report on the Papers of Joseph Chamberlain relating to the Jameson Raid and the Inquiry', *The Bulletin of the Institute of Historical Research*, XXV (1952).

DU PLESSIS, J. C. 'Investment and the Balance of Payments', *South African Journal of Economics* (December 1965).

DU PLESSIS, J. S. 'Die Onstaan en Ontwikkeling van die Amp van die Staatspresident in die Zuid-Afrikaansche Republiek (1858–1902)', *Archives Year Book for South African History* (1955) i.

EISELEN, W. W. M. 'Harmonious Multi-Community Development', *Optima*, ix, 1 (1959).

ENKE, S. 'South African growth: a macro-economic analysis', *South African Journal of Economics* (March 1962).

FALLERS, L. A. 'Are African Cultivators to be called "Peasants"?' *Current Anthropology*, 2 (1961).

Farming in South Africa, Festival Issue: 1910–1960 (Pretoria 2. 1960).

FRANKEL, S. H. 'An Analysis of the growth of the National Income of the Union in the period of prosperity before the war', *South African Journal of Economics* (1944).

GALBRAITH, J. S. 'The pamphlet campaign on the Boer War', *Journal of Modern History*, xxiv, 2 (1952), 111–26.

GARDINER, C. 'The Problem of the Day: Evils of Squatting and the Labour Question', *Farmers' Weekly* (6. 9. 1917).

GARSON, N. G. 'Het Volk', *Historical Journal*, ix, 1 (1966), 101–32.

—— 'The Swaziland Question and a Road to the Sea (1887–1895)', *Archives Year Book for South African History* (1957) ii.

GARTHORN, E. R. 'Application of Native Law', *Bantu Studies*, 3 (1927–9).

GERMOND, R. C. 'Economic Development and Land Reform in Basutoland', *South African Outlook*, 95 (1965).

GLUCKMAN, M. 'Analysis of a Social Situation in Modern Zululand', *Bantu Studies*, XIV (1940).

GRAY, J. L. 'The Comparative Sociology of South Africa', *South African Journal of Economics*, 5 (1937).

GUÉNALT, P. H., and RANDALL, R. J. 'Some Financial Aspects of Urban Native Segregation in South Africa', *Race Relations Journal*, VII, 4 (1940).

HAMMOND-TOOKE, D. 'Chieftainship in Transkeian Political Development', *Journal of Modern African Studies*, 2 (1964).

HARTMAN, W. 'Die Nuwe Afrikaner', *Huisgenoot*, 28 May and 4 June 1965.

HENDERSON, J. 'The Economic Condition of the Native People', *South African Outlook*, 57 (1927) and 58 (1928).

HOBART HOUGHTON, D. 'Men of Two Worlds', *South African Journal of Economics*, 28 (1960).

HOLLI, M. G. 'Joseph Chamberlain and the Jameson Raid: a bibliographical survey', *Journal of British Studies*, May 1964.

HORWOOD, O. P. F. 'Is Minimum Wage Legislation the answer for South Africa?' *South African Journal of Economics* (1962).

HUGO, M. 'Die Stemregvraagstuk in die Zuid-Afrikaansche Republiek', *Archives Year Book for South African History* (1947).

HUNT, D. R. 'An Account of the Bapedi', *Bantu Studies*, v (1931), 275–326.

HUNTER, M. 'The Effects of Contact with Europeans on the Status of Pondo Women', *Africa*, VI (1933).

HUNTLEY, J. K. 'The development of production control in South African sugar industry', *Agrekon* (5. 2. 1966).

HYAM, R. 'Smuts and the Magnanimous Gesture', *Historical Journal*, viii, 3 (1965), 380–98.

JORISSEN, J. A. T. 'The Native Labour Problem: why it is scarce and unsatisfactory on the farms', *Farmers' Weekly* (5. 7. 1911).

KATZEN, L. H. 'The case for minimum wage legislation in South Africa', *South African Journal of Economics* (1961).

KELLEY, T. H. *et al*. 'Economists' Protest, Dairy Produce and Maize Marketing Schemes: Memorandum of Objections', ibid. (6. 1. 1938).

—— ——'Economists' Protest, Marketing Act 1937, scheme relating to marketing of wheat: Memorandum of Objections', ibid. (6. 2. 1938).

—— —— 'Economists' Protest, the Operation of the Wheat Marketing Scheme 1938–39: Memorandum of Objections', ibid. (8. 1. 1940).

KOOY, M. and ROBERTSON, H. M. 'The South African Board of Trade and Industries; The South African Customs Tariff and the Development of South African Industries', ibid. 34 (1966).

KOZIARA, K. S. *et al*. 'The Rural Worker in America', *Monthly Labor Review* (June 1968).

KRUGER, H. J. P. L. 'International Commodity Agreements with special reference to recent developments and future possibilities', *Agrekon* (7. 1. 1968).

LANDIS, E. 'South West Africa in the International Court: Act II, Scene I', *Cornell Law Quarterly*, XLIV (1964).

LAWRIE, G. G. 'South Africa's World Position', *Journal of Modern African Studies*, II (1964).

LEISTNER, G. M. E. 'Patterns of Urban Bantu Labour', *South African Journal of Economics*, 32 (1964).

LESLIE, R. 'Paper Money and the Gold Standard at the Cape', *Report of the Fourteenth Annual General Meeting of the South African Association for the Advancement of Science* (Cape Town, 1917).

LEWIS, W. A. 'Economic development with unlimited supplies of labour', *Manchester School* (1954).

MACDONALD, J. D. M. 'The South African Wool Reserve Price Scheme and its Administration', *Agrekon* (7. 1. 1968).

McLoughlin, J. R. 'A defence of control in the marketing of agricultural products', *South African Journal of Economics* (6. 3. 1938).

Mafeje, A. 'An African Chief Visits Town', *Journal of Local Administration Overseas*, II, 2 (1963).

Manning, C. A. 'South Africa and the World: In Defense of Apartheid', *Foreign Affairs*, XLIII (1964).

Mason, P. 'Some Maxims and Axioms', ibid. XLIII (1964).

Mathewson, J. E. 'Impact of Urbanization on Lobolo', *Journal of Racial Affairs*, 10. 3 (1959).

Meyer, A. S. 'Die Rol van die Koöperatiewe Beweging in die Ekonomiese Vooruitgang van die Afrikaner', *Verslag van die Tweede Ekonomiese Volkskongres* (Bloemfontein, 1950).

Molteno, D. B. 'Urban Areas Legislation', *Race Relations Journal*, XXII, 2 (1955).

Mouton, J. A. 'Generaal Piet Joubert en sy aandeel aan die Transvaalse geskiedenis', *Archives Year Book for African History* (1957) i.

Mqotsi, L., and Mkele, N. 'A Separatist Church, Ibandla, lika-Krestu', *African Studies* (1945).

M'Timkulu, D. G. S. 'The African and Education', *Race Relations Journal*, XVI, 3 (1949).

Neal, M. 'The United Nations and the Union of South Africa', *Journal of International Affairs*, VII (1953).

Oppenheimer, H. F. 'The Orange Free State Goldfields', *South African Journal of Economics*, 18 (1950).

Ploeger, J. 'Onderwys en Onderwys-beleid in die Suid-Afrikaanse Republiek onder Ds. S. J. du Toit en Dr. N. Mansvelt (1881–1900)', *Archives Year Book for South African History* (1952) i.

Potgieter, J. F., Fellingham, S. A., and Neser, M. L. 'Incidence of Nutritional Deficiency Diseases among the Bantu and Coloured Population in South Africa as Reflected by the Results of a Questionnaire Survey', *South African Medical Journal* (40. 22. 1966).

Pretorius, P. J. 'The Clinical Nature and Extent of Protein Malnutrition in South Africa', *South African Medical Journal* (42. 36. 1968).

Principal, Lovedale, The. 'Where Lovedale Pupils Come from', *South African Outlook*, 57 (April 1927).

Rademeyer, J. I. 'Die Oorlog teen Magato', *Historiese Studies* 2 (1944) 79–122.

Reedman, J. N. 'Agricultural Surpluses and Social Policy', *Race Relations* (4th Quarter, 1941).

Richards, C. S. 'The "New Despotism" in agriculture: some reflections on the Marketing Bill', *South African Journal of Economics* (4. 4. 1936).

—— 'Subsidies, Quotas, Tariffs and the excess cost of agriculture in South Africa', ibid. (3. 3. 1935).

Riekert, P. J. 'Skakeling van die Stedelike Bantoe met hul Tuislande', *Triomf: Jaarboek van die Suid-Afrikaanse Buro vir Rasse-Anngeleenthede*, 1 (1966).

Ritchken, M. 'The Fisherfolk of Kalk Bay', *The Black Sash*, March–April 1965.

Roberts, M. 'High Commission Territories: In Pawn to Apartheid?' *Africa Today*, X (1963).

Robertson, H. M. 'The Cabinet Committee and the control boards', *South African Journal of Economics* (6. 1. 1938).

—— '150 Years of Economic Contact between Black and White', ibid. (2. 4. 1934; 3. 1. 1935).

Rottenberg, S. 'Income and Leisure in an Under-developed Country', *Journal of Political Economy* (lx. 2, 1952).

SCHAUDER, H. 'The chemical industry in South Africa before Union (1910)', *South African Journal of Economics* (December 1946).

SCHOLTZ, A. P. 'Die mieliebedryf in Suid-Afrika—Gevaartekens vir die toekoms', *Agrekon* (1. 1. 1962).

SCOTT, J. D. 'Conservation of Vegetation in South Africa', *Bulletin of the Commonwealth Bureau of Pastures and Field Crops* (No. 41, 1951).

SCOTT, P. 'Cape Town: a Multi-Racial City', *Geographical Journal*, CXXI, 2 (1955).

SENGHOR, L. S. 'Negritude, a Humanism of the Twentieth Century', *Optima*, 161 (1966).

SHANNON, H. A. 'Urbanization, 1904–1936', *South African Journal of Economics*, 5 (1937).

SHEPPERSON, G. 'Notes on Negro American Influences on the Emergence of African Nationalism', *Journal of African History*, I, 2 (Cambridge, 1960).

SMUTS, J. C. 'Problems in South Africa', *Journal of the African Society*, XVI (1917).

SONNABEND, H. 'Demographic Samples in the Study of Backward and Primitive Populations', *South African Journal of Economics*, 2 (1934).

'South Africa and Emergent Africa', *Africa Institute Bulletin*, V (1967).

'South African Sugar Industry, The', *South African Sugar Journal* (Durban, 1945).

SPENCE, J. E. 'British Policy towards the High Commission Territories', *Journal of Modern African Studies*, II (1964).

—— 'Tradition and Change in South African Foreign Policy', *Journal of Commonwealth Political Studies*, I (1962).

SPES BONA, 'The Native Labour Problem: a Few Remedies Suggested', *Farmers' Weekly* (30. 8. 1911).

STEENKAMP, W. F. J. 'The Bantu Wage Problem', *South African Journal of Economics* (March 1962).

STOKES, E. 'Milnerism', *Historical Journal*, V (1966), 47–60.

STULTZ, N. M., and BUTLER, J. 'The South African General Election of 1961', *Political Science Quarterly*, LXXVIII (1963).

SUMMERS, R. 'The Southern Rhodesian Iron Age', *Journal of African History* (1961).

THOMPSON, L. M. 'Afrikaner Nationalist Historiography and the Policy of Apartheid', *Journal of African History*, 3, 1 (Cambridge, 1962).

—— 'Constitutionalism in the South African Republics', *Butterworths South African Law Review* (1954).

TINLEY, J. M. 'Control of Agriculture in South Africa', *South African Journal of Economics* (8. 3. 1940).

TOMLINSON, F. R. 'The Importance of Agriculture in the National Economy', *SABC Economic Review* (1962).

TRAPIDO, S. 'African divisional politics in the Cape Colony, 1884 to 1910', *Journal of African History*, ix, 1 (1968), 69–98.

TRISKA, J. F., and KOCH, H. E. 'The African States at the United Nations', *Review of Politics*, XXI (1959).

VAN BILJON, F. J. 'The Economic Nature of the Challenge to South African Agriculture', *Agrekon* (5. 1. 1966).

VAN DER HORST, J. G. 'Two Conferences', *South African Journal of Economics* (1. 1. 1933).

VAN DER HORST, S. 'The Economic Implications of Political Democracy', supplement to *Optima* (1960).

VAN DER MERWE, C. and DU TOIT, S. J. 'The Contribution of the Agricultural Departments to Agricultural Development', *Agrekon* (6. 1. 1967).

VAN DER ROSS, R. E. 'Misery of Farm Trekkers', *Cape Times* (16. 7. 1959).

VAN DER WALT, A. J. H. 'Dr. Verwoerd's African Policy', *Africa Institute Bulletin* (1966).

VAN RENSBURG, H. J. 'Beheer Kragtens die Bemarkingswet', *Agrekon* (1. 1. 1962).'

VAN RENSBURG, W. C. J. 'Export of Eggs from South Africa', ibid. (6. 4. 1967).

VAN ROOYEN, T. S. 'Die Verhoudinge tussen die Boere, Engelse en Naturelle in die geskiedenis van die Oos-Transvaal tot 1882', *Archives Year Book for South African History* (1951) i.

VAN WAASDIJK, T. 'Agricultural Prices and Price Policy, 1933–1953', *South African Journal of Economics* (22. 1. 1954).

VAN WYK, C. A. G. 'Trends in Land Values in South Africa', *Agrekon* (6. 1. 1967).

VAN WYK, J. J. *et al.* 'Mechanize our Maize Harvesting Process', *Farming in South Africa* (June 1964).

VATTER, H. G. 'On the folklore of the backward sloping supply curve', *Industrial and Labour Relations Review* (vol. 14, 1961).

VILJOEN, D. C. 'Recent Developments in the Dairy Industry', *Agrekon* (6. 4. 1967).

VILJOEN, P. R. 'Planned Agriculture in South Africa', *South African Journal of Economics* (6. 3. 1938).

VILJOEN, S. P. 'Higher Productivity and Higher Wages for Native Labour in South Africa', ibid. (1961).

WEBB, M. 'Indian Land Legislation', in Hellmann, E. (ed.), *Handbook on Race Relations in South Africa* (Cape Town, 1949).

WHITEHEAD, P. 'When it's harvest time every-one goes', *Cape Argues* (18. 6. 1966).

WILDE, R. H. 'Joseph Chamberlain and the South African Republics 1895–1899: a study in the formulation of imperial policy', *Archives Year Book for South African History* (1956) i.

WILSON, M. 'The Principle of Maintaining the Reserves for the African', *Race Relations Journal*, XXIX, 1 (1962).

WITTMAN, W., MOODIE, A. D., FELLINGHAM, S. A., and HANSEN, J. D. L. 'An evaluation of the relationship between nutritional status and infection by means of a field study', *South African Medical Journal* (41. 27. 1967).

XUMA, A. B. 'Bridging the Gap between White and Black in South Africa', Paper read before the Conference of European and Bantu Christian Student Associations held at Fort Hare, June to July 1930.

UNPUBLISHED MATERIAL

ALEXANDRA HEALTH COMMITTEE, 'The Future of Alexandra Township—An Open Letter to the Citizens of Johannesburg' (Johannesburg, 1943).

BEHRMANN, H. I. 'A Study of the Economics of sugar-cane production in Natal' (Ph.D. Thesis, Pietermaritzburg, 1959).

BERG, E. J. 'Recruitment of a labour force in Sub-Saharan Africa' (Ph.D. Thesis, Harvard, 1960).

CARR, W. J. P. 'Influx Control as seen by the Administrator of Non-European Affairs' (Address to South African Institute of Race Relations, 1961).

DU TOIT, J. B. 'Plaasarbeiders: 'n Sosiologiese Studie van 'n Groep Kleurling—Plaasarbeiders in die Distrik Tulbagh' (M.A. Thesis, Stellenbosch, 1947).

HARINCK, G. 'Aspects of Mpondo history in the nineteenth century' (Seminar paper, U.C.L.A. 1966).

HATTINGH, D. J. 'Die verwantskap tussen finansiele sukses in Boerdery en Bepaalde sosiaal-kulturele faktore in die S2 en C5 Agro-ekonomiese streke in die omvanggebied van die Bo-oranje rivier' (M.Sc. [Agric.] Thesis, Pretoria, 1965).

HESSIAN, B. 'An Investigation into the causes of the Labour Agitation in the Witwatersrand, January to March 1922' (M.A. Thesis, Witwatersrand, 1957).

JOHNSON, D. H. 'The Legal Position of South West Africa' (Institute of Commonwealth Studies, London, 1964).

KAVINA, S. 'South West Africa—An International Problem' (M.A. Thesis, University of Edinburgh, 1967).

KIES, B. M. 'The Policy of Educational Segregation and some of its Effects upon the Coloured People of the Cape' (B.Ed. Thesis, University of Cape Town, 1939).

LANGA AFRICAN VIGILANCE COMMITTEE (Undated memorandum of evidence to the Fagan Commission 1946/8).

MAFEJE, A. 'Leadership and Change: A Study of two South African Peasant Communities' (M.A. Thesis, University of Cape Town, 1964).

MAYTHAM, Y. M. 'The Changing Position of the Coloured People' (Cape Town, 1966).

MBATA, M. B. 'The African in the City and his Family' (Address to South African Institute of Race Relations, Durban, 1960).

MSIMANG, H. S. (Address to Location Advisory Board Congress, Ermelo, 1951).

M'TIMKULU, D. G. S. 'African Adjustment to Urbanization' (Address to South African Institute of Race Relations, Johannesburg, 1955).

ORANGE FREE STATE MUNICIPAL ASSOCIATION, Statement at Kroonstad, 1932.

SAKER, H. 'The Langeberg Rebellion' (B.A. Hons. Thesis, Cape Town, 1965).

SCHREUDER, D. M. 'The second Gladstone Administration and the Transvaal, 1880–85: an analysis of policy' (D.Phil. thesis, Oxford, 1967).

SOUTH AFRICAN INSTITUTE OF RACE RELATIONS, 'The Challenge to Urban Family Life To-day' (Papers presented at Natal Conference, 1959)

UYS, A. 'Plaasarbeiders: 'n Sosiologiese Studie van 'n groep Kleurling-plaasarbeiders in die distrik Stellenbosch' (M.A. Thesis, Stellenbosch, 1947).

VERWOERD, H. F. 'More Powers for Coloureds' (Address to the Union Council of Coloured Affairs, Cape Town, December 1961).

WILSON, F. 'An Analysis of the Forces Operating in the Labour Market of the South African Gold Mines, 1936–1965' (Ph.D. Thesis, Cambridge, 1966).

ADDITIONAL BIBLIOGRAPHY

ABRAHAMS, P. *Mine Boy* (London, 1946).
—— *Return to Goli* (London, 1953).
—— *Tell Freedom* (London, 1954).
—— *Wild Conquest* (London, 1951).
African National Congress, Minutes of the Annual Conference of the (Bloemfontein, December 1940).
Africans' Claims in South Africa (African National Congress, Johannesburg, 1945).
BENSON, M. *The African Patriots : The Story of the African National Congress* (London, 1963).
BLOOM, H. *Episode* (London, 1956).
BUNTING, B. *The Rise of the South African Reich* (Penguin Books, 1964).
CALATA, REV. J. A. Presidential Address, Conference of Cape African National Congress (4 July 1938).
CARTER, G. M. *African Concepts of Nationalism in South Africa* (Edinburgh, 1965).
—— *Separate Development : The Challenge of the Transkei* (Johannesburg, 1966).
Congress Youth League Manifesto (March 1944).
DOLLARD, J. *Caste and Class in a Southern Town* (New York, 1937).
DUBE, J. L. *A Talk Upon My Native Land* (Rochester, 1892).
FEIT, E. *South Africa, The Dynamics of the African National Congress* (London, 1962).
FERRIS, W. H. *The African Abroad, or His Evolution in Western Civilisation; Tracing His Development Under Caucasian Milieu* (New Haven, Connecticut, 1913).
FIRST, R. *The Farm Labour Scandal* (Johannesburg, 1959).
FORMAN, L. *Chapters in the History of the March to Freedom* (Cape Town, 1959).
GANDHI, M. K. *Satyagraha in South Africa* (Madras, 1926).
—— *The Story of My Experiments with Truth* (Boston, 1957).
HILL, C. R. *Bantustans—The Fragmentation of South Africa* (London, 1964).
HOOPER, C. *Brief Authority* (London, 1960).
JOHNS, S. W. 'Workers' Challenge to White South Africa: Labor unrest and the Establishment of the I.C.U.' Paper presented to the African Studies Association (October 1966).
JOSEPH, H. *Tomorrow's Sun* (London, 1966).
KUPER, L. *Passive Resistance in South Africa* (London, 1956).
MAHABANE, Z. R. *The Good Fight* (Evanston, 1966).
MANDELA, N. *No Easy Walk in Freedom* (London, 1965).
MATTHEWS, Z. K. 'Late S. M. Makgatho—Great Teacher-politician', *Imvo Zabantsundu* (28 October 1961).
MBEKI, G. *The Peasants' Revolt* (Penguin Books, 1964).
MERCIER, P. 'On the Meaning of "Tribalism" in Black Africa', in P. L. Van den Berghe (ed.), *Africa : Social Problems of Change and Conflict* (San Francisco, 1965).
MODISANE, B. *Blame Me on History* (London, 1963).
MPHAHLELE, E. *The African Image* (London, 1962).
—— *Down Second Avenue* (London, 1959).
MSIMANG, H. S. *The Crisis* (Express Printing Works, 1936).
—— '50 Years on the Road to Liberty', *Contact* (3. 7. 2 April 1960).
—— 'South Africa's Freedom Struggle in Focus', ibid. (3. 15. 30 July 1960).
MUNGER, E. S. *Bechuanaland—Pan-African Outpost or Bantu Homeland* (London, 1965).
NGUBANE, J. K. *An African Explains Apartheid* (New York, 1963).
—— 'Should the Natives' Representative Council be Abolished?' (*The African Bookman*, Cape Town, 1946).
Non-European Conference, Minutes of the First (Kimberley, June 1927).
—— *Minutes of the Third* (Bloemfontein, January 1931).

PALMER, M. *The History of the Indians in Natal* (Cape Town, 1957).

POLAK, H. S. L. 'Early Years', in H. S. L. Polak and others, *Mahatma Gandhi* (London, 1949).

ROUX, E. *Time Longer than Rope: A History of the Black Man's Struggle for Freedom in South Africa* (London, 1948).

SACHS, E. S. *Garment Workers in Action* (Johannesburg, 1957).

SEGAL, R. (ed.). *Economic Sanctions against South Africa* (London, 1964).

SEME, P. KA I. 'The African National Congress—Is it Dead?' (1932).

—— 'Native Union', *Imvo Zabantsundu* (24 October 1911).

SIMONS, H. J. *African Women: Their Legal Status in South Africa* (London, 1968).

—— 'The Status of Customary Unions', *Acta Juridica*, 1961.

SKOTA, T. D. M. (ed.). *The African Yearly Register, Being an Illustrated National Biographical Dictionary (Who's Who) of Black Folks in Africa* (Johannesburg, 1932).

South African Native National Congress, Minutes of the Eighth Annual Conference of the (Queenstown, May 1919).

TABATA, J. B. *The All African Convention* (Johannesburg, 1950).

—— *Education for Barbarism* (n.d.)

TUROK, Ben. *The Pondo Revolt* (Johannesburg, n.d.)

VAN DEN BERGHE, P. L. (ed.). *Africa: Social Problems of Change and Conflict* (San Francisco, 1965).

—— *South Africa, A Study in Conflict* (Middletown, Connecticut, 1965).

INDEX

THE OXFORD HISTORY OF
SOUTH AFRICA

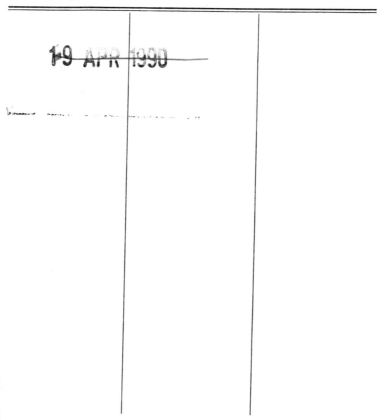